AVID

READER

PRESS

ALSO BY CHRIS HUGHES

Fair Shot: Rethinking Inequality and How We Earn

MARKETCRAFTERS

The 100-Year Struggle *to* Shape
the American Economy

CHRIS HUGHES

AVID READER PRESS

*New York   Amsterdam/Antwerp   London
Toronto   Sydney/Melbourne   New Delhi*

AVID READER PRESS
An Imprint of Simon & Schuster, LLC
1230 Avenue of the Americas
New York, NY 10020

For more than 100 years, Simon & Schuster has championed authors and the stories they create. By respecting the copyright of an author's intellectual property, you enable Simon & Schuster and the author to continue publishing exceptional books for years to come. We thank you for supporting the author's copyright by purchasing an authorized edition of this book.

First Avid Reader Press hardcover edition April 2025

AVID READER PRESS and colophon are trademarks of Simon & Schuster, LLC

Simon & Schuster strongly believes in freedom of expression and stands against censorship in all its forms. For more information, visit BooksBelong.com.

For information about special discounts for bulk purchases,
please contact Simon & Schuster Special Sales
at 1-866-506-1949 or business@simonandschuster.com.

The Simon & Schuster Speakers Bureau can bring authors to your live event. For more information or to book an event contact the Simon & Schuster Speakers Bureau at 1-866-248-3049 or visit our website at www.simonspeakers.com.

Interior design by Ruth Lee-Mui

Manufactured in the United States of America

1   3   5   7   9   10   8   6   4   2

Library of Congress Control Number: 2025000111

ISBN 978-1-6680-5017-0
ISBN 978-1-6680-5019-4 (ebook)

For David and Sophie, the lights of my life

Contents

Introduction

Several years ago, I sat on the set of CNBC's *Squawk Box*, one of the most watched morning business shows in the United States. We were in the middle of a commercial break, and under the large, black camera that faced me, a digital clock was counting down the seconds until I would be back on air.

I was there that day to talk about economic policy—the bourgeoning movement for robust antitrust enforcement and tax code reform. But what I remember most clearly was the off-air squabbling between the hosts. I constantly clashed with Joe Kernen, a co-host typically clad in suspenders who held court while reclining in his chair. Kernen and another co-host, Andrew Ross Sorkin, were debating a question so abstract that it felt surreal that it could provoke such intense on-set acrimony: Would more government regulation and antitrust action stifle American entrepreneurship? Seconds before the cameras rolled, the argument escalated into such a raucous dispute that part of me wondered if the peacock-labeled coffee mugs might start flying.

The intro music played, and the light above the black camera turned green. Becky Quick, the co-host playing the role of Switzerland in the debate, turned to me. With a calm smile, she lobbed me right into the fray: "So, what do you think? Do we need more government regulation, or should we trust free markets to create prosperity?"

I balked. Decades before, I had been part of the founding team of Facebook, but I had long since left Silicon Valley to focus on public policy and economics. This question felt personal, at least to me. Who was my favorite child: the entrepreneur or the policymaker? Both felt vital in the project of democratic capitalism. Meant to choose a side on set in real time, I stumbled through an answer that made the case for both. It satisfied no one, including me.

In the years since, in the halls of the Wharton School as I pursued a doctorate, in conversation with Republican and Democratic policymakers, and in the archives of history, I have attempted to answer this basic question. When do markets produce the most prosperity in a reasonably fair, equitable fashion? What are the ingredients that make that economic structure possible?

The dynamism of American capitalism doesn't stem solely from business-minded entrepreneurs or from government policy. The engine that often drives it forward is a distinct practice of managing and organizing our economic lives that I call *marketcraft*. This book offers a new way of thinking about political economy that discards the market-versus-government duality, replacing it with a vision for how entrepreneurial leaders in government can harness the power of markets to meet political and social goals. Much of today's American economy—its resilient strength and confounding structure—can be explained by the actions of marketcrafters of the past century. The stability in our financial markets, our resiliency to energy shocks, and our ability to develop vital new technologies to combat climate change—these are all a result of the institutions we have chartered and the leadership of individuals who run them.

This book tells the stories of the people who shaped and crafted markets over the past century. When these marketcrafters were successful, they used public power to structure business activity to contribute to the common good. Their names generally do not appear in economic textbooks or standard histories. A few achieved renown, but most faded into obscurity. There were among them a Texan millionaire, a Pakistani American immigrant, a teetotaling Missouri banker, a union organizer, and an economist or two. They were Republicans and Democrats, everyday Americans and elites, pragmatists and idealists. Their actions were often at least as impactful as the work of better-known politicians, businessmen, or Nobel Prize winners. Not all of them had sympathetic aims, and they certainly did not always succeed. We have much to learn from their triumphs, but even more from their failures. Studying their work can help us escape the zero-sum framework of regulator versus entrepreneur and improve upon a historical practice that uses private markets to accomplish public goals.

Many of these consequential figures have been forgotten, even though their work was hardly concealed at the time. Journalists covered their actions, and they were subject to the adulation and critique of politicians and voters, not to mention their own friends and family. But their power and influence, when recognized, was often misunderstood. Few people around them saw their work as an effort to organize markets for political or social ends. Instead, the marketcrafters were more likely to be considered technicians of industry, finance, or government, adjusting the wiring of the supposedly self-propelling engines of American capitalism. Their obscurity reflects more than just the natural dimming of reputation over time. It is an artifact of our conventional way of thinking about our economy, which causes us to see markets as sudden and complete manifestations of a natural order. This obstinate, almost religious habit prevents us from seeing markets as they are—dynamic, productive networks shaped and managed by the state.

In this book, we tour through the grand triumphs, petty spats, and personal conflicts of a dozen of these marketcrafters. As I sifted through their correspondence and spoke with them or their surviving family members, I felt like I got to know them as people first and policymakers second. Understanding their personal stories helps explain the professional decisions they made, placing them in the social and political context of their times. My hope, however, is that their stories add up to something bigger: a new way of looking at the economic life we share.

I want to be precise up front about the meaning of some of the words this book uses, since several are new to the lexicon. "Marketcraft" describes a practice that dates back to the start of capitalism hundreds of years ago: intentional, state-led efforts to organize and manage markets for social or political ends.[1] In foreign policy, we use the term "statecraft" to describe how a government pursues power and influence geopolitically. Similarly, marketcrafters employ the tools of the state to pursue economic goals. These can be noble ones such as prosperity, stability, and fairness, or they can be much darker. In the eighteenth and nineteenth centuries, policymakers used state power to categorize many Black Americans as property, shaping a market in slavery whose shameful legacy continues today. Fascist governments in Europe during the Second World War organized their economies to support genocide. Marketcraft is not a values-laden agenda, but a practice, an approach that policymakers use to make markets work in line with political goals.

Marketcraft exists between two better-known ways of thinking about political economy. In one, the "free-market" fantasy of laissez-faire economics, the state is limited to providing fundamental services, such as safeguarding property rights, enforcing contracts, and ensuring domestic security. At the other extreme, such as in the authoritarian state capitalism of contemporary China, political leaders plan the composition of industrial production and publicly owned companies dominate highly orchestrated markets.

This book argues that in America we strike a balance between these extremes. We organize many of our markets for the common good, choosing to cultivate and guide them rather than plan them outright. They do not function according to an ineffable logic of free-market impulses, and the state does not only step in to clean up the mess when they malfunction. Government leaders have shaped them, often from the start, to harness market forces for social or political ends. This work is a "craft" not unlike the work of a sculptor or painter, synthesizing the technical and the human. It is a practice that people can get better at over time.

Even if we haven't used the word, we have crafted many of the most important sectors of the economy. Health insurance, pharmaceuticals, banking, finance, and airlines make up nearly 40 percent of American economic output, and each of those sectors has a deep history of state administration and management. Energy markets, semiconductor design and manufacture, and automobile production have, as this book illustrates, also been managed extensively by the state. We often call each of these sectors a "special case." Banks hold our money and are prone to runs, so they need unique regulation. Everyone should be able to see a doctor, which means the state shouldn't allow exorbitant pricing in health-care markets. Semiconductors, unlike other goods, are essential to the growth of technology businesses and American national security, we say. Conservatives and progressives, despite their deep divisions, generally agree that each of these industries needs some special attention, although they diverge on what to do. When you take a step back and consider all of these "special cases," you start to see that managing and organizing markets is a core value and long-term practice in America. Without properly structured markets, the way of life we treasure would be impossible.[2]

✿

I didn't used to see it this way, because I thought in terms of the market versus government duality. I grew up the only child of a traveling paper salesman and public-school teacher in the Appalachian foothills of North Carolina. The son of centrist Republicans in the era of President Ronald Reagan, I was raised to be dispositionally skeptical of government, even if I was more interested than some of my peers in remedying the social and racial injustices of the South. I did well in school and got a scholarship to go to Harvard. Halfway through sophomore year, my roommates and I started Facebook, now called Meta, and my life took a major turn away from the study of history and current events and toward the world of business. In Facebook's early years, I felt out of place and restless, and with the impulsivity of a twenty-three-year-old, I quit the company three years after its founding to go work for Barack Obama during his first campaign for the presidency. In the years after, I moved back and forth between business and policy worlds, working at a venture capital firm, running a civic action nonprofit, and owning a magazine. In 2016, I made a turn toward work on economic issues, first at the Economic Security Project, a nonprofit I co-founded, and later as a researcher and academic.

Before I began a deeper study of economics, I generally believed that markets functioned best when left on their own, allocating private capital efficiently and creating plentiful jobs over the long term. I knew from my undergraduate economics coursework that markets had side effects, or "externalities," such as pollution or congested roads. They could be prone to disruptive panics, runs, and hoarding. In the fall of 2008 while working on the Obama campaign, I watched on as the Great Financial Crisis caused markets to implode in devastating fashion. Those moments of "market failure" merited government "intervention," I believed, buying into the traditional view. Government's role was to step in and set them back on course. Even as late as 2016, I still believed that the best thing the government could do to help American workers was to provide a "safety net" for people harmed through no fault of their own by market forces. With that helping hand, workers could jump back into the unpredictable but productive activity of the market.[3]

I soon came to see the flaw in thinking about economics this way. The stubborn persistence of the language of "market failure" and "government intervention" reinforces a faulty vision of how the economy works. There is no sequence where markets exist first, before a governance structure. Just as there was no state of nature where humans existed without a social order, there was never a time when markets flourished without a political order. The core flaw of the "market failure" paradigm is that it casts the government as a reactive parental figure—one who merely corrects missteps or offers aid after harm has occurred. In this view, the government's role is limited to "intervening" in markets only after problems arise, much like a parent scolding a child for misbehaving on the playground. This notion of state interference with natural market forces reinforces a false market-government dichotomy, sets up the state in the role of nefarious nanny, and constrains its capacity to foster widespread prosperity.

In 2016, the election of Donald Trump broke open the conventional way of thinking about economics for me and many others. A decade of economic stagnation, accelerating deindustrialization, and frustration with badly structured trade deals fueled the skepticism of many Americans that the promise of modern economics would ever be fulfilled. Later, the Covid-19 pandemic and ensuing supply-chain crisis further scrambled the conventional wisdom that government's role should be constrained to addressing "market failure." When I became a parent in 2017, I struggled to know what to do to stop my toddler from flicking the garbage disposal switch—or even more dangerous activities. I learned from friends and family that, when it works best, parenting is holistic and proactive—not confined to reacting when things go wrong. Shaping a child's behavior starts well before a meltdown strikes. As parents, we have less control over our children than we might like, but we can use what power we have to guide our children in the right direction. Similarly, why would we wait to "intervene" in markets when things go wrong instead of shaping them to be more stable, prosperous, and fair from the outset?

As I pursued my graduate studies in economics, I began to understand that there were schools of thought and intellectual traditions built around this question. In 2019, I joined the call for the reinvigoration of antimonopoly power—one of those dormant traditions—to take on global companies using their dominance to suppress innovation, raise prices, or lower wages. I had been working on the campaign for a guaranteed income for several years and had seen firsthand how futile cash transfers might be if corporate powers dominating housing, health care, or childcare markets hoovered up all the money. Because Facebook had been so instrumental to my own life, I felt like

I had to speak first to the need for structural separation, or "breakup," at that particular company, which I did in the pages of the *New York Times*. Notes of support and invitations to speak flooded into my inbox, and a year later the the Federal Trade Commission, led by a Chair appointed by Trump, filed suit against the company.

Through my study of antimonopoly, I discovered the importance of a positive vision of marketcraft more broadly. Marketcrafters employed a range of tools—public investment, licensing, regulations, and others—to shape a more prosperous, fair economy. Everywhere I looked in history, I began to see the stories of individuals who were combining technical expertise and personal knowledge to craft markets—not just stand by to "intervene" when they failed.

When I was a kid, my father tilled up a third of our backyard, transforming the green grass into a large vegetable garden. A swing set stood on one side, and a doghouse for our pet anchored the other. On the weekends in the spring and fall and daily on summer evenings, my dad hauled me outside to help him stake the tomato plants or pick green beans or yellow squash. I hated it—my fingers got grimy in the dirt, bugs swarmed, and these particular vegetables were not my favorite foods. I would have preferred to be inside reading a book or watching television.

Yet when I think about what marketcraft is, I return to the image of that vegetable garden, vibrating with the activity of plants, insects, and other animals as they vied for sun, shade, and the nutrients that fuel life. The DNA of those plants programmed them to transform nutrients into energy to grow and reproduce. Most of the plants were competing with one another for scarce resources, although just as humans succeed better when we cooperate, some flourished when grown near companion plants.

When our ancestors domesticated and cultivated plants that had otherwise grown in the wild, we began to produce more abundance. Harvesting seeds, drying them, and planting them at the right time of year aided my father in getting our vegetable garden to grow, just as it aided humans thousands of years earlier in their fight against famine. My dad would always create shade for plants that grew better without direct sunlight. He would enlist my help to weed the plant beds, water the plants, and sometimes spray to ward off pests. We made all kinds of mistakes, and some years our harvests were modest. But in others, we had so much produce that we passed much of it off to neighbors and family members who had no garden of their own.

Humans have the power to guide the natural world to make it work better. By moving plants out of the turbulent, uncontrolled wild and into the garden, we cultivate them to provide an incredible and enduring bounty. The history of human progress is premised upon our ability to develop the skills and knowledge to harness seemingly uncontrollable forces to work for us. Once small and bitter, watermelons are now robust with sweet, pink flesh inside thanks to human cultivation. Carrots, bananas, and tomatoes have all been transformed through our ingenuity, making our food tastier and, in some cases, more nutritious. The gardener's skill lies in the combination of insights from science and personal judgment, which is sensitive to the parcel of land, the year's climate, and the particular crop. At once technocratic and human, a gardener hones a craft.

Markets are similar. Technically speaking, markets allocate scarce resources dependent on consumer preferences, investor decisions, and social policy, but that doesn't capture what can feel like their ineffable magic. Adam Smith rightly celebrated the invisible hand's power to harmonize the uncoordinated, profit-seeking activity of many to produce wealth. Across recorded history, the persistence of markets suggests that certain features are nearly universal, transcending time and culture. Over centuries and civilizations, money has naturally emerged as a medium of exchange, workers have been both organized and exploited, and human specialization has driven an ever more intricate division of labor.

Yet for the most part, since the emergence of capitalism several hundred years ago, we haven't managed to produce enough. Abundant prosperity—the kind that provides the basic needs of food, shelter, and sanitation—has only occurred in the past century, and only then for certain people in developed economies. It was only when we figured out how to think about our economic activity like gardeners that we began to build real collective prosperity that could extend human life-spans and provide enough food and even some leisure time to the working class. A gardener does not "intervene" in a garden; she cultivates it. Without her ongoing attention, it would turn fallow and quickly be overrun. Without qualified people in government managing our markets, we have no assurance their growth will satisfy our social priorities.

Instead of wallowing in chaos, as if our job is to give the market what "it" demands, we can harness markets to work for our needs. "Capitalism needs to be cared for by policymakers," Secretary of State Marco Rubio recently wrote. "Our economy is supposed to work for our nation; our nation does not work for our economy."[4]

The comparison of a market to a garden runs the risk of being too bucolic and simplistic. It might suggest that marketcraft is always in pursuit of positive goals—who is against an abundant garden?—even though policymakers can harness markets to produce bombs of war or to cultivate industries that make people sicker or sadder. Even so, it illustrates the power of humanity to use our smarts to harness once uncontrollable forces in pursuit of what we want.

Many people are waking up to this way of thinking about economics. In recent years, there's been a surge of interest in one particular kind of marketcraft called industrial policy. That term has historically been used narrowly to describe government efforts to support the growth of specific sectors deemed important to American competitiveness or national security. Republicans and Democrats now compete to aggressively support American manufacturing to counter the rise of China. Yet "industrial policy" is too limited a term to capture the full breadth of America's market-shaping activities. It hardly seems fitting, for instance, to describe the role of the Federal Reserve in shaping banking and financial markets as industrial policy. Calling Medicare and Medicaid industrial policy is not just imprecise—it strains credulity given that health care is not just about supporting economic productivity. Creating an institutional framework to manage the oil crises of the 1970s was not industrial policy per se, but it was clearly an effort to organize energy markets for greater resiliency. Industrial policy is a kind of marketcraft that appears often in this book, but marketcraft is the larger, more encompassing idea of legislative and administrative action to configure markets to work in a certain fashion.

Some readers might wonder if marketcrafting is just "economic planning" dressed up in a new language. Libertarians often portray multiyear plans with production targets overseen by faceless bureaucrats as the antithesis of market-driven economies. But at no point in American history have we embraced that kind of command-and-control model.[5] As this book's stories reveal, policymakers have frequently steered markets toward political goals, but they have not orchestrated production over the medium or long term. The bogeyman of economic planning stands in stark contrast to what the marketcrafters in these pages envisioned.

You do not need much historical background to understand the stories and arguments I make in this book, but it is important to be clear about one pivotal historical fact: American marketcraft is as old as the Republic. Alexander Hamilton held that only an empowered, centralized state could engineer economic stability and build material wealth and geopolitical power. It would be an understatement to say this was controversial at the time. The British had used their own marketcraft to support state monopolies and prohibit colonial efforts to develop industry, and Americans had forged an identity in opposition to the quite visible hand of the British monarch. The constitution that Hamilton and others shaped provided the basis for a stronger, more effective American state. In the years before, General George Washington had charged the young Hamilton, his aide-de-camp, with the resupply of the geographically dispersed Continental Army with food, medicine, and weapons. While the army was at Valley Forge, the failure of states to deliver promised supplies contributed to a logistical collapse. That fomented a mutinous environment. "Our distress," Hamilton wrote privately at the time, "is infinite."[6] He moved to consolidate the army's authority and coordinate the logistics of the resupply efforts. That experience shaped him, leading him to favor a centralized, activist state with strong financial and manufacturing institutions that could fund and equip a robust military.

In the years after the ratification of the Constitution, Hamilton argued for the federal consolidation of state debt, the creation of a central bank to foster credit markets, and a program of tariffs and subsidies to nurture American industry. The only way to defend America's interests globally, he believed, would be to use political, legal, and military power to build a resilient, nationally integrated economy. He was not waiting for a "market failure," a term no one would have used at the time. Just as the American nation needed to be built, so too did the American economy. "The mission was, in short, development or death," said one writer summing up the Hamiltonian vision.[7]

Some of Hamilton's ideas made it into law. The federal government assumed state debt and increased tariffs, although it did not provide the industrial subsidies Hamilton favored. It chartered a central bank, but the bank's mandate expired in 1811. Twenty years after a second bank was chartered, Andrew Jackson destroyed it, and no central bank in America would exist again until 1913.

Even so, Hamilton's ideas did not fade. They took on new forms in the 1820s with the advent of Henry Clay's "American System," an ambitious developmental program that advocated high tariffs, a central bank, and publicly financed infrastructure. Debates about so-called internal improvements animated political discussions until the Civil War. Meanwhile, other market-crafting efforts were afoot. The American postal service was pursuing a road-building program that opened the frontier to settlement and investment. New York State, aided by federal land grants, funded the construction of the Erie Canal, which caused the cost of freight shipping to fall precipitously and reduced the travel time between New York and Buffalo by half. Decades later, Abraham Lincoln's Republican Party reshaped the American state, drawing inspiration from Hamilton and Clay. The federal government facilitated the construction of a transcontinental railroad through vast public subsidies and empowered citizens to settle the frontier by granting them land in exchange for a commitment to cultivate it. In both of these cases, government did not just manage markets to improve their function but created them where none had before existed.[8]

This book begins in 1932, but I considered starting it thirty years earlier in the formative years of the Progressive Era of the 1900s and 1910s. That was the moment when policymakers began to build institutions responsible for implementing the vision that Hamilton, Clay, Lincoln, and others had shared. The late phases of the industrial revolution had generated incredible wealth through mass production powered by electricity, steel, and oil. A new American aristocracy controlled record amounts of wealth and power, fueling a broad-based movement to get political leaders to set the country on a fairer path. Progressives believed in rational, scientific methods and the professional management of institutions. The development of technical knowledge, progressive reformers believed, could improve industrial efficiency and productivity if managers in the private and public sectors could use it smartly. Expertise was something to be celebrated, not feared. They created new institutions at the federal level, including the Federal Trade Commission and the Federal Reserve, which would become two of the central sites of market-craft in the decades to come.

I outline all of this prehistory because it gives some context for where this volume begins. This book picks up the story of American market-craft at the start of the Great Depression, with a focus on the man who created one of the most overlooked institutional innovations of the New Deal: an American national investment bank known as the Reconstruction Finance Corporation (RFC). The first three chapters examine how the RFC supported American finance and shaped housing and aviation markets in the 1930s and '40s. Chapters 4 and 5 tell the stories of two very different marketcrafters—a Fed Chair who created an orderly, liquid money market and a union organizer—who laid the groundwork for our byzantine health-care system in the 1950s and '60s. In the second section of the book, I tell the stories of three marketcrafters in the 1960s and '70s who fostered global financial interdependence, responding both success-fully and disastrously to twin energy crises, and figuring out how to fight inflation. The third section spans three decades, starting in the 1980s and ending in the Great Financial Crisis. These chapters reconsider the in-evitability of the Volcker shock and shine a light on Ronald Reagan–era industrial policy before tracing the work of marketcrafters to enhance fi-nancial innovation and efficiency. In the final section of the book, I take a different path. Over the course of five chapters, I chart the emergence of a new marketcraft, built on a commitment to public investment and competition policy. That story begins in the wake of the Great Financial Crisis and culminates with the economic programs of Donald Trump and Joe Biden. These later chapters are based on contemporary analysis and interviews I conducted rather than archival materials. In them, I illustrate how a growing cross-partisan consensus for shaping markets took hold. The conclusion considers what all this might mean for our future.

A foundational insight of this book is that marketcraft is not only a project of the American left. Half of the marketcrafters in these chapters were self-described conservatives, and several of them considered themselves libertar-ians. Conservatives and progressives alike have endeavored to make markets work for the common good, but they have often raucously disagreed on how to define that term. Frequently, but not always, conservatives and business-minded interests have preferred to organize markets for efficiency, prioritiz-ing financial innovation and unencumbered trade. Meanwhile, progressives have more often sought to use markets to ensure that essential goods, like health care, housing, or the technology to combat climate change, are both abundant and accessible.

In writing this book, I've had only one true enemy in mind: jargon. I have tried to minimize the world salad of highly technical language without sacrificing the rigor and thoughtfulness that comes with an academic inquiry. That said, I hope experts in history, economics, and political science can also engage with it. I've purposefully provided extensive endnotes as a method of encouraging further study and dialogue on any particular claim.

While I have not focused on the technical details of the tools of marketcraft, it is important to understand what they are at the start. These tools function as a kind of "vocabulary" for understanding how marketcrafters endeavored to accomplish their missions. They include public investment, competition and coordination policy, stockpiling and reserve management, government procurement, and taxation and subsidy. Regulation, by far the most often discussed activity of government economic management, is just one among a much broader set of tools through which policymakers organize markets.

This list is broad, and not all policies that affect markets add up to marketcraft, just as there are many geopolitical decisions taken that do not add up to statecraft. Marketcraft is active work by government officials to organize and manage markets toward a particular goal. Many well-known government programs with significant economic impact were not created to change our economy, even though they clearly have. For instance, since the 1950s, the Defense Advanced Research Projects Agency (DARPA) has supported risky research in support of American military power. It played a formative role in the development of the Internet, and many of its less well-known investments have had spillover effects, like voice recognition software, touchscreens, and global positioning systems. Yet this is not marketcraft. DARPA was not created with an economic mandate, and its leaders have not attempted to organize or manage a market for a political goal. A similar observation can be made for the National Institutes of Health, the National Science Foundation, and the National Aeronautics and Space Association. All have affected American markets, but none was constituted to point them in a certain direction. Similarly, roads, schools, and public safety forces all can affect market outcomes, but they are not created to guide markets toward particular ends.

Some government programs exist in a gray area. Are food stamps, unemployment insurance, and Social Security benefits guided by a humanitarian impulse to prevent destitution or to manage markets to be fairer and to stabilize aggregate demand? It's a bit of both. For the purposes of this book, I focus on efforts that are specifically about targeted, sectoral marketcraft. I've left a lot of marketcraft out—including the cultivation and coordination of defense contractors, the organization of telecommunications infrastructure, and direct investing by today's Energy Department in technologies to mitigate climate change. I have also skipped over the more subtle, quotidian elements of marketcraft. Agricultural subsidies, patent and copyright law, and the assignment of corporate liability in consumer technology are just a few examples. What is consistent throughout the stories I tell here is policymakers' intent to use state power to lead markets from the status quo toward a new configuration.

Some economists might squirm when reading this book. That's because I do not use the conceptual frameworks most common in the field. Neoclassical economic theory portrays markets as efficient systems powered by rational actors, guided by self interest, and operating in a world of scarcity, where every decision involves trade-offs. While some of these dynamics exist at times, any American who has recently bought a home, procured health insurance, or bought gas after an Organization of the Petroleum Exporting Countries (OPEC) production cut knows that the truth is more complicated. To be fair, economists have evolved in recent decades to incorporate insights about human behavior and take more seriously the study of undesirable side effects of markets, or "externalities." But this has not solved the fundamental problem that institutions come *after* markets in economic analysis. Even when centrist or left-leaning economists welcome government action, it tends to be in pursuit of managing consumer demand or compensating for market failures.[9] There is much to be said for these policies, but they offer us little help in thinking about why the cost of prescription drugs remains so high or why government keeps extending lifelines to banks and airlines in moments of crisis.

The foundational problem that economics struggles with—and this book hopes to change—is the inability to reckon with the role of institutions. To tell the story of the marketcrafters in this volume, I have chosen to lean on a lesser-known school of thought called institutional economics.

Popular in the earliest decades of the twentieth century, writers like Wesley Mitchell and John Commons revolutionized the field by focusing on empirical research. They believed that the world often didn't work the way a textbook full of graphs might imply, and only by studying the reality of market dynamics could an economy be understood or managed. Early institutionalist economists created the National Bureau of Economic Research and hatched the methodology to tabulate gross domestic product, a measurement of the size of the economy. Institutionalist economists believed that the size and function of corporations, the behavior of labor unions, and the role of government so deeply affected patterns of market activity that an economy could not be studied without taking them into account. In the first decades of the twentieth century, institutional economics dominated the field, but in the postwar years, the approach faded, overshadowed by the promise of Keynesian demand management and abstract, formal models driven by ever-increasing mathematical complexity. Only a smattering of development economists, usually focused on understanding the challenges of poorer countries, managed to carry the baton of institutional economics. They thought critically about how the state might steer an economy toward prosperity and stability. As interest in industrial policy surges today, the institutionalist outlook stands to make an important comeback. I hope this book can contribute to that resurgence.[10]

As an American, I've focused this volume on the history of the United States, but countries across the world share a similar approach. The French have a name for it—*dirigisme*—and the Japanese did it so successfully in the late twentieth century that many Americans worried the island nation would soon outpace us. In early fourteenth-century Venice, after bankers developed a system of credit, the state followed suit, issuing the first sovereign-backed bonds for military funding and internal projects. A few hundred years later, the joint stock companies of Amsterdam, chartered and managed by the state, powered Dutch trading routes across the globe. Economic development councils in England and France after the Second World War ushered in extensive cooperation between business and government.[11] A few decades later, East Asian economies such as Singapore and South Korea pursued policies to protect infant industries, provide domestic subsidies, and support close collaboration between government and business. Today many countries in Europe impose taxes on carbon and fund state investment banks to mitigate the effects of climate change. There is much to learn from all of these examples and to critique, but this volume focuses on the American experience.

At the risk of ruining the suspense, let me tell you where this book lands. Marketcraft can fail, or it can succeed. When it works best, it is usually because Congress invests a single institution with broad authority and discretion to accomplish a clear mission. That setup gives the marketcrafter the ability to build a team of experts—practitioners of a craft—who are responsive to market feedback and to the people charged with holding them accountable. This is a fundamentally Hamiltonian vision of a robust, empowered government that "is not the enemy of the private economy, but its sponsor and partner," as the historian Michael Lind has written.[12] Sorting out how to do that work effectively and fairly is often not clear, which is why the study of these historical contexts is so critical. But the good news for the marketcrafters of today is that there is a structure that works. We know what direction to head in, if we have the political will to do so.

Crises are particularly formative moments when Americans welcome state guidance of markets, as many of these stories illustrate. When we feel vulnerable, people move faster to line up behind a clear, short-term mission, despite their class, racial, and ideological divisions. We crave a stabilizing force to organize markets when they are in disarray. That commitment often falters when the crisis ebbs. Every now and then, we manage to build an institution in the wake of a crisis that endures. The Federal Reserve was created in the wake of the Panic of 1907, the worst financial crisis before the Great Depression. The Strategic Petroleum Reserve—a central reason we have not had a major energy crisis in decades—emerged from the crises of the 1970s. The CHIPS Program Office, the recent effort to spur semiconductor manufacture, emerged after a pandemic-induced chip shortage. One of the chief lessons of this volume should be that we need to build and fortify the institutions forged in crisis so that they can prevent future ones.

One of the most tragic facets of the stories in this volume is that we often undermine the success of our own institutions. More often than not, we have accepted a government of rules, but not of administrative expertise. Since the nation's founding, Americans have articulated a strong antistatist impulse when compared to other countries. Hamilton's rival Thomas Jefferson celebrated an agrarian republic made up of small farmers and merchants.

Working close to the land cultivated the virtues of hard work, self-sufficiency, and republican simplicity. Jeffersonians worried that the state was more likely to disrupt and harm this way of life than to support it. If farmers gave the government too much power, it might advocate for the freedom of slaves, the development of cities, and the advent of industry. Decentralizing power and setting up a multilayered federalist structure would limit the reach of the national government, ensuring that America would stay just as it was in the late eighteenth century. To be sure, this vision itself was marketcraft, a political effort to prioritize small farms over large companies, localized currencies over a national one, and the commodification of Black Americans. History would prove it profoundly regressive, but its legacy continues to drive an enduring suspicion of government power. Ironically, the enduring fear of a centralized government has given us more convoluted structures of bureaucracy and unnecessary waste, as we will see.

For some, the idea of marketcraft might sound too elite, intellectual, and detached from the lived experience of most Americans. Some activists and scholars, concerned that experts focused on technical policy work too easily lose touch with the concerns of everyday people, have argued for incorporating the "popular will" into the administration of government.[13] This is harder than it may seem. Injecting laypeople into complex, technical policy matters does not necessarily lead to better results. Giving local homeowners in suburbs more say in housing policy can restrain much-needed development, leading to higher prices and, in some cases, more segregated neighborhoods. A more democratic Federal Reserve could lead to chronically loose monetary policy, and a more participatory Federal Drug Administration (FDA) to premature drug approvals.

At the same time, blind trust in experts can lead to bad policy. Decisionmakers may lack critical information or insights. They may fall prey to "groupthink," avoiding the important process of wrestling with dissenting perspectives, and they can suffer from bias, blocking important ideas or people from consideration. We need accountability structures to ensure that the specialists at work in the quiet of a conference room remain responsive to human needs.[14] People elect representatives who create the institutions of marketcraft. Congress then hires the experts to pursue that work, with all three branches of government and civil society checking their power through ongoing action and oversight.

We have much to learn from our marketcrafting successes, but even more from our failures. History can be riveting to read for the simple pleasure of understanding the stories of the past, but this book is meant to provoke us to think about how public policy should work today and in the future. Understanding the history of American marketcraft can help policymakers, economists, politicians, and business leaders think about how to do it better moving forward.

To ensure the American economy serves the American people, we must guide its activity in the direction of what we imagine a prosperous future to be. This is an eminently conflict-ridden task, subject to the kind of messy political debates that democracy requires to develop a workable vision of the common good. But let's be clear. The real debate should not be a battle between pro-business and pro-government forces. It is about how to ensure that markets work for the common good—and what that entails.

AGE OF
THE NEW DEAL

1

"THE MARKET IS WHAT YOU MAKE IT"

JESSE JONES & THE RECONSTRUCTION
FINANCE CORPORATION (1932-37)

Early one morning in the fall of 1932, a fifty-eight-year-old Texan investor descended the limestone stairs of one of the buildings he owned on New York City's Upper East Side. Six feet three and dressed in a three-piece suit, the gray-haired Jesse Jones stooped into a waiting car and ordered the driver to head to Pennsylvania Station. They made excellent time. Three years into the Great Depression, millions of Americans were out of work and the city was eerily quiet, foreboding even.

Jones boarded a New York Central Railroad train, likely the express 20th Century Limited, and made his way to the luxury "parlor car." His destination was the state capital, Albany, three and a half hours away. There he would meet with New York Governor Franklin D. Roosevelt, whom the Democratic Party had just nominated as its presidential candidate. Roosevelt was running against Republican incumbent Herbert Hoover. Election Day was still three months away, but the deepening Depression had devastated Hoover's chances of reelection. It seemed very likely that Roosevelt would win. Confident but jittery, Jones knew that day he was likely meeting the next President of the United States. And he had a mission.[1]

The two outsized characters were no strangers. They had known each other for more than a decade. Back in 1924 they even worked in the same office in New York. Both men were wealthy and ambitious, and both men aspired to receive the affection and esteem of their peers. But there the similarities ended.

Jesse Jones was born in 1874 into a middle-class family of Tennessee tobacco farmers. He lost his mother to tuberculosis when he was six and dropped out of school after eighth grade. He would later boast that he read only one book in his life, a biography of Sam Houston, who shared Jones' Tennessee-to-Texas tangent.[2] He farmed the family's tobacco fields until his father died when Jones was eighteen.[3] Then he settled in Houston and began managing his extended family's money. An itinerant charmer with a keen eye for business, Jones helped propel Houston's explosive growth. At the age of twenty-eight, Jones had been living in Houston for only four years, but he had used that time to build a network of lumberyards and construction material shops. He had become a wealthy and popular bachelor. The Houston elite had begun a tradition a few years before called the Notsuoh Festival (flipping the word "Houston"), in which the town coronated a King Nottoc (flipping the word "cotton") as a celebration of civic pride. That year, the festival's organizers crowned Jones the festival's King, the highest honor. A photo from the celebration pictured Jones, in full regal dress with a pointy crown atop his head, surrounded by women and men, all playing at being eighteenth-century royalty.[4] By the age of thirty-three Jones was a millionaire.[5]

Jones had contributed generously to President Woodrow Wilson's 1912 election campaign, and Wilson asked him to join his cabinet in a newly created post: Secretary of Commerce. Jones declined, too focused on continuing to build his fortune. The Commerce job felt provisional, set up for failure. He did, however, move to Washington briefly during World War I to lead the American Red Cross relief effort. There he befriended Wilson and immersed himself in DC's clubby culture.

By the 1920s, Jesse Jones was one of America's wealthiest men. As a major Democratic donor, he attended the 1924 convention in New York, sitting in the booth next to Franklin Roosevelt. The party chair persuaded Jones to lead fundraising efforts for the Democratic presidential campaign that year of John Davis—a campaign that ended in electoral disaster. Four years later, Jones convinced party elders to host the Democratic convention in Houston, the first time any party convention had been held in Texas. At one point during the event, hundreds of balloons bearing the slogan "Jesse Jones for

President" accidentally floated down from the ceiling. The Texas delegates had nominated him for the top job, a reflection of their affection for him.

Houston soon proved too small for Jesse Jones, and he began to develop real estate interests outside of Texas, including several in New York. But he mistrusted the blue-blooded East Coast establishment. His frontier ways didn't fit in with the New York elite, and he blamed Wall Street's tight-money policies for disproportionately hurting the expansion of the South and West.[6]

Roosevelt, by contrast, was born into American aristocracy. Wealthy, confident, charming, schooled at Groton and Harvard, he built his political career by channeling the social capital his privilege bestowed on him. Focused on the presidency, he followed the course charted by his distant cousin former President Teddy Roosevelt to become Assistant Secretary of the Navy. But in 1921, when Roosevelt was thirty-nine, polio derailed his ambitions. He spent the rest of the decade physically recovering and getting his political career back on track. He succeeded. By 1928 he was elected Governor of New York, and four years later the Democratic Party nominated him as their presidential candidate. In an unprecedented move, Roosevelt accepted the nomination in person, flying to Chicago in the summer of 1932 to do so. On the brink of power, he promised a new kind of government. Exactly what that meant remained unclear.

So on that September morning, Jesse Jones brought one specific request to Albany: that Roosevelt support a new, fledgling federal institution, the Reconstruction Finance Corporation (RFC). Or at least, avoid impugning it in his presidential campaign. The previous January, President Hoover and Congressional leaders had created the RFC, a new, bank-like institution able to extend emergency credit to businesses teetering on the brink of bankruptcy and so prevent further collapse of otherwise-sound financial entities. Hoover's team modeled the RFC on the War Finance Corporation, which had provided emergency credit to American interests in World War I and continued to do so for a decade afterward, only shuttering in the late 1920s.[7] The RFC was its direct descendent, organized with the same eight divisions, the same thirty-three local offices spread out across the country, and several of the same senior staff.[8] The RFC might be able to show that the American state could shape financial markets to be more stable and prosperous, not just in times of war.

But that fall, the RFC was at risk of shutting down before it had even launched, and Jones had taken on the role of unlikely advocate. He had a history with the new institution. When private and public markets froze in the early years of the Depression, Jones had fewer moneymaking opportunities. While on a visit to Washington in early January 1932, he had discussed the idea of a national investment bank with several Congressmen who were working with the Hoover administration to assess how the idea might work.[9] Two weeks later, Congress passed legislation to create it, endowing the RFC with initial capital of $500 million provided by the Treasury, and the ability to lend up to $1.5 billion, about $690 billion in today's dollars.[10]

Hoover asked the Texan Speaker of the House, John Nance Garner, for a short list to fill the three Democratic seats on the board of the new RFC, and Nance handed him a piece of paper. It had only one name: Jesse Jones.[11] When Hoover called Jones to offer him the job, Jones accepted. He claimed later that he did it out of a sense of patriotism, but the market deep freeze likely influenced his decision. He knew so little about the position that he assumed it was part-time. When he realized that, by law, it required his full-time commitment, he rang his wife, Mary Gibbs Jones, who was still in Houston. "Pack your trunk and come on up," he told her. "I am stuck with a steady, 365-day-a-year job."[12]

Theirs was no ordinary marriage. The two had known each other since their twenties, but Mary Gibbs was then married to Jones' cousin. She divorced him at age forty-seven, after twenty-six years of marriage, and a year later married Jones. Given the social impropriety of their union, it was a hush-hush ceremony, held at home.[13] Now, more than a decade later, Mary made her way up to Washington, intending to persuade her husband to resign from the RFC. When he refused, she acquiesced and, in his words, "returned to Houston later, closed the home, had a good cry with the old Negro servants, and came back to Washington."[14]

Jones still had to figure out what his new job as a government banker entailed. His résumé was all in the private sector—real estate developer, newspaper and bank owner, and general investor. This was his first public service job. The only other RFC board member physically in Washington was Charles Dawes, who had formerly served as Vice President and US Ambassador to the Court of St James. The two of them went hunting for office space. They set off for the Treasury Building, intending to ask the Secretary for a room there. But on the way, Dawes had another idea. Thirty years earlier, he had been the Comptroller of the Currency, and he knew its offices well. The current Comptroller was away on business, so Dawes and Jones managed to convince his secretary to allow them to use his private office. They hauled in a second desk for Jones and pulled out the legislative text on the RFC to figure out what it was they were supposed to be doing. All they had to go on was the legislative rubric and Hoover's public statements about it.[15]

In a makeshift office, Jesse Jones embarked on what was to become for him a twelve-year odyssey to build the RFC into a national investment bank. Jones would oversee the investment of over $50 billion in public funds and profoundly alter America's financial foundations.[16]

Now, eight months since he first sat at that borrowed desk, Jones was on the train to Albany to see Roosevelt. In that time things had not gone well—not for Jones, and not for the RFC. Hoover had wanted the RFC to avoid helping large industrial organizations or banks. "Such institutions are amply able to take care of themselves," he said at its creation. The RFC "is created for the support of the smaller banks and financial institutions, and through rendering their resources liquid to give renewed support to business, industry, and agriculture."[17] Hoover's small-scale ambitions were typical of his approach to the Great Depression, and the RFC Directors found they had the tools to respond to larger emergencies.

At the RFC's very first meeting, the Directors approved a loan to Bank of America, one of the country's largest banks that was now teetering. Roosevelt, a newly declared presidential candidate, went on the attack. He used a national radio address, later known as "The Forgotten Man Speech," to thunder, "The two-billion-dollar fund which President Hoover and the Congress have put at the disposal of the big banks, the railroads and the corporations of the Nation is not for him." Him being the little man, the common man, the forgotten man.[18] The early Roosevelt brain trust had little interest in using public dollars to backstop large financial institutions, and Roosevelt himself was skeptical.[19]

The RFC's problems didn't end there. Unexpectedly few wanted to borrow its money. Banks, in particular, avoided borrowing from it for fear of the stigma. Any sign of distress for a bank risked provoking a panic. And the ones who were willing to borrow had to surmount stringent lending standards. Field offices could only approve loans up to $100,000. Anything more needed to be vetted by the Directors in DC, who were anxious not to set a bad precedent by lending to any banks or railroads at risk of not repaying. One of the few big loans the RFC did make went to a major Chicago bank, the Central Republic Bank and Trust, which had been founded years before by RFC President Charles Dawes. When it threatened to collapse, Dawes resigned from the RFC and rushed to Chicago to run the ailing institution. To prevent a panic among other Chicago banks, the RFC decided to extend emergency credit to Central Republic Bank and Trust. It was a bad look: propping up a major Chicago bank run by a former board member, at a time when Chicago's teachers were going unpaid. To make matters worse, the RFC had extended a loan to the struggling Missouri-Pacific Railroad, which simply used the money to pay back its creditor, J.P. Morgan. That made it look like the RFC was lining the pockets of America's wealthiest. These early missteps made the RFC a tempting target for further Roosevelt attacks.[20]

Though he hadn't supported all of these specific loans, Jones had become committed to the RFC as an institution. His goal on this trip to Albany was to persuade the future President to reform, rather than abolish, the RFC. In these hopes, Jones was not alone. After the Chicago drama, financiers quietly welcomed the RFC's support of distressed banks. They did not necessarily want to lend to borrowers, but they welcomed recapitalization for teetering banks. Jones believed government support would restore the confidence of banks and thus spur the new lending that American businesses needed. He believed in the power of the state to make markets work better. Unlike the good ol' boys of the antebellum South who distrusted most federal institutions, Jones was a businessman from the frontier, open to state action and marrying the power of private industry with public direction. In the early 1910s when he had yet to turn forty, Jones had used his status and charm to harness both business and government. He had collaborated with other Houston businessmen to drain the bayou and create the fifty-mile-long Houston Ship Channel. It was a vast project. Private business interests pooled their funds to pay half the construction cost and Jones convinced the federal government to pay the other half. He didn't just make the deal; he followed through to chair the Houston Harbor Board, which implemented it.[21] Completed in 1914, the Channel attracted dozens of new industries to

Houston. This development would not have been possible without government help. "Private industry and the common carriers, by land and water, will invest sums here compared with which our own public investment will appear infinitesimal," he said in a speech describing the effort, several years later. He was right. Within decades, Houston had become the nation's second-largest port by tonnage, boosting the fortunes of both the city and Jones himself.[22]

Two decades later, he used a similar strategy to organize fellow bankers to set up an emergency fund to rescue a failing Houston bank. Jones understood that panic prevention, like infrastructure building, required a leader to convince investors to take on excessive risk collectively, minimizing the chance of loss. The RFC, with its deep pocketbook and network, could support shaky institutions in a similar fashion and prevent the Depression from worsening. Now he just needed to convince the future President of the United States that he was right.

When he arrived at Union Station in Albany, Jones made his way to a grand Italianate house, built by a banker a half century before the state of New York bought it and turned it into the Governor's Executive Mansion. To exercise his polio-withered leg, Roosevelt had recently installed a swimming pool in the backyard.

After their greetings, Jones began to make his case, asking Roosevelt to lay off the RFC on the campaign trail: "I took with me to Albany a list of all applications for loans covering a period of weeks, and showed him that, instead of the Corporation being reproached for loans it was making, it could be more appropriately upbraided for not making loans. I knew we were not doing enough." Roosevelt seemed swayed, Jones reported, and agreed to avoid attacking the RFC. Jones left nothing to chance. A few weeks later, he heard that Roosevelt was preparing to criticize the RFC for making large loans to railroads, just to serve the interests of bankers. Jones made a second trip to dissuade him, this time to the President's private estate in Hyde Park. He seemed successful again, as Roosevelt held his fire.[23] After the election Jones intercepted Roosevelt's train back from a Florida vacation, just days after an assassin had attempted to take Roosevelt's life. "Will join you at Savannah," Jones telegraphed the President-elect. "Don't forget to stop."[24] Neither Roosevelt nor Jones could have known that the nature of how American

markets worked now hung in the balance, depending on what the RFC did
next.

Over the following twenty years, the RFC would reshape the relationship between government and markets in the United States, offering a clear
example of how centralized, independent, national authority can shape markets to make them work better. After strengthening the financial and business
backbone of the country in the early years of the Depression, the RFC went
further, creating new markets from scratch and providing investment capital
to support the industries critical to winning World War II. Its marketcrafting
power was to become so great that the press would dub it the "fourth branch
of government." Such success would also make it a prime target for postwar
abolition. But back in 1932, when the RFC was still dangling by a filament, a
serendipitous nationwide bank shutdown created the space for it to become
a bigger, bolder institution.

On Inauguration Day in March 1933, Roosevelt awoke in room 776 of the
Mayflower Hotel, with a view across the street of the White House, his new
home. The plans for the day followed in the tradition of presidential inaugu-
rations: a morning church service, the oath of office at noon, a parade along
Pennsylvania Avenue, and celebrations in the evening. But this Inauguration
Day was to prove quite different.

While Roosevelt had been sleeping, his successor as Governor of New
York had joined with the Governor of Illinois to declare bank "holidays" in
both states, shuttering the two major centers of the nation's banking system.
Just weeks before, a panic that started in Detroit had spread nationwide as
Americans, lacking deposit insurance, rushed to withdraw their funds, fearful
that their own banks might be the next to fail. This was just the latest chapter in the rolling banking crisis of the Great Depression. Between January
1930 and Inauguration Day, more than 5,500 banks had closed or merged
with stronger ones. Now the markets were going from bad to worse. The
New York Stock Exchange and Chicago Board of Trade suspended trading
altogether, effectively closing down American financial markets. Political and
financial leaders had little option but to shut down banks while they waited
to see what the Roosevelt administration might do.[25]

Roosevelt had plans. The day before the inauguration, he had met with
his advisers and Fed officials to develop a proclamation to close all the banks,

which was likely a legal overreach. On Inauguration Day, after the church service, Roosevelt rushed back to the Mayflower to confer again with his advisers on the deteriorating financial situation. In the lead-up to his inauguration, Roosevelt had spoken of the need for "action, action," and now he was ready to take it.[26] At 1:00 am on Monday, March 6, he issued Proclamation 2039, declaring a national banking holiday and closing all American banks for a week. A team of outgoing Hoover advisers and incoming Roosevelt officials worked together, round the clock, to create a structure for shoring up the banks during the holiday and then reopening them. The men had "forgotten to be Republicans or Democrats," Raymond Moley, a close Roosevelt adviser, later recalled. "We were just a bunch of men trying to save the banking system."[27]

The plan they devised would unfold gradually. First, bank supervisors would fan out across the country to inspect the books of as many banks as possible. Second, government officials would reopen solvent banks, in order of their importance to the financial system. Third and perhaps most critically, the RFC would be given the authority to buy equity in banks, handing the institution the power to become the nation's single largest investor in, and owner of, American banks. It would all happen in a matter of days. The aim was a stable restart, after which banks could not fail en masse. They would be more reliable and, if they wobbled, the RFC could invest capital in them directly, even taking a controlling interest if necessary. The RFC would no longer just be in the business of lending to shaky banks. It was now in the business of *owning* them. Such a dramatic and extensive move was unprecedented in the history of American capitalism.[28]

By Thursday, Roosevelt's team had drafted a bill authorizing the powers necessary to carry out the rescue and rehabilitation plan. Within hours of its introduction in Congress, both chambers passed it. The following Sunday, before the banks began to reopen, Roosevelt broadcast his first fireside chat by radio to the nation, explaining the inspections and the gradual bank-reopening schedule. Because of the government's efforts, "no sound bank is a dollar worse off than it was when it closed its doors last Monday," Roosevelt assured the American people.[29] American depositors had heard a new President assure them of the soundness of financial institutions by explaining a thorough plan for remaking the foundation of banking. Roosevelt's efforts worked. As banks reopened, deposits flooded back into the system.[30]

✿

Like most Americans, Jones was relieved. Since the previous summer he had
been asking Hoover to expand the borrowing capacity of the RFC and "turn
it loose" and received no response.[31] Hoover, like many Republicans, feared
excessive "intervention" in markets, believing that if the government provided a lifeline to failing businesses, it would create zombie companies that
should have been destroyed by the discipline of capitalism. Jones, however,
was more pragmatic, believing that the depth of the emergency required expansive policy moves that would restore confidence in the institutions of finance. Only the government could do that. In the last months of the Hoover
administration, even Republicans were coming around to the importance of
dramatic RFC action, including direct ownership of private bank stock. It
would provide banks with capital funds, helping them to meet withdrawal
demands and shoring up investors' confidence in their viability. Their earlier
allergy to government ownership of banks evaporated in the face of rolling
shutdowns and growing panic.[32] Now that Congress had authorized the action, the RFC's primary mission was to ensure that the nation's reopening
banks had the cash they needed—to avoid another panic, at any cost.

Jesse Jones was ready to transform the RFC from a defensive institution
responding to occasional bank failures to a national investment bank responsible for shoring up American banking and finance—a new marketcraft. In
the weeks after his inauguration, Roosevelt appointed Jones Chairman of the
RFC, elevating him from the position of influential board member to the
leader of the institution. That position offered him the chance to grow his
power, and he began the work of growing the RFC into a pivotal institution
of the New Deal with great flexibility and power—and into his own personal fiefdom. From the start, his genuine interest in righting the American
economy was often overshadowed by his personal thirst for admiration and
respect. "Quick to judge and slow to forgive, Jones gave no mercy to his opponents and no end of support to his friends, and he jealously guarded RFC
prerogatives," the historian James Stuart Olson wrote.[33] As long as he was
in charge, the RFC would be sure to flourish. What came after was of little
concern to him.

For now that worked just fine for his boss, Roosevelt. At the start of his
presidency, he was unconvinced of the need for a robust, powerful RFC, but
he did want Jones—with all his private-sector credentials—to be a happy

warrior in his unabashedly progressive administration. Jones stood ready to appease business critics of the New Deal whenever the President needed. A bonus was Jones' influence over the rebellious and often-skeptical Texas delegation of the Democratic Party, which included Roosevelt's own Vice President, John Nance Garner.[34] Their respective personal and political needs cemented the Roosevelt-Jones alliance. The RFC would be the principal beneficiary, at least until their relationship collapsed.

In early 1933, even though Roosevelt and Jones had stemmed the initial banking panic, Jones' problems were compounding. Railroads and farmers were still teetering on the edge of bankruptcy, and the banks that should have been extending credit to them were refusing to take the RFC's equity investments. They feared even partial government ownership, even though they were close to insolvency. In June, Congress passed federal deposit insurance, a safety net for bank depositors, protecting their funds in case of bank failure, which was meant to eliminate banking panics altogether. Roosevelt had feared such a sweeping program, anxious that it might create more risk. Congressional leaders enthusiastically favored it, and Roosevelt eventually acquiesced. For a bank to qualify for the insurance, it had to be certified as solvent by the Treasury by January 1, 1934. More than half of American banks needed capital infusions to solidify their cash positions to pass this stress test.

Now that banks had a deadline to get into shape, Jones saw his opportunity. In September, he traveled to Chicago to address the American Bankers Association. He was in enemy territory; several prominent national bankers had lobbied for his removal from the RFC chairmanship earlier in the fall. Jones used the opportunity to be direct. "Be smart for once," he told the bankers. "Take the government into partnership with you in providing credit which the country is sadly in need of."[35] The speech fell flat, and the bankers felt lectured to by an entitled Jones. A few hours later, after the customary bankers' dinner, Eugene Black, a member of the Federal Reserve Board, invited Jones back to the podium to modify his remarks. He agreed to come up, saying that he knew how much the bankers hadn't liked his earlier remarks. But once at the podium, Jones doubled down. "Half the banks in this room are insolvent," he warned, "and those of you representing these banks know it better than anyone else."[36] His message was clear: take our money or crumble.

Within days, National City Bank (the precursor to Citibank) sold $50 million of preferred stock to the RFC. Chase National followed, and the dam began to break. Bank executives knew that the need was pronounced across the finance industry and that any stigma of taking government funds would soon be shared. No one wanted government ownership, but they needed certification to qualify for deposit insurance, putting them in a bind that only Jones could help them get out of. Applications poured in, and the RFC invested over $300 million across hundreds of banks.

Three days before the deposit insurance certification deadline, Jones convinced Treasury Secretary Henry Morgenthau to certify virtually every bank, providing them all with deposit insurance. In exchange, over the following six months, through loans and investments, the RFC took on the responsibility of capitalizing any viable bank that was still short of the mark. By September 1934, the RFC was a partial owner of half the country's banks, having invested over $1 billion, or $478 billion in today's dollars. (For comparison, the entire size of the government's 2008 investment in American banks was $250 billion in today's dollars.)[37] The RFC would normally buy an amount of preferred stock that matched the outstanding common stock, doubling the bank's capital and giving the RFC the controlling interest.[38] Jones himself professed to having "no desire to control or manage the banks," although he didn't mind occasionally lowering exorbitant salaries or influencing bank leadership decisions.[39] The banks, increasingly well capitalized and now federally insured, saw their deposits continue to return. They grew by nearly 20 percent since the emergency banking shutdown, even though national economic growth was anemic. The banking crisis of the Great Depression was over. Disaster had been averted.

It was not the Federal Reserve or the nation's banking regulators who had saved the day. It was Jesse Jones and the RFC, working in collaboration with the Treasury and the new deposit insurance system. Jones had used the power Congress had invested in the RFC to capitalize banks, breaking the boundaries of state ownership to craft a market for stability.

In its twenty years of existence, the RFC had three distinct lives. Its first, defined by the banking holiday and its aftermath, was its most conservative. Between 1932 and early 1938, Congress restricted the RFC mandate to the conservative goals of stabilization and support. Jones and Roosevelt hewed to the traditional belief that government should assist commercial banks in the private allocation of credit—but not invest directly in nonfinancial businesses itself. This belief was grounded in the view that banks had a unique and pivotal role in the functioning of an economy. Their expertise in separating a promising business loan from a lackluster one would help the economy more efficiently allocate its resources, powering growth. Banks had to function for the economy to grow. The RFC's mission, in this first phase, was to reinforce the pre-Depression market order, rather than create a new one.

This conservative tack reflected Jones' own values. He described himself as a fiscal conservative, opposed to "wasting" government money and wary of any nonemergency government action to shape markets.[40] Fellow New Dealers often criticized Jones' innate conservatism. "[A] man of narrow business values, a haggler over pennies, and an apostle of the status quo," one former RFC employee wrote.[41] Jones' insistence that the RFC should not lose money was indicative of this narrow thinking. He agreed with his colleagues, like the Secretary of the Treasury, Henry Morgenthau, and the President himself, that they should avoid running up government deficits. The initial mandate in the first phase of the RFC was to use government's marketcrafting power to reinforce the existing market order, not reinvent it.

As the Depression deepened in the summer of 1933, Jones began to use the RFC's power to bring stability to nonfinancial markets. Farmers struggled to keep themselves afloat, given the collapse in demand for their products. Secretary of Agriculture Henry Wallace proposed a drastic idea to help some of those struggling farmers: the mass slaughter of 6 million pigs and the deliberate destruction of 10 million acres of cotton.[42] The idea was as shocking as it was heart-wrenching. Livestock farmers would kill healthy animals and dump their carcasses in mass graves. Arable farmers would be paid to plow under every third row in their fields, leaving the crops to rot beneath the summer sun. Haunted by the specter of poverty and the desperate pleas of struggling farmers, Wallace saw this sacrifice as an unavoidable evil. By reducing the supply of agricultural products, he hoped to drive up prices and provide support to farming families. The farmers themselves were shocked, but many reluctantly accepted. It did little good. Hog prices recovered modestly, and cotton prices continued to plunge.

Jones and Roosevelt, their rapport deepening as the banking crisis ebbed, now conspired to develop a different kind of program to help farmers. The model Jones suggested was based on an old idea in agricultural markets: collective stockpiling to buffer sharp rises and falls in the prices of commodities. American farmers had been struggling well before the Depression, and Hoover's first act as President had been to create government-sponsored "stabilization corporations" to buy and hold crop surpluses in periods of glut, waiting to sell until prices had recovered.[43] The program was modestly funded and decentralized, lacking the heft to make a real difference. Jones saw promise in the idea but knew it needed a strong national authority to work. He and Roosevelt worked out a plan: "One afternoon in 1933, President Roosevelt called me to the White House and, as soon as I entered his office, said: 'Jess, I want you to lend 10 cents a pound on cotton.'"[44] They had been working on a structure for an RFC-managed price stabilization program, one that launched in October, called the Commodity Credit Corporation (CCC).[45] "Before we had finished helping the farmer, the job had become second only to our bank rescue program. We loaned money to millions of farmers. We raised the price of farm commodities and came out ahead on the books," Jones later wrote.[46]

The plan did not directly subsidize farmers, nor did it require the kind of wholesale crop destruction Wallace had tried. Instead, the RFC worked with farmers and wholesalers to buffer market prices, guaranteeing a floor price to help farmers in the most challenging of years and selling into the market to manage a ceiling price. A farmer with cotton, corn, or wheat to sell now had the option of going to his normal bank or warehouse facility and pledging his crop for a low-interest loan at a guaranteed price. The CCC underwrote the process by committing to buy these loans from the banks.

For cotton in 1934, the government lent at twelve cents a pound, a few cents higher than the market price. The bank in turn sold the loan on to the CCC. A year into the program, farmers tendered 4.5 million bales in exchange for $1.2 million in loans, $493 million in today's dollars. So much cotton was tendered that the warehouses became brokers in the cotton market, selling the cotton on behalf of the farmers as prices floated above the twelve-cent floor. By 1935, the government had lowered its price to ten cents a pound, but the market price was clearing at twelve and higher, enabling the government to sell off its stocks. The CCC pursued a similar strategy with corn, buying in the early years of the Depression. When a calamitous drought struck in 1936, the surplus corn from previous years, which had been stored on farmers' properties rather than rotting unsold in frozen markets,

was put to use: "[M]any farmers simply reacquired their own corn by paying their notes, then took it from the unsealed cribs to feed their livestock,
or to sell to their neighbors."[47] The CCC pursued similar price stabilization
efforts for wheat, butter, and several other products, such as pecans in Georgia, prunes and grapes in California, and hops in Washington.[48] The RFC
was using multiple financial strategies—extending credit, stockpiling, and
buying and selling itself—to buffer farmers' finances from the gyrations of
the market. Eventually, Congress moved these operations from the RFC to
the Department of Agriculture, where the CCC continues today as a wholly
owned government corporation.

In addition to banking and agriculture, the RFC stepped in to support
railroads, which, like farmers, had been in major trouble even before the
Depression. Passenger revenue and the number of cars in service peaked in
the years after World War I and then declined with the rapid rise of automobiles and trucking. When the Depression hit, the bottom fell out. Freight
train revenues fell by nearly 50 percent between 1929 and 1932, and passenger revenues were down even more.[49] By 1934, 70 percent of the nation's
largest railroads were running at a loss.[50] The precarious financial position
of the railroads threatened the stability of other institutions, like banks, insurance companies, and private endowments that held nearly 70 percent of
outstanding railroad debt.[51] Investors had long considered railroad bonds
some of the most reliable, fueling these companies to acquire them as an-
chors in their portfolio. If railroads began to default en masse, the stability
of the financial system that Jones and his team were working so hard to restore would teeter. By 1933, Congress began implementing a rescue plan to
consolidate the rail lines. By suspending antitrust rules for railroad interests,
they hoped to minimize losses and bankruptcies.

Even with those moves, the Roosevelt administration needed the RFC's
help to address the railroad challenges given their depth and importance.
Initially, the RFC offered the companies short-term loans, but given the size
of the losses, that did little to stabilize the industry. Extending larger, long-
term loans ran the risk of lining the pockets of banks and other companies,
effectively moving money from the government to the wealthiest Americans
via the railroads. So Jones and the RFC began to work with railroads to refinance and restructure their debt, often by using the RFC's size and power to
force existing investors to take on more risk. The Great Northern railroad,

for example, had been paying 7 percent on a $115 million bond issue for over a decade and needed to roll over its obligation into new debt. Wall Street banks were offering to take it at 5 percent with an underwriting fee. Jones announced that the RFC would buy any unsold bonds at 4 percent with no charge, using the institution's size to shift the market. The banks capitulated, and the Great Northern sold the entirety of the $115 million to the public at 4 percent, without the RFC having to put a single dollar of capital at risk.[52] In some cases, the RFC was even more hands-on, buying up much of the debt of the Baltimore and Ohio (B&O) line and managing the railroad's finances to prevent bankruptcy until the 1940s when its financial position recovered.[53]

"The market is what you make it," Jones told Henry Morgan, the co-founder of Morgan Stanley.[54] Jones had embraced government's power to guide markets toward stability, strengthening bankers, farmers, and railroads to ensure the enduring functioning of capitalism. This was marketcraft—intentional use of state power to shape markets toward the political goal of stability. The alternative—cascading bankruptcies in the banking, agricultural, and railroad sectors—was out of the question. The state could stabilize these markets without suffocating the profit-seeking impulse of early twentieth-century capitalism. The Texan businessman continued to embrace supply and demand, but he believed the government must use its power to stabilize those markets.

Two years into Roosevelt's presidency, other New Deal institutions such as the National Recovery Administration and Public Works Administration began to wither, under assault in the courts and lacking clear early successes. Not the RFC. It stood out as an independent and powerful force for shaping markets to be more stable and prosperous.[55] Banks and farmers alike were on firmer financial footing. Railroads, while still challenged, were no longer hemorrhaging cash. By the end of 1935, the RFC had disbursed over $5.5 billion (about $74 billion in today's dollars) averaging about $1.4 billion a year. But as the RFC's power and influence grew, so did Jones' personal problems.

Three years after taking the train to Albany to ask Governor Roosevelt for help, Jones was now one of the most powerful men in the American government. With much of the New Deal under assault, Roosevelt, sitting in the White House, needed Jones and the RFC more than either man had anticipated years earlier. But both men still didn't understand the potential of the institution they had created. It would take another recession and world war to make that clear.

2

KING NOTTOC OF WASHINGTON

JESSE JONES & HOUSING MARKETS (1932–37)

Thirty years after being crowned King Nottoc of Houston, Jesse Jones claimed a new throne of sorts. This time, his domain was Washington, and instead of a cape and crown, his admirers entrusted him with billions to invest. The combination of his down-home bonhomie and wide discretion to use RFC funds made Jones enormously popular, particularly on Capitol Hill. Congressmen and Senators queued for an audience with Jones, soliciting RFC funds for projects in their home districts and states. Securing RFC funding did not require new legislation, and it didn't show up as an increase in appropriations, making it an almost magical source of funding. Given the loyalty of the board to its leader, all a Congressman or a Senator had to do to unlock the RFC treasure chest was to convince Jesse.[1]

Jones enjoyed the attention and loved the negotiations. His friend John Nance Garner, the former House Speaker and now the Vice President, invited Jones to use the vice-presidential office in the Capitol. Garner had been an influential Congressman, but now as Vice President, his power had been reduced. Many days, he hobnobbed in Congress, where he smoked cigars nonstop and claimed to be "living a good Christian life." He once bragged, "I don't get drunk but once a day."[2] Jones too enjoyed a snifter of fine whiskey and often paired it with a congenial game of poker, or occasionally bridge. In Garner's Capitol office, Jones would cajole and carouse with members, sharing off-color jokes and wrangling them to his side on any pending legislation that affected the RFC.[3] Garner said, "I guess it's our office. Jones uses it as much as I do."[4]

His jokes could be raunchy and off-putting, particularly to people of color and women. "He was a great big overpowering Texas man," the wife of a prominent RFC employee said. "He told nasty jokes. You know that kind of dirty jokes I feel like are so offensive to women, that make women the butt of [them]."[5] At one point, he sent the President a written copy of a joke that used a particularly offensive racial slur.[6] Members of Congress, almost all male and White, didn't seem to mind. They all wanted a slice of his largesse, and many ended up in his debt. Jones was adept at using this credit in service of expanding the size and scope of the RFC—and his own power.[7]

Over the course of the 1930s, the RFC swelled in size, fueled by recurring Congressional renewals and expansions of its mandate. By 1938, Congress had invested it with the authority to buy the debt or equity not just of banks, railroads, and agriculture, but of any business. But all this success didn't just create new friends for Jones; it made him enemies, on both the left and right. Agriculture Secretary and future Vice President Henry Wallace became an enduring antagonist, competing with Jones for authority and power, initially over agricultural issues and later in the preparation for World War II. Jones regularly antagonized lefty New Dealers who wanted an even more robust role for the state, including Rex Tugwell, Frances Perkins, and Adolf Berle. He called them "the free-spending, Santa Claus school of government reformers."[8] Jones insisted on making profitable investments, which made it harder for the RFC to support growth industries that were riskier or needed more time to develop. As one profiler put it, "To New Dealers, Jesse's insistence on maintaining the RFC's profit is heresy. To Jones, the profit is the line of credit on which the House of Jesse rests."[9]

On the right, the Treasury Secretary and close Roosevelt pal Henry Morgenthau—the most fiscally conservative member of the administration—pressed to abolish the RFC altogether, fearing its power would undermine private entrepreneurship. In 1933 Eugene Meyer, Jones' predecessor as RFC Chair, bought the *Washington Post* and used its pages to amplify the business-minded critique of Jones as a leader of "state capitalism," a description Jones reviled. Jones saw the RFC's interventions as making existing markets work better, with government enhancing their function in a moment of extreme duress. It was not the kind of robust planning effort that his critics on the left advocated, and Morgenthau knew better.

Yet by 1937, the biggest of Jones' problems did not come from these critics, nor did it come from the RFC's balance sheet. Depending on the accounting techniques used to evaluate it, the RFC could have been considered profitable. Almost across the board, RFC businesses were paying back the funds that had been loaned or invested in them, keeping overall RFC finances in the black. Instead, Jones' biggest problem was that while the RFC had saved many existing businesses, it had failed to spur economic growth. Policymakers, bankers, and the media applauded Jones and his team for preventing the systemic breakdown of American capitalism, which had been a real risk in the dismal winter of 1933. The RFC had spent five years strengthening the economy as it was—restoring the status quo ante—but it had not tried to reorganize or craft the economy anew. It had been a firefighter, not an architect. That was about to change.

A year after Roosevelt's reelection, some of the more progressive voices in Roosevelt's administration wanted to expand the first term's agenda to encourage economic expansion and reduce unemployment. American output in 1937 had only just edged above its 1929 level, and though unemployment had drifted downward, it remained stubbornly at 9 percent.[10] Jones did not believe that the RFC was the right New Deal institution to create active stimulus, and he was unsure if more was needed at all. Private industry should bear the burden of investment, since it was not the government's role to directly stimulate economic activity, he believed. Supporting otherwise-profitable businesses that had hit a rough patch did not challenge Jones' economic orthodoxy but selecting specific markets to nurture or directly investing in nonfinancial enterprises seemed like a different matter altogether.

When green shoots of economic growth appeared in 1936 and 1937, RFC loan volume began to taper. Jones was not initially bothered by the institution's fading influence. "I am not one who favors government in business, but when business runs amok, and private credit is no longer available, the government must step in. I favor the withdrawal of all these agencies, as soon as private enterprise is prepared to take up their work, and to furnish credit and work, for those who must have credit and work."[11] Even though the RFC had become the single largest investor in the United States, Jones wanted to pause its lending activity, believing that the economic recovery had

finally arrived. In the summer of 1936, he wrote to Adolf Berle, a left-leaning
New Dealer, explaining that the RFC was slowing down and he was fine with
that: "[T]here are no more emergencies, and the fewer things we do the better, perhaps. The record is good now."[12]

Roosevelt felt similarly. The previous fall, Roosevelt had won reelection
on a populist message. He told a crowd in New York's Madison Square Garden, "[N]ever before in all our history have [business] forces been so united
against one candidate as they stand today. They are unanimous in their hate
for me—and I welcome their hatred." The crowd erupted in applause, and
Roosevelt continued in a confident, vengeful tone. "I should like to have
it said of my first Administration that in it the forces of selfishness and of
lust for power met their match. I should like to have it said . . ." When the
crowd interrupted him with cheers, he implored them to let him conclude
his thought. "Wait a moment! . . . I should like to have it said of my second
Administration that in it, these forces met their master."[13] He won a resounding reelection, carrying every state in the nation but Vermont and Maine.

Roosevelt may have used the enmity of business and financial leaders to
win reelection, but within months of his second inauguration, he shifted back
toward Jones and the more conservative voices in his administration. With a
tepid economic recovery taking hold, Roosevelt wanted his government to
reduce government expenditures. In 1937, he moved to balance the federal
budget by reining in spending and raising taxes. Congress and the administration cut spending on public works and relief at the same moment that new
payroll taxes were levied to support the emerging Social Security program.
The Federal Reserve, anxious to return to a more normal financial environment, started tightening monetary policy in the fall of 1936. These moves
sent interest rates up and made it harder for businesses to borrow.

Even so, Roosevelt charged forward. In October of 1937, he wrote Jones,
instructing him to cease any further lending through the RFC.[14] The press
called it the "long-sought triumph by Secretary Henry Morgenthau over
RFC chairman Jesse Jones." But Jones did not seem to mind. A week before
the President's directive, he told bankers that "it is our purpose to discon-
tinue general lending for the very good reason that there is enough available
private credit to meet legitimate demands for all purposes. . . . Our country
has seldom been more prosperous."[15]

The combination of the actions of Roosevelt, Jones, and the Federal

Reserve plunged the American economy straight back into an avoidable recession. Unemployment, which had dipped below 10 percent for the first
time in seven years, was already increasing when Roosevelt instructed Jones
to stop lending. Now that the economy had begun to sputter once more,
many in Washington began to believe that restoring 1920s capitalism would
not be enough to encourage long-term, equitable prosperity. The more progressive New Dealer Adolf Berle, for one, could see what a terrible mistake
the retrenchment had been. "I wish the R.F.C. were staying in business," he
wrote in his diary. "The President put it out of business yesterday morning at just about the time when we need it most. The insane jealousy which
[Treasury Secretary Henry] Morgenthau has for Jesse Jones is at least partly
responsible—and not creditable."[16]

Berle's wish soon came true. Six weeks after his shutdown letter, Roosevelt confidentially asked Jones to restart lending to industrial firms if the
projects committed to hiring a lot of workers.[17] The limited, private decision
illustrated the President's growing concern that he had gone too far and had
undermined the very recovery that he'd spent the last five years chasing. Two
months later, in February 1938, the President publicly backtracked when he
reauthorized RFC lending. All of the nation's economic indicators were now
flashing red, and Roosevelt needed Jesse Jones to ignite the engines of economic growth.

The phoenix of the RFC rose from the ashes. Within hours, it notified
banks that it was back in business, ready to lend.[18] It had $1.5 billion of cash
on hand and was able to move fast. But it was now clear to Jones, Roosevelt,
and even the most conservative New Dealers that what the RFC had done
in the past would not cut it in the future. The new RFC would have to go
beyond salvaging teetering institutions. The goal of its marketcraft in this
second phase would change: it would have to foster and cultivate new markets to spur growth. The near death of the institution was a catalyst for its
new life, with a bigger, broader mandate: the RFC as a national investment
bank. Its second life was about to begin.

Jones and Roosevelt knew where they wanted to start when they brought
the RFC back to life in February 1938: housing construction. Jones, who
had made much of his fortune in real estate, had a personal appreciation for
the outsized role that residential home construction played in the American

economy. It helped that economists and politicians alike had now developed a consensus that, to create jobs, government would have the highest impact if it focused on supporting housing construction. The basis for their belief that no market could spur growth as powerfully traced back to the decades just prior to the Depression.[19]

In the years before the Depression struck, Americans had seen a housing bonanza, and nowhere was the boom as pronounced as it was in southern Florida. In the 1910s and 1920s, a wave of developers rushed to buy up land and create cities out of nothing. One entrepreneur, marketing maven and stuntman Carl Fisher, came to Miami in 1910 to pursue a new idea: transform the swampy sandbar of a barrier island that separated Biscayne Bay from the Atlantic into something habitable, even desirable. His major problem was not the hundreds of alligators or thousands of rats. It was the rattlesnakes. Before he could mow down the thick mangrove groves that proliferated around the island, he had to kill them all. "When you kill one, tie it to a stake, and another one will be coiled there the next morning," his friend reminded him.[20] After months of effort, Fisher had managed to thin the snake population enough to start building. He soon reaped the rewards. In the decade that followed, homebuyers poured in, buying up lots not only in Miami Beach, but all across Florida.

Before the Great Depression, Americans had bought homes in record numbers, particularly in states like Florida. The flood of homebuyers in that state alone in the 1920s demolished the records of the last biggest American land rush in California in the mid-nineteenth century. By 1925, one writer estimated that 4,000 people entered Florida by car each day and over 3,000 by train and ship. In total, some 2.5 million entered the state that year alone.[21] Not all would become permanent residents, but many wanted to buy homes. Developers like Fisher were more than happy to oblige. On one occasion in Miami, buyers literally threw checks at a builder, who rushed to collect them and stuff them in barrels.[22]

The rash of home buying did not happen just in Florida, even though the burgeoning bubble was most pronounced there. Between 1922 and 1929, nearly 800,000 new homes were built each year across America, well over twice the amount of the preceding decade, with a particular prominence in the rapidly growing suburbs that hugged cities.[23] Economic growth, expanded access to credit, and government policies like the new opportunity to deduct the interest expense from a mortgage from federal tax liability fueled the wave of home buying. Most Americans still bought their homes in cash, as mortgages required high down payments, often topping 30 percent, and came with short, five- to ten-year durations. Despite their difficult structure, mortgages tripled in volume over the course of the 1920s as Americans got used to buying their homes on credit. All those purchases fueled a historic rise in construction jobs.

The start of the Great Depression put a swift stop to the home-buying trend—and the jobs it created. In Florida, the market had slowed a few years earlier, thanks to mania-like price inflation, jammed transit, and a disastrous hurricane. By 1933, housing starts nationwide had fallen to 93,000, not even one-eighth of the 1920s level. Policymakers in Washington knew they needed to spur housing construction to get Americans back to work. The Hoover and Roosevelt administrations passed multiple initiatives in the early 1930s to provide short-term loans to mortgage lenders, refinance the loans they had, and push them toward a new longer-term, self-amortizing mortgage structure. In 1934, the Roosevelt administration created the Federal Housing Authority (FHA) to provide government insurance to mortgage lenders and to promote long-term mortgages, up to twenty years, with modest down payments. Despite these efforts, housing starts were still anemic in 1937, a third of the pre-Depression levels.

The economist John Maynard Keynes wrote to President Roosevelt in February 1938, arguing for a significant increase in federal expenditures to restart the American economy, with a particular focus on residential housing markets. "Housing is by far the best aid to recovery because of the large and continuing scale of potential demand; because of the wide geographical distribution of this demand; and because the sources of its finance are largely independent of the stock exchanges," Keynes wrote. "I should advise putting most of your eggs in this basket, caring about this more than about anything, and making absolutely sure that they are being hatched without delay."[24] Many in Congress also believed that housing was a high-leverage economic activity to support. With the support of Fed Chair Marriner Eccles, Congressional leaders passed a bill the same month to lower the down payments on government-insured mortgages to 10 percent and extend their terms from twenty to twenty-five years. Roosevelt agreed with the consensus, struck by the statistics that suggested that a third of the unemployed were in the building trades. "[Housing] would act as the wheel within the wheel to move the whole economic engine," Eccles wrote, describing Roosevelt's thinking.[25] Two weeks later, Roosevelt wrote Jones, asking him to bring the full force of the RFC to the problem and create a new market in government-insured home loans, with the goal of lowering the rate homebuyers would pay and inducing the banks to lend more freely.

Jones and his colleagues were ready. The RFC had experimented with housing initiatives before, including a subsidiary mortgage company (the RFC Mortgage Company) that provided low-interest loans to multifamily homes, hotels, and office buildings. But in line with a new, more aggressive conception of the RFC's mandate, it would need to go bigger. Within days, Jones created a new RFC subsidiary called the Federal National Mortgage Association—known, more familiarly, as Fannie Mae—to support housing growth. "A real building program will increase employment and stimulate business more perhaps than any other one thing that can be done," Jones said when announcing the program.[26] The RFC intended to create a market for cheap, government-insured mortgages by guaranteeing an ongoing baseline of demand. Fannie Mae would purchase long-term mortgages from the issuing local banks, making them more liquid and, indirectly, cheaper. Jones was not just supporting an existing financial product; he was birthing a new one and the market to support it.

Jones wanted to make long-term mortgages a standardized financial product that would serve the needs of American investors, not just homebuyers. Financial institutions and wealthy individuals who wanted reliable, consistent returns could buy long-term mortgage securities, now made significantly less risky because of government insurance. Jones had used the power of government to create a low-risk and relatively high-yield investment product. Now a New York banker could invest in Colorado mortgages and the local bank in Colorado would no longer be constrained in the number of loans it could make by the cash deposits of its local customers. More mortgages would mean more homes and more jobs.

Jones marshaled all of the housing efforts of the RFC behind supporting Fannie Mae and cheap mortgage provision. In Fannie's first year, the organization bought $38 million of mortgages, and the legacy RFC Mortgage Company increased its lending to $36 million in the same year. The RFC disbursed another $130 million to mortgage loan companies for additional capital loans, meaning that the RFC spent $200 million in total on housing initiatives in a single year. By 1940, the total amount spent on housing approached $1 billion, or approximately $264 billion in today's dollars.[27] For context, today's Department of Housing and Urban Development (HUD) has a total annual budget of $70 billion.

The market making worked. Private and public institutions alike began to seek out government-insured loans as a source of reliable return, seeing in the government guarantee investor protection from meaningful loss. If housing markets bounced back as many expected they would, they stood to make a sizable profit. The Comptroller of the State of New York, desperate for reliable securities for his own investment portfolio, came to Jones' office with an offer to buy all of the government-insured mortgages in New York State at the going rate of 1 percent above their face value. "I told him the price would be 101.5," Jones later wrote. "He protested, asking why, if we would sell him one mortgage at 101, we wouldn't sell him all we had at the same price, or even less. He bought them all—and paid 101.5."[28] Buoyed by the RFC, housing construction nationwide took off, increasing by nearly 20 percent each year for the next five years, aside from a pause when America entered World War II.

Even though Jones was quickly pivoting the RFC to focus on housing construction, Washington whisperers questioned whether Jones had the wherewithal to pursue the bigger, bolder, activist RFC. Fed Chair Eccles and Interior Secretary Harold Ickes even worried that Jones might sabotage the new institution or, at the least, hold it back from making the riskier loans and investments that might be required. Berle was convinced that Jones alone was in a position to take bold action, but he worried that he would not seize it given his disposition as a fiscally conservative businessman.[29] Yet Jones was a pragmatist, sensitive to the shifting political winds and personally convinced that the Depression had not been contained as he had hoped a year earlier.[30] King Nottoc of Washington could see that the RFC and his own personal leadership might actually be more necessary than he had thought. His influence could even grow.[31] Jones, initially a reluctant warrior, was increasingly convinced that the RFC needed to go bigger to combat the recession. If it embraced this broader mission, it might just endure.[32]

Over the next two years, Jones evolved the RFC into an activist institution that would have scandalized the 1933 version of himself. It helped that Congress gave him carte blanche to do so. Just two months after Roosevelt and Jones refired the engines, Congress gave it wide latitude to loan or buy securities directly from any kind of business, however large or small, and for whatever duration the RFC wanted. It also extended the institution's lifespan yet again. These changes were not marginal expansions of power or incremental appropriations for the RFC; they amounted to an invitation to do the work that banks, now nearly a decade into the Depression, were still refusing to do. Congress was explicitly asking Jones to accelerate, but he personally had to agree.

Jones had historically resisted significant direct lending during the RFC's first phase. Bankers would know how to more efficiently allocate scarce capital than a government administrator, he believed. By 1938, that reticence was fading, because banks were still not making the long-term loans needed to fuel investment and get businesses hiring, despite being well capitalized. Frustrated and impatient, Jones set aside any scruples about government "intrusion" in financial markets. Government investment, he decided, could act as a catalyst, spurring private investment and not crowding it out. Moving forward, the RFC would no longer merely stabilize existing market orders in banking, agriculture, and railroads as it had in its first phase. It would become the banker to the nation, supporting a broad range of businesses, including housing.

Jones wrote to the President in April 1938 that he wanted to get more aggressive and pursue direct lending. He asked Roosevelt if the RFC should pursue the more direct route in the service of economic expansion. Roosevelt endorsed the plan the next day, writing in the margin "especially in the case of small enterprises."[33] Jones announced the new aggressive approach in a speech in April 1938 on national radio, telling listeners that the RFC had consolidated and shortened its application forms to be more conducive to small business borrowing. It was ready to lend, and not just for the short term, but for five- or even ten-year loans. "Every business, however small, that is being honestly conducted is entitled to some line of credit."[34] Jones told business owners that if a commercial bank rejected their application, they should come to one of the RFC's thirty-three field offices and apply. He flung the doors wide open.

Over the next two years, the RFC transformed itself into the nation's largest lender to industrial and commercial enterprises. Authorized loans to nonfinancial businesses increased sixfold after the RFC came back to life. Between April 1938 and June 1940, the RFC lent over $214 million, or $57 billion in today's dollars. The RFC approved twenty-five to forty applications a day, and most were for less than $10,000. Nearly three-fourths were less than $75,000. Thousands of businesses that could not secure loans at a local bank were now getting the credit they needed to expand. Jones worked hard to keep the quality level high and continued to brag about the RFC's ability to stay in the black. Even so, it was lending more widely. Historically it had approved 30 percent of loans, but by the end of 1939 approval rates had reached 60 percent of received applications.[35]

The RFC's marketcrafting mission was clear: flood hiring-intensive businesses, particularly housing and small businesses, with affordable, abundant credit. Given the weak interest banks expressed in lending for the long term, the RFC stepped in, providing the public investment that the private sector failed to offer. This marketcraft fostered a revival of American housing and small business, guiding markets in the direction Jones and Roosevelt preferred.

By now, Jones had learned to sing a different tune about the relationship between government and industry. Gone were the days when the RFC could only be justified as an emergency response. Now American capitalism needed an institution such as the RFC to ensure broad-based prosperity. "It is as important for government and its representatives to realize the essential nature of business enterprise in this country as it is for business men to get it through their heads that government is in business to stay," he said in July 1939. "Both must realize that neither can get along without the other, and that more is to be gained through cooperation and restraint than by keeping constantly at each other's throats."[36] Business had little choice given how large the RFC had grown. Total disbursements by 1940 amounted to more than $11 billion. One of the country's largest banks, J.P. Morgan, by contrast, had underwritten $6 billion of loans between 1919 and 1932 when markets were raging.[37]

All of the robust lending and investing was helping to power the American economic engine, putting millions back to work. In addition to the RFC, a raft of additional New Deal investments and looser monetary policy had stimulated demand in the immediate prewar years. Between February of

1938 and June of 1940, the American economy added over 5 million new jobs, a nearly 20 percent increase in just over two years.[38] Unemployment began to fall again, and the American economy grew by 8 percent in 1939. America was increasingly back in business.

Despite the progress, some voices wanted to push the RFC and similar institutions even further. Eccles supported a proposal for the government to insure all business loans, and Berle continued to advocate for a new network of national credit banks. Other voices, concerned about corporate concentration, such as Tommy Corcoran and Ben Cohen, wanted the RFC to increasingly focus on small business investment to the exclusion of large business support. Jones resisted all of these calls, likely out of his desire to consolidate his own power.[39] None of the ideas took off, largely because the RFC was flourishing and America seemed to be emerging from its economic doldrums.

Jones was at the peak of his career, and the promotions kept rolling in. In July of 1939, in an attempt to streamline reporting and make government more effective, Roosevelt consolidated all of the federal government's credit-generating institutions—including the RFC, the Export-Import Bank, the Federal Housing Administration, and several others—to have them report to a single boss under the umbrella of a new Federal Loan Agency (FLA). Jesse Jones would be its leader. The mercurial Roosevelt announced the promotion at a press conference, without telling Jones ahead of time. Roosevelt was maneuvering, placating some of the Jones critics who wanted a more liberal leader at the RFC while at the same time recognizing Jones' important role in the administration and with the business community. But Jones knew an opportunity when he saw one. Kicked upstairs, Jones made sure that he placed a loyal devotee as the technical head of the RFC, retaining all of the power and influence over the institution that he had built. Jones kept the same desk and the same office. Despite what an org chart might indicate in the years to come, the RFC's head would remain Jesse Jones.[40]

For a brief moment, all of Washington joined in feting Jones. Notes of congratulations and flowers poured into his office. Even Treasury Secretary Henry Morgenthau, who had been working to eliminate the RFC for years, sent Jones a private note of praise. In the media, widely read columnists gossiped that Jones was considering a run for President in 1940—and that the idea wouldn't necessarily be crazy. Roosevelt—who wouldn't announce his ambition for a third term until almost a year later—was aware that Jones

had flirted with the idea of a presidential run. One of Roosevelt's sons, Elliott, had been promoting the idea a few months before to party members.[41]
Publications such as *Fortune* and the *Saturday Evening Post* were calling the
RFC a "fourth branch of government" with "vast power" that is "illustrative
of the dangers inherent in this governmental form." But fortunately, Americans did not have to fear this particular governmental power, they argued,
because the institution's leader was judicious and wise. "Now it so happens
that in Jesse Jones, who has run the RFC since 1933, the American people
have found the perfect man," a *Fortune* editorial on business and government marveled.[42] The former King Nottoc of Houston had become one of
the most celebrated leaders in Washington. Jones' vision of marketcrafting,
honed in the service of a local political economy, would now influence the
future of the United States and—as geopolitical tensions rose—the world.

3

EMPIRE, BUILT AND BROKEN

JESSE JONES, AVIATION & THE WAR (1939-45)

When the new year dawned in 1939, Franklin Roosevelt was in a bind. Democrats had suffered stinging losses just weeks before in the midterm elections. The American economy was only slowly exiting the second recession of the Great Depression, and a belligerent Adolf Hitler in Germany suggested that war in Europe was imminent. Most Americans had little interest in engaging in another foreign war, and the American army, including the reserves and air force, ranked sixteenth in size among its global peers, between Spain and Bulgaria.[1] Yet Roosevelt wanted to make sure the nation was prepared should war break out. "[T]he world has grown so small and weapons of attack so swift that no nation can be safe in its will to peace so long as any other powerful nation refuses to settle its grievances at the council table," Roosevelt said to Congress in his State of the Union address in January. "For if any government bristling with implements of war insists on policies of force, weapons of defense give the only safety."[2] What Roosevelt needed most was the ability to manufacture those "weapons of defense" without significant new Congressional investment.

The RFC offered him the unique flexibility to do exactly that. "[T]he President probably did not want to ask Congress for large appropriations for war purposes, nor would the Congress have been inclined to make them," Jones later commented. Jones himself hoped the United States could avoid another world war but soon recognized publicly that "adequate preparation for national defense" was now "the most pressing problem."[3] Roosevelt and Jones decided to use RFC loans, instead of Congressional appropriations, to support early American armament efforts. When the Japanese attacked Pearl Harbor, in December 1941, the political constraints disappeared and the American war machine swiftly mobilized. But during the eighteen months between Hitler's victory in Paris and America's entry into the war, the RFC led the preparation effort. "This jump on the Axis powers," Jones believed, "shortened the war considerably."[4]

Congress trusted Jones, but some on the Hill still balked at the scale of the RFC's war preparations. Jones had to sit through weeks of hearings as Congress considered investing more in the institution. Despite lawmakers' initial resistance, on June 25, 1940, Congress handed the RFC unprecedented power to "do anything that could be regarded as in the national defense."[5] The RFC could now purchase, lease, and build factories to manufacture planes or tanks, for instance, on behalf of the war effort. It authorized the stockpiling of essential goods and gave Jones wide authority to make investments even if they seemed tangential to the war effort. Loans and investments no longer needed to be "fundamentally sound," and the RFC could create subsidiaries focused on producing critical materials or for the construction of defense plants and equipment. Any sense that the RFC was not necessary to the functioning of American capitalism melted away, replaced with a recognition of how helpful a flexible national investment bank could be to cultivate and support new industries. "Some of the Senators seemed appalled [at our new power]," Jones later wrote. "My friend Arthur Krock, chief Washington correspondent of the *New York Times*, wrote in his column that I was asking for the dictionary. Congress gave it to us. Before the war was won we had thumbed almost every page of it."[6]

Between its start in 1932 and 1940, the RFC and its affiliates had loaned more than $2.5 billion, but over the next four years they would invest $37 billion more, dwarfing all previous activity.[7] Much of the RFC's work happened through the work of seven wartime subsidiaries, including most prominently the Defense Plant Corporation.[8] Over $8 billion alone went into facilitating the construction of 2,300 war plants in forty-six states.[9] By war's end, the RFC and its subsidiaries owned nearly all of the manufacturing capacity in the synthetic rubber, magnesium, and aluminum industries. The federal government would own nearly a quarter of the value of all the nation's factories, much of which had been financed by the RFC.[10]

No industry was more important to the RFC's national defense efforts than aviation. America would need tens of thousands of bombers if it ever were to face the German or Japanese military. In 1939, more Americans were employed in the confectionery industries than in aircraft and engine manufacture.[11] Only three small companies in the entire country manufactured high-horsepower aircraft engines.[12] The US Army Air Corps had less than half as many planes as Germany and nearly all American combat aircraft were outdated, whereas Germany had built virtually all of its fleet since 1936.[13] Hundreds of thousands of men worked for the German air force and associated industries by the end of the 1930s.[14] As Adolf Hitler began his march across Europe, it became clear to Jesse Jones that America's aviation industry would have to grow to win what now seemed to him and President Roosevelt like an inevitable war with Germany.

The American war mobilization, particularly in aircraft production, faced an immense challenge in both scale and urgency. Roosevelt and Jones had started to try to tackle this as early as the fall of 1938, when Roosevelt announced his intention to create an air force with 10,000 planes. In April 1939, Congress tripled the size of the existing Army Air Corps and flooded the aviation industry with over $100 million of new orders.[15] Jones and the RFC had already made some major investments, including a $5 million loan to Boeing to expand its plant.[16] Even so, a year later, the army and navy only owned 1,600 planes, still a fraction of Germany's stock. In May 1940, with Germany aggressively bombing London, Roosevelt set out a highly ambitious and somewhat implausible goal: the manufacture of 50,000 planes per year. A few weeks later, Congress agreed to half that, setting aside money for 24,000 new planes. The American aviation industry was not just small but also backlogged with foreign orders. In the prior two years, Britain and France had submitted major orders to American aviation companies, anxious to strengthen their defenses as Hitler became increasingly antagonistic. All that money had spurred some initial growth, but it was slow going. American aviation did not just need more money. It needed a market structure that facilitated knowledge sharing and supply-chain coordination, allowing companies to scale production swiftly and efficiently in the near term.

Birthing an American aircraft industry was not just about wartime. Jones hoped to lay the foundation for a new industry that would outlast the conflict, supporting American economic dominance and geopolitical power—and the legacy of Jesse Jones.[17] "After this war there will be a phenomenal boom in flying for all purposes—as phenomenal as the growth of the automobile and truck after the last war," Jones said at the time. He had always had a sixth sense for the long-term development trend of markets, which now informed where he guided the RFC to invest. "There can be no doubt that our future strength lies in air power and our ability to make sure of it."[18] To get there, the RFC would have to help support and craft a market that would thrive in war and peacetime alike. "There is no mystery about it. It is just as necessary to prepare for peace, as it is to prepare for war. They both mean work, and more work; planning, and more planning, as the scene changes," Jones said two years into the war.[19]

Jones and his team began to work the phones, facilitating the production and manufacture of all of the inputs that went into airplanes. Jones averaged eighty to ninety phone calls per day. A photo from the time shows him talking on a phone, surrounded by several others, while enjoying his lunch on a tray.[20] Rather than waiting to build new factories, Jones and his team maneuvered to transition existing industrial production to the new cause. Automobile manufacturers scaled back their car- and truck-manufacturing efforts and updated their plants to make planes. Ford Motor Company began to mass-produce Pratt & Whitney eighteen-cylinder engines at its River Rouge campus in 1940, made possible with a $90 million investment from the RFC wartime subsidiary. At the RFC's urging, Buick, Chevrolet, and Studebaker followed Ford, opening RFC-funded plants that eventually produced half of all aircraft engines in the United States during the war.[21] Perhaps no single aviation project was as extensive as the Dodge-Chicago plant, built in a cornfield southwest of Chicago, with the $176 million cost financed by the RFC.[22] The plant took up 6 million square feet spread over 145 acres and used over 4 million gallons of water a day.[23] By the end of the war, it had produced 18,000 aircraft engines alone.

All those parts needed to be assembled into planes, and the RFC funded the construction of 534 new aviation plants and assembly facilities across the country.[24] Many factory assembly lines operated twenty-four hours a day, seven days a week. In Michigan, the RFC owned the aircraft assembly plant at Willow Run, leasing it back to Ford, which by 1944 managed to churn out a plane an hour. An airport was built next door so that the planes could take to the skies immediately.[25]

It wasn't just the money that turbocharged aircraft production at River Rouge and elsewhere. The RFC facilitated the sharing of otherwise-siloed production techniques and performance insights, ensuring that engine and aircraft production was not stymied by corporate competition or an attempt to protect intellectual property. Jones and colleagues wrangled corporate leadership to share their learnings about how they were transitioning their infrastructure.

Planes need pilots, and the RFC helped take care of that as well. Eager to expand and streamline the pilot-training programs, many of which had been initially funded by Congress, the RFC's wartime affiliate outright purchased over sixty private pilot-training schools.[26] They made up a major portion of the nationwide civilian pilot education programs that ultimately trained 400,000 pilots by the end of the war, half of whom joined the American military.[27]

By March of 1943, the RFC and its affiliates had invested in aviation initiatives ten times the entire assets of all aircraft manufacturers before the war.[28] A year later, at the war's peak production, 2.5 million American workers were producing 110,000 planes a year. By the time the Axis powers capitulated, America had made a staggering 300,000 military planes, dwarfing production levels in Germany and Japan, with nearly three-fourths of the aviation expansion financed by the RFC.[29] "In one area of industry, that of aircraft, the extent of expansion, the need for speed, and the element of risk early suggested that no satisfactory alternative existed to RFC financing," wrote one former employee who became a historian of its wartime efforts.[30]

The RFC's wartime marketcraft did not stop at aviation. Just as it was birthing the aviation industry, it altogether transformed the existing market for rubber, a key input in the production of military equipment, particularly tires. One of Jones' first moves in June of 1940 after receiving Congressional authorization to prepare for war was to secure as much rubber as possible for the effort. Jones set up an RFC subsidiary exclusively focused on rubber and contracted with the British and Dutch cartel to buy all of the rubber available on world markets. Once the rubber was purchased, the RFC divided it up between the American companies that needed it, stockpiling some for potential war needs. Between the middle of 1940 and Pearl Harbor a year and a half later, the RFC's wartime affiliate amassed 600,000 tons of rubber, a record amount, but only enough to support a year of peacetime production needs.[31]

Once war broke out, all of Washington, including Jones, realized that much more was needed. In early 1942, Japan conquered all rubber-producing islands in the Pacific, cutting off any additional provision.

Jones and the RFC pivoted to focus on supporting the incipient synthetic rubber industry. If rubber couldn't be bought, it would have to be made. In September 1942, an official report documenting the growing pains of rubber production noted that it should "require a dozen years" to happen. "To compress it into less than two years is almost a superhuman task."[32] The RFC had made some early investments in synthetic production, but it was not progressing fast enough. Jones announced a major investment of $400 million to expand production, even though no one knew how it could be done. Over the following two years, the RFC designed and built fifty-one government-owned plants, operated by private companies, at a cost of $700 million.[33]

As with aviation, it was not only RFC funding that made the industry work. Jones and colleagues organized the existing rubber companies, including major oil and chemical companies responsible for synthetic rubber inputs, to pool patents and share research secrets, turbocharging the process by rewarding collaboration. The RFC induced the companies to share information in an ongoing fashion, organizing them around a clear mission of inventing a functional synthetic rubber as quickly as possible. Eventually, those efforts improved their collective efficiency.[34] Production ramped up in 1943, and by 1944, it blew past 700,000 tons. In 1945, plant capacity exceeded 1 million tons a year, producing a glut.[35] By contrast, German synthetic rubber production reached a peak of 109,000 tons in 1943.[36]

Birthing the aviation industry and inventing synthetic rubber were just some of the Herculean tasks the RFC completed during the war. German submarines were blowing up American oil tankers carrying energy supplies from Texas to the industrial Northeast, where much of the wartime manufacturing was happening. One of the RFC's wartime subsidiaries constructed a new pipeline from Texas to the Northeast that was larger and longer than any other in the world. Over the course of 350 days, workers completed the 1200-mile pipeline, laying pipe at a clip of over three miles each day, including Sundays. It was so successful the RFC financed a second pipeline to transport heating oil and gas along the same route. Meanwhile, it built and managed the wartime aluminum and magnesium industries and supported the growth of steel production.

Over the course of the war years, the RFC demonstrated that it could develop industry and markets to serve public purposes. It helped spur and manage the greatest turn in the American economy in its history, away from supporting peacetime priorities of housing, banking, and small business loans and toward war priorities such as aviation, rubber, critical minerals, pipelines, and munitions. Those efforts shortened the duration of the war and ensured Allied victory. American capitalism continued to function with private ownership of the means of production, but if the country's political leaders wanted, they could guide private efforts to serve the needs of the nation. As an institution, the RFC tripled the number of employees from its prewar size and set new records monthly for funds deployed. Its power and influence had never been greater.[37]

Ironically, it was just at this moment, the apex of the institution's power, that Jesse Jones started to unravel.

In August of 1940, Roosevelt again promoted Jones, making him Commerce Secretary in addition to his responsibilities as FLA Administrator. Technically, no one in government service could occupy two jobs, so Roosevelt had to get a joint resolution from Congress green-lighting the move. The White House left it to Jones to do the lobbying. Two Washington columnists wrote: "[The] reason Roosevelt was forced to give in is that Jones is the most powerful one-man lobby on Capitol Hill. He can get anything he wants out of Congress."[38] Only Senator Robert Taft protested, arguing that Jones "probably has more power than any other man in the government, with the single exception of the president." Even so, he supported the unusual dual appointment.[39] Jones was on the cover of *Time* in January 1941 with a single line under his portrait: "If jobs were wives, he would be the patriarch of polygamists."

All those jobs and all that power meant that Jones increasingly became a target for criticism from inside and outside the administration. He had always been able to parry these critiques, often by cutting deals as he went. In the tempest of war, Jones' dealmaking skills began to fail him. For some critics, the RFC was moving too slow. Congress had expanded the draft in August 1941 and German U-boats were increasingly confronting American ships in the Atlantic. Americans were coming to terms with what seemed like an inevitable mobilization, and given the RFC's central role in facilitating early armament efforts, it began to attract additional attention. For other critics, the RFC's emphasis on speed turned it into a subsidy for private business. An RFC deal with Alcoa, the aluminum monopoly, caused private criticism to bubble over in October. Panning the deal as a government handout, Missouri Senator Harry Truman organized other legislators in Congress to aim their fire at Jones, a first.[40] With Jones no longer holding the frequent press conferences he once did, his media coverage began to sour, with *Fortune* asking: "Is Jones of Texas a great national asset or is he in fact a bottleneck?"[41]

The following year, the criticism of Jones grew. In 1942, supplies of synthetic rubber were at historically low levels, in the months before the technological breakthroughs the RFC facilitated. Legislators and the media complained that Jones should have ramped up production even faster. "The chief reason for [Jones'] failure is boundless ambition for power that has led to his taking on more jobs than he can successfully manage," read an editorial in the *Washington Post*, owned by Eugene Meyer—Jones' predecessor in the RFC Chair role. Jones rarely took responsibility for failures that occurred within his purview, and he was not about to start now. Jones and Meyer had been lifelong rivals. After Meyer had stepped down from leading the Hoover-era RFC, he and Jones had competed against each other in an open-air bidding war on the steps of the *Washington Post* for its ownership. Jones owned a prominent Houston paper and enjoyed the notoriety and power it lent him. Meyer won, and now used the paper as a soapbox for criticizing the administration. "Blaming the other fellow is a confession of defeat—not a marker of merit," the Meyer-approved editorial opined about Jones. "The proof of an official's worth to his country lies in his ability to meet and conquer the kind of obstacles of which Mr. Jones complains."[42]

Jones was furious. The night of the editorial's publication, he attended an Alfalfa Club dinner at the Willard Hotel in Washington alongside Supreme Court justices, Senators, and businessmen. Meyer was also there, and Jones and he spent much of the evening glowering at each other from afar. When Meyer got up to leave, Jones left his seat and approached him directly, seething with frustration over the editorial. "With bulging eyes, [guests] saw the Administration's No. 1 money-man, Jesse Jones, shake the daylights out of Eugene Meyer, multimillionaire Washington publisher, and then saw Meyer swinging like a maddened walrus in attempts to connect with Jones' chin." Jones had shaken Meyer so aggressively that his glasses fell off, breaking, prompting Meyer to defend himself. "Jones sidestepped faster than a banker dodging a loan applicant. Meyer threw a right, which also failed to connect," wrote a syndicated columnist in the New York *Daily News*. "A wag in the crowd later said that Meyer had always been so conservatively Republican that he found difficulty in moving to the left." Onlookers scrambled and pulled the two apart, but not before their altercation had become the gossip of Washington.[43]

The dustup was too juicy for the press to drop it. Roosevelt, when asked about it a few days later, sidestepped getting involved, but his tolerance for Jones' outbursts was thinning. With the nation at war, the President's responsibilities had multiplied, and while the RFC remained important, Roosevelt had little patience for petty spats. Within days of the fight, the President shifted responsibility for stockpiling in the war effort away from Jones and toward Vice President Henry Wallace, another Jones enemy in the administration. Wallace and Jones had been competing for authority for years, most recently dueling for control over exports, imports, procurement, and stockpiling, and Wallace was now winning out. The press began to talk about "the crumbling empire of Jesse H. Jones," and the *Wall Street Journal* called the move the "fade-out of Jesse H. Jones as financier-in-chief."[44] Roosevelt's move was less impactful than it may have seemed at the time, and Jones and the RFC hung on to all of their power. But Jones would now have another boss between the President and him when it came to stockpiling, his rival Wallace.

Even if the journalists overstated Jones' demise, he could not seem to learn how to work with people who did not bow to his will. The Jones-Wallace rivalry simmered until it came to a head the following year, 1943, over supply-chain issues. Wallace accused Jones of "obstructionist tactics" in the war effort and claimed the RFC had "failed dismally." Jones shot back, saying that Wallace's statement was "filled with malice and misstatements."[45] The press covered their disagreement as if it were a soap opera. Roosevelt asked an aide to coordinate an in-person meeting at the White House to placate them. After two hours, the aide ended the meeting, fearing that Jones was about to physically assault Wallace. A few days later, the *New York Times* noted that three men had to sit between the two at the most recent cabinet meeting.[46] The President, frustrated with the public nature of their childlike antics, stripped both of power. A few months later, Roosevelt chose to dump Wallace as his VP from the 1944 presidential ticket and replace him with Truman.

Meanwhile, Jones would never regain the President's favor. Jones had made the RFC into one of the most successful institutions of the New Deal and war effort, but he could not get out of his cwn way to retain and leverage that power. That winter, back in Texas for the holidays, Jones was hit by a car while asking for directions at night, breaking both his legs. While recovering, he contracted the flu, then pneumonia, and eventually needed to have foot surgery, which required him to remain in bed for seven weeks.[47] His physical demise tracked his political downfall.

Jones' political career was coming to a close. While he was attempting to recover physically from his ailments, the husband of one of his nieces, George Butler, was leading a rogue contingent of Texas Democrats to oppose Roosevelt's move to secure a fourth term for the presidency in 1944. No President had served three terms, let alone pursued a fourth, and Butler and others were frustrated by the progressivism of the New Deal. Under no circumstances did Butler, the Chair of the Texas Democratic Party's Executive Committee, want its members to vote for Roosevelt. Rumors swirled in Washington that Jones was behind the effort to undermine the President, with one widely read columnist arguing that "it is inconceivable that [Butler] would act without Jesse's approval."[48] Meyer's *Washington Post* wrote an editorial questioning Jones' involvement in the effort, prompting Jones to write an article in the newspaper he owned, the *Houston Chronicle*, denying his involvement. He sent it to the President but heard nothing back. The denial didn't stick, and Jones later recounted that "certain troublemakers" swirling in Washington tried to convince the President that Jones was out to get him.

Their conflict peaked in a conversation with the President on June 13, 1944. When Roosevelt asked Jones what he was doing about the Texas insurgency, Jones said he didn't know. "Well, it seems to me you ought to know," Roosevelt fired back.[49] Trying to make the point that relatives cannot always be controlled, Jones brought up Roosevelt's son, who had sidestepped the President's wishes a few years before: "I reminded him that his son Elliott, over my protest, had persisted in his purpose to second my nomination for the Vice Presidency at the 1940 Chicago Convention, after the President had chosen Henry Wallace, and of Elliott telling me that his father did not know what he was doing in wanting Wallace." It was surely a subtle way of reminding the President that Jones had his own supporters, some of whom had made the case for challenging Roosevelt for the presidency itself. Roosevelt balked. A few weeks later, the President met with Jones' rival Wallace. Roosevelt had just engineered Wallace's removal as Vice President, but he still needed Wallace to stay on the campaign trail to appease the left wing of the party. Privately, Roosevelt told Wallace that after the election, he intended to "make a list of the folks we were going to get rid of." First on the list: Jesse Jones. Wallace quickly saw an opening and expressed interest in the Secretary of Commerce job, including RFC oversight, and the two agreed it would be "poetic justice" for him to take over Jones' role.[50] A few weeks later, in a private meeting with the incoming Vice President Truman, Roosevelt signaled that Jones would be toast after the election, drawing his finger across his throat.[51]

In November, a beleaguered nation chose not to switch horses midstream and reelected Roosevelt decisively, hoping for a quick close to the war. The inauguration, customarily held outdoors at the Capitol, was moved to the South Portico of the White House to accommodate the President's delicate health. On the day of the inauguration, a cold, wet snow fell in Washington. Jones came to the White House and attended the midday ceremony with the rest of the cabinet before returning home briefly for a pit stop on his way to a planned lunch. He found a letter, sent by messenger, waiting for him there. The President was asking for Jones' resignation. He intended to name Wallace as Secretary of Commerce.

The President's decision did not entirely surprise Jones, but the brusque and abrupt nature of it stung. Rumors had swirled for weeks that his political career might be ending. Shortly after he opened the letter, the phone rang, and the President's secretary asked Jones to come the following day at noon to meet with Roosevelt. Jones was told the President had a luncheon at 12:15, so the meeting would be short. It didn't matter; there was little to say anyway. Jones was fired, making way for Wallace, who, despite being kicked out of the VP slot, had campaigned loyally for Roosevelt. That dedication meant that he had now earned a top-notch cabinet job that Roosevelt had proffered the previous summer—and the chance to beat out a bitter rival. In their final meeting, Roosevelt floated other positions to Jones—ambassadorships to France or the United Kingdom, even the Chair of the Federal Reserve—but they all seemed hastily conceived. The President was "tired, unhappy, and annoyed," according to his assistant, who remembered that "Jones looked grim when he arrived and grimmer when he left."[52] Jones later wrote that "[o]ur last meeting was probably a mistake. Better he had let it go with the letter of dismissal, because it was not a happy occasion for either of us." Jones fired off a combative letter of resignation in which he argued against the decision, and promptly shared it with the press, along with the President's original note asking for his resignation. A few days later, he testified before the Senate that Wallace was uniquely unqualified for the job of Commerce Secretary given that he was a "visionary planner."[53] Jones wanted to be seen as the voice of business and moderation, compared to the supposedly socialist outlook of Wallace. His dramatic testimony garnered headlines, and Congress decided to remove the RFC from the future Commerce Secretary's purview. But it did not stop Wallace from taking Jones' job.

Jones packed up and left his office, never to return to government service. Two months after he was fired, he sent Roosevelt a package full of photos of the estate next door to Hyde Park. At Roosevelt's request, Jones had an insurance company owned by the RFC purchase Crumwold Farms, a 741-acre parcel of land, rather than letting it fall into the hands of a controversial Black pastor, who wanted to use it for congregant homes. The army used the site during the war, ostensibly for training and presidential protection, but it was a rare example of self-dealing at the RFC.[54] (Jones did resist other presidential larks, such as when Roosevelt asked him to purchase the struggling Empire State Building to consolidate federal government offices in New York in the tower.) The package from Jones to Roosevelt served as a not-so-subtle reminder to the President of Jones' true loyalty. "I am glad to have them and appreciate your kindness in sending them to me," Roosevelt responded, a line of communication between the two now open again.[55] But just weeks later, while having an official portrait painted, Roosevelt suffered a cerebral hemorrhage and died, less than a month before Allied forces won the war in Europe.

With Franklin Roosevelt dead and Jesse Jones out of government, gone were the two men who had built the RFC from an afterthought of the Hoover administration into one of the most powerful institutions in American government, a force that had lifted the country out of the Great Depression and prepared the country for war. But what *was* the RFC without Roosevelt and Jones? A hint of the trouble to come came from a journalist writing an in-depth profile of Jones just before the start of the war: "One suspects he would rather see the House of Jesse destroyed than in other hands."[56]

✿

In the years after the war, the RFC's mission continued to evolve. At first, Congress directed the bank to lend to several nations in the process of re-building and to the United Nations for its new headquarters in New York. Meanwhile, faced with a postwar housing shortage, its efforts to support and cultivate housing markets continued. By 1950, half of all new home mortgages were backed by FHA or the Veterans Administration, with Fannie Mae con-tinuing its operations to deepen the residential housing market.[57] The RFC also began to lend to businesses that produced prefabricated homes and hous-ing components for modern building sites, a way of accommodating the ex-ploding demand for new housing from soldiers in the aftermath of the war.[58] By 1950, Fannie Mae had grown so large that Congress moved it out of the RFC, setting it up to be a permanent fixture of American housing finance.

Even after the war, some progressives wanted to expand the RFC, turn-ing it into a fixture of American government that could outlast Jones and Roosevelt. In 1949, two Senators and a House member introduced a bill to enlarge the RFC to a loan fund of $15 billion (roughly the same budget as the contemporary Marshall Plan), with the funds deployed on the recommenda-tion of the White House's Council of Economic Advisers (CEA). "They envi-sioned loans to existing and new enterprises, to states to aid in their industrial development, and to regional authorities like the TVA," wrote one former RFC employee.[59] But these plans ran into opposition from business interests that were then making a concerted effort to diminish state power over invest-ment and finance, including at the RFC. Without a dedicated leader to make its case, the organization fell prey to conservative assault.

Congress struggled to find meaningful incidences of graft or corruption in the $40 billion the RFC had lent over thirteen years. But at the moment that scrutiny was ramping up, the postwar RFC made a disastrous loan to a company called Lustron to pursue mass production techniques to build affordable homes. The company mismanaged the funds and misled RFC of-ficials. When Congress began investigating, the RFC foreclosed on its loan, giving its critics an easy example of wasted taxpayer dollars.[60] In 1951, Con-gress reorganized the RFC and, at Truman's urging, appointed as administra-tor a military man to "clean house." He stopped all non-disaster lending.[61] In 1952, when Dwight Eisenhower became the first Republican in twenty years to win the presidency, he prioritized shutting down the RFC as one of his administration's early moves. In July of 1953, Congress abolished the institution, replacing it with a new Small Business Administration (SBA) to continue to facilitate credit.

Jones had never attempted to explain the RFC's mission in terms of its potential to guide and shape American capitalism. For him, it had been about building an empire of his own, and he would rather see it collapse than have another leader. Jones rapidly shifted from RFC champion to RFC critic after he was fired. He had always been criticized by his enemies for being more interested in his own power and position than in the work he was doing. Now he proved it to be true. While still at the helm of the organization, Jones had envisioned government partnering with the private sector for prosperity. "Private initiative alone cannot do it. In many instances government must continue to have a hand in business. It must make investments and take risks where private capital cannot afford to, just as government had to take risks and do most of the financing for expansion of our industrial facilities to meet the demands of war," Jones said in 1943.[62] Once outside of power, unable to imagine his baby being run by someone else, he sang a different tune. Without his wisdom, Jones believed, the RFC could veer off in a destructive direction. Better for it not to exist at all. In private correspondence to Arkansas Senator J. William Fulbright in 1950, Jones minced no words: "As for the future of the RFC, I think it should be given a decent burial, lock, stock, and barrel."[63] The following year, he testified to Congress, saying, "Having completed its original purpose, to meet the depression, and its vast expansion for the war job, it had entirely too much authority and power, most of which had been given it on my testimony and in the expectation that I would direct its affairs. I wanted to put it away."[64]

It wasn't just the RFC that was in Jones' sights. His dismissal had made him bitter, and in 1948 he endorsed Republican Thomas Dewey against Truman. Jones never forgot a grudge, and Truman had aggressively interrogated him in 1942 over challenges with rubber provision in the war. Four years later, he chose not to endorse in the race between Eisenhower and Adlai Stevenson. It would be the last election he would see. After a decade spent investing his fortune and pursuing local philanthropy with his wife, he died of kidney failure in June 1956 at the age of eighty-two. Presidents Eisenhower, Truman, and Hoover all published tributes, and Jones was laid to rest in his adopted home of Houston.[65]

As the RFC demonstrated, the most effective way to craft a market is for Congress to invest in an institution with a clear mission and give it the latitude to pursue it. The RFC could have survived the conservative turn in American politics in the postwar years. For that to happen, Jones would have needed to build an institution in the 1930s and '40s to outlast him, cultivating talent and practices that would endure. Congress also would have needed to give it a clear mission and mandate in the postwar economy. But the RFC failed to find a new raison d'être or a leader capable of steering it to success. It had touched the lives of millions of Americans throughout the Great Depression and World War II, rescuing banks, railroads, and farmers while shaping and supporting new markets like housing, aviation, and synthetic rubber. Yet the institution's leaders failed to make a compelling case for its value in a postwar world no longer defined by crisis and without Jones at its helm. Lacking ardent defenders and a viable vision for its future, it crumbled in the hands of a new administration.

Because of the critical nature of its work, many of the RFC programs did endure, even if the parent institution did not. In addition to Fannie Mae and the SBA, the Commodity Credit Corporation continues to exist today, as does the Export-Import Bank, a sibling financial institution that fell under Jones' administration after 1939. In the postwar years, with the aviation industry in sudden decline, Congress approved over $3 billion for plane procurement to minimize production and employment disruption. In the years following, the Pentagon continued to provide working capital and finance research and development in the aviation sector, and the tax incentives to spur aircraft production originally introduced by the Defense Plant Corporation became a permanent part of the fiscal tool kit.[66]

With the RFC's demise, the legacy of Jesse Jones, its architect, champion, and defender, crumbled as well. He had made himself synonymous with the bank, powering its growth in the early years as his Congressional dealmaking led to high levels of funding and an expansive mandate. But an institution that relies on a single leader for its success is not really an institution at all. Because neither Jones nor Roosevelt invested in it for the long term, one of the most consequential efforts of the New Deal and Second World War has been increasingly forgotten. Ironically, Jones' own shortsighted narcissism deprived him of the prominent place in the history of American capitalism he so longed for.

✿

Despite its eventual downfall, the RFC shifted the relationship between the American government and markets, demonstrating that a national investment bank could shape capitalism to work for the public good. Many economic historians believe the New Deal and war efforts succeeded because of the significant level of public investment. Political leaders and economists discovered over the course of the 1930s that government spending could stimulate demand and private economic activity, softening the blow of a recession. The writings of John Maynard Keynes have become a kind of shorthand for the economic takeaways of the period.

While largely true, these historical narratives have often missed the importance of American marketcraft in the Depression and 1930s. Major efforts in economic planning and public regulation such as the National Industrial Relations Act were struck down by the Supreme Court before they could flower. Economic planning never took root in America, but marketcraft did. The national investment bank, led by a moderate businessman, first proved it could *stabilize*, by backstopping faltering financial institutions. In its second, late-Depression life, it showed it could *shape* specific markets by ramping up its direct industrial investing and creating the institutions to foster more residential housing construction. Finally, its wartime investments in industries like aviation and rubber showed that it could *build* markets, setting the stage for their dramatic postwar expansion.

The RFC's approach was thoroughly American, embracing the dynamics of market competition but channeling the guiding power of the state to push them in a productive direction. There was no "socialist" takeover where state ownership of private companies squashed innovation and competition. Instead, it worked through private markets by reducing risk, enhancing liquidity, and providing stopgap funding when financial firms couldn't occupy this role. The RFC largely avoided using public policy to unduly enrich private actors. Even in war, the bank managed to make the fixed investments in plant construction, leasing them back to private companies at reasonable costs and frequently guaranteeing to purchase a certain amount of materials produced. Profits were effectively guaranteed, as long as the private actors used their expertise for the war effort.[67] The RFC used its streamlined decision-making power to become a leading example of government efficiency, embracing a culture of moving fast and cutting red tape wherever possible.[68] Agile, cooperative, and largely accountable to the public, the RFC stands as a useful example of how marketcraft can work at its best.

Jones' memory may have faded, but the impulse to use state power to nurture markets for political goals did not. Competitive markets and a muscular state could work together, if the institutional structure was right. That impulse soon took hold in an institution that had effectively been dormant for decades: the Federal Reserve.

4

THE ARCHITECT OF ORDERLY

BILL MARTIN & THE FEDERAL RESERVE (1951–65)

In the midst of a sweltering Memphis summer, a teenager named Bill Martin stood on a steaming tennis court on the cusp of a dream. Martin had just won his match in the semifinals of a prestigious junior tennis tournament for the first time and would compete in the final—a first for the young sportsman—the following day. One match away from victory, Martin might soon return to his home in St. Louis a champion.

The finals were scheduled for a Saturday, but fate intervened. A sudden summer storm rolled through Memphis, forcing the tournament to postpone the match by a day. Martin soon realized the full weight of the predicament before him. His family was made up of devout Presbyterians, and his father, Bill Martin Sr., the founding Chair of the St. Louis Federal Reserve Bank and later its President, had cultivated a particularly puritan household. All family members were forbidden to drink, dance, gamble, smoke, and play cards. Martin Sr. led his wife and two sons to church each Sunday and quoted the Bible at home. His rare indulgence was an occasional quote of Shakespeare. As a boy, Martin had sometimes secretly brought marbles to church, which his parents considered one of the "small victories" of the devil. On other occasions, when he and his brother argued, their father insisted that "no matter how much insult had been dealt or how serious the matter was, each boy had to address the other with 'Sir, I perceive that you are in error. Allow me

to explain. . . .'" In moments of pronounced disagreement, the boys were allowed to go further and say, "Sir, I perceive that you are in *gross* error."[1]

The family observed the sabbath, which meant no tennis could be played
on the Lord's day. This prohibition was not merely a household rule but a
testament to the values that shaped their lives.

As the Saturday storm passed, Martin faced a profound dilemma for a
competitive teenage tennis player. His parents were back home in St. Louis,
so he would have to make this decision on his own. He could defy them and
play the following day, indulging the young athlete's hunger for recognition.
Or he could heed the call of his conscience.

Martin forfeited the match. He let the tournament know and informed
the family that was hosting him of his decision. The father, who was the head
of Memphis' largest bank, confided in a friend of the family, "That young
man has no future."

Bill Martin later became the longest-serving Chair of the Federal Reserve, working through five presidential administrations. Perceived as a
paragon of conservatism, over the nearly twenty years of his tenure, Martin
designed and led a new kind of central bank, turning it into a core institution
of American marketcraft. The obsequious, tennis-playing teenager never let
go of his ambition, but he got a lot more comfortable with bending the rules
to get what he wanted.

Initially, Martin followed a conventional path. As a teenager, he imbibed his
father's passion for banking and finance. Martin sat down to family dinner
at home with Benjamin Strong, the legendary head of the New York Fed,
and Virginia Senator Carter Glass, who had been instrumental in the Fed's
creation and design in the early 1910s. After high school, he headed to Yale,
where he majored in English, the most vanilla of courses of study at the time,
graduating in 1928. He returned home to St. Louis after graduation to work
for the regional Fed bank where his father was a Director. The next year,
Martin's father became the Governor. (Congress changed the titles of reserve
bank leaders to President a few years later.) Martin Sr. reportedly grew uncomfortable with his son on the payroll of the reserve bank, so he found a job
for the young Martin in a local stock brokerage firm as a "board boy," where
Martin Jr. updated the stock prices on a big chalkboard in the office. A few
months later, he moved into the research department.

Martin was working at that brokerage firm when the stock market fell into its historic tailspin in 1929, leading to the Great Depression. In October of that year, he watched as the office devolved into chaos. As prices fell over the course of "Black Thursday," sell orders began to pile up on desks. The phone lines were blocked, and the stock exchange was physically unable to process orders quickly enough. The ticker tape fell behind as sell orders continued to flood in. Many remained unexecuted by the end of the day. Banks that had lent money to traders began to make margin calls, and Martin watched as the accounts of his firm's customers dwindled away to nothing, forcing many into bankruptcy.

Over the next two years, unemployment in St. Louis shot up to 24 percent, 50 percent higher than the national level. Roving bands of families sought out food scraps from the dumps.[2] For the young Martin, there was no virtue to be found in the chaos of 1929 and the start of the Depression. He saw firsthand that private markets might be effective vehicles for investment, but they could also become forces of profound destruction.

Marked by that early revelation, the otherwise-straightlaced Martin incorporated it into his political and economic outlook. Government could and should organize and guide markets to be fundamentally stable. Only then, with government and finance working hand in hand, could prosperity ensue.

If there were a single word that came to dominate the marketcraft of the mid-century American central bank, it was "orderliness." Bill Martin made it his mantra once he became Fed Chair in 1951, binding together the interests of his conservative allies, bankers, and Martin's more activist critics. A Fed mandate to create and manage orderly markets might sound foreign to free-market conservatism, but after the Depression and the war years, even conservatives believed in government's responsibility to organize and manage markets for the common good. Martin himself always claimed to believe in the virtue of free markets and free enterprise, but what he meant by those terms was quite different from how they're used today.

Fomenting orderly markets was not an altogether new idea in marketcraft. For centuries, even millennia, governments across the globe smoothed price volatility, particularly in agricultural commodity markets, in the interest of preventing shocks.[3] Nineteenth-century American activists had justified their calls for public control of transportation, communications, and credit networks by appealing to the need for government to ensure stable, orderly markets.[4] Jesse Jones' RFC had bought cotton, butter, and corn low and sold

it high in order to buffer markets from demand swings. That work built on
the calls of farmers in the 1910s and '20s for localized efforts to stockpile,
cushioning price movements.

But it was in finance and banking in particular where orderliness had
been a foundational imperative for government. Financial panics and recessions had occurred frequently since the nation's founding, but the Panic of
1907 had been particularly destructive, the worst before 1929. In its wake, reformers began to imagine the creation of a central bank, modeled on those in
Europe, that could mitigate the booms and busts of agricultural and business
cycles. It would do so by managing an elastic currency, tied to the underlying
value of gold, but with banks possessing the power to loosen or tighten the
money supply given market conditions. The nation had resisted the creation
of a central bank for decades. Two attempts in the early nineteenth century
had been dismantled by agrarian and populist concern about consolidated
banker power. By 1913, however, a coalition of agrarian and financial interests agreed that a network of regional central banks could stabilize the
American economy and mitigate the threat of deflationary or inflationary
periods. Congressional leaders, working with President Woodrow Wilson,
chartered the Federal Reserve System—a network of twelve regional reserve
banks with a coordinating board of member banks in Washington.

In the first two decades of its work, the Fed improved the reliability and op-
erability of the American banking system, but it failed to buffer the business
cycle from sharp ups and downs as many economists had hoped. Balkanized
and feuding, the reserve banks did little to contain the speculative surge in
the 1920s that led to the crash. Tighter monetary policy and more aggressive
bank supervision could have mitigated the initial downturn, but the relatively
few moves that the Fed made came too late to matter. Then, in the early years
of the Great Depression, the Fed enabled the wound to fester and deepen
by failing to use its lending power to shore up and stabilize the banking
system. In 1935, Congress reformed the Federal Reserve system to central-
ize decision-making power in Washington, setting the stage for a new, more
effective era that began with World War II.

The early roots of Bill Martin's marketcrafting Fed can be traced back
to the Second World War and the actions of one of Martin's predecessors,
Marriner Eccles. On December 7, 1941, just before 8:00 am, the Japanese air

force had initiated a blistering attack on Pearl Harbor, crippling the American Navy in the Pacific and guaranteeing the United States' entrance into the war. Eccles learned about Pearl Harbor that afternoon, and as soon as he did, he convened his fellow governors of the Fed to work on two problems that would have to be solved as a result: one short-term, and the other long-term. The Treasury was in the middle of selling its own debt in an auction, a customary event that occurred every few weeks before the 1970s. The Pearl Harbor attack happened on Sunday, and this auction had begun on Friday and was slated to last until Wednesday.[5] Given the shock of the attack and the permeating uncertainty about what would come next, the Treasury and Fed worried that interest rates might spike if lenders panicked. People might not want to buy government debt if that government was in chaos, on the precipice of war.

Eccles would not allow that to happen. On the phone that evening, he assured the Secretary of the Treasury, Henry Morgenthau, that the Fed would step in to buy government bills the next day in the market to calm nerves. Eccles told Morgenthau that the Fed intended to buy so aggressively that it would engineer an *increase* in the price, suggesting that investors were so confident in the government's borrowing capacity that they wanted more of its debt. That way, "it would look less like complete fixing," Eccles told Morgenthau in the secret conversation. In addition, the head of the regional New York Fed would tell government debt dealers that the Fed "will stand ready to give support to these long bonds."[6] The Fed was prepared to provide support across the government debt market, not just in the case of this financing auction. The Fed was using its power to engineer calm.

Fixing the bond markets was just the start. The next day Eccles and colleagues released a statement that hit the wires just before 5:00 pm, minutes after Congress declared war on Japan: "[The Federal Reserve] is prepared to use its powers to assure that an ample supply of funds is available at all times for financing the war effort and to exert its influence toward maintaining conditions in the United States Government security market that are satisfactory from the standpoint of the Government's requirements."[7] Behind the thicket of verbosity, the Fed was promising to do whatever it took to enable the US government to fund the war. If necessary, it would use its unique power to print money to buy the Treasury's debt and pay for the fight against Japan—and soon against Germany.

To do that, the wartime Fed shut down the market-driven system of interest rates and replaced it with an administered, centralized one that set both short- and long-term government rates by fiat. This move was akin to a market freeze and was unprecedented. During the First World War, the federal government borrowed at market interest rates and the Fed made no commitment to subsidize the Treasury's cost of borrowing.[8] In the peacetime order between the wars, the Fed implemented its monetary policy by adjusting the overall amount of money in the banking system. Banks themselves had the responsibility of allocating credit through their lending decisions. To fund its spending needs, the federal government collected taxes and borrowed from private investors. In that arrangement, the Fed could tighten or loosen the monetary supply, increasing or decreasing the cost of the debt, but private markets determined the exact rate at which the state could borrow.

Now, at the start of World War II, the Fed named the price. By April 1942, the Fed had implemented an interest-rate peg on short- and long-term government securities, starting at 0.375 percent for thirteen-week bills and rising to 2.5 percent for twenty-five-year bonds. Investors could still buy and sell government debt, but if they tried to sell too cheaply, raising rates, the Fed would bid higher to keep them stable. If rates drifted too low, the Fed could always shed some of the bills on its balance sheet, lowering the price and raising the rate. These bills had, in the words of Eccles, "ceased to be a market instrument."[9] The Fed embraced its power to peg interest rates and became an implementing partner to the Treasury rather than an independent regulating force, giving the US government a guarantee that it could borrow enormous sums of money at cheap rates to fund the war. There was a clear downside. In committing to set rates, regardless of changes in the economy or financial markets, the Fed had relinquished its discretion in making monetary policy. It could no longer meaningfully tighten or loosen the money supply in response to what was happening in the economy—unless it changed the pegged interest rate, which it never did.[10]

Total federal government debt quintupled from $57 billion in 1941 to $271 billion in 1946, reaching 119 percent of GDP by war's end. It wasn't just the Fed buying all that debt. While the Fed did end the war with a swollen balance sheet of $24 billion, nearly the entirety of the remaining $247 billion had made its way onto the balance sheets of America's banks.[11] Banks in the war years became an institutional vehicle for financing the state, with their business shifting from lending to private businesses toward harvesting

THE ARCHITECT OF ORDERLY   55

the guaranteed profits on government securities. By the end of the war, nearly 60 percent of the assets on the balance sheet of banks were government debt and securities and only 18 percent were private loans. (Government securities make up less than 10 percent of banks' balance sheets today.)[12] The banking system had deprecated one of its critical functions in the financial system— private credit allocation—to prioritize the needs of the government. "Interest paid on public debt became little more than a subsidy to private banks, keeping them afloat until the wartime emergency ended," wrote the historian Aaron Wistar.[13] The price of preserving the nation's banking sector was a tacit agreement between the Fed, Treasury, and bank to guarantee their profits.

Few believed this relationship should be permanent. Once the war ended, the demand to revert to a market-based system of banking and finance returned with force. But now the Fed, Congress, and bankers had all learned that the central bank had more awesome powers than anyone had known.

On a Monday in March 1951, Martin settled in at a table in a large, ornate room of the US Capitol. Eleven Senators sat across from him. Just days earlier, President Harry Truman had nominated the forty-four-year-old Martin to become the next Chair of the Federal Reserve. He had enjoyed a stellar ascent. After moving to New York in the early 1930s, he became the Chairman and President of the New York Stock Exchange at age thirty-one, a dark-horse, reformist candidate for the position energized by what he had seen during the Depression. While there, he worked with the new Securities and Exchange Commission (SEC) to stabilize the stock exchange. After serving in the army during the war, Martin became the head of the Export-Import Bank, which had spun out from the family of RFC institutions of which it had previously been a part. In 1949, Martin became the Assistant Secretary of the Treasury and played a pivotal role in negotiations between the Fed and Treasury to end the pegged-rate system that Eccles put in place after Pearl Harbor, giving the Fed more independence.[14] During those negotiations, the previous Fed Chair, Thomas McCabe, had resigned, and Truman's first choice was disqualified from serving. Truman landed on Martin, who, based on his track record, promised to be a reliable technician. No one expected him to redefine the institution.

What the Senators wanted to understand that day was just how Martin thought markets should work. They couldn't give him their blessing until they did. This might seem like a heady, abstract topic, but in the wake of the Second World War it was important to bankers, Congressmen, and Fed officials. Even though the war had ended six years earlier, the Fed had continued enforcing its administered interest rate on most government debt until the Fed and Treasury inked an agreement to give the Fed increased authority, signed just weeks before. Both government officials and bankers worried about the future. The Treasury wanted to keep the pegged interest rates on government securities for as long as possible. If the Fed dropped the wartime order, the government's cost of borrowing would skyrocket, making it much harder to pay down the sizable war debt. Escalating interest rates would also mean a sudden contraction of credit and a recession. That would not be good for bankers either. They welcomed the return of free markets, by which they meant significantly less government control—but only if they could avoid sizable losses in the transition. Should the Fed release the peg without any other action, the value of all those government bonds they had bought would plummet. Many of these businessmen, including the Chairs of Chase National Bank and J.P. Morgan, imagined a hybrid system where the Fed would continue to set short-term interest rates and buffer any dramatic rises or falls in the name of creating an "orderly market."[15] Most importantly, they wanted to avoid panic selling, which could lead to financial crises like in 1907 and 1929.[16] Bankers wanted to redefine a "free market" to mean one where the Fed would set the price of short-term credit and guarantee orderliness.[17,18]

But what would this new market—balanced somewhere between the pegged market of the war and the "free" market that preceded it—look like? In his testimony, Martin answered the question by weaving together a proactive role for government organizing and managing credit markets in pursuit of orderliness—under the *name* of a free market.

"I don't say we are ever going to have completely free markets, because markets are nursed along as children are nursed along," Martin told the Senators. "There are some people who carry this idea of a free market too far." Invoking his experience as the leader of the New York Stock Exchange in the Depression, he made the case that government was at its best when it prioritized orderliness in markets.[19]

Martin was articulating a middle way between laissez-faire and the wartime peg. His long-term belief in rules—those of the church or a good tennis game—could now be used to structure a market to prevent the kind of panic he had witnessed in the first months of his career. A market made orderly by the Fed would avoid the chaos of laissez-faire and the stagnation of pegged rates by ensuring regular transactions could occur at any moment without significant price movements. "I can say that certainly the Federal Reserve should assume the responsibility for an orderly market," Martin said. "When you have an orderly market, that doesn't mean you create a false market but you shouldn't have air pockets in markets. There should never be a point where people who have securities to sell cannot find buyers . . . it creates panic and fear in a market that shouldn't exist."[20] It had been twenty-two years since Martin sat in the brokerage firm office on Black Thursday, but he hadn't forgotten. The following day, the committee voted to advance Martin's confirmation. No committee member of either party opposed him. But now Martin had to figure out exactly how to implement his marketcraft.

Martin testified in Congress a few weeks into the job, explicitly explaining how he was going to go about managing the transition: "[We] don't intend to support prices of government bonds on a pin-point peg, nor let the market go completely on its own, without regard to orderly conditions," he said.[21] Business and finance were happy with what they were hearing. If the Fed was committed to preventing sudden dips in the value of their assets, it meant it would furnish a kind of insurance for their holdings—but one for which they didn't have to pay. The Fed's commitment to order, if it stood by it, would make the government security into a reliable, liquid, and abundant asset.[22] Martin was not motivated by a conspiratorial desire to enrich banker friends, but it was clear that a stable money market would reduce volatility and enhance banks' confidence to lend.

Martin believed that their confidence to extend credit would be the primary means for the Fed to help American workers. Orderly, stable markets would increase investors' confidence, making them more likely to provide credit. As credit became more abundant and cheap, businesses would grow and hire workers. Stable and abundant credit in the banking system would mean more jobs. When a crisis hit, the Fed's market support would ensure credit didn't dry up overnight, lessening the impact of a recession on labor markets and preventing unnecessary unemployment. Martin's Fed would use its power to structure financial markets to be orderly and stable, helping investors and American workers alike.

✿

In the beginning, Martin was intent on clarifying the Fed's mandate for order as a rare response to market chaos. He used the same language to describe his intentions that many use today. Markets would work "freely" on most days, and the Fed would "intervene" only in emergencies to prevent another 1929-style panic. Martin claimed the Fed would only work in short-term credit markets, so that medium- and long-term markets would only be indirectly influenced by the central bank's policy decisions. It would also avoid setting any short-term interest rate—as today's Fed does—and use its control over banks' reserves to tighten or loosen monetary policy. These may seem like insignificant technicalities with modest limits on Fed power, but the consequences were enormous. Moving forward, the Fed would not support Treasury financings, as it had previously. It would only "intervene" in the market in moments of significant disorder. "Under the hard choices left us in wartime, we had to dictate even some of the smallest details of our economic life, but that strait-jacketing of the economy is wholly inconsistent with democratic institutions and a private enterprise system," he said in a speech in 1953.[23]

But it didn't take long for him to realize that the markets couldn't work this way. Just a month after Martin's speech, the Treasury mispriced a large tranche of long-term bonds, causing speculators to buy in bulk. When prices failed to go up as expected and the speculators' expected profits evaporated, they dumped the government securities. Investors had taken Martin's speech about rare Fed intervention literally and assumed that the Fed would not come to their rescue. That prompted a panic in the market, putting the Fed's rhetorical commitment to free markets to the test. Martin stepped in to do exactly what he said the Fed would do in extraordinary circumstances. He concocted a fig-leaf cover—the Fed was vacuuming up long-term bonds to "give elbow room" to market actors. But in reality, the Fed pursued its most serious stabilizing activity in years by purchasing $150 million worth of short-term bonds, known as Treasury bills. As markets continued to slide over the coming days, Martin's Fed bought another $82 million of bills, this time in a single day. The Fed also bought nearly $4 million in the long-term bond market where Martin had promised not to trade, although technically as an agent of the Treasury. Markets calmed.[24]

This stabilization activity was just the beginning of the efforts to come. Once the Fed started guiding markets for orderliness, it couldn't stop. The moments of disorder came so fast and frequently that market participants and Fed governors realized that the Fed wasn't just stepping in at moments of crisis. It was constantly crafting. Martin had promised in 1953 only to intervene in the case of significant events, but by 1961 the charade of only rare "intervention" came to an end, at least to those in the know.

Several events had made it clear that the Fed was not interjecting only on rare occasions. First, the Fed had dropped the pretense that it wasn't guiding interest rates. When the Fed chooses to tighten or loosen the country's money supply, it has a few different ways to do so. The Martin Fed initially promised only to adjust bank reserve levels, but over time it adopted a significantly more precise procedure first pioneered in the 1920s called open market operations. The Fed participates in the government securities market as a buyer and seller, using its large balance sheet to guide the price of credit in the direction it desires. In the 1950s, the Fed began buying and selling government securities daily—not just in moments of distress—to keep interest rates stable and appropriately high or low given the market backdrop. These same open market operations are still a major tool in the efforts of today's Fed to guide money markets to its desired outcomes.

In addition, the Fed had taken so-called extraordinary action so often that market participants knew that the Martin Fed would always insure extreme downside risk. By 1961, the Fed had taken major action on four occasions in less than eight years. In 1955, after a Treasury financing event failed to attract sufficient private-sector buyers, the Fed stepped in to purchase Treasury debt despite its promise just two years earlier not to do so. It was a bad look, so the Fed deepened its use of "repurchase" agreements, or "repos," which gave Martin the power to inject money into markets without the public or Congress knowing the extent of the Fed's support.[25] Three years later, upheaval in the Middle East and uncertainty about the economic outlook caused demand for Treasuries to evaporate, sending the market into a downward spiral. With rates surging, the Fed "could not stand by and let the market move on its own" as one Reserve Bank President put it.[26] The Fed unanimously voted to authorize purchases of government securities "without limitation," eventually spending a record $1.2 billion.[27]

By 1960, the pattern of ongoing management of the market was so clear that politicians were increasingly demanding that the Fed push the boundaries of its mandate to preserve orderliness. They could see the Fed crafting markets for stability, so why couldn't it adopt even more explicit goals such as boosting domestic investment and strengthening the dollar? The Martin Fed agreed to an experiment, initiating a program of long-term bond purchases and short-term bond sales that came to be known as "Operation Twist."[28] The Fed was now shaping short- and long-term interest rates, without waiting for a market panic to precipitate the moves. Martin was testing the boundaries of the Fed's mandate to orderliness, experimenting with using monetary policy to go further to support the dollar's strength and incentivize long-term investment. This kind of collaboration between Martin and political leaders was rare, but it continued sporadically. In 1963, Martin even agreed to raise the Fed's discount rate, the amount it charged banks to borrow directly from the Fed, in coordination with President John F. Kennedy's legislative push for a tax cut. The *New York Times* described Martin's decision on the front page of the business section: "To the political observer, this marks an open liaison between the Federal Reserve System and the New Frontier," the name Kennedy had given to his domestic policy program.[29]

Rhetorically, Martin continued to describe the Fed's activity as supporting a "free market," which kept him on the good side of bankers and Congress. But his actions were louder than his words. Martin was redefining what a "free market" meant: one managed and guided by the Fed.

The savviest participants in this policy development were happy to call it what it was—a centrally managed bond market. Allan Sproul, President of the New York Federal Reserve and the second most powerful central banker in the country, privately made sure the Fed governors understood that this was far from a free market in a laissez-faire sense. He was also more willing to explain what was happening publicly. "So far as 'free markets' are concerned, I think we are all attracted by the phrase. It suits our habit of mind. But we haven't had a free market in money and credit, at least since the Federal Reserve System was established," Sproul said in a speech to the New Jersey Bankers Association. "[W]e haven't had a free market in government securities, and therefore a wholly free securities market, since the government debt climbed to the higher magnitudes, and open market operations by the Federal Reserve System came to be used as a principal instrument of credit policy."[30]

On the Hill, Texas Congressman Wright Patman named what Martin was doing as well. Patman was no friend of bankers or to the Fed, having used his postwar perch on the Banking Committee to make the case for government taking over the stock in the twelve reserve banks, which turned them into full government entities. After Martin took the helm and began to craft orderly money markets, Patman called out the commitment to orderliness as a pretext for ongoing government management. As historian Aaron Wistar writes, "Rather than using the smoke and mirrors of 'orderly markets' to disguise market support, Patman implied that if the Fed was going to support the market, it might as well return to explicitly pegging bonds at par."[31]

The Nobel Prize–winning economist Milton Friedman, whose influence in economic circles was just beginning to build, felt similarly. "'Orderly markets' has become a semantic cloak hiding the desire to resist all price declines," he testified to Congress.[32] For him, the Fed's maintenance of orderly markets distorted the price signals of a market driven by the forces of private demand. Friedman wanted a different kind of state management of money markets: a steady and reliable increase in the money supply, managed by the Fed, but without day-to-day guidance or crisis-induced changes.

As the 1950s gave way to the 1960s, it was increasingly clear that the Fed's commitment to supporting orderly markets in government securities was not going anywhere as long as Martin was Fed Chair. But Martin himself was evolving. Increasingly appreciative of the Fed's power to guide markets and shape industries, he began to pursue another kind of marketcraft. He pursued this one, however, in the shadows and far away from the scrutiny of the media and Congress.

Martin's affinity for rules had animated his professional success. It had defined his early career at the New York Stock Exchange in the Depression and the efforts to create orderly markets. He conducted meetings of the Federal Open Market Committee (FOMC) in the same fashion, creating a rule that each Reserve Bank President would speak first before he did. He took a break every day for a midday tennis match. He created a rule that he would avoid direct contradiction of a sitting President. Mandates such as these had worked well for him, driving his career success.

But Martin's appreciation for rules meant that when he met one that he *didn't* agree with, it could be maddening. There was one in particular that made his life, and the work of the Federal Reserve, particularly challenging. In the 1930s, Congress had created "Regulation Q," which required the Fed to cap the interest rates banks could pay for savings accounts. It also forbade banks from offering any return on demand deposits, such as those contained in a standard checking account. Legislators thought that competition for deposits had helped precipitate the 1929 financial crisis by forcing banks to pursue riskier investments to compensate for the high rates they were paying on deposits. Banning returns on demand deposits and capping those on savings would make banking more like a public utility—partially shielded from market pressures and operating with limited profitability.

Nearly thirty years later, those regulations felt antiquated and useless to many, including Martin. Few believed that interest-rate competition was what had set off the Great Depression, and the regulations were now making life difficult for the Fed. Because of the regulation, deposits were flooding out of standard commercial banks and moving into riskier, money-like financial products. This trend was a particular problem in moments of high interest rates when the trickle of deposit loss would turn into a flood. In these periods, because the rate of return was capped by the Fed due to Regulation Q, a depositor might only get 5 percent in a savings account at a commercial bank, yet they could get 7 percent by investing in a government bond or loaning the money overnight to a large, stable company such as General Electric. Why would they even bother to park money at a commercial bank given the lower return? As a result, the markets for money-like investment products like Treasuries, commercial paper, offshore dollars, and repurchase agreements were growing, just as the deposits in the commercial banking system were dwindling.

Legally, the Fed only had the power to regulate commercial banks. Other investment products were not in its domain, and some were not regulated in any meaningful way. Perhaps more importantly, the Fed's monetary policy relied on adjusting the reserve levels of commercial banks, largely through open market operations. As deposits in those very banks dried up, the Fed's tools to implement its monetary policy were at risk of becoming less effective.[33] (Today, the Fed's methods of implementing its monetary policy have changed, giving it more power over similar money-like products that exist in current financial markets.)[34] If the Fed were going to maximize its power to guide the economy, it needed commercial banks to remain the center of private credit creation and allocation.[35] Regulation Q was standing in the way.

But if Regulation Q was an ongoing headache for Bill Martin, it threatened to undermine the careers of many in finance, including the future CEO of First National City Bank, the precursor to Citicorp, Walter Wriston. The son of an economics professor, Wriston grew up in Connecticut, then served in the Second World War as an intelligence officer and returned home to begin work as a banker in New York. As he ascended the ranks at First National City, Wriston toyed with how to use financial innovation and technology to make banking more efficient. He was particularly infatuated by the idea of a cashless society, facilitated by credit cards and electronic transfers. Such a concept was more than a business strategy; it was a mission to democratize finance and unleash "free markets."

The problem was that New York banks like First National City were getting hit hard by the Regulation Q deposit flight. Total deposits in the United States had grown by $57 billion since 1947, but New York banks, historically the most powerful and dominant in the system, made up less than 3 percent of that growth.[36] The share of total deposits held by New York commercial banks within the national commercial banking system had shrunk by 40 percent over the past twenty years.[37] First National City had attempted to catch up by consolidating with other banking institutions and chasing more retail deposits. Both strategies failed.[38] By 1960, the pressure to circumvent the law was building. Market interest rates had exceeded Reg Q ceilings, and the deposit flight was accelerating. "You didn't have to be too smart to know you had to do something to survive," Wriston said when reflecting back years later. "We were hemmed in in this country, and the stagnation in New York led to the invention [of something new]."[39]

Martin and Wriston were interested in solving the same problem: sidestepping Congressional regulation to get money back into commercial banks. The question was: How to do this when it would be pushing the boundaries of the law?

Two New York Fed officials connected Martin and Wriston in their effort to sidestep government regulation: John Exter and Howard Crosse. Exter had spent his career in international finance, working as an economist at the Federal Reserve; at one point, he departed the Fed to set up the central bank of today's Sri Lanka. In 1959, Exter left his position at the New York Fed to work with Wriston.

Just a few months into his new job, Exter wrote a set of memos describing how a new financial product could avoid the troublesome interest-rate cap and solve the deposit leakage problem. Exter built the idea for the new financial product on the certificate of deposit (CD), which had existed for decades. Before Exter's invention, cashing in a CD before its maturity brought a meaningful penalty, making the funds illiquid and inaccessible for the depositor. (Banks benefited from the illiquidity by being able to issue longer-term loans since the deposits were less likely to flee.) Exter's innovation was to make the CD marketable. The so-called negotiable CD could be sold in a secondary market at any time before its maturity date. A CD that could be bought and sold at any time would make it a long-term, yield-bearing financial asset exempt from interest cap regulation *and* entirely liquid for the depositor. As long as the secondary market had abundant buyers, a depositor could have nearly immediate access to funds and enjoy the return not available on demand deposits. If savers could get liquidity and a high return, they would rush to transfer their money back into commercial banks.[40] Wriston could see the opportunity in Exter's idea. He began organizing the bank's leadership behind the negotiable CD and managed to get Exter promoted a few months later to Senior Vice President of the bank.[41]

Meanwhile, Exter's former colleague at the New York Fed Howard Crosse could see in Exter's brewing idea the key to dismantling Regulation Q. He knew that Exter's plan hinged on the creation of a secondary market for the negotiable CD. The Fed would have to approve that, and that decision in the short term would fall to him. Crosse was the Vice President in charge of banking regulation and supervision, making him the policeman for all New York banks. Despite that responsibility, Crosse showed a marked willingness to interpret the law selectively, prioritizing certain regulations and disregarding others.

A decade later a scandal would end his career, but already Crosse was dancing close to the ethical line in his relationships with private market actors. In 1960, Exter met with Crosse to discuss the plans for the negotiable CD and assess the Fed's interest in supporting the effort. Officially the New York Fed made no public statement, but a few weeks before the new product was announced, Crosse let slip in a speech that something big was coming. Banks had a choice: revert to an older, simpler business model or cook up new products to attract more deposits, he said. Crosse believed they needed to move toward "more flexible and competitive rates on time deposits" by creating new products to "aggressively" seek funds in search of return and liquidity. "[P]erhaps a nationwide market in 'prime bank certificates' will develop," he said. That label—"prime bank certificates"—was the confidential internal name for the negotiable CD that First National City had developed. He and Exter had been plotting the rollout, which would happen any day.

With the Fed and First National City in partnership, the only remaining major barrier to the launch was the creation of a secondary market. For the CDs to be liquid, each bearer certificate would need to be marketable to a buyer. A depositor would need confidence that they could sell the CD to someone else, providing immediate access to the funds. Wriston and Exter scheduled a meeting with Herbert Repp, the CEO of the Discount Corporation, a prominent government securities dealer. They pitched their new product, and Repp was intrigued. At one point in the meeting, Repp asked Wriston how large the market might be and Wriston responded by estimating "two to three billion dollars." Exter balked, interrupting his boss. "Walt, it'll go much higher than that," Exter said. "It will go into the tens of billions." Exter turned out to be right. By the end of the meeting, the pair had convinced Repp to become a dealer and make the market, although Repp did exact a commitment from First National City to break the bank's policy and lend $10 million unsecured to facilitate the setup. Wriston got his bosses to agree.

On February 21, 1961, First National City rolled out the negotiable CD. The *New York Times* covered the news in depth.[42] Wriston and Exter had convinced one of the prominent dealers in government securities to "make the market" by connecting buyers and sellers of the new product, and trades took off.[43]

Bill Martin was pleased. He convened the Fed's Board of Governors in Washington for an unplanned discussion a week after the negotiable CD's launch to evaluate the impact of the new product. Martin had been inundated with calls over the weekend since the announcement of the negotiable CD, asking for the Fed's position. The popularity of the product meant that he needed to wrangle his fellow Fed governors quickly to green-light the new market. The sense of the board was not hard to assess. The governors were supportive of First National City's move, partially because of its clever way to evade Regulation Q. If he had wanted, Martin undoubtedly could have stopped the negotiable CD in its tracks, on the grounds that it was an effort to pay interest on demand deposits in violation of the law. He chose not to do so.[44] Instead, sensing the momentum, Martin floated a more ambitious idea. The Fed could issue a public statement affirming a desire to remove Regulation

Q altogether. "Chairman Martin stated at this point that he would support a recommendation, if it should be made, for complete repeal of the statute requiring the Board to fix maximum rates on time and savings deposits," the minutes of the meeting read. Despite Martin's gusto, the governors were not quite willing to be so public, fearing that the Fed could be seen as overstepping its bounds. Martin tabled the idea, and Fed staff were assigned the fig-leaf task of "further study" of the negotiable CD.[45]

No regulatory action would be taken, making the New York Fed and First National City's marketcrafting project unstoppable. Over the years following, Martin and the Board of Governors nurtured the growth of the new negotiable CD market by increasing the interest-rate caps on all certificates of deposit. That attracted still more funds into the new instruments—and into the commercial banks that provided them. By 1962, not even two years after the creation, CD volume had reached $6 billion. For context, when the New York banks felt they were hemorrhaging deposits in 1959, they had lost $1 billion.[46] By 1966, total CD volume had reached $18 billion.[47] "The [negotiable] CD heralded a new era of growth for big money-center banks, enabling them not only to meet the financing demands of a booming economy but also to create demand by purchasing and selling money," Wriston's biographer Phillip Zweig wrote. "These events marked the transformation of banking from a public utility to a business, and of bankers from staid men with green eyeshades to gunslinging entrepreneurs."[48]

Wriston benefited enormously. His power in the bank grew, boosted by his claimed authorship of the product. Flush with deposits, First National City—later renamed Citicorp—became a domestic and global powerhouse.[49] Wriston became CEO in 1967. "By force of intellect, acerbic wit, and hobnail boots, he transformed Citicorp from a genteel utility, where golf scores counted for more than IQ, into a tough, arrogant corporate meritocracy that dragged the rest of the industry out of the era of quill pen banking," wrote Zweig.[50] The myth of Wriston became the story of a creative visionary who learned how to undermine or manipulate government regulations to build a world-class business. That narrative, in turn, was founded on his invention of the new financial product, the negotiable CD, that reversed the deposit outflow.

In 1963, the New York Fed's Crosse took public credit for the launch of the negotiable CD: "I have been very interested in the CD since I had something to do with its launching a couple of years ago."[51] Government and private interest had conspired to evade Congressional mandate, and Crosse couldn't help taking some of the credit. Ironically, this tendency to blur the lines between legal and illegal would cause his celebrated career to end in infamy: he left the New York Fed in 1965 to join the leadership team of a regional lender with global ambition, Franklin National Bank.[52] In 1974, after the bank pursued risky loans in the offshore dollar market, Franklin National went bankrupt, making it the largest bank failure in American history at the time. A few months later, Crosse pled guilty in federal court to falsifying the bank's records to hide significant losses. "I knew this was contrary to sound accounting principles and not the right thing to do," he said.[53]

Martin perhaps ended up being the biggest winner. Funds moved back into the commercial banking system, enhancing liquidity in the economy by making bank credit more abundant and accessible. The Fed's monetary-policy tools would continue to work as the Fed wanted, loosening or tightening the money supply when necessary. Wriston the entrepreneur may have gotten the glory for the negotiable CD, but it was the Fed's marketcrafting program that was the big winner. Martin had built an orderly market in government securities and managed to sidestep Congress to strengthen commercial banks and the power of the Fed itself.

Martin's top-line commitment to orderly markets seemed to have largely worked to spur investment-led growth. Interest rates remained relatively stable into the late 1960s. Periods of tight credit were modest, and investor confidence was never meaningfully shaken. That stability contributed to a rise in investment, as Martin had hoped. Private fixed investment averaged 7 percent per year between 1953 and 1971, and economic growth was similarly robust.[54] In the midst of all that success, however, signs of future instability were surfacing. By 1968, inflation threatened to disrupt the precious orderliness that Martin had cultivated. Government deficits—driven by social spending and Vietnam—were pushing inflation toward levels unseen since before the 1951 Accord. "I do not see how it can be any plainer than it is now that [orderly, functioning markets] cannot be provided by monetary policy alone," Martin said in a 1968 speech. "Nor can I see how it could be any plainer that, *whatever* course monetary policy may follow, there will *still* be prospects for trouble unless and until our Government's finances are brought into better control."[55]

With Congress avoiding paying for its expenditures, the responsibility for inflation fighting was falling on the Fed. It would need to keep markets orderly
while fulfilling its mandate to keep prices stable, a significantly more challenging task. But it would not be Martin who would have to solve that problem.

In October 1969, Richard Nixon informed Martin in a private Oval Office meeting that he intended to nominate Nixon's adviser Arthur Burns to
chair the Fed. Martin's nearly nineteen-year run was coming to an end. That
Christmas, his wife and he traveled to the Bahamas. In the gray mornings,
he walked the beach in his pajamas and a raincoat, admiring the view and
pocketing seashells.[56] At a celebratory farewell dinner hosted by Nixon at the
White House a few weeks later, Martin delivered grim news to the guests
attired in black tie and gowns. Inflation was surging, and he personally apologized for his role in its rise. "Uneasy applause" followed, before a dancing
troupe flooded into the room in an attempt to raise the spirits. Martin had
popularized the idea that the Fed, in tightening monetary policy, worked like
a party host who "took away the punch bowl" at a party before it grew too
raucous. At his own farewell party, he couldn't help doing the same.

Despite his despondency, Martin left the Fed stronger than he found it,
having shaped it into a preeminent institution of marketcraft. Using a new
mandate for "orderliness," he created a central bank that smoothed the gyrations of markets and set the price of short-term credit through direct market
operations. That marketcraft—the intentional use of the Fed's power to set
the price of short-term credit and stabilize markets—made him its most influential leader until Alan Greenspan's arrival decades later. When regulatory
frameworks challenged the operations of commercial banks and threatened
the power and effectiveness of the Fed, he worked with the private sector
to sidestep that regulation. His marketcraft fostered a strong commercial
banking sector and deep, liquid money markets. The consummate conservative rule follower grew into a practical leader who saw immense value in a
centralized, powerful central bank.

Unfortunately, neither his fellow governors nor his successor as Chair,
Arthur Burns, liked to think of the organization as one that pursued marketcraft. That reticence would make their work to strengthen the dollar and
fight inflation in subsequent years even more difficult than it otherwise could
have been.

5

CRAFTING HEALTH-CARE MARKETS

KATHERINE ELLICKSON & MEDICARE (1948–68)

Two years into the Great Depression, a young woman stood in the Kanawha coalfield of southern West Virginia, hands fixed behind her back, surrounded by hundreds of miners. Some sat on the ground, and others stood in the early summer heat. The miners were weighing whether to create a union, and they had come to hear her speak about their power to organize. Their wages were just cents a day, and 90,000 workers in the region were considering walking out. Spontaneous strikes had occurred in nearby coalfields, and Katherine Ellickson expected something similar to happen any day now. She was there to breathe confidence into the organizing effort and report back to labor leaders in New York and Washington on what was happening. "The miners here," Ellickson wrote from West Virginia, "are desperate, and like their mountaineer brothers in Kentucky, they can shoot."[1]

A twenty-six-year-old Vassar graduate, Ellickson had come to the region as a labor organizer, but she was also chronicling her experience for a journal of labor activity. The daughter of German Jewish immigrants, Ellickson grew up in a family that supported her education and union-organizing efforts. After college, she joined a small cohort of labor leaders fighting to challenge the pro-business consensus of the roaring twenties by organizing the masses of industrial workers who had been neglected by the nation's leading union, the American Federation of Labor (AFL). Millions of unorganized workers were "semiskilled," and many of them were immigrants or children of immigrants from southern and eastern Europe. At this moment, however, Ellickson stood in the West Virginia coalfields, surrounded by men whose families had worked for generations in the mines. A young Jewish woman who lacked legal protection for union organizing, Ellickson plowed forward unintimidated.[2]

It was this affinity for taking on high-risk gambits that drove Ellickson to become one of the most historic labor leaders in American history. Often overshadowed by the bombast of prominent men around her, Ellickson laid the plans for a wholesale reorganization of American health care. That work began a few years after her visit to the West Virginia coalfields. In 1935, Ellickson helped start the Congress of Industrial Organizations (CIO), a new labor alliance where she became the first employee. For decades, the AFL had focused on organizing skilled workers into specific craft unions, but by the middle of the Depression, a new set of voices wanted to go bigger and broader. Ellickson and several others split from the AFL, with the intent to create a new union that would include all workers within an industry. Whereas the AFL parceled autoworkers into existing unions of electricians, painters, and machinists, the CIO wanted to bring all of those unions, plus the masses of assembly line workers, into a single body, the United Auto Workers. This inclusive approach to the workplace also meant a more militant and politically progressive stance. By 1937, the CIO had won contracts with GM and US Steel, two of the largest enterprises in world history—and until then, union-free. Soon the CIO would represent millions of workers across industries.

By the early 1940s, Ellickson had begun to devote herself to what would become her life's work: using the power of the labor movement to create a broad social and health insurance system for all Americans. In 1942, Ellickson became the CIO's Assistant Research Director after a brief hiatus from the CIO to have two children. "I had the option of working for the labor movement when it paid very little, [an option that] somebody less fortunately placed might not have had," she said later. "My husband did not expect me to devote myself entirely to him or to the family. My working and accomplishments may have been a threat to him but he did not protest."[3] That kind of spousal support was uncommon, but not unique. By the 1940s, many policy experts belonged to "a sexually modernist, relatively feminist left-liberal scene in Washington," in the words of one historian.[4]

When she returned to the CIO in the 1940s, the nation was at war. With its attention elsewhere, she began to lay the conceptual plans and build the political coalition necessary to reimagine insurance markets. She envisioned building on the New Deal's creation of old-age insurance and unemployment insurance to go bigger and wider, protecting all American workers from the precariousness of mid-century American capitalism. No single thing was more important than access to affordable health care.

The idea of national health insurance started percolating early in the twentieth century, when activists in the Progressive Era proposed compulsory health insurance for industrial workers when sick, mirroring the calls for similar social insurance in western Europe. It would be a leap forward from the bandaid of employer-based insurance that helped cover sick leave by enabling all Americans to access preventative care and treatment for chronic ailments, reducing the collective burden of sickness. State legislatures debated the idea, but none managed to pass a program, largely because existing insurers and doctors mobilized against government involvement. During the New Deal, Roosevelt convened a set of his advisers to develop a social insurance scheme. The committee considered including a plan for national health insurance, but they dropped the idea, fearing organized resistance from the American Medical Association (AMA) and doctors. Instead, the committee proposed old-age pension insurance, which became Social Security in late 1935.

After the war, many expected that the first domestic policy priority would be health care. Before he died, Roosevelt had outlined an "economic bill of rights," including the right to adequate health care, and outside of recovery from the war, it seemed to be the most urgent domestic priority. In the first half of the twentieth century, medicine became a lot better—and a lot more expensive. New technologies and medical insights increased the number of procedures available to sick Americans—most of which needed to be performed in hospitals. Advances in anesthesia and antiseptic surgery, the proliferation of blood transfusions, the invention of insulin, and improvement in X-ray technology all meant that patients—mostly middle-class or rich—needed more medical procedures than ever.

Even though demand for medical services was growing, the number of providers was not keeping pace. In the early twentieth century, a movement to license doctors prompted most practitioners to join the AMA. Those licensing requirements set qualifications for who could practice and heightened the requirements of medical education, reducing the supply of doctors. More importantly, licensure required them to agree to a Code of Ethics, which blocked the creation of group practices and contract medicine. Doctors were largely self-employed, their numbers dispersed across the country. Any attempt to bind together and make service provision more efficient was punishable by expulsion from state and county medical societies. In a world where membership in county medical associations was normally a prerequisite for maintaining credentials with local hospitals or obtaining malpractice insurance, the requirement meant the code functioned as the contractual terms of a nationwide sellers' cartel.[5] Doctors were not allowed to work together, and they were obligated to support the national membership organization, the AMA.[6]

More demand and less supply meant escalating medical costs, which became particularly problematic for the middle class in the 1920s. In the past, Americans had paid for doctors' visits out of pocket, because they were simple and rare, and involved few hospital procedures. "Now, people who are economically secure, humanly speaking, against all ordinary demands, are not secure against the costs of sickness," said one prominent leader in the health-care fight in 1934.[7] Health insurance became a way of budgeting larger medical expenses for individuals, not just a fallback in case of extreme illness.[8]

Ellickson wanted to craft a different kind of market, and the CIO was at the center of those efforts. In the two decades following the war, labor became *the* most important social force backing the effort to redesign health care for the nation, not just for its workers. Before the war, labor had not always been supportive of the efforts for national insurance schemes, often preferring to focus on negotiated agreements between workers and employers. The CIO now intended to support the kind of sweeping social insurance programs that the AFL, which had preferred to focus narrowly on the needs of its discrete unions, had historically avoided.

Ellickson convinced her counterpart at the AFL, Nelson Cruikshank, to work together with her in the early years of the campaign. Elizabeth Wickenden ("Wicky" to friends), another well-connected Vassar graduate, moderated the discussions between Cruikshank and Ellickson to ensure that any

AFL and CIO rivalry didn't disrupt the united front. Ellickson and Cruik-shank developed enough rapport that they even considered forming a joint office to consolidate the separate campaigns, a rare overture of coordination in the rivalry between the two unions. In the end, the AFL held back because of reservations that the CIO might prove too radical, but even so, Cruik-shank had convinced his bosses that cooperation on this issue would likely bear fruit.[9] The two also brought in Wilbur Cohen from the Social Security Administration, who would become increasingly influential in the coming years. The core figures in this organizing unit "were in almost daily com-munication" in the early stages of the fight.[10] By 1943, they had engineered the introduction of a cradle-to-grave welfare bill, which included a plan for

• national health insurance. Its legislative sponsor told the idealists that the bill "would never be passed in anything like its original form," but Ellickson and her team knew that already. The point was to start building legislative momentum. "The function of the labor movement," she reflected, "is to keep holding up the goal of what is needed . . . even if it can't be attained."[11] Whatever its prospect, legislators could be confident that the progressive policy frameworks were supported by a united front of the CIO, the AFL, and prominent "technicians" within government.

After the war, Truman began the expected push for national health insur-ance, picking up on the call Roosevelt had made in his final State of the Union.[12] Ellickson and the "social security division" within the CIO began to mobilize for the idea. She had a worthy adversary in the AMA. Fearing any government involvement would constrain doctors' freedom and limit their economic upside, the AMA organized to block virtually any bill. When Truman surprisingly won reelection in 1948, the CIO escalated its efforts, initiating a major campaign to pass the national health insurance plan in 1949. "Only widespread popular demand can force action of even a mild kind by the present Congress," Ellickson wrote when she first began to lay the plans.[13] Now, she and her AFL counterpart, Cruikshank, began to coordinate a broad-based labor effort. For his part, Truman was willing to keep fight-ing on the issue, reflecting a naivete about the strength of the AMA—and a conviction for change inspired by the abysmal conditions he had witnessed as a county-level politician.

Within days of Truman's reelection, both the AFL and the CIO were conferring on strategy with top Social Security officials such as Arthur Alt-meyer, Wilbur Cohen, and I. S. Falk.[14] At one characteristic meeting in late December 1948, Ellickson joined Altmeyer, Cohen, and Falk for an audience with Truman's economic adviser Leon Keyserling.[15] The group discussed health insurance "and all other soc. sec. fields."[16] The walk from the CIO headquarters to the offices of the CEA was just a few minutes' stroll down West Executive Avenue. In the 1920s and '30s, Ellickson would later recall, she thought she would end up involved "maybe with a revolution or something." But she "never expected to end up in a marble, almost—palace, near the White House!"[17] The support of Ellickson and labor was becoming increasingly criti-cal to the effort. "[F]or the first time, a political base had been established for a broad legislative program. This base was the united support manifested by organized labor," wrote one leading scholar and activist at the time.[18]

Ellickson devoted an entire special issue of the widely read *Economic Out-look* pamphlet to national health insurance and distributed it to legislators, the media, and other influential voices. The CIO paid for a full-page ad in seventy-seven newspapers and waged a battle for support in the media.[19] The CIO's campaign wing also mobilized ordinary people to speak about their concrete experience. Prominent CIO leaders testified before Congress, but so did Anna Hilton, the wife of a union shipbuilder from Camden, New Jer-sey. When complications from acute appendicitis landed her husband in the hospital for months, the charges were over $5,000, or $65,000 in today's dol-lars. Hilton had a good union job, and the family even had voluntary medical insurance. But the insurance would cover only 12 percent of the total bill. Even for a family with more of a safety net than most workers, the conse-quences of routine illness could be catastrophic.[20] The local CIO officials guided the Hiltons to union support, and their story filtered its way up to Ellickson at national headquarters.

The nation's doctors brought even more firepower. The AMA levied an emergency twenty-five-dollar-per-member assessment to fund a vast lobby-ing and public relations fight against Truman's efforts.[21] By the time Truman announced his support for a robust national health insurance plan, it had hired a public relations firm for $1.5 million, more than any group had spent on a lobbying campaign before.[22] That firm in turn hired dozens of employ-ees to mount a nationwide campaign against the idea. "Who is for Com-pulsory Health Insurance?" one of the pamphlets it distributed asked. "The

Federal Security Administration. The President. All who seriously believe in a Socialistic State. Every leftwing organization in America . . . The Communist Party." It even quoted Soviet leader Vladimir Lenin as saying, "Socialized medicine is the keystone to the arch of the Socialist State."[23] There is no evidence of this statement, or anything similar, in Lenin's works. It didn't matter. With anti-Soviet rhetoric heating up in the early days of the Cold War, the AMA's criticism took hold much faster than the CIO's advocacy campaign. "This is medical dictatorship at its worst," one Senator said.[24]

The AMA's aggressive pushback worked. By the end of 1949, hopes for legislative passage of a national health insurance program faded. Congressional leadership did not even bring the issue to a vote. Truman continued to call for it in the remaining years of his presidency, but by 1951, most health policy experts and insiders had moved on.[25] "I have had some bitter disappointments as President, but the one that has troubled me most, in a personal way, has been the failure to defeat the organized opposition to a national compulsory health-insurance program," Truman later said.[26] It was a personal defeat for Ellickson. Almost forty-five, she knew how rarely the political window opened for sweeping change.[27] It had now closed, and she would have to find a plan B. The fight for Medicare began.

Marketcraft can sometimes feel like designing a house from scratch, as in the creation of global aviation or Treasury markets. But more often, it's like taming an overgrown garden—bringing order to complex, entrenched markets where corporate interests and consumer habits resist change. In these cases, like in health-care markets, where many prefer the familiar, effective marketcraft becomes especially challenging.

In the years after Ellickson's first defeat, Americans started paying more for health care with few results to show for it. Demand for doctor and hospital services continued rising, fueled by further scientific progress. By the 1950s, doctors had largely learned how to manage infectious diseases, and the bulk of medical attention turned to combating chronic diseases such as cancer, heart disease, and neurosis. Treating them was expensive, and private insurance plans grew quickly to manage the cost. In 1946, about a million Americans had private insurance plans, but by 1957, the number was up to 30 million, including dependents.[28] Two policy actions during the war had helped spur the growth of private insurance in the postwar years. Congress had incentivized corporations to invest in health-care funds for employees as a way for companies to avoid the excess-profits tax. Federal authorities had also allowed companies to offer health benefits despite wartime wage and price controls, making these benefits a way of attracting workers in the tight labor market of the war.[29]

After the collapse of the national health insurance effort in 1949, the CIO and other unions went "full blast" in pursuit of greater private insurance provision, aiming to press employers to provide it to workers.[30] A series of judicial and administrative decisions affirmed in 1949 that pensions and health care were legitimate objects of collective bargaining. Over the next five years, around 7.5 million workers gained health care through labor actions, equivalent to a more than threefold increase. By 1954, three out of every four union members had secured medical benefits.[31] In the early 1960s, over two-thirds of the American population had private health insurance. Unfortunately, these plans were often expensive and unreliable. Premiums were increasing by double digits, and insurers were abusing their power by telling some who filed claims that they would be dropped unless they downgraded coverage or waived other benefits.[32] As Ellickson explained in 1958, "Nearly 2 out of 3 aged persons had no form of health insurance whatever," and those who did carried policies that were subject to cancelation by the insurer.[33]

Even so, in the face of widespread private insurance, it became increasingly difficult for Ellickson and others to imagine a national health-care plan that would wipe out these agreements. What President or other elected leader would want to take something away from millions of Americans and replace it with a government scheme?

In 1952, Ellickson and the CIO downsized their ambitions to a more modest proposal than comprehensive national health insurance: providing hospital insurance to the elderly, soon to be known as Medicare. Truman's advisers and health policy experts had retrenched to that position in 1951. Social Security officials such as Wilbur Cohen, who was particularly respected by Washington insiders, sought a delimited program available only to those Americans over sixty-five who had paid into Social Security. Limiting the number of Americans who could use it would minimize the disruption to current medical providers and prevent a stampede of Americans from gumming up the offices and time of doctors. Incremental changes would be easier to manage.

Perhaps more importantly, Ellickson, Cruikshank, and Cohen bet that it would be politically attractive. Medicare would only support the elderly, a group of Americans more likely to be in need of health care and less likely to be covered by employer-provided insurance programs.[34] The children of the elderly, now grown adults, often ended up paying out of pocket for their parents' care. Their support could help build momentum for the new policy. Limiting the measure to hospital care would hopefully avoid triggering the overwhelming opposition of the AMA. Insurance companies were even sympathetic to the idea of having the federal government take care of insurance for the elderly, a group that worsened the risk pool for private group health plans.[35] Finally, tying the program to Social Security could help convince political holdouts, given the high levels of public support and administrative efficiency of that program.[36] This would not become a Soviet-style reimagination of medicine in America, but instead, a way to provide medical care "in a manner consistent with the dignity and self-respect of each individual," as Ellickson said.[37]

Ellickson was much more discreet about her long-term ambition to build on the passage of Medicare and gradually expand government-funded health insurance to all Americans. "[W]e expected Medicare to be the first step toward universal national health insurance, perhaps with 'Kiddiecare' as the next step," Cohen said years later, describing the understanding he shared with Ellickson and Cruikshank.[38] The group had reason to believe that gradual expansion over time might work. The Social Security program had been incrementally expanded after its initial passage in the mid-1930s to cover dependents, farmers and domestic workers, disabled workers, and the self-employed. The same might be possible with Medicare.

Soon Ellickson and Cruikshank would have the chance to see if that bet would pay off. In 1955, the two became colleagues, not just collaborators. As a result of declining membership and a convergence of organizational goals, the AFL and CIO merged into a single federation. For Ellickson, it meant that she would now work for Cruikshank. She chafed at the new arrangement, which shifted them from co-conspirators to a more hierarchical and formal relationship. Ellickson may have become the subordinate, but her power had grown, a result of the sheer size of the combined AFL-CIO. The union now represented 15 million Americans, making it one of the most powerful forces in American politics. Health care remained the top legislative priority, but

Ellickson and Cruikshank made a tactical decision to prioritize the expansion of Social Security insurance to cover disabled workers between fifty and sixty-five. The two wrote the bill, with Cruikshank describing it as "a kind of a wedding ceremony" for the newly merged federations.[39] A testament to the power of the new union, the bill passed in the summer of 1956. Cruikshank called the moment the best day of his life, and a colleague from the Social Security administration was "literally dancing in the aisles." Typically, the AMA fretted that this heralded the end of the Republic.[40]

Now it was time to aim for the real prize. Ellickson and Cruikshank drafted the legislative framework for Medicare, got it introduced, and began to lay the groundwork among Democrats for passage. They knew that, under Eisenhower, the legislation was unlikely to move, but they wanted to build the foundation should Democrats take back power after the next presidential election in 1960. That was the same strategy Ellickson had used during the war, and yet again, it worked, at first. "The old folks lined up by the dozen every place we went," one Senate staffer said. By 1960, legislators were receiving more mail on Medicare than any other topic.[41] That wasn't an accident. Ellickson and Cruickshank were mobilizing on a national scale, including in places with low union density.[42] As the political potential of seniors became clearer, more politicians in Congress embraced the cause.[43]

Senator John F. Kennedy felt that momentum growing and built on it, campaigning on the idea of Medicare in his 1960 race for the presidency. He had no interest in picking up where Truman left off with a sprawling national health insurance bill. Kennedy wanted to get behind something more modest and novel, something that was popular with both labor and elderly Americans.

After his victory, Ellickson saw the political window open again. The AFL-CIO had organized a Senior Citizens Committee for Kennedy, which now became the nucleus of a new organization that soon enrolled 1.5 million members. A little over a year into his presidency, polling showed that support for elderly hospital insurance had reached 69 percent.[44] That year, the President gave a speech at Madison Square Garden, rallying 17,000 people to the cause. As Cruikshank admitted, this social movement energy reflected Ellickson's traditions more than his own: "The CIO always believed a lot in big mass demonstrations, and bringing a thousand people into Washington and all that kind of thing. The AF of L didn't."[45] In this case, the public pressure seemed to be working.

The AMA, as expected, wanted to minimize any changes to health-care markets, and it waged an even bigger advocacy campaign than it had over a decade earlier. It advertised on nearly 200 television stations across the nation and rented out Madison Square Garden for a rally of its own.[46] It employed nearly a thousand people working on health-care legislation, a tally that did not include the additional advocacy efforts of health insurance companies.[47] Not satisfied with big rallies and mass media, the AMA asked physicians' wives to host coffee meetings with friends and neighbors to explain the threat of socialized medicine. Ronald Reagan, the former President of the actors' union, recorded an audio message that all the hosts played, warning against the legislation. "One of the traditional methods of imposing statism or socialism on a people has been by way of medicine," Reagan said, picking up the line inaccurately attributed to Lenin in the last campaign.[48] At the height of the Cold War, such messaging continued to resonate with both politicians and voters, and momentum swung. Congressional leaders blocked the legislation and defeated Medicare. This time, however, it was a temporary setback rather than a death knell.

After Kennedy was assassinated in late 1963, President Lyndon B. Johnson inherited his health-care agenda. Like Truman after Roosevelt, Johnson decided to build on the priority and momentum of his predecessor. His actions in 1965 shaped American health-care markets, expanding access but setting the country on a wasteful course by building on a byzantine and privatized structure.

Johnson won the presidential election in 1964 by the largest margin in three decades, dominating Barry Goldwater to win forty-four states. Johnson prioritized health-care reform during the campaign, and the National Council of Senior Citizens, a pressure group set up by the AFL-CIO to drum up support for health insurance for the elderly, called the election results a "magnificent mandate" for Medicare. Fourteen thousand seniors had marched at the Democratic convention to demonstrate their electoral power, and now they intended to use it.[49] Johnson made health-care reform one of his highest domestic priorities in the newly emerging "Great Society," and the AFL-CIO was again revving up the engines of its campaign arm behind the scenes. Even Republicans could see that health-care reform had some momentum, prompting them to pull together competing proposals that included a voluntary program to cover physicians' bills.[50] A window was opening for something big to happen, but efforts would soon run into the two forces that have stood in the way of well-administered marketcraft since the nation's founding.

From the start of the Republic, Americans have been wary of centralized government. Until the start of the twentieth century, most Americans lived on small farms, which Thomas Jefferson lionized as the ideal political economy for a self-governing people. They were convinced that their own hard work would be enough to create material abundance, and that agrarian interests would flourish as long as government remained modest in size and decentralized. As many Americans moved to urban centers and immigrants flooded into the country at the end of the nineteenth and start of the twentieth century, the Jeffersonian outlook faded—but it never disappeared.

At the heart of the small government, agrarian outlook, was a desire to prevent government from disrupting the racial hierarchy of the antebellum South. Centralized power could be used to even out the power differential between White and Black Americans. After the Civil War, White Americans used public policy to write Jim Crow laws enforcing segregation, voting restrictions to disenfranchise Black citizens, and discriminatory practices in housing, education, and criminal justice. Such policies created a pervasive system of racial inequality that touched nearly every aspect of American life, not only in the South. White Americans were more likely to gain access to housing, educational opportunities, and higher-paid employment than Black Americans or immigrants, not to mention the higher likelihood of inheriting generational wealth.

By the time of the Medicare debates in the 1960s, representatives in Congress from the South remained committed to preventing too much centralized power in Washington—or least the "wrong" kind of centralized power. They happily accepted, and avidly pursued, federal money for regional development and military contracts, so long as the programs did not provide a lever for reordering the racial hierarchy. Anything that might was dead on arrival. "[T]he actual line-up in the Congress started becoming quite hostile to progressive legislation in '37," Ellickson said, tracing the history of the southern resistance to Medicare to the New Deal. "[T]his was the Republican-Dixiecrat coalition, which continued to control the Congress until 1965." Many conservative Democrats were able to hold on to power because of the limited geographical reach of Ellickson's own CIO. "The unions had not succeeded in organizing the South, so they had not been effective in making a change politically in the South," she said. "That revolution is going on today [in 1967] actually. It's still going on, but it may finally be taking place."[51]

By the mid-1960s, Southern Democrats were on the defense. Black Americans were demanding the right to vote and the elimination of segregation in public spaces and institutions, including in hospitals and health-care facilities. If Dixiecrats allowed power of any kind to be consolidated in the federal government, federal administrators would be more likely to deliver on the promise of racial equality.

One Southern Democrat in particular stood in the way of progress. In 1938, Arkansas voters ·had elected a Harvard-educated lawyer and county judge named Wilbur Mills to Congress. Like other Southern Democrats, Mills railed against the New Deal, provoking the ire of Roosevelt, and later Kennedy and Johnson. By 1965, Democrats were a party full of contradictions. They at once supported the advance of civil rights, while dominating in the conservative South, where the Dixiecrats advocated for an economic populism that preserved racial segregation and states' rights. Mills sought lower tax rates for the middle class and Social Security expansion, but he had little interest in the further expansion of federal power, which might require racial integration. In 1954, after the landmark *Brown v. Board of Education* Supreme Court ruling, over a hundred Congressmen and Senators signed a so-called "Declaration of Constitutional Principles" against school integration, including Mills.

By 1958, Mills had climbed the ranks to become the Chair of the House Ways and Means Committee, the most powerful position in the House of Representatives at the time, outside of the role of Speaker. He used that position to block the creation of any kind of broad-based health-care marketcraft. Over the next seventeen years, he resisted efforts by labor and others to build a consensus around a health-care overhaul, including insurance for the elderly. There was an organic connection between Mills' interest in preserving White privilege and his opposition to health-care expansion. Southern opposition to federal power did not mean there was no government; it just meant that state and local elites remained in control of their communities. Health care should not be a federal issue. That view aligned perfectly with the AMA, which preferred organizing doctors at the state or even county level. According to the AFL-CIO's Nelson Cruikshank, private, decentralized control of medical decisions gave a local doctor "considerable power and prestige and status in the community, which he undoubtedly enjoyed." This included the power to decide, via pro bono work, which poor people deserved what kind of free medical care—care that he could easily distribute along racial lines.[52]

Mills was particularly deferential to the AMA. Decades earlier, he was "originally backed by a small group of doctors in Arkansas when he ran against the incumbent when he originally got his first seat. He never forgot that," recounted one health-care organizer.[53] Mills remained loyal to those doctors for decades. In an effort to defuse broader legislative momentum for health reform, he wrote and passed a bill in 1960 that provided funds for states to administer limited health-care aid to families on welfare benefits. The structure was so devolved and the benefits so modest that the vast majority of states did not bother to implement the federal program.

That legislation did not disturb the intimacy and sanctity of existing doctor-patient relationships, which the AMA brandished as its most potent weapon in the recurring legislative debates. "You would talk to a Congressman or Senator and so often he would say, 'You have no idea what political influence a doctor has in his local community, and I don't want to get them stirred up against me,'" said Oscar Ewing, who had once been Administrator of Truman's Federal Security Agency.[54] Those legislators were mainly talking about White, professional voters. The millions of Americans excluded from access to quality medical care had no doctor-patient relationship to preserve. "[T]here were various counties in the South where there was not a single Negro doctor and on the whole Negroes got short shrift from the white doctors," Ewing said in the late 1960s.[55] Groups like the NAACP had strongly backed health-care reform since Truman's early attempts to pass it, but Jim Crow restrictions on voting, which prevailed until the early 1960s, made it difficult for them to effect change.[56]

By the spring of 1965, Mills and the AMA had been backed into a corner. Johnson's resounding win a few months before, partially premised on the promise of hospital insurance for the elderly, meant that Mills and fellow Southern Democrats would burn large amounts of political capital if they chose to block any effort outright. The election had swept in new, less deferential members, who made clear they would work around Mills if neces-sary. Redistricting also brought unionized workers into his electoral district back home, giving the CIO new leverage over him.[57] "The election of the President in 1964 had the major impact, made the major difference," Mills later said of the passage of Medicare. "He had espoused it in his campaign, you know, and here he was elected by a 2 to 1 vote, which was a pretty strong endorsement of it, I thought. I thought the time had come to pass it."[58]

If something was going to pass, Mills was determined for it to be modest in scope and as decentralized in administration as possible.[59] Instead of work-ing across competing coalitions to piece together a single, coherent structure for health-care reform, Mills opted for a slapdash solution. He combined Ellickson's proposals for elderly hospital insurance with Republican coun-terproposals for the federal government to reimburse physicians for costs re-lated to treating the elderly. Finally, he added an expansion of the state-based program for the poor that he had passed years before. This three-layered cake, as it was called, became the basis of Medicare and Medicaid.

The result was a sprawling set of poorly coordinated programs with sig-nificant waste. When they passed the old-age insurance bill, legislators tacitly agreed that private insurers would continue to cover working Americans. But they created no requirement for private businesses to do so, inevitably leav-ing out millions of low-wage workers. When it came to Medicare, Congress set up a system where private corporations would handle claims for hospital insurance and physician reimbursements, rather than a government agency. Mills also failed to create any cost restraints on the amounts that hospitals or doctors could charge the government. The higher a hospital's or physician's costs, the more the government would pay. Finally, health insurance for the poor, now known as Medicaid, would be administered by states without any meaningful federal oversight.

The legislative hodgepodge was health-care marketcraft—but a piece-meal, sloppy version of it. Partially because it was so byzantine with little lack of federal coordination, it satisfied Southern Democrats, and two-thirds of Congress voted for it. President Johnson signed it into law in July 1965.

At first, Medicare and Medicaid seemed like a breakthrough for much of the left. "No longer will older Americans be denied the healing miracle of modern medicine," Johnson said when he signed the bill. "And no longer will this Nation refuse the hand of justice to those who have given a lifetime of service and wisdom and labor to the progress of this progressive country."[60] But the next half century would illustrate just how much a misstep of marketcraft it was.

Ellickson was not there to see the "victory." In 1962, she took a partial leave from the CIO to join a Presidential Commission on the Status of Women created by Kennedy and headed by Eleanor Roosevelt. When she asked for a full leave from the CIO, she was denied, and she resigned in response.[61] Her official reason was that, as legislative momentum heated up, labor had taken a secondary role in the legislative fight for health insurance. More likely, Ellickson's constant clashing with Cruikshank drove her away. When they started as equals at different organizations, they had worked well together, but when Cruikshank took over as her boss, the dynamic gave way to the typical power structures of the time. "As a woman it was certainly more difficult for me to function in the labor movement," she said later. "I was not one of the boys."[62]

Ellickson had long wanted to be more out front in the movement for health care. She testified on Capitol Hill on behalf of health insurance proposals, but Cruikshank forced her to take a backseat to him in Congressional negotiations and with the media. She was also pushing fifty-seven at the time, and a new twenty-seven-year-old woman named Lee Bamberger—a "brainy woman" as well a "gorgeous babe," according to Cruikshank—had joined the office. Cruikshank claimed that men were put off by Ellickson's "meticulousness," preferring Bamberger's "charm." "All her life Kitty had kind of felt that she'd been kept under, kept down, because she was a woman," Cruikshank said in an interview a decade later. To the men in the office, Bamberger's fast success seemed to disprove Ellickson's assumptions. "It got to where, I'm sure, it was an intolerable situation for Kitty. And I believe that this was the reason that she left."[63] Cruikshank did not mention that he had refused Ellickson's request for leave to serve on Kennedy's Presidential Commission on the Status of Women.[64]

Her departure was not just about office politics. Ellickson had spent twenty years of her life formulating policy and making the case for a robust expansion of social insurance in America.[65] As she put it in 1967, "Well, I for one was never converted to the idea of letting the private insurance companies in at all into a federal insurance program. This was a very heavy price to pay." She worried in particular about the potential for private interests to inflate costs: "Our feeling was that it was important to have the kinds of controls that would prevent costs from skyrocketing . . . this is a subject that hasn't been settled yet actually." Was it worth compromising that principle to pass the bill? Within the AFL-CIO, Ellickson remembered, "we had some pretty hot, searching discussions as to how far one could legitimately go in opposing the use of the insurance companies at all."[66] These debates crested around 1962, and not in her favor. Frustrated and overshadowed, Ellickson left the fight, making way for the Frankenstein compromise that Medicare and Medicaid became.

In the end, the AFL-CIO advocates in the final phase of the legislative fight did not support the provisions for private administration and uncapped costs, siding with Ellickson's private position. They pointed out that the lack of cost constraints on physician reimbursement and the use of private companies to administer the program would increase costs for consumers and likely build in unnecessary bureaucracy and waste.[67] Yet the AFL-CIO still supported the bill in the end. The leaders hoped that, because insurance companies would no longer have the burden of insuring the elderly, they might lower their prices and cover more low-wage workers.[68] That would not be the case.

It took little time for health-care prices to skyrocket after the passage of Medicare. As the legislation moved into its final stages, doctors and hospitals rushed to hike their prices so that the baseline for future reimbursements would be high. Hospital daily charges rose 17 percent in the year the bill passed, and internists' fees rose by 40 percent.[69] In the seven years before passage, medical costs were rising at 3 percent annually. In the five years afterward, they rose at nearly 8 percent. Government spending on health care rose 21 percent every year in the same period.[70]

The Medicare compromise created significant waste because of legislators' refusal to invest a federal institution with power and discretion in administration. No federal entity had the authority to manage the prices hospitals and companies charged the government. Legislators left it to private companies to evaluate claims and ensure that charges were consistent with prevailing rates. As long as a charge wasn't higher than the average charge in the geographic area, the doctor or hospital would almost always be paid. If a doctor or hospital didn't like its intermediary—perhaps because it was loath to reimburse high costs—it could switch at any time.[71] This outcome was just what Mills intended.

It was not just rapidly rising costs that posed a challenge. Millions of Americans remained without health insurance after Medicare's passage. Low-wage workers whose employers did not provide health insurance were particularly vulnerable, since they were also not sufficiently indigent to qualify for Medicaid. People with "preexisting conditions" that insurance companies found unprofitable were also blocked from coverage.

Medicare and Medicaid did do immense good in the decades after passage. Elderly Americans gained meaningful medical coverage, and they grew healthier and lived longer as a result. Medicare also became a force for racial integration, an ironic twist given the efforts by Mills and other Southern Democrats to avoid supporting any initiative with that goal. Leaders at the Social Security Administration, responsible for certifying which hospitals could receive Medicare reimbursements, could now require them to be desegregated. Many hospitals, especially in the South, continued to have separate rooms, or even wings, for Black and White patients. They couldn't, however, afford to lose out on the massive wave of federal funding for elderly patients. By 1966, 97 percent of short-term hospital beds in the United States were in facilities compliant with federal civil rights law.[72] One of the few provisions that had placed power in a federal government agency illustrated its ability to counter the enduring racial injustices of the time.[73]

Even so, the structural problems with Medicare meant that it would never serve as the foundation for a larger, more universal insurance program as Ellickson had hoped.[74] That original plan might have worked if Mills and other Southern Democrats had not refused to even consider a coordinating institution with discretion and power in the federal government. In a world where such an institution existed, with the ability to control costs and manage escalating claims, Medicare might have been able to serve as the foundation for future expansion that Ellickson had dreamed about.

Instead, the private administration and lack of cost controls doomed the program in the court of public opinion in its early years. By the time a new health-care debate reopened in the first half of the 1970s, exploding costs precluded meaningful expansion of existing programs. "Instead of serving as a foundation for national health insurance, Medicare functioned more like a prophylactic against it," the historian Paul Starr wrote. By 1975, the *New York*

Times reported: "National Health Insurance Now Considered Just Remote Possibility."[75] The failure to build in cost controls in the beginning meant that many came to believe that a universal program built on Medicare would be unaffordable.[76] Ellickson's colleague Cruikshank lived with that regret. "[W]e didn't think [Medicare] would put off other legislation in Social Security as long as it did," he said over a decade after its passage. "I'm not sure what the decision would have been, had we known what the price was at that time."[77]

Despite the incremental gains, the 1960s health-care compromise amounted to a failed marketcraft. It created a fragmented system of service delivery without granting the federal government enough authority to control costs or guarantee universal coverage. By resisting the need for a federal institution to manage a market providing such essential services, Congress constructed a byzantine system that continues to define our health-care options today.

Multiple Presidents and Congresses over the next half century attempted to reform the system, to modest effect. A few years after Medicare's passage, President Nixon proposed a national health insurance plan, but it fell victim to Watergate. Ted Kennedy led an effort to create a single, federal national insurance system, but it received minimal support in Congress or from President Jimmy Carter. President Reagan, who had been so critical of the programs in the decades before, moved to expand Medicaid while President in the 1980s. In 1983, his administration secured stronger regulatory authority to control the prices that Medicare paid hospitals.[78] Federal administrations would now standardize reimbursement rates based on patients' diagnoses, not the open-ended approach of the past. Yet hospitals' profit margins hit new highs as they lowered their costs and then received the guaranteed payments. Providers also gamed the system by moving covered services out of hospitals.

The changes rolled on through the years, some expanding government control and others empowering market forces. President Bill Clinton extended government health care to indigent children. George W. Bush partially privatized Medicare, allowing Americans to select a plan from a private insurance company that Medicare has approved. In 2010, President Barack Obama and a Democratic Congress passed the Affordable Care Act, providing access to Americans whose employers did not offer insurance, banning companies from refusing Americans with "preexisting conditions," and requiring all Americans to buy health insurance. That effort ensured universal coverage, but it did little to bring down the cost of health care. Like Medicare and Medicaid, it was a helpful marketcraft that broadened access but retained the balkanized, wasteful structure of American health-care markets.

Today Americans spend over $4 trillion a year on health care, or about $13,000 per person. We spend just shy of $1 trillion on Medicare and over $800 billion on Medicaid. More than 17 percent of the American economy is devoted to health care, 50 percent higher than any other developed industrial country.[79] Much of those extra funds are used for administrative costs in hospitals and insurance companies, the kind of bureaucratic bloat that most Americans want to avoid—and precisely the problem that Ellickson warned about six decades ago.

Today's US medical system is governed neither by "market forces" nor by the public interest. It illustrates what happens when large-scale government investment is not fused with a positive commitment to an institution with power and discretion to manage markets effectively. The long-standing fear of a centralized state power, the enduring legacy of racism, and the outsized power of doctors and hospitals stood in the way of the creation of a national scheme to provide affordable health care to all Americans. In the pursuit of less bureaucracy and waste, we got more of both.

RISE OF
THE GLOBAL

6

IN THE SHADOWS OF BRETTON WOODS

ANDREW BRIMMER & GLOBAL FINANCE (1963-74)

In August 1946, a nineteen-year-old Black man from Louisiana named Andrew Brimmer was stationed on the island of Oahu in Hawaii, just a few miles from Pearl Harbor. Drafted into the army in the spring of 1945, Brimmer first completed basic training and left with his unit for Japan. The Second World War was coming to an end in Europe but continued to rage in the Pacific. While en route, the leaders of his unit received orders to divert to Hawaii given a declining need for soldiers in the Far East. Stationed at Barbers Point, Brimmer watched as soldiers and officers who had been in the fight for years returned home. Given the churn, new recruits like Brimmer could ascend the military ranks fast. He arrived in Hawaii as a private in December 1945. Eight months later, he became an acting first sergeant, the third in a string of fast-moving promotions. That month, the last of the officers overseeing his 380-person, all-Black unit had departed, and it would be weeks before a new one arrived. Brimmer, not yet twenty, was in charge.

What he lacked in age and experience he made up for in grit and savvy. One of six children, Brimmer grew up on the Louisiana-Mississippi border on the land of a plantation where his ancestors had worked generations before. His grandparents had been sharecroppers, cultivating that land in a state of racial servitude. His father worked in an agricultural company, which owned cotton fields and gins, and his mother grew much of the family's food from a twenty-row vegetable garden behind their house. When his parents wed, they received from their families two cows, two hogs, and eighteen chickens—a foundation to begin their own lives. "We were typically poor, but not dirt-poor," Brimmer insisted, even into his seventies. When the Depression hit, he watched his father be forced to work odd jobs, at one point joining the Works Progress Administration (WPA) to build roads. During that difficult decade, the family worked seasonally in the cotton fields. His parents weeded in the spring, and he and his siblings harvested in the fall. "The rule was, you worked sunup to sundown, especially during the cotton-picking season," Brimmer recounted. That kind of work ethic propelled him swiftly up the ranks of the army.[1]

If work was a constant of young Brimmer's life, so too was racial segregation. He internalized the codified racial hierarchy of the South, stepping aside on a sidewalk when a White person passed and avoiding any trouble with "country boys." At the local drugstore where he later worked as a teenager, White customers refused his help. Brimmer went to a segregated, all-Black school through high school, where each school year was shortened by at least a month to allow the students to harvest cotton with their families. Students graduated after eleven grades, not the twelve grades the White school offered, and Brimmer's school remained unaccredited. Even so, he became a fastidious student, the result of a combination of innate curiosity and familial pressure. Brimmer brought his textbooks home at night, and his father would pore over them after his workday had ended: "I visualize my father, after a hard day's work, sitting in the kitchen with his kerosene lamp reading—particularly geography, history, and English. He said, 'You must be able to read, write, and figure.'"[2] Brimmer was clever and ambitious, and by the time he finished high school, he was ready to leave Louisiana. The war meant that he didn't have to wait.

Now, without any officer training, Brimmer was overseeing a company of hundreds of men thousands of miles from home. Most people would have just tried to keep the unit together, but that was not his intuition. Instead, Brimmer would make it better. "I tried an experiment," he recounted decades later. "If I could get 80 percent of the men to work seven and a half hours a day for four and a half days a week, we still could get our targets accomplished. I could give every man a day off a week, and I could give every man of sergeant rank or above a jeep and a three-day pass." At first, when Brimmer outlined his plan, the rank and file balked, fearful of any experimental changes to the military order. Brimmer, steady in his conviction, found someone who could convince them. In his company was a man named Jake Jordan. Barely literate, Jordan had served in the army for thirteen years, making him forty years old and highly respected by the other soldiers. He would often dominate the company in late-night poker games, waiting until the better players had weeded out the neophytes. Brimmer convinced Jordan to lean on the other troops to support his plan. That worked, and Brimmer started to implement his program. "We could get more work done at less cost and provide more opportunity for time off for the men," Brimmer said. Three weeks later, a White officer arrived to take control of the unit, his own first deployment. "You did a very good job here leading the company by yourself in the last few weeks," he told Brimmer. "I think it's time for us to go back to the Army," he said. "Yes, captain," Brimmer obediently responded.[3]

Twenty years later, Andrew Brimmer made history when he became the first Black man to serve as a governor on the Federal Reserve Board. But it was not his race alone that marked his legacy. Brimmer's willingness to conform when necessary belied an abiding commitment to make change. Over the course of his career, he gained access to some of the most elite institutions of America—Harvard, Wharton, the Department of Commerce, and the Federal Reserve. A Black man in a country struggling with the legacy of racism and slavery, Brimmer found a way to subtly challenge the rules, sometimes reshaping them to better serve the common good, just as he did in Hawaii at the end of the war. That drive made him a master marketcrafter who strengthened the global dollar and simultaneously dared the Fed to focus its attention on the neglected at home.

In late February 1966, Brimmer got a call from President Lyndon Johnson's appointment secretary. He was the Assistant Secretary of Commerce for Economic Affairs at the time, but this was not a routine work meeting. "The boss wants to see you," the secretary said. "Drive yourself over. Don't ask one of the Commerce drivers to take you because the President wants to see you privately."[4]

In the twenty years between Brimmer's army service and his eventual nomination to the Fed, he had become a well-known economist—and a respected colleague of the President's. After discharge, he completed a bachelor's and master's at the University of Washington, studied in India on a Fulbright, and earned his PhD in economics from Harvard in 1957. He worked for several years at the New York Federal Reserve, and then moved to academia, eventually taking a post at the Wharton School of the University of Pennsylvania. The school informed him—after he had accepted the role—that they could only pay him the lower salary of a more junior professor, despite a more senior title, evidence of the enduring racism prevalent in the academy. While at Wharton, after Brimmer delivered a lecture one day, a seven-year-old fan approached him, introducing himself as "Larry" and informing Brimmer that both his parents were economists, as was his uncle. The child's father, Robert Summers, was a colleague of Brimmer's, and young Larry Summers would later become Treasury Secretary.[5]

But true to his background, Brimmer remained a man on the move. Just two years after he joined Wharton's faculty, the Kennedy administration recruited him to work at the Commerce Department, where he began to develop a direct relationship with Johnson, who was Vice President at the time. After Kennedy was assassinated and Johnson won the 1964 election in a landslide, the new President promoted Brimmer to Assistant Secretary of Commerce for Economic Affairs in early 1965. That spring, Johnson trusted him to be his envoy in the effort to convince Reverend Martin Luther King Jr. to call off a business boycott of Alabama.[6] When Brimmer got the call from the President's personal secretary in February 1966, rumors were swirling that Johnson might nominate him to the Fed.

Brimmer drove to the White House, passed security, and entered through the door with direct access to the West Wing. He got into the elevator. "There was this very old black man operating the elevator. I'd seen him a number of times," Brimmer remembered. "The man closed the door, but before moving up, he turned to me, and said, 'Dr. Brimmer, I understand you may be getting a very important appointment.'" Brimmer demurred: "'You know how it is; all these rumors are going around.'" The elevator operator, who had seen presidential administrations come and go, mustered up a simple "Good luck."

The door opened, but Brimmer did not head to the Oval Office or a private study as he expected. A Secret Service agent led him to the private residence and opened a door. Brimmer walked into the President's bedroom. Johnson lay in bed, preparing to take a nap. But before his rest, he wanted to talk to Brimmer to test his appetite for the job. "If I end up appointing you to the Federal Reserve, that's going to be a real breakthrough," he told Brimmer from his bed. "That's what I want to achieve: breakthroughs in areas where the coloreds have not been represented."[7]

Nominating Brimmer was also a deft political move. At the time, Bill Martin was still Fed Chair, and Johnson and he were engaged in a heated, public battle over how tight monetary policy should be. Johnson had summoned Martin to his Texas ranch two months earlier to directly challenge his efforts to tighten money, worrying that it could slow economic growth and raise unemployment. Given the new vacancy on the Fed board, Martin rightly suspected that Johnson would choose someone who tilted toward loose monetary policy. He threatened to resign if the President did so. That would create drama that Johnson didn't need politically, so he devised a way around it.

In Brimmer, Johnson believed he had an "easy money man," and one whom Martin, for a clear reason, could not help but publicly support. Johnson told his primary domestic policy adviser that "Andy Brimmer hasn't forgotten what it's like to be Negro, to be a small farmer, to be a candy-store owner, to be a corner druggist, who needs to borrow money to keep his business going without paying exorbitant interest to the New York bankers."[8] (Brimmer did not turn out to fulfill Johnson's hopes on this count.) Johnson also knew that if Martin resigned over the nomination of the first Black governor, it would forever change his legacy. "The president has Martin in a box," the *Wall Street Journal* quoted a banker saying at the time. "If Martin resigned now, it would look like it was because he didn't want a Negro on the board."[9]

Johnson announced his nomination two days later, and Martin publicly supported it. The Senate confirmed Brimmer to the Fed a mere eleven days later. Johnson suggested to Brimmer that he ask Martin to swear him in, a sly way of rubbing the President's victory in Martin's face. Brimmer, unaware of the depth of their disagreement over his candidacy, agreed. On March 9, 1966, Brimmer's wife held the Bible while Martin administered the oath of office, the President at their sides. Brimmer's four-year-old daughter, Esther, looked on, witnessing history, a pink bow in her hair and white gloves on her small hands.[10]

✿

Brimmer was an ideal choice for Johnson because of his race and his supposed inclination for loose monetary policy. But there was a third, even more powerful reason that grew in importance over time: his expertise in international money markets.

At the request of the President, Sylvia Porter, an acclaimed financial journalist, consulted several of the most influential people in finance to get a sense of how they would think about Brimmer's appointment. The message that came back was clear: It wasn't Brimmer's race that made them supportive. It was his power to keep the dollar strong. Wall Street and other economists supported Johnson's pick because they had followed Brimmer's efforts at Commerce to strengthen the dollar in a world of increasing currency turmoil. In a phone call with the President, secretly recorded by the system Johnson had installed when he took office, Porter relayed the content of her private conversations, including with New York Fed President Alfred Hayes' "right-hand man." Brimmer was "bright, not radical, ambitious, and young and energetic," and nominating him would be an "astute move." While his race had come up in every conversation and several of the White business individuals were "worried about a chip on his shoulder because of his color," the consensus was cautiously supportive.[11] But Porter and Johnson spent the bulk of their time discussing Brimmer's efforts at Commerce to maintain confidence in the US dollar. A strong dollar was critical to preserving global financial stability and American economic power, and that required management of the country's trade balance and capital flows. Brimmer had been the "chief workhorse" behind the efforts to implement capital controls, which limited American investment abroad to keep dollars in the country. Even though some of Brimmer's moves risked thwarting the bottom lines of Wall Street firms, investors believed there was no question that he would be a qualified pick—and wanted a global currency expert at the Fed. "Lyndon Johnson said he appointed me not because I was black," Brimmer said years later, "but because he was convinced, based on my performance, my work on the balance of payments, and so on, that I was the right man."[12]

The task Brimmer faced, first at Commerce and then as a governor at the Fed, was one of the thorniest of problems for economic policymakers and politicians in the 1960s: how to preserve the global currency order, known colloquially as Bretton Woods.

Twenty years earlier, in 1944, representatives from forty-four countries came together in a New Hampshire town to sort out what the postwar international and financial system would look like. The participants, led by the American Harry Dexter White and the Briton John Maynard Keynes, sought to create a framework for international economic policy coordination that would foster exchange rate stability and global trade. These were long-standing problems. Economists and policymakers across the world had struggled with how to support their domestic markets with a stable, national currency *and* reap the gains of foreign trade. Relying on gold had helped many European nations in the half century before the First World War, but in the years after that conflict, attempts to return to the gold standard resulted in austerity, deflation, and high unemployment. While America thrived in the 1920s, much of Europe sank into deeper economic malaise, eventually leading to the rise of fascism. In 1944 at Bretton Woods, world leaders wanted to avoid repeating the mistake of a postwar snap back to gold, but abandoning the gold-based approach altogether also posed significant risks. Allowing currencies to "float" freely, as we do today, seemed experimental; the world had benefited from a clear global reserve currency of some sort since the eighteenth century. Any new system could elevate the risk for dramatic devaluations if investors suddenly lost confidence in a nation's currency. If a currency lost its value quickly, the wealthy and well-connected stood to lose the most. Most delegates to Bretton Woods did not want to be responsible for that.

The solution that the leaders at Bretton Woods came up with was novel. The countries agreed to peg their currencies to the American dollar, which meant, for instance, a British pound would convert at a set dollar price, determined by central banks and governments. Market forces might disrupt the peg in the short term—British individuals could offer to sell or buy pounds at rates the central bank did not like. To mitigate those disruptions, the central banks would use their gold and foreign exchange reserves to ensure that the peg held, working through banks or in markets to buy or sell gold or foreign exchange reserves to maintain the fixed rates. If a country needed more gold to keep the peg stable, it could turn to the United States, which would guarantee to sell an ounce at a fixed price of thirty-five dollars. Only dollars could be converted to gold. Because dollars were in plentiful supply and the United States would continue to print more, the global currency could be significantly more elastic than a return to a pure gold standard. If a country's balance of payments—the accounting of exports, imports, and financial flows—changed significantly, the country could devalue or revalue, which meant adjusting the peg to the dollar. Those kinds of valuation changes would hopefully be rare and would require the approval of the newly formed International Monetary Fund (IMF).

Bretton Woods created a system where a country could enjoy the stability of a global gold standard but focus on managing their currency's peg to the dollar. This avoided much of the need for austerity that had occurred after the First World War, enabling countries to rebuild and invest for the future. The dollar, through its connection to gold, became the world's reserve currency.

For America, this arrangement brought significant advantages. Countries across the world now required dollars, because only dollars could be used to settle balance of payment differentials, manage currency pegs, and finance trade in the same fashion that gold had been used in previous eras. That thirst for dollars blessed the American government with an exorbitant privilege, as the French called it. When countries other than the United States bought more in international markets than they sold, they had to settle those balances by buying dollars or gold. The United States could uniquely settle its deficits by printing more money rather than drawing down its gold reserves. Strong international demand for American debt enabled America to finance abundant government spending rather than hiking taxes. Countries wanted dollars, and America was more than happy to print and spend.[13]

Bretton Woods was fragile from the start, and by the time Brimmer was in government, it threatened to come apart. The system was premised on the political support of other major industrial powers for America's central position. The exorbitant privilege could dissolve if America took its spending too far, printing too many dollars and keeping monetary policy too loose. This wasn't a problem during the 1950s because the number of dollars circulating globally was relatively modest. Abundant American gold reserves meant no one ever questioned whether thirty-five dollars would buy an ounce of gold. But dollars began piling up throughout the industrialized world, facilitated by American investment abroad, international aid, and military spending. As American fiscal spending ramped up in the 1950s and '60s, countries began to worry that America's reserve of gold could be exhausted if all other countries were to simultaneously present thirty-five dollars for an ounce of gold. At some point, there would be more dollars in circulation than there was gold in reserve—a so-called dollar overhang——and the United States would risk not being able to guarantee the peg.

These first cracks appeared before Brimmer even began his work in government. European countries officially allowed their currencies to be freely converted to dollars in 1958, and only a year later the total amount of foreign dollar claims exceeded the official gold reserves of the United States for the first time.[14] The simmering anxiety turned into a speculative attack on the dollar in October of 1960, a month before the American presidential election. In response, Kennedy promised to pursue policy that would strengthen the dollar and ensure its convertibility to gold. When he took the oath of office a few months later, he "considered Cuba and the balance of payments to be the two most dangerous, the most demanding, and possibly the most intractable problems then confronting the country," as he told the Treasury official tasked with managing the problem at the time.[15]

Over the next ten years, Brimmer and other economic policymakers became increasingly focused on the goal of strengthening the dollar to hold together Bretton Woods and retain America's exorbitant privilege.[16] Three Presidents—Kennedy, Johnson, and Nixon—would do everything in their power to keep the dollar strong, and Brimmer worked at the Commerce Department and the Fed at the forefront of these efforts through the tenures of all three. Looking back, the whole attempt to keep Bretton Woods intact can seem pyrrhic, years of wasted effort to preserve a system whose foundation was flawed. But that judgment imposes today's knowledge on the past. "There was absolutely no acceptance of flexibility of exchange rates on the part of any responsible officials I knew," said a senior Treasury official in the late 1960s. "And there was not really much acceptance in the academic community. There was almost a total lack of support for them in the banking community. Now you had a few mavericks. But I can't recall any serious discussion on this; we didn't look at it all that seriously."[17] One government official, Paul Volcker, was determined, like Brimmer, to hold the system together. He believed that only its institutional arrangement could ensure foundational stability for global growth. Whatever its flaws, its signatories had committed to it as the best feasible option for global economic stability.

So what could be done? Most people believed officials had three options.

Brimmer, along with other colleagues at the Fed and on Wall Street, found a fourth way.

The standard three options were all bad: devalue the currency, tighten American monetary policy, or forbid American finance from investing abroad. All three threatened to hurt the American economy in the short term, even if they would keep the global system stable.

Devaluation was perhaps the simplest approach, and one that other nations such as Great Britain had pursued several times.[18] But President Kennedy feared that voters would see devaluation as an emasculating admission of economic mismanagement, calling "into doubt the good faith and stability of this nation and the competence of its President."[19] It would also anger the rich whose portfolios would take a hit. Some economists such as James Tobin and Paul Samuelson favored devaluation, believing that it would slow the gold drain in the short term and boost American exports in the longer term. A more skeptical group believed that a devaluation of the dollar would be followed by similar moves by other countries, creating a race to the bottom that Bretton Woods had tried to prevent. It would also undermine long-term confidence in the dollar. Countries that had trusted America and amassed large dollar reserves would be less likely to want dollars in the future. It also might disrupt international trade, given how much traders relied on a stable dollar for invoicing and short-term credit.[20]

If devaluation wouldn't work, what about tightening monetary policy domestically? Higher interest rates would strengthen the dollar by attracting more foreign investment, as investors sought better returns on their capital. That would in turn increase demand for dollars, boosting the value of the currency. In an open letter, David Rockefeller of Chase Manhattan Bank tried to impress on Kennedy "the hard truth" that the preservation of "the key role of the dollar in international monetary affairs" required higher interest rates.[21] New York Fed President Al Hayes agreed. However, such a move risked stifling American growth or even a recession for the sake of global stability. Walter Heller, Chair of the CEA, reminded President Kennedy and other senior leaders in the administration that "our basic goal was not merely to save gold, but to do it in a way that kept domestic expansion going and our liberal international policies intact as well."[22]

The third option, blocking foreign investment abroad, became the most preferred of the conventional options, and initially, Brimmer focused here. The theory was straightforward. Outside of government aid and military spending, the primary source of the outflow of dollars abroad was foreign investment. Turning off—or even just slowing—that spigot would relieve pressure on the dollar internationally by slowing the number of dollars going into circulation. The only people domestically who would suffer would be the wealthiest, as well as the financial industry. A mission as simple as its methods were complex, this agenda could stabilize the postwar monetary system, at least in the medium term.[23]

Brimmer was at the center of these marketcrafting efforts. In 1963, the Kennedy administration proposed its capital control program, and Brimmer oversaw its implementation at the Department of Commerce. Kennedy's White House designed the initial effort as a surcharge on the new issue of foreign equities and bonds sold in the United States. Business leaders begrudgingly accepted the policy, given that it was a "market-based" instrument rather than a direct ban on foreign investment as some had feared.[24] But the tax was not as effective as its designers had hoped, and with American capital still flowing overseas, the Johnson administration expanded the regulatory scope to impose a cap on foreign investment. That "voluntary" program became mandatory, dramatically restricting the use of dollars to invest in foreign companies. Banks were required to reduce short-term loans by 40 percent and cease renewing all long-term loans.

Brimmer managed the implementation of the initial Kennedy tax, and as Johnson ramped up the later efforts, he became the individual responsible for jawboning corporations to adhere to the government's supposedly voluntary policy. Charged with monitoring and managing what the nation's largest companies were doing, Brimmer kept the Commerce Secretary and the White House up to date on the program's effectiveness.[25] The Federal Reserve, however, handled requirements on banks, and when Brimmer joined the Board of Governors in 1966, he took over the Fed's management and enforcement of the controls there. Banks needed explicit approval for any foreign expansion plans, which meant they needed to ensure they curried Brimmer's favor. "[I]n the late 1960s, Federal Reserve Governor Andrew Brimmer's shadow hung over all banks," wrote one economist.[26]

The capital controls did work. By December 1965, Brimmer's efforts had resulted in a drop in direct US investments overseas, to $515 million in the third quarter of that year from $1.12 billion in the first quarter, as he explained in a speech at the time.[27] While overall foreign investment did increase despite the capital controls, this reflected borrowing in offshore markets, which did not show up as a drain in the balance of payments figures.[28] Even with the capital controls, though, global currency instability was deepening. Investors were growing increasingly skeptical that the United States could honor the commitment underpinning the Bretton Woods system.

So Andrew Brimmer did what he had done his whole life: he improvised. In Hawaii two decades earlier, he had used his newfound authority to rewrite the rules of the military. Now he used his new authority at the Fed to do something similar.

While working at Commerce, Brimmer had tracked the growth of a new, somewhat shadowy offshore-dollar market. Dollars held in foreign banks or the foreign branches of American banks don't work the same as dollars held domestically by American banks. (These offshore dollars are often called Eurodollars, even though foreign institutions around the world and not just in Europe hold them. There is no relationship to the Euro, the single European currency established in 1999. To prevent confusion, I use the term "offshore dollar" whenever possible.) When a depositor transfers money from Bank of America in San Francisco to Barclays in London, the dollars move out of the American commercial banking system and become a claim on a foreign bank. Foreign banks, however, are not subject to American banking law and do not have direct access to the Federal Reserve or the Federal Deposit Insurance Corporation (FDIC). If a depositor wants to withdraw these funds, the foreign bank turns to an American affiliate to access dollars. But, critically, as long as they remain in the foreign bank, the offshore dollars can be used to finance transactions outside of the American banking system, a short but important step away from official oversight.[29]

Investors had begun to move into offshore dollars as a way to increase their return on capital. In Brimmer's time, the Depression-era caps on how much interest American banks could pay were still in place. A sophisticated depositor could sidestep these by shifting his funds from a deposit account in the New York branch of a bank to the London branch of the same bank. Those funds could earn a higher return, since foreign banks weren't bound by American monetary policy and were free to pay market rates. This arrangement was not without risk. The offshore-dollar market lay largely outside the oversight and control of American law, leaving it, in practice, subject only to the rules of the private institutions that participated in it. Foreign banks were not subject to American reserve requirements or audit. If a foreign bank or foreign branch of a US bank were to collapse, their offshore-dollar depositors would enjoy none of the guarantees provided to depositors of domestic banking institutions by the Fed or FDIC.[30] "[T]he Eurodollar was able to operate as a contraband currency, not only held and used outside the country where it had the status of legal tender, but, more significantly, traded in a market which exists and operates outside the system of state sovereignty, and consequently, outside any national banking jurisdiction," wrote one historian.[31]

Brimmer had watched this market grow for another reason: It was a clever way to circumvent the capital controls he was responsible for enforcing. If an American wanted to invest abroad, he could route the money through offshore-dollar accounts and avoid repatriating any returns. Enterprising bankers in London even created dollar-denominated foreign bonds to simplify capital investment in Europe.[32] Offshore dollars could now help improve an investor's returns and also avoid the limits on foreign investment imposed by the capital controls. The market for offshore dollars unsurprisingly exploded in size in the 1960s, jumping from next to nothing at the start of the decade to $71 billion by 1971.[33]

Initially wary of the market, Brimmer came to understand that supporting these offshore dollars could actually help strengthen the dollar—not just in the short term, but even after Bretton Woods came apart. The reason was simple: if investors were using offshore dollars to fund investment activity, that meant they weren't using real dollars. Only dollars in the American financial system could be exchanged for gold. Keeping offshore dollars circulating abroad meant fewer real dollars would need to leave the American system. What's more: theoretically, all this foreign investment should develop these foreign markets further, strengthening their currencies and enhancing dollar demand.[34]

It was a game of musical chairs, but keeping the music going as long as possible would give Brimmer's Fed the time to manage the transition to a new and better system. Exactly what that would look like had not yet been sorted out.

Quietly, other officials at the Fed had come to believe that offshore dollars offered a useful stopgap as well. Several years earlier, the New York Fed had dispatched a mission to Europe to study the market's emergence, and their findings formed the basis of a foundational report. A few years later, the Fed even created a swap line with foreign central banks, standing by to exchange dollars for a foreign currency should a run occur. That assured investors that the offshore-dollar market was stable.[35] As Fed officials were coming to these conclusions, the Treasury was also untangling what role offshore dollars were playing in the global financial system.[36] Contrary to the belief of many economists and historians, there's no evidence of bankers having to convince Brimmer or Treasury or Fed officials to support the offshore-dollar market. When corporations decided to keep their foreign funds offshore, they were not flouting but in fact following government-sanctioned policy. As Brimmer said in a speech in 1966, "Under [the capital control] program, the companies are asked to borrow abroad to the extent feasible to finance their foreign programs. And they are doing so."[37]

Once he got to the Fed, Brimmer wanted to address the offshore-dollar market's stability. He argued that banks and companies moving monies into these accounts should be required to disclose that activity and keep a portion at home as a reserve requirement. By making the offshore-dollar market more secure, however, it could make it *more* attractive for investors to flood into. The governors agreed to give the proposal further study.[38] But around the same time, a severe "credit crunch" in the United States took hold, meaning that a mini-panic induced American investors to scramble to find lenders. The offshore-dollar market worked as a "safety valve," allowing banks access to desperately needed funds and preventing the crunch from turning into a crisis.[39] Worried that new regulations would be ill-timed, Brimmer decided to hold off on the reserve requirements and allow the offshore-dollar market to continue growing unrestrained in the short term.[40]

Not only was this economically useful; it was politically advantageous. The offshore dollars made the capital controls more porous, tamping down on the political pushback from companies and banks. "The capital controls of the United States," wrote a prominent financial analyst in a report sent to Brimmer in 1969, "could not have operated so smoothly—with a minimum restrictive effect on international trade and investment—if it had not been for the enormous expansion of the Euro-dollar market."[41] The offshore dollars were, perhaps ironically, stabilizing the American system, pleasing some investors and banks and helping keep Bretton Woods together.

In the end, the music did have to stop. Offshore dollars did not prove strong enough to save the Bretton Woods system, as we will see in later chapters. But they delayed its breakdown until the early 1970s and ensured that when it did happen, central bankers, investors, and policymakers were better prepared to handle the challenges it posed. For the decade prior to the breakdown, the United States seemed to be able to defy the laws of economics, using its unique international financial position to sustain domestic growth, finance meaningful fiscal deficits, and maintain stability in a global international economic order undergoing rapid transformation. For nearly nine years, from February 1961 to December 1969, America enjoyed the longest era of economic expansion in its history, largely thanks to the commitment made by Brimmer and others to preserving Bretton Woods.

Perhaps more importantly, Brimmer's moves helped solidify the dominance of the American dollar even after that system broke down in the early 1970s. After Bretton Woods came apart, investors had easy access to tens of billions of offshore dollars, not subject to American banking law, which greased the wheels of global investment. Particularly after the 1973 oil crisis, as more institutions and countries adopted the dollar for international transactions and reserves, a self-reinforcing cycle emerged, further cementing the dollar's dominance. Offshore dollars created a parallel international monetary system that reinforced the dollar's global role beyond what domestic US financial markets alone could have achieved. More than fifty years after the collapse of Bretton Woods, that market remains essential to the contemporary global financial system. The basic paradigm of the American central bank working with the central banks of industrialized countries to support offshore-dollar transactions endures. The offshore dollar market today is estimated to exceed $13 trillion, approaching the $18 trillion held within the U.S. banking system.[42]

In his seventies, Brimmer recounted a story from his first days in Washington. In the swampy summer heat of 1950, a twenty-three-year-old Brimmer stewed in the sun of the Rose Garden, just outside of the White House. For the past several months, he had worked as a summer intern at the institution responsible for implementing the Marshall Plan, a program of direct aid to Europe to aid in postwar economic recovery. President Harry Truman had invited all of the city's interns to join him at the White House for a celebration of their public service. The interns sipped punch and ate cookies, stewing as they waited for the President to arrive. When he finally did, over an hour late, Brimmer positioned himself strategically across from the President on the off chance that Truman greeted some of the young folks directly: "[T]here were probably 6 or 7 black students among the 350 to 400 students. I figured that Harry Truman is not going to walk past me, and that's what happened. He spotted me and came right over." Brimmer thanked him for his leadership on civil rights, and Truman assured him the fight would continue.[43]

But at the same moment as Brimmer was queuing to praise a President, he was also stepping out to question the country's failing record on racial equality. When he had a chance to meet Alabama Senator John Sparkman a few weeks earlier, the young Brimmer had minced no words. "Explain yourself, why you are not supporting the Civil Rights Act," he said. Sparkman chalked it up to pragmatism, saying it was a compromise to hold on to office.[44]

Having spent the first part of his tenure in government shoring up Bretton Woods, Brimmer focused the second half of his time as a Fed governor in the early 1970s on helping the most disadvantaged Americans. Brimmer had never been a social or racial justice activist on the front lines of the Civil Rights Movement, but he did have an abiding commitment to supporting Americans who had suffered from generations of oppression or exploitation.

As a Fed governor in the 1970s, Brimmer started arguing for a new, fairer approach to monetary policy. Specifically, he wanted the Fed to target its policies more narrowly by embracing its power to differentially price credit. That approach could make loans more expensive for finance and cheaper for small businesses or home builders, for instance.[45] His experience with the offshore-dollar market illustrated that the Fed, if it wanted to, could use its power domestically to make the American financial system work more in line with the wishes of its leaders, supporting industries that might be better for American workers over those that were less productive.

This argument was a provocative line of reasoning. Even in Brimmer's time, claiming that the Fed could make private credit allocation decisions was controversial. After the Fed regained the power to manage the nation's credit system after the war, many economists came to believe axiomatically that the central bank should not be involved in deciding *who* gets credit. They believed that work could quickly become "political" and should be left exclusively to private banks, which would have a purely profit-driven rationale. Most agreed that the Fed should manage the overall tightness of the monetary supply and regulate and supervise banks—it just should not make specific decisions about supporting certain sectors over others.[46] The official line was that an independent Fed pursued monetary policy and supervisory policy outside of politics. Chair Martin in 1955 suggested that the Fed's primary responsibility was "to act in the position of the chaperone who has ordered the punch bowl removed just when the party was really warming up."[47] It was not the Fed's business to decide what was in that punch or who got to partake while the party was going.

As the Civil Rights Movement had grown and Americans paid more attention to the winners and losers of capitalism, Brimmer began to question just how sacrosanct this principle must be. For Brimmer and others, there was no purely "market-based" system of credit. Large corporations had relatively easier access to lending facilities, even in high-interest-rate periods. In 1970, big banks could borrow cheaply given their large, distributed depositor network and their access to the offshore-dollar market, whereas small banks could not. When monetary policy tightened, big banks could continue to provide somewhat abundant credit, but small banks had to reduce lending. Because most of the big banks' customers were corporations, the practical effect of Fed tightening was a contraction in household credit, mortgage provision, and government loans issued by the small banks, while big business continued to flourish.[48] That wasn't explicit Fed policy, but it was the effect of the market structure within which the Fed operated.

Brimmer believed the Fed could craft a better market. "[T]he time has come for a thorough reexamination of the main tools and techniques of monetary control in the United States," Brimmer said in a speech in 1970 at the Fairmont Hotel in San Francisco. "[F]or a number of years, I have been concerned with the differential impact of monetary policy on different sectors of the economy. I have also urged that means be found to moderate these adverse effects." Specifically, Brimmer wanted a monetary policy that didn't tilt the field toward the biggest companies but instead made a purposeful decision around credit allocation: "In my opinion, we need a better way to assure that the overall objectives of monetary policy can be achieved without having a few sectors bear a disproportionate share of the burden of adjustment, while other sectors escape or significantly moderate its impact."[49]

It was Brimmer's experience crafting international money markets that made him confident that the Fed actually had the power to ensure fairer access to credit. He was able to rein in foreign investment activity with capital controls, proving that it was possible for government to shape a market. "[The capital control effort] was a credit allocation system in a sense. We told the banks the maximum amount of foreign loans they could have on the books of their head offices," Brimmer said. "I suggest that a new domestic credit allocation system could be patterned on the old foreign credit restraint program."[50] Specifically, Brimmer proposed that the Fed implement a system of "supplemental reserve requirements," which would tighten money disproportionately for the largest banks in periods of high inflation.

But around this time, a major shift had taken place at the Fed that proved a stumbling block for Brimmer's marketcrafting zeal. Bill Martin, the Fed Chair since 1951, disagreed with the new President, Richard Nixon, who wanted Martin to back down from the tight monetary policy he had been pursuing in the hopes of stemming inflation. Martin refused, so Nixon replaced him with his friend and counselor Arthur Burns. Brimmer began his campaign for supplemental reserve requirements about the same time, and within months Burns dismissed the idea, fearing that it would politicize the institution and make his job harder.

Brimmer was undeterred. He testified before Congress and gave speeches in support of action—even going so far as to push Congress to change the law to be even more explicit about the Fed's mandate, an aggressive step for the era. "What is important is a decision by the Congress to put in place some kind of instrument to assure that some sectors of the economy do not carry a disproportionate burden from monetary policy while others are affected much less severely," he said in 1972.[51] Brimmer was trying to use the power of the Fed to support small businesses and housing, disproportionately supporting American workers over finance.

As a result of Brimmer's zeal, Senator William Proxmire introduced legislation to give the Fed the authority to set supplemental reserve requirements. The increasingly influential Proxmire believed that the Fed should alter the price of credit based on a sector's relative importance in the economy and need of support, rather than allow the market to dictate this price as it had been. "This hands-off policy is really a throwback to the laissez faire economics of Adam Smith and has no place in a complex and highly developed country as the United States," Proxmire said. "Market forces do not allocate a limited supply of credit consistent with the public interest." Marketcraft was required. The solution, as Brimmer had imagined and Proxmire proposed, was an empowered Fed able to price credit more surgically by adjusting the prices of "commercial bank assets such as housing loans, poverty area loans, business loans, etc.," Proxmire claimed. "The Board [of Governors] can provide commercial banks with strong incentives to shift their lending in a way which benefits the public interest."[52]

Oddly, it was Brimmer's fellow Fed governors who would stand in the way of this proposed change in its mandate. In private meetings, the board split nearly evenly, ultimately breaking four to three against supporting the Proxmire proposal. Sherman Maisel—another Johnson appointee—was particularly inclined to support Brimmer, although he left the board in the midst of Brimmer's campaign.[53] Despite the meaningful private support for Brimmer's idea, Burns lied in subsequent testimony, telling legislators that the Fed governors "unanimously opposed the authority," even though Brimmer, Maisel, and J. L. Robertson supported it.[54] While Proxmire's legislative effort subsequently failed, Brimmer had unleashed an idea that refused to go back in the drawer. Senators and representatives continued to propose credit allocation programs for years, with nearly 100 bills considered in the 1974 legislative session alone.[55] Burns continued to oppose these efforts, and he eventually shaped the Fed board so that it would reflect his beliefs. By 1974, when a powerful House member, Henry Reuss, introduced a bill similar to Proxmire's, the Fed board voted six to one against supporting it. "I was the one, naturally," Brimmer said.[56]

In May of that year, though he still had six years left in his term, Brimmer announced he would step down from the board in the fall. He was not yet fifty years old. In his letter of resignation, Brimmer tactfully wrote: "I would like to stress that I am not resigning because of any policy disagreement with my colleagues on the board."[57] But there were clear hints to the contrary, drawing the picture of a visionary governor isolated by a confining Chair. One trade publication linked Brimmer's "unexpected" resignation to the fact "that Brimmer, more so than any governor, brought to the Board exceptional

innovative ideas which have been shunted aside, if not buried."[58] Another
well-informed industry journalist noted: "[I]t has been no secret that [Brimmer] has felt increasingly frustrated in his efforts to move the conservative-dominated board of governors to a more socially active stance." The article
mentioned the proposal for supplemental reserve requirements, adding that
"sources agree he has been disenchanted with Federal Reserve Chairman
Arthur F. Burns' refusal to provide even a modicum of support to the plan."[59]
Six months after he left the board, Brimmer was still on the case. He testified before Congress, saying that "the Federal Reserve in fact was allocating
credit" already. He listed several specific examples of distributive decisions
made under Burns' leadership.[60]

So why *did* Brimmer become stymied when he tried to apply these lessons domestically? Even the Fed governors had difficulty accepting just how
powerful they had become. They were increasingly in possession of potent
tools for managing the American economy, but they struggled to square this
power with the fickle and volatile nature of American politics. Rather than
embracing the immense and important marketcrafting power it had developed, the Fed in its next era would struggle to find its institutional voice.
Those stumbles contributed to one of the least stable and most disorienting
periods in twentieth-century financial history, the 1970s inflationary shocks.
At the center of this era stood one controversial and misunderstood man:
Martin's successor and Brimmer's detractor, Arthur Burns.

7

THE COST OF CONTROL

ARTHUR BURNS & INFLATION (1969-73)

On a Saturday morning in early December 1970, Arthur Burns sat in his office at the headquarters of the Federal Reserve in Washington anxiously listening to the sounds of his secretary tapping away at her typewriter. He had just revised a speech he planned to deliver the following Monday at Pepperdine University in Los Angeles. Burns had given countless public lectures in his career as an admired Columbia University professor, but he knew his address this week would be a pivotal moment in economic history. He was planning to outline the most aggressive marketcrafting agenda that a Fed Chair had ever dared to conceive.[1]

Down the street, President Richard Nixon was in a nasty mood. The midterm elections a month earlier had gone badly for him, and the country was grappling with a novel economic problem: a recession in the midst of surging inflation. He wanted the Fed to lower interest rates to boost the economy. Nixon had imagined this kind of moment when he had placed his old friend Arthur Burns in charge of the central bank a year earlier. He wanted a loyalist who would follow his directives.

But Burns was refusing to cooperate. Nixon had received word that in forty-eight hours his handpicked man would defy him by placing partial responsibility for inflation control with the White House rather than pinning the blame exclusively on the Fed.

Burns knew the President wouldn't like it, but he felt he had no choice. Just the day before, Nixon had attempted to box Burns in by falsely claiming that Burns was about to fall in line with the President's wishes. "He'll get it right in the chops," Nixon said to aides privately before delivering the message publicly.[2]

This was not a fight that Burns welcomed. The two men had a long-standing, amicable relationship, and Burns owed much of his public relevance to the President. The two had met in the 1950s when Burns worked in the Eisenhower White House as the Chairman of the CEA and Nixon was Vice President. In that role, Burns had forsworn politics altogether. "I had no political connections whatever. None," Burns said in an interview years later. "I paid absolutely no attention to a man's politics. I didn't know and I didn't care about that, and my judgment turned out to be right."[3] The role of a supposedly apolitical economist in the White House burnished Burns' credentials with Eisenhower's lieutenants, even if it undermined his ability to implement a political agenda. It also meant that Burns felt entitled to lecture Vice President Nixon about economics, as if he were a Columbia undergraduate. "Burns thought of Nixon as a protégé and treated him with what one friend described as 'slight condescension,'" wrote Burns' biographer.[4] Fifteen years later, Nixon won the 1968 presidential election, and the roles reversed. President Nixon flaunted his power, and Burns turned into the eager supplicant asking for a job. When he took office, Nixon first appointed Burns to a newly formed role, Counselor to the President, which came with an office in the Eisenhower Executive Office Building (EEOB) across from the White House. Clad in tweed suits and smoking his favorite pipe, Burns played the part of a disoriented, brilliant academic, oblivious to the power dynamics that built and broke careers in Washington.

In October 1969, Nixon informed then Fed Chair Bill Martin that he would not reappoint him to the position. He planned to nominate Burns, preferring to have a confidant in the role rather than the independent and conservative Martin. Nixon had always believed that he lost the 1960 presidential election to Kennedy because Martin's Fed had tightened money in the lead-up to the election. At the press conference announcing the nomination of Burns, Nixon joked about how Burns would handle his formal autonomy at the Fed, saying, "I respect his independence; however, I hope that he will *independently* conclude that my views should be the ones that should be followed." Nixon grinned, and the press corps cackled. Standing just behind the President, Burns grimaced and stared at the ground.[5]

By the end of his first year in the Chair position, Burns had become convinced he had no choice but to pursue a public confrontation with the White House. Inflation remained over 6 percent, and unemployment was climbing, reaching 6.1 percent in December 1970. Nixon's preferred policy—further loosening monetary policy—seemed likely to aggravate the problems by spurring inflation and only modestly helping lower unemployment. Burns had other ideas about how to engineer price stability, without unduly throwing millions out of work.[6]

Burns' secretary finished typing up his remarks, drafted in longhand, by 3:30 pm. As he was preparing to leave to catch his plane to California, the phone rang. On the line was the President with a clear message: "Don't you dare."

Burns wasn't surprised. William Safire, a journalist working as a special assistant to the President, had called the day before to offer "advice" for Burns' upcoming speech and express the President's concern. Nixon did not want a public war with his recently appointed Fed Chair. Now, as the President pushed for him to stand down, Burns sat on the other end of the phone trying to maintain a diplomatic tone. "I explained that I was fully sensitive to the need of avoiding any impression of a conflict between us," he wrote in his private diary of the conversation.[7] While he might have understood how the situation looked, he was also unwilling to compromise.

The professor lectured the pupil, hoping that his brilliant analysis would win him over. He read multiple pages of the speech to the President, forcing Nixon to sit on the other end of the phone and listen to his vision for a marketcraft in pursuit of price stability. The Fed could not and should not be expected to rein in inflation on its own, he argued. Relying on high interest rates to contain inflation would strangle economic growth and put millions out of work. Even so, rising prices did need to be controlled, and Congress was the institution that needed to step in.

Burns had been trained in institutional economics, a strand of the field that holds that patterns of economic activity depend on how institutions— businesses, government, labor unions, the central bank, etc.—interact.[8] With this pedagogical background, Burns put a particular emphasis on how Fed policy could work in conjunction with other public policy passed by Congress to promote economic goals. In this case, Burns believed the Fed needed to raise interest rates, but at the same time, Congress needed to pursue a legislative strategy to contain prices. This marketcraft needed to be an all-of-government effort, with Congress using its power to slow the pace of cost rises.

Burns intended to outline in the Pepperdine speech an eleven-point plan to check rising prices.[9] He would call for more vigorous antitrust enforcement to rein in large companies, the creation of job-training programs, the reduction of taxes on business investment, and lowering the minimum wage to bring more workers into the labor market.

One tool in particular, the most important in the proposed effort, particularly enraged Nixon: the creation of wage and price controls. Nixon had served during World War II in the Office of Price Administration, which convinced him that the government had no business dictating prices in the American economy. For years he publicly opposed such measures, clashing with Burns and others in his administration who supported them as anti-inflation tools. In public speeches, he derided "government controls that cause artificial market shortages," suggesting that he would never support them.[10] The Democratic Congress disagreed. They believed in targeted wage and price controls and saw public support on their side. In 1970, Congress gave the President the authority to freeze wages, rents, and salaries. Democrats wanted to embarrass the President by giving him broad price-fixing authority, which Congressional leaders believed he would not use. From Nixon's vantage point, his supposed loyalist Burns was backing Congressional Democrats, giving his political opponents more material that they could use to embarrass him. The President stewed on the other end of the line.

When the call ended, Burns rushed to the airport to make his flight. He thought that Nixon, infamously afraid of outright conflict, "seemed pleased" when he finished reading him his speech on the phone. "At least he said he was," Burns wrote in his diary.[11] It's difficult to imagine that was true, given the acrimony that came in the following weeks. The morning after he outlined his agenda at Pepperdine, the *New York Times* ran the news of the speech as its lead story of the day and reprinted Burns' words in their entirety. The editors marked it as a turning point, clarifying the still-new Fed Chair's vision for inflation control and the sources of disagreement with the Nixon White House. Their private quarrel was now a public dispute.[12]

The problem of high inflation only grew more urgent in the months and years after Burns' Pepperdine speech. If you stashed $100 under your mattress in January of 1968, fifteen years later that same $100 would be worth just $34. By the early 1980s, inflation had so depleted the purchasing power of American consumers that labor, business leaders, and retirees alike all agreed that no problem was more urgent to fix. Public polling in the summer of 1980 showed that over half of Americans believed inflation was the most important problem facing the country, and it remained at the top of the list of Americans' concerns until a Fed-engineered recession caused unemployment to take the top spot.[13] Arthur Burns served as Fed Chair for half of the Great Inflation, from the start of 1970 to early 1978.

The inflation that Burns combated in the 1970s had not, in fact, arrived unannounced on his watch. Government spending ballooned in the mid-1960s, a result of President Johnson's escalation of the Vietnam War and investment in a strong welfare state. Meanwhile, the government was taking in less money because of historic tax cuts that Democrats and Republicans passed in 1964. Large government deficits overstimulated consumer spending, and Martin's Fed was slow to tighten monetary policy. In 1968, President Johnson attempted to bring fiscal discipline by passing a onetime 10 percent surcharge on corporate and household incomes. That created a temporary surplus for the government, but it did little to stop inflation. In another attempt to slow price increases, Bill Martin's Fed tightened monetary policy at the end of the 1960s, sending interest rates to historic highs.[14] But inflation kept growing. Martin came to believe that he should have been even more aggressive. Nixon, sensing Martin's latent desire to hike interest rates, shunted him aside just in time.

As Burns took the oath of office in February 1970, high inflation was now occurring alongside economic contraction and accelerating unemployment. That combination defied what many economists believed possible at the time and soon went by the name stagflation. The problem for Burns was that restrictive monetary policy was not having the expected effect of bringing down inflation, and no one knew why. Tightening the vise could just make matters worse.

If anyone could squelch inflation, it would be Burns, most economists believed. No one supported Burns for Fed Chair more enthusiastically than

Milton Friedman, the emergent leader of the new Chicago School of Economics. Friedman had been Burns' student at Rutgers and called him "almost a surrogate father." His support for Burns did not stem only from loyalty; he believed that Burns would aggressively tackle inflation in a way that Martin had not. "He understands the monetary system and its relation to the economy at a depth and subtlety that has not been equaled by any past chairman of the board," Friedman said.[15] Burns had long argued for the importance of price stability, which Friedman knew. Inflation was dangerous and corrosive because of its effects on consumer spending power and business investment decisions, Burns believed. A central task for policymakers was to ensure business confidence, which in turn would stabilize private investment and prevent sharp swings in the business cycle. Inflation could undermine all of that.

In 1969, a year before he became Fed Chair and with inflation over 5 percent, Burns made much of this clear in an essay published in his book *The Business Cycle in a Changing World*. "Serious depressions are no longer the threat they once were, while creeping inflation has become a chronic feature of recent history and a growing threat to the welfare of millions of people," he wrote. "Not only is a creeping inflation unnecessary to the continuance of prosperity, but it can in time become a grave obstacle to it."[16] The question was how to control it. Today most economists believe that the only way to manage inflation is for the Fed to tighten the money supply. That was not the consensus in 1970, and for good reason. The inflation that occurred while Burns was Fed Chair was caused by a variety of factors, including elevated government spending, the eventual breakdown of Bretton Woods, and a set of commodity shocks, largely related to oil.[17] In other words, the inflation was caused by both supply problems and excess demand. Burns believed it would be wrong to expect a single tool—tightening the money supply—to be the *only* weapon the government should use to combat an enemy with such diverse causes. If policymakers waited on the Fed, expecting it to act alone, the central bank would have to raise interest rates so high that it would initiate a historic recession, destroy millions of jobs, and fuel the fire of voices in Congress anxious to rein in the Fed's autonomy.

Burns wasn't alone in thinking that inflation control should be rooted in a broader marketcraft. Leading Keynesian economists John Kenneth Galbraith and James Tobin believed that fiscal decisions—particularly tax hikes and cuts, along with adjustments in government spending—were the most powerful tools of demand management and affected inflation significantly more than monetary policy could. In addition, wage and price controls could supplement monetary policy to make it more effective.[18] For these Keynesian economists, the preferred answer to the inflationary surge in 1970 would be a permanent tax hike, draining money from the economy and reducing overall demand. (Some also believed that the problem of high inflation was overstated and smothering it was not worth the cost in lost jobs.)

Other economists believed that workers had too much power and that unions were responsible for bidding up wages, fueling inflation. Roughly one in three Americans at the time still worked in mining, construction, or manufacturing, and these industrial sectors were heavily unionized.[19] The argument went this way: When organized autoworkers faced higher prices, they naturally demanded higher wages. When employers granted the wage increases, they had to raise prices—at least if they didn't want to accept lower profit margins. The workers also had more money to spend, fueling a further increase in prices. All those higher prices meant that laborers demanded even higher wages in the next round of negotiations. Editorial pages were filled with debates about how much of a problem this so-called wage-price spiral actually was and whether decreasing the bargaining power of organized labor would help combat inflation. The compromise position for labor and business leaders that was gaining momentum in late 1970 and into 1971 was the idea of government-led controls on wages and prices. If government stepped in to arrest both prices and wages, the self-defeating cycle might be broken. By January of 1971, 62 percent of Americans responded in favor of a system of wage and price controls in a Harris survey, a thirteen-point increase from the previous summer.[20]

One final, insurgent group of economists who called themselves monetarists were skeptical of all these theories about inflation. Led by Friedman, they believed efforts to fine-tune the economy—whether they were initiated by the Fed or Congress—were destined for failure. Demand for money was fundamentally stable, in their view, and did not shift based on consumer or investor confidence. Only an increase in the supply of money, which the central bank had near total control over, could cause inflation. Friedman lectured students, policymakers, and everyday Americans with his maxim "Inflation is always and everywhere a monetary phenomenon." If prices went up, it could only be a sign of too much money circulating in the economy. Supply shocks—such as a precipitous drop in oil production—caused changes in relative prices, but they only had a persistent upward effect on the aggregate price level if the central bank accommodated the shift with additional money creation. The only real way to curb inflation was to take discretion away from the Fed and agree to a consistent, gradual increase in the money supply that corresponded to long-term economic growth expectations. That would put monetary policy on autopilot, they argued.[21]

Burns did not fit neatly into any of these economic camps, although he drew from each of them. He believed that deficit spending spurred inflation, and that Congress could hike taxes to dampen price pressures. He also believed that the central bank could tighten more aggressively if necessary to rein in inflation, although he feared the social and political consequences of going too far. Where Burns diverged from both the Keynesians and monetarists was his emphasis on an *institutional* economic vision, a marketcraft for the 1970s. Markets could be profoundly influenced by public policy, and Congress could change laws and regulations if it wanted price stability. He continued to revise and develop the ideas he had uncorked at Pepperdine. Some of the suggestions, like challenging labor unions to dampen wage demands and reducing the minimum wage, pleased conservative interests, while more aggressive antitrust enforcement and calls for local "job banks" or "productivity councils" appealed to the left. Some of his ideas were more developed than others, but they all shared in common a commitment to restructuring markets to reduce price pressures.

The most important of his proposals—and the major one to come to fruition under his watch—was the creation of wage and price controls. Historically, Burns had been skeptical of controls, aligning himself with conservatives who believed that the controls imposed during the Second World War and in the Korean War had twisted markets, disrupting the ability of the price mechanism to bring production and consumption into alignment. Once in the seat of Fed Chair, he surprised himself in coming to believe that they should be a supplementary tool to the implementation of monetary policy, a way to turbocharge Fed efforts to tighten money. Burns' views had changed as circumstances changed, and by the time of his phone call with Nixon, he believed that "the scope of an incomes policy" should be considered "quite broadly."[22]

The problem was that Burns was still thinking like an academic, developing a "wish list" of smart policies that he believed could stabilize the nation. Just as he had floundered in the Eisenhower and Nixon White Houses to sort through the politics of how to turn ideas into law, he struggled to move his ideas out of the realm of theory and into action.

It didn't help that the President was furious with him. Burns is often portrayed as a sycophant who refused to tighten monetary policy in 1972 out of concern for Nixon's reelection. He was lost at sea after Nixon's resignation, critics allege, too timid or inept to cure inflation with high interest rates.[23] In these narratives, Burns is cast as the foil to one of his successors at the Fed, Paul Volcker, who effectively tackled inflation.[24]

Burns did fail to rein in inflation, but not because he was buddies with President Nixon.[25] In the months after assuming his role at the central bank, Burns persistently made a public case for his ideas in speeches and Congressional testimony. It's easy to understand why this angered the politically sensitive Nixon. Burns' relentless call for elected officials to take action kept making it sound like the responsibility for the inflation lay with the President rather than the Fed. By the summer of 1971, Nixon decided he'd had enough, demanding that Burns stop his public campaign. Burns instead escalated the situation, rearticulating his vision in a Congressional hearing two days later.[26] "Nixon thought that he could appeal to my friendship and get his way," Burns wrote in his diary, clearly proud of his willingness to stand up to the President. He assured the President that he remained his friend, but he "owed it to the Congress to speak [his] mind honestly."[27]

Nixon would not be outmaneuvered. After a few drinks with Treasury Secretary John Connally aboard the presidential yacht, Nixon directed his staff to leak a rumor that Burns was seeking a doubling of his salary. (The presidential yacht served as a floating White House for American Presidents from Herbert Hoover to Jimmy Carter, who ended the tradition in 1977 to symbolize government austerity.) Rightly suspecting the White House was the source of the rumor, Burns wrote in his diary of his anger and frustration. Nixon, for his part, was tickled that he had rattled Burns, going so far as to phone up Connally to share the good news that their ploy had worked—a couple of schoolboys delighting in their prank.

Burns was not getting far with his marketcrafting wish list. He testified to Congress eleven times between May 1970 and August 1971, but lawmakers had not passed any of his proposed reforms with the exception of a law giving the President power to implement price and wage controls—a deliberate attempt from Congressional Democrats to embarrass Nixon and pin the blame for inflation on the President himself. Almost no one expected the authority would be invoked. The professor's view simply wasn't breaking through in Washington. "He would come testify in Congress and tell us what we needed to do or the President needed to do. Even though we agreed on some—definitely not all—of the things on his list, we didn't take it all that seriously," said the liberal economist James Galbraith, who worked on the staff of the House Banking Committee. "Burns' lists included a large share of anti-labor and budget-cutting measures that we opposed on the merits."[28] If those on the left found his proposals unfriendly to workers, monetarist economists on the right believed them to be a distraction from sounder solutions. His scientific pluralism rendered him politically inert.

By the late summer of 1971, Burns and Nixon were back on speaking terms. Economist Alan Greenspan, a friend to both, had played emissary between the President and the Fed Chair, eventually brokering a détente of sorts. Burns would quiet down his calls for a broader program to fight inflation if the President held off on further bullying. When the President called to apologize, Burns used the conversation to make the case for the price and wage controls that formed the central plank of his marketcrafting agenda.[29] Publicly, he stuck to the Greenspan accord. In private, he remained dogged.

Even so, the pair tentatively patched up their relationship just in time for a global economic crisis. Only days later, the two had to decide whether America should give up its decades-long commitment to the world to guarantee the value of dollars in gold at a fixed price. The long-feared breakdown of the Bretton Woods agreement forced Burns and Nixon to collaborate—and put a central element of the Fed Chair's marketcraft agenda at center stage.

On an early mid-August morning in 1971, President Nixon, dressed in a bathrobe and slippers, was walking between cabins at Camp David, the presidential retreat nestled in Maryland's Catoctin Mountain Park not far from the Pennsylvania border. It was 5:45 and Nixon had been awake since 3:15, dictating into a microphone the first draft of what would prove to be a defining speech of his presidency, and now he wanted to drop the tapes off at the cabin of his personal secretary, Rose Mary Woods. Doubting that anyone else would be up, the President didn't bother to dress. On the walk over to Woods' cabin in his robe, he ran across one of the security officers charged with guarding the facility taking an early morning dip in the pool. Nixon greeted the navy chief with a "Good morning," to which the swimmer reportedly replied, "Yes, ma'am." Likely both amused and incensed, the President asked the man to deliver the tapes on his behalf to Woods' cabin. Once the man was dispatched, Nixon went for a swim of his own. When the President's speechwriter Bill Safire arrived at Woods' cabin a little over an hour later to share with her his own first draft of the speech, he found her typing away. She annotated the President's directives and passed them off to Safire for incorporation into his own draft. It was barely 7:00 am, and breakfast had not yet been served.[30]

Early mornings for presidential advisers are not uncommon, but this was no ordinary weekend. Six days before, on Monday, August 9, the long-feared global run on the dollar began. The pressure had been building for years. In 1944, developed nations signed on to the Bretton Woods agreement to stabilize global currencies to support international trade. That financial order was premised on the postwar American commitment to convert dollars to gold at a fixed price. A little more than fifteen years later, the number of dollars in global circulation eclipsed American gold stores, raising the first questions of whether the United States could honor it. For most of the 1960s, the large industrialized economies, including West Germany, France, and the United Kingdom, agreed to avoid converting their dollars to gold. If they all had, there would not be enough to go around. In 1969 and 1970, Germany pursued a tighter monetary policy than many other countries, including the United States, causing investors to dump dollars for deutsche marks. As investors fled the dollar, its value continued to fall, and waves of speculation hit European exchange markets in the spring of 1971.

In that high-pressure environment, offshore-dollar holdings, which Fed governor Andrew Brimmer and others had cultivated to delay the Bretton Woods breakdown, became a problem for investors and American policymakers alike. Private holders of offshore dollars rushed to sell their holdings, with foreign central banks forced to take the other side of the trade. As they mopped up dollars in the system, central banks' holdings of dollars escalated to record levels—increasing by over 60 percent between September 1970 and June of 1971, even before the run started.[31] If America devalued, it would dramatically decrease the value of reserves in foreign central banks, weakening their power to keep their currencies stable. In May 1971, the central banks of Germany, the Netherlands, Switzerland, Belgium, and Austria officially dropped their commitment to support the dollar.[32]

Bretton Woods hung by a thread for much of the summer of 1971. One week before Nixon's Camp David dip, a subcommittee in the House recommended devaluing the dollar, and all hell broke loose.[33] The run began on Monday, August 9, and by Thursday, the Bank of England asked the New York Federal Reserve for "cover" for $3 billion of its dollar reserves. The ambiguous nature of the request suggested either that London was asking the United States to reimburse it in case the US government devalued the dollar *or* that it wanted to convert sterling for $3 billion worth of gold. Either way, such a request from the United Kingdom indicated that even America's closest friends no longer trusted America's commitment to its peg.[34] The global monetary order—and perhaps the entire global economy—was on the verge of collapse.

That afternoon, the President's chief of staff, Bob Haldeman, contacted the leaders of the government's financial institutions, including Burns, and told them to pack a bag to leave town for a few days. All were barred from telling friends or even family that they were headed to the presidential mountain retreat. Their mission for the next forty-eight hours: develop a plan for how to end the global monetary order known as Bretton Woods without causing chaos at home or abroad. The helicopter ferrying most of the advisers touched down on Friday around 3:00 pm, and the leaders quickly assembled for an initial conversation.[35]

Nixon and Burns were joined at Camp David by Treasury Secretary John Connally and Paul Volcker, the Under Secretary of the Treasury for Monetary Affairs. The two men had been planning for this moment. The turmoil had started in May when the Germans allowed their currency to appreciate beyond the limits prescribed by the Bretton Woods protocol. That unprecedented move ricocheted through markets and prompted Volcker to draft a plan for a controlled American devaluation that he shared with Connally. The two worked on the plan over the following weeks, and Connally began to preview the ideas with the President midway through the summer. The United States would announce that it would no longer convert dollars for gold at thirty-five dollars an ounce—or, for that matter, any price. This would take the world off the gold standard. The US government would then attempt to manage a *gradual* devaluing of the dollar in the months following the suspension of convertibility. To prevent a precipitous devaluation, the plan imposed a temporary 10 percent tariff on merchandise imports, strengthening the dollar for that period. To tamp down the inflation that would follow a devaluation, the plan outlined spending reductions in the federal budget and, to the surprise of many, wage and price controls. Nixon now had to weigh his enduring dislike for controls with the risk of a major inflationary surge on the heels of the closing of the gold window. He needed short-term domestic economic stability, and controls might offer that. A central element of Burns' marketcraft agenda was now on the table.

In their first meeting of the weekend, the President's economic advisers discussed the basic contours of the Connally-Volcker proposal. The President seemed inclined to embrace the world-changing nature of the decision to end Bretton Woods and initiate the kinds of programs under discussion. If America were going to devalue the dollar, Nixon wanted to pair that perceived weakness with an aggressive effort to control the fallout. Two participants were particularly wary of the idea of the dissolution of Bretton Woods. One was Burns, who argued that the proposed plan was strong enough that its implementation alone could be sufficient to shore up international support for the dollar. "These major actions will electrify the world," he argued, believing that they might be enough to stop the panic.[36] Plus, if Nixon closed the gold window, other countries could retaliate by pursuing their own devaluations, introducing chaos into the global economic system.

The second skeptic of the decision was Volcker, even though he conceived the plan. Volcker shared many of Burns' concerns and was keen to emphasize that he believed only a temporary suspension was merited. "I hate to do this, to close the window," Volcker said. "All my life I have defended [fixed] exchange rates, but I think it's needed."[37] Volcker meant for the United States to return to Bretton Woods once stability was regained. Nixon took Burns and Volcker's counsel into account, but by Saturday morning, he had decided to close the window permanently and implement the rest of the program. Burns agreed not to stand in the way. "I assured the President that I would support his new program [fully]," he wrote in his diary afterward. "I could not responsibly question what he did on gold—publicly. Moreover, I was aware of the margins of doubt on this question, and I could not be sure that my position was right and his wrong. In any event, as the meeting drew to an end, the President was obviously relieved to find that I would support him."[38] Burns also knew that the decision would create a back door for the price and wage controls he had been advocating for.

On Saturday night, still at Camp David, Nixon asked his political advisers to come to his cabin. His chief of staff, Haldeman, found the President in his study with the lights off and a fire roaring despite the warm night. "[The President] was in one of his sort of mystic moods," Haldeman recounted. He told the group that this was the spot where he developed his big ideas and he was formulating what he would soon say to the nation. Camp David had been where Nixon had gone to write his eulogy for President Eisenhower and where he made the decision to send troops to Cambodia in the spring of 1970. Now he had come to the conclusion that his speech must somehow invigorate Americans, even as his administration took an economic route that might indicate weakness, even an admission of failure. "We need to raise the spirit of the country. That will be the thrust and rhetoric of the speech," Haldeman recounted the President saying. A forward-looking, optimistic America would demonstrate to the world its economic vitality and strength: "Let America never accept being second best. We must try to be what is within our power to be."[39] What that meant was up to Nixon's speechwriters to define.

On Sunday, while his economic advisers scrambled to develop specific policies and inform foreign allies, the President took Marine One back to the White House. At nine o'clock that evening, he interrupted the popular television show *Bonanza* to give a primetime address from the Oval Office announcing the end of the gold standard and the imposition of controls. Wearing a gray suit, white shirt, and gray tie, Nixon sat at his Oval Office desk stiffly reading from seventeen printed pages, his eyes darting back and forth from the sheets of paper to the camera. "He stumbled over several words, and at one point he wiped what seemed to be a bead of sweat below his nose with the back of his hand," wrote one author who chronicled the weekend.[40] Nixon talked through his plan, including the suspension of convertibility and a ninety-day freeze on prices and wages. Calling the controls "temporary," Nixon pledged they would "not be accompanied by the establishment of a huge price control bureaucracy." He kept neither promise.

Over 46 million watched Nixon's speech, and despite his wavering delivery, the public response was one of broad support. Americans wanted economic stability and an end to inflation, and Nixon seemed to be offering them that. Nixon had managed to take the devaluation of the dollar and transform it into a political asset. Herbert Stein, the conservative Chair of the CEA who attended the Camp David weekend, later called the price controls "the most popular move in economic policy that anyone could remember."[41] A Gallup poll just after the President's announcement reported that 68 percent of the public supported the freeze, with only 11 percent opposed. Enthusiasm was bipartisan and enduring over the following months, with two-thirds of Americans still supporting the controls in November.[42]

Partially thanks to Burns' constant advocacy—in the press, at the Fed, and in front of Congress—a broad consensus had developed in the country for the controls. For Democrats, the controls were a way to show that they were standing up to exploitative business interests, limiting their profit margins to help American families.[43] For business leaders, such as David Rockefeller and former Fed Chair Martin—who was now working in the private sector—the controls could hold back the escalating wages that they saw as the primary driver behind inflationary surges. Without them, the breakdown of Bretton Woods could spell chaos. That all of Nixon's economic team aligned in agreement behind the price and wage freeze indicated the unusual level of consensus in the country. "There is no serious, coherent policy that is an alternative to the one the administration has initiated," Stein said a few months later.[44]

Burns may not have gotten his way on the gold window, but he left Camp David with a core piece of his marketcrafting approach in place. After nearly a year and a half of public dispute with the President, Nixon and his advisers had found their way to Burns' impassioned demand for price and wage controls. Now they had to make them work.

For a year or so, it looked as if the controls might succeed. Core inflation receded in the fourth quarter of 1971 to 2.3 percent, despite the breakdown of Bretton Woods. By the first half of 1972, unemployment began to decline, and growth accelerated. To many it felt like the American economy had turned a corner.

Most Americans attributed that tentative success to the controls. Even though Nixon's post–Camp David price freeze was technically supposed to be in effect for only ninety days, it proved so effective and popular that no one in Washington considered abandoning it. Instead, the administration institutionalized it, expanding the initial Cost of Living Council to include three new agencies. A new Price Commission of seven members was charged with regulating what companies could charge for goods and services. A fifteen-member Pay Board—split between representatives of labor, business, and the public—monitored and restricted wage growth.[45] Burns chaired a third implementing institution, the Committee on Interest and Dividends.[46] Despite the creation of these institutions, the federal government spent less than $100 million each year implementing the suite of controls, less than a quarter of the cost of operating the Federal Reserve system.[47]

The controls of 1972 were largely successful at holding down inflation, keeping it to 3 percent for the year.[48] As the price and wage controls settled in, the economy flourished, growing at nearly 5.3 percent, its most robust year since 1966.[49] The one area of significant concern was the continued growth in wages, which were increasing at more than double the rate of prices. Burns, siding with other economists and business leaders, worried that higher wages could augur more inflation to come. He claimed that the Pay Board was failing to do its part. As it got more aggressive in reining in wages, the labor representatives on it walked out. The President took the opportunity to downsize it, trying to make it easier to hold down worker pay. The drama with the board made little economic difference. With low inflation, increasing wages, and skyrocketing growth, most Americans found little to criticize in the controls.

It was in the midst of this frothy economy that Burns made a move that would define the inflationary struggle for the rest of the decade. Given receding unemployment and accelerating growth, Burns could have gradually but decisively tightened monetary policy. The controls were providing the Fed with a window of opportunity to tighten while the economy was robust. He had argued for years that price and wage controls should be paired with restrictive monetary policy from the Fed, saying clearly that the controls were not a long-term solution.[50] Now when he had his moment to implement that vision, he failed. Instead, Burns led the FOMC to make only modest tightening moves, with the prime rate increasing by just over a single percentage point to 6 percent in December 1972.[51]

Burns was not alone in his decision to only modestly tighten. Many law-makers, economists, and journalists heeded the siren song of effective price controls, becoming convinced that high interest rates or tax hikes could be delayed indefinitely into the future. "We all thought 'We're a long way from full employment, we still have a lot of room for expanding the economy, and the inflation rate is low,'" recounted CEA Chair Stein. "We misinter-preted."[52] In the midst of 1972, one of the most influential Senators, William Proxmire, even pushed Burns toward pursuing a more stimulative monetary policy. On Wall Street, the Fed's decision to keep rates stable garnered little criticism.[53] The consensus supported Burns' decision to hold off on mean-ingfully tightening money.

Instead of focusing on getting monetary policy right, Burns continued to stump for the rest of his marketcrafting program. In the midst of 1972, he testified to the Joint Economic Committee on Capitol Hill. The Fed will continue its "path of moderate money growth," he said, but he wanted Con-gress to do the work of implementing his other Pepperdine ideas, including zero-base budgeting, a ceiling on fiscal expenditures, and more robust anti-trust enforcement against businesses and unions alike. "The Federal Reserve is in a favorable position to continue pursuing a path of moderate monetary growth," Burns testified. "The fundamental problem . . . is how to regain control over federal expenditures."[54] Once again, Burns managed to turn off just about everyone listening. This time he didn't have an international crisis to help his ideas gain traction. Of all of Burns' suggestions, the only one to receive real consideration was the spending ceiling. Nobody saw any reason to tinker with an economy that seemed to be working just fine.

None of Burns' ideas ended up going anywhere, and it was not only be-cause Burns failed to organize effectively for them. Many of the specific ideas that Burns advocated for could have been impactful, but they were without any viable institutional context to deliver on them outside of Congress. He prof-fered countless ideas but failed to explain which institutions might be charged with delivering on their promise. Nor did he want the Fed to be responsible for the elements of his marketcraft. That approach pushed the boundaries of believability: Congress was supposed to enact smart economic policy because it was right on the merits, nimbly passing new legislation as economic variables themselves changed.

Meanwhile, rumors about the Burns-Nixon relationship swirled. Nixon was up for reelection in the fall of 1972, and some wondered if Burns was purposefully keeping monetary policy loose to aid the President. Two years later, a *Fortune* journalist wrote an article reporting that Burns had asked the FOMC to keep rates low to goose the President's reelection chances in 1972. The FOMC supposedly shirked its independence and gave in, according to the article. No evidence supports that claim. Even Andrew Brimmer, who voted several times to raise rates in periods when Burns did not and harbored little personal affection for the Chair, found the idea preposterous. Years after Burns' death, Brimmer continued to denounce the claim. "Arthur was not holding down the discount rate explicitly to help get Nixon reelected, although some people presumably thought so," Brimmer said.[55]

Regardless of why Burns chose not to tighten monetary policy, the critical fact is that he did not. "If a restrictive monetary policy had been imposed at the same time that controls were used, we could have avoided both the vacillating nature of the program and the disappointment we experienced when controls were lifted and we discovered that inflation was as much a problem as ever," wrote the economist and price and wage controls expert Hugh Rockoff a few years later.[56] At the same time, Congress did not significantly rein in its own expenditures. The fundamental dynamics of the macroeconomy endured.

The controls worked like a dam, holding back price pressures. But without policy to reduce aggregate demand, draining the reservoir, they could only hold off the flood for so long. After his reelection in the fall of 1972, Nixon's administration began an across-the-board phaseout of price and wage controls except in food, medical care, construction, and rent. It disbanded the Price Commission and Pay Board, assigning their responsibilities to the Cost of Living Council. Policymakers from both parties were torn: they were interested in returning to a market-driven pricing system but hesitant to remove controls that had proven effective. As soon as Nixon announced the wind-down of controls, consumer expectations shifted and prices began to lurch upward. A bad harvest in the fall of 1972 meant food prices were the first to come under pressure.[57] Overall inflation doubled from 2.8 percent in the first quarter of 1973 to 5.6 percent in the second. Unemployment continued to recede, but now inflation felt as though it had only been dormant during the controls. It was now returning with a vengeance.

The progress Burns had made with his controls was disappearing as fast as they were being repealed, and he knew it. By the summer of 1973, the Fed started tightening money aggressively, but Congress, still convinced of the power of nonmonetary solutions to inflation even as the problem threatened to spiral out of control, debated how they might slow or stop the Fed's rate hikes. Burns continued sermonizing, and his agenda now included a further tightening of price and wage controls, reduction in federal spending, and a compulsory savings plan for individuals. Meanwhile, gas shortages were growing as 1973 progressed, provoking Nixon to implement another of Burns' early recommendations: ending oil import quotas. Inflation kept rising even so. Nixon wanted to institute a price freeze just as he had done nearly two years before to such impressive political and economic results. "You can't step in the same river twice," Stein told the President that spring, invoking the Greek philosopher Heraclitus. "You could," Nixon snapped back, "if it was frozen."[58] In early June, Nixon issued a second price freeze, this one for sixty days on all retail, including food. It didn't work. Prices were frozen below production cost in some cases, and shortages were common. Public opinion was as hostile to the second freeze as it had been enthusiastic about the first. The Nixon administration initiated an effort to gradually lift the remainder of the controls, but the country had given up on them, making enforcement increasingly difficult as the system broke down. Controls ended officially in April 1974, except on energy products like natural gas and oil.

Price and wage controls had worked exceptionally well in the early stages, but Burns and Nixon had failed to build on that success to achieve lasting price stability. They did not understand that the all-of-government approach required controls and monetary tightening to be used in tandem, the left and right hand working simultaneously to bring prices down. Monetary tightening would have constricted credit provision, cooling economic activity while the controls kept prices stable. This would have no doubt required a delicate balance, but it could have illustrated how monetary policy might work alongside controls in moments of crisis. Some economists at the time, including the libertarian-leaning Hugh Rockoff, understood this. As Rockoff wrote, controls "are a medicine to be used to dull the pain and tranquilize the patient while monetary restraint and reform of our fiscal affairs work the fundamental cure. To renounce controls completely would subject the patient to needless pain. . . . But to rely on controls to work the whole cure, or to continue their use after health was restored, would create more problems than it would solve."[59] Because of the Nixon-Burns failure, the general acceptance of price controls as one aspect of a larger tool kit faded from popular consciousness. Tightening monetary policy would increasingly be seen as the only viable alternative to controls, rather than a complement.

Burns' inability to deliver price stability made him a failed marketcrafter. The trouble was neither his economics nor his personality. He did not lack the courage to stand up to Presidents. Burns served under Nixon, Gerald Ford, and Jimmy Carter, and continued hammering his plans with all three administrations and Congress. And his all-of-government approach to mac-roeconomic management had both theoretical elegance and analytical rigor. But his inability to make the case to Congress for investing the Fed—or any other institution—with the power to implement his broader marketcrafting vision doomed his program. The tweeded, pipe-smoking professor lacked the political skills to organize people in Congress or the White House to support his ideas, and he failed to imagine how the administrative state might implement them. As a result, his recurring demands for Congressional help often sounded like an excuse for Fed inaction. With little bipartisan agree-ment or appetite for new marketcrafting policies in Congress, the ideas went nowhere. Burns' failure left the American economy vulnerable to both the most painful and enduring inflation in US history and gave license for an ultimately brutal cure.

Because even as inflation was spinning out of control, a related crisis was already erupting. In late 1973, OPEC's world-shaking decision to cut off oil exports to the United States threw the American political and economic system into chaos. The response would not fall to Burns or any economist at the Fed. It would fall to a libertarian crusader, one of the unlikeliest market-crafters yet.

8

CRISIS ARCHITECT

BILL SIMON & ENERGY MARKETS (1973-80)

Bond trading at Salomon Brothers was not a particularly glamorous affair. The buyers and sellers of government debt were the truck drivers of 1960s finance—brusque, impulsive, and tightly wound—and Bill Simon was the ultimate bond man. Simon ran the trading department at Salomon, barking orders as he roamed the floor while sipping jug after jug of ice water. It may not have been the most highbrow work, but it was important: US Treasury rates served as the benchmark for lending throughout the economy. The bond market, powered by the traders' ongoing decisions to buy and sell, set those prices. "Don't try to get intellectual in the marketplace. Just trade," Simon told his team.[1] He once ordered a junior trader to tidy his desk. The next time Simon passed by, it remained cluttered, so Simon swept his arm across it, knocking all of the items to the floor.[2]

Simon was demanding, but he was also one of the savviest traders in the business. That afforded him immense respect and loyalty, from colleagues and employees alike. On one occasion, a team member came to him complaining that every time he attempted to borrow funds in the bond market, the cost jumped. Unable to execute his buy trades, he was stuck. "Be the seller," Simon told him. That directly contradicted the trader's original mandate, but he did as he was told and lent money that he didn't have. Those moves sent borrowing costs in the market back down to a manageable rate, and the trader quickly bought back the money he had lent and executed the original trade at the lower cost. "That was how a Salomon trader thought: he forgot whatever it was that he wanted to do for a minute and put his finger on the pulse of the market," the author and journalist Michael Lewis wrote. "If the market felt fidgety, if people were scared or desperate, he herded them like sheep into a corner, then made them pay for their uncertainty. He sat on the market until it puked gold coins."[3]

Now, at the age of forty-five, for the first time in his life Simon was considering a career move. Feeling slightly apprehensive, Simon boarded a presidential fleet helicopter in Washington, DC, in the brisk post-Thanksgiving air of November 1972. The helicopter lifted off and turned to head west, whisking Simon and a few companions to the secluded presidential retreat Camp David. Despite his financial market expertise, Simon had not spent meaningful time in the halls of government, let alone on a presidential aircraft. That lack of government experience was of little concern to President Richard Nixon, who, at least Simon believed, was about to interview him for a cabinet position for the upcoming second term. Simon had memorized a few ideas he knew he wanted to share and was hoping to leave Camp David with a job offer.

Within the hour, he was sitting across from Nixon, who was anxiously pushing Simon to accept an iced tea with pineapple. "That's how we drink it down here, you know," he said invitingly. The President settled in across from Simon in the relatively relaxed environs of a Camp David cabin and launched into a meandering monologue on history, politics, and the balance of power. Simon, unsure of how—or whether—to interrupt a President, listened attentively, waiting for a pause. It didn't come. "I felt like an invisible observer and had a strange feeling that President Nixon's dissertation would have continued unabated whether I was there or not," he later wrote.[4]

Simon had traveled to Camp David believing that he was in the final stages of being vetted for the job of Secretary of Housing and Urban Development (HUD). A few days earlier, however, Treasury Secretary George Shultz had overheard a conversation in the White House mess about Simon's potential appointment. Simon had served on an advisory committee to help the government with its debt issuance, impressing Shultz with his willingness to speak plainly and cut through jargon. Shultz had wanted to bring Simon into government during the first term, but Nixon had balked at having another East Coast finance man in the mix. But in the weeks after Nixon's successful reelection, as his aides were drawing up personnel plans, they circled back to Simon, this time as the top pick for HUD. Shultz, overhearing the plans in the mess and determined to have Simon under his wing, walked over to the aides and picked up a sheet of paper that said: "Simon: Secretary, HUD." He politely asked for a pen and then crossed out "HUD" and wrote in "Treasury," adding the word "Deputy" in front of "Secretary."

Now a few days later, the President, still sitting across from Simon in the Camp David cabin, interrupted his own monologue: "You know, this is a very important job. You realize this is tantamount to running the department." Simon had been silent until that point, but he could not conceal his confusion. He stumbled his way through the conversation unsure of whether he was already being demoted and feeling too deferential to confess that he wasn't sure what they were discussing. Within minutes, he left Camp David, "bewildered, unclear of precisely what I had gotten myself into." Soon Simon learned he would not be Secretary at HUD, but rather Deputy Secretary of the Treasury, a powerful position more in line with his experience. Nixon had signed the document approving his nomination days before the unaware Simon had even stepped foot on the helicopter. Within weeks, the Senate confirmed him, catapulting him from the position of a municipal bond trader on Wall Street to the operational leader of the Treasury overnight. "I don't belong in this league," Simon said to himself at the time. "There was a tremendous amount to learn about economics, energy, imports, exports, monetary policy, and government in general."[5]

According to Simon's telling, until he entered government service in January 1973, he had never had much interest in ideas, public policy, or government. His success at Salomon Brothers had come about almost despite himself. Simon was born into a wealthy, Catholic family in New Jersey; his father had inherited a multimillion-dollar fortune from the sale of silk mills that his parents had developed. As a young child, Simon watched his father use the family's wealth to live the life of a "bon vivant," joining fabulous parties and traveling the world. When Simon was eight years old, his thirty-four-year-old mother died unexpectedly from an infection she caught while recovering from appendicitis, throwing his childhood into chaos. Previously a well-behaved kid, he now struggled to follow rules of any sort, becoming, as he put it, the "original 'problem child.'" He bounced from school to school, earning a string of polite expulsions along the way, and through his mid-twenties, his life barely stayed on track, largely thanks to extensive efforts by friends and family to keep him moving.[6] Eventually he graduated from high school and completed a brief military service. Afterward, his father leaned on a friend who was a trustee at Lafayette College, a well-regarded liberal arts school in Pennsylvania, to accept the young Simon. He enrolled and, while a student, married and had his first child.

After college, the social capital of being born into privilege started to yield increasing dividends. He secured a job in a Wall Street firm, the result of a spontaneous recommendation from a friend's father and bonding with the interviewer over shared fraternity experiences. Simon was never under any illusions about the root of his good fortune: by his own assessment, he rode the wave of Wall Street expansion in the 1950s and '60s, eventually growing into a leadership role on the municipal bond trading team.[7] "Much of the success, however, can be attributed to being in the right place at the right time," he wrote in a memoir later in life.[8] Lucky or not, Simon did manage to channel the restlessness of his teenage years into a drive to work and earn, motivated by the desire to set himself apart from his father, who was always "spending rather than saving, consuming rather than investing."[9] The fastidious son would achieve the wealth and renown that the indulgent father never could. By 1967, Simon was "a not-quite-forty-year-old millionaire with a beautiful wife and seven wonderful children."[10] He appeared to embody the American dream: if not quite a self-made man, then at least a man of ingenuity and ambition, able to overcome his father's indolence through tenacity and grit.

But despite his financial success, Simon felt unsatisfied, and he yearned for a bigger and more important stage on which he could prove himself. His success on Wall Street meant that he was increasingly asked to join or even lead commissions and advisory groups to wrestle with public policy. He chaired a committee charged with tempering New York City's rapidly escalating debt, and he provided expert testimony to Congress and advisory assistance to the Treasury on the growth of municipal bond markets. These experiences whetted his appetite for the power work in government could afford.

Simon was also increasingly outraged by the dangerous social and

political trends that had begun in the late 1960s. A lifelong Catholic, Simon
worried that the cultural revolution of the 1960s, with its unabashed challenge to authority and tradition, risked the dissolution of his way of life. In his
view, the disparate voices of "collectivism" challenged the social and cultural
order of the time. "There has never been such freedom before in America to
speak freely, indeed, to wag one's tongue in the hearing of an entire nation;
to publish anything and everything, including the most scurrilous gossip; to
take drugs and to prate to children about their alleged pleasures; to propa-
gandize for bizarre sexual practices; to watch bloody and obscene entertain-
ment," he wrote later, describing the legacy of the 1960s. The country was
moving in the wrong direction, and Simon believed that he could help turn
it back. In 1968, he was an "enthusiastic supporter" of Nixon's campaign on
behalf of the "silent majority."[11] When Nixon ran for reelection in 1972, he
organized his associates at Salomon to give over $100,000 to the campaign
(over $700,000 in today's dollars) and volunteered to help vet and interview
officials for a potential second term.[12]

Some historians see in Simon a lifelong avowed libertarian who entered
government service the same way he ended it: an ideologue determined to
dismantle the state and minimize its role in markets.[13] In reality, Simon's
"philosophical views were just beginning to jell" at the moment he entered
government, as he himself later said. Nixon had surprisingly embraced Arthur Burns' price and wage controls and overseen the creation of the Environmental Protection Agency (EPA), revealing the administration to be far
more state oriented in its economic policy than many had expected.

That didn't matter to Simon. He knew he was a Republican, as much
because of the party's stance on social and cultural issues as its economic
agenda. "My battles in youth, however, were conducted on . . . nonphilo-
sophical fronts," Simon wrote.[14] "I had a code of values, but I didn't fully
understand the philosophical and pragmatic implications and ramifications
until after my arrival in Washington several years later."[15] When the Nixon
administration broached the idea of his coming to work in government, he
said yes without even knowing which position he was being offered.[16] "It
was then that I began to fully appreciate that ideas have consequences," he
wrote in his memoir.[17] Power had come knocking at the door, and Simon
jumped at the opportunity to improve his status and support the conservative
cause. If Simon held any economic ideology at the time, it was rooted in his

opportunistic pragmatism, which would soon shape his approach to policy far more than any political beliefs.

President Nixon took the oath of office for his second term on a Saturday in 1973, and Simon was sworn in to his new position by Monday morning. Within days, his problems began to pile up, the most looming concern among these being growing instability in American energy markets. Several months earlier, in the fall of 1972, advisers across government, including in the White House Office of Emergency Preparedness, began to register early warning signs of a meaningful shortfall in American oil supplies.[18] Some predicted that heating oil, which millions of Americans in the Northeast relied on to heat their homes, could be in short supply that winter. By January of 1973, former Treasury Secretary John Connally, then overseeing energy policy for the Nixon administration, told the President, "This energy crisis is much deeper, much broader, much more severe than anybody in this country realizes."[19] He believed rationing might even be required by the summer.

Within days of Connally's warning and Simon's swearing in, Treasury Secretary George Shultz, who had secured the position for Simon, stopped by his office with a question. "What do you know about the oil import policy in the United States?" Shultz asked.

"Nothing," Simon replied.

"Well, the President wants you to take a look at it. He decided that you should be the head of the Oil Policy Committee," Shultz responded. A bewildered Simon wasn't being falsely modest. The municipal bond trader from Salomon knew nothing—absolutely nothing—about energy markets, which he relayed to Shultz. "You'll learn," was just about all Shultz could muster in response.[20]

Nixon and Shultz were not just casually choosing Simon to lead the Oil Policy Committee. They needed someone just like him—a neophyte with no ties to any existing factions in the oil or gas industries—to wade into the tricky political territory of American energy policy. Simon's job would be to shepherd the committee toward a critical policy recommendation that Nixon already knew he wanted, which was the eradication of oil import quotas. The nation needed more oil fast, and domestic production was not keeping pace. Nixon understood that the increasing urgency of the supply issues could ironically offer him a political opportunity—a way to resolve the raucous debate that had plagued his first term over whether to end the fifteen-year-old policy limiting the amount of oil from foreign producers. The *New York Times* had called that decision "as complex and as politically troublesome as any he will confront during his Presidency."[21] Throughout his first term the debate had raged, with big oil producers wanting to preserve limits on the amount of oil American refiners could import, while scientists, foreign policy voices, and economists all pushed for the quotas to be relaxed in order to lower prices and meet America's surging demand. Nixon's cabinet was divided on the question, and he had decided to punt the decision until after the 1972 election. Now that oil was in short supply, it looked more certain that the quotas would at least have to be meaningfully relaxed, if not eradicated, regardless of the protests of big oil companies. Even though Simon was being set up to take the inevitable heat on the administration's behalf, it placed him on a critical path toward becoming the nation's marketcrafter on energy policy at one of the most pivotal times in the history of the issue.

American policymakers had been shaping energy markets for decades. Even before World War II, the federal government had used the tax code to support American fossil-fuel producers by incentivizing the risky business of exploring and drilling new wells. Beginning in the mid-1920s, Congress created an "oil depletion allowance," lowering the taxes that oil and gas companies had to pay on new well construction. But it was in the years after the war when policy support for fossil-fuel production became more critical. Energy production before the war had kept pace with accelerating industrial demand for coal, oil, and natural gas, but wartime brought unprecedented demands. Between December 1941 and August 1945, US wells produced 6 billion barrels of oil—a volume equivalent to one-fifth of the entire output of the US oil industry since 1859.[22] After the war, consumption continued to rise, as oil increasingly displaced coal as the fuel powering the ascendant American military, as well as the country's robust economic growth.[23] Policymakers subsequently moved to structure domestic energy markets to provide abundant, cheap energy at stable prices. The Federal Power Commission used its rate-setting power to control the price of natural gas, a source of energy particularly popular with American industry in the mid-century period.[24] Most importantly, in 1959 President Dwight Eisenhower imposed the oil import quota, capping imports at 12 percent of domestic production. The move allowed American multinational companies to drill in foreign countries

and sell those fossil fuels all around the world, but only a small portion could
be imported back into the United States. That decision tied American gasoline prices to the level of American oil and gas production. "The adoption
of mandatory quotas in March 1959 was the single most important energy
policy in the postwar era," wrote the economist Richard Vietor. "It ushered in
a decade of stasis in policy that ignored continuing changes in energy supply
and demand."[25]

The result of these marketcrafting policies was a long period of energy
abundance throughout the 1950s and '60s. Oil was free-flowing and inexpen-
sive, easily keeping pace with accelerating energy consumption in the United
States. In 1972, the year before Simon moved to Washington, the price of gas
had been stable for three years straight at thirty-six cents a gallon, the lowest
price in the history of oil when controlling for inflation.[26] But in the midst
of the glut, the first signs of shortage appeared. Skeptical that prices would
rise enough to justify the high costs and under the impression that many of
their existing oil fields were declining in capacity, American oil producers
gradually reduced their investment in exploration and drilling. At the same
time that investment in production was ebbing, enduringly cheap oil and gas
spurred consumer demand. American energy consumption increased by over
50 percent in the 1960s, compared with only 36 percent in the decade prior.[27]
Meanwhile, outside of Alaska, energy producers were struggling to identify
new tracts of undiscovered oil. American oil production peaked in 1971 and
1972, and few businessmen or policymakers understood just how precarious
a position American energy markets were in. "As late as 1971, there was no
consensus within industry or government, nor scarcely any warning, that a
crisis was imminent," Vietor wrote.[28] By the time Simon took on the portfolio in early 1973, industry and government alike agreed that signs of danger
were all around.

Simon realized he was ill-equipped to face the looming challenge of a
domestic oil and gas shortage. He had to get smart fast. Simon recruited
experts inside and outside of government to help him grasp the basics of how
energy markets function. "For three months, we met nights and weekends
as my 'tutors' generously educated me on energy—oil, gas, imports, exports,
shipping, transportation, trucking, pipelines, petrochemicals, thermal energy,
water falls, the mandatory import quota policy—and the international implications of the most complex, intricate industry on earth," he wrote. "We

survived on greasy hamburgers and pizzas, delivered to my office at 10 p.m. and consumed into the wee hours of the morning."[29] Over the course of those tutoring sessions, the warning signs became clear that America was headed for choppy waters. By March 1973, commercial gasoline production levels were 10 percent below where they were the previous year, and some wholesalers were struggling to find sellers in the market.[30] Responding to the brewing crisis, Simon's committee recommended the removal of all oil import quotas, and the President announced their end in April. Simon had completed the first task the President had assigned him.

Nixon's decision, however, emphasized the new reality of energy markets: America now relied on foreign powers to fuel its lights, cars, and heat. Between 1972 and 1973, American petroleum imports jumped by 32 percent with three countries in the Middle East—Saudi Arabia, Iran, and Libya— holding outsized sway.[31] Those countries and their allies had been preparing for this moment for years. Since the mid-1950s, foreign producers had conspired to guide the global price of oil by coordinating their production and pricing decisions through a new organization, OPEC, which they created in 1960. Given the relative abundance of global energy supplies in the 1960s, they had seen little success up to that point. But as events began to turn in 1971 and 1972, several countries, including Libya and Saudi Arabia, nationalized oil production and negotiated new ownership positions for foreign-held firms licensed to drill. National Security Advisor Henry Kissinger reported to President Nixon that regional leaders were becoming increasingly aggressive, eager to brandish their new "oil weapon."[32]

In April, the same month that Simon and Nixon decided to lift the import quotas, a State Department official named James Akins published an influential article in *Foreign Affairs* arguing that oil-producing countries would soon use their power in energy markets as leverage over American foreign policy. "The vulnerability of the advanced countries is too great and too plainly evident," he wrote.[33] In a secret oil study he had recently penned at the State Department, he was even more explicit: "By 1975, and possibly earlier, we will have entered a permanent sellers' market, with any one of several major suppliers being able to create a supply crisis by cutting off oil supplies."[34] The headline of his *Foreign Affairs* piece emphasized the point: "The Oil Crisis: This Time the Wolf Is Here." Foreign producers could now exploit their power, and it was only a matter of time until they did.

In the late spring and early summer of 1973, with Akins' warning ringing in their heads, Simon worked with colleagues in the Nixon administration and Congressional leaders to develop an approach that could prevent
a full-blown crisis. As gas levels declined precipitously, the Secretary of the
Interior, Rogers Morton, asked Americans to stop making unnecessary trips
in cars, drive slower, and use mass transit whenever possible. These were all
voluntary entreaties, and not binding in any way. Simon had come to believe
that a marketcrafting strategy of rationing and government allocation could
be required eventually—a sentiment shared by Senator Henry "Scoop" Jackson, one of the most influential Democrats on Capitol Hill on energy policy.
The two agreed that only through rationing could the administration guarantee to all Americans that supplies would be sufficient, preventing a disastrous run of panic buying. "[N]ew ration coupons would provide assurance
that each citizen would get his due," one historian wrote of the thinking at
the time.[35] Simon even went so far as to leak to the press that the administration was considering mandatory allocation to certain sectors and regions, but
that move received blowback from the President and other administration
officials in public.[36] Despite Nixon's willingness to pursue price and wage
controls, he did not want to go as far as mandatory allocation or rationing,
fearing that it reeked of government planning. On top of that, Nixon's attention was being consumed by the snowballing Watergate scandal. On April 30,
1973, he asked for the resignation of his chief of staff, another top aide, and
the Attorney General—and fired the White House Counsel.

But the energy crisis spiraled even faster than Nixon's political problems.
By June, half of all gas stations polled by the American Automobile Association (AAA) were limiting hours or days of business or restricting supplies.
Every station in the Northeast had shortened their hours of operation.[37]
Gas remained cheap, at thirty-eight cents a gallon, but the President himself began to ask Americans to conserve and companies to invest. By June,
President Nixon had grown frustrated with the balkanized energy policy in
his administration and was anxious to tap a single leader who would have
outsized control. Nixon and his new chief of staff had a private meeting in
the Oval Office with John Love, the Governor of Colorado, to convince him
to take the job: "Your responsibility will be directly to me with direct access,
because I cannot have other people making end runs at me. I can't have Rogers Morton, George Shultz, Bill Simon . . . and a lot of other people. What

you have, John, is an unusual opportunity."[38] Love accepted, resigning the governorship and moving to Washington.

Shultz informed Simon that he had been layered through the appointment of Love, but Simon refused to give up the portfolio. Within days, Simon attempted to organize Love to his outlook, pushing him to join his effort to create a framework for a mandatory allocation program, but Love demurred. Considering that Simon's efforts had met with resistance from the administration, Love was wary of falling out of the President's favor before he'd even made his way in. Simon bided his time and continued his campaign, arguing in September that "a mandatory program is inevitable and we should get out in front of Congress on the issue," despite Shultz and Love's opposition to the idea.[39] It seemed for the moment that Simon was waging a futile campaign.

On the afternoon of October 6, 1973, Israeli eyes turned to the skies as hundreds of Egyptian and Syrian planes launched a surprise attack on targets in Israel. The day was Yom Kippur, the holiest day in the Jewish calendar. Thousands of mobilized soldiers, armed with heavy artillery, attacked Israel's northern and southern borders. It would become known as the Yom Kippur War, and the Israelis and Americans alike were caught by surprise. They had watched for months as the Egyptian President, Anwar Sadat, amassed troops on the Israeli-Egyptian border and began military exercises, but up until the attack, the Secretary of State and National Security Advisor Kissinger considered Sadat "more actor than statesman."[40] That incorrect assessment, shared by many in the American and Israeli governments, meant that the Israeli army was caught unprepared. As Israel retreated in disorder, the Syrians and Egyptians moved deeper into Israeli territory.

For the Nixon administration, the attack was no less than "an energy Pearl Harbor," in the words of one adviser.[41] For years, American policymakers had attempted to balance the interests of multiple Arab governments, Iran, and Israel to keep the fragile peace that emerged after the Six-Day War in 1967. America's interests in the region were organized around more than just oil production: they prioritized Cold War dominance and the desire to limit Soviet power. Now, with Israel under attack, American leaders felt they had to help their chief ally in the region, but they also had to balance this with the country's new reliance on foreign oil. All that oil was coming from allies of Israel's attackers.

Attempting to walk a thin line, Nixon approved a Kissinger-led plan to deliver supplies to the Israeli government covertly within a few days of the invasion. The military prepared several large cargo planes, but given their size and heavy load, they needed to refuel on their way to Israel. High winds at the refueling stop in Portugal prevented them from leaving America on time, which in turn made a night landing in Israel under the cover of darkness difficult. "Instead, they came lumbering out of the sky on Sunday during the day, October 14, their immense white stars visible for all to see. The United States, instead of keeping to its position of honest broker, was now portrayed as an active ally of Israel," wrote one historian.[42] The OPEC producers, angered and mobilized, were ready with a response—an immediate and dramatic pullback in oil supply. The "wolf" that State Department official Akins had warned about six months before was now at the door, and the crisis that Simon had been preparing for began.

Within forty-eight hours, six of the major oil producers announced an immediate hike in the price of oil by 70 percent, to over five dollars a barrel. The following day, oil producers agreed to reduce production by 5 percent each month for every month Western countries continued their support of Israel, with selective allotment by country. Undeterred and anxious to display American leadership, Nixon announced a $2.2 billion aid package to Israel on October 19. The Saudis and other Arab oil exporters countered with a blanket oil embargo: all shipments of oil to the United States would cease. Kissinger, enraged by the betrayal of the Saudis, who were an American ally, called it "political blackmail."[43] It didn't help matters that, on the same day of the embargo, Nixon fired the special prosecutor, Archibald Cox, who was investigating the Watergate scandal and had just subpoenaed the President's secret office tapes. The Attorney General resigned in protest. That day would live in infamy as the "Saturday night massacre."

Reeling from the potent combination of domestic and foreign disasters, policymakers in Washington watched with horror as oil prices in global markets began to rise. By the first week of November, Arab oil producers announced a further 25 percent cut in production levels. The American government estimated that American oil supplies would fall between 10 and 17 percent short of demand over the following months.[44]

Despite the challenges of the Watergate inquiry, Nixon administration officials started to work with Congress to develop plans for a new nerve center that could guide energy markets through the turmoil. Roy Ash, the Director of the Office of Management and Budget, convinced the President's chief of staff to create a new institution, invested with significant authority to manage energy markets. "Whether we like it or not, we must temporarily inject the government into the private sector in ways reserved only for emergencies," Ash wrote. "We've got to do so by starting with a state of mind *a la* the War Production Board," the organization that managed American output levels in the Second World War.

The administration and Congress coalesced around the idea of an energy agency on the cabinet level responsible for pricing, allocation, and managing domestic production. In mid-November, Congress took a little-noticed but pivotal step when it chartered the Federal Energy Office (FEO) to organize and manage American energy markets in the crisis. The decision to create a semi-independent institution, consolidating several departments working on energy policy from across the federal government, meant that the nation's energy agenda could be streamlined and unified, an enormous advantage in a fast-moving crisis situation with divided government. Just as Jesse Jones and FDR had met the Great Depression and World War II with a strong institution able to coordinate marketcrafting efforts, a new organization would help steer America through this skid.

Who would lead it? Former Governor Love had offered no vision for how the state could manage the energy crisis over the late summer and early fall, even before it became acute in the wake of the Yom Kippur War. He had made no meaningful plans for allocation, controls, or conservation, and Nixon, increasingly impatient, needed someone who believed in leveraging state power in energy markets and who would not be afraid to do it. Heeding the advice of Treasury Secretary Shultz and others, Nixon asked Simon to lead the new FEO. Love, demoted a mere five months after giving up the Governor's mansion in Colorado, resigned abruptly, telling an Associated Press reporter, "To be honest, it's been difficult to try to do anything meaningful and even to get the attention of the President," a veiled reference to Nixon's Watergate challenges.[45] Simon, for his part, was at once pleased to have the faith of the President and wary about the big new role. Not even a year into government service, he was now responsible not just for tailoring policy, but for leading the response to an unprecedented shock to American life that would require a delicate balance between political, economic, and geopolitical priorities.

✿

Most people who look back on the energy shocks of the 1970s see little to admire in government action, including Simon himself, who believed that the
American government failed to develop a workable energy policy that served
the country's interests. They see a befuddled and rudderless government, ac-
cusing three presidential administrations in a row of failing to adapt to a
rapidly changing energy landscape. This conventional wisdom has seared an
image in the minds of many Americans that government missteps contributed to widespread gas shortages and the resulting, precipitous inflation. But
a closer look at the history shows that view to be mistaken, the result of a
tendency to lump fifteen years of energy policy into a superficial, generaliz-
ing judgment that overlooks the profound impact of Simon's marketcrafting
leadership.

In the fall of 1973, panic gripped Americans as a severe global crisis caught them off guard. In May of that year, 62 percent of the population thought things were going well in the country, but by November, only
27 percent agreed. The ebullience that characterized the American economy
in 1972 turned dark as inflation soared with the relaxation of wage and price
controls in 1973. The deepest recession since the Great Depression began
in November of that year, and the instability of energy supplies and rise in
prices exacerbated the challenges.

With his own leadership in question because of Watergate, Nixon was
desperate to project strength and resolve in response to the disorienting
uncertainty. For Nixon, that meant leaning into the marketcrafting power
of the state. Over the course of his presidency, whenever a major challenge
arose, Nixon reacted by embracing state power rather than diminishing it,
including the development of price and wage controls and the creation of the
EPA. Nixon did the same with the FEO, the semi-independent institution
Congress had chartered to guide energy markets. When introducing Simon
to his cabinet as the head of the new institution, Nixon emphasized how
thoroughly he wanted to empower him by invoking the example of Albert
Speer, the Minister of Armaments and War Production in Nazi Germany.
"The president told the cabinet that if Hitler had not given Speer the power
to override the German bureaucracy, the Nazis would have been defeated far
earlier, and indicated I would have comparable power," Simon recounted in
his memoir.[46] It was a bizarre comparison, but for Nixon, it made sense. The

prime example of FEO leadership was a German who harnessed the power of the state to fulfill a political end, albeit a dark and disastrous one in the midst of war. Better examples could have been found at home. Nixon was setting up Simon to follow in the path of Jesse Jones and Bill Martin to lead a federal institution invested with discretion and power to steer markets toward stability.

Backed by Congress and the President, Simon now had nearly total control over how energy producers sold their products, including to which refineries, which regions, and which dealers. Congress had mandated that the FEO develop an allocation program by industry and region. Now it was up to Simon to revise and expand his plans from the summer for official implementation. In addition to directing refining capacity and allocation, Simon also controlled the price of oil, the power to institute a system of rationing if need be, and even the mix of products that refineries made—for example, the balance between needs for home heating oil versus gasoline. With over 1,300 federal workers in his employ at the FEO, he had the mandate and people power to shape energy markets in a historically unprecedented fashion.[47] Simon's new informal title, both inside and outside the administration, became the "energy czar."[48]

In this early period, there was little trace of the ideologue Simon would later become. He confidently charged ahead, ready to wield his new power. He believed that the market left to its own devices would not enable Americans to weather the oil shock. "I have been asked by the President to manage the immediate emergency as well as to develop the longer term solution to the energy problem. I emphasize the word manage because that is exactly what must now be done," he testified to Congress in December. "[W]e clearly recognize that the federal government must exercise leadership. We must manage the energy problem mainly because it is so complex and so interwoven with vital interests which we cannot allow to be threatened or harmed." In his remarks, he asked Congress to expand existing authorities and create a permanent agency with the power to control prices, set import and export controls, and invest federal dollars in research and development. All of this required "strong government leadership," in Simon's view.[49]

Simon used all that state power to formulate a marketcrafting program with two core goals: conserve and control. The first priority was an immediate reduction in Americans' energy usage. "Actions must be taken to stimulate a long-term energy conservation ethic," Simon wrote the President in early January.[50] Because oil and gas had been so abundant and cheap for so long, even modest conservation efforts up front stood to have a significant impact at a small cost. In November, Nixon moved to lower the speed limit on highways to 50 mph and asked Americans to reduce the temperatures on their home thermostats. He encouraged gas stations to close on Sundays to discourage weekend road trips, and for Americans to take additional voluntary measures to reduce their energy consumption.[51] Once Simon took over at the FEO, he went further, announcing an immediate reduction in gasoline supplied to retail stations (only 5 percent, to start) and limiting drivers to a maximum of ten gallons of fuel per week. Simon sent out millions of decals, "Don't Be Fuelish," to put on light switches to encourage people to turn off the lights.[52] As the holiday season approached, Simon banned outdoor light displays and Nixon decided that the White House would only activate 20 percent of the normal decorations, setting a precedent for other public displays.

A warm December gave the marketcrafters a moment to breathe. Demand for heating oil, which was critical for homes in New England, fell from historical levels given the milder temperatures and conservation efforts. Gas stations did not report significant cutbacks in service or lines in December, meaning that for most Americans, the immediate effects of the Middle East war took time to appear. "In the last weeks of 1973, disruptions at the pump turned out to be bothersome but no greater than those in June, well before the boycott," wrote historian Jay Hakes. "Most data on oil turned out much better than expected, making it legitimate to ask whether the country had dodged a bullet."[53] It had not.

The warm weather and fast-moving conservation efforts were already helping with Simon's second marketcrafting goal: controlling the level of energy production and its cost in order to prevent shortages and price spikes. Initial estimates of a double-digit deficit of oil supplies meant that Simon needed to reduce deliveries to the market to help stockpile and conserve for the later winter months, when shortages would become more pronounced. Simon capped refinery output at 75 percent of its 1972 base, with public transit, the military, and agricultural interests receiving all of their fuel requirements. While trying to ensure other essential industries had the energy they needed, he tilted toward retaining higher stock levels throughout the early winter, even as retail gas stations began to experience more shortages.

Better to have moderate shortages each month, he thought, than abundance in December and January with significant strain from February onward. No one knew how long the production cuts would last, and seasonal demand for gasoline peaked in the busy summer months. Simon had to think ahead. He also moved to ensure that home heating oil production remained a high priority. It would be better for drivers to wait in gas lines than for people in the Northeast to risk freezing in their homes.[54]

Perhaps the most powerful and effective tool in Simon's marketcrafting toolbox was the ability to control prices. While he would later claim he had always opposed controls on principle, Simon made a strong argument against deregulating energy prices. As he explained to Congress, "the abrupt nature and magnitude of current shortages could, in a free market, cause the price of crude oil to shoot substantially above the levels required to bring supply and demand into balance." Beyond a certain point, higher prices would not bring any additional oil supplies online.[55] Blind faith in libertarian microeconomics would undermine the goal of price stability without contributing to the goal of abundance.

To be sure, Simon did want gas prices to rise, bringing them more in line with global prices and incentivizing conservation, but he wanted them to do so gradually. He believed that higher prices would dampen consumer demand and incentivize domestic oil producers to pursue additional exploration and drilling, which could once again be profitable. While that wouldn't help with the immediate shortage, it would contribute to American energy resilience in the longer term. At the same time, gas prices couldn't rise so precipitously that they disrupted economic activity or incited an explosive political blowback, which meant that Simon needed to orchestrate a gradual creep upward, avoiding price spikes along the way.

At first, this balance seemed to be working. In the initial months of the crisis, gas prices rose by a modest two cents a gallon, despite oil prices on the global market increasing by 36 percent.[56] But in late December, OPEC producers, increasingly determined to brandish their power, doubled the price of oil again from $5.12 to $11.65 a barrel, over three times the prewar price of $3.12.[57] OPEC increased overall production levels out of a desire to capture the financial windfall from the higher prices and fear that too drastic a reduction in supply could incite a worldwide depression. Even so, the additional price shock rattled global markets.

By the end of January 1974, Americans were no longer wondering if they had "dodged a bullet," and Simon's FEO was fielding all kinds of inbound complaints about shortages. About a sixth of gas stations were out of fuel, and many in the Northeast and Northwest implemented binding quotas on customer purchases, often closing by midafternoon.[58] In February, truckers, frustrated by escalating prices for their gas and excessive government regulation, staged a nationwide strike that reached forty-two states, creating an atmosphere of national pandemonium. They used their trucks as barriers, blocking highways and interstates, and occasionally embraced violent tactics to intimidate any truckers not joining in the strike. "Arsonists set aflame fuel tanks and big rigs, and gunmen opened fire on noncomplying trucks," the historian Meg Jacobs wrote. Over the following week, there were hundreds of highway shootings and even a bombing on the Pennsylvania Turnpike, and the strike provoked shortages of essential goods, including meat, milk, and eggs.[59] The Secret Service stepped in to protect Simon, who had started to receive death threats. His wife, Carol, took to "skulking around in a shawl and dark glasses," refusing to use the credit card with her name on it for fear of being identified.[60] "The psychology of hysteria took over," Simon said of the time.[61] By the end of February, 20 percent of gas stations nationwide had no supplies. In Pennsylvania and Florida, it was 40 percent, and in the Carolinas, half. Prices for gas nationwide had increased from the precrisis price of forty cents a gallon to forty-nine cents, a 23 percent rise in four months.

Despite the mounting anger and disorder, much of it directed at him personally, Simon held his ground, and in the early weeks of February, his team felt that they were turning a corner. Import levels, while depressed, were down less dramatically than energy analysts had initially feared. Total shortfalls were estimated at 1.2 million barrels a day, about 20 percent lower than the September levels. Conservation efforts—and the developing recession—were having a meaningful effect, with demand for oil falling faster than many had expected. Seeking to calm the boiling anger in the country, Nixon pushed Simon to release more fuel from the reserves, despite the risk that the winter could worsen or that production levels could fall further still. "I really nailed him to the cross," Nixon said of a mid-February conversation with Simon. "I said I want those service stations filled up so we don't have those damn lines."[62] Simon's staff advised against it, but

Simon, loyal to the President, followed Nixon's instructions and released significant allocations for the hardest-hit states.[63]

Within weeks, the shortages abated, and the number of gas stations with no gasoline fell from 40 percent to 5 percent by March 12. A few days later, on March 18, the Arab oil producers agreed to end the embargo on oil to the United States, believing the relaxation necessary to support American efforts toward further disengagement of the conflict. Global oil prices remained high, but any American who wanted gas could get it.

By the spring of 1974, the United States had made it through the first oil shock better than many had expected. Outside of two weeks in February, oil and gas supplies stayed largely stable, even with the global production cuts. Americans had taken the imperative to conserve seriously, shifting their habits out of civic concern as well as in response to rising prices. Americans drove nearly 10 percent fewer miles in 1974 than 1972 and turned down their thermostats. "Homeowners were installing insulation, adjusting thermostats, and buying wood stoves, just as they were reporting to pollsters," Hakes writes.[64] Energy needs were so significantly reduced that oil and gas inventories did not even dip below the levels of previous years. There was no shortage of home heating oil, which meant that no American froze to death, a fear real enough heading into the crisis that Simon's FEO had diverted oil refining from gasoline to home heating oil. Buoyed by Americans' efforts to conserve, inventories for home heating oil were actually up from a year earlier. Meanwhile, the administration's price controls delivered the gradual, escalating increase in prices that Simon had been targeting.[65] The 23 percent surge in prices at the pump was a meaningful increase for Americans used to cheap gas, but when compared to a 125 percent rise in global crude oil prices, it was relatively modest.[66] Prices at the pump in the United Kingdom, Japan, and Italy, by contrast, nearly doubled between 1973 and 1974.[67] Inflation in the United Kingdom jumped to 16 percent in 1974, a postwar record at the time. Because of effective management of energy markets in the United States, "[t]he oil weapon had packed a wallop but by itself delivered far from a knockout punch," Hakes writes.[68]

In comparison, the "unfettered market" alternative could have been bleak. Without mandatory conservation efforts, consumption of oil and gas would have likely stayed much closer in line with historic levels. Factoring in the supply shortfall of close to 20 percent, shortages would have arrived in the mid- to late winter and likely would have lasted far longer. Decontrolled prices would have shot up precipitously, mirroring the experience internationally and ensuring that upper-class consumers could manage to continue their day-to-day lives and careers while working-class Americans would have struggled. The combination of significantly higher prices and shortages would have meant delays in shipping networks and the grounding of some commercial air travel. If the violent trucker protests that took place over modest hikes were any indication of the potential for civil unrest, it's reasonable to expect that a doubling of gas prices and widespread shortages would have augured a much darker, more chaotic time in American history.

Even as the Nixon administration deployed its marketcrafting policies with success, Simon and colleagues experienced significant challenges in the first acute phase of the crisis. The shortages and resulting strikes, while brief, damaged Nixon's popularity, as did the accelerating prices. Polls also showed that Americans believed oil companies and governments were the ultimate drivers of the crisis, more so than the war in the Middle East. Gas prices remained high even after the embargo ended, and Nixon's approval ratings continued to fall, though much of that had to do with mounting concerns about his personal involvement in Watergate. But for those inside the administration aware of how destructive the crisis could have been, it was hard not to feel anything but a sense of relief. Vice President Gerald Ford defended the administration's policies, saying, "[We] chose between unemployment lines and gas lines. We made the right choice." Simon echoed the sentiment. "People . . . would rather wait in line for gas than spend a couple of months or longer waiting in line for unemployment checks."[69]

Simon had succeeded as the country's first-ever energy czar by skillfully wielding the discretionary power of his institution in the pursuit of governing. In his telling of the story, his success was a result of his willingness to "impatiently bypass the bureaucracy, violate its procedures, and outrage the Civil Service mentality."[70] But Simon was pushing those boundaries in pursuit of effective marketcraft—using the administrative power of a new institution to guide markets through the crisis. His success led to the ultimate conversion of the FEO into a permanent institution of government: first as the Federal Energy Administration, and later as the Department of Energy.

More importantly for Simon's career in the short run, the embattled Nixon was so happy with his leadership that within weeks of the end of the oil embargo, he elevated Simon to the role of Treasury Secretary. (Simon's patron George Shultz had left government for the private sector.) But before Simon could move on to the work of laying long-term plans to ensure another crisis did not occur, the house of cards that was Richard Nixon collapsed.[71]

A little before nine o'clock on the evening of August 8, 1974, Simon stood in the hallway outside the Oval Office, waiting for the President. Nixon was slated to give a nationally televised speech to address the whirling rumors that he would soon resign, and Simon had passed the time waiting for this momentous occasion by splitting a bottle of Scotch with another counselor to the President. At 9:01 pm, Nixon began to deliver the first and last resignation speech an American President has ever given. "I have never been a quitter. To leave office before my term is completed is abhorrent to every instinct in my body. But as President, I must put the interest of America first." he said. "Therefore, I shall resign the presidency effective at noon tomorrow." Nixon did not apologize for any actions and admitted no crime. Having completed the speech, Nixon got up from the desk, tears streaming down his cheeks, and walked past his tipsy Treasury Secretary en route to the privacy of the White House residence. "I was frozen in my spot, overcome with grief and disbelief," Simon said. "Do we know, I wondered, do we really know what we have done?"[72]

A few weeks after the resignation, Simon made a trip to California to visit the ex-President, whom he found unexpectedly relaxed. The two tossed a football, "first in his living room and then on his back lawn," Simon recounted. "Go out for a pass," the former President told the current Treasury Secretary. Simon complied, and as the two men played catch like boys, they chatted about history and politics. He left the former President's home as befuddled about Nixon's core motivations as he had been at Camp David the day Nixon had offered him his first job in government. "A walking contradiction, I thought at the time, a man so complex and unusual that I'm not sure anyone could truly figure him out or really understand what makes him tick, including himself," he later wrote.[73] Even if he couldn't quite grasp the man, Simon was loyal to a fault, and that meant he would overlook the President's unethical actions and support him through his darkest moment.

But Simon didn't have much time to spend on Nixon's plight. After the new President, Gerald Ford, was sworn in the day following Nixon's speech, he asked Simon to stay on in his role of Treasury Secretary and to collaborate with administration officials to develop an energy policy road map. Americans were consuming less oil than they had a year before, but because global production remained lower than before the Yom Kippur War, they were paying more for it. Prices began falling by the autumn of 1974, but only modestly. The combination of persistently high energy costs, significant inflation, and a deep recession meant that Americans were angry about the economic state of the country.[74] The occupant of the Oval Office might have changed, but it was still up to Simon to mitigate those problems and ensure another energy shock did not occur.

Simon's preferred method to shape energy resiliency in the long term was the imposition of a sizable gas tax of twenty cents a gallon. Such a tax would incentivize conservation and enhance efficiency, while raising $17 billion in revenue to be split between deficit-reduction measures and cash rebates to the poor. But as simple and elegant as the idea was, the administration judged it politically unpalatable.[75] Ford wanted a broader, bigger agenda. Within weeks of taking power, he sent the outlines of an energy plan to Congress. It did not include Simon's gas tax, and instead focused on federal investment in research and development, the expansion of mass transit, ending price controls on natural gas, and enacting a windfall tax on oil producers. The message was clear: the Ford administration wanted to focus on a broad legislative effort to build on Simon's crisis-induced, marketcrafting successes.

The same month that Ford outlined his energy policy to Congress, an influential and popular economist—who would have a significant impact on not just energy policy, but American history—arrived in the West Wing. In the summer of 1974, Nixon needed to fill a vacancy to lead the CEA, which was, at the time, the primary White House institution for the development of economic policy. Simon suggested the New York economic analyst Alan Greenspan. "It was Bill who originally asked me to come down to [Washington]," Greenspan recounted later. Simon and Greenspan had been friends for years, and Greenspan even joined the Simon family for Christmas in the midst of the oil shock in December 1973. "In fact, he called me twice. The first time, I said 'No.' I did not want to go; I had a thriving private business ... He called me back and said that I was the only one they wanted. It was Bill who was actually the strongest proponent of my coming down."[76]

Simon was not alone in supporting Greenspan's candidacy. An old friend of Greenspan's, Fed Chair Arthur Burns, encouraged the White House to make him the offer and then called Greenspan to convince him to accept. "This government is paralyzed," Burns told Greenspan. "But there's still an economy out there and we still have to make economic policy. You owe it to your country to serve."[77] That both the sitting Treasury Secretary and Chair of the Federal Reserve aggressively recruited Greenspan for the position testified to the reputation he had made for himself in New York as a brilliant empiricist, a savant who could interpret and synthesize large datasets to parse the present and predict the future. (He correctly assessed early on in the first oil shock, for instance, that the shortages would be more modest than some had feared.) He had been at once a supporter of Nixon in the campaign and later an avid opponent of the former President's price and wage controls. Now that those had been lifted—with the important exception of energy markets—he was willing to serve. Between the submission of Greenspan's appointment to the Senate and his confirmation, Nixon resigned and Ford became President. Greenspan, excited by the prospect of the power of the West Wing, was undeterred by the changing of the guard. He started his job in September of 1974.

Simon and Greenspan forged a strong partnership, an unlikely duo of self-styled libertarians at the center of an insurgent "counter-intelligentsia." Simon began to take on his increasingly ideological orientation beginning in the fall of 1974 when Greenspan arrived at the White House. The two were in frequent contact with the economist Arthur Laffer, Citibank CEO Walter Wriston, former Treasury Secretary George Shultz, and economist Milton Friedman, all of whom were forming an increasingly tight-knit bond as they developed and refined a "free-market" agenda. In April 1975, Simon made an official visit to the Soviet Union, which he claimed inspired an epiphany. "I had never, until then, thought philosophically about my own feelings about freedom," he wrote. Around the same time, he published an article against big government in *Reader's Digest*, the popular magazine whose imprint would eventually publish his memoir. That project began to take shape while Simon was still in government in 1976. The ghostwriter was Edith Efron, a former disciple of the writer Ayn Rand.[78]

Even though Simon's social circle was increasingly stridently libertarian, he and Greenspan continued to use the power of government to craft markets for political ends. Their rhetoric was not always a reliable guide to the policies they pursued. "[Bill] was very much an activist," Greenspan was able to say about Simon in a moment of candor. "He was one of the people instrumental in changing the way government works."[79] For his part, Greenspan could deprecate his libertarian values for more immediate political ends, as one of his biographers, Sebastian Mallaby, later noted: "Greenspan's specialty as a political actor lay in a sort of manipulative genius." In 1975, he recommended to President Ford that he support a sizable tax cut that would grow the deficit without reducing the size of government. "Greenspan had become the enabler for a policy that contradicted his principles," Mallaby wrote. "He had insisted that budget deficits were the cause of inflation; now he ignored his own lectures."[80]

When it came to energy independence, Simon and Greenspan both wanted the state to have a heavier hand in guiding markets to create long-term energy resiliency. In addition to conservation and efficiency measures, both advocated for the creation of a state-run stockpiling authority, called the Strategic Petroleum Reserve (SPR). Policymakers had debated such an idea for decades. Harold Ickes, a Secretary of the Interior in the Roosevelt administration, had proposed a crude oil stockpile program as far back as 1944, and President Truman's minerals commission had supported a similar idea in the early 1950s. The concept resurfaced over the following decades but each time went nowhere because America had plenty of oil and too many business interests opposing the idea.[81] By early 1973, Senator Jackson was proposing the creation of a reserve, and the FEO published a seminal report called "Project Independence" outlining how the United States might build energy independence and resiliency. The report argued for a "storage program [to] provide a buffer against the disruption of that supply." It modeled out how such a stockpile could help foster American economic resiliency in the face of sizable market disruptions.[82]

Simon and Greenspan embraced the idea. They agreed that if America could dip into oil reserves, it could more easily weather supply shocks. The existence of the stockpile might also dissuade foreign powers from pursuing an embargo as they had done in 1973. Business leaders were warily supportive, favoring a government-run buffering and stockpiling program over the possibility that they might have to shoulder the burden of maintaining reserves. With Simon and Greenspan's help, the proposal began to gain momentum as the cornerstone of a long-term energy policy. It signaled the next iteration of Simon's marketcrafting efforts, a state effort to buffer markets that might endure in a way that price controls never could. The existing market structure, Simon said, promised recurring "political and economic spasms." Measures like the strategic reserve concept would allow Americans to "regain a great deal of control over the situation" and even to "control . . . our own economic destinies."[83]

To reassure libertarians, the concept could be presented as a response to OPEC's "political" manipulations. But alongside such rhetoric, one could find straightforward statements about marketcraft. One government report, which Greenspan approved and signed, declared that structural changes in the economy "may require a more sophisticated, more responsible role for Government in interpreting and supplementing market signals." This applied not only to oil but potentially to other basic materials, "span[ning] a wide range of market structures and of Government involvement." None of this meant that market forces could be abolished or ignored. To the contrary, "decisionmakers will have to be aware of forces which affect prices in each market." In this vision, markets and state decision-making would be complements, not substitutes.[84]

Others in the Ford administration, such as Kissinger, considered going even further than stockpiling by creating a price floor for oil. They wanted government to agree to significant purchases of oil whenever the price hit a sufficiently low level, effectively using its power to guarantee a minimum sale price for domestic producers. Confidence in the minimum price would theoretically encourage producers to pursue additional exploration and drilling activities. Simon and Greenspan were both wary of an outright floor, despite their support for the SPR, but the idea was in line with their efforts to use state power to stabilize markets.[85] Vice President Nelson Rockefeller also proposed an RFC-like investment authority, providing funding in energy projects that were too risky or capital-intensive for private-sector investment alone. Neither the price floor nor the investment authority gained traction, but by the end of the year, the SPR became a reality. Congress included it in December legislation along with an extension of price controls and greater energy efficiency standards. The stockpile would be large enough to replace crude oil imports for ninety days—about 500 million barrels of storage capacity. Ironically, Greenspan and Simon recommended the President veto the ultimate bill, because they had hoped for more narrow legislation embracing their favored provisions, including the SPR. Ford, however, decided to sign it. Even if the legislative efforts were broader than they would have liked, Simon and Greenspan secured their marketcrafting priority.[86]

The following year, President Ford lost his reelection campaign to Georgia Governor Jimmy Carter. Simon remained at Treasury until Ford's last day. Within months of his exit from government, Simon began to fashion a new identity for himself: part businessman, part public intellectual. His first book after government service, *A Time to Choose*, became a bestselling manifesto for the emerging "neoliberal" outlook. Focused on spreading the gospel of "free markets" and deregulation, Simon lectured across the country and built a new financial empire of his own as a pioneer of the leveraged buyout. He never missed a rhetorical opportunity to fault big government liberals for the destruction of America, pitting government against business, with the two in a head-to-head competition. Government regulation and tax-and-spend policies designed to help the poorest Americans led to a less fair and less prosperous country. Bureaucracy got in the way of the businessman's impulse to invest and build, he believed. Despite his years in government service, Simon wanted none of the credit for the Nixon and Ford administrations' energy policies. His anti-government crusade is part of what has led to the confusion over the role he played in these events and the misconceptions about how the initial energy crisis was handled.

Yet Simon had in fact harnessed the power of government to steer markets for political and social ends, making him a marketcrafter par excellence. Simon's work while in government illustrates that government can shape markets for the better with the right institutional configuration. To make his past leadership consistent with his contemporary ideology, Simon had to undertake a wholesale reimagination of his earlier marketcrafting efforts at the FEO, which had gotten him the Treasury Secretary job in the first place. This change in attitude was nothing short of a "metamorphosis," as one historian called it.[87] Simon now castigated all forms of oil price control and allocation, refusing to recognize the FEO's—and his own—success in using them to weather the first shock. He called voluntary conservation efforts "unadulterated nonsense," even as he had supported Nixon encouraging just that.[88] Even Democratic proposals for additional import fees on oil—a method to raise domestic prices and reduce consumption—incited his ire, despite his robust support for a domestic gasoline tax throughout his time in government service. When in government, Simon had found ways to use its power to enhance and improve the stability and functioning of markets. That pragmatism faded as his laissez-faire ideology surged.

How can we explain this turn? Simon was not the kind of nuanced thinker interested in resolving competing impulses; he thought in the crusading colors of black and white. Despite his government service, he was still the gruff bond trader on the floor of Salomon who dissuaded his traders from thinking too hard. If he did not fight against an increase in the scope of government, it would continue to grow, spending more and more on social services and increasing taxes on men like himself. Bureaucracy was bad, as was taxing and spending. He let that perspective overshadow the statist marketcrafting efforts that he led. Faced with a choice between a crusade to downsize the state and one to strengthen its marketcrafting power, he chose the libertarian road.

He was not alone. Simon was part of a close-knit group of former administration officials and academics—among them Shultz, Greenspan, and Friedman—who were shaping the ideological framework that, within a few years, would become conventional wisdom: markets solve problems more effectively than government. It was as if as soon as Simon left behind his position at the FEO, he had to excise the demons of his leadership in it. Simon went on to write a second libertarian book, *A Time for Action*, and flirted with running for President in 1980. A year later, he became the head of the Olin Foundation, a philanthropic effort to undermine the role of government in shaping markets.

With Nixon in disgraced retirement and Simon uninterested in taking any credit for the successes of 1973–74, the political story of the initial oil shock became increasingly about government ineptitude rather than marketcrafting success, a demonstration of how effective marketcrafting could get obscured by an ideological gloss. If Simon buried his own successes, the second oil shock of 1979 threw even more dirt on the grave.

The first oil crisis had been caused by the weaponization of oil: oil-producing nations wanted to punish the United States, and that was a lever they pulled to do so. To a certain extent, the fact that the second oil crisis was *not* a targeted aggression against the United States—that it was a result of geopolitical instability—made it even more confusing and threatening, as it pointed to just how sensitive and volatile this crucial system had become.[89] By the time Iranian revolutionaries overthrew the Shah of Iran in January 1979, America was even more reliant on foreign oil than it had been in 1973.

Neither Presidents Ford nor Carter made meaningful headway toward energy resiliency. In 1977, a major pipeline in Alaska came online, significantly contributing to domestic output, and Alaskan production ramped up in the following years. But the simultaneous drawdown in production from older wells meant there was no meaningful boost in domestic supplies. Oil imports continued to increase dramatically, doubling between 1973 and 1979.[90] Meanwhile, the most significant public-policy lever that could help build independence in the medium term—the SPR—was taking several years to become operational. It required procuring significant amounts of oil, identifying multiple sites for the construction of new salt caverns in which it could be stored, and getting it into the ground. SPR administration made significant progress in three years, with over 90 million barrels in storage by 1979, but it was still slower than its leaders had hoped.[91] Between 1972 and 1979, the economy grew 25.9 percent, factoring in inflation, but thanks to conservation and efficiency efforts, US oil consumption was flat.[92]

After the revolution in Iran, the country's oil production came to a standstill, pulling 5 million barrels of oil off global markets. Other countries increased production, which ultimately amounted to about 3.5 million barrels a day, roughly in line with the first oil crisis when accounting for the growth in global demand. But in the second shock, rather than adopt the conserve and control strategy that Simon had utilized in 1973, the Carter administration failed to pursue a coherent marketcrafting approach at all, exacerbating the crisis. As prices surged in March, Carter announced in an executive order that he would begin a phased *decontrol* of oil prices in June, trusting markets to ensure shortages did not occur. That move enraged many on the left, including Senators Jackson and Edward Kennedy, who would go on to challenge Carter in the presidential election the following year, winning twelve primaries. Carter made no meaningful attempts at new fuel allocation provisions, and when it came to conservation, he pleaded with Americans to voluntarily reduce their consumption but took no legislative or administrative action. "The only thing that would help was to let prices rise and get the government out of the energy business. Conservatives, of course, agreed," the historian Meg Jacobs wrote.[93]

Carter's market-driven strategy immediately led to widespread shortages and panic buying. By the end of April 1979, global prices for oil had doubled since the start of the year. In June, as Carter's decontrol program took effect, the shortages grew worse, with 90 percent of gas stations in New York closed by the end of the month. The lines continued through July, only ebbing as Iranian production clawed back to the prerevolution levels and global demand adjusted to the higher prices. Meanwhile, Carter made symbolic gestures a kind of ritual at the White House, putting solar panels on the roof, unscrewing every other lightbulb, and turning off the air conditioners. The root problems of America's multiple crises were "self-indulgence and consumption" and the "piling up of material goods," not his administration's failure to plan or manage a crisis.[94] Rather than public policy, Carter believed that personal responsibility would somehow be the solution to this crisis. Meanwhile, at the pump, the price had exploded from sixty-eight cents in January to ninety-one cents by July. By the end of the year, the average price was in excess of a dollar, an important psychological marker—it meant that gas-station signs needed to be updated to include three figures instead of two. Carter's approval rating plummeted, and it never recovered.[95] When Carter took office, the average price of a gallon of gasoline was $.63; by the time he left, drivers were paying $1.30.[96] Americans were paying $85 billion a year for imported oil, double what they were paying four years before.

A frequent critic of the Carter administration, Simon had no sympathy for its approach. He believed that the Democrats needed to deregulate the oil and energy industry further to spur production. "All of this is lost on bureaucratic Chicken Littles, who keep telling us the energy sky has fallen in for natural reasons," he wrote. No amount of unscrewed lightbulbs in American homes could fix the markets: the government needed to step in to deregulate and right the ship. "The 'energy shortage,' in other words, is a creation of the federal government," he wrote. "Price controls are only a part of it. The government has taken numerous other steps to close off petroleum production while increasing consumption, including refusal to lease offshore lands for drilling, imposition of environmental standards that prevent construction of refineries, mandated emission and safety features on automobiles that require greater oil consumption."[97] On its surface, Simon was making the case for a government retreat. But it was a retreat that would require new legislative and administrative action to make markets operate more smoothly. This kind of "deregulatory" agenda would not make markets free, reverting them back to a neutral or natural position. Instead, Simon called for policy choices that would require government action to recalibrate the market's balance of permissions and restrictions, enhancing business autonomy through state action. Even in his libertarian tirades, Simon was still marketcrafting.

The second energy shock effectively ended Carter's presidency. Ronald Reagan took the general election with 489 electoral votes, compared to Carter's mere 49. It did, however, build more momentum for expanding the SPR. Like Carter, Reagan embraced the idea of stockpiling crude oil, and in the wake of the second crisis, Congress authorized the SPR to acquire oil reserves at a significantly faster rate. A bill in 1982 authorized still more purchases. By 1985, the stockpile held just shy of 500 million barrels, enough oil to last a remarkable 115 days. Meanwhile, twelve years after that first crisis, Americans were using less oil and gas than they had before 1973, even factoring in significant economic growth over the decade. (Absolute consumption increased in the late 1970s before decreasing in the early 1980s.)[98] Thanks to the major efficiency gains since 1974, imports had fallen from their peak in the 1970s. By 1985, with more oil in storage and moderated demand, America was on a surer energy footing than it had been in fifteen years. This was not the full-fledged independence from foreign oil that Nixon had promised when the first oil shock had hit, but it was a new kind of resiliency, achieved through gradual marketcrafting.[99]

The broad record of government policy in energy markets between 1970 and 1985 is checkered, but the dominant narrative that government failed to navigate the energy challenges is not right. Ironically, the conservatives of Nixon's administration, led by Bill Simon, more effectively used the power of government to navigate the first energy shock than Carter's administration did in the second. Yet because of Nixon's resignation and Simon's refusal to own the success of the FEO, the marketcrafting efforts of the first oil shock faded into a grand narrative of government ineptitude in the 1970s. The Carter administration's inability to manage the chaos of the second oil shock reinforced the perception of government incompetence.

The mistakes in the second crisis and Simon's revisionism of the first should not obscure the evidence that the state showed that it could manage energy markets to be more stable, as long as policymakers embraced the tools. Much of Simon's success in the first crisis resulted from Congress' willingness to charter a new institution, and Nixon's decision to charge Simon with considerable discretion. That created a situation in which Simon could guide energy markets through a period of deep dislocation and turmoil. Gasoline shortages were brief, homes did not lack for heat, and planes continued to fly. Domestic prices stayed significantly lower than global levels, smoothing the adjustment to a higher-priced future. Congress doubled down on Simon's control and conserve strategy in landmark 1975 legislation that enhanced energy efficiency standards and created a massive state-run stockpiling effort that remains in use today. It took the suffering and pain of the chaotic second crisis to convince American policymakers to more deeply embrace some of the long-term plans for energy resiliency, particularly the SPR, that Simon and others laid in the wake of the first crisis. Since that reserve was adequately supported in the early 1980s, no energy crisis has occurred since.

From the 1930s through the 1970s, the march of marketcrafters illustrated both the immense promise of effective market administration and the catastrophic downsides of failure. In the decades ahead, the free-market fantasy of Bill Simon would grow in prestige and dominance as the New Deal order faded. Yet when policymakers tried to let markets take care of themselves, even the most libertarian voices discovered the need for a guiding hand to ensure stability and prosperity.

THE LIBERTARIAN FANTASY

9

THE FIGHT FOR DISCRETION

NANCY TEETERS & THE VOLCKER SHOCK (1979-84)

They didn't even know what to call her at first. On September 18, 1978, Vice President Walter Mondale swore in his friend and fellow bridge club member Nancy Teeters as the first female governor of the Federal Reserve. Members of Congress, the press, central bankers, and her family watched on as Teeters, forty-eight, dressed in a pink, satin-blend dress, raised her hand to take the oath of office in the Roosevelt Room of the White House. Fed Chair William Miller christened Teeter's appointment with a joke. "We had a big debate this morning at the Board," Miller said to the room. "There was one of our Governors who all his life had wanted a Governess, and he is going to have to be satisfied with a Governor, I think. We're delighted to have you here."[1] Chuckles and cringes rippled through the room.

Teeters had been navigating her profession's characteristic chauvinism for decades. As late as 1973, only 6 percent of the economics faculty at American universities were women.[2] Born in 1930 in a small Indiana town, Teeters was a bright child who often completed her older brother's homework for him while churning through nearly a dozen books each week that had been specifically set aside for her by the local librarian. After high school, she enrolled at Oberlin College in Ohio, where she met her husband. Oberlin forbade students from marrying, so the two waited until just after graduation. She had planned to enroll at the University of Michigan for graduate work in economics that fall, but when she arrived with her husband, the school rescinded her scholarship: only unmarried women could receive financial support. (Her new in-laws happily provided a direct loan.) In 1956, after she completed her graduate studies, the couple moved to Washington, and Teeters secured her first job as an economist in the government finance division at the Fed. Two years later, she became pregnant with her first child. The Fed's policy at the time required women to stop working after six months of pregnancy, so Teeters lied about how far along she was, giving birth to her daughter, Ann, several months "early."[3]

After six weeks at home with their infant, Teeters confronted her husband on the porch of their Cleveland Park home one day when he returned from work. "I can't do this," she told him. "I want to go back to work." He agreed. Teeters' boss, Stephen Axilrod, managed to finesse the Fed's bureaucracy to accommodate a temporary shift to part-time work for Teeters. "I like to think that I helped to prove that part-time employment of women with young children was mutually productive for both the employer and employee," she wrote years later.[4] Teeters had two more children as her career advanced. In 1962, she moved over to the White House to work on Kennedy's CEA, returning to the Fed the following year. By 1966, anxious to climb the ladder at the Fed, she turned to Axilrod for advice. "Steve was absolutely convinced that I couldn't get a job anyplace," she recounted. "I asked [him] why, and he said, 'You have no place to go.' This was in the morning, and by three o'clock that afternoon, I had a new job."[5] Teeters decamped to the Bureau of the Budget, the precursor to today's Office of the Management of the Budget. Afterward, she joined the Brookings Institution and later became the chief economist of the House Budget Committee. By the time Teeters returned to the Fed in 1978, over a decade later, it was as a governor. Axilrod now worked for her.

There was universal agreement within the Carter administration that the Fed board seat opened up by the departure of Arthur Burns should be filled by a woman. In the memo recommending Teeters to the President, several voices commented that she was "aggressive" and "her own person [who] has no compunction about telling you what is on her mind."[6]

That was fine with Carter, who believed Teeters would be ideologically in line with the administration. As the New York Times reported, "Mrs. Teeters, chief economist for the House Budget Committee, has been described

as 'a Humphrey Democrat,' as 'pragmatic and eclectic,' and as 'a sophisticated Keynesian'"—qualities Carter valued for his economic team.[7] In addition to the sterling résumé, Teeters was politically connected, friendly with
Democrats and Republicans alike. The Democratic Chair of the Senate committee in charge of her nomination, William Proxmire, was a neighbor, and
one of the Republican members, Richard Lugar, was a cousin. Vice President
Mondale was also a family friend; their children ran back and forth from
one another's houses after school. She sailed through her Senate confirmation.[8] At her first meeting of the FOMC at Fed headquarters, Teeters wore
a lipstick-red dress, a jolt of color in a sea of gray and black suits. When the
other governors looked stunned, she smiled and said, "You don't want me to
look like you, do you?"[9] She settled into the same literal chair that Burns had
made for himself and took up her work.[10]

Over her six-year tenure at the Fed, Teeters faced not one but two intractable problems: how to be a trailblazer in a sexist culture and how to subdue
runaway inflation. Her story has been largely overlooked, as historians and
economists have chosen to focus on the leadership of Fed Chair Paul Volcker. That has been a disservice, not just to Teeters' own legacy, but also to
an important path not taken: a marketcraft that could have restored price
stability at less cost to American workers.

The "Volcker shock" has become foundational economic lore. Between 1979
and 1982, precipitous monetary tightening restored price stability after fifteen years of volatility—and created the deepest recession the United States
had endured since the Great Depression. Economists and bankers generally
reflect on this harsh medicine with approval, while American manufacturing
workers remember the recession of the early 1980s as the moment that jobs
began to disappear for good. In the years before the Volcker shock began,
however, the consensus was clear: Americans hated inflation more than anything else. For decades, the nation's political and economic leaders had debated how to balance the competing needs for robust employment, stable
prices, financial stability, and growth. When Carter nominated Teeters, inflation hovered around 7 percent, significantly higher than the 5 percent low of
a few years earlier and nearing the levels seen after the first oil shock earlier
in the decade. Even to many liberals who prioritized employment over price
stability, it felt like enough was enough. Prices had to stop going up.

But in Teeters' first months at the Fed, shortages in energy and global food markets compounded the inflation problem, much as they had on Burns' watch five years earlier. This time, it was the revolution in Iran in January and February of 1979 that shocked the world and shut down Iranian oil fields, causing global fuel production to fall. Caught unprepared, American leaders believed that they had few tools at hand to address this second energy shock. Carter removed controls on oil prices that had been in place since the early seventies, at just the moment that global prices were doubling. The spot price for crude oil from West Texas surged by 165 percent in a year.[11] Those energy price increases showed up in the cost of secondary goods, exacerbating inflationary pressures.

In another stroke of bad luck, domestic food production unexpectedly and dramatically declined in the same period. A bad winter in 1978 cooled the production of everything from fruit to poultry, and food prices across the board spiked. The dollar also experienced a sharp drop in value, which increased the prices of imported agricultural products. Another challenging winter in 1979 exacerbated America's food problems, while a disappointing Soviet grain crop sent global wheat prices soaring.[12] With energy and food prices surging, workers demanded higher compensation to keep up with the rising prices. The industrial and service sectors of the economy passed along these various cost increases by raising their own prices further, pushing inflation still higher.

The economist Alan Blinder, who served as a Fed governor from 1994 to 1996, spent decades investigating the primary causes of the inflationary surge of the 1970s. Blinder concluded that the entirety of the inflationary surge from 1978 to 1982 was due to the effects of "supply-side" crises—the run-up in oil, food, and housing costs—rather than loose monetary policy or excessive fiscal spending. Other economists disagreed, seeing instead a reinforcing system where loose monetary policy combined with the oil and food shocks to start an inflation spiral. Once inflation expectations were "unanchored," business and consumers alike planned for a world of permanently high inflation, exacerbating the cycle. Still others pinned the entirety of the blame on the central bank, which, they argued, accommodated the price rises with loose policy. That minority view was difficult to reconcile with the clear and sharp uptick in commodity prices, and most Fed leaders agreed that oil and food shocks were a central cause.[13]

Whatever the ultimate cause, American voters looked to their government for relief. Congress had not created any institution outside of the Fed charged with using the different economic policy tools available to the federal government to stabilize prices. No one at any agency was responsible for evaluating the performance of commodity stockpiling efforts that had been used several times over the previous decades to buffer extreme price movements. The wage and price controls office had been shut down, and the successor to the FEO had not developed a new framework to ensure adequate distribution of energy resources in short supply. The SPR was not yet meaningfully operational, and Congress had little appetite for fighting inflation through tax hikes or budget cuts. The only institution with the mandate and tools to step in and squash inflation seemed to be the Fed.[14]

Teeters believed that it was far from ideal for the Fed to be taking on inflation alone. Because high oil and food prices drove much of the inflation of 1979, relying on monetary policy—without the help of other coordinated public- and private-sector efforts—was like starting a forest fire to eliminate a single invasive species: it could work, but with significant collateral damage. The situation called for a more surgical approach. "[F]oreign oil price increases set off wage/price spirals in the United States," she wrote privately to a Congressman in March 1980. "[The Fed's] macroeconomic policies can restrain the spiral process. In fact, they could probably stop it completely, if severe enough. However the price, in terms of unemployment, could be extremely high."[15] The problem was that the government lacked the tools to target the real causes of inflation narrowly: energy and food prices. Teeters had advocated for the creation of new facilities, such as an institution that could coordinate federal credit programs to help buffer sectoral price movements. Congress had not acted.[16]

Given her background, the press expected Teeters to be a "dove," preferring relatively loose monetary policy, but in her first year at the Fed, she joined the other governors in favor of significant tightening. In late 1978, the board raised the interest rate at which banks could borrow from the Fed from 7.8 percent to an all-time high of 9.5—and they left it there through the first half of 1979. Teeters was struggling with her own personal finances. That year, she was forced to refinance her home at double-digit mortgage rates to send her two oldest children to college.[17]

But in the late summer of 1979, the situation rapidly deteriorated. By

July, prices at the pump were exploding, increasing from sixty-eight cents a gallon in January to ninety-one cents.[18] President Carter's approval rating was in free fall, and Americans reported feeling a new and pervasive pessimism about the future. Wanting to take headline-grabbing action, Carter gave a nationally televised speech about the growing "crisis of confidence" in America and then fired five cabinet secretaries at once, including the outgoing Treasury Secretary, whom he replaced with Fed Chair William Miller. Carter now had to find a new boss for the Fed, and after Bank of America's President declined the role, Carter considered offering it to his second choice, New York Federal Reserve Bank President Paul Volcker.

When Carter invited Volcker to the White House to interview him for the job, Volcker was direct about his plans. "'You're thinking of making me Chairman of the Federal Reserve?'" Volcker asked the President, according to his recollection in 2008. "'You've got to understand that I'm going to have a tighter policy than Mr. Miller, and I feel very strongly about the independence of the Federal Reserve.' I went home and had dinner in a restaurant with a couple of old friends of mine, and I said, 'Well, I'm not going to be Chairman of the Federal Reserve.'" A few days later, the President offered him the position. Carter believed Volcker could end the inflationary spiral, once and for all. Administration voices, finance, and even labor supported the move. Despite Volcker's warning, Carter might not have been prepared for just how far Volcker would go. "At that moment, few in the White House appreciated what would become obvious in the next few years, that this was the most important appointment of Jimmy Carter's Presidency," the journalist William Greider wrote in a landmark book on the Volcker Fed. "The choice had occurred by accident, driven by political panic and financial distress. In time, it would profoundly alter the landscape of American life."[19]

Volcker loomed in more ways than one: in addition to his imposing reputation, he stood six feet, seven inches. Many government, Fed, and finance leaders personally knew him, given that he had moved between policy and finance circles in New York and Washington for decades. Like Teeters, he had begun his career as an economist in the Federal Reserve System, although he had worked for the New York Reserve Bank instead of the Board of Governors in Washington. He joined Chase Manhattan Bank before becoming a deputy under secretary at the Treasury Department. In 1969, he became Treasury's Under Secretary for International Monetary Affairs, where he managed the world's transition away from the fixed exchange rate system outlined by the Bretton Woods agreement. He parlayed that experience into one of the most powerful positions in economic policymaking as President of the New York Fed, making him the Federal Reserve system's delegated policymaker most entrenched in the day-to-day decisions of banking leaders and earning him the respect and trust of bankers on Wall Street as well as his colleagues at the central bank.

As President of the New York Federal Reserve Bank, Volcker joined the FOMC, the primary policymaking body for monetary policy at the Fed, in 1975, as its vice chairman.[20] Teeters had joined in 1978, meaning the two had worked together for about a year by the time Volcker was elevated to Chair in 1979. Despite the similarity in their careers, their paths had not meaningfully intersected before. To outsiders, they seemed to stand for different approaches to monetary policy. The *Wall Street Journal* wrote that Volcker had a "world-wide reputation as a determined advocate of anti-inflationary policies" and in his confirmation testimony he reaffirmed the clear message that he had communicated to the President: his top priority would be the eradication of inflation.[21] Teeters' views were less clearly known, but given her left-leaning politics, most assumed that she would tilt toward looser policy.

Within weeks of Volcker's elevation to the top job, the media was pitting the two against each other, with Volcker saying "we must and we can" squelch inflation while Teeters argued for patience to let the recent rate rises take effect.[22] The gender stereotypes could not have been more blatant. "The Fed is a kind of family," one close observer said at the time.[23] Volcker, the stern father, stood ready to discipline an indulgent nation that had lost its way. Teeters, the judicious mother, sensitive to the damage the suffering might cause, favored moderation. The "real" experts knew that the father's steadfast resolve was what was needed. "Mrs. Teeters—bright, articulate and 50—is less warmly regarded within the Fed, no doubt partly because she is a woman in an institution still overwhelmingly male but more important because she is seen as representing an economic point of view whose time is past," wrote Steven Rattner in the *New York Times*.[24]

But like most marriages, the stereotypes belied a more complicated reality. The two, in partnership together, would soon deliver an unexpected shock to the financial system. Volcker embraced a new, experimental marketcraft in order to ensure price stability, while Teeters favored a more moderate, discretion-based marketcraft. Only in the months and years afterward would their distinct visions of the Fed's marketcrafting role become clear.

Since the chairmanship of Bill Martin in the 1950s, the Fed had committed itself to crafting and managing orderly money markets. It had become accepted wisdom that an orderly market in short-term Treasury debt in particular would increase investor confidence and make credit abundant and cheap. That commitment endured throughout the 1960s and '70s, and in the years before the Volcker shock, the Fed had stepped in on two dramatic occasions to soothe money market turmoil. In 1970, after the bankruptcy of Penn Central, the nation's largest railroad, the Fed took emergency action to stabilize commercial paper markets and the banking sector.[25] It intervened again in 1974 in support of offshore-dollar markets after one of the nation's largest banks, Franklin National, collapsed. These dramatic moves garnered attention, but they overshadowed the real effect of the Fed's commitment to orderliness: the ongoing use of its balance sheet to ensure that interest rates did not fluctuate too dramatically. In moments of calm and instability alike, the Fed bought and sold government securities, preventing interest-rate spikes and falls from disrupting the Fed's monetary policy. Preventing extreme volatility and the market turmoil that came with it gave investors the confidence to make medium- and long-term bets, the kind of investment needed for mid-century capitalism to thrive.

Volcker, with the help of Teeters and other governors, shredded this commitment to orderliness barely two months into his tenure as Chair with a deliberate jolt to markets in October of 1979. People tend to think of the Volcker shock as a discrete, decisive intervention, as if Volcker flipped a switch that squelched inflation. In reality, the shock lasted three long years and was full of twists and turns, including a credit crunch, two recessions, and a historic tax cut. But the first eight weeks of Volcker's tenure as Chair crucially set the course. Within weeks of taking the helm, Volcker established the focus of the coming eight years of his chairmanship: building and retaining credibility for the Fed. "Economic policy," Volcker said in his first meeting as Chair, "has a kind of crisis of credibility."[26] Volcker believed he had a short, unique window early in his tenure to set a clear policy direction, telegraphing to fellow FOMC members and the market what his ultimate priorities would be. If market actors—whether they worked in finance,

corporate America, or small- or medium-sized businesses—expected inflation to continue to rise, they would adjust their prices to be in line with those
expectations, converting those expectations into self-fulfilling prophecies.
Something had to change to get people back to assuming that prices would
not increase by 10 percent the following year. If the Fed lacked credibility in
its fight to anchor prices, it would fail as an institution.

Volcker might have hoped that his appointment alone would begin to
build that credibility, but financial markets soon sent him a different signal.
In a Board of Governors meeting on September 18 just weeks after his appointment, the board voted four to three in favor of a half-point increase
in the discount rate, the second half-point increase since Volcker had taken
the helm. Teeters opposed the hike, believing it was too aggressive. Even
so, Volcker had a majority and raised interest rates to historic levels only a
month into the job. With surprise, Volcker watched markets fall the following day as traders tried to piece together what had happened in the meeting
and why the vote was so close. Their concern was simple: a Fed reluctant to
implement a half-point rate hike when inflation was over 10 percent would
not likely be a Fed ready to do whatever it took to restore price stability. The
margin was too thin, suggesting that monetary policy would tighten much
more gradually than many had imagined. The *Wall Street Journal* warned of
"increasing opposition" to tighter monetary policy, and the *New York Times*
characterized the Teeters-Volcker split as "a fundamental division within the
Board over whether inflation remains a more pressing problem than recession."[27]

Despite the media's coverage and their looming policy differences, Volcker
and Teeters were developing a personal rapport. When he stepped into the role
of Chair, Volcker told Teeters he wanted to join her on a planned trip to China,
which remained almost entirely closed to Westerners. "That morning, we'd
sworn in Volcker. We had lunch," Teeters remembered. "About two o'clock in
the afternoon, Paul came down to my office with a piece of paper in his hand.
He said that it was the only thing on his desk. [Former Chair] Miller had literally taken everything off the desk, and the only thing that was on his desk was
a piece of paper about my trip to China. Paul said to me, 'I'm going along.'"[28]
The next summer, the two headed to Beijing, joined by four other Fed officials,
including a translator. In an era when China lacked developed physical infrastructure or meaningful tourist accommodations, Teeters and Volcker forged

a special connection through the shared adventure. As Volcker said upon his return, "The trip was the kind of thing that gives rise to stories around the campfire."[29] But it would be some time before this bond paid dividends, and in the meantime, Volcker was intent on taking dramatic action to counter the emerging narrative that his Fed wasn't strong enough to tackle inflation.

Betting his chairmanship on building a reputation of a determined inflation fighter, Volcker needed a tactic to tighten monetary policy that could *also* win broad, enduring support from the board, ensuring that markets would trust the Fed's commitment to maintaining tight money. He turned to an idea that had been brewing at the staff level for years. Volcker would reprogram *how* monetary policy functioned, shifting the implementing framework in a way that would tie the Fed's hands, reducing discretion and sending interest rates soaring.

It's important to understand what Volcker—and Teeters initially—agreed to do in order to recognize the better path not taken. Over its long history, the Fed had used various tools to implement its monetary-policy goals. Its ultimate target, however, had always been to maintain a specified amount of tightness or looseness in "money market conditions," a purposefully vague term of art that retained ongoing discretion at the FOMC level to adjust policy in response to what was happening in the economy. A set of intermediate targets—specific variables the Fed would use as indicators of "money market conditions"—developed over time, many of which focused on the price of money. Short-term interest rates were the most reliable and commonly used benchmark.[30] In the 1970s, an alternative view known as "monetarism" emerged, arguing that instead of focusing on "money market conditions," which required discretion to assess, the Fed should pursue consistent, gradual increases in a single, targeted category, the money *supply*. Specifically, the monetarists believed the Fed should commit to a low and stable growth rate in the money that banks directly controlled, regardless of macroeconomic conditions. They disagreed with the prevailing Keynesian policy consensus of the time, which held that loose monetary policy during a recession could minimize the impact of a downturn without creating inflationary pressure. To the monetarists, any discretionary increase in the money supply would cause inflation. Only by *constraining* its discretion and mechanistically delivering a predetermined amount of money to the economy could the Fed reliably control inflation in the long term.

As radical as the idea may have sounded, the Fed had considered moving to a model that focused on regulating the money supply over money market conditions just a few years before, in 1976. Volcker had opposed the change at the time, but now he realized that it could be his opening. Volcker did not experience any sort of ideological conversion; he was not a monetarist and did not agree with many of the school's policy recommendations. While he acknowledged some limited value in the monetarists' insights over the years—such as the point that inflation has "something to do with money" as he said—he had consistently rejected the overarching theory.[31] But Volcker saw monetarism as a tactical opportunity to break free of the norms of gradualism plaguing the FOMC's current procedures and shift to a significantly tighter and more rigid posture. It would be just the right kind of surprise, experimental but not unfamiliar, delivering the jolt to markets he believed they needed.

Within days of the divided September meeting and subsequent market fallout, Volcker called in Teeters' previous boss Stephen Axilrod, now the FOMC's staff director for monetary and financial policy, and another Fed official, Peter Sternlight, and asked them to hatch a plan for implementing the new policy framework. Axilrod and Sternlight were familiar with the FOMC's existing research on procedures for money supply targeting, which meant they could work quickly, delivering the first, highly confidential draft of the memo to Volcker on September 27.[32] They outlined how the so-called "new operating procedures" would work. Instead of using a dashboard of various money market indicators, the Fed would prioritize a single target: how much money existed in the economy. To control that single variable, the Fed would add money to the banking system by buying government debt from banks or drain money from the system by selling government debt to banks. This practice was not new, but now the Fed would pursue these so-called open market operations to achieve a specific money supply growth target rather than a certain level of tightness or looseness in "money market conditions."

Axilrod and Sternlight acknowledged that the move was not without major risks. Focusing primarily on how much money existed in the economy meant that the Fed would cede its long-standing control of interest rates, a key tool in the institution's policy-setting apparatus. Rates could rise or fall, and the Fed would not be able to control or even guide them. Adopting such a radical new program also implied an abandonment of the Fed's decades-long commitment to stable money markets. Bill Martin had staked the identity of the institution on its commitment to orderliness, and there was no precedent for allowing money market rates to fluctuate so dramatically.

As if those downsides weren't big enough, the Fed might have a hard time hitting its new targets, for two reasons. First, the Fed affected the money supply only indirectly, through its control over "bank reserves"—how much money banks hold in their vaults or in their accounts at the Fed. And while reserves are an important determinant of the money supply, the precise relationship between the two—known as the "money multiplier"—is affected by numerous factors and can fluctuate. Second, the money supply itself is difficult to measure precisely. Policymakers, bankers, and economists had trouble even agreeing on the definition of money, let alone how best to measure it. As a result, the official measurements of total money in the economy themselves—referred to as the "monetary aggregates"—added uncertainty to the task of money supply targeting rather than making it clearer or more manageable.[33] By committing to money growth rate targets, the Fed would be giving up its discretionary power to fine-tune short-term interest rates and relying on an untested methodology to implement its monetary policy.[34] Looking back on their memo, Axilrod believed they underestimated the downsides: "I didn't fully realize the enormity of what we were doing. We were putting in place something that had never been done before."[35]

If the risk was worth taking, it was largely due to political considerations. "We could have just tightened," Volcker later told the journalist Greider, "but I probably would have had trouble getting policy as much tighter as it needed to be. I could have lived with a more orthodox tightening, but I saw some value in just changing the parameters of the way we did things."[36] Moving to the new model would upend market expectations, allowing rates to go wherever supply and demand took them. The practical implication was that short-term rates could adjust by several percent in a single day, meaning that Volcker would not have to turn to his colleagues for every 25 basis point increase. Money could get very tight, very fast. In switching to the new procedures, Volcker would show investors and bond traders that the Fed was serious about restricting the money supply and letting the chaos begin.[37]

While Axilrod and Sternlight worked out the details, Volcker approached

Teeters and other governors one-on-one to talk through the idea. Historically, the Chair of the Federal Reserve had not lobbied fellow board members before meetings. Bill Martin had favored a consensus-driven approach,
while Burns preferred something more akin to a seminar on monetary policy
that he could dominate, with the other governors serving as his apt pupils.[38]
In both cases, the sense of the FOMC was developed through a gentlemen's
discussion in committee rather than political maneuvering beforehand. But
Volcker sensed that his proposed rupture was too dramatic and too important to take it to the committee without securing the support of at least some
FOMC members first. If markets caught wind that the FOMC was divided
on the topic, it would undermine his credibility further, weakening his chairmanship before it had even got off the ground. Volcker had a clear mission in
these private conversations: win over potential doubters on the FOMC, including several traditionalist hawks who feared such a dramatic move. One of
these doubters, Volcker would have had reason to suspect, would be Teeters.

No record exists of these one-on-one talks between Volcker and Teeters
and fellow governors, but it's not hard to imagine what was said given the
public transcripts of the official meetings that followed. Teeters was no monetarist and did not intuitively favor the rigid approach to reserve aggregate
targeting. "The monetarists who were in the academic world were coming in
and telling us we were doing the wrong thing. They were terrible," she later
said. "These guys would come in and they'd give a little speech. It was their
point of view of what our role was. We didn't pay any attention to them."[39]
Evidence from the time shows that they did, particularly when it became
politically useful to cherry-pick some of their ideas in the service of a market
jolt. It turned out Teeters agreed with Volcker that resetting market psychology would be useful. While she was concerned about the likely increase in
interest-rate volatility that would result from the new policy procedure, she
also knew that rates would probably have to move up relatively quickly even
if they stuck with the old procedures. This arrangement could be a faster way
to accomplish the same end, akin to ripping off a band-aid. Another feature
of the new regime would be that Teeters, Volcker, and the other Fed leaders
would have plausible deniability that the Fed was responsible for the high
rates. Because the new system would mean that the Fed would cede control
over interest rates, high rates would be markets' fault, not a result of surgical Fed action.[40] "I wouldn't call it a cover, but I don't think anyone on the

committee would have been willing to vote to push interest rates as high as 20 percent," said one fellow governor.[41] It was this lack of discretion and control that alienated another governor, Henry Wallich, who was wary of any policy that reduced the Fed's power. "It's a pact with the devil," Wallich told Volcker. "Sometimes, you have to deal with the devil," Volcker replied.[42]

Teeters was inclined to agree with Volcker at this early stage. She had favored a slow and steady tightening cycle, but given that rates were already at historic highs and inflation was still raging, she felt that it might be better to apply a brief and powerful jolt to the system, a onetime dramatic action along the lines that Volcker was proposing. There was another important and related advantage to the new procedure that was particularly attractive to Teeters: it could lead to sharp drops in interest rates as well as sharp rises. If the economy were to fall into recession—leading to decreased demand for money and credit—market interest rates would naturally fall. And with the Fed allowing rates to fluctuate without day-to-day guidance from the central bank, rates could drop quickly, thereby providing an automatic expansionary effect, potentially allowing for a faster recovery.[43] Taking a decisive action might minimize the long-term pain. If the other governors and FOMC members were all supportive, she would be open to the change.

Volcker called an unusual FOMC meeting for Saturday, October 6, asking the Fed governors and Reserve Bank Presidents not to tip off the press. Fearing a leak that the FOMC was having an unscheduled, in-person meeting, he instructed those coming in from out of town to stay at different hotels and to enter the Fed's headquarters through the back door. In the forty-eight hours leading up to the meeting, Volcker continued to work his internal politics. On Thursday, he held an unscheduled meeting with the six other governors based in Washington in the Special Library at the Fed, a more intimate room conducive to frank conversation than the traditional boardroom. The group seemed to be moving in his direction.[44] The next day, he convened a conference call for the full FOMC to give the governors a preview of the meeting agenda and distribute a final version of the Axilrod-Sternlight memo, which laid out how the new monetary-policy framework would function.[45]

On Saturday morning, the FOMC members gathered for the pivotal discussion. Volcker laid out two choices: aggressive moves to tighten monetary policy using the status quo operative framework or a shift to "new operating procedures" that would target growth in the amount of money in the economy. The element of market surprise of the latter approach appealed to the dovish and hawkish members of the board alike. Governors Charles Partee and Emmett Rice, who had voted with Teeters against Volcker not even three weeks before, announced their support, with Rice arguing that the "psychological impact of a change in operating technique will be strong."[46] The conservative wing also wanted to do "something dramatic."[47] "[W]e are dealing with an essentially psychological situation, both abroad and here at home," said Chicago Reserve Bank President Robert Mayo. "[N]ow is the time for us to take the plunge."[48] Volcker allowed himself to hope that market actors might start to believe the Fed took inflation seriously. If they did, he told the board, interest rates might not need to move as high as they otherwise would, getting the Fed "more bang for the buck."[49]

Teeters was largely silent in the meeting. Perhaps no individual vote was more important than hers, given her symbolic contrast with the Chair and the expectation that she might oppose the move. When Volcker conducted a straw poll of participants at the end of the meeting, he found twelve governors and Reserve Bank Presidents in support of the move and five opposed.

Teeters raised her hand in support, and Volcker, seemingly wanting to make sure she was landing on his side, asked for confirmation. "You're in that camp, Nancy?" he asked. "I feel queasy about it," she replied. Not all the participants in the meeting technically had a vote because of the FOMC's complicated organizational structure, so Volcker conducted a second straw poll of only the voting members, including Teeters, asking for a show of hands for those who have a "strong preference for moving in the new direction."[50] She raised her hand yet again. "I'm in," she said. A few moments later, the FOMC unanimously voted to adopt the new monetary-policy framework, shifting the Fed's policy regime to look primarily at money supply growth. "She understood the economy was in bad shape, and something had to happen," her daughter, Ann Teeters Johnson, later recounted. "She was willing to give it a limited trial."[51] The Volcker shock had begun, and Nancy Teeters' problems began in earnest.

Markets went haywire. When they reopened after the announcement, the federal funds rate jumped an eye-popping 2.5 percent, from 11.5 to 14 percent in a day. Just the previous week, analysts were marveling at a 1 percent rise over the past two months, and now the market had moved two and a half times that in a single day. (Today the Fed Funds rate may move by .01 or .02 percent on any given day.) This was just the beginning of historic gyrations. "The Fed Funds rate, which money traders watched as their key barometer," wrote Greider, "moved like a Yo-Yo—perversely unpredictable. It went as high as 18 percent one day, then back to 14 percent the next, then up again to 16 percent, then plunging briefly as low as 11 percent, then back up again."[52] When the Fed made the decision to move to its new framework, it specified a ceiling for interest rates, even though it wasn't technically controlling them anymore. If the market broke through that level, the FOMC agreed to assemble in an emergency meeting to sort through what to do, if anything. Not even two weeks into the new operating procedures, the rate threatened to break through the barrier, and Volcker convened a conference call. But even with the volatility, the FOMC members, including Teeters, agreed to allow the market rate to move higher, acknowledging that the volatility was an expected feature of the new operating framework. (Teeters did ask for an additional conference call if the higher rates persisted.)[53] As 1980 dawned, the Fed Funds rate remained near the record high level achieved directly after the announcement, and it would climb further in the months to come.

Teeters got the historic jump in interest rates that she wanted, but she was already nervous about how high the rates were moving and how unstable markets had become. Like Burns a decade before, she understood that tightening the money supply was a blunt instrument that put the entire economy in a deep freeze. Sometimes this might make sense when aggregate demand was running hot thanks to tax cuts or excess government spending, but this inflation was driven almost entirely by energy and food price shocks. Even so, with no other institution in the American government charged with the power and discretion to tackle inflation, it fell to the Fed. Teeters understood this laid immense responsibility on the institution she helped lead, but there were limits to how far she was willing to use the Fed's powers. By January of 1980, just three months after having authorized the jolt, she was already signaling to her colleagues a reluctance to be more aggressive. "We [are not] the sole source of the inflation. But it's like playing poker with the other players always pulling all the wild cards. We're playing with OPEC, and we really have no control over oil prices," she said to her colleagues at an FOMC meeting. "To say that we're consistently going to reduce inflation in a situation where we don't have control over inflation is, to me, going out on a limb. There may be a time, if this so-called recession turns very deep, when we might want to reverse our policies completely."[54]

Although Volcker didn't entirely disagree, he also knew he would favor higher rates and tighter policy for longer than Teeters likely would. Now that the Fed had promised to use this new framework, there was no option but to embrace it—anything less would threaten the Fed's credibility. That didn't mean he couldn't bemoan the situation privately. At several points during the three years that the Volcker shock lasted, the Chair lamented that the Fed was the only institution in town sufficiently insulated from political pressure to take on inflation. "The danger that I see, and I put it very crudely, is that everybody will be committed to an attack on inflation but it's entirely up to the Federal Reserve to perform," he told his colleagues.[55] In a meeting two years later, he was even more explicit: "Nobody else can think of anything else to do so they say that the monetary authority must have control over all these things and if they press the right button everything is going to come out right. The presumption is that there's a right button to press; I'm not sure there is. Some problems don't have that simple an answer."[56] Teeters and Volcker agreed that Fed interest-rate hikes alone were far from ideal, but that they were left with little other choice. The difference between the two came down to the pivotal questions of discretion and moderation.

While Volcker stood firm in support of the new operating procedures and the increasingly high rates they created, Teeters began in early 1980 to chart a separate path. The first year of the jolt was full of zigs and zags. President Carter asked the Fed to impose credit controls, which the governors agreed to do reluctantly. They initiated a sharp recession in the spring and summer of 1980, before the Fed moved to relax them. The economy bounced back unexpectedly in the late summer and early fall. Teeters was unconvinced that the recovery would be strong, and she began the first of two periods of principled dissent during the Volcker shock. "I am . . . strongly of the opinion that rates are already too high. We have already killed the housing market. We are depressing the automobile market. We have continued pressure on business fixed investment, and it's to a point where I think it will stall out," she told her colleagues during an FOMC meeting.[57] A year into the Fed's experiment, she'd seen enough to want looser policy and less volatility. Volcker and many of the other governors disagreed.

Yet Teeters was no dovish ideologue. In the first period of the Volcker shock, she hedged. After the chaos of the first year, the Fed maintained a tight monetary policy throughout the second year of the shock, 1981. Volcker was determined to snuff out inflation and organized the governors to keep monetary policy tight even as the economy was in free fall, defying monetary-policy orthodoxy. The consequences for American workers were horrific. From mid-1981 into late 1982, 2.9 million Americans lost their jobs, sending the unemployment rate into the double digits.[58] Estimates of the cost in terms of foregone output vary widely, but even using the most conservative assumptions, the recession destroyed around 20 percent of GDP.[59] But inflation was starting to ease, and many of the Fed's governors attributed it to their tight policy. Teeters was more wary. For her, it seemed as if the governors were inaccurately attributing the fall in inflation to their own actions. In July 1981, she told her colleagues, "May I remind you that we shouldn't take too much credit for the price easing? I never thought we were totally at fault for the price increases that we suffered from OPEC and food; and I don't think the fact that OPEC and food have calmed down has a great deal to do with monetary policy per se, except in the very long run." The implication of her position was that the Fed should be loosening policy, albeit gradually. "[W]e're really tearing at the fabric of the financial world and the economy. If we persist in having very high interest rates over very long periods of time, we're going to cause a disaster in this country. It may not be next month and it may not be next quarter, but it's going to be a severe problem and it's going to come down on our shoulders for having pushed the economy over the edge."[60] Over the ensuing months, the recession worsened, just as Teeters had predicted.

Surprisingly, despite her warning, Teeters did not buck her colleagues and continued to vote to support restrictive policy—for the time being. The explanation has more to do with her experience on Capitol Hill than at the Fed. Before she had returned to the Fed as a governor in 1979, she worked in Congress, analyzing how fiscal decisions affected output, employment, and inflation. That experience had given her a sophisticated understanding of just how pronounced an impact legislation could have on the American economy, which she would soon apply from her seat at the Fed.

Ronald Reagan's administration, which began in January of 1981, shepherded a dramatic tax cut through Congress that lowered the marginal income tax rates on top earners to the lowest levels in nearly fifty years.[61] There were no accompanying cuts in government expenditure, setting the stage for ballooning deficits, which conservative policymakers claimed would not climb as high as many predicted. They invoked a new, thinly supported economic theory that the tax cuts would spur so much growth that the additional taxes from the prosperity would outweigh the cost of the initial cuts. George H. W. Bush had called the ideas "voodoo economics" while he was running against Reagan in the 1980 campaign but changed his position after joining the ticket. Reagan administration officials admitted in 1981 that there was little empirical basis for the fantastical claims. "None of us really understands what's going on with all these numbers," the young head of the Office of Management and Budget, David Stockman, told Greider in a blockbuster article for *The Atlantic*.[62]

Teeters and Volcker foresaw that the significant tax cuts would stimulate the economy and increase inflation at the exact moment that the Fed had committed to raising interest rates high enough to rein it in. Volcker had publicly opposed the tax cut when Reagan campaigned on it in 1980, warning in his speeches of "a clash" between fiscal and monetary policy and throwing cold water on the idea that the tax cuts would somehow decrease the deficit. "Let us not be beguiled into thinking there are quick and painless solutions," he said in the fall of 1980.[63] But after the election, he increasingly kept his frustration private. Teeters likewise understood that in the wake of the tax cut, it would be nearly impossible to favor loosening monetary policy, even if the economy was falling into a recession. To do so would be to counteract all of the tightening she had already supported. Given that Congress seemed set to pass the stimulus early in 1981, the Fed had to hold the course. Teeters explained in private correspondence that the Fed had "reluctantly" agreed to keep interest rates high, reducing aggregate demand.[64] But even with her support for high rates in the Reagan tax cut period, she wanted to make it clear to her colleagues that this level of restrictive policy couldn't last much longer. She told them in November, "[W]e don't have complete control and . . . we could do extreme harm if the economy continues to run at these very low levels of real utilization."[65]

Rage was brewing in the country, and the Fed was increasingly the target. The Fed had historically been a behind-the-scenes institution, surrounded by a mystique of complexity and authority. Now with intense coverage of its historically tight monetary policy, it was increasingly front and center, seen as responsible for the millions of lost jobs that resulted from its quest to stabilize prices. Before the Volcker shock, Americans had shared a strong consensus that inflation was the country's top problem. As soon as the recession began in the second half of 1981, they suddenly changed their minds, now citing unemployment as the top concern—even though inflation remained elevated, despite recent improvements.[66] Americans could blame corporations, labor unions, and Congress for high inflation, but they had only one institution to blame for tight money and the resulting recession—the Federal Reserve. Construction workers sent two-by-four pieces of lumber inscribed with pleas for help, and auto dealers filled coffins with the keys to unsold cars and shipped them to the Fed's headquarters.[67] In December 1981, while the Board of Governors was meeting, a man wearing a trench coat entered the building with a revolver, a sawed-off shotgun, and a hunting knife in his backpack. When denied access at the entrance, he ran past security to the second floor of the building and approached the room where the governors were meeting. He removed the revolver from the bag but then took a seat outside the meeting room. When he put the gun in his pocket for a brief moment, security lunged and disarmed him.[68]

At the center of the Board Room in the Fed's headquarters in Washington stands a twenty-seven-foot-long mahogany table that can seat more than twenty people. It is surrounded by dozens of additional chairs for senior staff. A 1,000-pound brass chandelier hangs from the two-story-high ceiling, illuminating the granite inlaid on the surface of the table. At one end of the room stands a marble fireplace with a golden eagle hovering on the wall above. The grand setting can give FOMC meetings a theatrical feel, even though they are structured as group discussions. In the opening months of 1982, as Volcker's tight-money regime began to come apart, Nancy Teeters took center stage.

That February, as her colleagues on the board and Fed staff looked on, Teeters began an epic and prescient campaign of principled dissents. Steeled by her experience and convinced that she was right, Teeters informed her colleagues that she was finished, both with the operating procedures that had kept interest rates unusually volatile and with the tight nature of monetary policy. "We have bounced this economy all over the mat for three years with no growth," she said, and it had to stop.[69] As the meeting became increasingly heated, Teeters didn't budge, persisting in her calls to drop the new operating procedures and the high rates they had ushered in. After two and a half years of collaboration with only occasional dissents, Teeters now assumed the role of the strident antagonist to Volcker. She believed his policies had gone too far, and she was willing to step out of line and speak her mind, even if nobody else at the Fed would.

She wasn't entirely alone. Congress, the media, and the markets had also begun to urge Volcker to loosen policy, but he was determined to charge forward, committed to his increasingly quixotic quest. Volcker worried that releasing the vise too early might restart inflation. Any crack at the Fed could be seized upon by outsiders to strengthen their case for loosening. Given that she stood largely alone inside the FOMC, Volcker decided to make an example of her in the February meeting. After Teeters argued for increasing the permissible ranges for the monetary aggregates—a way of loosening monetary policy within their new operation procedures—Volcker met her with disbelieving dismissal. "I think monetary policy is much too tight for the state of the economy," she replied.[70]

Countering Teeters' push to loosen were several governors and Reserve Bank Presidents who were anxious to stand firm or even tighten further still. Consensus in the FOMC had fractured. By the end of the meeting, Volcker managed to cobble together a loose consensus to keep monetary policy tight but not intensify it.[71] Volcker knew that the move would deepen the recession, accelerating the rise in unemployment, but he continued to believe it was too risky to change course at this stage. "The decision was perhaps the single gravest error that the Fed policy makers committed during the liquidation of 1981–1982," wrote Greider. "It was as if the central bank had decided to start the recession all over again."[72] Teeters alone dissented, her "No" vote echoing in the cavernous, two-story room. "Eleven for, one against, Mr. Chairman," the Secretary recorded.[73]

By voicing her dissent, Teeters opened up space for her colleagues to question how long the Volcker shock should endure. A few weeks after the meeting, Frank Morris, the President of the Boston Reserve Bank and the longest-serving Reserve Bank President in the system, gave an unusually critical speech, effectively backing Teeters' position. Morris was not able to vote on the February directive because of the rotating nature of voting on the FOMC, but he could still use his position at the Boston Fed to express his opposition. His primary concern was even simpler than Teeters': the FOMC was stubbornly insisting on using the monetary aggregates for its decisions, but these very indicators were increasingly deeply flawed. Legal changes meant that deposit accounts could now pay interest, a seemingly small change that meaningfully scrambled the calculation of the monetary aggregates, making the numbers out of line with the historical methodology. "Just in time for their star turn, monetary aggregates had become unstable," Jennifer Burns wrote in a biography of Milton Friedman. "Aggregates had long been a meaningful measure of economic activity. But now a surge or fall in money was nearly impossible to interpret. . . . [A] rise in M1 could be a sign of monetary ease, or it could be a by-product of changing consumer behavior. The aggregates could not be controlled, or even predicted."[74] For these reasons, Morris argued that the Fed needed to drop its new operating procedures and return to assessing money market conditions more broadly, which would almost certainly prompt a loosening in monetary policy. While New York Fed President Anthony Solomon was unwilling to go as far as Teeters and Morris in the first months of 1982, he was also becoming increasingly skeptical of the utility of the monetary aggregates.[75]

After her February dissent and Morris' public support, Teeters felt increasingly emboldened to make her case. The press called her a "Fed maverick," and she was happy to explain her rationale for her dissent in public.[76] By the time the May FOMC meeting rolled around, Teeters was ready to prosecute her case more aggressively. Even though it was increasingly unreliable, data on the monetary aggregates had come in high for the year. If Volcker stuck with the new operating procedures, this would mean still more restrictive monetary policy, even though unemployment was approaching 10 percent. "[W]e are in the process of just pushing the whole economy not just into recession, but into depression," Teeters said to the FOMC members at their meeting. "As far as I'm concerned, I've had it with the monetary experiment. It's time to put this economy back together again and to get us some stability as to where we're going and how our interest rates are going to operate. I have very little respect for the long-term aggregate [ranges] and I don't feel we have to prove ourselves any more. I think it's time to operate as rational people and to try to get the economy at least started on a tentative recovery."[77]

It wasn't just the depth of the recession and unemployment that worried her. The financial system was teetering as well. The day before the meeting, a nearly 100-year-old stock and bond trading firm, Drysdale Securities, went bankrupt, spooking financial markets. By raising the price of money, the tight monetary policy heightened pressure on the riskiest financial actors, making it costlier for them to face short-term challenges by borrowing. Teeters rightly believed that high interest rates were putting an increasing number of financial institutions under pressure, threatening a broader financial crisis. "It's time just to say we [have] finished one job and to start the next one," she argued. No one else agreed. The vote was yet again eleven to one.[78] In retrospect, FOMC Vice Chair Solomon and Governor Rice said they regretted their May decision.[79]

Within months, Teeters' warnings of a deepening recession and financial fragility began to prove true, shifting the sentiment of the committee in her direction. For Volcker in particular, everything changed in the summer of 1982. Inflation was rapidly cooling, down to just over 5 percent, a result of a dramatic slide in oil prices from their 1980 peak as well as the restrictive Fed policy.[80] But even with falling inflation and unemployment at a postwar high, the FOMC met the following day and left monetary policy unchanged, with Teeters again the sole voting member dissenting. For the first time, the tone of the conversation began to shift as anxiety crept into the FOMC deliberations. In July, all of the mounting pressure threatened to break the financial system. Penn Square, a small but well-connected bank in Oklahoma, went bankrupt, igniting concerns about the balance sheets of other banks, including one of the nation's largest, Continental Illinois. At the same time, American banks had lent heavily to the Mexican government, which was increasingly struggling to meet its financial obligations, exposing the banks to significant problems if the country defaulted. The Fed extended $900 million to the Mexican central bank to stabilize the peso, a second package that built on aid provided earlier in the year.

Meanwhile, political pressure on the Fed to follow Teeters' recommendation to loosen was growing. Congress adopted a resolution in favor of fiscal and monetary policy coordination, a threat to the Fed's much-vaunted decision-making authority. The resolution suggested that the House might move on legislation to tie the Fed's hands by requiring it to adjust its monetary targets based on the budgetary impacts of Congressional decisions. The

Treasury Secretary, Don Regan, frustrated by its historically high borrowing costs and looking nervously toward the midterm elections, wanted to restore the Treasury Secretary to the Board of Governors and FOMC. At the White House, James Baker, a senior adviser to President Reagan, explored how Congress might constrain Federal Reserve independence by subordinating it to the Treasury.[81]

The financial fragility, deep recession, and political pressure were too much. At the July FOMC meeting, the dam broke inside the Fed. The FOMC members felt they had to make some gesture to accommodate the stress in markets and in Washington. "Caught between the two positions— political pressures, legislator threats, and fear of crisis on one side and concern about their credibility and the need to maintain the appearance of independence on the other—Volcker made a first small change in policy to lower rates," wrote the historian Allan Meltzer.[82] FOMC members decided to break with the new operating procedures they had been using for nearly three years. They also loosened monetary policy even though their guidelines, which remained primarily focused on the money supply, specifically did not allow for such discretion. Volcker, complaining of the overly "mechanistic" requirements of the operating procedures he had led the FOMC to adopt, urged the committee to adjust the reserve aggregates to ease policy modestly. The other members followed the Chair's recommendation, and markets took note. Within three weeks, the federal funds rate was down by 3 percent, making it significantly easier to borrow.[83]

But that discrete move would not be enough to stem the growing criticism of the Fed. In August, Senator Robert Byrd introduced legislation that would have required the Fed to lower rates to "normal" levels, and long-standing governors began to worry about Congress limiting the Fed's power. One governor believed that a continuation of ultra-tight monetary policy "would risk a second decline in the economy and we wouldn't survive that as an institution."[84] That month, Volcker began to speak more frankly inside the cocooned walls of the confidential FOMC meetings about his frustration with the extreme volatility that the new operating procedures had introduced. (The transcripts of the meetings were not public at the time.) "I, frankly, cannot live in these circumstances, given what is going on in the money markets, with violent moves in short-term rates in either direction. It would just be so disturbing in terms of expectations, market psychology, and fragility that it's just the wrong policy, period, during this particular period."[85] Even with the decision to loosen monetary policy in July, unemployment continued to rise for months, reaching 10.8 percent by the end of the year.

In October 1982, the Volcker shock came to an end. The FOMC gathered in the august Board Room for its regular meeting, and Volcker led with a bleak overview of the global economy. "[W]e haven't had a parallel to this situation historically except to the extent 1929 was a parallel," he said.[86] Three years of tight monetary policy and minimal discretion had led to persistent interest-rate volatility. When the Fed stepped back from guiding the money markets toward stability, they were prone to spiral into a state of dysfunction. Supply and demand could not function smoothly with the money market in chaos. The political pressure from Congress and the White House on the Fed to right the situation had never been stronger. "[I]f one wants to put it in terms of risk to the institution," Volcker said at the meeting, "if we get this one wrong, we are going to have legislation next year without a doubt. We may get it anyway."[87]

With growing political pressure, Mexico on the precipice of bankruptcy, unemployment climbing, and financial stress in the banking sector, few on the FOMC were interested in extending the volatility or the record tight monetary policy. If the committee was going to finally loosen, the Fed had to choose between using the existing procedures that had been established in 1979—which entailed uncontrolled interest rates and potentially high volatility in money markets—or returning to their previous approach, which allowed greater control over rates and volatility. The committee opted for the latter. This time, the vote was nine to three, with Volcker joining Teeters in the majority. In the meeting, she said little. She didn't have to. She had won.

Throughout the Volcker shock and her tenure at the Fed, Teeters became a sort of modern-day Cassandra, watching her accurate predictions dismissed by her colleagues. There is little doubt that those colleagues refracted her prognostications through her gender. Because she was often the lone voice in disagreement with her colleagues on the FOMC, the other members could see her as soft or even nagging. "She was sounding the alarm about unemployment in a way that irritates people," one staff member told Greider. "Of course [the governors] were humane and they were concerned about unemployment, but they didn't need anyone lecturing them on that. It was her tone, her mode of argument."[88]

Despite the dismissals, she persevered, perhaps strengthened by her experience, and she began to seek peers who could understand the unique challenges she faced. During the second half of her term, Teeters began a new tradition of a monthly lunch with the newly confirmed—and first female—Supreme Court justice, Sandra Day O'Connor. "They would compare notes on what it was like to be the only woman in these old institutions," Teeters' daughter remembered.[89] Those lunches almost certainly reinforced her willingness to stand up for what she believed in, even if she was in a minority of one. Toward the end of her service at the Fed, Teeters sent a memo to a fellow governor who had overstepped by interrupting her at an FOMC meeting and mischaracterizing her comments. "When you misrepresent what I've said, I will interrupt you. I also intend to bring it to your attention when you interrupt me . . . ," she wrote, carbon copying the letter and sending it to all fellow FOMC members. Nancy Teeters would not be dismissed.

Over the course of 1983, the Fed continued to loosen money policy and adopted a new implementation framework more akin to the one it had used for decades prior. With two rare exceptions, Teeters was now consistently back to voting with her colleagues and the Chair. Even so, the intense stress of her Fed tenure started to take a toll. Teeters and her husband separated for six months in 1983. Her husband received a melanoma diagnosis, his second, and had surgery to remove it. Her mother died in the fall of 1983, and her own ongoing back problems became more significant and debilitating. Eventually, Teeters and her husband reconciled, and she had surgery to help with the back pain, requiring her to miss FOMC votes in February of 1984.

As Teeters expected, Reagan chose not to renominate her to continue on at the Fed, preferring a Republican appointee. Her tenure ended by the summer of 1984. She landed a top job at IBM, and she and her husband had a fresh start in Connecticut. She retired at sixty and spent several years traveling the world and spending time with family. A year before she died, Teeters returned to the Fed for a luncheon to commemorate the 100-year anniversary of the institution. She was seated at a table with seven other women, including Janet Yellen, who was awaiting Senate confirmation to become the first female Fed Chair. "It was the first time I've been seated at a women's-only table and been the envy of the room," she said afterward.[90]

Many in economics and finance glorify the Volcker shock, seeing in it the ultimate conquest of inflation. It might be easy to look back on the legacy

of Nancy Teeters and see a stubborn holdout, a dissenter who tried in vain
to resist the painful but necessary medicine of high interest rates. That assessment aligns with the conventional—and gendered—typecasts that many
who look back approvingly on the Volcker shock have used, lionizing Volcker
at Teeters' expense. It also does not match what happened. Teeters aligned
with Volcker and voted for the new operating procedures, knowing that they
would raise interest rates precipitously in 1979.[91] She voted consistently with
the FOMC throughout 1981 for the most restrictive monetary policy in
American history. Even when she was aggressively dissenting in early 1982,
in her private correspondence she was still defending Fed actions, arguing
for a gradual loosening of monetary policy rather than something more dramatic.[92]

Despite these periods of support for tight money, Teeters took a principled stand for a monetary policy marketcraft that embraced two core
values—discretion and moderation—that Volcker and the majority of her
colleagues did not support. Through her actions, she showed that another
way was possible. Her initial vote with her colleagues for the new operating
procedures reflected a shared belief in the value of a onetime jolt, but not
necessarily a three-year period of restrictive policy. "I'm very uncomfortable
about the period we've been through. We choked the horse. Now, do you
want to completely strangle him or do you want to be able to ride him a little
further down the line?" she once asked.[93]

Most importantly, the Fed should not have given up its power to interpret the growing empirical data that revealed the relative strength of
the economy and financial markets. Whereas her colleagues wanted to tie
monetary policy to the mast, subjecting it to mechanistic actions that followed from formulae, she understood that indicators and models were all
programmed by humans, meaning that they could be flawed. It was the Fed's
responsibility to inquire, synthesize, and adjust the direction of its policy
decisions that made it such an important and unique institution. Teeters
made the case for returning to a monetary policy of discretion focused on
strengthening money market conditions, even before it became clear that
the Fed's measures of monetary aggregates were significantly off. When the
time came to loosen in early 1982, she was courageous enough to stand
alone in her recommendation. She favored doing so gradually and moder-
ately, snuffing out the last embers of inflation while supporting American

workers. Teeters was no obstinate objector, but rather a pragmatist who believed that the use of Fed discretion and moderation would be the best tools to crush an inflation largely caused by supply-side pressures.

In the history of marketcrafting, the Volcker shock is one of the clearest moments of public policy steering financial markets toward an outcome chosen by a particular set of leaders. Free markets did not create a disastrous recession and restore stable prices; the Fed did. There were other options. The recession could have been mitigated if policymakers had created and invested in institutions responsible for stabilizing the sources of inflation. The prices of energy and food are particularly prone to swings, yet no life or economy can function without them. The SPR, the primary institution responsible for stockpiling and buffering swings in energy markets, was not yet operational, and no similar system for addressing food price volatility yet existed.

Given the lack of options, policymakers turned to a single institution, the Fed, to use its power over the money supply to conquer inflation, whatever the cost. Teeter's marketcraft embraced that power. She did not just want to loosen faster than Volcker; she believed in a monetary policy that embraced the Fed's human power to interpret incoming data to decide what monetary policy to pursue. These seemingly subtle differences of marketcraft approach might have made a remarkable difference when it came to the depth and duration of the deep recession. If the Fed had more quickly embraced Teeters' outlook, reclaiming its mantle of discretion and moderation, it might have shortened the duration of the downturn while continuing to meet its inflation-fighting goals.

For her part, Teeters wondered if her primary legacy might be her battle against sexism. She wrote early in her tenure at the Fed: "I have been the *first* woman on *so many* all-male groups that I have frankly lost count of them. Maybe that is the most important thing that I have done—made it easier for women coming after me."[94] With the benefit of hindsight, it was not only her gender that made her tenure on the Fed so important. It was her steadfast dedication to the principles of discretion and moderation, values that would become a cornerstone for the work of future Fed leaders. Volcker returned to a policy that prioritized orderly, stable money markets, just in time for the Fed to manage a series of international and domestic financial crises. Even more in line with the Teeters focus on discretion was Volcker's successor as Chair, Alan Greenspan, who prioritized empirical analyses of economic activity to inform a policy of "fine-tuning." That effort to consolidate power and embrace discretion would make Greenspan one of the most effective marketcrafters ever.

As the Volcker recession began to fade, a different set of marketcrafters seized the stage—this time, not to restrain, but to build. Whereas Teeters had wielded her influence within an established institution, these business leaders shaped a Reagan-era industrial policy that created a new institution to strengthen America's economic power in the digital age. That work had started a few decades before in the flowering orchards of Palo Alto.

10

SAVING SILICON

ROBERT NOYCE & SEMICONDUCTOR
INDUSTRIAL POLICY (1983-93)

On a sunny day in 1959, a black limousine pulled into the parking lot of Fairchild Semiconductor, the leading manufacturer of the semiconductors that powered the early years of the digital revolution. Groves of apricot and plum trees surrounded the retrofitted warehouse that served as Fairchild's headquarters in Palo Alto, California. The concrete jungle of highways and office parks that became Silicon Valley would take another fifteen years to emerge. "Nobody had ever seen a limousine and a chauffeur out there before," wrote the journalist and novelist Tom Wolfe in *Esquire* in 1983. The engineers of Fairchild left their workbenches and desks to cluster at the front windows and gawk.

For the Fairchild employees, it wasn't just the car's appearance that made the day memorable. "It was the fact that the driver stayed out there for almost eight hours, *doing nothing*," Wolfe wrote. "He stayed out there in his uniform, with his visored hat on, in the front seat of the limousine, all day, doing nothing but waiting for a man who was somewhere inside." The driver was waiting for the chief executive officer of Fairchild Semiconductor's parent company, who lived "back east" in New York. He had come for the day to learn more about the growing subsidiary that would soon overtake the parent company in value and size. For Fairchild's tight-knit team, this glimpse of

New York corporate culture was not just unusual in the verdant landscape of the Santa Clara Valley. It felt foreign—and wrong.[1]

Robert Noyce, the boss of Fairchild Semiconductor, disdained the institutions of the East. Born in a small Iowa town, Noyce was one of four sons of a Midwestern Congregationalist preacher and a stay-at-home mother. As Noyce was growing up during years of economic depression and war, his family wandered about the plains in search of a welcoming community and a reliable income. They landed in Grinnell, Iowa, a college town of 7,000, which doubled as the center of the Congregationalist faith. Both of Noyce's grandfathers and his father were all preachers who propagated the nonhierarchical, communitarian tradition of their denomination. The Noyce parents expected their boys to reflect the values of the family and their faith each day, which meant being courteous and proper, attending Sunday school, and becoming Boy Scouts.

But Noyce did not want to be the predictable, well-behaved preacher's son. He wanted adventure and the respect that came with it. Noyce became a tinkerer, the kid who built a box kite to lift a person into the air from the instructions of *Popular Science* magazine—and then convinced other boys to try it with him. When the box kite failed to take off after he ran with it across the roof of a barn, Noyce tied it to the rear bumper of a neighbor's car, which lifted the thirteen-year-old into the air for a full thirty seconds. His clever childhood exploits earned him the attention and esteem of his peers and provided him a temporary escape from the yoke of religious duty.

Noyce enrolled at Grinnell College after high school and staked out a reputation as a well-liked, high-achieving golden child. That "halo" would follow him for the rest of his life. "Bob really was ten feet tall. He just appeared five-foot-eight to the untrained observer," said one colleague.[2] In college, he became a muscular young man, with a strong jawline and thick brown hair. He took up diving on the Grinnell team, sang in the chorus, and sailed through his coursework. Math and physics were his specialty, and the faculty at Grinnell rewarded his curiosity and acumen with special attention.

Powering all that success and charm was the same drive for attention and esteem that had caused him to push boundaries as a child. As a young adult, though, Noyce soon learned that it could take him to darker places. In May 1948, when Noyce was a college junior, he learned that his girlfriend was pregnant and he was the father. She soon decided to have an abortion. A few days later, he and some of his friends hosted a luau-themed party. They wanted a roast suckling pig with an apple or pineapple in its mouth to serve as the centerpiece of the gathering. Noyce and a friend took on the responsibility of procuring the main attraction. That night, the two crept onto the land of a neighboring farm and stole a twenty-five-pound piglet. Back at the dorm, the college boys figured out how to butcher it in a third-floor bathtub. "A frantically squealing animal, intoxicated young men with knives—the ruckus was such that students all over campus immediately knew something untoward was happening in Clark Hall," wrote Noyce's biographer Leslie Berlin.[3] Within hours, they had their prize: an apple in the pig's mouth and applause all around.

Noyce's religious impulses kicked in the next morning. He felt a wave of guilt that he attributed to stealing the pig, likely heightened from the news of the unwanted pregnancy. In the state of Iowa, livestock was a major social and economic asset and stealing an animal was a felony, with a minimum penalty of a year in prison. Noyce turned up at the farmer's home and apologized, but he had chosen the wrong farm to steal from. The farmer prosecuted the case, reporting the crime to the sheriff, who in turn informed Grinnell administration. Threatened with arrest and expulsion, Noyce was called to account for his boyish ways. A college administrator and friend of the family brokered a peace: the university would suspend Noyce for one semester and he would serve no jail time. Noyce spent the months of his suspension in New York, studying to get his actuarial license, a job he decided he never wanted to pursue.[4] The following spring, he completed his coursework at Grinnell and left Iowa for good.

In the years to come, Noyce's career took off. While at Fairchild, Noyce invented the integrated circuit, making possible the digital life we know today. Later, he co-founded Intel, making him one of the most respected tech entrepreneurs of the twentieth century and the "Mayor of Silicon Valley," according to the local press.[5] Noyce came under national scrutiny as he became increasingly successful, and the luau story grew to a mythological status in Noyce lore. Journalists and academics depicted it as a story of a daring, good-looking kid with a moral conscience who learned the important lesson of just how far he could push boundaries. For Noyce, however, there was a deeper lesson at play. His creative ingenuity and clever inventions may have won him admiration from peers, giving him independence from the strict oversight of school and church. But in the end, those same institutions kept him on track. If you're charming enough, the authorities will step in with help when times get tough. That insight proved invaluable decades later, when he turned to Washington to save Silicon Valley.

The invention of the semiconductor in the late 1940s was one of the most pivotal moments in the history of human civilization, on par with the invention of electricity or the nuclear bomb. The word "semiconductor" refers to a material with the capacity to regulate the flow of electricity between a conductor, such as copper, and an insulator, such as glass. But the real significance lay in the tiny devices that could be constructed with these materials.

William Shockley invented the most basic semiconductor, the transistor, in 1947, using a new material called germanium. Noyce learned about Shockley's work from a professor at Grinnell and decided after college to head to the Massachusetts Institute of Technology to study the new invention and get a PhD in physics. While there, he developed little affection for the traditions of academia and drifted away from his religious faith. During a brief post-degree stint in Philadelphia, Noyce married and had his first child while working in the small semiconductor research group of a radio and television manufacturer. He quickly became disillusioned, frustrated by only modest corporate investment in semiconductor work and unchallenged by his colleagues. One day Shockley himself called Noyce's home out of the blue. Impressed by Noyce's presentation of some of his research at a conference a few months earlier, he invited the younger man to California to interview for a job.[6] Within days, Noyce, who was charmed by the opportunity to make a name for himself in a place unencumbered by tradition and hierarchy, uprooted his family and moved west.

When Noyce signed up to work for Shockley, he joined a community of cutting-edge researchers pushing the frontiers of physics. Just a year later, Shockley's erratic and autocratic management style and refusal to invest in silicon (as opposed to germanium) transistors provoked Noyce and seven others—later known as the "Traitorous Eight"—to leave the company and form a new one of their own. To secure financing, Noyce had to head back east to New York, where he worked with a banker who approached twenty-two investment firms on his behalf before finding one that was willing to risk supporting the start-up. The Fairchild family made an initial investment and negotiated an option to buy the company at any time in the next eight years for $3 million.[7] That decision proved lucrative. Two years later, while leading Fairchild Semiconductor, Noyce and his team invented something almost as original as the transistor itself: the integrated circuit. By embedding multiple transistors into a single silicon chip, Noyce made it possible to miniaturize and mass-produce complex electronic systems.[8] That single innovation opened up endless possibilities, eventually making possible human travel to space, mobile phones and personal computers, and today's advances in artificial intelligence.

Decades before Google and Facebook, Americans had already fallen in love with the idea of a solitary entrepreneur in a California warehouse creating the future. But Noyce's innovation would have never happened in the first place—or later taken hold—without the involvement of the American government. Beginning in the Second World War, the Department of Defense funded academic and industrial R&D efforts to give the American military a tactical advantage. That early support contributed to Shockley's breakthrough invention of the transistor, but in the two decades afterward government support of chip manufacturing became increasingly critical.[9] From the late 1950s to the 1970s, federal funding accounted for nearly half of all research and development in semiconductor manufacturing.[10] The American military wanted better, smaller, lighter semiconductors for missile guidance and other advances in aviation—especially after the Soviets launched the first man-made satellite in late 1957. Noyce always said he hated taking government research dollars for Fairchild's work. "Government funding of R&D has a deadening effect upon the incentives of people," he said. "This is not the way to get creative, innovative work done."[11] These comments reflected Noyce's desire for autonomy and his visionary grasp of the potential civilian market in electronics. But historians have concluded that military contracts were crucial all the same. As one Fairchild veteran remembered, "We carefully chose [government projects] so that the government needed the product and it was work that we needed also in order to promote the commercial aspects of the product."[12]

Even more valuable than the government's research dollars was its commitment to be the first customer for the private sector's products. Over 80 percent of the items manufactured by Fairchild went to the military in 1960.[13] Reliable revenue gave manufacturers like Fairchild the confidence to move from ideas to production, and to survive the learning curve through which new products could become cheap enough for price-sensitive civilians. As late as 1962 the government was the *only* customer for integrated circuits.[14] By 1965, however, government purchases had fallen to a mere 55 percent of total microchip sales.[15] Business computing, such as IBM's breakthrough System/360, now constituted the fastest-growing market for chips.[16]

Noyce continued to rail against the "bullshit, waste, make-work, lack of incentive" of government agencies and the military, even though they were his most important customers. So as soon as he could sell to other customers, he did, and by 1963, he claimed that he was transitioning away from government contracts.[17] This may have been true regarding direct government contracts, but Noyce himself predicted that in 1965 "over 95%" of microchips would ultimately be used in the military or space programs.[18] Thousands of miles away from Washington, DC, Noyce's Fairchild, like other semiconductor-manufacturing companies, could not disentangle its business from government support.

Robust funding for research and development and big government procurement budgets did not add up to a marketcraft. American legislators were not attempting to grow or broaden the semiconductor industry in the 1960s, even if the military was spending lavishly to secure its products. The semiconductor revolution may not have been possible without government support, but it was not until the 1980s that Noyce and policymakers in Washington began to shape the semiconductor market to meet political goals. In the heyday of the 1960s, when Noyce was growing Fairchild and making millions for himself, government was the enemy to be tolerated, not the partner it would become.

In 1968, for the first time, humans saw the dark side of the moon. The new spacecraft, powered by the chips Noyce had pioneered, carried three Americans out of the Earth's orbit and into the moon's. The *Apollo 8* crew circled the celestial body ten times, taking an iconic image of Earth rising over the darkened lunar horizon, before the astronauts escaped the moon's gravitational pull and returned to Earth. Noyce and his colleagues may not have been feted on the nightly news, but they knew that voyage was only possible because of their work on the semiconductor.

What else might their innovation enable, if given proper support?

Impatient with recurring trips back east and frustrated that Fairchild's parent company was not investing enough in semiconductors, Noyce decided to leave. That year, Noyce and an old friend and colleague, Gordon Moore, resigned from Fairchild to start a new company of their own. They wanted to work at the cutting edge of semiconductor development, prioritizing risky research into memory storage and microprocessors over more conventional refinements of existing chips. They named their company "Intel." Noyce became the CEO.

Noyce intended to make the culture of Intel the antithesis of the East Coast establishment. Even while at Fairchild, he had loathed the idea of hierarchy and preferred to foster a culture of committees and shared efforts, an echo of the Congregationalist impulse to prioritize collaboration. Fairchild employees had worked in a warehouse with simple worktables and threadbare cubicles. There was minimal senior staff and no clear top executive team, and the doors of offices and meeting rooms were always open. Noyce made sure that there was no dress code, a contrast to the jacket and tie requirements of the East. "Sharp, elegant, fashionable, or alluring dress was a social blunder," Wolfe wrote. "Shabbiness was not a sin. Ostentation was."[19]

At Intel, Noyce took his campaign against hierarchy and signals of social status further. He dispensed with cubicles, forcing all employees to work together in the same room—the birth of the open floor plan. Virtually all engineers and employees received stock options in the company, and Noyce was at pains to avoid the creation of management teams. One of the first employees asked Noyce for Intel's organizational chart. "Noyce drew an X in the middle of a circle, and then drew seven more Xs along the perimeter of the circle," wrote Berlin. "As the amazed employee looked on, Noyce proceeded to connect the center X to each of the other Xs in the system so the drawing resembled a wagon wheel. The X in the center, said Noyce, was the employee asking the question." The other Xs were the executives.[20]

Whether it was because of this unorthodox culture or in spite of it, within years Intel had developed a pioneering memory chip and the microprocessor. The company grew in size and value, going public in 1971 only three years after its founding, which enriched Noyce further. Running a highly valued public business with thousands of employees and minimal hierarchy was not easy. Representatives from separate divisions inside the company, such as engineering and marketing, convened endless meetings to work out problems among themselves. These "councils" lacked vested power, working through issues by airing grievances and forging compromise.[21] To some, Noyce's radical attempt to dismantle hierarchy just fanned the flames of conflict. Andy Grove, who later became Intel's CEO, said Noyce let "people bite into each other like rabid dogs" in meetings.[22] Conflict averse, Noyce watched on with a "pained expression" as his employees fought. Even though he had been a corporate leader for more than a decade, Noyce never fired anyone until 1971.[23] But it also turned out that the labor-intensive aspects of production—perhaps the biggest potential sites for workplace conflict—were physically separated from the "nonhierarchical" campuses in the Valley, demonstrating that there was a limit to which Noyce's ideology could be taken. The emphasis on collaboration and participation risked interfering with physical production.[24] It was not hard to imagine that the supposed revolution in corporate style was a fig leaf covering the competing impulses in Noyce: to stick it to the voices of hierarchy and tradition back east, without losing the admiration of the people around him.

By the early 1980s, a new threat had emerged that overshadowed any challenges that Noyce's management style had created. Noyce had succeeded in realizing his long-held vision of a mostly civilian market in microelectronics. Government purchases accounted for only 10 percent of all integrated circuits sold.[25] Yet American semiconductor manufacturing was in free fall. The United States stood to lose what had been a booming market to a new, aggressive competitor: Japan.

A little over ten years after starting Intel, in 1979, Noyce left his operational responsibilities at the company. At the age of fifty-one, divorced and remarried with his children now in college, Noyce had become a mini-celebrity, one of the richest and most widely respected individuals in Silicon Valley. He intended this next phase of life to be filled with investing in new start-ups, doing occasional board work at Intel, and flying his planes to skiing destinations. But a growing anxiety in Silicon Valley punctured that idyllic dream: Japan might soon eclipse American economic dominance. Japan's economy had quadrupled in size over the past twenty years, growing at 7 percent a year.[26] Even though its growth leveled out in the 1980s, nearly half of Americans believed that Japan would supplant America as the globe's leading economic power by the end of the decade.[27] Japanese power threatened the success of Intel and semiconductor manufacturers in particular. In 1975, the American share of the global semiconductor-manufacturing market stood at 60 percent, but by 1987, it had fallen to below 45 percent. Industry predictions suggested it could be half that a few years later.[28] The leaders of the chip companies just had to look around to see what their future might look like: by 1987, the largest steel company in the world was Japanese, as was the largest bank.[29] America's trade deficit with Japan had grown to $56 billion, quadrupling from a decade earlier.[30]

This concern was not an abstract one for Noyce. He was responsible for keeping the chip industry afloat. In 1977, while still at Intel, Noyce had agreed to become the leader of a new industry-wide effort, the Semiconductor Industry Association (SIA), to encourage collaboration between manufacturers. Noyce and other CEOs could see the Japanese threat on the horizon. "Their intent is quite clear," he told *Fortune* magazine in an article on Japanese "spies in the Valley" a year after he took the role. "They are out to slit our throats, and we'd better recognize that and do something about it."[31] Noyce and others were incensed at Japanese economic policy, which closed their market to American fabricators. As the 1980s began, Noyce and other leaders in the Valley became increasingly convinced that the Japanese chipmakers were "dumping" their products in international markets, selling them below the cost of production to gain market share and snuff out American competitors. The American semiconductor industry shed tens of thousands of jobs, and Intel lost money for the first time in 1986. Other companies were losing even more.[32]

At first, Noyce and others in the semiconductor industry held tight to their libertarian instincts. The best action government could take, they believed, was to unleash more venture capital by allowing pension funds to invest in riskier assets.[33] Noyce also advocated for lowering the capital gains tax rate that investors paid to boost the industry, claiming that Intel would not exist had it not been founded before capital gains taxes were raised in 1969.[34] By 1981, though, the "less regulation and lower taxes" posture was beginning to change. "We all believe in motherhood and the open market," said Charles Sporck, who had been Noyce's deputy at Fairchild and shared Noyce's responsibility at the SIA of organizing the industry against the Japanese threat. "I dig the laissez-faire free market approach myself, but the world isn't going along with it," he continued. "Back three years ago, I was anti-government and viewed all politicians as a bunch of bastards. I have to say that is not the case now."[35]

Over the next four years, Noyce and other leaders in the semiconductor industry transformed into activists for a robust federal marketcraft. Sporck was the first to get there— "We must have an industrial policy," he said in 1981—and Noyce wasn't far behind.[36] With declining market share and disappointing revenues, the SIA convened industry leaders to discuss what could be done. Like the old meetings Noyce ran at Intel, they created much space for debate, but there was little agreement on how to proceed. Noyce was not going to impose a plan from the top.[37] Yet between 1981 and 1984, the industry continued to see its global market share decline, and IBM, anxious to partner with other industrial heavyweights to turn the industry around, joined the SIA, enhancing the organization's power. In 1985, Noyce expressed the consensus of corporate leaders that chipmakers were experiencing "the worst recession in the history of our industry," and Japan bypassed America in global semiconductor market share that year.[38] As they became more desperate, Noyce and industry leaders settled on a strategy: they needed direct, targeted government support to survive.[39]

Within months, the industry group Noyce led became one of the best organized and most powerful lobbying outfits in Washington. The chip industry's newfound consensus meant that they could speak with one voice on an issue of global competitiveness and national security. Noyce began to make regular trips to the capital and recruited his fellow CEOs to join him. Their first order of business was to support the passage of a cooperative research act to loosen antitrust restrictions on joint ventures of research and development.[40] The success of that effort in 1984 whetted their appetite, and Noyce and Sporck began to think concretely about what government policy they wanted for semiconductors in particular. The turnaround from disdain for government to admiration was remarkable. Jeff Bingaman, the Senator from New Mexico, had joined Noyce and other leaders from Intel at a dinner in 1983 at which they claimed to be handling the challenges just fine. But only two years later, they showed up in Bingaman's office with a list of specific requests to help the industry. "Their opinion about the value of government involvement had changed dramatically," Bingaman said.[41]

Over the coming months and years, Noyce led the effort to secure government support for American semiconductor manufacturing. His agenda had two prongs: first, take Japan to task for "unfair" trade practices, and second, earmark hundreds of millions of public dollars for semiconductor research and development.

The antiestablishment California entrepreneur had evolved into an aspiring marketcrafter. Noyce spent half his time in Washington in the mid-1980s, lobbying Republicans and Democrats, accepting awards, and joining cocktail parties and dinners around town.[42] Invited to serve on a commission that President Ronald Reagan set up to explore how to boost American "competitiveness," Noyce used the perch to make the case for an industrial policy focused on "industries of the future," including semiconductors, rather than "sunsetting" industries like steel, which were also seeking support. The SIA petitioned the United States Trade Representative (USTR) to review Japanese tariffs and the dumping of chips. The discovery of a "smoking gun" memo from Hitachi that discussed conquering the American market with artificially low prices catalyzed Reagan's team to take action.[43] Noyce's SIA was so involved in the efforts to apply pressure on the Japanese that his team was given a room in the USTR building to work from while the negotiations took place.[44] As a result of American pressure, Japan dropped their tariffs on American chips in 1985, opening their market to semiconductor imports. The following year, Japan agreed to stop selling their chips below cost to American firms and to help secure 20 percent of the Japanese semiconductor market for foreign firms within five years. These commitments, if fulfilled, stood to help Noyce and his peers. When the Reagan administration judged that the Japanese were not complying a year later, it slapped 100 percent tariffs on $300 million of Japanese imports.[45]

The second step for Noyce was securing government funding for better chips. The semiconductor companies began to sketch out what form a public-private research effort might take. In 1985, with Noyce in Washington, Sporck took on the shuttle diplomacy to convince chip manufacturers to pool their money and knowledge into a centralized vehicle for research and development dubbed Sematech, shorthand for semiconductor-manufacturing technology. The recent change in antitrust law meant that companies could share "precompetitive" research insights, and Sporck and Noyce believed that collaboration could speed up the pace of chip development. By the end of the year, White House aides were circulating SIA memos mentioning cooperative research.[46] Soon the Department of Defense set up a

Science Board Task Force to review its supply chain for critical technologies, including semiconductors. Noyce joined that group too.

By 1987, the deal was done, and Sematech was born. Sporck and Noyce had secured the agreement of fourteen chip manufacturers, representing 80 percent of American semiconductor-manufacturing capacity, to create a joint research effort to boost the sector's performance. Each company agreed to pay 1 percent of their semiconductor sales revenue—at least $1 million and no more than $15 million—per year.[47] The companies considered pursuing their goals without government support, but Noyce and Sporck believed they needed matching funds from the government to make it work. Noyce used his position on the Defense Science Board to convince the Pentagon that its supply chains could not rely on foreign chip production to power its weapons. If the American military wanted to preserve its global power, American chip manufacturers had to thrive.[48] Noyce knew what form Pentagon support should take: telling the White House and Congress to fund the new R&D consortium. In late 1987, Congress agreed, appropriating an initial $100 million to Sematech to match the $100 million from the private sector. Austin, Texas, won a competitive bidding process for Sematech headquarters, and state and local officials chipped in another $50 million. Congress continued to fund at the $100 million annual level for the next five years.

In prioritizing collaboration and seeking government support, the American companies were copying much of what the Japanese had done over the past two decades to boost their own companies, enhancing the quality of production and bringing down their R&D costs. "[We are] adopting some of the elements of the Japanese model, a model that seems to be working better than our own," Noyce said.[49] Government and tech leaders needed to work together to make the market work for their shared interests. A year after Congress committed its first tranche of funding, over a thousand people attended the opening of Sematech's campus in Austin. The Austin Symphony Orchestra performed on a red, white, and blue platform with an enormous American flag hoisted above, and jets from Bergstrom Air Force Base flew overhead in an aerial salute.[50]

A few months before the Sematech opening celebration, Noyce stood on a peak at the Continental Divide in the Rocky Mountains outside of Aspen, wrestling with an important decision. It was the summer of 1988, and he had hiked to the mountaintop with his wife, Ann Bowers, whom he had first met when she was at Intel. Noyce was sixty years old and worth over $100 million. He owned multiple planes, a 6,500-acre California ranch, and a vacation home in Aspen. Despite all of his success, he felt like his legacy hung by a thread. As American chip manufacturing faltered, so too might what people thought of Robert Noyce. "I prefer not to see all of [my] life's work go down in flames," he told a friend.[51]

For the past six months, Noyce, Sporck, and another colleague had been overseeing Sematech's setup, but they had struggled to find a CEO, despite considering hundreds of candidates. The defense agency responsible for dispensing Sematech funds was threatening to withhold the money given the delay. After a visit to Sematech's construction site, Noyce sat next to Sporck on the flight back to California. As they sipped Beefeater gins, Noyce floated the idea that he should take on the CEO role.[52] That would require the kind of singular dedication to a start-up more typical of someone hungry for early career success. It also would mean he'd have to leave his longtime home in California. Sporck supported the idea, and Noyce mulled it over for a few days. Perched at the Rocky Mountain summit, the wind howling in their faces, Bowers agreed to make the move with her husband, and Noyce decided to take the job. The next week, the two flew to Washington for the announcement, and another week later, they arrived in Austin.[53]

Noyce's first order of business was to get specific about Sematech's mission. Congress and industry had vaguely charged it with recovering semiconductor market share from the Japanese, but no one, including Noyce, had a clear vision of how to do that.[54] Before Noyce became CEO, Sematech's initial leaders decided to build a state-of-the-art chip fabrication facility. Sematech planned to induce firms to pool their knowledge about how to produce cutting-edge chips, creating new insights and efficiencies in the process. In thirty-two weeks, a record for the industry, Sematech built and made operational a "clean room" fabrication facility, and the fourteen member companies sent some of their best engineers to live in Austin and begin work together.[55]

Within months of taking control, Noyce shifted Sematech's focus. Like other industries of mass production, semiconductor manufacturing required precise and customized equipment. A company like Intel, focused on end-product manufacturing, had to buy this equipment from a firm that specialized in equipment design and manufacture. In early 1989, a Sematech employee reported back the results of a broad industry assessment: "The chip makers' biggest headaches stemmed not from technological problems but from difficulties with suppliers."[56] The consortium's own member manufacturers expected to buy less than 40 percent of their equipment from American suppliers; the rest would come from the Japanese.[57] This was a sharp reduction from previous years, and potentially a far more serious problem than Japanese dominance of end-product manufacturing. If Japanese firms dominated the market, they would decide which technologies received investment, leaving American manufacturers with little say over their direction. Japanese suppliers would likely favor their domestic counterparts, further disadvantaging the US industry. To take an example that Noyce might have considered: if Intel's managers wanted to produce a special new chip, say to use in a personal computer, they would be at the mercy of a Japanese equipment supplier who might also happen to own their own semiconductor fabrication plant and their own personal computer business. Why would they help Intel? And how, operating like this, would the United States ever eclipse Japan?

More times than he could count, Noyce had promised Congress and Pentagon officials that government support would secure American semiconductor independence. But without a coordinated effort to strengthen the equipment makers, the industry could be out of business.[58] Noyce realized that the urgent need for Sematech was not end-product manufacturing—it was coordinating firms such as Intel with their upstream suppliers.[59]

Within weeks of getting the report, Noyce dropped Sematech's initial mandate to encourage "horizontal" collaboration for cutting-edge manufacturing practices. He also canceled plans to build a second fabrication plant.[60] Sematech's goal became shoring up a fraying supply chain, encouraging "vertical" collaboration between the hundreds of equipment companies spread across the United States and the manufacturers who used their products to make the chips.[61]

This new strategy had little of the sparkle of cutting-edge technology. It wouldn't generate headlines like building a brand-new factory in record-breaking time. Instead, the action would take place out of the spotlight, as the consortium assembled best-in-class engineers to collaborate effectively. Talent flocked to Austin, inspired by the ambition of the project and Noyce's commitment. Engineers usually came for two years and thrived in the environment of high standards and strong talent—nearly all said they would do a second tour of duty if asked.[62]

Led by Noyce, Sematech worked with the equipment manufacturers and business leaders to develop a "road map" for what the next ten to fifteen years in the industry might look like. Identifying the most difficult technological challenges and roadblocks, Sematech forced the kind of cross-sector communication that had never happened before, enabling companies to prioritize the development of the technologies most likely to be useful—and lucrative. Leaders met several times a year to update the road maps, revising goals and timetables given the changing industry dynamics. The road map for the industry became an operational plan for Sematech itself, with the organization making decisions about where to focus its attention and funding based on it.[63] Sematech gradually narrowed its active projects, decreasing from sixty in 1990 down to twenty just three years later, preventing investment in initiatives unlikely to succeed or unnecessary duplication.[64] In addition to the road maps, Sematech developed industry-wide standards for hardware and software to help manufacturers and suppliers use a common language to evaluate the function and value of products.[65]

As they identified priority technologies, Sematech brought equipment providers and manufacturers together to refine how the products might work in concert. Sematech engineers procured test equipment and brought its designers into direct collaboration with the chip-manufacturing teams who would eventually use it. Meeting together in Austin, often in the "clean room" facilities, the combined teams tested the technology under normal and stressed conditions, identifying errors and slippages or new innovations to improve its effectiveness. Semiconductor manufacturers were soon able to bring their plants online faster, decreasing the number of unexpected problems and shortening their production cycles.[66]

The sleek, state-of-the-art fabrication facility of Sematech's early days was useful, but not for the reasons that many had first expected. Cutting-edge innovation had been eclipsed by something much more prosaic: good communication. "The new research agenda has shifted the consortium's focus from the development of a complete state-of-the-art production process in its Austin facility to knowledge diffusion and technology transfer," wrote several researchers who studied how to best spur collaborative research.[67] By the early 1990s, Sematech leaders were earmarking half of the R&D budget for equipment production improvement, leaving the advanced manufacturing fabrication facility working at only a little more than half capacity.[68] All of Noyce's emphasis on councils and collaboration at Intel and Fairchild in the decades prior had set him up to prioritize cross-sector collaboration in the final phase of his career.

The workers on Sematech's campus seemed to orbit around Noyce's charm. Employees saw in him a godfather of the semiconductor industry and an advocate for their work in Washington and around the world. In May of 1990, an equipment supplier told a California newspaper that Americans needed to "change their idols," and nominated Noyce to become part of a new American pantheon. When Noyce returned to Austin from giving a talk in California, he arrived at the Sematech headquarters to discover the employees had designated it "Bob Noyce Day." They had printed out T-shirts for the surprise event with Noyce's photo and the phrase "Bob Noyce, teen idol." A photo from the day shows Noyce crouching with a grin, surrounded by thirty-five women wearing the T-shirt.[69]

Two days later, Noyce went for a morning swim. Feeling unwell afterward, he lay down for a nap, suffered a heart attack, and died. He was sixty-two. A thousand people attended his memorial service in Austin, and over two thousand in Silicon Valley.[70] Without him, the progress the American semiconductor industry had made—premised on his ability to orchestrate many different players and interests—was at risk.

President George H. W. Bush called Noyce's wife, Ann Bowers, to offer his condolences. She thanked him, and then pivoted to a request. It was no secret that Bush wanted "to scale back projects smacking of an 'industrial policy.'"[71] The grieving widow told the President that the best way to honor Noyce's legacy was to continue to support Sematech. Bowers suggested he get clear with his staff about his commitment, just to be sure there were no misunderstandings.[72] The day after Noyce's California memorial, Bowers flew to Washington to meet with government officials with whom Noyce had warm relationships. Noyce may have been dead, but Bowers, like many others in the chip industry, was determined to lock in government support to see his final mission through.[73]

A new CEO at Sematech, William Spencer, arrived at headquarters a few months later and told its employees that "Bob Noyce set a vision for us, and it's up to us to implement that vision." After the pep talk, he boarded Noyce's

plane to head to Washington to ensure support continued.[74] Spencer did not
have the same charm as Noyce, but he supported Noyce's strategic approach
and managed to ensure that the government-industry partnership endured.
In February 1991, Bush submitted a budget request. Whatever his ideological reservations about industrial policy, the President recommended that
Congress renew Sematech's funding at the full $100 million per year level.[75]

Four years after Noyce's death and six years into Sematech's life, the United
States regained its position as the world's top manufacturer of semiconductors. In 1994, America made 48 percent of the world's chips and Japan's share
had fallen to 36 percent.[76] American chipmakers were also making a lot more
money, and concerns about their imminent demise had faded.[77] Two years
later, all of the jobs lost in the 1980s had returned.[78] The upstream equipment suppliers rallied as well. When Intel bought $300 million worth of
equipment for a new plant in 1992, 60 percent of it came from American
sources. Before Sematech, the company had expected to be buying 70 percent of its equipment from Japan.[79]

   Even Sematech's most fervent admirers never claimed that the consortium was the only factor in the resurgence of American chip manufacturing.
Japan's decision to change its import and industrial policies under intense US
pressure boosted demand for American chips and raised the price of those
made in Japan. A deep economic recession in Japan that began in 1991 also
undercut the country's efforts to keep up with American innovation. Those
macroeconomic factors handicapped the Japanese, but most analysts and the
leaders of the American chip companies themselves believed that Sematech
had made the difference.[80] Intel claimed it had saved up to $300 million from
greater production efficiencies as a result of its $17 million of investment in
Sematech. That estimate may have been an outlier, but empirical analysis
showed that for every dollar that companies invested in the initiative, they
gained between $1.40 and $2.80 in return.[81] Researchers analyzing R&D investments found cost savings of nearly 10 percent.[82] Given the importance of
semiconductors to Silicon Valley and the military, lawmakers in Washington
were generally satisfied with the returns. By 1993, the US government had
invested $500 million, a rounding error in an annual budget over $1 trillion.

   There were some failures. The Sematech team invested heavily in
lithography, the technology that transferred intricate patterns of circuits

onto the silicon chip. One Massachusetts-based company alone, GCA, received $75 million to support its technological advancement. But the company went bankrupt in early 1993.[83] The setback highlighted ongoing challenges with high-tech marketcrafting. At the level of pure technology, historian Chris Miller writes that "GCA delivered far beyond expectations." The problem was a lack of guaranteed demand for brand-new products—exactly the problem that NASA and the Pentagon had solved for Bob Noyce in the 1960s.[84] In principle, there was no reason the government couldn't have offered a demand guarantee to GCA. But the end of the Cold War, which some had hoped would usher in a new age of explicitly civilian-oriented industrial policy, instead created serious political obstacles for more assertive state action in the economy. Inaction created new problems decades later.

The same year GCA failed, three of the initial fourteen companies that had joined Sematech left the consortium, a result of Sematech's decision to focus on more efficient equipment production over advanced chip production itself. Ironically, the departure of a few dissatisfied companies signaled the success of the effort as the Sematech strategy came more clearly into focus. Noyce was empowered with enough money and discretion—by both the corporate members and the government—to pursue a strategy that he believed would best support the semiconductor industry. The strategy would not satisfy all of the companies in the industry, but by the early 1990s, it seemed clear his approach had largely worked. "It would not be an understatement to say Sematech saved the industry," said the chairman of Silicon Valley Group, the second-largest US semiconductor equipment supplier.[85] Even a representative from one of the departing companies had to admit that "'[Sematech is] good for the industry—it's just not necessarily good for us."[86] In 1993, the *New York Times* reported that "[W]hen its president and chief executive, William J. Spencer, goes to Washington these days, it is not so much to ask as to bask."[87]

By the time the United States retook the lead in semiconductor manufacturing in 1994, the world was changing. The dissolution of the Soviet Union led to a period of globalization, and American political and military leaders became less concerned about having an entirely American supply chain for critical equipment. Silicon Valley's future seemed increasingly tied to the software revolution rather than the manufacture of hardware such as chips. Having succeeded in attaining their goal of retaking the lead in global market share, the Sematech board in 1994 decided to decline additional federal funding.[88] That decision helped them prepare for the coming political backlash to Sematech's work. The Republican Congress elected in 1994 and led by Newt Gingrich put Sematech directly in its sights. By 1996, all government funding had ceased.[89] At the same time, the Japanese created a new R&D consortium modeled on the American effort, and one company petitioned to join Sematech directly. In 1996, Sematech opened to foreign members.[90]

In the decades that followed, semiconductor companies in the United States began to focus on design, outsourcing the production of chips to overseas foundries. As the supply chain for increasingly advanced chips became more global, American companies became the architects of chips rather than the fabricators. This trend hit an inflection point after the tech recession of 2001, when domestic fabrication capacity collapsed and never recovered fully.[91] Shareholders also balked at the cost of building new fabs, which ballooned from hundreds of millions of dollars in the 1980s to tens of billions today.[92] Sematech's close integration of equipment suppliers and chip fabricators was increasingly irrelevant, even though the United States had continued to dominate the global market for semiconductor equipment.[93] American policymakers and military leaders were content to preserve America's lead in semiconductor design and allow for chip manufacture to happen largely overseas. In 2015, the State University of New York Polytechnic Institute absorbed the last remnants of Sematech.

Sematech's successful model might have been developed and extended to other American industries. In the early 1990s, other business leaders, including those in the American automotive industry, toyed with creating a similar research consortium.[94] If Noyce had lived, he might have championed a more general application of marketcraft, grounded in his own experience of saving Silicon Valley. "Sematech is unique, but the idea of getting government, industry and academia together for a national purpose is not at all new," Noyce said before he died, citing support for American farmers and aerospace technology.[95] Industrial policy, he admitted, "carries a lot of political baggage with it." But Sematech "might be a model that would be, or could be, endorsed by a lot of Americans. Even if they are violently opposed to industrial policy."[96] His conversion from avowed libertarian to collaborative marketcrafter might have sketched a pragmatic path for other business leaders to follow, and reminded policymakers that effective industrial policy was possible.

Instead, a new story about how markets work emerged in the 1990s, premised on the idea that minimizing state involvement would bring more prosperity. Sematech's successes faded as policymakers began to focus on fostering financial innovation to enhance the efficiency of "self-regulating" markets. But at the same time as the deregulatory rhetoric took hold, the practice of American marketcraft continued to flourish and develop, this time through the work of another supposed libertarian—Alan Greenspan.

11

THE MAESTRO'S MARKET

ALAN GREENSPAN & FINANCIAL INNOVATION (1993–2006)

On a warm summer day in 1959, a thirty-three-year-old Alan Greenspan was cruising down the highway that lines the east side of Manhattan at the wheel of his brand-new black Buick Electra convertible. It was a beauty, with red interior leather seats and all the latest features, including air conditioning. "It did cheer me up driving on highways with J.S. Bach loudly pouring out of my car radio speakers," he later wrote. Greenspan loved his cars. A year later, he upgraded to a blue Cadillac El Dorado, also a convertible. The only problem was the cops. Greenspan regularly got speeding tickets on the morning commute. Given his surging financial success, he just paid them and kept on accelerating.[1]

Greenspan had grown up sharing a two-room apartment in northern Manhattan with his grandparents and mother. The single child of Jewish immigrants, he was obsessed with baseball and trains. He spent long hours in solitary study of the players' statistics and the timetables of modern railroads. He completed his undergraduate and master's degrees at New York University in economics, playing saxophone in downtown clubs on the side, and then started a PhD at Columbia. His mentor Arthur Burns inspired Greenspan with his sharp economic analysis and research methods. In 2011, after Greenspan was well into retirement, he pulled down from the shelf an old copy of Burns' 1946 book, *Measuring Business Cycles*, which was full of graphs and tables chronicling the rise and fall of interest rates, railroad stock prices, and coal and iron production. "It was a window on the economic thinking of a different age, and he wanted me to see where his love of statistics had come from," his biographer Sebastian Mallaby wrote.[2]

By the time Greenspan was driving down the Manhattan highway in his new Buick convertible, he was the wealthy owner of an investment advisory firm. A frequent guest at the house parties of the libertarian émigré and writer Ayn Rand, the introverted Greenspan was beginning to enjoy a rich social and cultural life in New York. At cocktails and dinners, he cultivated a personal style of pursuing respectful but provocative disagreement, peppering his monologues with abundant empirical detail.

Greenspan differed from his peers in the Randian salon and from his colleagues on Wall Street. More than his intellectual prowess or his quantitative skills, his success lay in balancing ideology with pragmatism. Greenspan spent his life making short-term decisions to build his own personal power or stabilize the economy, while at the same time pursuing a values-laden theory of how financial markets should work. Committed to financial innovation and efficient markets, Greenspan used the Federal Reserve's tools to shape markets according to his beliefs, illustrating that "self-regulating" markets needed cultivation and management to flourish. This ability to implement a big-picture vision through highly technical actions in government made him a successful marketcrafter.[3]

The same year he bought his first convertible, Greenspan presented his first major paper, "Stock Prices and Capital Evaluation," at a conference a few days after Christmas. The American Finance Association's annual gathering took place at the Shoreham Hotel in Washington, DC. (Katherine Ellickson was just down the hall, participating in a session on statistics and health care. Jesse Jones had lived upstairs while he ran the RFC twenty years prior.) Even though Greenspan had suspended his efforts to earn a PhD, he was conducting original research and wanted to publish it. In his presentation, Greenspan argued economists had overly focused on government spending to smooth the business cycle. They had failed to see that the value of assets—like stocks, bonds, homes, or companies—shaped the decisions that investors and consumers made. Robust valuations could spur investment or encourage consumers to buy more, just as weak valuations could lead to periods of extended stagnation. The implications for public policy were clear: to build a prosperous and stable economy, central bankers should be guided by the value of the stock market in addition to price stability and unemployment.[4]

To many today, this idea may sound self-evident. But in 1959, when banking and finance were still relatively conventional fields, Greenspan believed in the need to support financial innovation to enhance market efficiency. The stock market transformed illiquid ownership interests in companies into shares to be bought and sold freely. The more these assets circulated, the more confidence investors had in a market price. As investors were increasingly able to invent ways to market assets, the value of those assets would become more precise in a well-functioning market. The economists John Gurley and Edward Shaw used those premises to argue that financial innovation held the key to making markets more efficient. Greenspan, building on their work, observed that it was not only banks that created money, but any firm that was able to make an asset more liquid and marketable. Even risk might be made into an asset and traded at a market price. "Gurley [and] Shaw showed me that all financial intermediaries can be thought of as doing the same thing. They improve the economy by reducing risk through diversification," Greenspan said. When intermediaries make an asset marketable, they improve the efficiency of the financial system. "Gurley [and] Shaw allows you to cut through all the complexity and get to the essence of finance."[5] Finance became particularly valuable for its ability to create ever more efficient ways to enable exchange.[6]

Greenspan later became known as a champion of deregulation, but that is only part of his story. Driven by his faith in financial innovation, Greenspan wanted to nurture and cultivate the financial sector's efforts to increase leverage and distribute risk. The 1959 speech became the foundation of his eventual PhD dissertation and the driving force behind his marketcraft.[7]

In the decades that followed, Greenspan vaulted to the top of the American economic establishment. In the 1970s, he became the Chair of the CEA, agreeing to join in the weeks before President Richard Nixon's resignation and staying on under the leadership of Gerald Ford. He had partnered with his friend Treasury Secretary Bill Simon to shape energy markets to be more resilient and reduce regulations on several industries, including airlines and trucking. Over time, Greenspan became an increasingly vocal activist for "free-market" policies. He joined Simon and others in encouraging

Republican leaders, including Ronald Reagan, to run on a pro-market, anti-government agenda.

Neither Simon nor Greenspan was a pure libertarian in practice in the 1970s, but that did not slow the ascent, rhetorically at least, of free-market ideology in the 1980s. The economic and political instability of the two prior decades—ongoing high inflation, two energy crises, the withdrawal from Vietnam, the Civil Rights Movement, the impeachment and resignation of a President—had made many Americans wary of government action and inclined to reduce the imprint of federal rule making in particular. Greenspan said he wanted the same. A group of academics, economists, and lawyers—later called "neoliberals"—had undertaken the project of creating a modern operational framework for governing based on these ideas. With Reagan's election in 1980, they saw their opening to offer a simple story. Groups of people could not be trusted to solve problems collaboratively unless they were following the individual profit motive. The "invisible hand" coordinated the pursuits of individual avarice, creating enduring prosperity through competition. The role of government was to ensure that markets could function by guaranteeing property rights, a stable currency, and a generally educated citizenry—and stop there.[8] Many left-of-center neoliberals, who eventually dominated the Democratic Party, expected government to redistribute a share of the gains from economic growth to the poor and middle class, creating "equal opportunity" and a safety net for unlucky individuals. For many on the right, even those redistributive moves would likely lead to a bloated government that would slow growth and harm the poorest through its bumbling maneuvers to improve circumstances. Rhetorically, voices on all sides agreed that boosting prosperity required relying more on private markets than government action.

By the 1990s, neoliberalism had become so permeating and commonplace that it had transformed international trade, law, and finance by dismantling antiquated regulatory frameworks, encouraging the creation of new free-trade agreements, and lowering the overall tax rate.[9] "When the neoliberal consensus first formed in the 90s, think of everything Washington got done: the deregulation of finance and banking, welfare reform, NAFTA, the creation of the WTO, integration of China into global markets, and even the invasion of Iraq," said Oren Cass, Mitt Romney's policy director in 2012 and the leader of center-right think tank American

Compass. "They couldn't stop agreeing on things that we might, in hindsight, say weren't so great."[10]

In 1987, Ronald Reagan was on the hunt for a Fed Chair who would embrace the deregulatory efforts of his administration. Fed Chair Paul Volcker was resisting Republican efforts to encourage consolidation in the banking sector and allow nonbank corporations to be able to own banks. Anxious for new leadership at the Fed, Reagan nominated Greenspan. Greenspan told the *New York Times* just before his interview with the President that "I do not have a fear of undue concentration of banking powers."[11] Not only did he not have a problem with it; he later set out to create the specific institutional form—a full-service or universal bank—that he thought best. He sailed through his confirmation with only two Senators voting against him.

Within weeks of his becoming Chair, the extent of Greenspan's libertarian view of government was tested. On Monday, October 19, 1987—known ever since as "Black Monday"—equity markets cratered, with the Dow Jones losing 22.6 percent in a single day. With heads spinning in the United States and abroad, Greenspan issued a terse press release committing the Fed to using its tools "to serve as a source of liquidity to support the economic and financial system." The statement was as broad as it was short, word-smithed to create a sense that all options were on the table for emergency stabilization. Former Fed Chairs Bill Martin, Arthur Burns, and Paul Volcker had never responded to a drop in the stock market so forcefully, but Greenspan had built his early reputation as a researcher and economist on the idea that the stock market needed to be robust and stable for the economy to grow. He was now wielding the power of the nation's central bank to stabilize gyrating equity markets.[12] His statement, alongside some behind-the-scenes coordination with investors, worked magically, initiating a rebound and calming markets.

Greenspan had broken with his libertarian mentor Ayn Rand now in two major ways. He had become a central banker, recognizing the need for government to provide a stable currency and financial system. Now he was abandoning fixed rules and favoring discretionary central bank action. Ideology gave way to triage, just as it had for marketcrafters in the past. Greenspan told the journalist Bob Woodward that he "was prepared to go further over the line," even if it was legally ambiguous.[13] Government was not to be minimized or erased at all turns; it could be relied upon at the most crucial and difficult of junctures to make a financial system work better.

Greenspan could act quickly because he had been closely observing related government efforts in recent years. Three years before he became Fed Chair, he'd watched as first Penn Square and then Continental Illinois, one of the nation's largest banks, collapsed under the weight of portfolios of risky assets that had only become more toxic as interest rates remained high and volatile. Fearing that the failure of Continental Illinois posed a "systemic risk" to the financial system, Paul Volcker's Fed had partnered with the FDIC and Treasury to take the unprecedented step of guaranteeing all the deposits in the bank.[14] The move failed to save the bank but set a new precedent for what the government might do to protect large institutions in the midst of a panic. Greenspan, at the time in the private sector on hiatus from public service, supported the moves, saying on television that the Fed's actions "may well have been necessary given the potential dangers of a major run."[15] But he continued to oppose government-issued rules that would require banks to hold more capital as a buffer against similar shocks. It was the first glimpse of his approach, which had evolved from the free-market fixation of libertarianism and been tempered in the fires of economic pragmatism: empower financial actors with free rein, but support them with a powerful government backstop. "Greenspan continued to favor the deregulation of finance; but it grew obvious that government safety nets were there to stay—financiers would not pay for their errors," his biographer Sebastian Mallaby wrote.[16] Systemically important financial institutions would not be allowed to fail, but this guarantee was no reason that they should be forbidden from taking big risks in pursuit of private returns.

Greenspan's 1987 press release set the tone for what came next. Earlier in the decade, financial institutions chartered to support mortgage lending, called savings and loan banks (S&Ls), struggled to stay solvent, and their challenges compounded as interest rates stayed high in the 1980s. In 1989, Greenspan worked with the Bush White House to support a $90 billion bailout for the S&Ls, the largest in American history at the time. A few years later, the Mexican government was unable to service the large and expensive debt burden it had taken on, risking default. That would spell disaster for the Mexican people and economy, but more importantly for Greenspan, for the many American financial institutions that held the sovereign debt. In 1994, the Fed and Treasury joined the IMF to prevent the nation's default by mobilizing $47 billion in emergency lending.[17] As crises accelerated, Greenspan became so active in the work to stabilize markets that investors gave the new approach a name: the "Greenspan put." In finance, a put option guarantees to a seller that there is a floor below which an asset cannot fall in value. Greenspan had used government to stabilize markets so often and forcefully that investors now named a no-cost public sector, macroeconomic insurance policy after him.

Historians often point to Greenspan as the ultimate expression of free-market libertarianism, citing his early friendship with Rand as evidence of his anti-government fervor. That view of Greenspan the ideologue, however, ignores Greenspan the pragmatist.[18] "Presidents can talk about the virtue of small government as much as they like," Greenspan later wrote, but every President, including Republicans, still oversaw an increase in the size and scale of government as America's economy grew larger. Greenspan as Fed Chair was no different.[19]

Instead of seeking to prevent crises, the proper role of the state was to foster financial innovation, taking care to step in and clean up any mess it might cause. Greenspan took a two-step approach to encourage financial innovation: deregulation and marketcraft. With one hand, reduce the scope of the regulatory power of the Fed and other government agencies. With the other, use that state power to nurture financial innovation and hold together the system if it ever threatened to break.

On a cloudy April afternoon in 1998, the most powerful people in the American political economy, including Greenspan, filtered into Treasury Secretary Robert Rubin's private conference room. A sovereign debt crisis in several Asian countries was sowing chaos in financial circles, and the nation was beginning to indulge its obsessive curiosity for the details of an affair between the President of the United States and a White House intern. The agenda for the meeting that day did not have to do with either of these topics. Instead, principals across government were coming together to determine how heavily to lean into the Greenspan theory of how markets should work. Greenspan's agenda for the meeting in Rubin's private conference room at the Treasury in April 1998 was a straightforward application of the first of these principles: protect the blossoming, opaque market in derivatives from the hands of government regulators. Only later on would he use his marketcraft to hold the system together and further nurture the financial innovation he wanted to see in the system.

The meeting of the President's Working Group on Financial Markets was summit-like with participants from across the government. Rubin, a former Goldman Sachs banker, brought with him his Deputy Secretary of the Treasury and trusted confidant, Larry Summers. Then came Greenspan, as well as the Chair of the SEC, Arthur Levitt. As the official meeting time approached, a few more power brokers arrived: the heads of the New York Fed, the Office of the Comptroller of the Currency, and the Office of Thrift Supervision. George Washington peered out from a Gilbert Stuart portrait hanging over the mantel as they settled into their chairs.

One participant stuck out: Brooksley Born, the lone woman, who was the head of a smaller institution of government, the Commodity Futures Trading Commission (CFTC). Decades earlier, Born had been the first female editor of the *Stanford Law Review* and had worked her way up to lead the derivatives practice at one of Washington's most prestigious law firms. Accomplished and smart, Born could also be a bit politically maladapt, and she and her lionized counterparts in the room had a strained relationship. One journalist, Michael Hirsh, who chronicled the meeting, reported that the participants felt "she had no sense of place, no respect for who they were." A former Fed official put it more candidly, saying the group thought her to be a "light-weight wacko."[20]

Born's recent actions required the group's immediate attention. For over a year, she had been working to reorganize the booming and largely shadowy market in derivatives, a broad term encompassing the class of financial products whose value derives from some other underlying asset. A derivative might be a futures contract, which is an agreement to buy or sell something at a predetermined price at some point in the future. It could also be a swap, an agreement between two parties to exchange cash flows or financial instruments over time. These are often highly specialized and sometimes customized agreements made between sophisticated financial actors, and they would go on to play a "central role" in the Great Financial Crisis, according to Congress' official Financial Crisis Inquiry Commission.[21]

Greenspan and Born agreed on the goal of supporting financial market stability, but they disagreed on what kind of public policy was necessary to achieve it. Greenspan and most other participants in the meeting believed that financial innovations like derivatives brought speed, liquidity, and flexibility to the market, distributing risk and making markets more stable. The first step of Greenspan's two-step marketcraft was to deregulate, which meant in this case that government should leave the derivatives market alone—unless and until it needed support in a crisis.

Born, by contrast, believed smart regulation was necessary to ensure stability and resiliency in financial markets. "She was defying the zeitgeist," according to Hirsh. "She was fighting an idea so powerful, so intoxicating, that ten years later it required the worst crash since the Great Depression to tarnish it."[22] It was not that Born was an opponent of derivatives as such. She was fascinated by their promise and had been instrumental in the rise of the derivatives market over the past two decades, building her career by helping companies to structure them legally. She believed that derivatives could have a generative power to better allocate risk, allowing investors to hedge an investment by purchasing insurance against significant declines in the value of an underlying investment. But at the same time, the use of derivatives with no government oversight could create its own risk, and Born had become increasingly concerned about the ramifications. Investors who believed their bets were hedged were often tempted to make larger and riskier loans. If the investors selling protection were not required to post any collateral when they took those bets, the risk that they failed to meet their obligations was magnified. Without appropriate safeguards in place, derivatives created the possibility for firms to be on the hook for exorbitant losses, especially in the case of a serious financial crisis.[23]

By 1998, the market for derivatives had grown meaningfully in size. It wasn't any particular new technology that enabled this growth. It stemmed from public-policy decisions in the years before Born's arrival that licensed private market actors to enhance the riskiness of their bets. In the decade leading up to the fateful meeting, Born's predecessors at the CFTC had twice issued, once in 1989 and again in 1993, guidelines that encouraged the creation of more opaque, complex derivative products, relaxing the use of the oversight functions the agency and its forerunner had employed since 1930. In her last days on the job, the outgoing CFTC head under George H. W. Bush, Wendy Gramm, signed an order exempting most over-the-counter derivatives—transactions conducted directly between two parties—from oversight. "Up until then, the statute had provided that derivatives, with a few exceptions, had to be traded on a regulated exchange," Born recounted.[24]

These moves gave investors a green light to pursue risky bets that had previously been legally uncertain, and they flooded in to make them—often without understanding what exactly they were buying. In 1994 and 1995, the effects of a series of financial events—interest-rate hikes, the bankruptcy of Orange County, and an emergency US-Mexico financing agreement—were magnified by the increased frequency of derivative use. In the wake of those crises, bipartisan pressure had grown for tighter financial regulation, including of derivatives. Greenspan stepped in to make sure that didn't happen, testifying that "it would be a serious mistake to respond to these developments by singling out derivative instruments for special regulatory treatment."[25] The Fed, White House, and Treasury largely supported the financial industry's desire to avoid new regulation, and all the bills in the early 1990s failed.[26] As a result, the derivative market's notional value grew from an estimated $4.5 trillion in 1993 to $28 trillion in mid-1997.[27]

Given that growth, Born was now seeking regulation to stabilize and streamline the market. She did not, however, want to extinguish it. The other participants had attempted to dissuade her from taking any action. Before the meeting, Greenspan had invited her to lunch to explain his view that these instruments helped the system self-regulate. To him, the derivatives market was a crisp example of financial innovation distributing risk, making the system more efficient and safer. Treasury Secretary Rubin also met with Born and her team several times to discuss his concerns with her proposals. Rubin later claimed to be broadly supportive of derivatives regulation, but at the time, he wrote the chairman of the Senate Committee on Agriculture arguing against Born's actions. The culture of dismissing Born permeated his office. One of his aides at Treasury predicted the flow of an earlier meeting that mirrored the April standoff, saying, "Born will do about a 10 minute presentation laying out her position, after which she will probably get taken apart more or less politely by everyone else in the room."[28] Meanwhile, SEC Chair Levitt had even made a move to ostensibly rein in derivatives, a cynical attempt to claim the torch and undercut Born's campaign.[29] This provocation galvanized Born to put the issue on the top of that day's meeting agenda, making the standoff inevitable.

After the leaders settled into their seats and attended to some brief housekeeping, Rubin gave Born the floor. She laid out her high-level plan to reorganize the derivatives market, giving her agency more power in the process. Her proposal was purposefully inchoate: she intended to issue a "concept release," a draft of which she had circulated, to begin a public engagement process to strengthen the legal framework governing this market. "[We do] not want to suppress derivatives," she said. "We want to encourage them by giving greater legal certainty."[30] The participants in the room could barely suppress a synchronized eye roll.

It turned out that, as often happens in Washington, the real meeting had taken place before Born ever entered the room. Earlier in the day, Greenspan had left the Fed to huddle with Rubin, Summers, and Levitt at the Treasury to develop a plan for how to handle the threat of Born's actions. Leaders at the Fed, including Greenspan, cherished the institution's independence from prying Presidents and activist legislators. They argued that the Fed pursued its monetary policy and financial regulation agenda "above politics."[31] In reality, Greenspan was a master politician, conveniently setting aside any commitment to stay above the political fray when the issue became important enough. He visited President Clinton in the Oval Office early in his first administration to make the case against additional social spending and for a deficit-cutting budget, which Clinton pursued.[32] As a result, Greenspan appeared in Hillary Clinton's box at her husband's first Congressional address, a public move to show his support for the administration's deficit-reduction plan. At multiple points during his chairmanship, he weighed in publicly in favor of tax cuts, which are not part of the Fed's purview. He advocated for the privatization of Social Security and opposed the expansion of Medicare to cover prescription drugs. By the time of the Born meeting, he had grown accustomed to collaborating with administrations on fiscal and regulatory policy, often privately, to achieve his ends. According to the plan the group hatched in the pre-meeting to the Born standoff, Greenspan would play the role of ideological advocate and Rubin would play the role of professional counsel, reflecting his legal background. The group as a whole would unite behind a concern that Born's moves could harm already fragile markets.

After Born's opening remarks, Greenspan pounced, rolling out his long-standing argument that new derivatives regulation would suffocate economic innovation and should not be pursued. "Any regulation should enhance the development of financial institutions," Greenspan said in the meeting. "[This] regulation might suppress the over-the-counter derivatives market."[33] The swaps, futures, and options invented over the past several decades had delivered remarkable advances in finance, distributing risk more efficiently and enabling financial institutions to serve the economy more effectively, Greenspan argued. The risk of one party's failure to fulfill their obligations was priced into the transactions, and government should nurture companies' efforts to make these deals. By doing nothing, government would make it possible for markets to regulate themselves, as investors hedged their bets. Any proposed actions to make derivatives harder to procure or trade would only handicap the market's potential to grow and self-regulate, not protect it.

Born was unsurprised. In a lunch with Greenspan at the Fed several months before, he had reportedly ribbed her, saying, "Well, you probably will always believe there should be laws against fraud, and I don't think there is any need for it." Born had been flabbergasted, but the comment was memorable. In Greenspan's view, it was in the self-interest of a businessperson to deal honestly and reliably, which would naturally lead any duplicitous market participants to imminent ruin.[34]

Rubin spoke up, trying to play the role of diplomat. While Treasury Secretary, Rubin was fond of reminding colleagues that "markets are good, but they are not the solution to all problems."[35] A lifelong Democrat, he did believe in limited government regulation of financial markets and safety-net policies to help the poor. Rubin had expressed occasional theoretical concern about the risk that derivatives introduced, but he was unquestionably aligned with Greenspan. He believed that investor confidence needed to be strong to build economic prosperity—and to ensure the government could continue to finance its deficits at a reasonable cost. Rubin's top priority as Treasury Secretary and in his previous role as the Director of the National Economic Council (NEC) was to ensure government actions made investors confident and happy. Highly liquid, fast-moving markets—with government standing by to help in emergencies—generally improved investor sentiment.[36] Derivatives regulation, by contrast, would make no one happy in the short term. At the moment of the meeting, markets were already brittle because of the cascading challenges of the international debt crises. Rubin made a decision to prioritize market sentiment over market stability that day. Markets would be "petrified" if Born moved to rein in derivatives without legal clarity that she had the power, Rubin argued. Born should stand down.[37]

Surely chaos and ambiguity created less stable markets, Born retorted. If the government did nothing, the derivatives markets would become a time bomb. No government agency existed to ensure that the investors who were buying and selling could actually fulfill their commitments. It was a crisis in the making, she argued. As the conversation grew more heated, Greenspan tried to steer everyone toward what he presented as a sensible observation. "You can't put the cork back in the bottle," he said. Nothing could be done to rein in an exploding market of new financial products. There may be contradictions in the law, but the lack of clarity "shouldn't induce us to do things that will undercut the system that we are beholden to serve." The experienced hand was checking the upstart's naïve idealism. His outlook was clear: financial markets were the ultimate sources of authority and discipline. "Thus, the real question is not whether a market should be regulated. Rather the real question is whether government intervention strengthens or weakens private regulation," Greenspan had said earlier.[38]

By the end of the meeting, Born was on an island. Rubin offered the slightest cover for an awkward end: Let's get our lawyers to circle up and work it out later, he suggested. The participants packed up and left. A few days later, Summers reportedly called Born to say that if she moved forward in her efforts, she risked precipitating a profound financial crisis, worse than anything since the Second World War. Rubin stopped taking her calls. In later years, meeting participants and onlookers claimed that Born had lacked "a concrete or plausible plan" to achieve what she suggested, as future Treasury Secretary Tim Geithner wrote.[39] The people who made this claim were the same people who had shut down any attempt to develop one.

For a moment more, Born charged forward. In May, her agency released the concept document, a simple statement saying it was considering changing its previous guidance on derivatives markets. The release posed seventy-five questions for comment and made no immediate new claims for authority. Markets had no discernible reaction, despite Summers' warning. In response to her announcement, Greenspan, Rubin, and Levitt issued a rare coordinated public rebuke of Born. "We have grave concerns about this action and its possible consequences," they wrote.[40] By then, the press was fully embroiled in reporting a presidential sex scandal unlike any other, and America took little notice of the dispute between the institutions of government. Born's plan went nowhere.

Five months later, the world's largest hedge fund, Long-Term Capital Management (LTCM), led by Nobel Prize–winning economists and seasoned traders, imploded. The fund's global investment strategy relied heavily on derivatives, such as interest-rate swaps and equity options, to amplify small price differences in global bond and equity markets. When Russia defaulted on its debt, LTCM found itself deeply overleveraged, triggering massive losses for the firm. Because of its size, its impending bankruptcy threatened the stability of the financial system. The New York Fed encouraged the leaders of virtually all major American financial institutions to piece together a private bailout. They complied, offering a nearly $4 billion parachute to LTCM to allow it to fail gracefully. Neither the Fed nor Treasury contributed government money, but the crisis foreshadowed a much larger one to come: an unregulated market in derivatives had created systemic risk, which only an emergency, government-mediated rescue package could manage.[41]

The dramatic collapse of LTCM did not shift momentum in Born's direction, a testament to the power of the deregulatory voices across government. She resigned the following summer. A few months afterward, Summers, now Treasury Secretary, managed to get Congress to slip into an omnibus appropriations bill a rider that ensured that derivatives, including credit default swaps, could not be regulated by Born's agency, the CFTC. Greenspan notched his victory.

Even though Greenspan's deregulatory impulse is generally well understood, few people have paid enough attention to his proactive marketcraft. Greenspan did seek to get rid of existing regulations in some cases, like in the derivatives market, but in many others, he supported writing new ones. As Greenspan's tenure as Fed Chair progressed through the 1990s and early 2000s, he became increasingly active in using the power of the Fed and Congress to nurture and support financial innovation. This was a marketcraft of reregulation, often using the state's power to support new financial products and institutions and always stepping in to save failing institutions if their failure threatened sizable collateral damage.

Even though it had crystalized decades earlier in the 1950s, Greenspan's theory of financial innovation grew increasingly refined during his two decades in power at the Fed. The master goal was to make it easier for investors to buy and sell a wide variety of assets. As assets became increasingly liquid, market transactions could occur more easily, thereby creating more information about the assets' value. In theory, transaction costs would approach zero, making it frictionless for investors to trade. The faster and more often transactions occurred, the more up-to-date and accurate price signals became.

The engine to enhance market efficiency was financial innovation—products or practices that reduce friction when buying or selling an asset.[42] Electronic trading systems of the 1990s, made possible by growth in computing power and network speed, enabled investors to split up trades and take advantage of price discrepancies in previously less integrated markets. Similarly, consumer trading platforms made it easier for more traders to participate in market exchanges. To be clear, not all the innovation Greenspan welcomed came from technological advances. He also wanted financial firms to create new assets to be bought and sold. The development of new insurance products, for instance, could distribute risk around the financial system more effectively, Greenspan believed, decreasing the effects of the failure of any one particular institution.[43] Securitization of mortgage loans could make it easier for investors to hedge their risk and fuel credit provision to individuals who might not otherwise have been able to secure it.[44]

All of this innovation would make markets safer, Greenspan genuinely believed. With more precise price signals and abundant information, if a bank or company was teetering, an investor would be able to see that risk earlier and decide if it deserved a lifeline. "No market is ever truly unregulated," said Greenspan in a speech in 1997. "The self-interest of market participants generates private market regulation."[45] In Greenspan's view, the government's purpose was to leverage its power to unlock these self-regulating tendencies. The Fed's job—the mission of its marketcraft—was to encourage, embrace, and celebrate financial innovation's ability to make markets more flexible and efficient, unlocking their natural potential to self-regulate.

Greenspan also believed that America's global lead in finance enhanced the nation's economic and geopolitical power, a back-door, finance-focused industrial policy. New financial firms and products unlocked capital for nonfinancial businesses, enabling them to make the kind of investments that drive economic growth and improve living standards. In addition to seeing financial markets as founts of nonfinancial development, Greenspan also viewed the financial sector itself as a strategic pillar of the US economy—one that, unlike manufacturing, was too vital to be outsourced. He often grounded his argument against derivative regulation, for instance, in a concern that regulation would shift the market to London. In Greenspan's finance-centered industrial policy, the financial sector itself was both the means and the end of economic strategy.

Strengthening American finance meant supporting finance's efforts to invent new financial products that could increase leverage, distribute risk, and speed up trading. As one report from Rubin's Treasury in 1997 put it, "Government has no choice but to regulate financial markets, but it must do so in a way that gives markets plenty of space for innovation and adaptation. Often regulation is appropriate, but it should be designed, whenever possible, to maximize the benefits of innovation."[46] It was certainly not just Treasury officials and central bankers who shared this innovation obsession. *Wired* magazine ran a cover story in the summer of 1997 titled "The Long Boom: A History of the Future, 1980–2020." The article envisioned a future in which technological progress created a new "networked economy." "We have entered a period of sustained growth that could eventually double the world's economy every dozen years and bring increasing prosperity for—quite literally—billions of people on the planet." The engine for this transformation was new "information technologies to create the smaller, more versatile economic units of the coming era," it read. "Nearly every facet of human activity is transformed in some way by the emergent fabric of interconnection. This reorganization leads to dramatic improvements in efficiency and productivity."[47] *Wired* magazine may have exhibited a particularly naive, futuristic idealism, but its editors were far from alone. Economists, journalists, policymakers, and, to some unknowable but real degree, millions of voters had all come to believe that innovation-powered markets would usher in a new era of resilient prosperity.[48]

Greenspan's Fed supported the growth of two innovations in particular: credit default swaps and special purpose vehicles (SPVs). Financial firms created both, and Greenspan's marketcraft fueled their rise. Initially Greenspan and others believed these tools better distributed risk around the financial system, but in reality, they created interconnected, fragile money markets that made a lot of people a lot of money before they broke down spectacularly.

Banking lore places the birth of the credit default swap at a June 1994 J.P. Morgan retreat in Boca Raton, Florida. Between alcohol-filled parties, broken noses resulting from frat-style brawls, and late-night dives in the pool, the bankers spent their days attempting to invent new ways to drive profits.[49] Beginning that weekend and accelerating over the ensuing months, the derivatives team at J.P. Morgan hatched and refined a new financial product that could provide insurance in case of the default of a given security.

Using derivatives to insure against default risk had been tried a few times before, but no bank had ever invested in its success in the way that the J.P. Morgan team did over the following months and years. The primary obstacle that had doomed earlier forays into credit insurance by other banks had been its low profit margins. By 1997, the J.P. Morgan team solved that problem by figuring out how to scale it up. Instead of seeking investors for each individual transaction, they would take numerous insurance policies for different assets, pool them together, and then slice up the pool into tranches with different levels of risk. Investors had been securitizing mortgages, corporate bonds, and loans since the 1970s, but now, the J.P. Morgan team had created a securitized credit insurance product that they could sell widely. Banks that purchased the insurance could reduce the risk on their holdings of debt and debt securities, opening up new capital to invest elsewhere. The institutions underwriting the insurance products found a new revenue source that would only incur costs at some point in the distant future and only if things went bad. For the most reliable assets they were insuring, such as home mortgages, things would have to go *really* bad, on the order of a financial system meltdown, for them to be forced to pay. The chances of that were next to nothing. "In financial terms this was equivalent to taking thirty different home insurance contracts, bundling them together, and persuading a bigger consortium of outside investors to underwrite the risk that losses might affect those thirty homes," wrote Gillian Tett, the financial journalist who chronicled their rise.[50]

The timing was not coincidental. An international agreement in Basel, Switzerland, known as Basel I, had made banks increasingly constrained by requirements to hold a certain amount of capital. According to long-standing tradition in finance, American banking law, and now international agreement, banks needed to hold adequate levels of capital to provide a reliable source of funds in case their assets declined in value. The higher requirements specified by Basel took effect in 1992. They made the new credit default swaps particularly attractive by enabling banks to issue loans but avoid carrying the risk on their books. That, in turn, reduced their capital requirements and freed them to make more loans and thus more money. The bankers at J.P. Morgan—and soon other banks as well—benefited from the fees that they earned on these deals.

The financial creativity did not stop there. To further reduce the amount of capital they needed to hold, banks created SPVs. Like credit derivatives, banks had used SPVs for off-book activity for some time, but in the 1990s and 2000s, they supercharged their reliance on them. The vehicles became the engine of securitization, driving much of the buying, selling, and processing of a wide range of credit assets, including, eventually, credit default swaps. By conducting their business off the official balance sheets of the sponsor bank, the vehicles allowed that bank to minimize the held capital to meet regulatory requirements. Only modestly capitalized, these banks within banks borrowed aggressively in short-term credit markets, often collateralizing that borrowing with mortgage-backed assets. Crucially, this business model was only profitable if the SPVs held a top rating from the credit-rating agencies, allowing them to borrow money at very low rates. Ratings agencies required banks to commit to making good on payments to investors in the event the SPV could not. Conveniently, the ratings agencies believed the banks had ultimate responsibility, but regulators could not be sure that was true given that the vehicles were excluded from their framework that tallied capital requirements. This dizzying institutional arrangement created a so-called shadow banking system, a network of institutions with short-term liabilities and longer-term assets engaged in the borrowing and lending of trillions of dollars daily—all with minimal government oversight.[51]

As the bankers built this increasingly complex, interlinked structure, Greenspan's Fed hustled to support its growth. Greenspan was using his power as Fed Chair to craft markets to encourage financial innovation, which he believed made them more efficient and stable. As the J.P. Morgan team gained traction with credit default swaps, other banks moved into the market as well. In August 1996, Greenspan signaled his support for these efforts. The Federal Reserve issued official supervisory guidance that enabled banks to use credit default swaps to move risk off the balance sheet, effectively lowering their capital requirements and enhancing their profit potential. In effect, the Fed was allowing the market to determine the appropriate level of bank capital: if banks found the market price for reducing their capital requirements attractive, they were free to purchase the reduction. That decision facilitated an explosion in the production of credit default swaps, with levels increasing from $40 billion in 1996 to $300 billion two years later.[52] The bankers were "thrilled."[53] As a J.P. Morgan report from three years later recognized, regulators had "fueled" the "rapid growth of the credit derivatives market . . . over the last two years."[54] In the same report, Blythe Masters, J.P. Morgan's thirty-year-old global head of credit derivatives marketing, said that the growth of the new asset class was creating "enormous opportunities to exploit and profit from."[55] In 1998, LTCM imploded, the result of its heavy reliance on derivatives, particularly interest-rate swaps, options, and credit default swaps, to leverage its positions and enhance returns. Greenspan's response was to encourage more derivatives, by supporting the development of voluntary, private sector–led efforts to smooth their trading and make market activity more transparent. Market actors—nudged, if necessary, by the Fed's moral authority—would theoretically ensure risky firms could not go too far.[56]

Separately, the Greenspan Fed blessed the SPV, which made it possible for banks to create these separate bank-like subsidiaries. The parent bank could issue a loan in the form of a short-term liquidity line—to the SPV. Critically, the parent bank did not need to hold any capital reserves for the entity. These loans were functioning as credit guarantees, signaling to ratings agencies and others that the parent bank stood behind the obligations of the SPV.[57] This kind of financial innovation provided banks with significant additional flexibility to borrow short and invest long.

At the same time as Greenspan crafted markets to reward the financial innovation behind the credit default swaps and SPVs, he also worked with others in the federal government to enhance the risk—and returns—in the financial system. In 1999, banks were awash in new, high-quality credit assets with only modest returns. The Comptroller of the Currency, in coordination with the Fed, issued guidance to lower capital requirements on assets perceived to be reliable and stable, including mortgage-backed securities, reducing them from 8 percent to 1.6 percent. For every $1 billion of high-quality loans on their books, banks would now need to only hold $16 million of capital. In 2001, as the ecosystem of SPVs became increasingly important, the Fed and OCC reduced capital requirements for securitized products, such as mortgage-backed securities, freeing up space on the balance sheet for riskier investments.[58] That same year, the Treasury issued revised guidelines on how much capital banks needed to hold, lowering the amount in reserve against highly rated credit assets. It justified this move based on self-regulation: "The agencies expect that banking organizations will identify, measure, monitor and control the risks of their securitization activities (including synthetic securitizations using credit derivatives) and explicitly incorporate the full range of risks into their risk management systems."[59]

Some regulators pushed back on the campaign to reward the institutional innovation in the banking system. They argued that banks should be forced to reflect their SPV commitments on their own balance sheets so that regulators and investors could get a true picture of the risks involved. According to these critics, all of the byzantine rules that allowed banks to move supposedly high-quality assets around the financial system were creating unnecessary complexity and high levels of risk—not diluting risk as Greenspan claimed. In 2001, the energy company Enron collapsed as a result of its own duplicitous accounting practices, including the use of off-balance sheet vehicles. Two years later, the private-sector Financial Accounting Standards Board issued guidance that, from a bookkeeping perspective, the finances of SPVs must be consolidated onto the balance sheets of their parent institutions. The Fed clarified that these accounting practices did not affect regulatory requirements. In 2004, it specified that SPVs remained distinct from sponsor banks for regulatory purposes. The only concession made to the concerns about growing risk was a paltry increase in capital requirements for short-term liquidity lines.[60] It was window dressing, an inconsequential move that did little to enhance market stability. As a result, the total assets of SPVs reached $1.4 trillion in 2007.[61] According to the economist Barry Eichengreen, the face value of CDOs, the assets that pooled debt obligations and sliced them into tranches, reached $15 trillion by 2005. "[I]n truth no one really knew the value," he wrote.[62]

Perhaps no set of decisions was as emblematic of the public policy commitment to financial innovation as the government-wide movement to let banks sidestep the public regulatory structure by using their own private, proprietary models to assess their risk. New "value at risk" models developed by banks in the early 1990s promised to predict how much firms could gain or lose as market prices fluctuated. They relied on historical data to compute the risk, even during a period of significant financial innovation. Many of the assets and derivatives they used in their models hadn't even *existed* historically.

This discrepancy didn't stop the policymakers or bankers from putting their faith in them. In 1996, policymakers amended Basel I to allow banks to use their own risk models to inform how much capital they needed to hold on to, subject to approval from their national supervisors. Greenspan's Fed moved to license the banks to use these models to inform their decisions.[63]

Doubling down on this approach, federal banking agencies decided in 2001 to begin to accept investment quality ratings developed by private credit ratings firms and, in some cases, by a private firm's own internal risk-rating system.[64] In 2004, a second Basel agreement, outlined and negotiated by Greenspan and his disciples, permitted banks to use their own models to calculate the required level of capital for operational risk and, under certain conditions, for credit risk as well. Banks had every incentive to structure their models to seem more stable than they were. Greenspan handed "the teenagers the keys to the Mercedes" in the words of his biographer.[65]

While the Fed was blessing the creation of new financial products and asking banks to police themselves, Congress was busy facilitating the creation of financial innovations and larger banking and finance conglomerates. In 1999, legislators passed the Gramm-Leach-Bliley Act, repealing the 1930s Glass-Steagall law that divided commercial and investment banks. The basic idea behind Glass-Steagall was simple: A bank that accepts deposits from individuals or businesses, who expect their money to be safe and accessible, shouldn't be allowed to use those funds for riskier activities, like underwriting securities offerings. The law divided banking into a steady and somewhat sleepy commercial banking sector and a riskier investment banking one. Greenspan's Fed had been working for over a decade to erase this distinction, seeing in it a relic of the marketcraft of a century earlier. Stability would not be found through government regulation; more innovation and flexibility would provide that. Greenspan oversaw the granting of escalating exceptions to institutions blurring the lines between commercial and investment banking. Congress made it official in the passage of the new law. (Its passage did not happen without controversy. Armies of finance industry lobbyists mobilized to push the bill over the finish line, an effort capped off by a personal and direct appeal from Citigroup's Sandy Weill to President Clinton.)[66] The justification for the change was simple: more innovation to fuel prosperity and stability. "The Gramm-Leach-Bliley Act makes the most important legislative changes to the structure of the U.S. financial system since the 1930s," said President Clinton after its passage. "Financial services firms will be authorized to conduct a wide range of financial activities, allowing them freedom to innovate in the new economy."[67]

The market order that emerged after all of these changes was at once a result of Greenspan's deregulatory impulse *and* his marketcrafting efforts to nurture and amplify the innovation that he believed improved the financial system's operation. Deregulation alone is not a marketcraft; it does not use state power to shape a market toward a particular political or social goal. But Greenspan's efforts to foster financial innovation and provide a backstop to the global financial system amounted to an explicit marketcraft. Encouraging the growth of credit default swaps and SPVs required affirmative government action. Over the course of Greenspan's tenure, staffing at the Federal Reserve system increased by 30 percent and spending more than doubled. Government expenditures on financial and banking regulation ballooned by 58 percent between 1990 and 2005.[68] Nor did the complexity and size of the regulatory framework meaningfully shrink. In some cases, there were more regulations than ever: the Basel II agreement, running to 347 pages, was more than ten times as long as Basel I. Bigger budgets and expanding rule books do not necessarily mean more onerous regulation, but they symbolically dispel the idea that the regulatory state entirely shriveled under Greenspan's leadership. It took more people, more money, and more rules to implement Greenspan's marketcraft. Greenspan had a clear theory—more efficient markets would be more productive and stable—and he used his power at the Fed and with Congress to change the rules of how markets worked.

Just before the start of the Great Financial Crisis, the majesty of a world driven by financial innovation was on full display. The total assets of the finance sector were just shy of $73 trillion, having doubled since the era of financial innovation went into overdrive in 1999.[69] The global market value of derivative products exceeded $14 trillion, with an eye-popping $596 trillion of notional amounts outstanding—a way of describing how many bets investors had placed in the largely unregulated market.[70] Meanwhile, the models banks and regulators had embraced put the risk of a system-threatening financial meltdown at less than 5 percent—not nothing, but not worth turning the lights on to end the party. The smartest minds in finance believed they had engineered a prosperous economy where no one actor in the financial system held disproportionate risk, fulfilling a long-standing Greenspan dream.

The wave of financialization that Greenspan ushered in disproportionately enriched the wealthiest Americans. As profits soared in the financial sector, compensation packages for executives and traders mushroomed. The surge in asset prices also exacerbated income and wealth inequality, as those who already owned significant assets reaped the benefits, while those without such holdings fell further behind. The income share going to the top 1 percent rose from 10.7 percent in 1987 to over 17 percent in 2006.[71] Meanwhile, the broader workforce saw stagnant wages and diminishing economic security.[72] This inequality may not have been purposeful, but it was unmistakably the result of dedicated marketcraft to support finance with no similar agenda for American workers.

A few months before he stepped down as Fed Chair, Greenspan gave a valedictory speech that explained his two-step approach of deregulation and marketcraft: A "loosening of regulatory restraint on business" had improved the "flexibility of our economy." The decisions he and others had taken to enhance the freedom of market actors had created a new kind of "private regulation," reducing the need for government regulators. Those changes had spurred more innovation, stabilizing markets. "[R]ecent regulatory reform, coupled with innovative technologies, has stimulated the development of financial products, such as asset-backed securities, collateral loan obligations, and credit default swaps, that facilitate the dispersion of risk." The creation of these new, promising products required the public and private sectors to collaborate, and Greenspan's Fed had worked to nurture these innovations. "These increasingly complex financial instruments have contributed to the development of a far more flexible, efficient, and hence resilient financial system than the one that existed just a quarter-century ago."[73]

In 2006, after nearly twenty years as Chair, Greenspan handed over the reins of the Fed. The annual central banker meeting in Jackson Hole, Wyoming, became a grand fete of the so-called Maestro's legacy. His former rival Alan Blinder went so far as to say that "we think he has a legitimate claim to being the greatest central banker who has ever lived."[74] At the gathering, only one person, Raghuram Rajan, questioned Greenspan's legacy publicly, worrying that much of the financial innovation of the past two decades, particularly the emergence of credit default swaps, had made the financial system more fragile. Larry Summers rose from the audience to impeach Rajan's research credentials and defend Greenspan.[75] A few months later, Ben Bernanke, a mild-mannered, historically minded economist from Princeton, took over as Fed Chair. Little appeared likely to change with the shift: Bernanke shared his predecessor's foundational beliefs. "Financial innovation and improved risk management . . . have provided significant benefits," Bernanke affirmed just a month into his term. "Borrowers have more choices and greater access to credit; lenders and investors are better able to measure and manage risk; and, because of the dispersion of financial risks to those more willing and able to bear them, the economy and the financial system are more resilient."[76]

Maybe things were now actually different? The collapse of the Soviet Union had signaled the "end of history" geopolitically, and could it be that Greenspan, with the support of Rubin and Summers, had ushered in a new kind of economy that the world had not previously known? To many, it seemed possible that financial and technological innovation, when combined with the deregulatory agenda, had created this newfound period of prosperity and stability. The lack of a serious recession and unexpectedly low unemployment between 1994 and 2007 caused widely respected publications such as *The Economist* to wonder aloud: "Could the new economy defy history?" The Internet promised a revolution in knowledge sharing, collaboration, and productivity. It seemed at least plausible that its capabilities and insights, when combined with the right economic orthodoxy of less government, might mean a newly stable and prosperous economy. Nothing seemed quite powerful enough to rattle the machine that Greenspan had built.

Even on the rare occasions when something did cause a disruption, like the implosion of LTCM, government was always ready to respond. That brush with financial collapse seemed to confirm the system's essential stability. A year later, when the bubble burst in equity markets after the dot-com boom, there was no meaningful recession. The contested Bush-Gore election, the September 11 attacks, the bankruptcy of Enron and WorldCom— none of these events had managed to come close to shaking markets, as many might have expected. Greenspan, recognizing that "we need flexible institutions that can adapt to the unforeseeable needs of the next crisis," stood by to provide whatever government support was needed.[77] Economist and future Obama administration CEA Chair Christina Romer pointed to the Fed's policy approach in September 2007 as a driving reason for the newfound macroeconomic stability, arguing that "better policy, particularly on the part of the Federal Reserve, is directly responsible for the low inflation and the virtual disappearance of the business cycle in the last 25 years."[78]

It seemed as if Greenspan had crafted the perfect American economy.

Slowly at first, and then all at once, that Teflon-strong, self-regulating financial system collapsed. The greatest financial crisis in a century began.

12

THE PURIST'S PITFALL

HANK PAULSON & THE GREAT FINANCIAL CRISIS (2008)

The weekend that Lehman Brothers collapsed, Treasury Secretary Hank Paulson stood alone in the bathroom of his hotel room at the Waldorf Astoria in Manhattan. It was late on a Saturday night in September 2008, and Paulson, the former CEO of Goldman Sachs, was at once wired and exhausted. He had spent the last two weeks trying to prevent the American economy from collapsing. Six days prior, he had nationalized Fannie Mae and Freddie Mac, the two semiprivate institutions that underwrote 90 percent of American home mortgages. For the past two days, he had been hustling to save the teetering investment bank Lehman Brothers, either by finding another bank to buy it or by jawboning his friends and colleagues who ran stronger banks to use their own private money to bail it out—or both. When he had left the office that Saturday night, a deal looked close to happening, but nothing was for sure.

Now, alone in his room at the Waldorf, he stood in the harsh light of the bathroom. He pulled down a bottle of sleeping pills from the vanity, opened the container, and placed one in the palm of his hand, rolling it around. "As a Christian Scientist, I don't take medication, but that night, I desperately needed rest," he later recounted.[1] For Christian Scientists, medication cannot heal, even in the short term—only prayer can.

But these were not normal circumstances, and he had been given the bottle before he left Washington the day before. One single night of restorative sleep would do wonders for his ability to make important decisions the following day. He would feel sharper, more lucid, and likely more confident in the momentous decisions he would inevitably make, which would have major consequences not just for him, but for the world. The choice was clear: make a practical decision for the sake of health or hew to a rigid moral framework.

For decades, Paulson had held on to a midwestern, straight-laced demeanor. A farm boy from Illinois, he became an Eagle Scout before heading to Dartmouth, where he played football. During frat parties in college, he drank orange juice and ginger ale while the other students drank beer. As an adult, Paulson and his wife, Wendy, whom he had met while she was still in college, shared a modest two-bedroom apartment in New York, even though his pay packages meant he could afford something palatial. They tried to get to bed by 9:00 pm if possible and spent their free time on the weekends birdwatching in Central Park. Like Fed Chair Bill Martin a half century before, Paulson's faith and commitment to a moral order animated his personal life—and explained much of his professional one.

Before he became Treasury Secretary, Paulson had spent most of his career at Goldman Sachs, where he became the investment bank's President and later CEO in the 1990s. Ambitious and hardworking, he had been wise to moments when crises—inside and outside the firm—opened up new opportunities for him to advance. At times, he'd had to make brutal decisions, like when he forced the resignation of his co-CEO, Jon Corzine, in 1998. Corzine had stepped out of bounds when he initiated merger talks with Mellon Bank without telling Paulson or Goldman's management committee. The two men had grown to despise each other, and Paulson, sensing Corzine's weakness, organized Goldman's Executive Committee to authorize a surprise "palace coup," stripping Corzine of his title and power.[2] Despite his upbringing, Paulson was not so much a midwestern nice guy as he was an ambitious, aggressive leader with an unflappable sense of right and wrong. By the time Paulson left to become Treasury Secretary in 2006, he had led Goldman through its initial public offering, transforming it into the most highly respected investment bank in the country, if not the world. He'd also pocketed hundreds of millions of dollars in the process.

Those decades of hard work felt like they had somehow led to this moment at the Waldorf, and there was little question about what decision he would make. He tossed the sleeping pill into the toilet. Never one to do something subtly, he then picked up the bottle, held it over the toilet bowl, and poured out the rest. The pills tumbled down into the water. They swirled for just a moment before he flushed them away. "I longed for a good night's rest," Paulson wrote years later. "For that, I decided, I would rely on prayer, placing my trust in a Higher Power." Paulson had gotten this far by following a clear moral code of right and wrong. It was too late to change course now.[3]

A few hours later, in the early light of Sunday morning, Paulson left the Waldorf and headed back downtown to the New York Federal Reserve, the emergency headquarters that he was operating out of while in New York. Paulson never shared how he slept that fateful night, but it seems safe to assume it came in brief, restless bouts, if at all. Entering the grand Italianate building a bit before 8:00 am, he headed to the thirteenth floor, where he huddled with the two men in government he had been coordinating with all weekend: the President of the New York Fed, Tim Geithner, and the head of the SEC, Chris Cox. The Chair of the Federal Reserve, Ben Bernanke, had chosen to stay in Washington for the weekend, underestimating the severity of the crisis or not wanting to get embroiled in any decisions perceived as "political." Bizarrely, he had not even spoken to Paulson or Geithner since early Friday.[4]

All three men believed that the clock was running out to find a solution to the crisis of confidence in Lehman. They anticipated that Lehman could run out of the cash needed to continue its operations as early as Monday. To prevent chaos in the markets, they hoped to announce that the bank had been acquired by the time Asian markets opened around eight o'clock Eastern time on Sunday evening. A beleaguered and frustrated Paulson had spent the days leading up to the fateful weekend of Lehman's collapse repeating one simple idea to anyone who would listen: "I won't be Mr. Bailout."[5] The Fed and Treasury had worked together earlier in the year to broker an emergency acquisition of another failing investment bank, Bear Stearns, and Paulson was determined not to do that again. Over the summer, investors, the press, and Paulson himself knew that after Bear's collapse, Lehman could be next. Paulson encouraged the Lehman CEO to sell the company over the summer and tapped a close former colleague of his at Goldman to coordinate inter-agency efforts in case Lehman went bankrupt.

But now that he had nationalized Fannie and Freddie, Paulson felt that he could not appear to be doing the same for Lehman. He told members of Congress, the press, his colleagues at Treasury and the Fed, and, perhaps most importantly, everyone on Wall Street that he refused to use any of the resources of the federal government to assist Lehman Brothers. "I could hear the influence of [Paulson's] political advisers," Geithner later wrote of the period, "who had been trying to steer Hank away from supporting any Fed role, urging him not to let me talk him into another Bear." Paulson invoked "no public money" again and again as if it were a religious mantra, even as Fed and Treasury staff and private bankers pushed him to reconsider. On a phone call with Bernanke, Geithner, and staff on Thursday evening, Paulson said it again: "I can't be Mr. Bailout." His red line was so strong that he refused even to consider alternatives to the false choice he had cooked up: Lehman would either be sold in a fire sale or go bankrupt.[6]

That philosophy, which many policymakers, analysts, and Americans of both parties shared, hung on a single, pivotal idea: for innovation to enable markets to self-regulate, markets must penalize the losers. Reckless firms, no matter how large, how important, or how central, have to fail to disincentivize other firms from taking on too much risk. Because this keyed into an old, laissez-faire conventional wisdom—businesses fail every day; government can't and shouldn't stop that—it became insidious. It took on a strong moral dimension: the careless must get what they deserve for the economy to work well.[7] Crucially, the moral argument had purchase on both the free-market right and the anti-corporate left. Opposition to further bailouts had become one of the few areas of consensus uniting the two candidates running for President, John McCain and Barack Obama.

When Paulson had left the office Saturday evening, all suitors for Lehman but one had dropped out of the bidding process. The one bank that remained, London-based Barclays, would require roughly $30 billion of support from other private banks to facilitate the acquisition. Paulson and Geithner were attempting to wrangle those banks to make the deal work. That Sunday, Paulson's task for the day was as ambitious as it was straightforward: finalize the terms of a private acquisition of a global investment bank, clear it with all related governments and regulators, and announce it to the world by the early evening. But only a couple hours after arriving at the office, Paulson and his colleagues hit a major snag. A little after 10:30 am, Geithner charged into the makeshift office that Paulson was using and

found him in dialogue with Cox. Geithner had just hung up with Callum Mc-
Carthy, the head of the Financial Services Authority, the United Kingdom's
primary bank regulator. McCarthy's message had been clear: by British law,
Barclays' acquisition would be subject to a shareholder vote, which would
take thirty to sixty days to organize. McCarthy had no power to waive the
vote, thus making it significantly harder to complete the transaction. The
American team would have to engineer a soft landing to keep Lehman on life
support for thirty days. "I asked him if he was saying no," Geithner said to
Paulson and Cox. "He kept saying that he wasn't saying no."

Cox left the room to try McCallum again. Minutes later, he returned,
pale. "They're not going to do it," he said. Or at least, they weren't going
to do it on the snap timeline the American team was demanding. Paulson,
refusing to take no for an answer, moved up the chain of command in the
British government. He called Alistair Darling, the Chancellor of the Exche-
quer, who himself had been in conversation with Gordon Brown, the Prime
Minister, about the deal. The answer was the same. "He's not going to do
it," Paulson said to a much larger assembled group. "He said he didn't want
to 'import our cancer.'" They discussed asking President George W. Bush
to call the Prime Minister, but Paulson decided against it. Brown's answer
would almost certainly be the same, even if it was the President of the United
States on the other end of the line.

"Okay. Let's go to plan B," Geithner said. Fed staff had pieced together a
basic framework for a government lifeline. Paulson refused to even consider
it. Lehman had to go down.[8]

Policymakers, economists, and everyday Americans have a range of explana-
tions for why the Great Financial Crisis took place. Often people want to
blame a single particular product or policy. The most popular culprits are
the explosion of subprime financing in housing markets, unregulated shadow
banking, or the Fed's decision to keep interest rates low in the years before the crash. Housing in particular often takes much of the blame, with
the softening of the housing market in 2006 exposing a house of cards that
banking leaders and policymakers had created. The proliferation of subprime
mortgages was a real problem, but the collapse of that industry should have
harmed the financial institutions issuing those mortgages and not necessarily threatened the financial system. The modest size of the riskiest home

mortgages drove Fed Chair Ben Bernanke to say in Congressional testimony as late as March 2007 that the subprime crisis would not threaten the broader economy.[9]

The subprime crisis was the spark that caused a highly integrated, fast-moving, and leveraged financial system to melt down. As some mortgage-based assets began to go bad, the financial institutions that had insured them by purchasing the derivatives known as credit default swaps began to worry about whether they were actually insured. The relatively low-rate environment of the years prior had encouraged significant borrowing across the financial system, including on the balance sheets of households. Housing-based assets functioned as collateral for borrowing for many banks, and when those prices collapsed a panic began. Gradually at first, and then all at once, everyone needed cash to cover their losses, and no one was willing to lend.

It's not wrong to say that subprime housing, low rates, and excessive leverage contributed to the crisis, but nor does it capture the root cause. By 2007, Greenspan and others had structured the American financial system to encourage historic levels of financial innovation in support of more market efficiency. Any program of marketcraft is only as good as the theory behind the mission. The crisis exposed the misguided logic of the obsession with innovation and efficiency, revealing the fundamental fragility that marketcraft had created.

Despite Paulson's starring role in the Great Financial Crisis, he was an acolyte of Greenspan's marketcraft rather than an architect. Greenspan had created a fundamentally flawed financial structure, believing that markets would naturally self-regulate. If crisis hit, he could always step in to help. Paulson believed in the simpler idea that the profligate should be punished. Whereas Greenspan had understood the power government held to nurture innovation and stabilize markets in moments of crisis, Paulson's lifetime in the private sector had led him to believe in a simpler laissez-faire story. His outlook was more conventional and more authentically libertarian than Greenspan's. In this case, Paulson believed that the failures of banks, even a major institution like Lehman, could on some level be helpful to the markets, proving, once and for all, that the government was only willing to go so far. "For market discipline to constrain risk effectively, financial institutions must be allowed to fail," Paulson said publicly in July 2008, just months before the

Lehman collapse.[10] Lehman would have to be made a memorable example for the market discipline of the "free market" to work in the future.

Lehman was not just an unlucky financial institution, Paulson believed. Its leadership had played fast and loose and had refused to confront the weakness at its core, laid bare in the months between Bear's collapse and Lehman's own demise. This kind of cavalier, rule-defying behavior could not be indulged. Paulson had decided that if no buyer was willing to acquire Lehman without government assistance—still his preferred option—it would have to become the example for the world to see. "I am a firm believer in free markets, and I certainly hadn't come to Washington planning to do anything to inject the government into the private sector," Paulson wrote years later.[11]

At times, Greenspan's rhetoric had resembled Paulson's. But the logic of Greenspan's policymaking was not Paulson's moralistic framework. Instead, it was the pragmatic one of a central banker intent on guaranteeing stability. If an institution's failure threatened the system, some combination of the Fed and other public- and private-sector leaders had a responsibility to prevent the crisis from occurring—or step in to mitigate the effects. "We are not here to see the economy destroyed in the interest of not bailing somebody out," Fed Chair Paul Volcker had said a generation earlier, and that ideology had guided Greenspan in the decades following.[12]

Paulson was not alone in his belief in a simpleminded version of free-market ideology. There was substantial political opposition to any kind of government support for private companies, which permeated popular opinion and in the halls of Congress. In the summer of 2008, Greenspan privately pushed Paulson to lobby Congress to give the Treasury the authority to manage the winding down of a failing institution. From his perch in retirement, Greenspan anticipated that Paulson might have to handle more bankruptcies, and ever the pragmatist, he wanted to make sure Paulson had the tools to do it in an orderly fashion. That meant getting the legal authority for an orderly wind down of an investment bank, for instance.[13] Paulson tried to get that authority from lawmakers, but he got little traction. Congress was already authorizing the Paulson-led Treasury to coordinate a bailout or takeover of the nation's largest mortgage-financing companies, Fannie and Freddie. Giving Paulson still more power to unwind a failing bank felt like it risked empowering a former Goldman banker to extend a taxpayer-funded lifeline to his friends. That was a step too far.

✿

In early September, the mounting anxiety that had gripped financial markets throughout the summer began to turn into a panic. Fannie and Freddie were buried under the weight of an enormous portfolio of mortgages and unable to secure short-term financing or longer-term investment to keep them afloat. Paulson, having foreseen this part of the crisis for months, invoked his newfound authority from Congress and nationalized the entities. He and his team believed that these moves would prevent additional chaos, but the decision provoked a torrent of criticism across partisan lines, including from both presidential candidates John McCain and Barack Obama. In calls to members of Congress that week to brief them on the decision, Paulson heard a consistent message back from them: "no more bailouts." One particular op-ed struck a chord: "We'll Protect Taxpayers from More Bailouts" was the headline in the *Wall Street Journal*. The authors were fellow Republicans John McCain and Sarah Palin. "All punditry could talk about was moral hazard, as if it were some sort of emerging disease that had just reached pandemic proportions," the journalist Andrew Ross Sorkin wrote of the mood in Washington. "Bail out Lehman, the thinking went, and you will make bailouts the default solution at a time when no firm seems safe."[14] Rather than working with Fed and Treasury officials to find a middle way or to buy more time, Paulson fell into the same logic. Either someone would have to buy Lehman, or it would fail.

After Paulson and Geithner had gotten the bad news about the failed Barclays acquisition of Lehman, they decided it was time to inform Lehman's executive team of the need to declare bankruptcy. At 1:00 pm, Lehman executives got word that the crisis team at the New York Fed needed to talk to them in person immediately. Once they arrived, Thomas Baxter, the general counsel of the New York Fed, informed them that Paulson was ordering Lehman to declare bankruptcy.[15] The New York Fed would not allow Lehman to access a newly set-up liquidity facility, meant to serve as a lifeline to other investment banks. The Lehman participants were blindsided. Before the meeting, they were under the impression that the Barclays deal was still viable. Pushing back on the decision, they asked for further clarification. No one had ever heard of the federal government telling a company to file for bankruptcy. Lehman's leadership hastily called a 5:00 pm board meeting at its offices in New York to discuss its options. As it began, its Directors were still trying to make sense of the situation. They made little progress and adjourned an hour later. At the New York Fed, Paulson, Geithner, and SEC Chair Cox were struggling to understand what the Lehman board was doing, and Paulson in particular was getting agitated as the minutes ticked by. By 7:00 pm, he was pacing the halls, anxious to get Lehman to file. "This guy is useless," Paulson reportedly said to his chief of staff about Cox, who technically was charged with the communication with the board. Paulson walked over to Cox's office and slammed the door. "What the hell are you doing? Why haven't you called them?" he shouted. "You guys are like the gang that can't shoot straight! This is your fucking job. You have to make the phone call."[16]

Cox complied and picked up the phone. The Lehman board had reconvened just before 8:00 pm, and now Cox dialed into the board meeting. Lehman CEO Dick Fuld put him on speakerphone. Cox made clear the government's belief that an immediate bankruptcy would be in the best interests of the nation and would help calm the market. The New York Fed's general counsel reinforced the message, saying that the Fed agreed with the SEC. Lehman's Directors pushed back, perplexed by what was happening. One asked directly, "Are you directing us to put Lehman into bankruptcy?" Cox paused, unsure of himself, and suggested he needed to confer with his colleagues. Moments later, he returned: "The decision on whether to file for bankruptcy protection is one that the board needs to make. It is not the government's decision. But we believe that in your earlier meetings with the Fed, it was made quite clear what the preference of the government is." The board discussed its options. Frozen out from the Fed's emergency facilities and unable to get immediate clearance for the Barclays deal, it saw little choice but to declare bankruptcy. At 1:45 am, Lehman's lawyers filed the papers.[17]

The next morning, the plaudits streamed in. The *New York Times* lead editorial on Monday began with the simple idea "It is oddly reassuring that the Treasury Department and Federal Reserve let Lehman Brothers fail." To have done otherwise would have been a show of "weakness."[18] On the right, candidate McCain championed the move, saying, "I am glad to see that the Federal Reserve and the Treasury Department have said no to using taxpayer money to bail out Lehman Brothers." Investors, however, understood how central Lehman was to the global financial system and how dangerous its bankruptcy would be given the deep integration. The markets went into a tailspin.

In the days afterward, Paulson made it clear that he had never even bothered to consider a stabilizing action other than fire sale or bankruptcy. "I
never once considered it appropriate to put taxpayer money on the line in
resolving Lehman Brothers," he told reporters the day after its collapse.[19]
He extended short-term lifelines to Lehman's competitors, finding a middle
way that avoided a robust taxpayer-funded bailout and bought more time
for those banks to survive. But he had no interest in doing that for Lehman.
Making a pragmatic decision to stabilize Lehman would not exact the market
discipline that he believed appropriate. It would be like a Christian Scientist
taking a sleeping pill before a difficult day—a confession that the ideological
system guiding his behavior may be fundamentally flawed.

A little over a month later, on the morning of October 23, 2008, Greenspan
settled into his seat at a long wooden table in the Congressional hearing
room of the Committee on Oversight and Government Reform. Over the
course of his career, Greenspan had testified to Congress dozens of times
and had a reputation for artful obfuscation. He was known to wander lan-
guidly in his answers, lacing mini-lectures to Senators with financial jargon.
Occasionally he would insert a sly joke or clever aside to provoke a chuckle
or a smile. "He was dense, circuitous, and difficult to follow," his biographer
Mallaby writes. "[Y]et somehow his listeners were encouraged to believe that
the difficulty was their fault."[20] Despite Greenspan's retirement as Fed Chair
two years earlier, angry legislators hauled him back in front of Congress that
October as markets collapsed all around them. Journalists, investors, and
policymakers—not to mention American workers whose jobs were on the
line—all wanted to hear how the wise man would make sense of what was
happening and how he'd speak to his role in the crisis.

Spoiling for a fight, the Chair of the House Committee on Oversight and
Government Reform, California Democrat Henry Waxman, opened with a
set of aggressive questions for Greenspan. Now eighty-two, his hair thinning, Greenspan sat behind a long table across from the legislators, dressed
in his classic black suit and professor glasses. He brushed back Waxman's
questions, one by one, as he was known to do. "What I wanted to point out
was that the—excluding credit default swaps, derivatives markets are working
well," Greenspan said. In response, Waxman grew more aggressive. "Well,
where did you make a mistake then?" he asked.

Greenspan had come prepared, knowing his audience would want to see some humility in the wake of such disastrous events. He didn't hesitate. "I made a mistake in presuming that the self-interest of organizations, specifically banks and others, were such that they were best capable of protecting their own shareholders and their equity in the firms," Greenspan said. "So the problem here is something which looked to be a very solid edifice, and, indeed, a critical pillar to market competition and free markets, did break down. And I think that, as I said, shocked me."

A few moments later, Waxman pressed his point, quoting Greenspan himself saying that "free, competitive markets are by far the unrivaled way to organize economies." "Now, our whole economy is paying its price," Waxman said. "You feel that your ideology pushed you to make decisions that you wish you had not made?"

The Maestro, as his admirers had called him when he was at the height of his powers, again sidestepped. But then, with the world watching on, he continued, more slowly. "I found a flaw. I don't know how significant or permanent it is, but I've been very distressed by that fact," he said.

"You found a flaw in the reality . . . ?" Waxman asked.

"A flaw, a flaw in the model that I perceived is the critical functioning structure that defines how the world works, so to speak," Greenspan replied.

"In other words, you found that your view of the world, your ideology, was not right, it was not working?" Waxman pressed.

"Precisely," Greenspan replied. "That's precisely the reason I was shocked, because I had been going for forty years or more with very considerable evidence that it was working exceptionally well."[21] For a brief moment in October 2008 in the midst of the maelstrom, he wondered aloud if his devotion to market efficiency and belief in private market discipline might just be the mirage it was. For a moment, he seemed to acknowledge the work he had done to make markets more efficient had amplified financial instability rather than mitigating it. The next day, the *New York Times* ran a close-up shot of Greenspan's anguished face on the front page, above the fold, with the caption "Looking Back in Disbelief."[22]

If he had remained in power, Greenspan might have found a way to smooth Lehman's fall. He inherited from Volcker a commitment to bring massive firepower to stabilize teetering financial institutions, ensuring an orderly downfall when they had to collapse. Even in that counterfactual, the depth of the crisis would still likely have been enough to chasten him. After his testimony in the fall of 2008, Greenspan returned to his previous postures. He began to file the Great Financial Crisis away as a "tail event," an event with such low probabilities that it would certainly not reoccur.[23] That enabled him to keep his ideological system largely intact.

After the Lehman bankruptcy and the profound instability in markets it precipitated, Paulson and colleagues got serious fast about stabilizing the rest of the financial system, even if their books were as bad as—or worse than—Lehman's. Market discipline went out the window as America's most powerful financial and political leaders shifted into firefighting mode to restore financial stability.

On Tuesday, two days after Lehman's bankruptcy, the Fed and Treasury bailed out the insurance company AIG to the tune of $85 billion. On Wednesday, money market funds collapsed as investors withdrew twenty times the amount normally withdrawn in a week. The Fed and Treasury set up emergency programs to shore them up. The following Thursday, Washington Mutual, with over $300 billion of assets, failed—still to this day the largest bank failure in history. The FDIC took it into receivership. The stock market collapsed, and soon the largest automakers reported that they would go bankrupt without government action.

By the first week of October, any trace of a desire to exact market discipline on firms that had taken on too much risk had evaporated. Congress passed the Troubled Asset Relief Program (TARP), which authorized Paulson's Treasury to purchase $700 billion in troubled assets, primarily illiquid mortgage-backed securities, from financial institutions. His team used the wide-ranging authority from the TARP legislation to inject capital directly into banks, a measure designed to shore up their balance sheets and restore confidence in the banking system. Paulson chose to buy preferred stock in the banks, which did not come with voting rights, thinking that as long as the government didn't directly control management, his critics would not call it a nationalization. Many called it that anyway. (Over the course of the crisis, Citibank received more financial assistance from the government than any other financial institution. Robert Rubin served as the head of its executive committee until August 2008.[24]) The same month, the FDIC offered to guarantee all current and future unsecured debts of shaky banks, a sweeping and historic move.[25] Congress, two months later and a few weeks into the new presidential administration of Barack Obama, passed a major stimulus package, injecting $787 billion to stimulate economic activity and job creation through a mix of spending programs and tax cuts.

Meanwhile, Ben Bernanke's Federal Reserve was following Greenspan's precedent, reinventing itself as the provider of short-term financing to the global banking system. It uncorked a half-dozen facilities that lent cash to domestic banking institutions in exchange for illiquid assets.[26] These programs had the effect of stabilizing money market funds and the commercial paper market, which had seen a stampede of investors attempting to exit. The Fed went further by quietly creating "swap lines" with fourteen foreign central banks, using a structure invented a half century before in the era when offshore dollars first emerged.[27] It provided them nearly unlimited dollars in exchange for their currencies. That helped those central banks support their own fledgling financial institutions that wanted the stability of dollars in an uncertain time. The collection of these programmatic advances was a "truly spectacular innovation," according to the financial historian Adam Tooze.[28] Fed officials seemed not to worry about any legal barriers that might have prevented this kind of pragmatic activity. As one *New York Times* reporter wrote, "Often when the Fed says that it cannot do something, what it really means is that it does not want to. Laws can be stretched."[29] The central bank went from being a lender of last resort to providing a promise to the financial system: no major market would be allowed to come apart and cease functioning. If necessary, the Fed would step in as a buyer for even the most illiquid assets. Many of these programs would be restarted and expanded twelve years later in the fallout from the Covid pandemic.[30] The Greenspan put had grown into a systemic guarantee.

Even with these measures, by March of 2009, when markets bottomed out, the S&P 500 was down 57 percent from its precrisis peak, and nearly two-thirds of the drop had come after the Lehman implosion. Companies continued to shed a record number of jobs over the following months. By 2010, 9 million Americans had lost their jobs.

In the weeks after the Lehman collapse, journalists, businesspeople, and politicians began asking hard questions about whether the Lehman debacle could have been avoided. Paulson, anxious to avoid making it seem as if they had made any choice at all, invented an argument that the Fed and Treasury could not have helped Lehman because they lacked the legal authority. "We didn't have the powers," Paulson insisted in his first major interview on the topic with the *New York Times* a month afterward. The Fed could only help Lehman with a loan if the bank had worthy assets to serve as collateral, he claimed. "If someone thinks Hank Paulson could have made the Fed save Lehman Brothers, the answer is, 'No way,'" he said about himself.[31] Bernanke, who was not even close to the decision-making process that fateful weekend, adopted the same explanation: "[W]e essentially had no choice and had to let it fail."[32]

These claims weren't true. The day after the bankruptcy, Bernanke told the Fed's FOMC that policymakers had had "to make a judgment about the costs" of intervention, including "from a moral hazard perspective."[33] A bailout of Lehman would have been incompatible with the laissez-faire expectation of market discipline. He also said that the Fed and Treasury made their decision partially because private market actors had already "priced in" the possibility of a Lehman collapse. As Bernanke said, "the troubles at Lehman had been well known for some time, and investors clearly recognized . . . that the failure of the firm was a significant possibility. Thus, we judged that investors and counterparties had had time to take precautionary measures."[34] On a more personal level, it was clear that Paulson was feeling the heat to avoid extending a lifeline. "The negative publicity is really getting to him," Bernanke said a few days before the bankruptcy. Emails sent by top Treasury staffers confirm that the question was one of will, not legal authority: "I just can't stomach us bailing out lehman [*sic*]," read one email. "Will be horrible in the press."[35] Another email reported: "[J]ust did a call with the WH [White House] and usg [US government] is united behind no money. No way in hell Paulson could blink now."[36]

If Paulson or Geithner had chosen to "blink," they had a menu of options to prevent a spectacular implosion at the center of the financial system. Lehman might have been past the point of rescue, but it could have had a much softer landing. Greenspan's cultivation of innovation and risk-taking had always gone hand in hand with dramatic rescue operations, and Lehman could have been just another one of those seminal events—if Paulson and crew had shared Greenspan's belief that markets needed ongoing state action to be stabilized. The experienced contingency planners at the New York Fed had made the case for a Lehman stabilizing program, but Paulson refused to even consider it.

What would that stabilization program have looked like? By the fateful September weekend, Lehman Brothers was indeed in dire financial shape, unable to sell its assets to secure the cash it needed to conduct its business. Lehman did have more than $100 billion of assets on its books, but in the panic, there were no buyers for them. The challenge for any potential acquirer of Lehman in such a chaotic moment was to assess the "true" value of the assets, which was likely higher than the unsettled market believed but lower than the prices these assets would have recently fetched in a more stable environment. Whether Lehman was truly insolvent and beyond the hope of repair depended almost entirely on the valuation of those assets.

The problem is that the Fed and Treasury never did the math to find out, instead relying on the approximate valuations of potential acquirers, who had every reason to underestimate Lehman's strength. In 2010, the general counsel of the Federal Reserve, Scott Alvarez, confirmed in testimony to the Financial Crisis Inquiry Commission that neither the New York Fed, the Fed's Board of Governors in Washington, the Treasury, nor the SEC did an assessment to find out if Lehman was solvent: "Folks had a pretty good feeling for the value of Lehman during that weekend, and so there was no memo prepared that documented why it is we didn't lend."[37] Chair Bernanke confirmed Alvarez's testimony in front of the same commission, saying, "I don't have a study to hand you. But it was the judgment made by the leadership of the New York Fed and the people who were charged with reviewing the books of Lehman that they were far short of what was needed to get the cash to meet the run. And that was the judgment that was given to me." Bernanke, of course, had not bothered to go to New York to coordinate that fateful weekend. There is no evidence that he even talked to Paulson or Geithner until several hours after Paulson had ordered Lehman to file for bankruptcy. In one of the most fateful decisions the Fed and Treasury made in their institutional histories, no one bothered to examine the numbers.[38]

If they had, they would have seen an institution on the brink, but not beyond the scope of assistance. The economist Laurence Ball conducted a book-length forensic analysis of Lehman's financial position at the time of its bankruptcy and concluded that Lehman was indeed solvent, although just barely.[39] Its challenge was that it had no access to short-term liquidity, meaning there were no buyers for the assets it would normally be able to sell to meet its obligations.

Even if Lehman had been insolvent, the Fed and Treasury still had the economic and legal power to act. At the time, the law required a loan to be "secured to the satisfaction of the Reserve Bank," allowing significant discretion for lending in "unusual and exigent" circumstances. Paulson, Geithner, and Bernanke knew this, as their actions over the following days and weeks showed. The day after Lehman filed for bankruptcy, Paulson suddenly changed his tune and supported the New York Fed in making the $85 billion loan to AIG, which was secured by privately held equity of highly uncertain and volatile value—even more so than the assets Lehman had held. The decision nationalized AIG, making the Treasury the primary shareholder with 79.9 percent of the company's equity. (The loan size would later increase to $142 billion.) Geithner, at least, had found the strength of his conviction that market stabilization in this moment outweighed market discipline. "After Lehman, I lost whatever minimal tolerance I might have had for letting moral hazard or political considerations impede our efforts to attack the crisis," he later wrote. These actions, while bold, were not without precedent either; in the forty years before Lehman's collapse, government had organized or provided an emergency parachute to systemically important failing institutions on three separate occasions.[40]

If Paulson had not been driven by ideology, the Fed and Treasury could have stabilized Lehman, at least long enough to complete the Barclays acquisition. Lehman had failed a New York Fed liquidity stress test in June, and in the aftermath, Fed officials had developed a plan to provide emergency cash to Lehman or a similar investment bank if it were to suffer a sudden loss. "If we think it can be sold, then proceed as in [Bear Stearns]," one planning email suggested. "If not, discuss with Treasury its appetite for a permanent addition to the government's balance sheet by lending to the distressed firm."[41] In the Bear Stearns deal, the New York Fed had extended a loan of about $30 billion to a vehicle that would absorb the most toxic assets of the bank, allowing J.P. Morgan to purchase the remaining Bear assets. Lehman was a larger bank than Bear had been, and Bank of America wanted a $65 billion package to entice it into acquisition. It was still theoretically possible for the government to finance a graceful Lehman failure, which Geithner and his team knew when they chose to let it implode dramatically.

There were other options as well. Paulson and Geithner had set up an emergency liquidity facility in the spring so that financial institutions, including investment banks like Lehman, could trade stable collateral like Treasuries in exchange for short-term cash from the Fed. It was an emergency credit line limited only by the amount of high-quality collateral a borrower could post. On Sunday afternoon of the Lehman weekend, the Fed expanded the program, allowing banks to post a broader range of collateral, including riskier assets, like subprime mortgages, and get cash in return. This seemingly small change was radical and powerful because of its promise to turn toxic, illiquid assets into liquid ones—for the banks that were able to take advantage of it. Paulson and Geithner barred Lehman from accessing this facility, allowing only Goldman and Morgan Stanley the privilege. If Paulson and Geithner had included Lehman, the bank might have survived an extended tumultuous period. Assuming a dramatic drawdown would continue, Lehman would have needed about $80 billion to stay in operation over the following weeks, which it could have borrowed from the financing facility using $114 billion of acceptable assets.[42] More likely, it would have been a lifeline for the Barclays deal or another potential acquirer to buy the bank for next to nothing.[43]

Fed officials and business interests who understood the history of financial crises saw promise in a government-assisted acquisition and access to liquidity facilities for Lehman. Fed staff in particular surfaced their planning documents multiple times in the days leading up to the collapse, including on Sunday afternoon.[44] Meanwhile several bank leaders organizing the private bailout fund had been pushing for some government participation for days. Geithner in his memoir hints that he knew all along that the government could have pursued a different policy. "All week long, Hank had stuck to a consistent message in his private calls to the market: the government will not subsidize the purchase of Lehman," he wrote. "As a private negotiating posture, I thought that made some sense. . . . But whatever the merit of no-public-money as a bargaining position, I didn't think it made sense as actual public policy. The Bear intervention had been a well-designed solution to a serious problem."[45] This vantage is either selective rewriting of what Geithner felt at the time or a confession that on some level he knew that other options were viable and did not argue enough for them. Paulson shot down the idea of a government-assisted acquisition for a final time on Sunday afternoon.

Greenspan appeared Sunday morning on the television talk shows, taking no official position on a Lehman bailout. "I don't know enough of what is going on. I would have to have very detailed information of what's on the Lehman Brothers balance sheet . . . and what the repercussions would be with any particular solution," he said.[46] Even if his answer was noncommittal, the contrast with the categorical anti-bailout position taken by Paulson was clear. Greenspan's framework, unlike Paulson's, would likely have been profoundly practical—a careful look at the numbers to find some way to stabilize the bank and avoid the implosion to come. This would have involved, in Greenspan's words, "very difficult decisions." But whatever decision he would have reached, it would have been just that—a considered decision—not a rigid proclamation against government meddling.

When observers consider Washington's role in the financial crisis, they often point to what is regarded as a complacent regulatory system, run by unsophisticated regulators too simpleminded to see the risk that was building within it. The economist Alan Blinder argued that regulators across the board were "asleep at the wheel" in the years leading up to the crisis: "They were a deregulation-minded bunch of regulators who probably also got swept up in the euphoria of the day."[47] Paulson liked this story too. Testifying to the Financial Crisis Inquiry Commission (FCIC) in 2010, he enumerated the multiple causes of the 2008 crisis, but perhaps most importantly, he emphasized that government administrators were balkanized, confused, and unresponsive. "The result was that regulators were often unable to supervise the firms they oversaw adequately," he said. "They did not see the impending systemic problems that progressed towards the crisis. They did not have the tools to contain all the harms that unfolded as institutions began to collapse." In Paulson's telling, markets went bonkers and regulators, bewildered and disempowered by the previous regime, could do little but watch.

Paulson was criticizing Greenspan and his campaign of financial innovation, which had been signed off on by plenty of other luminaries. But Greenspan had not been telling regulators to sit idly. Greenspan as well as the other politicians and policymakers aligned with him relied on these regulators to implement the mission of financial innovation, which would, they believed, create more stability. Congress revised regulations, and Fed officials developed supervisory guidance in line with what Greenspan directed them to.

Regulators had done what they were told: encourage financial innovation because it would make the system more resilient.

Greenspan and others might have acknowledged the important role for government in shaping innovation-powered, efficient markets. He could have proactively differentiated his approach from the conventional laissez-faire narrative, which he had helped to spin and Paulson had come to believe. If he had, his marketcrafting program might have continued through the chaos of 2008. Instead, Greenspan often did the opposite, playing up the rhetoric of self-regulating markets and eliding the practical work he did to stabilize teetering institutions.

As a result, the libertarian story that minimized government's role in political economy became the dominant idea that political and economic leaders used to understand the world in the midst of the crisis of 2008, even though it wasn't true. The flawed ideological belief that markets operate according to some spontaneous internal logic led Paulson and others to push Lehman into bankruptcy, fulfilling the promise that only failure can discipline market actors. The one principal in the firefighting crew of the Great Financial Crisis who might have had a more practical view, Geithner, did not stand up for a plan B to soften Lehman's demise. In the decades prior, he had watched Greenspan develop and implement that approach, but he did not implement it when the critical moment arrived.

Instead, the governing consensus that Greenspan had worked so assiduously for decades to create broke wide open, a victim of his own obscurantist mythologizing. The "free-market" consensus depended on a powerful marketcraft, the success of which paradoxically made it possible to imagine that the state had withered away. By mistaking this rhetoric for reality, Paulson broke the spell and unleashed a crisis that would wash away old institutions and assumptions. From the rubble, a more explicit marketcraft would gradually begin to take shape.

A NEW MARKETCRAFT

13

THE REALIGNMENT

BRIAN DEESE & THE AUTOMOTIVE INDUSTRY (2008-10)

In mid-November 2008, Brian Deese, the thirty-year-old economic adviser to the President-elect, Barack Obama, sat down at a large table at the center of an all-glass conference room in a high-rise in downtown Chicago. Obama, who had won the election less than two weeks before, was waiting in the seat across from him. Given the free fall in markets and surging job losses, the President-elect was navigating the highest-stakes presidential interregnum since Hoover had given way to Roosevelt. As one of Obama's economic advisers, Deese would have to help him find a way through the storm.

Deese was an unusual choice to be advising Obama on economic policy. He lacked experience in government or an advanced degree of any kind. He sported a beard and had a chummy demeanor that read more like fraternity brother than economist. A few months earlier, he had joined the campaign as deputy to the chief economic adviser, the Harvard-trained Jason Furman. Now, with the nation in crisis and the President-elect in need of advice, Deese, Furman, and a handful of other advisers were beginning to sketch out a plan.

Deese would help develop and implement the rescue efforts over the next several years. But that would just be the start of his legacy. Over the next fifteen years, Deese transformed how Washington believed markets work and left a broad and deep mark on the American economy. He pioneered a new way of thinking about economics with lasting consequences for American industry and workers. But first he had to solve a discrete but enormous task: saving the American automobile industry.

Deese had spent much of the past decade getting as close as possible to the center of power of the Democratic Party. Born in Belmont, Massachusetts, in 1978, he grew up in a family of intellectual, policy-oriented personalities. His mother was an engineer who studied at MIT and later worked for the Massachusetts Environmental Protection Agency. His father, a political science professor at Boston College, studied how intergovernmental collaboration could manage international trade. Deese's older sister studied physics as an undergraduate before earning a PhD in oceanography. In this family of high achievers, Deese preferred spending his time on sports, theater, and singing while in high school.[1]

When he enrolled at Middlebury in 1996, a bookish streak took hold. He studied philosophy and political economy, shunning the empirical work of economics in favor of wrestling with bigger-picture questions about how government and markets should work. He studied abroad in Argentina, right when it was on the precipice of a devastating economic crisis in late 2001 that resulted from rising public debt and an overvalued peso. While there, Deese lived with a family on a fixed salary and watched as the communities around him slid into poverty, the result of economic collapse and hyperinflation. The Argentine government had failed its own people, but it also seemed that the medicine the Washington consensus prescribed to Argentina—a more open economy, significant cuts to government spending, and the privatization of state-owned companies—would not solve the underlying problems. They might even exacerbate them. There were no clear answers, but Deese had discovered the question that would guide his career: How could countries "create agency," as he put it, in a globalized world?[2]

Deese's first job after college was at the Center for Global Development, a nonprofit led by the economist Nancy Birdsall. Researching international economics was stimulating, but he wanted influence in Washington. The pace of life at think tanks was too slow and the subject matter often drifted toward the theoretical. "I wanted to be in the middle of the action as much as I could be," Deese said. An astute observer of how Washington worked, Deese had realized that he needed to tie his fortunes to someone with growing political power. He fell into a role working for Gene Sperling, the former Director of the NEC under President Bill Clinton. Sperling told a small set of friends that he'd buy a television for whoever could help find him a talented research assistant. One of them suggested Deese, and within weeks, he had endeared himself to Sperling by turning out detailed analysis and policy memos on whatever Sperling needed. It was 2004, and Sperling was informally advising Jason Furman, chief economic adviser to John Kerry's presidential campaign. "Gene was producing multipage, bulleted, bolded stuff of a higher quality than I'd ever seen him do before. My question was, who was doing it?" Furman said. "One day, Gene brings the guy doing all of this into the office and says, 'Please be nice to him. He's really smart. He's a really good guy.'"[3] It was Brian Deese.

The young Deese became a bullpen volunteer for the rest of the campaign, pitching in to help Furman and Sperling with whatever they needed. That decision put him at the center of a network of economic policymakers who would define the Washington consensus for the next decade. "These were the people I grew up with," Deese remembered.[4] They loved him for his smarts, his humility, and his reliability. "Brian was obviously very talented," Furman recalled.[5] Virtually everyone agreed. "This is somebody whose greatest joy is that swift arc up the learning curve," said Sperling. "He has both this amazing policy I.Q. that he can bring to any issue as well as the humility to reach out and find and listen to every expert on the planet on that issue."[6] By saying he was reaching out on behalf of the Kerry campaign, Deese discovered that he now had the power to call up virtually any Senator, academic, or business leader to answer his questions. He didn't hesitate to use it.

Despite his smarts, work ethic, and ambition, there was one thing Deese was lacking—a professional degree. It might be enough for him to learn at the feet of the smartest minds in political economy, but without academic training, his career would hit a wall, he believed. After John Kerry lost the presidential race in the fall of 2004, Deese submitted applications to America's top law schools. While he waited for their admissions decisions, he packed up and traveled the world with his soon-to-be wife. In the spring of 2005, Yale Law School offered him admission, and he enrolled in the fall.

Just as he was restless in the think tank world, Deese was never content leading a purely academic life. Just months into law school, he drifted back into public-policy fights. He teamed up with his classmate Wally Adeyemo,

as well as their law professors, to sue the state of Connecticut, arguing that it
was failing to meet the educational needs of its citizens. That same fall, Deese
organized against the confirmation of Supreme Court nominee and Yale law
alumnus Samuel Alito. He later spent a summer interning for the NAACP
Legal Defense Fund. By the time the next presidential election started to
rev up in early 2007, Deese was ready to return to politics; he started casting
about to see if he could advise a candidate early in the primary. The Obama
team brushed him off, but he had personal connections in Hillary Clinton's
orbit. He became an economic policy adviser there, even though he had another year left at Yale Law.

After a grueling primary, Clinton conceded in the spring, and Obama
became the Democratic nominee. Within days, the Senator from Illinois offered Furman the role of leading his campaign's economic policy efforts. As a
parent with young children and a burgeoning career, Furman said he would
only do it if he could bring along a deputy. The campaign balked, but Furman insisted. With the American economy on shaky ground and Obama's
thin economic experience a vulnerability, the campaign caved. Furman called
Deese, who quickly accepted and moved to Chicago for the role.

A few months later, Lehman Brothers filed for bankruptcy and the American economy began to collapse. Senator John McCain, Obama's opponent,
said at a rally that the "fundamentals of the economy are strong." He opposed
the bailout of AIG and then reversed himself a day later. Obama proceeded
more carefully and avoided issuing a statement that applauded Treasury Secretary Hank Paulson's decision to let Lehman fail. Furman and Deese organized a group of big economic names, including former Fed Chair Paul
Volcker, former Treasury Secretary Larry Summers, the economist Austan
Goolsbee, and investor Warren Buffett, to develop the campaign's response.[7]

Two months after the Lehman collapse, when Deese sat down with Obama
in Chicago in mid-November, he needed to deliver bad news to the
President-elect, who was already swimming in it. In the weeks since the implosion of Lehman and AIG, President George W. Bush's administration and
Congress had extended emergency lifelines to a broad set of banks and insurance companies, as one pillar of American capitalism after another threatened to collapse. Stock market losses for the year would total $7 trillion,
and unemployment was rising fast.[8] Estimates at the time suggested that the

American economy was contracting at a rate of 6 percent in the fourth quarter of 2008, a level not seen since the Great Depression.

The bad news Deese needed to share with Obama was more specific. Two of the nation's three largest auto manufacturers, GM and Chrysler, needed an emergency infusion of cash to avoid bankruptcy, and the third, Chrysler, was in rough shape as well. The three companies were losing over $150 million *a day* in late 2008.[9] Furman had assigned Deese to sort through how to respond, even though Deese had no experience in automotive manufacturing and was still technically a Yale law student on leave for the campaign. "Battlefield promotions come fast," surmised Larry Summers, who within weeks of the meeting became Deese's boss at the NEC.[10]

Obama and Deese had not yet spent significant time together, but Deese understood that his job in briefing the President-elect was to hew as closely as possible to the facts. He shared his analysis of what was happening to American automakers and the questions that the administration would soon need to answer. Obama did not need to make any particular decision that day; that would come later, after the selection of a Treasury Secretary and other key officials. But Deese needed Obama to be aware that if the auto companies collapsed, which could happen any day now, nearly a million people could be out of work. Estimates at the time suggested another 2 million would likely lose their jobs in related industries.[11] The auto companies had requested a $34 billion federal aid package. As Deese outlined its terms and how to respond, all he could think to himself was, "This is basically just darkness."[12]

Over the next few weeks, the automotive companies' problems compounded. In early December, Congress failed to authorize an auto bailout, forcing the Bush administration to come up with a patchwork solution to keep the companies on life support. It extended a $17 billion loan to GM and Chrysler, preventing immediate bankruptcy by using funds that Congress had initially appropriated for bank bailouts. Many people viewed this as the government bailing out elites, eliciting a populist backlash. It had started with Wall Street's largest banks and then moved to insurance companies. "I'm a strong believer in free enterprise, so my natural instinct is to oppose government intervention," President Bush told the nation in September as he called on Congress to save the banks, jettisoning the usual "let them fail" rhetoric that had animated Hank Paulson and others at the start of the crisis. "But these are not normal circumstances. The market is not functioning properly.

There's been a widespread loss of confidence. And major sectors of America's financial system are at risk of shutting down. . . . We must not let this happen."[13] Congress agreed, passing a landmark bailout package that made the federal government a major owner of America's banks. Now it seemed as though car manufacturers were next. Vice President Dick Cheney argued to Republican Senators that they must step in to save the auto companies: "If we don't do this, we will be known as the party of Herbert Hoover forever."[14] The liberal columnist Nicholas Kristof wrote a few days later: "For the first time in human history, I agree with Dick Cheney."[15]

By the time the Bush administration made its $17 billion loan, the Obama economic team was taking shape. Obama named Tim Geithner to be Treasury Secretary and Summers to direct the NEC. Given their focus on banks and finance, it would take both men weeks to fully understand the problems facing automotive manufacturing. For the moment, it fell to Deese alone to lead the team charged with coming up with a response. He roped in several volunteers to help with financial analysis and economic modeling. Waking at 5:00 am each day, Deese sidebarred with members of the team before convening a group conference call at 10:00 am and again at 8:00 pm to assess their collective progress and formulate next steps. If the incoming administration did not coalesce around a solution fast, Deese would take the fall, ending his up-and-coming career before it even started. "There was a time between Nov. 4 and mid-February when I was the only full-time member of the auto task force," he later said. "It was a little scary."[16]

In January 2009, as Barack Obama prepared to take the oath of office, his team was racing to put together their plans to address the nation's multiple economic crises. After his initial conversation with Deese in Chicago about the auto industry, Obama had a series of meetings with Summers, Geithner, and Deese to sort through how to respond to the growing recession and potential bankruptcy of American automotive companies. The first step was making sure he would have the right team in the White House. Summers tapped Jason Furman, Deese's boss on the campaign, to be Deputy Director of the NEC. Summers and Furman asked Deese to join the team, and Deese accepted so quickly that there was barely a meaningful discussion of the role he might play. Obama decided to create a senior position tasked with responding to the auto crisis, and in the first week of January word leaked that the front man for the administration's auto bailout efforts would be Steve Rattner, a former journalist and private equity investor. He could not start for weeks until his financial and ethical vetting was complete. As that process dragged on, Rattner waffled, unsure whether to join the administration. "I was still terrified. While Detroit melted, I dithered," he later wrote. Only in late February did Rattner commit.[17] While Rattner wrung his hands, Deese was tasked with outlining a temporary relief package for the American auto industry.

But first, he had to address a more prosaic problem: Where would he sit in the White House? Days before Obama was sworn in, Summers instructed his chief of staff to find blueprints of the second floor of the West Wing. He wanted to create a seating chart for the NEC staff to avoid wasting a single minute during those critical early days. Summers believed that, in Washington, proximity signaled status and power and a seating chart was like a map of who mattered. At one point during a meeting with Vice President Biden, Summers, unimpressed that the Budget Director had seated himself next to the Vice President, summoned a staffer and had him moved several seats away, securing the spot for himself.[18]

The challenge was squeezing enough bodies into the NEC's cramped quarters. The West Wing is notoriously tight on space, and Summers' own office measured just four feet by four feet—barely enough room for both him and a desk. A white parapet, only two feet away, blocked the office's single window. Outside, in a former waiting room, stood a handful of desks for Summers' deputies and maybe one or two others. The rest of the NEC staff had to work in the neighboring EEOB—just minutes away on foot but symbolically and politically miles from the center of action. Deese knew he had to be in the West Wing.

As the team settled in after the inauguration, Deese discovered that the desk assigned to him was in a "coat room." "I would be watching everybody walk back and forth to the bathroom all day." So, he improvised, commandeering a desk just steps from Summers. He fully expected to be evicted, but no one ever came to move him. Meanwhile, Rattner, who joined weeks later, was assigned a desk in one of the 566 rooms in the neighboring EEOB along with the rest of the auto bailout team. "Always wise, Deese also understood the value of proximity and elected to remain in a location that gave a huge boost to our efficiency," Rattner later wrote.[19]

It wasn't luck that prevented Deese from being exiled after his savvy choice of seat. Summers had taken to Deese, likely seeing something of himself in his young staffer. Twenty years earlier, Summers had been one of the golden boys of Washington. The nephew of influential economist Paul Samuelson, he started college at MIT at sixteen and received his PhD in economics from Harvard in 1982. A year after earning his PhD, at age twenty-eight, he became one of the youngest tenured professors in Harvard's history. Almost immediately, he decamped to work in the Reagan White House under the guidance of his mentor Martin Feldstein. Later, he became the chief economist of the World Bank and then a senior official in the Clinton Treasury Department, where he worked with Treasury Secretary Robert Rubin and Fed Chair Alan Greenspan. At the end of the 1990s, Clinton promoted Summers to Treasury Secretary at the age of forty-four, a remarkable achievement in a still-rocketing career. In the years afterward, Summers landed himself in public controversy while serving as President of Harvard for a series of boorish comments he made and ongoing conflict with faculty. Despite that, he managed to make it into Obama's inner circle on his campaign, positioning him for a senior role in the administration.

While colleagues and journalists consistently described Deese as "whip smart" and "a wunderkind," he also seemed to have people skills that Summers at times lacked. "Brian was really smart and really good with people," Summers recounted. "Although he was young, he was highly effective while never seeming threatening to people."[20] Deese held on to those people skills over the next decade, but he gradually left behind the habits of the duty-bound, loyal staffer that he was in his early days.

Summers, who was by then fifty-four, had often embraced a deep personal relationship with the young, bright minds he recruited to work for him. That made Deese part of a tribe. Working for the highly demanding economist required the junior partner to imbibe Summers' unique blend of economic analysis, frank demeanor, and high standards. Once an up-and-coming young person had earned his esteem, he or she was in the family, for life. The intensity of Summers' commitment to his protégés was a major reason he had built as much influence as he had in economic and government circles. "Summers' biggest strength was the mentor-style relationships he formed with students at every stage of his career," the *Harvard Crimson* said when Summers became the university's President.[21] Summers gave Deese a nickname in the early days of their White House relationship: "boy czar." The media had called Steve Rattner the auto czar, an echo of the "energy czar" title Bill Simon took in the early 1970s and the "drug czars" who had overseen American drug policy.

Now in the White House in the midst of a collapsing economy, Deese had to prove himself to Summers before he could advance. By March 2009, Rattner and Deese had been working with the rest of the auto bailout team for weeks to formulate a plan. After Bush threw the companies a lifeline, Deese, Summers, and Rattner began to think through what they might demand from the auto companies in exchange for additional financial support. The Big Three companies submitted restructuring plans in mid-February, and the team knew that their response would be a pivotal moment. "There's an old saying in finance called the golden rule of bankruptcy: He who has the gold makes the rules," Deese later wrote.[22] In this case, his team had all the gold.

On Thursday, March 26, the auto task force decided that the restructuring plans the companies had submitted were not viable. Obama convened his advisers in the Roosevelt Room to discuss what came next. Deese and Rattner had concluded that GM needed to undergo deeper cuts than the companies had proposed and that Chrysler needed to be acquired by Fiat to survive. "I had a Fiat in college," Obama said during the meeting, expressing some resignation about the decision. "It was in the shop all the time."[23] Some of the President's political advisers like David Axelrod—the administration's messaging guru—were also wary of another bailout, but Geithner and Summers insisted that the government had to step in.[24] Deese sat in the back row, and the one comment he made became a memorable joke, which Obama later described in his memoir. "Having seen his side prevail and feeling swept up in the moment, though, Deese started pointing out all the potential upsides of the decision I'd just made—including that a Chrysler-Fiat tandem could end up being the first U.S.-based operation to produce cars capable of getting forty miles to the gallon. Except in his nervousness, he said 'the first U.S.-produced cars that can go forty miles an hour,'" Obama wrote. "The room was quiet for a moment, then broke into laughter. Realizing his mistake, Deese's face, cherubic beneath his mustache and beard, turned bright red. I smiled and rose from my chair. . . . I walked around the table, patted Deese on the arm, and turned back as I was heading out the door. 'The people at Chrysler thank you,' I said, 'for not making that particular argument until after I made my decision.'"[25]

In the end, Obama green-lit the massive restructuring of the American auto industry that Deese and Rattner had proposed. Both GM and Chrysler were given a matter of weeks to develop new plans that would cut even deeper to get additional government money. Undiscussed with the President, but agreed upon by the team, was the need for a change in corporate leadership as well. After the meeting, Rattner fired the CEO and Chairman of GM, Rick Wagoner, as a requirement for additional bridge financing while GM made its plans for deeper cuts. "The challenge was to set up a framework that kept us at arm's length and out of the business of running a car company, yet held senior management accountable for its decisions and allowed us to protect the precious taxpayer dollars we had invested," Deese later wrote.[26]

Despite Deese's youth and inexperience, or possibly because of it, he was on the verge of designing a bailout that would set the auto industry on a new course—and would teach him a critical lesson about the power of marketcraft.

Three days later, on Sunday evening, the team was preparing to announce the government's plan for the restructuring of the American auto industry the following morning. Deese, Rattner, and Summers gathered in the Oval Office with President Obama while he made courtesy calls to legislators on the Hill and others, previewing the announcement he would make the next day. Many were nervous, expressing reservations about the plan's scope. Deese and Rattner ran a challenging briefing call with a hundred members of the media, who seemed preoccupied with the firing of Wagoner. Frustrated by the journalists' focus on the CEO drama, Deese and Rattner went in search of an alternate storyline that would help Americans understand how the sizable government investment would help them.

Deese had an idea: create a financial incentive for Americans to trade in vehicles with particularly bad fuel efficiency, like SUVs and large trucks, for cleaner vehicles. The program, called Cash for Clunkers, would spur the purchase of new cars and simultaneously support the administration's goal of mitigating climate change. The team had discussed something similar before but had dismissed it because it would need Congressional approval. But this time, that seemed a price worth paying to solve the conundrum they faced. "Let's try it," Summers said.

Deese and his colleagues stayed up through the night to put together the plan so that it would be ready for the President the following morning.[27] Six weeks later, the House and Senate approved the program, eventually appropriating $3 billion, which Americans used to purchase over 500,000 new vehicles, reducing emissions and stimulating economic activity. "It was an extraordinary success, far beyond anything we had imagined," Rattner wrote.[28] Deese didn't stop there. As he went about implementing the administration's program, he used the newfound government leverage to impose the first federal greenhouse gas emissions requirements on auto manufacturers and significantly increase fuel efficiency for new cars.[29] Those efforts would set the auto industry on a new, climate friendlier development path.

By the summer, GM and Chrysler had begun to recover. Record-fast bankruptcy proceedings meant that GM emerged quickly from its restructuring, with the US Treasury owning 60 percent of the company. Fiat bought Chrysler, and the Treasury took just shy of 10 percent of its shares. Private creditors lost almost all of their investment. Over the following four years, as auto manufacturers rebounded, the government gradually sold its shares, returning the companies to private hands. The government lost $10 billion on the investment, but it saved significantly more in foregone unemployment and health-care support payments.[30] American auto manufacturing recovered. In the summer of 2009, just over 600,000 Americans were employed in motor vehicle and parts manufacturing. By 2024, the number was over 1 million, close to the same level as in 2006, before the crisis began.[31]

Summers and Deese came away from the auto bailout with different lessons. For Summers, the success of the effort resulted from the government's light touch. The collapse of GM and Chrysler had been a market failure, the result of bad decisions by its leaders and private creditors who had not exercised sufficient discipline. Market failure required the government to step in—at least when the companies were systemically important or critical politically—to resuscitate them. But that, in Summers' mind, should be the end of it. "We said that we were going to run this as much as possible like a commercial restructuring," Summers said. "The basic idea was this was not going to be a sandbox for the Labor Department to do experiments in labor management and the [EPA] to push its electric car agenda. Nor were we going to try to do more than the minimum necessary to move them through restructuring."[32]

The experience proved formative for Deese, but not in the way Summers might have imagined. Temporary nationalization of two of the largest auto manufacturers left Deese with an appreciation for the power of the state to craft a market. "I came away with this enormous sense of the potential for government intervention to do good," Deese said. "We created a structure, and we asked the right policy questions. We organized effectively with our focus on the public purpose."[33]

Hundreds of thousands of Americans kept their jobs, and the government created a new structure for a more climate-friendly car industry that endured. The *New York Times* said at the time that Deese was "rewriting the rules of American capitalism," setting new precedent for government action and devising ways to help American workers, mitigate climate change, and stabilize a vital industry at once.[34] Deese had little interest in seeing the state own any industry, nor did it seem wise to leave the private sector unchecked. But he did see value in the auto marketcraft, intentionally using state power to achieve the political goal of shoring up the critical industry. Government did not just need to temporarily address market failures—it could shape a market to make it work better. "Brian's successful handling of the auto crisis gave him an understanding of what policymaking can and should do—of how possible, indeed necessary, it is to direct the gaze of markets, especially in a crisis," said Jen Harris, the Senior Director on the Biden NEC and National Security Council (NSC). "That animated his later willingness to go against the grain of various economic orthodoxies."[35]

For the moment, Deese was uninterested in breaking ranks with his mentors. Indeed, he needed them to continue to support his work to advance his career, and Summers had an unconventional demand. "This summer you are leaving," Summers told Deese as the bailout work was finally stabilizing. "You cannot come back until you have your degree, but you can come back as soon as you have it." Deese had yet to finish at Yale Law School. While Summers didn't see the law degree as a requirement for working on his NEC, he did want Deese to have the necessary credentials to ensure long-term career advancement. Deese took the advice: "I drove up to New Haven and spent four days in the law library, writing papers and doing tests."[36] Yale conferred his degree in the fall of 2009. A year later, Deese got the first of several promotions on the NEC that would eventually propel him to the top of government, where the lessons from the auto bailout would take center stage.

14

REVOLUTION IN THE RANKS

LINA KHAN & ANTIMONOPOLY (2015-16)

In August of 2014, a twenty-five-year-old incoming Yale Law student wandered around the ballroom of the Omni New Haven Hotel, a ten-minute walk from the law library where Brian Deese had finished his exams five years before. Classes had not yet begun, and Lina Khan was already unsure if she should even be there. Another meandering attendee, Gilad Edelman, struck up a conversation with her, and, in a moment of candor, she told him that she was already thinking of dropping out. Khan had chosen to enroll at Yale Law over accepting an offer from the *Wall Street Journal* to cover antitrust, and now she worried she had made the wrong choice. "I told Khan that journalists were indeed cooler than lawyers, but since she was already at Yale she should probably give it a shot," Edelman said. He later ended up working as a journalist covering Khan's specialty, antitrust.[1]

According to peers and professors, Khan seemed uncomfortable in her first months at Yale. The highly selective "finishing school" of the American establishment reeked of elitism and conventionality, and Khan felt like an outlier. Born in the United Kingdom in 1989 to a Muslim family of Pakistani immigrants, she grew up in London's diverse Golders Green neighborhood until the age of eleven, when her parents moved the family to Larchmont, a well-to-do suburb north of New York City. Her father worked as a management consultant and her mother at Thomson Reuters. After high school,

Khan went to the small, prestigious Williams College, where she studied political theory and edited the campus newspaper. Her senior thesis focused on the work of the German American philosopher Hannah Arendt. Khan argued that her concept of alienation could help people understand the lack of American civic activism. "Resignation frequently surrounds politics, a feeling that there is little any one person or group of people can do to effect meaningful political change," Khan wrote. "Indeed, structures of power do limit citizens' reach—but political indifference persists disproportionate to the influence ordinary people do and can have in the public realm." Khan would not succumb to such "political indifference." She dedicated her work to her parents, thanking them for teaching her "the value of tempering idealism with realism, but not so as to extinguish it."[2]

Like Deese, Khan headed for Washington after graduating from college in 2010, landing a job at the Open Markets Institute, a research group within a think tank called New America. Unlike Deese, Khan chose a mentor, Barry Lynn, who was closer to being a political outcast than to the center of power. Ten years earlier, while Lynn worked as an executive editor at a small business magazine, an earthquake in Taiwan disrupted the global semiconductor supply. That event provoked an epiphany for Lynn about the dangers of industrial concentration. After the magazine folded, Lynn joined New America and wrote two books on the risks of a hyperconcentrated economy. The problem was that few agreed with him. Lynn was going up against thirty years of legal and economic orthodoxy that held that corporate concentration, as long as it did not raise consumer prices in the short term, did little harm to Americans.

After the Great Financial Crisis, Lynn's solo efforts to challenge the antitrust consensus were falling flat, and he needed help. He aimed to assemble a team to produce original research and journalism exposing the risks of corporate concentration more broadly. To start, Lynn wanted to bring on someone without formal economics training, who was presumably free from the biases that came with it. With only modest funding, he needed to find someone early in her or his career whom he could mentor and show how corporate concentration harmed American workers and suppressed innovation. Khan became Lynn's first hire, even though she had never thought about competition policy in a meaningful way. "When she walked in that door, she had no idea what this entailed or what she would become," Lynn later said.

"She was just a fantastically smart person who was very curious."[3] Over the following three years, Khan invented a new role for herself: part researcher and part journalist, producing long-form analysis in the magazine *Washington Monthly* on topics like the creep of private arbitration and the consolidation of poultry farms.

It is hard to overstate how insignificant the Lynn-Khan outlook was at the time. Antitrust scholarship, never known for its riveting subject matter, had become unfashionable in the academy and public-policy circles following a concerted effort to narrow its scope. Antitrust enforcers had historically enjoyed a broad mandate: Between 1890 and the 1970s, antitrust law was used to ensure markets were broadly competitive and open, hemming in the abuse of concentrated corporate power. But starting in the 1970s, courts and enforcement agencies subscribed to a novel view, associated with economists at the University of Chicago, that mergers and acquisitions should be permitted unless there was clear evidence of higher prices for consumers. Khan and Lynn were part of a small group of lawyers well outside the mainstream who believed the new approach from the 1970s and '80s had emboldened a historic consolidation of economic and political power in global corporations. Increasingly powerful, the multinational businesses were harming American workers and suppressing innovation. Khan and Lynn also believed that the new antitrust approach could lead to political corruption by creating private institutions that rivaled the scope and power of the public ones. In 2010, nearly the entire antitrust field was debating whether Comcast's acquisition of Time Warner Cable should be allowed, given that it might add twelve cents to subscribers' monthly bills. The field's insurgents, Khan and Lynn, considered that dispute hopelessly narrow.

Khan and Lynn gradually began to expand their ranks. In early 2014, Fordham law professor Zephyr Teachout took a fellowship at New America and was joined by Matt Stoller, who had built an outsized reputation as a left-leaning writer and firebrand. "I got enough money to get these two rooms at New America," Lynn recounted. "Lina and I sat in the big room, and I bought for $200 an Ikea black, fake leather sofa. We hung a nice big whiteboard above the black sofa."[4] On it, the group diagrammed a twenty-five-year plan to "bring back antimonopoly," favoring the broader term "antimonopoly" over "antitrust" to emphasize the many ways state action could corral and manage private, corporate power.

Feeling emboldened and inspired, Teachout decided a few months later to make a long-shot run for Governor of New York, primarying the incumbent, Andrew Cuomo, from the left on an antimonopoly message. She had given electoral politics little thought, but she plunged into an unexpected campaign. She tapped Columbia Law School professor and former Obama administration official Tim Wu to run as her lieutenant governor. Khan took the role of policy director. The campaign raised less than $1 million, making it a long-shot bid against a powerful and popular governor. But Teachout and Wu's focus on an antimonopoly message translated the wonkery of ivory-tower legal debates into the language of the stump. They pledged to rein in corporate greed and ensure competitive, fair markets, lowering prices and creating jobs. They lost, but Teachout took a surprising 34 percent of the vote and Wu, 40 percent.

Election Day came two weeks after Khan started at Yale, no doubt playing in the back of her mind as she wandered around the Omni ballroom. But like Deese, she had decided that to get ahead in Washington, she needed a credential to command respect. She overcame her reservations and stayed in school, her eyes on a bigger prize ahead.

Khan and Deese did not know each other at the time, but the two of them were part of a new generation of policy leaders who flooded into Washington over the course of the 2010s and began to flex their power at the end of the decade. This was not a new trend. Every few years, going all the way back to the 1930s, a cohort of new arrivals brings to Washington a fresh understanding of how the world works, overturning the preexisting conventional wisdom. The political and policy minds of Washington feted the men and women who ushered in the New Deal, just as they celebrated the "brilliance" of young strategists who led America into Vietnam and the eager proponents of Reaganomics years later. The allure of youth and novelty often puts any skeptics of the new wave on the wrong side of history, whatever the merit of their critique.

No one captured the description of these waves of newcomers better than the journalist David Halberstam in his 1972 book, *The Best and the Brightest*. Usually under forty when they first attain significant power, they are "of truly uncommon industry and discipline, the brightest boy in the school," he wrote. Often familiar with one another from shared, elite educational experiences, they forge quick bonds in Washington and hastily climb the ranks of power, charming allies and inspiring jealousy in rivals. They are "intelligent, but more respectable than restless, more builders than critics," confident in their abilities and intellectual powers. Each is understood to be uniquely qualified to tackle complex policy issues by virtue of their untiring work ethic, dexterous capacity for analysis, and collaborative demeanor. Lack of experience in government or international relations is an asset that enables the new generation to see matters fresh, clearing out the underbrush of tradition to hatch policies that are clever and practical.[5]

Deese and Khan were at the forefront of a wave of the best and brightest who arrived in Washington after the Great Financial Crisis and invented a new kind of marketcraft. Their approach would prioritize public investment and competition policy—"build" and "balance" as it would later be called— but in the 2010s, the ideas were still in development. The accelerating deindustrialization of America and the economic shock of the financial crisis deeply shaped the outlook of this generation that was largely born in the late 1970s and 1980s. Some of its leaders, like Deese and his friend Jake Sullivan, the future National Security Advisor who would play a pivotal role in the development of the Biden economic agenda, began in government in the years after the financial crisis. They tended to rise to power a decade later, after the formative events of Donald Trump's election and the global pandemic. This particular wave of leaders crossed the partisan divide, united in its skepticism of the "free-market" orthodoxy that birthed the Great Financial Crisis and offered little in response to deindustrialization or pandemic. Despite deep disagreements and meaningfully different value systems, they shared a common belief in the need for the American government to guide and manage markets to serve human ends.

Every one of them passed through the gates of one of two educational institutions: the law schools of Yale and Harvard. Deese trained at Yale, as did Sullivan. When Deese hired three deputies at the NEC to run the nation's economic policy, all were under forty-five and all were graduates of Yale Law. Khan graduated from Yale, as did Jen Harris, one of the most influential White House staffers responsible for Bidenomics. The Republican think tank leaders and Senators making up this new wave, including Josh Hawley and J. D. Vance, shared the same profile: they too came to power before they turned forty and had been profoundly shaped by their experiences at Yale and Harvard.[6]

What made those elite institutions hotbeds of a new marketcrafting impulse? They unsurprisingly nurtured sharp minds and cultivated incredible ambition. "Half of the students want to be President one day, but it's not cool to say that," said one faculty member at Yale. "So they all say they want to be Attorney General." But their impact on this new wave of marketcrafters ran deeper than just cultivating zeal: the postrecession wave of the best and brightest learned at Yale and Harvard how to be just provocative enough. Conventionality is not rewarded in their classrooms or around the dining hall tables; the trick is to say something original or even radical, but without going too far.

Khan and Deese's cohort rejected the orthodoxy of self-regulating markets, seeing in the Washington consensus a false guarantee that had continually failed to deliver on its fundamental promise of widely shared prosperity. They rejected that stale premise and offered a novel understanding—just provocative enough—of how markets and government interact. It would not be a fundamental rupture in American economics, because it still relied on a market-based framework for its legitimacy. But it would be a radical break from what men like Summers and Greenspan had long argued, and it would impact the lives of millions.

At the same moment Khan was settling in at Yale, Deese's career was taking off. By 2015, he had an office of his own just down the corridor from the Oval Office. When Summers left the NEC in 2011, Gene Sperling, Deese's first mentor, became Director, and he promoted Deese to Deputy Director. After two years in that role, Deese moved to the Office of Management and Budget to take the Deputy Director role there. Then, in February 2015, he returned to the White House as a senior adviser to the President. By then, the emergent challenge of the Great Financial Crisis had ebbed, but Americans were enduring the slowest economic recovery from a recession since the 1930s. It took over six years for American workers to regain the jobs lost in the wake of the financial crisis, and unemployment remained higher than it was before the fall of 2008. Median wages remained flat, and deindustrialization continued to undermine manufacturing communities. An opioid crisis raged, leading to a surge in "deaths of despair," as a pair of economists called them in 2015. Macroeconomic indicators were no less bleak: productivity, a key reflection of technological progress, was particularly muted. Despite an extended period of historically cheap credit, business investment remained lackluster.

Something was wrong in the American economy, and Deese was coming to believe that the approach to economic policy he had grown up with was part of the problem. Contrary to Summers' faith in a light touch, Deese increasingly thought that government might need to take a heavier hand in organizing markets to make them more prosperous and stable. If the premise seemed novel, it had already survived a major political test: Democrats in Congress had taken that approach to health-care markets when they passed the Affordable Care Act in 2010. Obama had left much of the policy design to Congressional leaders, setting the stage for another byzantine set of legislative compromises similar to what happened fifty years earlier with the creation of Medicare. Summers resisted the most aggressive proposals, such as providing a public option of health insurance to all Americans and caps on the profits of private health-care companies, calling them "dumb." "Why aren't we jumping up and down about that, telling them how stupid it is?" he asked his colleagues, referring to the public option. His deputy, Furman, answered with another question: "Would it reassure you to know that they don't care what we think?"[7]

Congress eventually agreed to a convoluted structure in which individual states would run their own health-care markets offering private insurance to most Americans, paired with federal subsidies to lower costs. More poor and lower-middle-class Americans would be able to access Medicaid, and new regulations would hopefully slow the growth of health-care spending. The bill capped the profits of health insurance companies, required them to cover preexisting conditions, and mandated that Americans purchase insurance. This was undoubtedly marketcraft, but not the kind that invested a federal institution with a clear mission and the discretionary power to deliver it. The economic minds in the administration, including Summers, only reluctantly supported it.

The inability to embrace a coherent philosophy of how the state should manage and guide markets left many, including the President, lacking meaningful answers for what to do about the economic malaise. In his major speech on economic policy during the 2012 reelection campaign, Obama impugned the deregulatory, low-tax agenda of the opposition, but he offered few new economic policy ideas.[8] The biggest economic initiative of his second term would become the negotiation of a new trade agreement with the countries of the Pacific Rim, known as the Trans-Pacific Partnership (TPP). Addressing the simmering rivalry with China may have been prescient geopolitically, but even the most optimistic estimates for its impact on American growth and employment were modest.

Deese was beginning to build his own theory of how public policy could make American markets work better. When he returned to the White House in 2015 from the Office of Management and Budget, he took on a new mission: mitigate climate change. "It's not the harrowing urgency of the economy falling off the cliff," Deese told the *New York Times* after starting the job. "But it's the urgency of, 'We have a limited amount of time left to change the trajectory on a really urgent crisis. . . . It's a different kind of emergency.'" Deese again lacked deep subject matter expertise, just like in 2008 when he tackled the problem of the American auto industry. But he made up for it with enduring loyalty to the President. Obama had officials at the State Department to lead the charge on international negotiations and he had plenty of scientific experts on call. He needed someone with economic experience and personal loyalty to him, working in the West Wing, crafting the agenda. By 2015, Deese was one of the longest-serving members of the administration, outlasting Summers, Geithner, and Rattner, and in the process earning Obama's trust and affection.

Deese's two-year focus on climate policy built on the lessons he had learned from the auto restructuring and laid the foundation for the massive efforts he would undertake years later in the next Democratic administration. He believed that the government had to support the development of emerging technologies in order to slow the pace of climate change. "Some of the biggest opportunities," he later told the *Times*, "were at the intersection of strategic procurement, what some people would call straight-out industrial policy, and the work we needed to do as a country to scale markets for clean-energy innovation."[9] The jargon masked a simple but powerful idea: this was a significant shift from the approach that Summers had favored a few years earlier. In 2010, to combat climate change, Summers had wanted to pass a carbon tax or a "cap-and-trade" framework for carbon emissions. These approaches would embrace the wisdom of markets and minimize government involvement to the imposition of a tax. If the state created a framework to price the true cost of carbon emissions, private actors could sort through how to minimize their pollution. "Among economists, the issue is largely a no-brainer," wrote the conservative Greg Mankiw.[10] Politically, however, the idea never took off. Taxes that would raise the price of gasoline were just as unappealing in 2010 as they were when Bill Simon proposed them in the 1970s. A bipartisan legislative effort collapsed in late 2010, never to be revived.[11]

Obama pivoted to a new, two-pronged climate strategy: implement new regulations in energy markets and use international diplomacy to convince polluting countries to do the same. At home, the EPA issued rules and guidance to limit emissions from existing power plants and strengthen ozone standards to improve air quality and public health. Abroad, the Obama administration forged an agreement with the Chinese government to set top-line emission-reduction targets and ratchet down the production of hydrocarbons.

Deese was not the architect of these efforts, but he became the primary point person responsible for implementing the emerging climate agenda once Obama's previous climate adviser left government. Deese's most influential work in the role—and the most formative event for him—was negotiating the 2015 Paris Climate Accords. Five years earlier, an attempt to forge an international consensus to reduce emissions had collapsed in Copenhagen when participating countries failed to agree on a framework. Now Deese, alongside Secretary of State John Kerry and his deputy Todd Stern, was in charge of picking up those pieces and forging a new consensus for a binding international agreement at the next global meeting in Paris.

Deese and his team built on the momentum that the American-Chinese agreements had created over the prior two years, demonstrating to the world that two of the globe's most powerful countries were willing to use regulatory policy to reduce emissions. After two weeks of marathon negotiations in Paris, representatives of nearly 100 countries agreed to an international treaty to limit global warming to two degrees centigrade above preindustrial levels. The agreement required all participating countries to set voluntary emission-reduction targets, established a framework for financial assistance to developing countries, and encouraged international collaboration to develop new technologies to fight climate change. Deese had spent those two weeks moving in and out of endless negotiations, horse-trading with diplomats from across the world. "The Sunday morning after the agreement had been signed," Deese recalled a few months later, "there was a blur of headlines on cable news, characterizing the agreement that had just been inked as 'historic and unprecedented' and at the same time as 'insufficient and inconclusive.' Both descriptions are right."[12]

The climate agenda that Deese oversaw, which combined the regulatory power of the EPA with the fruits of coordinated international diplomacy, structured energy markets to enhance the production of cleaner energies and limit fossil fuels. This approach dumped the cap-and-trade and carbon-tax frameworks favored by Summers and other economists and embraced a mix of public investment and regulation. Deese knew even then that those steps, important as they were, would be insufficient without further technological progress. The world needed private capital to invest in the field of green technologies. "For me, one of the most striking things about the last year was the American private sector's near unanimous view that a long-term, international climate framework was in their business interest," he said a few months after the agreement was signed. Government regulation to limit emissions would only get us so far. The state had to use its power to cultivate new markets, harnessing the power of entrepreneurship and innovation to develop novel technologies that would make it possible to meet the goals outlined in Paris.

Just as the economist-favored carbon-tax approach was fading, so too was the cross-partisan agreement that more trade was better, regardless of how it was structured. Some of the economic leaders in the Obama White House hoped to create a Pacific free-trade zone through passage of the TPP. Obama himself believed that a new free-trade zone around the Pacific would strengthen America's ties to counter China's growing influence. But the air was leaking out of the free-trade balloon. Voters, particularly in the industrial Midwest, felt burned by the string of free-trade agreements that had hollowed out their communities and facilitated the rise of global megacorporations. Even Obama's Vice President, Joe Biden, expressed private reservations about the trade deal. "Don't fucking ever ask me to do a TPP event unless it comes from President Obama. That's the only time I'll do it," Biden told his staff in a moment of frustration.[13] Hillary Clinton and Donald Trump agreed in the 2016 presidential campaign that the Pacific deal as negotiated would not work for American workers. The United States never ratified it.

The Washington consensus had sustained support for "obvious" policies like a carbon tax and free trade for decades. The shifting political winds left Democrats and Republicans alike on the hunt for policies that put more control in the hands of the state to navigate a different course and reinvigorate American capitalism. Nothing illustrated that openness to new ideas as much as the sudden popularity of the new antitrust movement, soon to be led by Lina Khan.

The invitation landed in Khan's inbox in February 2016, just two months after Deese and his team had inked the Paris Agreement. The sender was Ganesh Sitaraman, former policy director for Senator Elizabeth Warren and a visiting professor at Yale Law. Would Lina be willing to help curate a small, private dinner to talk with Warren about the past and future of anti-monopoly policy? Sitaraman had reached out to Khan because of her reputation, growing in the worlds of New Haven and Washington, for advocating a broad and aggressive rethink of competition policy. She had the same lawyerly demeanor and the contrarian, provocative intellectual tilt that many had associated with Warren. Sitaraman had a sense the two would hit it off. "Lina really stood out among her peers," said one of her professors, Amy Kapczynski. "She was deeply committed to her own vision. She came in with her interest in antimonopoly at the start and followed it aggressively."[14] Her faculty adviser, David Grewal, had also been taken aback by Khan's seemingly unencumbered, crusading nature. Many would have expected her to take the safe route to keep climbing the public-policy achievement ladder: a clerkship for an appellate judge, perhaps followed by another clerkship for a Supreme Court justice, private practice, and then a move into government. "She didn't do that," Grewal said. "She went for the intellectual jugular."[15] Aware of Khan's acumen and boldness, Sitaraman knew that Warren needed to talk to her.

On a Friday morning in March 2016, Khan boarded a train bound for Washington, DC. When she had accepted the invitation a few weeks before, she made sure that her old boss Barry Lynn could join, along with an antitrust lawyer in private practice named Jonathan Kanter. Rohit Chopra, a Warren acolyte and future commissioner of the Federal Trade Commission (FTC) and Director of the Consumer Financial Protection Bureau (CFPB), joined for drinks before dinner. Afterward, the small group settled into Warren's private office for the meal and to talk shop. Khan immediately took to

Warren, seeing in her a biting intellect sensitive to the risks of concentrated corporate power.

Warren was charmed as well, and the message from Khan and colleagues seemed to resonate with her. Several weeks later, Warren gave a speech that outlined a new approach to antitrust that drew heavily on the influence of Khan and Lynn. "[A]nyone who loves markets knows that for markets to work, there has to be competition. But today, in America, competition is dying," Warren said, before reciting a jeremiad of the harms of corporate concentration. The consumer welfare approach to antitrust law had allowed companies to grow bigger and bigger.[16] Khan might as well have written the speech. "She actually named names—the company names," Khan said. "Lawmakers are often reluctant to do that because it makes it so much more pointed. It took on an additional force because she was willing to go there."[17]

Warren's speech was not about antitrust law, as narrowly practiced in the courts. Instead, Warren was tapping into a much broader school of thought, better understood as antimonopoly, premised on the foundational view that government should craft markets to ensure that no private entity has unchecked power. "Market structure is deeply political," Khan had explained in an article co-written with Teachout in 2014. "The structure of a market at any given time is the product of political decisions—made and not made—about how players in that market will be allowed to use their power." Highly concentrated markets were particularly problematic because certain companies "can assume enough power to restrain, and even control, the actions of others."[18]

Antitrust was one targeted way of checking that power, but a broader antimonopoly approach would craft particular markets to get the right mix of private competition, public investment, and administrative rule making. Antimonopoly action rejected the myth of a preexisting, natural market, and highlighted the need for state action to make markets more open, fair, and competitive. Each market developed within a specific context, taking on a unique shape and character based on the type of good or service being sold, the nature of the demand, and the urgency of people's needs. Government action was often required to secure the right balance between competitive forces and prevent the abuse of market power by the biggest companies. Khan and now Warren were arguing that a reinvigorated antimonopoly movement would lower prices, spur innovation, help workers, and limit lobbying power in the halls of Washington.

The reinvigoration of antimonopoly did not usually mean breaking up existing companies. Most of the time, it meant that the two agencies charged with antitrust enforcement—the FTC and Department of Justice (DOJ)—would step in to prevent mergers and acquisitions *before* markets became unduly concentrated. It meant ensuring that workers could move from one job to another, making labor markets more competitive. It also meant preventing enormous companies such as Walmart or Amazon from using their size to force suppliers into unfair contracts. They could also use their regulatory power to make sure that platform businesses treated all vendors fairly, preventing them from giving special treatment to those they prefer. Antimonopoly action would not just be a job for the twin regulators, the FTC and DOJ, charged with enforcing antitrust laws, but a theoretical approach that administrators across government could use. Congress and the executive branch could also create government-backed alternatives to private companies—so-called public options—to ensure universal access to essential services, ensuring appropriate levels of competition.[19]

The spring and summer of 2016 turned out to be the moment that the antimonopoly movement began to build real momentum. A few weeks after the dinner in Warren's office, *Politico* published a "road map" for a new approach to enforcement at the FTC. Authored by Khan, it called on the agency to take its responsibility much more seriously.[20] The same day as Warren's speech at New America, the center-left think tank the Center for American Progress released its own report called "Reviving Antitrust." A few weeks after that, Democrats unveiled a new plank in their platform, "promoting competition by stopping corporate concentration." Meanwhile, Obama's CEA, now led by Jason Furman, published a report on how to spur competition. In the often-static world of Washington ideas, momentum was building.

A bevy of think tank papers and a White House report might not change the world, at least not on their own. A juicy David versus Goliath story, however, could move the fight to rein in corporate power out of the realm of the abstract and technical and into the headlines. Throughout 2016, Khan was quietly working on something that might just do that. She had one of the nation's biggest companies in her sights.

But before she could put her plans into action, the world shook.

A little before 11:00 pm on Election Day, 2016, television networks declared that Donald Trump had won Ohio and Florida. By 2:30 am, Trump had prevailed in Pennsylvania and Wisconsin as well, giving him the electoral votes he needed to become President. Clinton called Trump to concede, and a few minutes later Trump walked onto a stage in Midtown Manhattan, declaring victory and promising a new direction for America and the world.

Where Deese and Khan had been working to challenge the economic assumptions comprising the Washington consensus, Trump's election overturned the conventional wisdom undergirding much of American politics. He had run on a thin policy agenda, heavy on populist rhetoric that was fundamentally anti-elite and anti-ideas. America was rotting at its core, he argued, because rich politicians and government bureaucrats had consolidated power in remote institutions insensitive to the needs of most Americans. Republicans and Democrats alike were running a rainbow oligarchy of global capitalism premised on open borders and free trade. Those ideas had led them to use government to enrich themselves and hollow out the American middle class. Trump's misogyny, bigotry, and questionable business acumen made little difference to voters. Nor did it matter that he offered few specific plans to fix things. Clinton won the popular vote, but voters in the states that mattered for the electoral college wanted a disruptive heretic, not another stable, establishment politician.

In the wake of Trump's victory, American politics broke wide open. Even though the election had delayed Deese and Khan's chance to shape markets from the executive branch by four years, it also proved that ideas once at the fringes could now be seriously discussed. If Trump could win, what else might be possible?

15

THE ODYSSEY

FELICIA WONG, JULIUS KREIN & JAKE SULLIVAN (2016-20)

At night in the desert, not far from Death Valley, Felicia Wong tilted her head back and let the stars wash over her. Here, a hundred miles from the nearest city lights, the cosmos spilled across the sky in a way that made earthly concerns—even the political upheaval that had driven her here—feel distant and small. "Great leaders in all ages have sought the desert and heard its voice," L. L. Nunn had written when he founded Deep Springs College on this remote cattle ranch a century earlier. "For what came ye into the wilderness?" For Wong, president of the Roosevelt Institute and one of the Democratic Party's leading economic thinkers, the answer was both escape and revelation.

Wong had convinced her board at the progressive think tank to grant her a six-month sabbatical at the start of 2017, in the aftermath of Trump's victory. Rather than retreating to the confines of an Ivy League fellowship, Wong chose Deep Springs, where twenty-six young men (the college did not begin to enroll women until 2018) practiced a form of educational self-governance—admitting their own classmates, hiring their own professors, and working the ranch between seminars. The students, with their mix of intellectual rigor and skepticism toward modern capitalism, had welcomed Wong as an instructor. But it was the isolation that had truly drawn her: with no cell service and strict limits on technology, there would be nothing to do but teach a single class and contemplate what had gone wrong in American politics—and what she could do to help fix it.

The answer for progressives like Wong could not just be "pivot left." Wong herself had tried that already. The previous summer, when it seemed likely that Clinton would beat Trump, Wong had been featured in a glowing profile in the *New York Times*. The writer put the left-leaning Roosevelt Institute at the center of the Democratic Party, crediting this achievement to Wong's leadership. "She has thick, artfully unruly cataracts of black hair and moves with a long, darting, buoyant stride," he wrote. "In meetings, she spends much of her time profusely, sweetly and genuinely thanking people for their thoughtful recommendations of white papers she has already read, studies she has already digested, arguments she could recite by heart, academics she already funds or would like to, funders who already donate and, often, information or ideas she herself has originated." The Clinton campaign had adopted many of Roosevelt's policy proposals, even going so far as to incorporate the title of a seminal Roosevelt report, "Rewriting the Rules," into campaign speeches. After being challenged in a long primary by the insurgent democratic socialist Bernie Sanders, Clinton had run the most progressive policy campaign in a general election since 1988. She argued against the ratification of new free-trade agreements such as the Trans-Pacific Partnership and made a proactive case for free college for students from families making less than $125,000. She campaigned on ending mass incarceration by reforming mandatory sentencing laws that her husband had signed just twenty years prior.[1]

If any other Republican besides Trump had beaten Clinton, it would likely have set Wong and her ideas back years, if not decades. The new economic progressivism that had been adopted by the Clinton campaign would have been defeated by another coherent ideology, one unmistakably more conservative. Instead, most Americans understood the election to be a rejection of the Clinton-Bush-Obama orthodoxy that had come before, not the endorsement of any particular economic road map going forward. When Trump shattered the playbook of "reasonable" policies for both liberals and conservatives, it created an opportunity for Wong to articulate something novel. She just had to figure out what that would be.

The Trump presidency ushered in a period of extreme polarization in American politics, with Republicans and Democrats ratcheting up their rhetoric to levels not seen since the Civil War. Within a week of taking office, Trump instituted a travel ban on several predominantly Muslim countries to the United States. In the months and years that followed, he appointed justices to the Supreme Court who eliminated the right to abortion. He used racist rhetoric to excuse White supremacy. He politicized the administrative state by firing civil service leaders he didn't like and demanding loyalty pledges from those he hired. He threatened to withhold American aid to a foreign government if it did not investigate his challenger in the presidential race. By the end of his presidency, Trump undermined the results of a democratic election he lost and encouraged his supporters to storm and occupy the US Capitol. American institutions had never been more embattled or fragile.

In the midst of the historic polarization, however, the first signs of an unexpected cross-partisan convergence on a new marketcraft, grounded in public investment and competition policy began to appear. In economics at least, Republicans and Democrats who profoundly disagreed with each other on other existential issues were moving toward a similar way of thinking about how government might help markets work better. Wong soon led the left's effort to sort out what a new marketcraft might look like.

One day in the brief period between Election Day 2016 and her sabbatical in the wilderness, Wong stood at a salad bar at Airlie, an institutional retreat center in rural Virginia. The 300-acre facility felt like a cross between a bare-bones hotel and a summer camp. In this case, the William and Flora Hewlett Foundation had invited dozens of civil society leaders to consider the future of democracy, and Wong was late to lunch. Hustling to fill her plate, she ran into someone else running late: Larry Kramer, the former Dean of Stanford Law School, and the head of Hewlett. "I said to myself, that's the President of Hewlett," Wong recalled. "I have to introduce myself—it's weird not to, right?" Clutching at leaves of romaine with the ubiquitous black salad tongs that unite every institutional dining hall in America, Wong introduced herself.

"Felicia?" Kramer answered. "Everyone says I need to talk to you. Word is that you think neoliberalism is over."

"Well, that's true," Wong replied. "I do think that—intellectually at least."

"Come sit with me," Kramer said, and he steered the two over to a side table. Kramer challenged Wong: "So describe to me why you think it's over."[2]

The two launched into a conversation about the persistence of the myth of a self-regulating market, and Wong's growing certainty that people were beginning to question whether the economic policies of the past forty years had provided the prosperity they had promised. In Wong's view, trade agreements designed to favor investor interests, combined with other political trends like hostility toward unions and a lack of public investment, had driven American capitalism into crisis. Propping up the bipartisan consensus that had pursued these policies was the flawed belief that governments should let markets work their magic, minimizing any "intervention." Responding to the anger of the American voter, policy wonks were waking up to the flaws in their ideology.

Kramer was open to Wong's argument but needed more research to be convinced. He asked Wong to hold a meeting in New York a few months later, where a small group of left-leaning leaders could try to knit together a bigger story about how the economy works. Inspired by Wong's ideas, Kramer became increasingly convinced that the effects of neoliberalism had fueled the populist anger at political elites that threatened the functioning of democracy itself. Something had to be done.

Kramer teamed up with a wing of eBay co-founder Pierre Omidyar's philanthropic empire, the Omidyar Network, to begin a major grant-making effort for individuals and institutions considering a "post-neoliberal" paradigm. The vagueness of the charge was an asset, Kramer and Wong believed. Wong had the first assignment: read everything, talk to everyone, and make us a map of what everyone believes. That was when Wong headed to the desert, a suitcase full of books in tow. A few months later, she co-authored a thick report replete with diagrams of how "new structuralists" differed from the "economic democratists." It was the dense and self-referential language of think tanks, but it was a start.

In May 2018, Wong followed up on that first paper with a long essay in *Democracy Journal*, co-authored alongside former Congressman Tom Perriello, bearing the provocative title "Bold vs. Old." In it, Wong pushed past what the Clinton campaign and her own Roosevelt Institute team had been advocating for eighteen months earlier, at the time of their defeat by Trump. "For half a century now, a neoliberal, free-market consensus has governed our politics, forcing progressives into a reactionary crouch, particularly on economics. But both the 2008 financial crisis and the 2016 election demonstrate that market fundamentalism has failed on its own terms," she wrote.

America did not need more aggressive redistribution of the fruits of the economic pie. The idea that markets work best on their own, with government providing at most a cushion for the unlucky, had run its course. "[W]hichever party responds with bold ideas has the opportunity to define the axis of politics for a generation," Wong and Perriello wrote.[3] A month later, Alexandria Ocasio-Cortez won a surprise victory in a Democratic Congressional primary in New York against centrist party insider Joe Crowley, a concrete example of the argument Wong was making. Bold had beaten old.

Yet, as Wong herself intimated, progressives had no exclusive claim on originality and ambition. Bold ideas had led to the New Deal and the Great Society, but they had also led to fascism in 1930s Italy and Germany. Reagan had been a bold leader, who had articulated a mythical vision of unfettered markets. Bold did not necessarily mean better. With Trump in the White House, the winning formula for boldness was up for grabs. And it wasn't only Democrats who were taking a hard look in the mirror, imagining what came next.

In his 2016 campaign, Trump ran against much of the core Republican agenda of the past forty years: free markets, free trade, and corporate freedom. He channeled the anger of White working-class Americans, who felt overlooked, but without filling in a clear new direction outside of anger and rage. When Trump won, Republicans faced the challenge of developing a platform *after* it had been approved by voters. At the beginning of his presidency, Trump did not have a deep well of political and policy advisers who shared his outlook and could staff his administration. The most experienced Republicans largely bought into the older Republican orthodoxy. Mitt Romney's 2012 policy director, Oren Cass, observed years later that "an earthquake knocks down everything that was outdated and poorly built. It offers an opportunity to modernize and update. But the earthquake itself doesn't build."[4] The savviest thinkers on the right saw an opening to define the future of the Republican Party.

In late February 2017, just a month after Trump's inauguration, Julius Krein, a thirty-one-year-old intellectual who had spent the past decade stuck in middling finance jobs, threw a party at the Harvard Club in New York. He chose the spot, with its wood-paneled walls and Gothic ceilings, not because it was hip, but because it suggested gravitas. Krein had corralled some of the most influential writers and thinkers in the nation into the room for a conversation he would moderate between billionaire tech investor Peter

Thiel and New America President Anne-Marie Slaughter on the effects of globalization.[5] The real point of the party, however, was to create "buzz" for the launch of a new, right-leaning journal called *American Affairs*. Name tags were laid out for the conservative columnist Peggy Noonan; William Kristol; the editor of the *National Review*, Rich Lowry; the historian and New America founder Michael Lind; the left-leaning *New York Times* editor Sam Tanenhaus; the quixotic columnist Andrew Sullivan; and Trump megadonor Rebekah Mercer.[6] It was an eclectic, cross-partisan group.

Krein himself sat at the intersection of the American heartland and the elite world he was recruiting for the party. He grew up in a small town in South Dakota but made his way to Harvard, where he studied political philosophy with the critic of liberal democracy Harvey Mansfield. After graduation, he went into finance with stints at Bank of America and the Blackstone Group. During some of the Obama years, Krein worked in Afghanistan with a division of the Department of Defense that had been created to promote private-sector investment in the Afghan economy. "The goal was to turn Herat into the quote-unquote 'Bangalore of Afghanistan,' and it was a complete disaster," he told a journalist. "They were buying internet from Iran at exorbitant prices, and the children of the largest Afghan drug lords and warlords would come and surf the internet for a few hours. This was packaged as a great triumph of American foreign aid and capitalism and free markets."[7] In the spring of 2016, as Trump was securing the Republican nomination, Krein had started a blog affiliated with the conservative think tank the Claremont Institute that attempted to provide scholarly context for Trump's ideas. What was initially a lark of a project exploded in popularity, with hundreds of thousands of readers and references in the *Wall Street Journal*. Krein and colleagues shut it down. "We'd rather have our jobs than have a blog," he said.[8] He deleted all of the archives before starting *American Affairs*.

Krein's goal at the Harvard Club was to launch a new initiative that would define the future of Trumpism. The media came because they loved the idea of a young, irreverent thinker ready to overturn orthodoxy, but they also seemed anxious to understand what Trumpism stood for. "Running underneath, through, and beyond these gaps between normal politics and Trump politics, is the Trump Conundrum," wrote two analysts in the *Columbia Journalism Review*. "How should the press cover a showman who turns out to be deadly serious—and who refuses to play by the rules of the long-running game of presidential press politics?"⁹ Some journalists wondered how to even ask the right questions, let alone interrogate or imagine what would be the abiding values and economic framework of a Trump presidency. Krein saw this confusion as an opportunity. "We in America no longer have any idea what the future should be, much less how to build it together," he told the *Times*. "A lot of people on the right are looking back and seeing an agenda that is a complete failure, presided over by a bunch of nonentities. It's a joke."[10]

It took hubris to think that a new intellectual journal could set the course of the Trump agenda, but Krein believed it might. Trump's governing approach seemed void of foundational beliefs that could serve as heuristics for the people now responsible for implementing policy. Krein's acquaintances and friends might fill the ranks of the Trump administration with ambitions to write their own ideas into Trumpism. *American Affairs* could serve as the ideological foundation. Krein circulated about the room, his red tie paired with dark black, circular glasses, peppering cocktail conversation with clues about where he wanted to take *American Affairs*—and what he envisioned for the Republican Party under Trump. "We hope not only to encourage a rethinking of the theoretical foundations of 'conservatism' but also to promote a broader realignment of American politics," Krein told one journalist at the party.[11] The media played into his hands. Despite a small initial print run of 300 copies, Krein's party landed him in-depth articles on the launch of *American Affairs* in the *New York Times*, the *New Yorker*, *Politico*, and *The Nation*.

Over the next several years, Krein's journal served as one of the first and most influential efforts on the right to think about a new marketcraft. "*American Affairs* really became the lodestar of the realignment right," said Cass, who founded an ideologically aligned think tank called American Compass three years later. "In those early days, there was no vocabulary for any of this and nothing to be a part of. You had a conversation with someone and mentioned *American Affairs*, and if they also knew what *American Affairs* was, then that was the secret handshake. It was the samizdat in that respect."[12]

Krein's influence grew as he and his colleagues developed a new conservative world view that was less reliant on Trump. Many in the Republican Party felt caught between the traditional, neoliberal posture of the Republican establishment and the unpredictable neo-populist impulses of Trump. Krein offered a third way. "At this point, expanding 'free markets' no longer has anything to do with classical American capitalism," he wrote in the first issue of the journal. "It is simply the further emancipation of the managerial elite from any obligations to the political community."[13] Krein and colleagues developed a vision for a new economic nationalism, grounded in the idea that a muscular state should manage and organize markets to help the working class. In its first few issues, it called for a new federal agency to pursue a manufacturing-focused industrial policy, the creation of a postal bank to ensure universal access to financial products, and the reinvention of the Commerce Department into a Department of Economic Growth and Security.[14] Legacy think tanks and journals on the right looked on aghast, their deep-pocketed donors anxious to steer them away from the activist policy positions of Krein's crew.

Despite *American Affairs'* growing influence, it was not managing to become the in-flight magazine of Air Force One. In the late summer of 2017, after a White supremacist rally in Charlottesville against the removal of a Robert E. Lee statue turned deadly, Trump said there were "very fine people on both sides." Krein took to the pages of the *New York Times* to say he regretted his past support of Trump. "Rather than advance a vision of national unity that he claims to represent, his indefensible equivocation can only inflame the most vicious forces of division within our country," he wrote.[15] Krein wasn't sacrificing much. His vision of economic nationalism had not gotten the early traction in the Trump administration that he had hoped. Trump's domestic economic agenda was shaping up to prioritize massive tax cuts on capital, very much in line with the Washington consensus that the President had claimed to be overthrowing. Trump did later renegotiate the North American Free Trade Agreement (NAFTA) and levied significant tariffs on Chinese imports. While he pursued those heterodox policies, he also aimed to gut the administrative state—repeating his call to "drain the swamp" and purge the bureaucrats from Washington. Steve Bannon said explicitly that the administration was focused on the "deconstruction of the administrative state."[16] Krein and colleagues, by contrast, wanted to reform and improve that administrative state to implement their economic program. It turned out that, for Trump, any coherent ideology got in the way of the highest priority: Trump himself.

Even so, *American Affairs* continued to build momentum behind a new economic theory. Though the institution stayed small, the ideas it propagated

Each year, the civic leaders of turn-of-the century Houston named one of their own "King Nottoc" (cotton, spelled backwards). At twenty-eight, Jesse Jones won the honor in 1902. He is pictured in full regalia, surrounded by family.

As the head of the Reconstruction Finance Corporation (RFC), Jesse Jones insisted on eating lunch at his desk most days. He worked the phones between bites of his favorite meal: soup, lamb chop, salad, rye crisp, and coffee.

3

The defense division of the RFC funded the construction of airplane production facilities across the United States. Here, B-24 Liberators are pictured on the production line at Ford's Willow Run plant in Detroit.

4

The longest-serving Fed Chair, Bill Martin, crafted mid-century financial markets to be more orderly and liquid. Here, Martin before the Senate in 1958.

In the Martin era, the most important "money market" transactions consisted of personal interactions in specific physical locations. Here, traders line up to submit bids for a new offering of short-term Treasury securities at Window 31 of the Federal Reserve Bank of New York, on Liberty Street in the Financial District, c. 1959.

Katherine Pollak (later Ellickson) speaks to mine workers in the Kanawha coalfield of southern West Virginia. November 1931.

7

Federal Reserve Chair William McChesney Martin swears in Andrew Brimmer, the first Black governor, on March 9, 1966. Brimmer's wife, Doris, and their daughter, Esther, look on. President Lyndon B. Johnson stands at right.

8

Counselor to the President Arthur Burns, left, and Federal Reserve Board Chairman Bill Martin, right. The two were attending a retreat of the Business Council in Hot Springs, Virginia, when President Nixon announced Burns as Martin's replacement. October 17, 1969.

The leaders of the nation's economic institutions gather at Camp David in August 1971. Within hours, Nixon announced the closure of the gold window and the creation of sweeping price and wage controls.

Front row, left to right: Undersecretary of the Treasury Paul Volcker; Assistant to the President Peter Peterson; Federal Reserve Chair Arthur Burns; Council of Economic Advisers member Herb Stein; Council of Economic Advisers Chairman Paul McCracken; Secretary of Treasury John Connally; and Office of Management and Budget Director George Shultz. In the background are senior staffers.

Treasury Secretary Bill Simon, left, aboard Air Force One disclosing a secret agreement between the US and France to stabilize erratic dollar fluctuations. Alan Greenspan, then Chair of the Council of Economic Advisers and eventual Chair of the Federal Reserve, is seated, right. Secretary of State Henry Kissinger, center.

11

The first woman governor of
the Federal Reserve, Nancy
Teeters, in her office in 1979.

12

Robert Noyce as an undergraduate
at Grinnell College, where he
earned his BA in 1949. Noyce
later invented the integrated
circuit, co-founded Intel, and
became the CEO of Sematech.

Sematech employees celebrated "Robert Noyce Day" in honor of the CEO just days before his death.

The evening before the White House announced the restructuring of American automotive companies, Barack Obama's economic advisers gathered in the Oval Office to inform legislators, journalists, and corporate leaders. From left, Harry Wilson, Treasury official; Ron Bloom, Senior Counselor for Manufacturing Policy; Steven Rattner, Counselor to the Secretary of the Treasury and lead auto industry adviser; Brian Deese, Special Assistant to the President on the National Economic Council; Gene Sperling, Counselor to the Secretary of the Treasury; and Larry Summers, Director of the National Economic Council.

Federal Trade Commission Chair Lina Khan, right, and Senator John Hickenlooper, left, meet with Colorado farmers to discuss federal legislation to affirm farmers' right to repair their own machines. July 26, 2024.

Director of the National Economic Council Brian Deese became the architect of a new marketcraft to spur clean energy investment, domestic semiconductor manufacture, and a reinvigoration of competition policy. Deese, left, in conversation with President Joe Biden, right, in the Diplomatic Reception Room of the White House in October 2022.

kept winning adherents, birthing a cogent economic nationalist outlook on the right inspired by Trump, which gradually began to flourish despite his early failure to embrace it. By 2019, Krein's efforts to reinvent the conservative political economy would graduate from cocktail parties and cult journals to the halls of the US Senate.

Just after Labor Day in 2017, an email landed in Felicia Wong's inbox containing a memo, titled "Grand Strategy for the Middle Class." It had been co-authored by one of Washington's "best and brightest," Jake Sullivan. Unlike Wong and Krein, Sullivan had spent much of the last eight years on the inside working for the Obama administration, just like his friend Brian Deese. After leaving the administration in 2014, he became the architect of Hillary Clinton's domestic policy agenda, and if she had won, he was expected to secure a senior role in the administration.

Like Deese, Sullivan had spent his life using his intellect and charm to gain influence. After growing up in Minnesota, the son of a college professor and a high-school guidance counselor, he headed off to Yale for college, where he edited the *Yale Daily News*, became a nationally ranked college debater, and interned at the Council on Foreign Relations. In his senior year, he won three of the most lauded fellowships in American higher education: the Rhodes, the Marshall, and the Truman. It was "the academic equivalent of horse racing's Triple Crown," as the *Bulletin of Yale University* put it.[17] Sullivan opted for the Rhodes, then returned to Yale for law school, a few years before Deese. After graduating, he clerked for Supreme Court Justice Stephen Breyer. In 2008, Sullivan joined the Clinton campaign and became one of her most trusted confidants, pitching in with debate prep and showing his intellectual sophistication and flexibility. Afterward, Clinton hired him as her deputy chief of staff at the State Department, before he became the Director of Policy Planning at age thirty-four, the youngest ever.[18] Philippe Reines, the longtime political strategist and Clinton adviser, called him a "once-in-a-generation talent."[19]

By 2012, Clinton dispatched Sullivan on several occasions to conduct secret talks with the Iranians, eventually leading to the 2015 nuclear deal.[20] Later in Obama's second term, Sullivan considered running for Congress back home in Minnesota, but the President called Sullivan from Air Force One to ask him to serve as Vice President Biden's National Security Advisor.[21]

Sullivan accepted. In 2016, when he married fellow Yale Law School graduate Maggie Goodlander at Battell Chapel on Yale's campus, Hillary Clinton
read from the book of Romans, while former President Bill Clinton, Supreme Court Justice Stephen Breyer, and future Secretary of State Antony
Blinken watched on.[22] But that same year, Sullivan's once unstoppable career
hit a wall when Clinton lost to Trump. Friends and colleagues said he took
the defeat personally. He emailed chastened notes of condolence and apology
to colleagues and retreated from Washington life. He and his wife moved to
New Hampshire, where she had grown up, and Sullivan joined a consulting
firm to advise companies on foreign policy. Sullivan's friend Deese also left
Washington, moving to Boston with his young family, where he worked first
at Larry Summers' think tank and later at BlackRock, the world's largest asset
manager.

Even in New Hampshire, Sullivan couldn't shake the need to sort out
what went wrong. Clinton had pivoted left, responding to the populism of
Sanders and Trump and aligning with the likes of Wong; why had it not
been enough? What did American voters want? Was Trump just a historical accident, or was he the harbinger of something new to come? "For me,
[Trump's win] reflected the exhaustion of a post–Cold War economic model
that rested on two flawed assumptions: that markets have all the answers,
and it was the end of history for geopolitical competition. Both were wrong,"
Sullivan later said.[23]

Sullivan's challenge, as he saw it, was to fuse together a domestic and
foreign policy agenda to support American workers. Since the end of the
Cold War, American economic policy had been largely viewed as a domestic issue. Policymakers focused on maintaining a stable, growing economy
by creating safety nets, regulating effectively, and ensuring macroeconomic
stability. From the 1980s onward, those in positions like Sullivan's believed
that the best way for foreign policy to support these domestic goals was to
expand global trade. More trade, they argued, would result in cheaper goods
and eventually lead to better, higher-paying jobs. Trump took a different approach, blaming free-trade agreements and the rise of China for wage stagnation and the decline of blue-collar jobs.

To put together a new agenda to match or beat Trump's, Sullivan wanted
to understand firsthand what Americans workers were experiencing. Yale
Law School and the experience gained in elite policy positions had created a

distance that he wanted to bridge. He assembled a bipartisan group of twelve to develop a "foreign policy for the middle class." Organized under the aegis of the Carnegie Endowment, Sullivan spent the next two years talking to Americans in three focus states—Nebraska, Colorado, and Ohio. "At least he's doing something," an Ohio voter told the group, referring to Trump's anti-China tariff policy.[24] The final Carnegie Report made modest calls: "tackle the distributional effects of public policy" and "broaden the debate beyond trade," vague descriptions of where public policy might go.

Personally, though, Sullivan went further. First, in a major essay for *Foreign Affairs*, he made clear that the link between globalization and shared prosperity was broken. More trade did not mean a more stable, more prosperous America.[25] That diagnosed the problem; writing the prescription would be harder. While Wong was collecting her ideas for her essay in *Democracy Journal*, Sullivan started writing his own for the same publication. In his case, the essay became an organizing vehicle to build consensus among many of the best and the brightest. Sullivan shared a Google Doc with several of his former colleagues to get their thoughts and feedback. Brian Deese and he discussed its argument extensively. "That was written, or at least edited, by a kind of committee socially," said one person with access to the document. "Jake was testing out what was there against the input of a bunch of different people." As they shared comments and edits, the Obama-Clinton crew began to think about going "bold," like Wong was calling for. "[T]he free market alone will not serve the public interest without checks against abuse, corruption, and unacceptable levels of inequality," Sullivan eventually wrote. The antidote was a more muscular state, prepared to make surgical investments in struggling regions, coordinate directly with businesses to support the growth of new, globally competitive industries, and reinvigorate antimonopoly policy to tackle abusive companies and the concentration of wealth.[26] This agenda was not radical, but it mattered because Sullivan and colleagues were beginning to apply the principles of statecraft, which put an active state at the center of a dynamic system, to economics.

Watching from the side, Larry Summers—the doyen of the old model that Sullivan and Wong now sought to overthrow—was growing increasingly concerned. "The attempt by Jake Sullivan to marry Hillary's political problems to some set of emerging economic problems and call them one dogma was substantially misguided," one of the voices of the Washington consensus told me. "The green policies and the resilience policies are not the right answers to the Democratic Party's problems with the rust belt. Those have much more to do with cultural and social issues."

Although Sullivan was a long way from having a robust vision for a new marketcraft, he knew that the old cocktail of free trade and crisis-driven bailouts was not a winning agenda. What he wanted, as evidenced by the title of that initial memo to Wong, was a "grand strategy" to strengthen American workers. That term had originated in the interwar period to encapsulate an old idea: a nation should have a clear set of military, economic, and political goals on the international stage—and then operate through existing institutions to pursue them. America could in theory refuse to act on the global stage, but ceding that power would undermine its long-term interests. Sullivan applied that kind of thinking, more common in statecraft, to domestic economics. Americans had needs not met organically by contemporary markets—such as economic stability for families, a more resilient climate, and the cultivation of future-facing industry like semiconductor manufacturing. If government did nothing to guide domestic markets, America would be worse off, running the risk of being consumed by internal strife or threatened by a foreign power. America needed to embrace its power to steer markets and set a grand strategy for economic prosperity, just as it had for global power.

What Sullivan didn't anticipate was a coming convergence of the left and right around these issues, fueled by two events over the next two years: the rising popularity of the antimonopoly movement and powerful Republicans who began to transform into economic nationalists.

In the summer of 2017, Lina Khan's phone would not stop vibrating. A *New York Times* editor wanted her to write an op-ed, and television and radio hosts wanted her on their shows. Khan had gone from law-school nerd to cult celebrity, because she had picked a fight with one of America's largest and most beloved companies, Amazon.

When Khan arrived at Yale Law School two years earlier, she came with a folder on her hard drive filled with hundreds of files about the e-commerce, logistics, and cloud computing giant. While working with Barry Lynn, she had conducted dozens of interviews on Amazon's business practices with entrepreneurs, workers, and investors, exploring whether the company was abusing its dominant market position. Two years into law school, Khan synthesized that research into a long-form essay that the *Yale Law Journal* published in January 2017. It clocked in at ninety-six pages and 24,000 words and argued that traditional antitrust frameworks, focused narrowly on consumer welfare and low prices, failed to address the anticompetitive practices of dominant platforms such as Amazon. The dense and sophisticated piece of academic writing went viral. "Most of my colleagues would give their little finger for a piece that got that much attention," said her adviser David Grewal.[27] The *New York Times* and *The Nation* covered the article, and the preeminent antitrust conference held each year at the University of Chicago invited her to speak.[28]

At first, Amazon reportedly thought all this attention would blow over. Executives there had read Khan's essay but didn't think that a single law review article could change much. In June, the company's general counsel brought four colleagues to meet with her in a kind of reconnaissance mission to better understand how she thought about the company.[29] They still did not take her particularly seriously, given that she had just completed law school.

Then, just days after their meeting with Khan, Amazon announced the acquisition of the grocer Whole Foods in June 2017. What Amazon executives hadn't realized was how extensively Khan's article had been traveling. That burgeoning familiarity with antimonopoly fueled a tsunami of criticism when the company announced its plan to move into groceries. "That was when my phone started blowing up, when people were really putting Amazon and antitrust in the same sentence," Khan said.[30] Within days, she had published an op-ed in the *Times*, boiling her law review argument down to something bite-sized for nonexperts.[31] The *Washington Post* and *The Atlantic* covered her efforts to rethink antimonopoly, starting with Amazon. The next month, Khan passed the bar.

Its customers may have loved Amazon, but its scale as a business seemed to be approaching something akin to Standard Oil or AT&T, both of which the government had broken up as a remedy for their abuses of power. Amazon was not just a retailer, but a cloud computing provider, a producer of television and films, a book publisher, a logistics and delivery company, and even a fashion designer and hardware manufacturer. Perhaps most importantly, it had become a platform with the power to dictate the terms of how thousands of small businesses secured access to America's customers. It owned the proverbial mall, operated the biggest department store inside it, provided the power for the building, and was increasingly fabricating what was sold. Now it wanted to own the grocery store as well. This level of power was unnerving.

In the midst of the political realignment in the wake of Trump, here was Khan, offering something concrete and clear, a way to rein in corporate power that used existing institutions rather than reinventing the wheel. "Antitrust is dead, isn't it?" Richard Posner, the Appeals Court judge and scholar, had wondered out loud when he shared a stage with Khan at a conference that spring.[32] If it was, it was getting the Lazarus treatment.

In the wake of the Whole Foods announcement, Democrats rushed to put antimonopoly and corporate oversight at the core of a new populist economic message. In 2017, their legislative proposals included multiple calls for "cracking down on corporate monopolies." Specifically, Democratic leaders wanted to invest antitrust officials with more power to conduct merger reviews and base their judgments on a broader set of criteria than short-term price hikes.[33] At the suggestion of Senator Chuck Schumer, Trump nominated former Elizabeth Warren adviser Rohit Chopra to be one of the five commissioners on the FTC. Trump was following tradition in nominating a Democrat for a Democratic seat, but Schumer had chosen a firebrand who came in with an agenda: show how a muscular federal agency could make companies work better for Americans.

Once confirmed by the Senate, Chopra started pushing boundaries, including by calling Khan to ask her to come work at the FTC. She joined him in the summer of 2018 as a fellow, her first meaningful work experience in government. "Khan spent a ton of time at the agency library, where she pored through tomes, studying how the FTC historically pursued antitrust cases," wrote a *Wall Street Journal* reporter about Khan's experience.[34] "Importantly, during this stint, she learned that many of the tools at the FTC's disposal had been little used or abandoned by contemporary agency regulators." Soon it was not just the FTC commissioners who wanted her time—antitrust leaders in Congress turned to her as well. Early in 2019, the House Antitrust Subcommittee, led by Democrat David Cicilline and Republican Ken Buck, began a bipartisan investigation into large tech companies for potential abuse of power. They hired Khan to work for the committee, which promptly made her "public enemy number one for the world's tech titans" according to the *Financial Times*.[35] The committee's report, published in the midst of the 2020 presidential election, reached the conclusion that the companies held monopolies in many markets and engaged in anticompetitive practices to maintain their market dominance. What should be done about it? The committee set forth several recommendations to strengthen antitrust laws and the power of enforcement agencies. The *New York Times* called it "the most significant government effort to check the world's largest tech companies" in decades.[36] The recommendations served as the basis for new legislation in the following Congress.

Khan had written much of the report, and her name was listed at the top of the first full page just after two Congressmen and the subcommittee's chief counsel. She had become one of the leading voices articulating what the government could do to craft and structure the markets of today to be more competitive, open, and fair. And as she went on this journey, I took a parallel one.

In the spring of 2019, I published a long essay in the *New York Times* calling for the breakup of Facebook, a company I had co-founded fifteen years earlier.[37] Mark Zuckerberg, Dustin Moskovitz, and I batted around the idea in our dorm room in the winter of 2004 at Harvard. We first restricted access to college students and only years later made it possible for anyone to join. I worked at the company for three years in product development and communications roles before I left to run digital organizing for Barack Obama's 2008 presidential campaign. Facebook's rapid adoption by hundreds of millions of people around the globe meant that its 2012 initial public offering changed my life, transforming the son of a high-school math teacher and traveling paper salesman into a multimillionaire overnight. In the years afterward, I began to feel a sense of unease about what the company had become. At dinners with friends, I would join in the Facebook pile-on, faulting the company for spreading misinformation about elections, contributing to a public mental-health crisis, and abusing its power by suppressing competition and harming innovation. If I was saying all that privately, why would I not publicly?

Around the same time, news broke that Facebook had allowed Cambridge Analytica, a political data firm, to harvest the private information of 50 million users. The company then used that information to support Trump's campaign. Democrats, worried about the threat to privacy and the weaponization of data to win elections, were outraged at Facebook. Republicans were not far behind, albeit for a different reason. They were increasingly sensitive to the power of coastal elites to set the standards of what speech was permissible on the platforms. Facebook was becoming a target on both sides of the aisle.

As the sentiment against Facebook was growing, I had been wrestling with many of the bigger questions about the structure of the American economy that animated Wong, Krein, and Sullivan's work. Beginning in 2016, I started advocating for the provision of monthly checks to poor and middle-class Americans, a guaranteed income that would wipe out poverty and provide the basis for economic mobility. As that work developed, I came to believe that direct cash transfers, while enormously beneficial, could also entrench a particular market structure. We could give people thousands of dollars every year, but if we didn't structure housing, health-care, or childcare markets to keep costs down, all of that money would go straight to the top, undermining the aspiration of a guaranteed income to foster stability and fairness.

The answer, I was beginning to discover, must be in some blend of policies that at once ensured purchasing power as a means to freedom—through labor markets and cash transfers—*and* crafted markets to be competitive, fair, and stable. I had a sense of how to pursue the work in labor markets and in support of a guaranteed income, but the institutional marketcraft was more of a black box.

In the fall of 2018, while pursuing graduate work in economics, I began to understand that all the pent-up rage directed at Facebook was not just about a single social media company. The concentration of economic power in a small number of American companies was contributing to economic stagnation, restricting consumer choice, hurting workers, and slowing productivity. Corporate concentration was not the sole cause of the problems in the American economy, but it was an important one to expose and examine. The antimonopoly tradition used state power to craft markets to make them work more fairly. It did not, as a rule, pick unfairly on entrepreneurs as some business voices claimed. Understanding the historical context and the economic rationale for reinvigorated antitrust, I charged forward with the essay in the *New York Times*. Its warm reception, at least outside of Facebook's headquarters, gave me a taste of what Khan must have been feeling in the wake of her Amazon critique. Even more than that, I felt the satisfaction of having discovered, like Khan, the beginnings of a new marketcraft.

At the same time that the left was finding the building blocks of its new economic program, so too were many unexpected voices on the right. *American Affairs* had engaged several legislators in conversation, but one Republican in particular expressed deep interest in rethinking conservative assumptions about political economy—Marco Rubio, the Cuban American Senator from Florida. "You started to have a number of Republican Senators who wanted to do something other than cut taxes. Marco Rubio was really the first," Krein said.[38] During his 2016 run for the presidency, Rubio had seen the extent of the deindustrialization in America—and the incredible wealth that finance had created. After losing the nomination to Trump, he began to invent a new ideology for himself and for other Republicans. His work on the Senate Select Committee on Intelligence also gave him the opportunity to see up close how China was using its own state capitalism to give its companies an advantage over American firms.

Concern about an increasingly strong and bellicose China began to change American politics starting in the early 2010s and gained steam over the decade. In 2012, the Republican candidate for President, Mitt Romney, who was advised by figures like Oren Cass, adopted a tough stance on China. His rhetoric was so strident that "other business-friendly Republicans warned it could spark a counterproductive trade war."[39] Simultaneously, the Obama administration lodged a complaint with the World Trade Organization (WTO) against China's handling of rare earth mineral exports and imposed tariffs on Chinese solar panels. But, in retrospect, these actions appear as minor bits of electioneering that reinforced rather than challenged most aspects of the Washington consensus. Obama's warning that public debt was akin to "taking out a credit card from the Bank of China" aligned with Rubin-style fiscal orthodoxy.[40] Through 2016, the primary strategy for containing China's influence was trade expansion, epitomized by the TPP, which its advocates marketed as essential to national security.

While American growth hovered around 2 percent, the Chinese economy grew at quadruple that rate. By 2018, China's nominal GDP surpassed that of the Eurozone. State action drove much of this growth, especially under the leadership of Xi Jinping, who came to power in 2013. This was not marketcraft as much as full-on state capitalism. Public policies subsidized critical sectors of the Chinese economy, like real estate development, and automobile and solar panel manufacturing. State-owned enterprises dominated the energy, telecommunications, and finance sectors. The Chinese state imposed tariffs on foreign agricultural products, automobiles, and luxury goods, and maintained tight control over the banking system and capital flows. A large, young labor force rapidly moved to cities, leaving large swaths of the countryside to stagnate. Beyond China's challenge to US economic power, American political strategists on both the right and left increasingly agreed on two points: First, China's growth relied on a model that repressed consumption and depended on export demand from the rest of the world. Second, contrary to expectations, China's integration into global capitalism did not lead to political liberalization but to an increasingly uncompromising dictatorship under Xi, who created for himself the opportunity to become President for Life when the Communist Party removed presidential term limits in 2018. The combination of these two events meant that China was dumping more and more below-cost goods onto global markets while manipulating its currency to keep its exports as cheap as possible. Rather than crafting markets, the Chinese government directly administered the most critical ones.

In the name of free trade, America watched on. "They argued that capitalism was going to change China. Now we stand here 23 years later and realize capitalism didn't change China—China changed capitalism," Rubio said in a speech on the Senate floor. "This is not the story of what China's done to us. This is the story of what we've done to ourselves. Because we've allowed the system of globalization to drive our economic policies and our politics."[41]

Rubio's solution was to use economic statecraft to sever as many ties with the authoritarian Chinese government as possible. After losing to Trump in the Republican primary, Rubio became increasingly sensitive to how antipathy toward China resonated with voters. He was soon one of the most hawkish anti-China voices in Congress. His tools for arresting China's rise were largely economic. "[W]e need to fundamentally realign the assumptions and the ideas behind our economic and foreign policies," he said.[42] Rubio called for robust tariffs to shut down imports, penalties for American companies doing business in China, and banning Chinese technology firms from operating within American borders. Perhaps most importantly, it meant pursuing global trade agreements only if they protected American workers. Trade was useless unless it worked to make American families stronger in the short term, Rubio argued, contradicting the consensus that had prevailed for decades before Trump.

Rubio's China critique flowered in the second half of the Trump presidency. He broadened it to encompass the business interests that he saw as increasingly responsible for American stagnation. Corporations had become exclusively focused on an insatiable drive for profits, regardless of the impact of their business model on workers, customers, or communities. American elites had destroyed small towns and stable families as they shipped jobs overseas, seeking to maximize profit above all. Those decisions had at once empowered the rise of China and undercut American workers. "We have a free market, but that free market operates under the conditions created for it by policymakers," Rubio told the *Washington Post*. "Those conditions should reflect our national priorities. And one of our top national priorities should be creating strong and stable jobs upon which strong families and strong communities can take root."[43]

Rubio was not alone among Republicans emphasizing the need for state power. Perhaps unsurprisingly, the best and brightest on the political right emerged from the same assembly line of cooperative contrarians as their liberal counterparts. With degrees from Stanford and Yale Law School, Josh Hawley arrived in Washington with the same ambition and appetite for rethinking orthodoxy as earlier Yale grads like Sullivan, and later ones like Deese and Khan. Hawley handily beat incumbent Democrat Claire McCaskill in a 2018 Senate election in Missouri. Polarization was driving the left and right further apart, but Hawley himself scrambled what it means to be conservative in Washington. As an undergraduate at Stanford, Hawley had written his senior thesis, later expanded into a book, on Teddy Roosevelt and the possibility of values-driven government to foster communitarian sentiment. In recent years, American conservatives had mistakenly surrendered government to the elites who believed that it should be downsized, neglecting its power to help build the nation. Their use of public policy to foster international trade and financial innovation made these elites richer, destroying the soul of America, according to Hawley. "The new aristocrats seek to remake society in their own image: to engineer an economy that works for the elite and few else, to fashion a culture dominated by their own preferences," he said in his first speech on the Senate floor.[44] Neoliberalism looked more like kleptocracy to Hawley than true conservatism.

Economic nationalists such as Hawley and Rubio wanted a more active government focused on supporting local communities and families over top-line economic growth. They supported Trump, but they also wanted a new ideology that was bigger than one person. Politically, they were trying to channel the populist energy Trump had tapped into, while offering the cogent and workable economic policy approach that he lacked. "We must put aside the tired orthodoxies of years past and forge instead a new politics of national renewal," Hawley said. In his vision, government would not pursue economic growth at any cost. State power would be channeled toward national greatness, built upon stable, virtuous families: "We must begin by acknowledging that GDP growth alone cannot be the measure of this nation's greatness, and so it cannot be the only aim of this nation's policy. Because our purpose is not to make a few people wealthy, but to sustain a great democracy, and so we need not just a bigger economy, but a better society."[45] Markets should work for us, not the other way around, he said.

The pair of Senators were translating the wonkery of Krein's *American Affairs*—its articles were often dry, long, and homework-like—into the language of the stump and legislation. In 2019, Krein worked with Rubio's office to introduce a proposal to encourage companies to boost investment by equalizing the tax treatment of share buybacks and dividends. Rubio also cited the work of the Roosevelt Institute in a Senate report on the topic.[46] That effort failed in 2019 but eventually became law during the Biden administration's second year. Rubio and Krein's early efforts were similar to what Zephyr Teachout, Tim Wu, and Lina Khan had done a few years before. They too had developed experimental, provocative ideas in abstract policy papers and long articles, and then refashioned them into campaign-friendly sound bites and policy proposals. Just as the Khan crew built momentum on the left, so too did the new economic nationalists on the right. As their approach gained steam and clarity, more powerful voices joined, including Senator Todd Young of Indiana, and Yale Law School–trained Senator J. D. Vance of Ohio, the eventual Republican vice president. In 2024, Republicans Dave McCormick, Jim Banks, and Bernie Moreno channeled a similar economic nationalism on the stump. "When you look at people 25 to 40 years old, all of the most motivated, competent, promising people across the right of center are going in this direction," Cass said.[47]

In 2019, as Rubio and Hawley were finding their voices on a new marketcraft, Cass was laying plans to fill in the agenda with actionable legislative ideas. After his stint advising Romney, Cass started his new think tank, American Compass, in early 2020 to outline a state-centered, conservative policy program. Republican establishment donors remained largely uninterested in a post-neoliberal approach to markets and government, which meant that American Compass' largest start-up funding came from the Hewlett Foundation. Hewlett provided Cass nearly $2 million over three years, a third of American Compass' initial operating budget. The Omidyar Network supplemented with half a million.[48]

These were the same networks funding Felicia Wong. What did it mean that they were also funding the cutting edge of conservative political economy? According to Hewlett, it was part of the larger quest to forge a viable post-Trump marketcraft. "American Compass is in our Economy and Society Initiative portfolio, in part, because of their work to move conservative thinking in a more worker-friendly direction," Hewlett said in a 2023 statement. "We support organizations across the political spectrum where our views align on a given issue. That doesn't mean we agree with our grantees on everything, nor require them to agree with all of Hewlett's positions. We believe that kind of dialogue across difference is critical to our democracy, and our bedrock commitment to democratic principles remains unchanged."[49]

But there was another major curveball to come. In March 2020, Americans found themselves huddling in isolation in their homes as the Covid-19 pandemic began its path of destruction. Left-leaning Democrats, including Wong, watched with concern as Joe Biden, already seventy-seven, came from behind to win the Democratic primary. He was the "old" that "bold" had been fighting against. To add insult to injury, Biden's top advisers on economic policy were people like Larry Summers, Brian Deese, and Jake Sullivan. Those three had all worked either for Obama or the Clintons and continued to be perceived, from the position of Wong and her cohort, as ideologically identical. The optics for Deese were particularly bad. While progressives like Wong and Khan had been inventing a post-neoliberal future, Deese had been working at BlackRock, one of the largest financial institutions in the world.

Yet there he was, on the precipice of power again. For Wong and Khan, all of the intellectual progress of the previous years felt like a sandcastle at risk of being swept away by the tide. In reality, Deese—with the help of Sullivan, Khan, Wong, and a new generation of Republicans—was now preparing to become the architect of a new marketcraft.

16

BIDENOMICS

BRIAN DEESE & JAKE SULLIVAN (2020-22)

In late April 2020, an impatient Joe Biden, the presumptive Democratic nominee for the presidency, interrupted a conference call with his economic advisers. "I want you all to expand your thinking," he barked into the speakerphone, sounding exasperated.[1] The economic crisis triggered by the Covid pandemic was dwarfing the 2008 Great Financial Crisis in speed and depth, and Biden believed that it might eclipse even the Great Depression. In the six weeks since shutdowns began, 30 million Americans had been laid off, and one Federal Reserve Bank President warned that the unemployment rate might soon reach 30 percent.[2] Many of the jobless could not access unemployment benefits, given that the systems had not been designed to handle so many cases at once.

Biden, sequestered in his basement in Wilmington, Delaware, had Franklin D. Roosevelt on his mind. The pandemic had ended in-person campaigning just days after he had become the Democratic nominee, and his top advisers had scattered to their personal hideaways. William McKinley once famously campaigned from his front porch; now Biden was doing it over video conference and speakerphone.

That meant Biden had a little more time to read. He pulled down from the shelf a volume on Roosevelt's first hundred days.[3] Channeling the New Deal ambition, he demanded his advisers think on the scale of the American response to the Great Depression. "The blinders have been taken off because of this COVID crisis," he told dozens of donors on a video fundraiser a few weeks later. "I think people are realizing, 'My Lord, look at what is possible,' looking at the institutional changes we can make, without us becoming a 'socialist country' or any of that malarkey."[4] His interest in claiming the Roosevelt legacy endured over the coming months. A week before the election, Biden traveled to Warm Springs, Georgia, where Roosevelt often went to convalesce from the paralysis he suffered from. After his victory, Biden asked a historian who had written a volume on Roosevelt to help draft his inaugural address. Once he moved into the Oval, he put a portrait of Roosevelt in the most prominent position above the fireplace. Months before that, in the lockdown spring of 2020, however, Biden desperately needed a set of economic and policy advisers who could match the ambition of Roosevelt.

Brian Deese, who was still working at BlackRock on renewable technologies, got the call. His friend Jake Sullivan had recently rejoined his old boss Biden to serve in a broad policy adviser role on the campaign. Biden had specifically charged Sullivan with "updating Roosevelt for modern times."[5] Sullivan wanted Deese to come on board to do that. "We are going to have to do more, push further, be more creative coming out of this once-in-a-century pandemic—no doubt about it," Sullivan said.[6] Deese agreed to volunteer, joining campaign calls and managing the effort to consolidate support behind Biden across the progressive and centrist wings of the party.

Sullivan had called Deese in particular because he knew that the two shared a similar policy vision. In the weeks before Biden secured the nomination, Sullivan published another essay building on his previous writings. This one pieced together an economic *and* foreign policy world view, titled "America Needs a New Economic Philosophy." Deese and he had discussed the ideas behind it at length, but Sullivan had turned to an old colleague to co-write it with him, Jen Harris. The two had worked together at the State Department years before and later on the Carnegie effort to develop a foreign policy for the middle class. Harris was a brilliant, hard-charging introvert whom the *New York Times* later called the "queen bee of Bidenomics."[7] With the support of her boss Larry Kramer and colleagues at another foundation, the Omidyar Network, she funded the people and institutions behind the bubbling ferment of the new marketcraft, including Felicia Wong, Julius Krein, and Oren Cass.

Sullivan and Harris argued in the pages of *Foreign Policy* that the practice of statecraft could be applied to domestic political economy. The American government needed to set a clear goal of widely shared economic prosperity and use the political, economic, and military tools at its disposal to accomplish it. Trade agreements must be structured to protect American workers and for a reinvigoration of antitrust, they believed. This was not just a move further left—the sort that had already happened during Clinton's 2016 campaign—but a synthesis of America's foreign policy and domestic economic priorities into one coherent philosophy. Sullivan and Harris argued that America would lose out to an ascendant China if it did not take a more muscular role in directing the focus of markets. "It was a little bit of 'If you can't beat them, join them,'" Harris told me. "Put differently, we can have an industrial policy of our own, or we can import China's."[8] Given his experiences in government, including the auto bailout and the efforts to mitigate climate change, Deese largely agreed that the US needed to take a significantly more active role in shaping markets.

There was, however, a major problem standing in the way of the group's efforts to fulfill Biden's call for a new Rooseveltian vision: Deese's old mentor Larry Summers. In the decade since he had left government, economists and activists alike had blamed Summers for the sluggish recovery from the Great Recession. He had supported an insufficiently robust stimulus, advocated for finance-friendly policies, and failed to bail out American homeowners as he had the banks, they said. Ironically, he had spent much of his tenure since the Obama administration reinvigorating a progressive theory that called for significant levels of public investment to jump-start the sluggish American economy.[9] That was a sharp turn from his position while within government, but he remained skeptical of the industrial policy efforts that Sullivan and Deese were developing. Despite all the controversy surrounding Summers, the Democratic nominee still wanted his counsel.

Many others, however, did not. The first major demand that two left-of-center groups, Justice Democrats and the Sunrise Movement, made during the postprimary party unity negotiations that Deese oversaw was to dump Summers from his economic advisory team.[10] Several other voices inside the campaign quietly agreed. As spring turned to summer and Covid continued to spread, Summers gradually disappeared from the conference calls. The state-led economic approach favored by Deese, Sullivan, and Biden himself became the dominant paradigm inside the campaign. Summers didn't fade altogether. "We would still check Larry's instinct or gut," one senior official on the calls told me, and it was Deese who often got the assignment to check in with his mentor. But Summers' voice was fading, as the "best and brightest" were taking over. The question now became: Could they avoid a repeat of 2016 and actually get the opportunity to implement their policies?

Deese and Sullivan moved quickly to get their big ideas into more concrete policy proposals. Over the following months, the pair, with the help of former NEC Director Gene Sperling, developed an economic policy agenda, dubbed "Build Back Better." In three speeches in July, Biden made the case for massive public investment to update American infrastructure, counter the threat of climate change, and provide affordable childcare and eldercare to all American families. This was not yet a new marketcraft, but it sent the message that a Biden administration would put meaningful public investment at the center of its agenda, particularly in support of efforts to slow climate change and to provide cheaper and more abundant care for children and the elderly. "The core things that have animated [the President] since, you can trace back to that. For Joe Biden as President, it was foundational," Deese said.[11]

The Trump administration was not sitting on its hands either, and it seemed as if the 2020 election could become a referendum on which candidate would be more aggressive in his support of the spending power of American households. In March, Trump worked with a Democratic Congress to send over $500 billion of cash to the American people.[12] Twenty-two million Americans had lost their jobs in March and April, and millions more were afraid they would be next. The checks were designed to help families and to boost the macroeconomy. They cushioned the rapid and significant fall in demand so effectively that the downturn that began in February lasted only through the summer, when growth returned. By the first quarter of 2021, the economy had eclipsed its prerecession highs, even though vaccines were just starting to become available.

Perhaps the most important project of the Trump administration was the government-led vaccine development program, Operation Warp Speed. In early 2020, the administration earmarked nearly $10 billion of the CARES Act that Congress passed in March to support the research, clinical trials, and manufacturing of promising Covid vaccine candidates. Several pharmaceutical companies, including Moderna, Pfizer/BioNTech, Johnson & Johnson, and AstraZeneca, entered into contracts with the federal government to provide millions of vaccine doses once developed, effectively guaranteeing market demand and incentivizing significant additional private investment in research and production. Meanwhile, Operation Warp Speed worked to address potential bottlenecks in the vaccine supply chain to ensure availability of glass vials, syringes, and other essential materials. By coordinating with suppliers and manufacturers, the government helped ramp up production capacity and prevent shortages that could have hindered the vaccination effort. By December, less than a year after the pandemic began, the FDA issued emergency use authorizations for the Pfizer/BioNTech and Moderna vaccines, green-lighting their provision to the public. Over the following months, tens of millions of doses were distributed, and by the spring of 2021, any American willing to be vaccinated could easily access one. Operation Warp Speed was not without its flaws. It left production decisions in the hands of private companies and failed to require them to share the intellectual property that government funding had made possible.[13] But it succeeded in speeding the development and distribution of vaccines to Americans.

Despite their popularity, neither the cash transfers nor Operation Warp Speed demonstrated the broader ideological shift happening on the right. George W. Bush's administration had also embraced direct cash transfer in moments of downturn, though the size and scale of the transfers the Trump administration supported was significantly larger. Unlike the vaccine and cash programs, the Trump administration's support for one of the most significant industrial policies advanced in years signaled how much thinking on the right was changing: the return of American semiconductor manufacturing.

Conservative interest in the topic predated the pandemic. By the fall of 2019, the American lead in semiconductor manufacturing had vanished. The United States made only about 10 percent of global semiconductor supplies and none of the most advanced chips.[14] In the two decades since public investment in Sematech had trailed off, American manufacturers had expanded their overseas fabrication facilities. The most sophisticated chips were still designed in the United States, but a single company, TSMC, located in Taiwan, dominated their production.[15] China did not threaten American economic preeminence with its own chip-manufacturing industry, but it could attack Taiwan, halting much of the production of an increasingly necessary good in the global supply chain.[16]

That threat spurred Keith Krach, Trump's Under Secretary of State and the former CEO of Docusign, to spearhead an effort to support and grow American chip manufacturing. Krach convened Senate leaders and business voices in the hopes of fostering cross-partisan political consensus around reshoring American semiconductor production. "We all believe in the free market. But when somebody doesn't play by the rules, the market is no longer free," he said of the new approach.[17] Krach was doing a similar two-step to the one Greenspan had employed for decades: embracing the rhetorical conceit of self-regulating markets and in the same breath calling for state action to shape them. Julius Krein's *American Affairs* was less subtle, calling for significant public investment in semiconductors to rival the investments China was making. "China understands that developing the most advanced semiconductor technology will position its chip makers not only to dominate the future market but also to give it a leg up in a third area of the conflict: artificial intelligence (AI)," one essayist argued.[18] America had to invest to win.

Krach worked with Congressional leaders—Democrats as well as Republicans—to draft legislation to create regional tech hubs with $10 billion of public investment and to allocate $100 billion to a new national entity investing in technology research. American Compass was pumping out reports offering an array of ways to support American private industry, including semiconductor manufacturing, filling in the details for legislators.

The following year, the coronavirus pandemic began, intensifying anti-China sentiment and exposing America's reliance on global supply chains. Politicians from both parties began to call the reshoring of chip production an urgent national priority. Todd Young, the Republican Senator from Indiana, introduced an expanded bill in May 2020, arguing that the government needed to convince hardware manufacturers to come back to the United States in support of national security.[19] His proposal garnered bipartisan interest in both chambers and the personal support of Democratic Majority Leader Chuck Schumer, which augured well for its viability in the next administration, no matter who won the White House. "Republicans want to talk about national security and China and maybe your left-wing people want to talk about inequality. But from my perspective, you get to the same place," Krein said at the time.[20]

This new bipartisan thrust signalled the resurgence of an old idea in the American political economy: "industrial policy." The term had been popularized in the late 1970s and '80s as a shorthand for government support for certain industries. It was unwieldy and imprecise, conjuring up the idea of government inartfully picking winners and losers in machine-dominated industries. In reality, industrial policy was just a specific type of marketcraft, something that had been practiced in the United States since its founding. Government efforts to shape finance, aviation, real estate, and energy markets were a recurring feature of American governance since the 1930s. "The United States, along with every other advanced and emerging economy, has always pursued industrial policies," wrote Jared Bernstein, a vice-presidential aide to Biden who was now advising the campaign, in July 2020. "The question is not whether the country should have such policies, but whether it is willing to be transparent about them." The American government, Bernstein noted, had created abundant rewards for finance through its regulatory policy and emergency infusions of capital whenever a crisis struck, an approach that had started in the New Deal and endured through the Covid crisis.[21] He rolled through other historical examples of government support for agricultural firms, defense and aerospace, and technology companies. "The United States might as well get it right by being transparent and smart about these policies," Bernstein wrote. "Anything else would not only be embarrassing and naive—it would also be bad for Americans and the U.S. economy."[22]

Biden defeated Trump in early November. Over the course of the campaign, a focus on public health and household finance had expanded into a larger reckoning with the enduring racial injustice in America and what a post-pandemic, inclusive American economy might look like. Given the desire for new, diverse economic and political leaders, it was a little surprising that within days of Biden's victory, Deese was fielding calls about whether he might join the administration. The position that the President was considering him for was a big one, the same one his former bosses Larry Summers and Gene Sperling had occupied—Director of the NEC. Aside from Treasury Secretary, it was the most powerful economic position in the government. Deese huddled with his wife to assess their family's interest in returning to the demanding requirements of a position in the White House. "It was daunting. It was the middle of Covid, and we lived in Boston and had two little kids," Deese told me. Even so, by the time the offer came, he was ready to accept. At forty-two, he became the youngest ever to occupy the role.

But before he could even begin to think about a policy agenda, Deese was fighting for his own political survival. Two days before Thanksgiving, news leaked that he was being vetted for the role, and the progressive left aimed its fire. His decision to spend the last four years at BlackRock had put him on a "hit list" for many liberals skeptical of corporate-minded appointees. "The Biden administration can't talk out of both sides of their mouth when it comes to fighting for economic justice," one activist said. "Are you serious about re-orienting our economic policy and priorities to fight climate change and will you commit to having dedicated public servants who will end Wall Street profiteering from the planet and BIPOC communities? Or are you not?"[23]

Deese had built goodwill with some progressives through his work on the unity coalitions the prior year, and he could also defend himself by point-ing to what he actually did at BlackRock. Deese had run the environmental, social, and governance (ESG) investment strategy, working with BlackRock's leaders to identify and develop financial products that environmentally minded investors could purchase. In addition to its environmental products, the company put together index fund–like investment vehicles, which effec-tively bought the entire market to replicate the performance of a benchmark. When progressives complained that BlackRock was investing in fossil-fuel companies, they didn't care that the products they were critiquing were at-tempting to replicate market outcomes broadly, not make active investment decisions. BlackRock might have been the world's largest owner of fossil-fuel assets, but it was also a major owner of almost *every* large corporation.

Deese managed to survive the onslaught from the left, and he wasted no time in demonstrating to influential progressives that he would staff the NEC with a new set of policy experts who reflected the collective impulse to be bold. "I saw his name in the news, and then I got a phone call. It was that fast," said Felicia Wong, the Roosevelt Executive Director. "He wanted to find the right people, and so we started sending him names. Some of the first people he hired were from the Roosevelt staff or our larger network."[24] Within weeks, Deese had named Bharat Ramamurti, a former policy direc-tor for Elizabeth Warren and Roosevelt alumnus, as Deputy Director of the NEC and Joelle Gamble, another former Roosevelt employee, as a special assistant to the President.

Meanwhile, the President appointed Jake Sullivan as his National Security Advisor. His charge was to work closely with Deese to oversee "the integration of foreign policy and domestic policy." The new administration's agenda would expand the burgeoning marketcraft by synthesizing the foreign and domestic, which Sullivan declared a "hallmark" of their new approach.[25]

Deese had to move fast. In the days after his victory, Biden had promised another Covid relief package to support American households, small businesses, and local governments, and in addition to building a team, Deese had to decide what to include. At first, it was not clear to anyone how big they might go, given that control of the Senate hung in the balance of a runoff election in Georgia. When two Democrats narrowly won there in early January, Democrats secured a rare governing trifecta with control of the House, Senate, and White House for the first time in twelve years. The big, inchoate ideas that had been bandied about during the Trump years could now theoretically become real, if Deese and Sullivan could pin down the details and get Congressional Democrats on board.

A week later, Biden announced a $1.9 trillion spending package of additional stimulus checks, unemployment benefits, and public health investments. In many ways, this first package did not reflect a new marketcraft, outside of a general desire to go big and be bold. The large spending bill was designed to pad the pockets of American households and support state and local governments.

It was the structure and size that bothered Deese's old mentor Summers. In late January and early February, Summers started calling Deese and other friends in the West Wing, cautioning them that the relief package they wanted was too large. Summers worried that generous spending would give legislators less financial room to make more durable public investments and could trigger inflation. For the moment, he was sharing these concerns privately. "I was strongly of the view that there was a big error being made on the size of the stimulus," Summers later told me. "They were seized with the political imperative around the legislative dynamics."[26] The President and his advisers, including Deese, were not listening to cautionary voices, Summers believed. They were riding high on the political opportunity to go big and wanted to use it, even if something more modest would do.

Summers was the worst person imaginable to deliver the message to go smaller. Twelve years earlier, during the 2008 financial crisis, he had recommended an $890 billion stimulus, which Obama and his advisers downsized to $775 billion. In the years since, conventional wisdom had concluded that the Obama stimulus was too meager for the demand shortfall, and its relatively modest size was a key factor in the sluggish recovery from the recession. Biden himself bought into that argument. During the transition, David Kamin, a lawyer who later became one of Deese's deputies in the White House, conducted an oral history of the Obama stimulus to avoid making the same mistakes. Summers had been pegged as the culprit for the modest size, because of a perception that he had overruled other administration voices advocating for a larger investment. Summers admitted that he believed a big package in 2009 would never have been viable in the Senate, so he did not present it as a serious option to Obama or others.[27]

Now Summers was back, ringing everyone he knew in the Biden West Wing, arguing for smaller. He could sense the skepticism on the other end of the line. As he watched his mentee Deese proceed despite his warnings, Summers decided to take his argument to the court of public opinion.

Much of Washington functions on a gentleperson's agreement that if you're on the same team as the people in power, you voice your concerns privately rather than spilling them publicly in ink. Summers himself was keen on such discretion. In April 2010, while NEC Director for Obama, he invited Elizabeth Warren to dinner at the Bombay Club, an upscale Indian restaurant just a few blocks from the White House. He wanted to discuss Warren's plans for a new agency focused on consumer protection. "Late in the evening, Larry leaned back in his chair and offered me some advice. By now, I'd lost count of Larry's Diet Cokes, and our table was strewn with bits of food and spilled sauces," Warren wrote a few years later. "Larry's tone was in the friendly-advice category. He teed it up this way: I had a choice. I could be an insider or I could be an outsider. Outsiders can say whatever they want. But people on the inside don't listen to them. Insiders, however, get lots of access and a chance to push their ideas. People—powerful people—listen to what they have to say. But insiders also understand one unbreakable rule: They don't criticize other insiders. I had been warned."[28] Warren, the consummate outsider, chose her lane.

Ten years later, Summers changed lanes himself, fashioning a new role as the surly outsider. For several years after his stint at the NEC, he had vied for positions of power in Washington, specifically in 2013 for Chair of the Federal Reserve and later to be President of the World Bank. He failed to secure those roles, but used his research perch at Harvard to make the case for more robust public investment to combat economic stagnation. In July 2020, the journalist Robert Kuttner wrote a long-form takedown of Summers in the *American Prospect*, chalking up his recent research efforts to a "rebranding exercise."[29] The critique was not entirely fair; Summers had a long track record of interest in the topic and a deep research base to explain why. It did, however, reinforce the idea that a certain set of left-leaning thinkers would never embrace Summers again, even when his priorities aligned with theirs. The world was moving on from Summers' ideology, and he had a choice: reinvent himself to again hold powerful positions in government, or abandon his insider status, holding firm to his convictions. In August 2020, at an event at the Aspen Security Forum, he said for the first time, "My time in government is behind me and my time as a free speaker is ahead of me."[30]

Two weeks after Biden's inauguration, Summers took to the pages of the *Washington Post* to argue against the stimulus proposal that Deese was working to shape and pass. "Bold measures need to be accompanied by careful consideration of risks and how they can be mitigated," Summers wrote. "[M]uch of the policy discussion has not fully reckoned with the magnitude of what is being debated." Summers thought the proposal so large that it risked setting off a wave of inflation. It was also not sufficiently focused on the kind of enduring public investment that would fuel long-term growth, in his view. "After resolving the coronavirus crisis, how will political and economic space be found for the public investments that should be the nation's highest priority?" he questioned.[31] A few weeks later, Summers called the legislation the "least responsible" economic policy in forty years—the period that included the Reagan deficits, the subprime mortgage boom, the Bush tax cuts, and Trump's trade war.[32] According to Furman, now a professor at Harvard himself, Summers was just saying the quiet part out loud: "[It] was what a lot of people were saying privately, what was being whispered by people without his voice or without his platform who were nervous about going public."[33]

Inside the White House, the article went off like a bomb. One of the most respected voices among the party establishment was echoing the concerns of Republicans and undermining what might be the single biggest chance for passing legislation. For Deese in particular, the public criticism landed hard.

His former boss and mentor was throwing rocks from the outside. Deese and Summers discussed his concerns privately, but they were at an impasse.

The President himself was frustrated. "President Biden does not like economists," Ben Harris, an economist himself and a policy adviser on the 2020 campaign, told me. "He just had this kind of disdain for the profession because he felt as though they were out of touch with the actual experiences of the American people, that they were using models or math to tell mis-truths."[34] Summers, the preeminent economist who had not gone far enough in 2009, had his sights on Biden's first major piece of legislation. It was too rich. "Instead of brushing aside the criticism, or wrestling with it, Biden called Summers and unloaded on him," one journalist reported.[35]

In the end, Summers' critique didn't matter as much as he may have liked. Biden had too much momentum, and Democrats virtually unani-mously agreed that they had done too little in the wake of the Great Reces-sion. Congress passed the American Rescue Plan on March 11 on a party line vote. "The fact that people like Lawrence Summers have been ignored in favor of progressives," the Roosevelt Institute economist J. W. Mason wrote at the time, "isn't just gratifying as spectacle. It suggests a big move in the center of gravity of economic policy debates. It really does seem that on the big macroeconomic questions, our side is winning."[36]

Even if Summers' argument didn't change the course of policy, it did change Deese and Sullivan. Summers had brought an implicit conflict to the surface in a way that the younger marketcrafters had carefully avoided—and then Summers lost. For Deese, who planned to advance an agenda of tar-geted industrial policy and reinvigorated antitrust, he was embarking on a personal rebellion—a tall task for someone who had staked his career on being a loyal, kind partner to the Summerses of the world. "One of the things that was challenging for me being NEC Director in this period was that our policy framework for doing that felt like I was the kid who was disobeying his parents," Deese said.[37]

To those looking in from the outside, it seemed to be more than disobe-dience, something more akin to an oedipal struggle. Deese was developing policies that broke all of the rules of the Washington consensus and, if suc-cessful, might create a new consensus to eclipse everything he had learned at the feet of Summers. "It was a break in economic paradigm," Deese said. The question was what to do with the pieces left on the floor.

After the recovery package had passed in March, Deese and colleagues turned their attention to building a foundation for a new marketcraft. The moment was ripe. In the spring of 2021, Americans were still reeling from the Covid pandemic, which had entered its second year. Its disruptions were compounding, not resolving. Supply chains worldwide had been scrambled, forcing many Americans to face, often for the first time, the global financial integration that made modern living possible. For a moment, Americans worried that they might not be able to secure basics like ibuprofen, much of which was made in China. A shortage of semiconductors fabricated in Taiwan and South Korea caused the cost of cars to skyrocket. Even the reliable provision of fresh produce on grocery shelves seemed threatened, a casualty of migrant workers unable to enter and move about the United States. Suddenly markets were not magical and self-propelling; they needed government to smooth their gyrations, resolve bottlenecks, and ensure basic, day-to-day operation.

At the same time, anti-China sentiment was reaching a crescendo, galvanizing interest in a more hawkish flex of American economic power. Because the virus had originated in China, Americans grew distrustful of a state actor that had become increasingly antagonistic in the years leading into the pandemic. Rubio and Trump had learned early the political value of taking China on, but that message now spread to the lips of some of the most left-leaning Americans. "The kind of story that we were made to believe from the Dick Cheneys of the world was that China would surpass some income to GDP threshold, and it would naturally grow in the direction of puppies and capitalism and democracy, in a mutually reinforcing fashion," Jen Harris said.[38]

Instead, China had grown significantly richer and more bellicose. Deese had lived a personal evolution on China policy. He had worked with Chinese partners on the bilateral and global agreements to reduce emissions back in 2015, but since then, China's economic statecraft had become more combative. Its leaders were pursuing such an aggressive industrial policy that Deese, like Sullivan and Harris, worried that it would dominate markets critical to its geopolitical power.[39] For years, American progressives had been clamoring for bold policies, and now in the wake of the pandemic and with anxiety about Chinese power growing, they had their opening.

Deese's plans came into focus in the three-month period between the passage of the Covid relief package in early March and June. The new marketcraft was founded on two pillars: public investment in critical industries and taking on concentrated corporate power. Jen Harris later coined the terms "build" and "balance" to describe the twin impulses.[40] Sullivan and Deese hired Harris away from the Hewlett Foundation, creating a new role for her in the White House that jointly appointed her to the NEC and NSC. There she bridged the foreign and domestic domains, while also fusing together the "build" and "balance" mandates. The connection between the two was not immediately clear. Deese and Sullivan aimed to strengthen critical industries like semiconductor manufacturing and renewable energy to address climate change and counter China, but they wanted to avoid a future where a few large companies dominated American markets. They confronted a fundamental tension: these strategic industries needed the massive research budgets and capital investments that only large institutions could provide, yet allowing corporate consolidation risked stifling innovation, concentrating economic activity in coastal regions, and enabling private interests to capture government policy.

The first of the two pillars was a new industrial policy, or "build," premised largely on government financial support for critical industries. Deese believed government funding could be a catalyst: by absorbing some of the initial risk in socially critical industries, public investment could create the certainty needed to unlock much larger pools of private capital, enabling breakthrough technologies that market forces alone might not support. Specifically, he wanted to make it easier for investors to profit from industries such as electric vehicles and semiconductors. Like iron filings to a magnet, public investment in clean-energy industries would theoretically attract additional resources that, from a social perspective, should have been there all along. "While traditional markets are fine for many, even most, things, the weight of experience over recent decades suggests they can miss some essentials— decarbonization, a stable manufacturing base, sufficient quantities of quality housing and childcare—and need to be organized and supplemented by active government policy," Harris later explained.[41] Deese and his team were searching for a middle way between the state capitalism of China and the neoliberal story. Government would not own industry outright, nor would it cede the field to careening markets. Rather, it would focus on guiding certain sectors, based on political goals.

Who got to decide which industries were most important? The answer could only be determined through politics, whether confrontational or co-operative. For Deese and the left, the most urgent focus was climate change. Republicans had little interest in supporting that goal, but their overlap with Democrats on other priorities was extensive. Both parties wanted investments in American infrastructure, semiconductor fabrication, and the reinvigoration of domestic manufacturing to create jobs for people in the heartland. Despite the partisan rhetoric, on economic priorities there was more overlap than disagreement.[42]

The *New York Times* was beginning to pick up on the Deese and Sullivan approach and to put it in its historical context. "While industrial policy is by no means foreign to the United States—any federally subsidized or man-aged expansion of an industry might qualify (think military contractors)—the caricature that comes to mind, even for many liberals, is Soviet-era central planning. The term carries with it a whiff of stigma," wrote one journal-ist in the *Times* about the burgeoning economic plans.[43] Deese, steeled by the support of Sullivan, Jen Harris, and the President himself, leaned in. By June 2021, he took to the stage of the Atlantic Council in Washington to confidently describe the administration's approach as a "twenty-first century American industrial strategy." "No one firm has incentive to invest in the kind of game-changing technologies or the kind of connecting infrastructure that fosters long-term economic competitiveness at the industry, the region, and the nationwide level," he said.[44] The American government had to make big, foundational investments to get the private money flowing.

Summers, apparently savoring his newfound outside role, rose once again to wage an assault on Deese's agenda. The more headlines Summers garnered, the more gas he gave his critique. "There's just a shortage of careful thinking," he said about the administration's economic approach. Ironically, thirty years before, Summers himself had written approvingly of the value of industrial policy for economies attempting to "catch up" quickly with the developed world.[45] He stood by his own research on the topic. "There's a lot to look at in the Asian experience, particularly with catch-up development. If you look at the catch-up of Japan after the Second World War or if you look at the experience of South Korea or Taiwan, it's hard to escape the conclu-sion that those were extremely favorable and that there were active and se-lective government policies focused on developing particular industries," he told me.[46] Whereas Deese argued for "catch-up" policies to address climate change and Chinese power, Summers disagreed that the learnings from development economics were relevant for the United States in 2021.

Even so, as he grew more comfortable in his public-facing role, Deese was becoming more confident and even combative, leaning into the contrast with what he had learned at the feet of Summers. *New York Times* columnist Ezra Klein, interviewing Deese during the pivotal 100 days, reacted like someone seeing an old friend for the first time in decades. "You and I have known each other for a while now," Klein said to Deese. "You were the young guy in the Obama administration. Now you're the grizzled old guy running the National Economic Council," he said.

"I have a hard time thinking of myself as the old guy," Deese replied.

"Sorry, man."

"I get it, I get it," Deese replied. Gathering his thoughts, he weighed in on the generational transition in ideas, "The space of thought has really broadened. We have people who are really disciplined about making sure we're thinking smartly about [the new industrial policy] but open to a much broader range of potential outcomes." This was a mark of strength of the program. Under Deese's leadership, orthodoxy was out, and pushing boundaries was in.[47]

Few people on Deese's team liked to push boundaries as much as Tim Wu, the person he chose to organize the second pillar of the new marketcraft, later known as "balance." An antitrust lawyer, *New York Times* columnist, bestselling author, and onetime candidate for New York lieutenant governor, Wu was just irreverent enough to think creatively about how to focus the Biden administration's attention on corporate power. After Wu's run for lieutenant governor in New York with Teachout and Khan in 2014, he had joined the Obama administration, where he worked on antitrust policy and got to know Deese. Over time, Deese had warmed to Wu's perspective, as he began to see how public investment, if not carefully structured, could entrench the dominance of powerful corporations in already consolidated industries. Major public investment in concentrated markets ran the risk of making big business even bigger if the companies positioned themselves to receive the bulk of the funding.

Deese was not the only one who had come around to being worried about the abuse of concentrated corporate power. It was a surprise to many that the core decision-makers in the Biden White House saw themselves as twenty-first-century trustbusters. The President himself had tepidly supported efforts to rein in corporate concentration over the decades while a Senator, but it was never his priority. As bipartisan concern grew during the years of his presidential campaign, Biden began to speak to the issue more directly, but few expected it to become a pillar of his presidency.[48] Some of the most important people around him, particularly White House chief of staff Ron Klain and his deputy Bruce Reed, had spent most of their careers as exemplary Democratic centrists. Klain had worked as a venture capitalist in the early 2010s with Steve Case, the former AOL chief executive and founder. Reed had started as the policy director for the triangulating Democratic Leadership Council in the Clinton era and later chaired the Simpson-Bowles deficit-reduction commission. In the years since, the two had watched as the technology giants Facebook, Amazon, Google, and Apple grew increasingly large, leveraging their power to lock down their markets. Simmering sympathies for holding big corporations accountable for their mistakes were now bubbling up to the surface. "It's not an accident that we ended up with Wu, Khan, and Kanter," one senior official told me.

The senior team at the White House asked Deese to assess whether Wu might consider joining the administration. Few knew antitrust better, and even fewer combined expertise with Wu's experience in the White House. When Deese broached the topic, Wu made it clear that his portfolio needed to encompass competition policy across all industries—not just Big Tech. Deese agreed, and after a few conversations, Wu accepted, calling it "a leap of faith."[49]

Within weeks, Wu drafted a memo humbly titled "The Grand Unified Theory of Antitrust Revival (and a Plan for Action)." The memo explained that presidential administrations had, for decades, allowed the scope of antitrust enforcement to narrow. According to Wu, this "approach of leaving matters entirely to the technocratic experts" became a political problem for the Obama administration. "[A]s industries consolidated, big mergers went unchecked, and things that the public cared about, like EpiPen price hikes or Big Tech's rise, seemed completely outside of the White House's purview."[50]

Wu argued that the new guard—the Biden administration's economic team, led by Deese—had to do something different. He laid out a road map for the administration to revive aggressive antimonopoly policies. He recommended appointing lawyers educated in the field of antitrust to the bench, advocated for legislative change, and encouraged relevant agencies to pursue existing rule-making power. As a first step, Deese authorized Wu to move forward on drafting an executive order to call on the FTC and Justice Department to use all of their antitrust powers more robustly. The order would also compel other departments of the government to dust off old laws that gave them the power to prevent abuses of corporate power. Wu's idea was to draft this executive order like it was the Declaration of Independence, detailing a big list of complaints and putting forward an ambitious new direction. "More thought went into the drafting of that document than almost anything in my whole life," he said.[51] It still wasn't clear, however, how far the President himself would be willing to go.

It wasn't just Wu who recognized the opportunity of the moment. Behind the scenes, Elizabeth Warren was placing her acolytes into two key government agencies, the CFPB and the FTC. Warren believed that "personnel is policy," and she knew who she wanted where—Lina Khan as a commissioner at the FTC and Rohit Chopra as the head of the CFPB. Deese, Klain, and Reed were open to both. The decision on Chopra came first. In January, the White House announced that Chopra would vacate his commissioner seat at the FTC and move to lead the CFPB. That move meant that there were two empty slots at the FTC that needed to be filled with Democratic commissioners. Once Chopra was announced, it became increasingly clear to Khan that the administration was likely to put her forward for one of the empty seats.

The President announced Khan's nomination on March 22, surprising many who had not picked up on the political evolution of onetime moderates like Deese, Klain, and Reed and didn't expect to see them back someone like her. "Lina was aligned, energetic, out of the box. She had cross-issue and cross-party appeal," Deese said, explaining their thinking at the time. Tech interests balked at the nomination, but given the frenzy of the initial few months of a new presidency, the early decision didn't make the front pages. Biden also would need to choose one of the five commissioners to be its Chair—by far the most powerful position at the institution. Most assumed that Biden would elevate Rebecca Slaughter, the acting Chair, to take the Chair spot permanently.

Then came the real surprise: without informing Khan, Deese and Klain conspired to make her the next Chair of the FTC. The difference between commissioner and Chair was dramatic. The Chair directed personnel, set the agenda and tone for the institution, and had ultimate say over which cases to pursue. Elevating Khan to the role would signal the administration's interest in pursuing the most ambitious antitrust agenda in decades. It was clear to Deese and Klain that Khan would move to dust off long-dormant antitrust powers, rewrite merger guidelines, and exercise rarely used rule-making authority. Big companies, particularly in tech, wouldn't like it, but progressive Democrats would celebrate. Best of all, the Senate wouldn't even have to know. Because the President had the exclusive authority to name one of the FTC's five commissioners as Chair, he could do it right after the Senate confirmed Khan as commissioner.

This arrangement could only work, of course, if the President agreed. On board Air Force One on a flight to Europe in early June, Deese managed to get some extended time with Biden. He made the case for Khan as Chair, as well as for the robust executive order that Wu hoped would reinvigorate the White House's focus on antitrust. Biden was in. "That was the moment when Deese turned the President into the trustbuster," said Wu.[52]

In June, the Senate confirmed Khan as FTC commissioner. Twenty-one Republicans voted yes, including Josh Hawley. Rubio did not vote. Sensing the cross-partisan momentum behind antimonopoly and tech oversight, Hawley seized the moment to make clear how important he believed antitrust to be. In April, he had introduced legislation to expand the power of the antitrust authorities. He proposed updating century-old regulations by shifting the burden of evidence from the government to businesses, which would now have to prove affirmatively that their mergers were *not* anticompetitive. Hawley's proposal would also codify the rejection of a narrow interpretation of antitrust focused on consumer prices by requiring that regulators protect economic competition, not just low costs to the public. "While Big Tech, Big Banks, Big Telecom, and Big Pharma gobbled up more companies and more market share, they gobbled up our freedom and competition," Hawley said. "American consumers and workers have paid the price."[53] His bill garnered some Republican support, but it did not move.

Although Hawley's bill did not make it far, nearly half the Republican caucus decided to support Khan. What few Senators, if any, knew at the time was that within hours Biden would name her as Chair, officially putting her at the head of the new antitrust movement. "It came as a surprise to everybody," Khan said.[54] In the hours between her confirmation to a commission seat and the announcement of her as Chair, the White House made some courtesy calls to antitrust leaders on the Hill, including Minnesota Senator Amy Klobuchar. An Amazon executive happened to be testifying in front of Klobuchar's Senate Judiciary Committee, which meant the Amazon public-policy team had gathered to watch remotely. They had tracked Khan's confirmation with surprise and trepidation. At one moment in the questioning, Klobuchar blurted out the news: "Lina Khan was just named the Chair of the FTC," she said. The Amazon executives, startled, looked at one another to see if they had misheard, before letting out a collective, "What the fuck?"[55] The lowly law student they had brushed off four years earlier was now the chief antitrust enforcement official in the country. The Biden administration rushed to make the official announcement, and that evening Khan was sworn in as Chair. Senate Republicans, despite their support for Khan, felt burned, calling the move "very sneaky, deceptive even."[56] The administration hadn't consulted them, and some questioned her preparedness for the Chair role given her age and relative lack of experience. Khan herself was thrilled but wary of the task ahead. "There was just no time to prepare for being Chair," said one supportive FTC official.[57]

Three weeks after Khan's elevation to Chair, on July 9, Biden took to the White House podium to announce his executive order on competition, which had grown out of Wu's Grand Unified Theory of Antitrust Revival. If elevating Khan to Chair had not convinced the critics that Biden was all in on antitrust, this announcement would. "Capitalism without competition isn't capitalism; it's exploitation. Without healthy competition, big players can change and charge whatever they want and treat you however they want," the President said.[58] The executive order was sweeping. It initiated seventy-two actions across a dozen federal agencies to spur competition in multiple industries and directed the FTC and Justice Department to revise their merger guidelines to prevent harmful combinations. The President also called on the antitrust authorities to limit noncompete agreements, contracts that employers used to prevent workers from changing jobs or negotiating higher wages. Finally, Biden created a competition council to provide an ongoing forum for agency heads to report to the President on their efforts to rein in corporate power. It was now clear that Biden's marketcraft was not so much about tech accountability as a broader interest in spurring competition across health-care, transportation, and agricultural markets.

The administration made clear that their concern was not the sheer size of companies, but how they were using that size to corner markets. "We do take the view that market structure matters, and that we need to be concerned about highly concentrated markets—particularly in an environment where our antitrust agencies have been under-resourced for so long," Deese said. "But that's different from fighting bigness for bigness's sake."[59] It was a subtle distinction, but one meant to bring along centrists like Jason Furman.

Summers didn't agree. He took to the social network X to say Khan's "populist" FTC would "make the US economy more inflationary and less resilient."[60] And a few days after Khan's elevation to Chair, he was back on television hitting Deese and the administration again. "I part company completely with the legal scholars who frankly in many cases are not very familiar with economic reasoning in its intricacy," Summers said. "We need new approaches, possibly new laws, but they need to be ultimately grounded in an economic approach that is based on having a more functional and efficient economy and [not] the idea that big is bad per se . . . that is the way to American failure."[61]

Deese took the fire in stride. "Larry and Jason [Furman] acted like, 'We are not an interest group to be managed. We are the carriers of the truth,'" one of Deese's colleagues told me. Not unlike annoyed parents telling their adult child they're doing it wrong, their advice seemed to have little effect on Deese or the administration's policies, even if it was grating. "It was a constant challenge," another senior economic official in the administration said.

The new build and balance marketcraft nearly failed to launch. In June of 2021, Sameera Fazili, one of three Deputy Directors of the NEC, approached the podium in the White House briefing room. Fazili had been at the Treasury and the Atlanta Federal Reserve before moving back to Washington to work for Deese. On this particular day, she hoped to explain the administration's efforts to address compounding problems in global supply chains and the recent surge in inflation. At the time of the press conference, inflation had reached 4.4 percent, higher than it had been in thirty years. A persistent journalist wanted to get the NEC on the record for what it expected in the future. Fazili, whose team was hustling to clear up ports as fast as possible, articulated the official position that would become a constant refrain in the coming months: "We still expect this to be transitory in nature. We're going to keep an eye on it, but we think it should resolve in the next few months."[62]

Instead, inflation accelerated. By December, it climbed to 6.2 percent, peaking in June 2022 at 7.1 percent. The accelerating prices showed up across the board. Initially, goods inflation led the way, as Americans sought out new homes—and stuff to fill them with. Demand for lumber climbed as people built decks and home offices, a reaction to the shift in lifestyle wrought by the pandemic. But it wasn't just housewares. A used car that cost $10,000 in July 2020 cost $15,000 by July 2022. New car prices jumped by 17.5 percent in the same period.[63] Car manufacturers had miscalculated at the beginning of the pandemic when they meaningfully throttled back production as sales plummeted. They reversed course when demand surged, but it was impossible to restart the supply chain quickly enough. New car production relied on semiconductors, the chips that Robert Noyce had helped invent and build and the American government had supported decades before. Demand for semiconductors had surged in the pandemic as consumers spent money on new electronics. Chip manufacturers shifted to prioritize these higher-margin products, which made it difficult for the automotive sector, reliant on chips for car manufacturing, to ramp up production.[64] It wasn't just household items and cars that drove inflation however. In early 2022, as people became more confident that the coronavirus no longer posed the same danger that it once had, inflation spread to services outside of the home, including restaurants and travel.

People had money to spend. The stimulus checks that Summers worried about had the effect of providing the financial cushion that politicians intended. That spurred consumer demand, causing the recovery from the pandemic recession to be fast and robust.[65] Yet the Fed, under the leadership of its Chair, Jay Powell, made the error of continuing to pursue monetary stimulus through the middle of 2021, despite the robust fiscal spending and percolating price rises. Then they waited until March 2022, when inflation was above 6 percent, to begin raising rates. Meanwhile, in late February of that year, Russian autocrat Vladimir Putin launched a full-scale invasion of Ukraine, sending global energy prices higher. As in 1973, a period of relatively high inflation fueled by loose monetary policy and robust government spending was exacerbated by a geopolitical crisis, causing prices to reach record levels. It was the perfect recipe for an inflationary surge.

Despite the multiple and complex causes of the inflation, Summers claimed victory, pinning it on the stimulus. Headlines asked: "Was Larry Summers Right about Inflation?"[66] He thought so, writing that Powell was delusional to think that price levels would soon come down.[67] Summers had warned of inflation risk from the relatively large size of the administration's relief package, but he had not predicted the severity of the supply disruptions, the Ukraine war, or the failure of the Fed to move faster. Those details mattered little to his analysis. For Summers, the only way for inflation to come down would be if more Americans lost their jobs: "We need five years of unemployment above 5 percent to contain inflation—in other words, we need two years of 7.5 percent unemployment or five years of 6 percent unemployment or one year of 10 percent unemployment."[68] That would spell disaster for American families—and for Deese, who would see his economic plan crumble by the widespread discontentment that would result.

The persistence of inflation made it hard for Deese and his team to focus on their affirmative vision for marketcraft. Even so, he was notching some wins. In October 2021, more than 140 countries agreed to implement a global minimum tax, an initiative that had been brewing for years but needed American support to get over the finish line. Deese's team renewed and expanded Trump-era tariffs on steel and electric vehicles. The White House competition council, Wu's invention, met for the first time in September of that year. But these steps forward looked modest as consumer sentiment fell thanks to escalating prices, and they received little coverage in the media in comparison to the monthly inflation reports.

Deese and his team bet that inflation would soon abate, doused by the resolution of supply-chain bottlenecks and the normalization of consumer demand thanks to widespread vaccination. Consumers would spend down their savings as the Fed raised rates, and the combination would alleviate price pressures. Deese focused on landmark legislation that he hoped would solidify the new economics, which was particularly ambitious given the fifty-fifty split in the Senate. His team wanted Congress to pass a large infrastructure package, a burst of public investment to fight climate change, health-care and prescription drug reform, new programs for child- and eldercare, and an initiative to reshore semiconductor production.

In November 2021, Congress made the first step happen. Nineteen Republicans in the Senate and thirteen in the House teamed up with all Democrats to invest $1.2 trillion in American infrastructure. Trump's team had spent years attempting to craft something along these lines, so much so that the recurring announcement that it was "infrastructure week" during his administration became a punch line. But Trump's groundwork made it easier to garner Republican support for Biden's legislation, given that there was a loose consensus from both parties on how it might work. The legislation included billions of dollars for roads and bridges, passenger and freight rail, power grid improvements, and broadband access. The last time Congress passed such ambitious infrastructure legislation was the National Interstate and Defense Highways Act over sixty-five years earlier.

The White House intended the legislation to be paired with a second bill to make a massive investment in climate, health care, and child- and elderly care. Everyone expected that bill would proceed on a party line vote, given Republicans' skepticism that climate change posed a significant threat and their lack of interest in supporting care work outside of limited tax credits. But Democrats could not even reach agreement among themselves. Within weeks of the infrastructure bill passing, support for climate investment collapsed inside the Democratic Party. Joe Manchin, the Senator from West Virginia and one of the most conservative in the Democratic caucus, was a pivotal vote. Ironically, Deese had followed Felicia Wong's mandate to go bold, but he worried that the administration may have gone too far. Just before Christmas, Manchin told Fox News' Bret Baier that he was walking away: "I've always said this, Bret, if I can't go home and explain it to the people of West Virginia, I can't vote for it."

"You're done? Is this a no?" Bret asked.

"This is a no on this legislation. I've tried. I mean, I really did."

The President and his team seethed. The President's press secretary went so far as to say that Manchin had betrayed Americans—and the President. Biden called Manchin, but his phone was off. "Joe," Biden said in a voicemail, "how can you do this to me—and at Christmastime?"[69]

Deese was intending to reshape American capitalism, but many of those legislative plans depended on the vote of a single man from West Virginia whom the administration had just publicly alienated. Meanwhile, at the FTC, Khan's early moves had also not gone over well. Within weeks of taking the helm, Khan rescinded a policy statement from the Obama era that said the FTC would not use its legal authority to issue regulations against "unfair methods of competition." That seemed a straightforward action in line with expectations, but Khan had given little notice of her intent, even to FTC staff. For existing commissioners and career staff, it suggested their voices mattered little and Khan had it all figured out. That initial concern was confirmed as staff attorneys and economists were dropped from decision-making meetings. When they did offer opinions, Khan at times overruled their judgment. The Chair's office would edit press statements and court filings to layer in new language that Khan favored.

It was inevitable that Khan would anger career staff at the FTC. She did, in fact, disagree with the way they had been working over the past several decades. Yet it was the style of the changes that seemed to aggravate the initial resistance. Instead of explaining the direction she wanted to take the FTC in and bringing staff along with her, she was imposing her decisions from the top, they said. Staff described her leadership as "irritated, impatient, and dismissive" to the *Washington Post*. "She didn't know what she didn't know," one person said.[70]

But as both Khan and Deese struggled to take the new marketcraft from rhetoric to reality, a lifeline soon arrived from the unlikeliest of sources. In the middle of March 2022, Deese received an unexpected invitation. Two cabinet secretaries were planning to head to West Virginia to discuss economic development with the President of West Virginia University and Senator Manchin. The trip would include a visit to the New River Gorge, a new national park, where the group would spend the night.

Manchin didn't just want the cabinet secretaries to come—he wanted Deese to join as well, only a few months after he had torpedoed Deese's prize legislation. "At first, I said, I don't need to join—we don't need to overload this," Deese said. Manchin's staff responded, "No, really. He would like you to come."[71] Despite Manchin pulling his support for climate investment, he and Deese had built a rapport over the previous year, with Manchin growing to appreciate Deese's frank, collaborative demeanor. As with some of Deese's progressive critics, Manchin associated Deese with the more moderate, practical wing of the party. Deese checked with the President, who agreed that he should go but directed him to keep the conversations "low key."[72]

There was a larger rapprochement between Biden and Manchin in the works. A few weeks earlier, Gina Raimondo, Biden's Commerce Secretary and the former Governor of Rhode Island, organized a dinner for Chief of Staff Klain and Manchin. She cooked roasted pork, eggplant Parm, and cannolis—with Scotch to wash it all down. Klain apologized to Manchin for the public lashing in December, and Manchin agreed to rejoin negotiations on the big legislative package that Deese had been pushing. But he would still be the same demanding negotiator.

"You're never going to agree to what I want," Manchin reportedly warned Klain.

"Try me," Klain replied.[73]

Now it was Deese who was headed to West Virginia at Manchin's invitation to see how far the conversations might go. His job was to deploy one of his most finely honed skills: listening attentively enough to figure out how to get a man in power to yes. Before he left Washington, Deese sent Manchin an outline of the climate and energy provisions of the legislative initiative the House had passed in the fall. He was priming the conversation.

In West Virginia, the cabinet secretaries and Manchin paraded through political events, which promoted the stimulus and infrastructure package. Later in the day, Deese and Manchin donned harnesses and helmets to zipline in the new national park. They posed for a photograph afterward, two buds out for a good time in the West Virginia woods.

In spare moments, Deese and Manchin dug into the Senator's concerns about the legislation. There were few "big-picture" problems about the nature of public investment or the need to manage energy markets. Manchin fixated on the finer details, such as the method of funding and the scope of tax refunds. Driving with the Senator between events and relaxing by the bonfire at night, Deese got a better sense of what he was grappling with. These were modestly sized problems that could be addressed. Manchin was testing Deese's willingness to compromise, particularly on the more progressive proposals, like a new Civilian Conservation Corps.

In a meeting after the trip, Deese brought along a list of policies that he imagined Manchin could accept. They were right on target. The Senator's team did not want to officially open a new negotiation with the White House, but they confirmed to Deese that he had nailed down the core items. They might just be able to figure this out together.

Over the next several months, Manchin's staff met privately with Majority Leader Schumer's staff to put a deal back together. Deese and the White
House were kept abreast of the conversations, but they had agreed that the
Senate staffers should lead. Through the early summer, the negotiating teams
worked through the fine points of what had become a climate bill, with provisions bolted on to improve prescription drug pricing. "The whole time I
felt like we could get it done, and yet on an hour-to-hour basis, it always felt
like we weren't going to get it done," Deese said. "It was constantly slipping
away."[74] Of all people, Larry Summers was helping Senators come around; he
distinguished the new climate investments from the large size of the initial
Biden stimulus, arguing the climate efforts were necessary and paid for.[75]

Just as they were closing in on a deal, new record inflation numbers
emerged in mid-July 2022. They were too much for Manchin. "I'm not
going to do something, and overreach, that causes more problems," he told
Schumer by phone on July 13. Exhausted and outraged, the negotiators and
most members of the President's team believed that the deal had failed yet
again.[76]

Only Deese had a sense that it wasn't true. From Thursday to Sunday,
everybody in the White House, including the President, thought it was dead.
Deese, however, had a hunch that Manchin would be back. He knew that
Manchin did, in the end, believe in the fundamental need for public investment to expand clean energy capacity. "On Monday morning, I was sitting at
my desk and I got a call from Manchin. He says, 'Will you come up and sit
with Lance and Petrella? We want to walk you through something,'" Deese
recalled. He left the White House and went down to the Capitol to meet
with Lance West, Manchin's chief of staff, and Gerry Petrella, Schumer's lead
negotiator. West distributed a few papers that contained the parameters of a
deal and said tersely, "This is all we could do."

Deese read through the terms, with Petrella scanning them at the same
time. "Lance, this is the deal. What do you mean this is all you can do?"
Deese asked. "This is what we've been talking about the whole time."

"Yeah, I know," West said, with a wry smile. "This is all we can do." They
had a deal.[77]

Over the following ten days, the negotiators finalized the terms. "It was the
only secret that really held in Washington," Deese said. On the afternoon

of July 27, they announced the substance of the deal, with Manchin affirming the terms. The proposed legislation would be confusingly called the Inflation Reduction Act (IRA). Even though the legislation was not primarily
concerned with lowering the cost of living, the name would signal to voters
that the White House shared their top-line concern. Congressional leaders
and the White House worked up the legislative text and passed the bill. On
August 16, 2022, President Biden signed it into law.

Deese had accomplished a feat that would have been unfathomable just a
few years earlier when he carried the climate portfolio for the Obama White
House. The law invested at least $350 billion of public funds into indus-
tries that mitigated the effects of climate change. Tax credits incentivized
the acceleration of renewable energy projects, including hydrogen production, solar and wind power, and carbon capture projects. It expanded tax
credits for consumers who purchased new, American-made electric vehicles,
and it invested in vehicle-charging infrastructure. Homeowners got money
for investing in solar panels, heat pumps, and energy-efficient windows and
doors. The bill provided funding for domestic manufacturing of solar panels,
wind turbines, batteries, and critical minerals, fostering the development of
domestic clean-energy supply chains. All together, the legislation was the
largest investment in clean energy and emission-reduction efforts in history.
Alongside the climate provisions, the bill also empowered Medicare to ne-
gotiate prices for certain high-cost prescription drugs and capped out-of-
pocket drug costs for elderly Americans at $2,000 annually.

One aspect of the policies that Deese pursued that made his marketcraft so
powerful—and so different from historical precedent—was the breadth of
the mission. At the same time as he was working with leaders in Congress to
forge a legislative package to tackle climate change, Deese, along with other
administration officials, was also attempting to reinvigorate American semiconductor manufacturing.

The same July morning that the climate deal was announced, Congress
passed legislation to reshape the semiconductor-manufacturing sector. Even
though the semiconductor legislation had originated with Republicans in
2019, Deese and other Democrats could see the substantive opportunity to
craft a critical market. In the spring of 2022, Deese and Gina Raimondo, also
his partner in the Manchin wooing, accelerated their efforts on the Hill to

pass a semiconductor industrial policy bill. Raimondo was more than happy to build on the plans laid by Republicans if it was in the best interest of the country. "You've got to give credit where it's due," she said about her predecessors at Commerce.[78] Deese and Raimondo reached out to former Trump officials, including Mike Pompeo, Trump's Secretary of State. "I'm always happy to help a fellow Italian," Pompeo told Raimondo when she called.[79] For all their wariness about public investment when it came to mitigating climate change, Republicans on the Hill were more than happy to spend government money in support of national security. "A resurgence of investment in domestic semiconductor capacity and innovation will require significant public spending, through a vehicle sure to be imperfect," wrote Republican Oren Cass. "But imperfect does not mean ineffective. Anyone can find an excuse to say no to any piece of legislation, but progress on rebuilding domestic industry will depend on sufficient courage to say yes."[80]

By the summer, Congressional leaders believed they had a consensus bill in hand, known as the CHIPS and Science Act. But despite the Republican origins of the bill and its widespread support in the party, Senate Minority Leader Mitch McConnell had little interest in handing a legislative victory to Biden. McConnell threatened to block the bill if Democrats moved forward with their climate program. Schumer had a plan, and it managed to turn the lemons of Joe Manchin's resistance into legislative lemonade. He would mislead McConnell into believing that the climate bill was dead, clearing the way for the CHIPS and Science Act. Only then would he announce the progress on what was soon to be called the Inflation Reduction Act.

It was a high-wire act that he barely managed to pull off. The morning of July 27, the Senate passed the CHIPS and Science Act, which set aside $52 billion for public investment in semiconductor research and manufacturing. Sixteen Republicans voted for the measure, with several more withholding their support out of conviction that it did not go far enough. The legislation left it to the Commerce Secretary to divide those funds up between R&D efforts and direct investments or grants to corporations that would open new chip foundries in the United States. The bill also funded workforce-training programs and regional tech hubs. Even the conservative American Enterprise Institute hailed it as "Far from Perfect, but Still Very Good."[81] That same afternoon, Schumer announced the breakthrough on the IRA. Biden signed both initiatives into law just weeks later.

Deese watched the roll call votes in the summer of 2022 on his laptop, which was perched on one of the many cardboard boxes filling his Washington home. His wife and two young children had spent a year and a half in the capital, but they were itching to leave. "Washington never really felt like our place," Deese said. Their home in Portland, Maine, beckoned. Deese planned to stay in Washington for another six months in his current position and commute to New England on the weekends to see his family. It would be grueling, but at least his kids would enjoy a full year of uninterrupted schooling and a more settled home.

Given the personal transitions, it took some time for Deese to appreciate the magnitude of his success. Between the stimulus package, the infrastructure bill, the climate bill, and CHIPS, Deese's NEC had overseen the appropriation of over $4 trillion of public spending—more than four times the size of Obama's stimulus. Roughly half of the funds were earmarked for relief—direct cash payments, support for small business and schools to navigate the pandemic—and the other half for public investment in infrastructure and climate. It would take years for the investment funds to be deployed, but even so, the level of peacetime public investment had only one historical parallel: the New Deal. Spending during that period eclipsed even the post-pandemic programs in size. But Deese and others would argue that the full scope of their marketcraft couldn't be measured by federal budgets alone. Government funds should work as a catalyst, significantly boosting the amount of private capital deployed into the sectors most in need of support. And by that measure, they succeeded: by 2024, private investment in new factories was about $150 billion greater—two and a half times larger—than the pre-Biden norm.[82]

As ambitious as the public and private investments were, mitigating climate change will cost significantly more. Climate experts estimate that the current flows of climate finance globally add up to about 1 percent of global GDP. To meet the targets necessary for mitigating the worst impacts of climate change, annual climate finance must grow fivefold by 2030 and continue to rise in the decades afterward.[83] Given existing budgets, the public sector will have to find still more ways to attract private investment to see the technological breakthroughs necessary to mitigate and manage climate challenges. Their legislation provided a solid start, but Deese and his colleagues understood that they had a long journey ahead of them.

Legislative accomplishments are always the result of many people and events. Policy elites and academics develop and refine proposals, while activist groups and lobbyists push for these policies in both the court of public opinion and the corridors of power. Legislative dealmaking then helps bring the initiative to fruition. In the case of the 2022 climate bill, however, with razor-thin support, it is easier to make claims about the role of individual actors. The IRA and CHIPS would not have happened without Brian Deese. A different leader would have never agreed to such ambitious marketcraft in the first place, and few others had the political skills to turn ideas into policy reality. "In a scenario where you had a moderate as chief of staff and someone else besides Brian heading the NEC, a lot of this just would not have gone through," a senior administration official told me. After his long first tour of duty, Deese came to power with a clear idea of how he wanted to use the power of government to shape and craft markets. And he made it happen.

In the fall of 2022, as the midterm elections loomed, Biden returned to the campaign trail and Deese hit the road promoting the administration's economic agenda. Inflation was beginning to decline, but it was still near 6 percent, which meant Biden's economic program was polling negatively. Over the coming months, inflation would fall back toward normal levels without the skyrocketing unemployment of 7-plus percent that Summers had prescribed. Unemployment remained below 4 percent, lower than in decades.

So what did cause the inflation, and its resolution? Several scholars studied the question, and most rejected Summers' simple "excess demand" theory that put all the blame on too much spending from Congress. Perhaps the most widely respected and conventional assessment was written by former Fed Chair Ben Bernanke and Olivier Blanchard, who had initially joined Summers in 2021 in warning that Congressional spending was excessive and labor markets dangerously tight. Writing two years later, Bernanke and Blanchard cited a convergence of factors, particularly the rapid shifts in what people wanted to spend money on, quick rises in food prices, and the energy shock of the Ukraine war. The elevated desire for nicer housing and automobiles in particular drove the shock. Many analysts believed that the

Fed had been too slow to end its quantitative easing and begin to tighten. Other scholars documented how corporations with large levels of market power were able to raise their prices disproportionately, although few experts agreed this was a major driver of the price rises. Economists disputed the extent to which tightness in labor markets had contributed to the inflationary spike. Congressional spending, what Summers had been most concerned about, had boosted household savings and spending power, contributing to the price run-up. But it was hard to cite it as the primary, and certainly not the sole, cause.[84]

For all of the diverse causes, the response to the inflation was clear. Voters did not like it, just as they had hated it in the 1970s when it raged at even higher levels and for longer. Deese had to strike a delicate balance between acknowledging that pain and defending the administration's success in reshaping the American economy. In a speech to regional business interests in Cleveland, he embraced the ambition of his marketcraft: "This combined endeavor—infrastructure, innovation, clean energy—is no less ambitious than the Erie Canal, the transcontinental railroad, rural electrification, or the interstate highway system were in their time."[85] But on cable news, all the hosts wanted to ask about was inflation, and whether Summers had been right.

The fall midterm campaign did not turn out to be a referendum on Deese's program. In the spring of 2022, the Supreme Court reversed nearly a half century of precedent and struck down constitutional protection for the right to abortion access, which mobilized Democratic voters and boosted the party's performance at the polls. Even though other issues overshadowed economic policy, the Biden team read into the election results a broader validation of his presidency's economic agenda, despite the challenges that inflation still posed.

Summers found a way to support many of the administration's economic policies while criticizing the ideology that had made them possible. "The best generals are reluctant warriors who hate war but know it is sometimes necessary. The best industrial policy advocates see industrial policy as a last resort when there are clear reasons why markets will fail and a strong basis for believing government can be effective," Summers said to me.[86] He would have preferred if Deese had focused on policies to address "market failures" rather than market-shaping initiatives, imitating Summers' own approach in the Clinton and Obama years. Summers' opinions, while they ricocheted around social media, had faded in importance to Deese and the White House. Their vision for how to organize American markets had won out legislatively, with an ironic assist from Summers himself. The next challenge would prove harder: matching the ambition of the new marketcraft with the short-term needs to lower the cost of living for American households.

17

THE NEW MARKETCRAFT

MICHAEL SCHMIDT, BRIAN DEESE & LINA KHAN (2022–24)

In the late summer of 2022, Mike Schmidt was navigating a maze of cardboard boxes littered across his Washington living room. A senior adviser at the Treasury Department and young father of two, Schmidt was part of a wave of exhausted political appointees preparing to step away from government service after eighteen grueling months. He had spent his time working under Deputy Treasury Secretary Wally Adeyemo, an old law school friend of Brian Deese's, shepherding one of the administration's most prominent initiatives: the expanded child tax credit in Biden's stimulus package. But now, with the credit left out of the summer's legislative victories and his energy depleted, Schmidt was ready to close this chapter of public service.

In the midst of his packing, Schmidt's phone vibrated, and the caller ID lit up with Deese's name. A few days earlier, Schmidt had gotten a similar unexpected call from the office of Commerce Secretary Gina Raimondo, who had asked if he had interest in administering the new CHIPS Act. He hadn't thought much of it. "I didn't know anything about semiconductors, and I was on my way out of DC," he said later. He declined to even meet with anyone from Raimondo's team.[1]

A call from Deese was different. The two were roughly the same age and had come up through the Obama administration together. Schmidt had worked in the Obama Treasury Department before leaving to enroll at Yale

Law School, just like Deese. His earnest, lawyerly demeanor lent him an aura of trustworthiness and dedication, a conscientious public servant committed to making government work better. During the Trump administration, he had worked for Governor Andrew Cuomo of New York before becoming the state's tax commissioner. In 2021, when he was headed back to Washington, he had spoken to White House officials, including Deese, about a job there but had landed at Treasury.

Now Deese was recruiting him for something new. "Mike, you have to go and take the meeting," he said. "I'm not telling you that you have to do the job, but you need to go hear Raimondo out." Deese worried that many Democrats were underestimating the importance of the semiconductor legislation, because its passage had been overshadowed by the climate change initiative. He compared leading CHIPS implementation to his own breakthrough career moment. "This is like the impact of the auto bailout, but several times over," Deese said.

Schmidt agreed to consider it. He called Raimondo's team back and, a few days later, sat across from her at the Commerce Department. Raimondo pitched him on the role, and when Schmidt cited his lack of industry experience, she leaned in. "We'll find the chips experts. I want someone who knows how to operate in government," she told him.[2] Days later, Schmidt repurposed some of those packing boxes and moved the few items left on his desk at Treasury to his new desk in Commerce. He was the first employee of a brand-new government agency, and his family's move back to New York would have to wait.

As summer turned to fall, Schmidt began to build a new institution of marketcraft, walking in the footsteps of Jesse Jones in the 1930s and Robert Noyce in the 1980s. Raimondo recruited Todd Fisher, a former private equity executive with extensive investment and administrative experience, to work alongside Schmidt as the Chief Investment Officer of the CHIPS fund. Fisher had already been working in government for a little over a year, helping the Commerce Department implement the economic development provisions of the early stimulus bill.[3] Congress had given Schmidt and Fisher a clear mission—boost domestic semiconductor manufacturing to enhance American geopolitical power and create jobs—and had allocated $52 billion to the Commerce Department for the work. Raimondo decided to set aside

$39 billion in a fund to subsidize direct private-sector investment and put the remaining $11 billion into research and development. (The balance of the funds went to the Defense and State departments.)[4] In addition to those funds, Schmidt and Fisher could deploy $75 billion in low-cost loans. Tax credits could further subsidize their pitch to companies. Schmidt and Fisher effectively had over $100 billion at their disposal to convince global companies to set up semiconductor manufacturing in the United States.

Just after Labor Day, the two showed up to an empty office. Whereas Jesse Jones' temporary headquarters had been inside the Treasury, Schmidt and Fisher's was at Commerce. It wasn't just the office that was a blank slate: "There was nothing," Fisher said. "There were no people, processes, sets of rules, and no one focused on executing." The two hatched a plan. In February 2023, they released a vision paper that outlined the intention to build new, state-of-the-art computer chip factories and become a world leader in advanced chip packaging, while also increasing production of older, more commonly used chips.[5] They refined the big-picture mission Congress had given them to be a little more precise: make sure the United States was producing abundant, high-quality memory chips, developing new memory technologies, and working with friendly nations to create a stable supply chain of essential chips. To get going, Schmidt and Fisher "were maniacally focused on building a team, hiring," bringing on 200 people within months. A quarter of them came with investment and dealmaking experience gained from working at companies like JPMorgan, Goldman, and McKinsey.[6]

Over the next two years, Schmidt and Fisher disbursed the bulk of the money Congress had appropriated, awarding grants and loans to twenty-seven projects across sixteen states.[7] All of the major leading-edge semiconductor-manufacturing companies in the world began to build factories in the United States, with clusters of activity in Texas, Arizona, and upstate New York. The US was on track to have five leading-edge logic and memory chip manufacturers operating in the country, while no other nation in the world had more than two. In the fall of 2024, TSMC began to fabricate the advanced A16 chips that power the iPhone at its Arizona facility.[8] The production yields at that facility exceeded similar factories back in Taiwan, a promising sign about what might be possible for TSMC and its competitors.[9]

For every big-name semiconductor manufacturer receiving support, there were several others providing the materials, equipment, and packaging necessary to support a full domestic supply chain. CHIPS invested in a company in upstate New York to produce dry vacuum pumps, previously not manufactured in the United States, and sites in Indiana and Texas to develop the "packaging," the protective casing and structural support, for the semiconductor chip. By October 2024, Schmidt and Fisher's team had invested over $30 billion and loaned an additional $30 billion.[10] By contrast, total government investment in the Sematech consortium that Robert Noyce ran in the 1980s to spur American semiconductor manufacture was just shy of $500 million, or $2.8 billion in today's dollars.[11]

Those public funds made up only about 10 percent of the total cost of the construction of the new manufacturing facilities, with the balance coming from private investment. The CHIPS team activated over $300 billion of private funds, leading to more investment in electronics manufacturing in the two years after the CHIPS Act passage than in the previous twenty-six years combined.[12] "In 2022, the United States did not produce any advanced logic chips," said a report by the SIA. "By 2032, the United States will produce nearly 30% of all logic chips [globally] at processes newer than 10 nanometers."[13] Experts estimate the CHIPS program investments will create over 100,000 jobs.[14] Challenges remained. One of the most prominent recipients of CHIPS funding, Intel, struggled to convince investors that it was moving fast enough to fabricate cutting-edge CHIPS. In many locations, a shortage of skilled construction workers caused delays in the construction and operation of factories. Schmidt and Fisher worked to mitigate the problem by investing $250 million into workforce training and education programs to ensure that the facilities can be built in a timely fashion and staffed by highly qualified workers. The growing number of facilities under construction and TSMC's initial successes point to promising long-term returns on this strategic investment.

With the CHIPS Act's success, a cross-partisan consensus for supporting semiconductor manufacture had taken hold. Senator Todd Young, the Indiana Republican, touted the bill's success at home and in Washington. "[Surging semiconductor demand] means more jobs, higher wages, and a more significant contribution to our defense economy, but also more broadly to our economic growth," Young said at one of several events promoting the law in Indiana.[15] Democratic Majority Leader Schumer took a victory lap as well: "Without the federal incentives funded by the CHIPS and science law I led to passage . . . major chips projects in New York and around the country would not be happening at the transformational scale that is occurring."[16] When Speaker of the House Mike Johnson suggested at a 2024 campaign event that Republicans might repeal the law, the response from his Republican colleagues was swift, and within hours, he said he had misheard the question. Instead, he wanted to improve the bill to enhance the speed of construction.[17]

There are two main reasons why the CHIPS initiative worked, and both are important lessons for how to craft markets. First, Congress created a clear mission to onshore semiconductor manufacturing, but it avoided assigning meaningful constraints or narrowly limiting the kind of investments it made—their structure, duration, or geographical focus.[18] This move gave wide latitude and discretion to agency leaders to make informed decisions responsive to the most promising opportunities for investment. Second, Raimondo recruited experts in their fields—both government administration and private investing—to head the effort. The CHIPS office became a relatively autonomous, unencumbered dealmaking unit with experts motivated by a public purpose. "We combine urgency with purpose. We bring humanity to work. And we treat bureaucracy like a dance partner, not a roadblock," Schmidt said in describing the values he and Fisher fostered.[19] Skeptics might doubt that sentiment—Elizabeth Warren, for instance, pushed back against the hiring of so many finance and investment banking experts.[20] But Schmidt and Fisher's ability to blend public- and private-sector expertise made their marketcraft successful, just like a similar partnership had powered Robert Noyce's efforts a generation before.

There are voices calling for additional investment in CHIPS, which might fund more semiconductor manufacturing or even a broader mandate to support the development of other cutting-edge technologies. Deese has said privately that Congress will probably want to renew or expand its initial $40 billion investment, and Raimondo would like to see additional funding. "I suspect there will have to be—whether you call it CHIPS 2 or something else—continued investment if we want to lead the world," she said in February 2024.[21] Unsurprisingly, industry voices are also supportive. "It doesn't get fixed in one three- to five-year program," Patrick Gelsinger, the recently retired chief executive of Intel, told the *New York Times*. "I do think we'll need at least a CHIPS 2 to finish that job."[22]

Building off the success, Congress has the opportunity to transition a temporary fund into a permanent institution. It could serve as the core of a new national investment bank, like the RFC, focused on particular sectors. While President Trump was vaguely skeptical of the initiative during his 2024 campaign, despite the fact that it originated in his administration, he was supportive of a sovereign wealth fund that might make similar investments. The CHIPS office's existing expertise on semiconductor manufacturing might be retained and expanded to support industries likely to be important to the future global economy, create jobs, and enhance American geopolitical power. Without additional investment, it will be difficult to retain the talent and culture that the CHIPS team has assembled at its start. Given the relatively modest size of the initial investment—less than half of 1 percent of the annual federal budget—much could be gained for a modest price.

As the CHIPS office gained momentum, so too did the FTC in the implementation of its own program of marketcraft. In the fall of 2020, the world's largest chip designer, NVIDIA, announced its intention to buy ARM, the largest designer of chips for mobile devices. Both are the architects of the chips that technology companies need to procure in their hunt for more processing power. The merger was set to be the largest ever in the chip sector, and it threatened to give NVIDIA a clear monopoly on the design of chips that power artificial intelligence computation, among other uses. In December 2021, Lina Khan's FTC moved to block the merger, arguing that it would lead to higher prices and stifle innovation. The vote was unanimous, with the Republican commissioners lining up with Khan. Two months later, NVIDIA dropped the plan, and the following year, ARM went public in the largest offering of 2023. After Khan's early struggles, the results were a clear victory.

In the courts, the FTC began to win cases and reach strategically beneficial settlements. In May 2023, Khan's FTC sued to block the pharmaceutical company Amgen's $28 billion acquisition of an emerging biotech firm, Horizon. A few months later, they reached a settlement, which allowed the merger in exchange for Amgen's agreeing to get FTC approval before acquiring certain new products and commitment not to bundle them to customers. In December of that year, the FTC sued to block a pharmaceutical giant from squashing a competitive product that would make it easier to treat Pompe disease. Within hours, the acquirer dropped its plan.[23] Just a week later, the

FTC won another victory in the case of Illumina, a California genomics company that had acquired Grail, a company with cutting-edge cancer detection tools, two years earlier. The FTC, concerned about higher prices and reduced innovation, sued to unwind the merger, and a federal court largely ruled in its favor. Given the regulatory and financial uncertainty, Illumina agreed to reverse the acquisition.[24] Meanwhile, Khan's FTC pushed pharmacy companies to lower the prices of inhalers and refunded hundreds of millions of dollars that Epic Games allegedly tricked Fortnite players into spending.[25] Perhaps most significantly, in December 2024, courts blocked Kroger's $25 billion deal to buy Albertsons, a rival grocery chain.[26] That decision was immediately followed by another victory that blocked the consolidation of two luxury fashion retailers. To be sure, Khan's FTC also lost some high-profile cases, including its attempts to prevent Microsoft from acquiring the gaming company Activision Blizzard. Even so, by August 2024, of the complaints pursued under Khan's leadership, the FTC had won over 90 percent.[27]

Khan's imprint on the FTC was not just on the cases she pursued. At the end of 2023, the agency, along with the DOJ, updated its merger guidelines. Lawyers at the enforcement authorities use these standards to determine whether a proposed merger should be allowed. Moving forward, legal counsel at the FTC and DOJ will take a broader view of the structural nature of a market, using lower standards for what counts as a concentrated market. They will also examine the potential effects of a merger or acquisition on wages, innovation, the supply chain, consumer prices, and market access.

A few months after issuing the new guidelines, the FTC issued a ban on legal arrangements that enable employers to prevent an employee from working for a competitor. These "noncompete" agreements restrict tens of millions of Americans from easily moving jobs.[28] The sandwich maker Jimmy John's can no longer prevent its employees from jumping ship to Subway, for instance. Industry groups sued to block the noncompete implementation, and the courts will get to decide if the FTC decision stands.

Regardless of what happens in that case, Khan's impact on corporate consolidation has been felt on Wall Street, in Silicon Valley, and elsewhere. Mergers and acquisitions are highly cyclical and dependent on the macroeconomic environment, including interest rates and intensity of demand. But they also depend significantly on expectations about government oversight.

In the two years after Khan took the helm, the value of all M&A transactions was lower than it had been in a decade, despite a booming economy.[29] Increasing interest rates were naturally moderating acquisition activity, but investors had also become significantly more wary of combinations. In 2024 alone, dozens of potential mergers were abandoned out of concern that they might trigger antitrust scrutiny.[30] If a merger looked like it might corner a market, the new assumption was that government regulators would not approve it. "Why even try?" one private equity investor told me. "[Lina] could turn out to be one of the most consequential regulators since Greenspan," Deese told me. "By definition, she's having an extraordinary impact—otherwise [her critics] wouldn't care."[31]

But Khan wasn't just having an effect on the practice of antitrust law. She was demonstrating how the new marketcraft could take hold, appealing to Democrats and Republicans alike. In March 2024, she returned to the Yale campus that she had stepped onto a decade earlier, unsure if she should even be a lawyer. Now she was welcomed back as one of the nation's most renowned attorneys and received rock-star treatment. Several law-school organizations, left and right leaning alike, had invited her to speak about the new antitrust approach that she was pioneering as the FTC Chair. They had booked a large room at the law school for a midday talk, but so many students and faculty turned out that the room was overflowing. A second room reached capacity, and the organizers scrambled to open up yet another overflow room so that dozens more could watch online from down the hall. Students posed for selfies with her afterward.

Khan also sat down with two dozen members of Yale's Federalist Society, the campus branch of the nationwide organization of conservative legal scholars. This was not unusual for Khan. Whenever she visited law schools, she sought out progressive and conservative students alike, making sure that she was not just talking to predictable fans. The previous fall, she took to the main stage at the national Federalist Society's 2023 conference, which played host to hundreds of legal professionals, with the theme "Originalism on the Ground." In a fireside chat with a George Mason law professor, she explained her vision for the future of competition policy and the work of the FTC. Like at Yale, conservatives took to her message there, with many seeing in her a champion of their own distrust of concentrated power. "If you didn't know she was working for the Biden administration, you wouldn't be able to tell," said one of the attendees at the national conference. "I think there is a lot of alignment with what we in the Federalist Society believe should be the right direction of our country."[32]

The shift on the right toward a more active antitrust posture predated Khan. Under the leadership of Trump appointees, the FTC and DOJ filed suit to prevent the AT&T–Time Warner merger and to force Facebook to divest Instagram and WhatsApp. Sensitive to the increasingly bipartisan interest in antitrust, Khan prioritized engaging Hill Republicans in dialogue. She made a habit of holding closed-door conversations with members of Congress to explain what she was doing and listen to their concerns. In addition to some of her early supporters, like Senator Josh Hawley and Congressman Ken Buck, Khan managed to woo other Republican voices who tend to be younger and insurgent, like Congressman Matt Gaetz and Vice President J. D. Vance. Enough Republicans had become her fans that they dubbed themselves "Khanservatives." "Lina Khan [is] one of the few people in the Biden administration that I think is doing a pretty good job," Vance said in early 2024.[33] These new voices were, in some cases, supporting Khan with more than just their rhetoric. At the end of 2022, thirty-nine Republicans joined with Democrats to vote to boost FTC funding by increasing the fees on companies when they merge.

Perhaps most telling of how far antitrust ideas had moved on the right by 2024 was the blueprint for policy in a potential second Trump administration published by the conservative Heritage Foundation. The document, called Project 2025, imagined antimonopoly in the Jeffersonian, libertarian tradition of providing accountability to the biggest corporations. "Beyond undermining small businesses and reducing their salubrious moral effect on American civil society, concentration of economic power facilitates collusion between government and private actors, undermining the rule of law," the blueprint said. To be sure, the fuel for Republican antitrust passion was often "woke" corporations that sought to cultivate and spread left-leaning political values. They imagined using antitrust law to prevent corporations from pursuing ends that strayed from the creation of profits. "Antitrust law can combat dominant firms' baleful effects on democratic institutions such as free speech, the marketplace of ideas, shareholder control, and managerial accountability as well as collusive behavior with government."[34] Project 2025 also promised to "assemble an army of aligned, vetted, trained, and prepared conservatives to go to work on Day One to deconstruct the Administrative State."[35] Despite the contradictions implicit in the document, it illustrated that few voices were arguing for a simple return to the consumer welfare standard.

There were still plenty of voices, particularly on the right, uncomfortable with Khan, but they tended to be the voices of the dying Washington consensus. The *Wall Street Journal* editorial page had a particular axe to grind, criticizing Khan over 100 times in the initial three years of her tenure.[36] Resistant members of the House opened an investigation into Khan's FTC, and one of her former colleagues, a Republican commissioner, resigned in a huff with a public article declaiming Khan's lack of deference to the rule of law.[37]

For every critic who remained unconvinced, there were several who came around.[38] "Antitrust will be in a better place when she finishes," Jon Leibowitz, an Obama-era official resistant to Khan's early moves, told the *Washington Post* in early 2024. The former Republican Chair of the FTC William Kovacic went further: "The antitrust establishment still doesn't know what hit them. She has built an awareness of the issue and a political constituency for it. I greatly admire what she has done."[39]

The early successes of the CHIPS office and Khan's FTC highlight several of the conditions required for effective marketcraft. Both were relatively unconstrained institutions, invested with power and discretion that provided some independence from the piecemeal interest-group politics of the legislative branch. Both had dedicated leaders and expert staff, anxious to work through the bureaucracy of government administration to accomplish their goals. And they both had clear missions—to onshore semiconductor manufacturing and to make particular markets more competitive—and the legal authority and tools to get the job done.

The IRA, though borne of the same vision for revived marketcraft, offers an instructive contrast. It provided no centralized administering institution for green technology investment, instead preferring to take a purely legislative approach to marketcraft, like Congress had done with mixed success in health-care markets in the 1960s and with Silicon Valley in the 1980s and '90s. The IRA's public investment provision was funded through the tax code, even though companies could receive many of the tax credits even if they had no tax burden. Manufacturers of solar panels or geothermal wells, for instance, qualified for a "tax rebate" even if they were losing money, meaning that the process of filing taxes became an application for subsidy. This put the Internal Revenue Service in the unusual position of qualifying private companies for public funds, even though it had no particular expertise in clean energy. (To compensate, Congress appropriated $80 billion to the IRS, but with a focus on improving enforcement, rather than building up specific capacity to execute industrial policy.) Politically, tax "credits" for companies and individuals had been a much easier sell—to lawmakers like Manchin and to voters—than appropriations for a new "bureaucracy."

The history of marketcrafting efforts illustrates that to manage markets effectively, a coordinating institution needs to be in charge. The lack of one in the IRA could signal potential future problems. As energy markets change and evolve, no mechanism exists for prioritizing the kind of clean-energy investments that are most needed. The IRA put no caps on how much could be spent, sidestepping any guidelines for how to balance investments in different green energy sectors. Significant public dollars could go toward minimally helpful projects or ones that would have happened anyway, leading to overinvestment in some actors and underinvestment in others. The provisions for a "green bank," to be housed within the EPA, envisioned a level of decentralization inconsistent with comprehensive investment strategy.[40] Clean-energy supply chains may require particular attention to prevent bottlenecks or overcapacity, but no one in government is responsible for managing the balance—or even monitoring it. That stands in sharp contrast to the administrative power invested in Mike Schmidt and Lina Khan.

Nor is it clear how much public investment the US government is committing through the IRA. At the time of passage, the Congressional Budget Office estimated that the climate provisions of the IRA would cost just shy of $400 billion over ten years. Because the legislation lacks caps, outside analysts, like the Brookings Institution and Goldman Sachs, have predicted that the actual cost could be two to three times higher.[41] The additional funds could be used to spur new technological breakthroughs—or just be wasted overinvesting in categories with little chance for success. We don't know where the money will go. Neither Congress nor the executive branch has the means to guide it. Some individual or institution in the American government should be able to steer the investment and manage the overall cost.

Deese, for his part, was unworried. In early 2024, he noted that the federal investment for all of 2023 netted out to $34 billion, one-half of 1 percent of total federal expenditures.[42] According to IRA champions like him, the real lever of policy change is not immediate public dollars deployed, but private money invested. When the law passed, he estimated it would mobilize $3.5 trillion over ten years.

The early signs suggest he may be right that public dollars are disproportionately attracting private ones. By the end of September 2024, businesses invested $272 billion in clean-energy production over the past year, which accounted for over 5 percent of all American private investment in structures, equipment, and durable consumer goods—a 25 percent boost from the previous year, which was already at a record level.[43] Virtually all major categories—from ground-level energy production to the fabrication of consumer-facing technologies like electric vehicles and heat pumps—showed signs of significant growth. For the first time in years, climate scientists were reporting that America was close to meeting its long-term goals for emission reduction. In 2023, nine research teams modeled the effects of the IRA and published their conclusions in *Science*.[44] While preliminary, the estimates suggest that the IRA will double the pace of emissions reductions, causing them to fall to 45 percent below peak 2005 levels by 2035, just shy of the 50 percent pledge President Biden made after taking office. It is still a long way to meeting the Paris benchmark of keeping global warming to two degrees Celsius.

The IRA undoubtedly set America on a stronger path to climate mitigation, but its structure suggests that without modifications, it runs the risk of repeating the mistakes of health-care marketcraft. If Congress had invested an institution in government with a clear mission, discretion, and the power to build expertise, American efforts at managing climate change would likely be even more successful.

Even with challenges on the horizon, the sea change in American economic thinking bodes well for the future. The most significant shift in American marketcraft has not been specific policy moves, but rather, the cross-partisan recognition of the need for a muscular state to shape markets to serve political ends. The parties may diverge on many of those goals, but they no longer deny they have agency or power.

Deese's successor at NEC, Lael Brainard, reflected this shift in outlook. As planned, Deese stepped down from the Biden administration in early 2023, completing two years of service and joining his family in Maine. The

President chose Brainard, the Vice Chair of the Federal Reserve, to replace him. Brainard had gotten her PhD in economics at Harvard, in 1989. Later, as a professor at MIT and Under Secretary of the Treasury, Brainard had advocated a view that minimized government "intervention" in markets and emphasized the need for redistribution to manage any inequities. Brainard considered Larry Summers a mentor, even though he was only a few years older. In the Clinton White House, Brainard had been a fierce advocate for bringing China into the WTO. "We are able to sustain such high living standards, in part, because Americans engage extensively in international trade," she said in a 2000 speech to the Consumer Federation of America. "WTO accession will advance market-oriented economic reform, the rule of law, and economic freedom in China. It will more deeply integrate China into a rules-based global economic system, which will in turn increase its stake in peace and stability," she said. "As the President says, it is an economic no-brainer."[45] A year later, she was even more explicit, stating that the Clinton team saw "advancing open trade as an economic policy in its own right."[46]

Two decades later, Brainard's attitude had changed. "We saw what happened in the wake of the first China Shock, which harmed factory towns all over our country," she said in a May 2024 speech to the Center for American Progress. "China's share of global manufacturing is now approaching 30%, enabled by a combination of non-market practices, including forced technology transfer and intellectual property theft, and discriminatory rules."[47] Integrating China into the global economy without the proper guardrails had undermined American jobs, and Chinese state capitalism had put American industry on the back foot. Something had to be done.

In the same speech, Brainard announced the imposition of aggressive tariffs on Chinese imports, including on electric vehicles, solar panels, and battery technology. Brainard was now intent on using tariff policy to nurture certain industries in the United States. "Imposing tariffs in selective sectors under Section 301 of our trade laws ensures the investments and jobs in EVs, batteries, vital medical equipment, steel and aluminum, semiconductors, and solar spurred by the President's historic laws are not undercut by a flood of unfairly underpriced exports from China," she said.[48] Brainard and Biden were building on the Trump-era tariffs, refuting the idea that markets work best when trade is "free" and instead evaluating what *kind* of trade best served American interest.

Even if Brainard now supported a new marketcraft, it was Jake Sullivan who remained in the administration and became the leading voice for the outlook after Deese's departure. Just a few months after Deese left, Sullivan gave a landmark speech explaining the economic framework that he had helped make conventional wisdom in Washington. He put a punctuation mark on the break in how people think about economics. "[T]he postulate that deep trade liberalization would help America export goods, not jobs and capacity, was a promise made but not kept," he said. Now the challenge was to craft existing and new institutions to fulfill the new promise of managing the American economy for workers: "America needs a deliberate, hands-on investment strategy to pull forward innovation, drive down costs, and create good jobs."[49]

In the summer of 2023, Oren Cass commandeered the Kennedy Caucus Room in the Russell Senate Office Building on Capitol Hill for an important event in the history of modern conservatism. On a stage flanked by enormous red velvet curtains and columns of white marble, four Republican Senators, including Marco Rubio and J. D. Vance, explained in a series of sequential speeches and interviews their new approach to economics. Senator Todd Young invoked the story of the Erie Canal to make the case for more public investment. Josh Hawley made the case for greater antitrust enforcement. J. D. Vance argued that some of the nation's most highly skilled individuals follow the logic of markets, leading neuroscientists to improve social media algorithms instead of solving problems like Alzheimer's, for instance. Capital and talent move toward short-term, profitable but less socially valuable opportunities unless industrial policy can better align incentives with addressing real challenges. "We need to direct our country's resources to solving real problems as opposed to fake problems," he said.[50]

But perhaps the most passionate of the speakers that day was Marco Rubio. Years of refining his ideas had led him to a clearer position: "A market is a tool. It is a tool that we use to strengthen America and improve American lives. It is a better tool than socialism and government, but it is a tool," Rubio said. "The end game here is to support the country and our people, not to serve the market."[51] Rubio argued for a public investment–led marketcraft, even if he disagreed with the specifics of how Deese and Sullivan had gone about it. Rubio called the IRA's climate provisions "the left's attempt to force green energy and EVs on an unwilling public" and said that he believed the CHIPS Act was not aggressive enough on China.[52]

The Biden administration's mistakes did not suggest a need to stop managing markets; Rubio disagreed with Sullivan and Deese on the *what* of the new marketcraft, but not the need for it. "Throughout our history, our leaders have enacted targeted industrial policy to foster productive growth, supply-chain resilience, well-paying jobs, and military strength," he wrote in the spring of 2024. "When designed properly, these policies have succeeded. There's no reason we can't follow in their footsteps today." Instead of Deese and Sullivan's emphasis on climate, Rubio and other conservatives want to shore up the defense industrial base and support critical domestic industries like mining, oil and gas, and agriculture. "Many on the right err . . . by allowing a healthy skepticism of government to morph into a hostility toward all government action," Rubio wrote. "A more balanced and, I would argue, more conservative view recognizes that government is often essential to identifying, organizing, and funding national projects beyond the scope of private initiative."[53]

A little over a year later, Lina Khan stood in the same Kennedy Caucus Room, in front of the same enormous red velvet curtains and glistening white marble columns. Instead of conservative policy wonks from DC, her audience that day was made up almost entirely of farmers from the National Farmers Union. Cowboy hats perched on many of the heads in the crowd. This was Khan's third time speaking with members of the group. Just months before, she had joined a smaller roundtable in Denver, Colorado, to better understand the challenges the farmers were facing and explain what the FTC might do to help.

Khan's message on Capitol Hill that day was a more concrete version of the vision that the Republican senators had articulated a year before: the FTC was in the business of crafting markets to work better for farmers, a historically critical voice behind antimonopoly efforts. "Because of the advocacy that we saw from the farmers 150 years ago, protesting the railroad monopoly and the discriminatory tactics that were allowing them to pick winners and losers—that is what resulted in Congress ultimately passing the antitrust laws and making sure that we have rules in place to protect against concentration of power," she said. To help farmers today, Khan's FTC had brought suit against two pesticide makers, arguing that their payoffs to distributors to exclude generics from their offerings illegally raised prices for farmers.[54] She was also working to ensure farmers had the power to repair their own products, like tractors and harvesters, expanding an initiative that the former Republican FTC Chair had started.[55] Khan closed after a few questions, and the crowd jumped to their feet to give her a standing ovation. As she stepped down from the stage, Khan pointed out an FTC colleague waiting to document the specific challenges with large corporations these farmers were experiencing. Within minutes, the line snaked into the hallway.

Four months later, just down the hall, Donald Trump was inaugurated president a second time, a historic political comeback after his 2020 re-election loss. Behind him stood the most influential tech billionaires in the world, including Tesla's Elon Musk, Amazon's Jeff Bezos, Meta's Mark Zuckerberg, and Alphabet's Sundar Pichai. They had all rushed to Trump's home in Mar-a-Lago in the days after his victory to heap praise and money on the incoming President. Their newfound enthusiasm was publicly shared by most other corporate leaders who expected an increasingly business-friendly climate in Washington.

Those hopes may be artificially high. While Trump does favor lower taxes on big businesses, many of his administration's economic policies may conflict with corporate profit-making. Tariffs threaten to raise input prices and snarl supply chains, and his picks to lead the government's antitrust efforts may be more aggressive than some expect. Khan's replacement at the FTC, Andrew Ferguson, supported several of Khan's actions while a minority member of the FTC, including a successful lawsuit to block an acquisition in the luxury goods market. Trump's nominee to lead antitrust at the Justice Department, Gail Slater, worked at the FTC for a decade and served as an economic policy advisor to Vance. Trump announced both of the personnel moves on X. "Big Tech has run wild for years, stifling competition in our most innovative sector and, as we all know, using its market power to crack down on the rights of so many Americans, as well as those of Little Tech!" Ferguson echoed the sentiment: "We will end Big Tech's vendetta against competition and free speech."

There are deep and meaningful differences between the left and right on how to shape and manage the American economy. Ferguson, for instance, did not join Khan in supporting one of her last moves, a lawsuit against John Deere for forcing farmers to use only authorized dealers for critical repairs. But a new generation of leaders in Washington is debating *how* a muscular state should craft markets for the common good, not *whether* it should do so. As fraught as these debates are, they illustrate that policymakers increasingly realize that the success of American capitalism relies on the smart decisions of entrepreneurial leaders in government—not a magical, self-regulating market.

Conclusion

When I began research for this book in 2021, I thought I was writing a history of the Federal Reserve. For years, I had been transfixed by how central bankers reinterpreted the institution's mandate, expanding and refining it over time. Economists were always telling me that monetary policy was a "science," and I'd respond with a quizzical look. Given the evolving nature of monetary policy, that assertion sounded to me more like a tactic to minimize critique rather than a description of reality. My skepticism fueled a quest to understand how Fed policy had changed over time.

But as I started writing, there was an explosion of interest in industrial policy in Washington and across the world. Over the prior two decades, particularly after its entrance into the World Trade Organization in 2001, China's system of state capitalism vaulted it into the ranks of the world's greatest military and economic powers. China's rapid ascent fueled concerns that its gains had come at the expense of American prosperity, sparking a national debate over how to reshape our economy to be more dynamic and competitive. Then the Covid pandemic exposed the fragile and global nature of modern supply chains. Within weeks of taking office, Joe Biden's administration began to build its policy agenda around a new "industrial strategy" to strengthen America geopolitically, support clean energy development, and expand domestic manufacturing.

Now everyone wanted to know what industrial policy was and how it could be made to work. I had studied similar moments in history, which led me to believe that the current conversation was far too narrow. Every time I read an article quoting someone saying that government shouldn't be in the business of "picking winners or losers," I wanted to throw my phone across the room. American policymakers have been shaping markets for at least a century, if not longer. Their work has gone significantly further than simply picking a particular company to win or lose in the marketplace. The Federal Reserve, for example, shapes financial markets to be "orderly" and sets the price of short-term credit. In many other markets, including health care, energy, and tech, policymakers have used political power to change how those markets function and what interests they serve. "Industrial policy" felt like far too specific a term to describe this tradition, yet there was little written for general audiences chronicling the efforts I call marketcraft. My project turned.[1]

This book has told the story of how businessmen, politicians, and government administrators have shaped markets for political goals time and again. Congress gave Jesse Jones the power to build a national investment bank, which supported teetering lenders, spurred housing development, and cultivated new markets in the Depression and World War II. Lawmakers created and expanded the Federal Reserve, investing it with the responsibility to ensure financial and price stability, develop global financial markets, and manage domestic unemployment. Congress gave the Federal Energy Office the power to stabilize erratic energy markets, which the libertarian bond trader Bill Simon used to navigate the first oil crisis. In the 1980s and again in the early 2020s, Congress chartered new institutions—Sematech and the CHIPs Office—to ensure America led the world in semiconductor manufacturing. In recent years, the Federal Trade Commission has used its authority to check concentrated corporate power, ensuring that key markets are competitive. The goals of marketcraft can be contentious and debatable, but its practice has endured over time.

For all the successful marketcrafting efforts, there are many examples of failed attempts to organize and steer markets effectively. Fearful of investing in a national institution with too much authority, legislators in the 1960s created a byzantine public-private health-care market that causes Americans to pay more for health care today than any other advanced economy. A few years later, Federal Reserve Chair Arthur Burns failed to quash inflation largely because he was unable to coordinate a strategy across different branches of government. Alan Greenspan implemented his deregulatory agenda and marketcraft of financial innovation, only to watch as the financial system collapsed as a result. Treasury Secretary Hank Paulson and others believed that markets operated "freely" through the self-regulation of firm destruction, seeing little history of useful state management of markets. They let Lehman fail, deepening the financial panic that became known as the Great Financial Crisis. That event led to the most pronounced recession in nearly a century and, ironically, made possible the resurgence of an affirmative marketcraft that many on the left and right are reimagining today.

Successful marketcraft requires three essential ingredients: a clear mission, a coordinating institution we can hold accountable, and the investment of power in that institution to accomplish its work. By choosing not to micromanage the *how* of policy implementation, lawmakers enable these institutions to attract diverse experts—from business, activism, academia, and public service—who can develop nimble approaches to achieve their objectives.

Despite today's skepticism toward government and experts in general, we cannot afford to abandon our institutions simply because they're imperfect. Improving them requires rethinking outdated mandates and granting institutions the autonomy to pursue well-defined objectives. The oversight that Congress, courts, and the press provide is critical, but true accountability requires policymakers to ensure the institutions are producing the outcomes that we need.

If there's one idea I want readers to take from this book, it's this: When policymakers successfully shape markets to serve the public good, they do so by empowering institutions with clear missions and the flexibility to achieve them. Building state capacity isn't about writing more detailed rules—it's about setting clear objectives and giving skilled people the tools to achieve them.[2]

Donald Trump's first election in 2016 shocked the world by showing how frustrated many Americans had become with their government. Trump's campaign was an anti-elite crusade arguing that the existing institutional order was not working for most Americans. His victory—along with the surprising strength of democratic socialist Bernie Sanders in the Democratic primary and the Brexit referendum in the United Kingdom—signaled the end of an era of global consensus that self-regulating markets would improve the lives of everyone.

But political change and institutional development do not always move in tandem. At the start of Trump's first term, Republicans scrambled to sort out what their protectionist and nationalistic economic agenda might look like. Over the years that followed, Trump's economic policy showed signs of the enduring legacy of the neoliberal order, particularly in the aggressive tax cut his administration oversaw. Those efforts were paired with victories for protectionist trade policy, including the renegotiation of NAFTA. Policy wonks spent much of the first Trump administration rushing to catch up with the emerging ideological outlook.

For his second victory in 2024, the scene was set differently. Unlike in 2016 when he won only an Electoral College victory, Trump won the popular vote with almost every corner of America shifting in his direction. This was not a landslide election, but it was a clear signal that a plurality of Americans embraced his brand of pugilistic economic nationalism.

In the eight years since his first win, many Republicans had reinvented themselves, channeling Trump's rhetoric to argue that they represented the needs of America's working class. Up-and-coming Republican leaders— including J. D. Vance, Marco Rubio, Josh Hawley, and others—put their rhetorical focus on kitchen table policies to support American workers and families. They downplayed sympathy for corporations, and trumpeted a belief that public policy could help create reliable jobs with good pay. They developed a stable of policies—an expanded child tax credit, targeted tariffs to support domestic industry, and antitrust action against some large corporations, particularly in tech—that appealed to many working-class Americans. To be sure, a legacy wing of the party, more oriented around corporate economics, endured.[3]

Trump, however, remains an inconsistent and chaotic force, too unfocused to launch a new and enduring marketcraft that would require relying on effective state institutions. His strongman politics is driven by personality, not program. After reading this book, some might wonder why Trump's tariff policies and his other more statist measures do not add up to marketcraft. It's worth spelling out, since understanding Trump's relationship to marketcraft also clarifies the concept.

It may be helpful to think of marketcraft on a spectrum. On one end is the intentional use of state power to organize or manage a market for a public policy goal. On the other end of the spectrum might be more general policies that affect all markets and often without policymaker intent. The real world is messy, and many public policy decisions *affect* markets, but not all of them change or guide them to satisfy a political end. Many policies sit in the middle.

Let's take an idea Trump ran on in the 2024 campaign, an across-the-board, 20 percent tariff. The imposition of that policy would affect American economic activity profoundly, but it is not a marketcraft. Economists estimate it could raise consumer prices by as much as 5 percent and shave $1 trillion off annual economic production.[4] It might spur some domestic production here at home, but there is no proposal to help particular domestic industries expand to meet ongoing demand. A broad policy meant to reduce imports across the board does not craft a particular market for a political goal. (It also happens to contradict Trump's supposed social goals of lowering prices, an irony for a president who partially owes his election to frustration with inflation.) Similarly, Trump's 2017 tax cuts, which disproportionately helped the wealthy and corporations, broadly affected America's economy. But a policy with the macroeconomic aim of boosting private investment and economic growth is not marketcraft: it is not designed to harness market power to achieve a specific public policy objective.

Trump's first-term trade policies fall in the middle of the spectrum. Some, like the 2017 tariffs on steel and aluminum, were narrowly focused on bolstering industries perceived as vital to American identity and military strength. The renegotiation of the North American Free Trade Agreement prioritized efforts to help the American auto industry. But at the same time, many other trade policies were broader in scope. Tariffs on Chinese imports were applied widely and served as leverage in the pursuit of a Sino-American trade agreement. Negotiators rewriting NAFTA introduced broad labor standards to protect American workers from the competitive threat of cheaper Mexican labor.

The collection of these efforts altered the trajectory of trade policy in the United States. While some initiatives—particularly with steel, aluminum, and autos—reflected deliberate marketcraft, others served broader geopolitical and economic goals, like redefining trading relations between other countries and the United States.[5]

More surgical, targeted marketcraft emerged in the Biden administration. Biden officials believed European steel was more climate-friendly, and his administration reduced tariffs on it, while preserving the tariffs on dirtier Chinese steel. The administration imposed new tariffs on electric vehicles, semiconductors, and solar cells made in China, each of which laddered up into the goal of encouraging domestic production of clean energy and semiconductors in the US.[6] With the support of Congress, Biden altered the tax code to encourage Americans to invest in solar panels for their roofs, geothermal to heat their homes, and electric vehicles to park in their garages. The administration intended its tariff and subsidy policies to support green industries, making their products cheaper and encouraging job growth. This is clear marketcraft: government organizing and supporting clean energy technologies through the tax code.[7]

In his second term, Trump has suggested he might pursue a strategic reserve for Bitcoin, requiring the Treasury to make purchases of crypto assets. That would expose the balance sheet of the United States to significant risk, given the volatility of crypto as an asset. It would, however, be a major boost to the crypto industry. Its leaders were major donors to Republicans in the 2024 election, and they could reap significant financial rewards. That would be marketcraft, but of a kleptocratic kind. A state-backed reserve for Bitcoin to stabilize its value would be a profound irony for an industry built on skepticism of the need for a sovereign to manage a currency. If Trump pursued the idea, it would adopt Bill Martin's ideal of orderly markets, in this case, to serve a particular interest group.[8]

Some readers might get caught up in a parlor game: What's in and what's out of the definition of marketcraft? That misses the point. Public policies rarely fit into neat categories. The wager of this book is that the marketcraft framework illuminates important aspects of our political reality, which have been obscured by more conventional ways of talking about economic policy. If some readers finish this book questioning whether a certain policy constitutes marketcraft, they're already engaging with the deeper question of identifying when and how policymakers actively shape markets to serve the common good. The question alone marks a departure from viewing markets as self-regulating forces beyond human influence. And that, in itself, is progress.

There are some signs of a promising new marketcraft on the horizon, despite the headwinds of Trump's personal disdain for state institutions.

On the morning of December 6, 2022, dozens of attendees filtered into a nondescript meeting room at the Marriott Marquis hotel in Washington, DC. The day's off-the-record meeting—which several of the most influential policymakers in America would attend—bore the unremarkable title "Investing in a Stronger America." The event's co-hosts, Julius Krein's *American Affairs* and Employ America, a left-leaning nonprofit led by Skanda Amarnath, hoped to create a neutral and unthreatening meeting space a few blocks from the Capitol and White House. Krein and Amarnath intended to use the day to nurture bipartisan interest in an incipient idea: a national investment bank. To do so, they were bringing together the left—members of the Biden administration and Senator Chris Murphy—and the right, including Senators Todd Young and Marco Rubio and future Republican Senator David McCormick.

Since the earliest days of the Republic, Americans had talked about the value of a national investment bank to guide markets, but it was Republican Herbert Hoover who created the first, the Reconstruction Finance Corporation (RFC), in 1932. Over the following twenty years, Congress expanded the RFC, increasing its investment capital and giving it the flexibility to support a range of industries. The RFC backstopped American banking and finance, stimulated housing lending and production, and fostered the growth of new industries such as aviation and synthetic rubber. After the war, some Democrats pushed for the RFC's expansion, but in the early 1950s, that effort fizzled and the RFC closed. It fell victim to the failure of its leader Jesse Jones to establish a lasting institution, and to a broader rightward shift in post-war American politics.

Even so, the dream of a national investment bank endured. In the 1950s, Congress reauthorized two initiatives related to the RFC, the Export-Import bank and the Small Business Administration. The pair of institutions provided credit to meet the political goals of countering communism and supporting start-up enterprises, respectively. Two decades later, Republican Vice President Nelson Rockefeller floated the idea of an investment fund to spur the development of clean energy. Congress introduced bills in the late 1970s and early 1980s for the creation of a national investment bank, although the idea didn't gain immediate momentum.

Then, in 2005, President George W. Bush signed a bill to create the Energy Loans Program Office, a bank-like institution in the Energy Department charged with providing federal financing in the form of loan guarantees for clean energy initiatives. After Congress expanded the office in 2009, it made controversial investments in Solyndra, a solar panel manufacturer that eventually went bankrupt, and Tesla, the electric vehicle manufacturer now one of the world's largest companies. The Bipartisan Infrastructure Law and the Inflation Reduction Act, both signed by President Biden, expanded its mandate and boosted its loan guarantee authority to $400 billion. By the end of 2024, the Loan Program office had provided $50 billion of financing with over $300 billion under review.[9]

The Loan Program Office is not a national investment bank, given that it primarily issues loan guarantees to mitigate risk for private investors rather than lending or investing itself. Its financing is constrained to focus on energy policy goals with a commitment to guarantee loans for projects that commercial banks wouldn't otherwise make. But it's a start. Like the other initiatives outlined, it shares the same foundational belief in using the government's financing power to support the growth of strategically important markets.

Trump and other Republicans are wary of the idea of focusing on clean energy, but they are broadly supportive of the idea of using federal financing power for political goals. In 2018, a Republican-led Congress, with the support of Trump's White House, created a similar institution called the Development Finance Corporation, to provide credit internationally in line with American geopolitical priorities.

Now some believe the time has come again for a full-fledged bank. A year before the 2022 event, seven Democratic senators had proposed a national investment bank to be included in the climate bill the Biden administration favored. The *Atlantic* magazine profiled the effort with a headline that claimed the bill "could truly, actually bring back U.S. manufacturing and help the climate, too."[10] Their effort didn't make it through the legislative process, but it did garner interest on the left and right alike. Krein and Amarnath aimed to build on that interest, convening the cross-partisan event just weeks after the midterm elections and before the next Congress was sworn in. That day's conversations kicked off a flurry of behind-the-scenes organizing activity. A few months later, Oren Cass' center-right think tank, American Compass, came out in support, and momentum grew in Congress behind a revised bipartisan bill.

In the summer of 2024, Senator J. D. Vance planned to introduce legislation to create that national investment bank. Republican Senators Marco Rubio and Todd Young intended to co-sponsor the bill, as did another half dozen Democrats. The new institution's mandate would be to support industries critical to American economic development and geopolitical dominance. After Trump selected Vance to be his vice presidential nominee, Vance paused all his legislative efforts, including the effort for the national investment bank.[11] But a month after Vance joined the ticket, Trump proposed a similar idea, which he called a sovereign wealth fund, to support the development of highways, airports, manufacturing hubs, and medical research.[12] After his remarks, the Biden White House informed journalists that National Security Advisor Jake Sullivan and others had been laying plans for a similar investment vehicle, but with more of a focus on "supply chain resilience, technological pre-eminence and energy security," according to the *New York Times*.[13] Two weeks after the inauguration, Trump directed the Treasury Secretary and the Commerce Secretary to develop a plan to create a sovereign wealth fund in support of economic stability and geopolitical dominance.[14] A sovereign wealth fund might function differently than a national investment bank, or it could just be the name Trump himself prefers for the policy framework that Vance and Democrats have been developing. We will only know in time.

Creating a national investment bank would be a transformative step in the history of marketcraft. Like the RFC, it could capably guide markets to achieve public policy goals. If the bank had the structure that bipartisan negotiators were formulating in 2024, Congress would initially capitalize it with $50 billion, giving it the authority to extend credit, purchase minority equity stakes in companies, and provide loan guarantees to businesses. The bank could lever its capital up to $500 billion of total liabilities.[15] Congress might give the bank a mandate to pursue economic development, as it did in the later stages of the RFC, or it might choose to narrow its mandate to support key industries. If it took the second route, it would have many options. Republicans and Democrats might agree to support semiconductor manufacturing, mining of critical minerals, battery technology, or drone design and production. Congress might task it with making investments that secure America's leadership in artificial intelligence, another area of some cross-partisan agreement.[16]

The national investment bank would have the power to extend credit and make equity investments to private sector actors in pursuit of these goals, without the expectation of profit for the government. With the right institutional culture, it could invest in high-risk efforts, acknowledging that some might fail while others will succeed.[17] The bank could be helpful in supporting companies through the "valley of death," the period after a start-up gains some traction but struggles to attract private capital due to extended development cycles and commercial uncertainty.[18]

A bank of this scale could cultivate deep expertise in its focus areas, developing a portfolio of investments that adapts to technological shifts and changing market dynamics. It could also evolve as the nation's political priorities change. The bank would be subject to the political direction of Congress—an asset, not a liability. When America faces its next major geopolitical conflict, the bank would be there to ensure that enough public capital was available to support the industries needed to win the war. If that sounds utopian, consider the story of the RFC's success in preparing for World War II.

To be sure, the bank could also run the risk of becoming a tool for corporate kleptocracy, should Trump and his allies design it in a way to make that possible. But Congress could mitigate the dangers of co-optation and capture by insulating the bank from executive influence—appointing directors to staggered terms, establishing an independent inspector general, and enshrining robust whistleblower protections. With smart design, a national investment bank could harness markets for social and political goals while building durable institutional expertise that outlasts any single administration.

As I was finishing this book, I described the argument to an up-and-coming congressman looking for new ways to talk with voters about how to make the economy work better. "I love the idea of marketcraft," he told me, "but that will never work on the stump." I mustered a smile and said, "Right, but that's your job, not mine."

Marketcraft is unlikely to be the rallying cry for any politician, whether left or right. Much like industrial policy, it's a technical concept—a framework for channeling markets toward political goals. Voters, with good reason, expect candidates to focus on outcomes, not the intricate details of how those outcomes are achieved. A national investment bank may not be a talking point fit for the stump, but the results it promises certainly could be. We can create abundant jobs in industries of the future, stabilize prices without resorting only to interest-rate hikes, and ensure the country is secure and geopolitically strong. To deliver on those promises, policymakers—alongside journalists, businesspeople, and government administrators—must understand how marketcraft works best.

The US has navigated periods of profound challenge by harnessing the power of markets to meet public policy goals. At one moment of particular crisis, Jesse Jones put it plainly: "The market is what you make it." It was classic Jones bluster, but his comment points in the right direction. We can craft markets to satisfy many of our needs. History shows us how.

Acknowledgments

People sometimes say that writing a book is a solitary task. This one was not. From its very beginning, I benefited from the expertise, criticism, banter, and personal support of colleagues, friends, and family. Barely a day went by when I was not engaged in conversation about the people and ideas that animate these pages, and I am deeply grateful to the community of people who joined me in the effort to research and write this book.

When this book was a germ of an idea, some of the earliest and best advice I got came over lunch with a good friend, the author Zach Carter. I had sent him a draft of the book proposal, and as we settled into our seats, he handed over a printed version with his feedback. The draft was littered with comments—whole pages struck through and comments spilling into the margins. He even insisted that I drop the sans serif typeface. Thank you, Zach, for your early encouragement, ongoing counsel, helpful edits, and insistence that I write in a serious typeface.

Six months later, I sat at another restaurant across the table from the historian Meg Jacobs. I described the project and the working title, which was *Marketcrafting*. Her brows furrowed. "If it's about the people, why wouldn't you just call it *Marketcrafters*?" she asked. After a brief moment of consideration, I replied, "You're right." I wrote the publisher the next morning. Thank you, Meg, for your helpful edits, archival tips, friendly dialogue—and for titling the book.

I am in deep debt to many other friends who helped with the conceptual development of the book and took the time to review sections of the manuscript. In addition to Zach and Meg, particular thanks go to Peter Conti-Brown, David Dryer, Y. J. Fischer, Natalie Foster, Peter Godwin, Taylor Isenberg, Kevin Lincoln, Sebastian Mallaby, Lev Menand, Sabeel Rahman, Cathy Rampell, Noah Rosenblum, Dan Schwerin, Lucas Wittman, Felicia Wong, Josh Younger, and Julian Zelizer.

My thanks also go to the many archivists who helped me access, organize, and parse large amounts of historical documents. In particular, I want to thank the archivists and librarians at the Baker Library of Harvard Business School, Carnegie Mellon University, the Gerald Ford Presidential Library, Lafayette College, the Library of Congress, Oberlin College, the Schlesinger Library at Harvard, and the Walter P. Reuther Library at Wayne State.

For several months after I signed on to work with this book's editor, Ben Loehnen, I would furtively ask friends in publishing when the "honeymoon period" between an editor and the writer was likely to end. Nearly two years later, it hasn't yet. Throughout this process, I have been supported by Ben and the stellar team at Avid Reader Press. Thank you for believing in this book from the start. I'm also thankful for the support of my agent, Howard Yoon, who made the concept strong enough to be attractive to the Avid team in the first place.

This book would not have happened without the personal support and assistance of Melissa Lopez, who made it possible for me to find the time to actually research, write, and edit. Thank you for defending those "research" blocks on my calendar at all costs. I am also grateful to the psychoanalyst Larry Saul, who helped set me on a path to pursue my passions and weather the inevitable storms. Our time together made this entire project possible in the first place.

Deep thanks go to my husband, Sean Eldridge, and our two children who have been enduringly patient with me as I stole away on weekends and family vacations to get in a few hours of writing. Thank you, Sean, for your investment in this work and willingness to edit the manuscript. Your exacting standards and intellectual companionship have made this book so much stronger than it otherwise would have been.

I want to thank several individuals who helped me piece this book together day after day. I am grateful to Peter Spiegler for the many conversations as we developed an early and workable definition for marketcraft in the first months of the project. I am particularly appreciative of your partnership as we explored the machinations of finance and banking. That work left an indelible mark on the manuscript and on me. I am also grateful to Teal Arcadi, who avidly helped in the closing months to integrate disparate chapters into a cohesive volume.

Finally, my deep thanks go to Tim Barker, whose historical expertise, archival skills, and editorial judgment were indispensable at every stage of the research and writing process. It was a joy to untangle the complex psyches of the subjects of this book together while making sense of the political and economic times they inhabited. Your dedication to this project has touched me greatly.

If any book was ever a truly social effort, this one was. Thank you, all.

Abbreviations

AFBP   Andrew F. Brimmer Papers

FDRPL   Franklin Delano Roosevelt Presidential Library

FOMC   Federal Open Market Committee

FRASER   Federal Reserve Archival System for Economic Research

ISFP   I. S. Falk Papers

JCPL   Jimmy Carter Presidential Library

JHJP   Jesse H. Jones Papers, Library of Congress

KPEP   Katherine Pollak Ellickson Papers

NHTP   Nancy H. Teeters Papers

Notes

Introduction

1. The political scientist Steven Vogel coined the term in the 2010s. Steven K. Vogel, *Market-craft: How Governments Make Markets Work* (New York: Oxford University Press, 2018).
2. Mike Konczal, *Freedom from the Market: America's Fight to Liberate Itself from the Grip of the Invisible Hand* (New York: New Press, 2021).
3. The 1990s and 2000s witnessed the rise of "public-private partnerships" and the advent of demands for corporate social responsibility. These efforts pushed certain corporations to make more ethical decisions or to partner with local governments to improve public goods like parks or roadways. In some cases, they had limited success, but in others, they hollowed out state capacity, turning over decision-making to private-sector actors rather than cultivating expertise in government. Marianna Mazzucato, *The Big Con: How the Consulting Industry Weakens Our Businesses, Infantilizes Our Governments, and Warps Our Economies* (New York: Penguin Press, 2023).
4. Marco Rubio, *Decades of Decadence: How Our Spoiled Elites Blew America's Inheritance of Liberty, Security, and Prosperity* (New York: HarperCollins, 2023), 43.
5. In two periods in American history, the New Deal and the late 1970s and early 1980s, policymakers considered how we might use statistical insights to support particular industries, planning their product development and delivery to market. Yet, outside of a brief and unsuccessful attempt in the early New Deal, no institution of the American government has attempted to develop the kind of multiyear plans with production targets that are common in authoritarian regimes. The closest we have approximated this structure was during the Second World War, and even then, the experience was limited and brief. For a summary, see Robert B. Reich, *The Next American Frontier* (New York: Penguin Press, 1984); and Otis Graham, *Toward a Planned Society: From Roosevelt to Nixon* (Oxford, UK: Oxford University Press, 1976).
6. Christian Parenti, *Radical Hamilton: Economic Lessons from a Misunderstood Founder* (New York: Verso, 2020), 34.
7. Parenti, *Radical Hamilton*, 7.
8. For an overview of nineteenth-century marketcrafting, see Stephen S. Cohen and Brad DeLong, *Concrete Economics: The Hamilton Approach to Economic Growth and Policy* (Cambridge, MA: Harvard Business Review Press, 2016); and Michael Lind, *Land of Promise: An Economic History of the United States* (New York: Harper Paperbacks, 2013).
9. In this view, premised on the mid-century "neoclassical synthesis," economic policy should

focus on minimizing unemployment and achieving long-term price stability. Once those goals are accomplished, "the usual virtues of free markets come to the fore," writes Paul Krugman. Krugman is quoted in Adam Tooze, "The Gatekeeper," *London Review of Books* 43, no. 8 (April 22, 2021), https://www.lrb.co.uk/the-paper/v43/n08/adam-tooze/the-gatekeeper. See also Paul Samuelson, *Economics: The Original 1948 Edition* (New York: McGraw-Hill, 1997); Paul Krugman, *Arguing with Zombies: Economics, Politics, and the Fight for a Better Future* (New York: Norton, 2020).

10. For a thorough history of institutional economics, see Timothy Shenk, "Inventing the American Economy" (PhD diss., Columbia University, 2016); Yuval Yonay, *The Struggle over the Soul of Economics: Institutionalist and Neoclassical Economists in America between the Wars* (Princeton, NJ: Princeton University Press, 1998); Malcolm Rutherford, *The Institutionalist Movement in American Economics, 1918–1947: Science and Social Control* (Cambridge, UK: Cambridge University Press, 2011); Geoffrey Hodgson, *The Evolution of Institutional Economics: Agency, Structure, and Darwinism in American Institutionalism* (London: Routledge, 2004); and Otis Graham, *Losing Time: The Industrial Policy Debate* (Cambridge, MA: Harvard University Press, 1992), 65–69.

11. Astrid Ringe and Neil Rollings, "Responding to Relative Decline: The Creation of the National Economic Development Council," *Economic History Review* 53, no. 2 (May 2000): 331–53; and Charles P. Kindleberger, "French Planning," in *National Economic Planning* (New York: National Bureau of Economic Research, 1967), https://www.nber.org/system /files/chapters/c1426/c1426.pdf.

12. Lind, *Land of Promise*, 13.

13. Paul Sabin, *Public Citizens: The Attack on Big Government and the Remaking of American Liberalism* (New York: Norton, 2021); Amy Kapczynski and Joel Michaels, "Administering a Democratic Industrial Policy," *Harvard Law & Policy Review* 18, no. 2 (Summer 2024): 279–343; Sabeel Rahman, *Democracy against Domination* (Oxford, UK: Oxford University Press, 2018); and Sabeel Rahman and Hollie Russon Gilman, *Civic Power: Rebuilding American Democracy in an Era of Crisis* (Cambridge, UK: Cambridge University Press, 2019).

14. "It is easier to plot a way through a labyrinth of detail when it is done in the comparative quiet of a conference room than when it is attempted amid the turmoil of the legislative chamber of a committee room," James Landis, a foundational scholar of the administrative state, wrote wisely in the 1930s. James Landis, *The Administrative Process* (New Haven, CT: Yale University Press, 1938), 70.

AGE OF THE NEW DEAL
1: "The Market Is What You Make It"

1. For more on the Albany trip, see Bascom N. Timmons, *Jesse H. Jones: The Man and the Statesman* (New York: Henry Holt, 1956), 247–48; and Steven Fenberg, *Unprecedented Power: Jesse Jones, Capitalism, and the Common Good* (College Station: Texas A&M University Press, 2011), 218.

2. James Stuart Olson, *Saving Capitalism: The Reconstruction Finance Corporation and the New Deal, 1933–1940* (1988; repr., Princeton, NJ: Princeton University Press, 2017), 49.

3. Fenberg, *Unprecedented Power*, 22–23.

4. Fenberg, *Unprecedented Power*, 40.

5. Fenberg, *Unprecedented Power*, 45.

6. Fenberg, *Unprecedented Power*, 160; Timmons, *Jesse H. Jones*, 146–49.

7. Olson, *Saving Capitalism*, 13–14.

8. Olson, *Saving Capitalism*, 15.

9. Timmons, *Jesse H. Jones*, 162–64.

10. When I convert to contemporary dollars, I calculate the historical dollar figure as a percentage of GDP rather than use a standard inflation calculator. This methodology provides a better sense of the scale of the financial investment as a portion of overall economic activity. In this case, $1.5 billion was approximately 2.5 percent of 1932 GDP of $59.5 billion. I use the 2023

estimate of nominal GDP of $27.4 trillion. The source for all of these GDP figures is the Bureau of Economic Analysis National Income and Product Accounts series.

11. Fenberg, *Unprecedented Power*, 187.
12. Timmons, *Jesse H. Jones*, 165.
13. Fenberg, *Unprecedented Power*, 40–41, 91, 100.
14. Timmons, *Jesse H. Jones*, 165.
15. Timmons, *Jesse H. Jones*, 166.
16. According to the RFC's final report in 1959, the RFC issued a total of $51 billion in notes to the Treasury and $3 billion in notes to the public. Secretary of the Treasury, *Final Report on the Reconstruction Finance Corporation* (Washington, DC: U.S. Government Printing Office, 1959), May 1959, FRASER, https://fraser.stlouisfed.org/files/docs/publications/rcf/rfc_19590506_finalreport.pdf.
17. Herbert Hoover, "Statement about Signing the Reconstruction Finance Corporation Act," January 22, 1932, The American Presidency Project, https://www.presidency.ucsb.edu/documents/statement-about-signing-the-reconstruction-finance-corporation-act.
18. Franklin D. Roosevelt, "Radio Address from Albany, New York: The Forgotten Man Speech," April 7, 1932, The American Presidency Project, https://www.presidency.ucsb.edu/documents/radio-address-from-albany-new-york-the-forgotten-man-speech.
19. In addition to "The Forgotten Man Speech," Roosevelt criticized the RFC by name in his September 1932 speech at the Commonwealth Club of San Francisco, drafted by Adolf Berle. Rumors swirled that Roosevelt remained privately opposed to the institution, with one journalist writing in August: "The Reconstruction Finance Corporation has come in for a lot of grief lately, and is going to see a lot more. I learned that Governor Roosevelt, like many other people, thinks that the Corporation has been negligent, and he will probably say so publicly in the near future." Adolf Berle, *Navigating the Rapids, 1918–1971: From the Papers of Adolf A. Berle*, ed. Beatrice Bishop Berle and Travis Beal Jacobs (New York: Harcourt Brace Jovanovich, 1973), 62–67; L.M.N. "Not on the Ticker Tape," *New Republic*, August 3, 1932.
20. Olson, *Saving Capitalism*.
21. Fenberg, *Unprecedented Power*, 47–48, 59.
22. Timmons, *Jesse H. Jones*, 83, 90–91; and Fenberg, *Unprecedented Power*.
23. Timmons, *Jesse H. Jones*, 247–48.
24. Jones to FDR, telegram, February 15, 1933, 8:37 p.m., Presidential Personal File (PPF) 703 - Jones, Jesse H., Franklin Delano Roosevelt Presidential Library, Hyde Park (hereafter FDRPL).
25. Christina D. Romer, "The Nation in Depression," *Journal of Economic Perspectives* 7, no. 2 (1993): 19–39.
26. David M. Kennedy, *Freedom from Fear: The American People in Depression and War, 1929–1945* (New York: Oxford University Press, 2001), 135.
27. Raymond Moley, *After Seven Years* (New York: Harper, 1939), 148.
28. The first and second Banks of the United States were taxpayer capitalized, but the RFC's ownership positions were significantly broader.
29. Franklin D. Roosevelt, "Fireside Chat on Banking," March 12, 1933, The American Presidency Project, https://www.presidency.ucsb.edu/documents/fireside-chat-banking.
30. Peter Conti-Brown and Sean Vanatta, "The Logic and Legitimacy of Bank Supervision: The Case of the Bank Holiday of 1933," *Business History Review* 95, no. 1 (2021): 87–120.
31. Timmons, *Jesse H. Jones*, 174–75.
32. Olson, *Saving Capitalism*, 39.
33. Olson, *Saving Capitalism*, 49.
34. Olson, *Saving Capitalism*, 61.
35. Jordan Schwarz, *The New Dealers: Power Politics in the Age of Roosevelt* (New York: Knopf, 1994), 73.
36. Schwarz, *New Dealers*, 73.
37. Olson, *Saving Capitalism*, 81; U.S. Department of the Treasury, "Troubled Asset Relief Program (TARP)," https://home.treasury.gov/data/troubled-asset-relief-program.

38. Olson, *Saving Capitalism*, 124.
39. "Jones Says Stocks Will Be Used, If Necessary, to Protect Investments," *New York Times*, June 17, 1934, section 9, 73.
40. Jones to Captain James A. Baker, October 14, 1940, box 2, folder: General Correspondence B, May 6, 1938–February 21, 1940, Jesse H. Jones Papers, 1916–1960, Library of Congress (hereafter JHJP).
41. Gerald T. White, *Billions for Defense: Government Financing by the Defense Plant Corporation during World War II* (Tuscaloosa: University of Alabama Press, 1980), 88.
42. Kennedy, *Freedom from Fear*, 204.
43. Kennedy, *Freedom from Fear*, 18.
44. Jesse H. Jones, *Fifty Billion Dollars: My Thirteen Years with the RFC* (New York: Macmillan, 1951), 88.
45. The Commodity Credit Corporation (CCC) should not be confused with another popular New Deal program, the Civilian Conservation Corps, which is often abbreviated as "CCC" as well.
46. Jones, *Fifty Billion Dollars*, 88.
47. Jones, *Fifty Billion Dollars*, 100.
48. Jones, *Fifty Billion Dollars*, 88–104; Olson, *Saving Capitalism*, 144.
49. Olson, *Saving Capitalism*, 97.
50. Olson, *Saving Capitalism*, 117.
51. Olson, *Saving Capitalism*, 100.
52. Olson, *Saving Capitalism*, 121.
53. Olson, *Saving Capitalism*, 122.
54. Samuel Lubell, "New Deal's J. P. Morgan," *Saturday Evening Post*, November 30, 1940, 9–10.
55. Olson, *Saving Capitalism*, 42–43.

2: King Nottoc of Washington

1. His colleagues on the RFC board were dedicated loyalists. "'When Mr. Jones favored something,' one of them once said, 'it never occurred to any of us to oppose it.'" Arthur M. Schlesinger Jr., *The Coming of the New Deal* (Boston: Houghton Mifflin, 1959), 431.
2. Anne Dingus, "John Nance Garner," *Texas Monthly* 24, no. 11 (November 1996): 226.
3. Olson, *Saving Capitalism*, 53; Fenberg, *Unprecedented Power*, 215.
4. Timmons, *Jesse H. Jones*, 264.
5. "Interview with Virginia Foster Durr," in Southern Oral History Program Collection (#4007), University of North Carolina at Chapel Hill, https://docsouth.unc.edu/sohp/html_use/G-0023-3.html.
6. Jones to FDR, no date [c. 1936], PPF 703, FDRPL.
7. Olson, *Saving Capitalism*, 44.
8. Jones, *Fifty Billion Dollars*, 51.
9. Lubell, "New Deal's J. P. Morgan."
10. Olson, *Saving Capitalism*, 116–17 and 123–25. For unemployment, see Robert A. Margo, "Employment and Unemployment in the 1930s," *Journal of Economic Perspectives* 7, no. 2 (Spring 1993): 41–59, https://pubs.aeaweb.org/doi/pdfplus/10.1257/jep.7.2.41. For output, see Bureau of Economic Analysis Data, U.S. Department of Commerce, "Table 1.1.6. Real Gross Domestic Product, Chained Dollars," https://apps.bea.gov/iTable/?reqid=19&step=2&isuri=1&categories=survey&_gl=1*ymoe2r*_ga*MTg5NTMxNDU3MS4xNzA5OTIxOTEw*_ga_J4698JNNFT*MTcwOTkyMTkxMC4xLjEuMTcwOTkyMjAoNy41Ni4wLjA.#eyJhcHBpZCI6MTksInNoZXBzIjpbMSwyLLDMsMTosImRhdGEiOltbImNhdGVnb3JpZXMiLCJTdXJ2ZXkiXSxbIk5JUEFfVGFibGVfTGlzdCIsIjYiXSxbIkZpcnNoX1llYXIiLCJxOTI5IlosWyJMYXNoX1llYXIiLCIxOTUwIlosWyJTY2FsZSIsIio2IlosWyJTZXJpZXMiLCJBIl1dfQ==.
11. "Speech Delivered at Convention by Mr. Jesse H. Jones on the Evening of June 25, 1936," box 217, JHJP.
12. Jones to Adolf Berle, August 18, 1936, box 1, folder: "B" Miscellaneous, 1927–1937, JHJP.

13. Franklin Delano Roosevelt, "Address at Madison Square Garden, New York City," October 31, 1936, The American Presidency Project, https://www.presidency.ucsb.edu/documents/address-madison-square-garden-new-york-city-1. Audio available at: https://miller center.org/the-presidency/presidential-speeches/october-31-1936-speech-madison-square -garden.
14. Jones, *Fifty Billion Dollars*, 266.
15. Fenberg, *Unprecedented Power*, 293.
16. Berle, *Navigating the Rapids*, 142.
17. Olson, *Saving Capitalism*, 199.
18. Jesse H. Jones to "Banks and Bankers," February 23, 1938, box 68, JHJP.
19. "Bicentennial Edition: Historical Statistics of the United States, Colonial Times to 1970," Series N 156-170, Nonfarm Housing Starts: 1889–1958, U.S. Census Bureau, https://www .census.gov/library/publications/1975/compendia/hist_stats_colonial-1970.html.
20. Christopher Knowlton, *Bubble in the Sun: The Florida Boom of the 1920s and How It Brought About the Great Depression* (New York: Simon & Schuster, 2020), 51, Kindle.
21. Kenneth L. Roberts, *Florida* (New York: Harper & Brothers, 1926), 19.
22. Knowlton, *Bubble in the Sun*, 204, Kindle.
23. "Bicentennial Edition." All further homebuilding stats refer to this Census data.
24. John Maynard Keynes to FDR, February 1, 1938, FDRPL, https://www.fdrlibrary.org/doc uments/356632/390886/smFDR-Keynes_1938.pdf/e6a5bbc6-db07-4d65-8576-e4ea 058c5641.
25. Marriner Eccles, *Beckoning Frontiers: Public and Personal Recollections* (New York: Knopf, 1951), 144.
26. "Housing Loan Body Is Set Up by RFC," *New York Times*, February 11, 1938, 3.
27. Olson, *Saving Capitalism*, 213.
28. Jones, *Fifty Billion Dollars*, 150.
29. Berle, *Navigating the Rapids*, 171.
30. Olson, *Saving Capitalism*, 204.
31. Jesse H. Jones speech to the 26th Annual Meeting of the US Chamber of Commerce, May 4, 1938, 6, box 221, JHJP.
32. Olson, *Saving Capitalism*, 194.
33. Fenberg, *Unprecedented Power*, 311.
34. Fenberg, *Unprecedented Power*, 311.
35. Olson, *Saving Capitalism*, 212.
36. Olson, *Saving Capitalism*, 226.
37. Lubell, "New Deal's J. P. Morgan," 88.
38. "Employees in Nonagricultural Establishments for United States," 1929–1939, Federal Reserve Bank of St. Louis, https://fred.stlouisfed.org/series/M0868AUSM148NNBR; "Employees in Nonagricultural Establishments for United States," 1939–1969, Federal Reserve Bank of St. Louis, https://fred.stlouisfed.org/series/M0868BUSM175NNBR.
39. For more on this debate, see Ellis W. Hawley, *The New Deal and the Problem of Monopoly: A Study in Economic Ambivalence* (New York: Fordham University Press, 1995); Olson, *Saving Capitalism*, 210.
40. Jones, *Fifty Billion Dollars*, 531; Fenberg, *Unprecedented Power*, 333.
41. Fenberg, *Unprecedented Power*, 330.
42. "Editorial: Business and Government," *Fortune*, May 1940, 46–57; Lubell, "New Deal's J. P. Morgan," 9.

3: Empire, Built and Broken

1. White, *Billions for Defense*, 1.
2. Franklin D. Roosevelt, "Annual Message to Congress," January 4, 1939, The American Presidency Project, https://www.presidency.ucsb.edu/documents/annual-message-congress.
3. Jones quoted in Fenberg, *Unprecedented Power*, 346.

4. Jesse Jones to Bernard Baruch, August 29, 1946, 2, box 3, folder: Baruch, Bernard, JHJP. Fenberg, *Unprecedented Power*, 543.

5. Jones to Baruch, August 29, 1946, 2.

6. Jones, *Fifty Billion Dollars*, 341.

7. Olson, *Saving Capitalism*, 220.

8. Secretary of the Treasury, *Final Report on the Reconstruction Finance Corporation* (Washington, DC: U.S. Government Printing Office, 1939), 18, 30, FRASER, https://fraser.stlouisfed.org /files/docs/publications/rcf/rfc_19590506_finalreport.pdf.

9. White, *Billions for Defense*, 10; Jones, *Fifty Billion Dollars*, 315.

10. Mark Wilson, *Destructive Creation: American Business and the Winning of World War II* (Philadelphia: University of Pennsylvania Press, 2016), 62.

11. White, *Billions for Defense*, 2.

12. White, *Billions for Defense*, 19.

13. Wesley Frank Craven and James Lea Cate, *The Army Air Forces in World War II*, vol. 6, *Men and Planes* (Washington, DC: Office of Air Force History, 1948), 175, 270; and Adam Tooze, *The Wages of Destruction: The Making and Breaking of the Nazi Economy* (New York: Penguin, 2008), 316.

14. Tooze, *Wages of Destruction*, 165.

15. Wilson, *Destructive Creation*, 57–58.

16. Fenberg, *Unprecedented Power*, 351.

17. Jenifer Van Vleck, *Empire of the Air: Aviation and the American Ascendancy* (Cambridge, MA: Harvard University Press, 2013), 169.

18. Fenberg, *Unprecedented Power*, 433–34.

19. Jesse H. Jones, "Post-war Problems," speech to the New York Board of Trade, September 30, 1943, 1, box 227, speech file, JHJP.

20. Lubell, "New Deal's J. P. Morgan," 9–11.

21. Wilson, *Destructive Creation*, 74.

22. Jones, *Fifty Billion Dollars*, 337.

23. "Dodge Plane Plant Now in Production," *New York Times*, March 25, 1944, 22.

24. Jones, "Post-war Problems"; and White, *Billions for Defense*, 68–71.

25. Wilson, *Destructive Creation*, 73–74.

26. Secretary of the Treasury, *Final Report on the Reconstruction Finance Corporation*, 131.

27. Van Vleck, *Empire of the Air*, 105–6.

28. "1,022 Plants Built by U.S. Are Running," *New York Times*, March 21, 1943, 2.

29. Van Vleck, *Empire of the Air*, 105; and White, *Billions for Defense*, 68.

30. Gerald T. White, "Financing Industrial Expansion for War: The Origin of the Defense Plant Corporation Leases," *Journal of Economic History* 9, no. 2 (November 1949): 164.

31. Jones, *Fifty Billion Dollars*, 396–400.

32. Bernard Baruch, James Conant, and Karl Compton, *Report of the Rubber Survey Committee* (Washington, DC: U.S. Government Printing Office, 1942), 24.

33. Jones, *Fifty Billion Dollars*, 415.

34. "A History of the US Government's Natural and Synthetic Rubber Programs, 1941–1955," *The Government's Rubber Projects*, vol. 2 (Washington, DC: Federal Facilities Corporation, 1955); Clay Johnson to Bradley Dewey, November 5, 1943, box 204, folder: Rubber. Correspondence, JHJP; Jones, *Fifty Billion Dollars*, 407.

35. Jones, *Fifty Billion Dollars*, 402.

36. Jones, *Fifty Billion Dollars*, 414.

37. Secretary of the Treasury, *Final Report on the Reconstruction Finance Corporation*, 31, 213.

38. Fenberg, *Unprecedented Power*, 359.

39. Fenberg, *Unprecedented Power*, 359.

40. Fenberg, *Unprecedented Power*, 391.

41. Albert Furth, "The War Goes to Mr. Jesse Jones," *Fortune*, October 1941, 91.

42. "Mr. Jones' Excuses," *Washington Post*, April 9, 1942, 12.

43. George Dixon, "Star Gallery Sees Jones, Meyer Mix It Up in Hotel," *Daily News* (New York), April 10, 1942, 122.

44. Fenberg, *Unprecedented Power*, 413.

45. "Wallace Accuses J.H. Jones of Obstructing War Effort," *New York Times*, June 30, 1943, 1, https://timesmachine.nytimes.com/timesmachine/1943/06/30/issue.html.

46. "Wallace and Jones at Cabinet Meeting," *New York Times*, July 10, 1943, 11.

47. Fenberg, *Unprecedented Power*, 489.

48. Drew Pearson, "Washington Merry-Go-Round," June 13, 1944, American University Library, Special Collections, https://digitalcollections.american.edu/Documents/Detail/the-washington-merry-go-round-june-13-1944/136900.

49. Frank Freidel, *Franklin D. Roosevelt: A Rendezvous with Destiny* (Boston: Little, Brown, 1990), 532.

50. Benn Steil, *The World That Wasn't: Henry Wallace and the Face of the American Century* (New York: Avid Reader Press/Simon & Schuster, 2024), 265.

51. Jones, *Fifty Billion Dollars*, 288.

52. Grace Tully, *F.D.R., My Boss* (New York: Charles Scribner's Sons, 1949), 190.

53. Steil, *The World That Wasn't*, 273.

54. Fenberg, *Unprecedented Power*, 507–8.

55. FDR to Jones, March 24, 1945, PPF 703, FDRPL.

56. Lubell, "New Deal's J. P. Morgan."

57. Schwarz, *New Dealers*, 86.

58. Secretary of the Treasury, *Final Report on the Reconstruction Finance Corporation*, 22–23.

59. White, *Billions for Defense*, 136.

60. Douglas Knerr, *Suburban Steel: The Magnificent Failure of the Lustron Corporation, 1945–1951* (Columbus: Ohio State University Press, 2015).

61. C. P. Trussell, "Symington Named to Head New R.F.C.," *New York Times*, April 18, 1951, 1, https://www.nytimes.com/1951/04/18/archives/symington-named-to-head-new-rfc-senate-group-will-examine.html.

62. Jones, "Post-war Problems," 3.

63. Fenberg, *Unprecedented Power*, 554–55.

64. Jones, *Fifty Billion Dollars*, 286.

65. Fenberg, *Unprecedented Power*, 547, 567–68.

66. Tim Barker, "Cold War Capitalism: The Political Economy of American Military Spending, 1947–1990" (PhD diss., Harvard University, 2022), 147–50.

67. White, *Billions for Defense*, 81–82.

68. In October 1941, a survey showed that nearly a quarter of lease agreements were negotiated and signed within twenty-four hours. White, *Billions for Defense*, 59.

4: The Architect of Orderly

1. Robert P. Bremner, *Chairman of the Fed: William McChesney Martin Jr. and the Creation of the Modern American Financial System* (New Haven, CT: Yale University Press, 2004), 12.

2. Bremner, *Chairman of the Fed*, 20.

3. The practice dates back well over 2,000 years. For context on its emergence in China, see Isabella M. Weber, *How China Escaped Shock Therapy: The Market Reform Debate* (New York: Routledge, 2021).

4. William J. Novak, *The People's Welfare: Law and Regulation in Nineteenth-Century America* (Chapel Hill: University of North Carolina Press, 1996), 101; Robert Wiebe, *The Search for Order, 1877–1920* (New York: Hill and Wang, 1967).

5. The bills were dated December 10 even though bidding started on December 5. By December 9, the sale was oversubscribed with more than $400 million in application for a $150 million offering. "Bulletin of the Treasury Department," U.S. Department of Treasury, January 1942, FRASER, https://fraser.stlouisfed.org/files/docs/publications/tbulletin/1942_01_treasurybulletin.pdf?utm_source=direct_download.

6. Telephone call between Henry Morgenthau and Marriner Eccles, December 7, 1941, 7:53 p.m., transcript included in *Diaries of Henry Morgenthau, Jr.* 470 (December 7–9, 1941): 35–37, Federal Reserve Bank of St. Louis, FRASER, https://fraser.stlouisfed.org /archival-collection/diaries-henry-morgenthau-jr-6880/volume-470-635050?page=45.

7. Press release, December 8, 1941, quoted in "Federal Reserve Bulletin," Board of Governors of the Federal Reserve System, January 1942, FRASER, https://fraser.stlouisfed.org/title /federal-reserve-bulletin-62/january-1942-21041.

8. By the end of the First World War, government securities made up 5.7 percent of the total assets (discounts, advances, loans, and securities) held by the Federal Reserve Banks. In June 1944, government securities represented more than 99 percent of the Fed's total earning assets. Allan Meltzer, *A History of the Federal Reserve*, vol. 1, *1913–1951* (Chicago: University of Chicago Press, 2003), 87–89; and Anna Youngman, *The Federal Reserve System in Wartime* (New York: National Bureau of Economic Research, 1945), 19–31.

9. Aaron C. Wistar, "Disorderly Markets: The Federal Reserve, the Banking Lobby, and the Government Securities Market, 1920–1961" (PhD diss., University of California, Santa Cruz, 2021), 148.

10. The Fed did have other, subtler tools to implement monetary policy, particularly through supervisory actions. Peter Conti-Brown and Sean Vanatta, *Private Finance, Public Power: A History of Bank Supervision in America* (Princeton, NJ: Princeton University Press, 2025).

11. "Federal Reserve Bulletin," Board of Governors of the Federal Reserve System, October 1945, 1021, FRASER, https://fraser.stlouisfed.org/files/docs/publications/FRB/1940s/frb _101945.pdf?utm_source=direct_download. Total reserve bank credit outstanding is an analog to "Total Factors Supplying Reserve Funds" in the present-day "Federal Reserve Balance Sheet: Factors Affecting Reserve Balances—H.4.1," Board of Governors of the Federal Reserve System, https://www.federalreserve.gov/releases/h41/.

12. "Assets and Liabilities of Commercial Banks in the United States: Series H.8," Board of Governors of the Federal Reserve System, https://www.federalreserve.gov/releases/h8/current /default.htm.

13. Wistar, "Disorderly Markets," 103.

14. The full text of the agreement was one sentence: "The Treasury and the Federal Reserve System have reached full accord with respect to debt-management and monetary policies to be pursued in furthering their common purpose to assure the successful financing of the Government's requirements and, at the same time, to minimize monetization of the public debt." *Thirty-Eighth Annual Report of the Board of Governors of the Federal Reserve System*, Board of Governors of the Federal Reserve System, 1951, 98, https://www.federalreserve.gov/mon etarypolicy/files/fomcropa19510302.pdf.

15. "Aldrich Favors Modifying Pegs on Long-Terms," *New York Herald Tribune*, December 29, 1948.

16. R. C. Leffingwell, "How to Control Inflation," originally published in *Fortune*, October 1948, reprinted in *Commercial and Financial Chronicle*, October 7, 1948, 6, FRASER, https://fraser .stlouisfed.org/title/commercial-financial-chronicle-1339/october-7-1948-554900.

17. Testimony of McCabe, *Hearings before the Subcommittee on Monetary, Credit, and Fiscal Policies of the Joint Committee on the Economic Report*, 81st Cong., 1st Sess. (2024), FRASER, https:// fraser.stlouisfed.org/files/docs/meltzer/jecmon1950a.pdf?utm_source=direct_download.

18. Wistar, "Disorderly Markets," 155–59.

19. Nomination of William McChesney Martin Jr. *Hearing before the Committee on Banking and Currency, United States Senate*, 82nd Cong., 1 Sess. (March 19, 1951), 10.

20. Nomination of William McChesney Martin Jr., 12.

21. "Martin Says Reserve Won't Peg Prices of US Issues on a Specific Level," *Wall Street Journal*, May 11, 1951.

22. The Fed chose short-term Treasury markets simply because of their size. Before World War II, monetary policy had not been conducted primarily through the government bond market. At the time of its founding, the Fed was barred from even purchasing government debt. Over the course of the 1930s, as government debt began to expand, the Fed increasingly used its financial

power to buy and sell in that market to affect prices. Given the large size of debt in circulation at the end of the war, it offered a clear and efficient way for the Fed to manage the interest-rate structure in the economy. Wistar, "Disorderly Markets," 228–29.

23. William McChesney Martin, "The Transition to Free Markets," April 13, 1953, FRASER, https://fraser.stlouisfed.org/title/statements-speeches-william-mcchesney-martin-jr-448 /transition-free-markets-7780.

24. Martin, a year later, looked back on the chaos of the late spring and chalked it up to markets not understanding what he meant by a return to a free market. "The money supply was quite adequate, in my judgment, in the spring of 1953, until the expectations of the people regarding the Federal Reserve concept of a free market and the administration's intentions with respect to interest rates on treasury securities just carried people away," he said.

   Investors wrongly thought that the Fed "was just going to abdicate so far as supplying and absorbing reserves was concerned." They had read the Fed reports and Martin's speech on free markets and believed that he had meant a return to the Fed's traditional functions: providing an elastic currency in seasonal periods, regulating the banking system, and functioning as a lender of last resort. They had been wrong. In reality, the Fed had redefined a "free market" to mean a managed one, with the Fed conducting significant and ongoing open market operations to loosen or tighten the monetary supply and ensure that even minor periods of instability did not occur. Wm. McC. Martin Jr., "Monetary Policy and the Federal Reserve System," in *Proceedings of the Fifteenth Annual Pacific Northwest Conference on Banking*, April 8, 9, 1954, Federal Reserve Bank of St. Louis, FRASER, https://fraser.stlouisfed.org/files/docs/historical/martin /martin54_0408.pdf.

25. Lev Menand and Joshua Younger, "Money and Public Debt: Treasury Market Liquidity as a Legal Phenomenon," *Columbia Business Law Review* 224 (2023), https://scholarship.law .columbia.edu/faculty_scholarship/4093/.

26. Kenneth Garbade, *After the Accord: A History of Federal Reserve Open Market Operations, the US Government Securities Market, and Treasury Debt Management from 1951 to 1979* (Cambridge, UK: Cambridge University Press, 2021), 230, quoting Watrous Irons, FRB Dallas, on July 18, 1958.

27. Garbade, *After the Accord*, 230.

28. Bill Martin, as Fed Chair, took many of these stabilizing actions reluctantly. The "bills only" or "bills preferably" policy he initiated in 1953 indicated a desire to constrain Fed activity to short-term bond markets and to minimize any assistance to Treasury at the moments of financing. The policy, controversial from the start, broke down in 1961 after eight years of frequent suspension. The Fed's actions to manage money markets were more robust than Martin desired, but he consistently authorized the actions, including the elimination of "bills only." Martin may have said he preferred a less active Fed, but he expanded its power dramatically in pursuit of orderly, liquid, and global markets.

29. Edward Cowan, "Federal Reserve Takes Bold Step," *New York Times*, July 21, 1963, 85.

30. Allan Sproul, "Central Banks and Money Markets," May 6, 1954, FRASER, https://fraser.stlou isfed.org/title/statements-speeches-allen-sproul-6743/central-banks-money-markets-618867.

31. Wistar, "Disorderly Markets," 279.

32. Friedman's testimony quoted in Wistar, "Disorderly Markets," 279.

33. Much of the discussion of this goal among the leaders and staff of the Fed was centered around the Fed's ongoing desire to enhance banks' "funding liquidity," that is, the ability for banks to access cash in an efficient manner. This is distinct from a separate goal of the Fed's to enhance "market liquidity," or the ability to transform an asset into cash.

   For more on the Fed's goal in enhancing funding liquidity, see Howard D. Crosse, "Bank Liquidity and Time Deposits," *Proceedings of the Thirteenth National Credit Conference*, January 1961, 103–114; Board of Governors of the Federal Reserve System and the United States Treasury Department, *The Federal Reserve and Treasury: Answers to the Questions from the Commission on Money and Credit* (Englewood Cliffs, NJ: Prentice-Hall, 1963), Federal Reserve Bank of St. Louis, FRASER, https://fraser.stlouisfed.org/files/docs/historical/federal%20re

serve%20history/frs_treasury_answers_money_credit_1963.pdf; and Robert Roosa, *Federal Reserve Operations in the Money and Government Securities Markets* (New York: Federal Reserve Bank of New York, 1956).

34. Since the Fed flooded the economy with reserves through its response to the Great Financial Crisis and its quantitative easing (QE) program, it no longer conducts monetary policy through the adjustment of the level of bank reserves. The Fed now operates under an "ample reserves" framework, in which monetary policy is implemented through direct adjustment of key interest rates that determine the cost of money to financial institutions. Jane Ihrig, Zeynep Senyuz, and Gretchen C. Weinbach, "The Fed's 'Ample-Reserves' Approach to Implementing Monetary Policy," Finance and Economics Discussion Series, Board of Governors of the Federal Reserve, February 2020, https://doi.org/10.17016/FEDS.2020.022; and Michael Ng and David Wessel, "The Fed's Bigger Balance Sheet in an Era of 'Ample Reserves,'" Brookings Institution, May 17, 2019, https://www.brookings.edu/articles/the-feds-bigger-balance-sheet-in-an-era-of-ample-reserves/.

35. As two New York Fed officials put it: "The lodging of these funds outside the banks has also been an important factor making finance companies, and through them, consumer credit, relatively unresponsive to general monetary restraint." Howard D. Crosse and George Garvy (FRBNY), "Federal Interest Rate Ceilings on Deposits," 41, memo enclosed in Crosse to Allan Sproul, July 11, 1962, series 1: box 2, folder 23: Crosse, Howard D. 1962–1965, Allan Sproul Papers, Bancroft Library, UC Berkeley.

36. John Exter, "We Need Deposits" memo, September 1959, 2, author's possession, courtesy of Phillip L. Zweig.

37. "The large New York banks watched their share of total deposits melt away from some twenty-five per cent of all commercial bank deposits in 1941 to less than fifteen per cent in 1960." George W. McKinney Jr., "New Sources of Bank Funds: Certificates of Deposit and Debt Securities," *Law and Contemporary Problems* 32, no. 1 (Winter 1967): 72.

38. The 1955 acquisition by National City Bank of First National Bank gave it a boost in these efforts and precipitated the name change to First National City.

39. Phillip L. Zweig, *Wriston: Walter Wriston, Citibank, and the Rise and Fall of American Financial Supremacy* (New York: Crown, 1996), 113.

40. Exter, "We Need Deposits," 1.

41. Ironically, Exter would later in life come to regret his role in developing the negotiable CD, believing that it became an engine of inflation by enabling banks to provide abundant, longer-term credit. In an interview with Wriston's biographer Phillip Zweig, he expressed such regret for his role that Zweig says "he viewed himself as a kind of devil's accomplice." He became increasingly invested in the gold standard, eventually leading to his departure from the bank and a break with Wriston. Zweig, *Wriston*, 144.

42. Coincidentally, it was the same day that the Fed announced the end of its "bills only" policy, embracing its marketcrafting power to ensure orderly markets. The two stories competed for coverage. Richard E. Mooney, "Reserve Ending 'Bills Only' Rule," *New York Times*, February 21, 1961, https://timesmachine.nytimes.com/timesmachine/1961/02/21/101449570.html?pageNumber=49.

43. Zweig, *Wriston*, 141.

44. "Financial regulators could have rather easily stopped the negotiable certificate of deposit in its tracks," writes the sociologist Pierre-Christian Fink in his outstanding study of midcentury money markets. "They possessed more power over banks than over other firms that had begun to issue new forms of money. Yet the regulators did not stop the commercial banks, and even encouraged the development of the negotiable certificate of deposit." Fink, "The Rise of the Money Market: The U.S. State, New York City Banks, and the Commodification of Money, 1945–1980" (PhD diss., Columbia University, 2020), 74.

45. Meeting Minutes, Board of Governors of the Federal Reserve System, February 28, 1961, 14, Federal Reserve Bank of St. Louis, FRASER, https://fraser.stlouisfed.org/title/minutes-board-governors-federal-reserve-system-821/meeting-minutes-february-28-1961-515685.

46. Zweig, *Wriston*, 111.
47. McKinney, "New Sources of Bank Funds," 75–76.
48. Zweig, *Wriston*, 143.
49. Other New York banks did well too. By 1965, just shy of half of the $11 billion of negotiable CDs were liabilities of banks in the New York Federal Reserve District. McKinney, "New Sources of Bank Funds," 79.
50. Zweig, *Wriston*, 1.
51. Crosse quoted in Fink, "Rise of the Money Market," 84.
52. Within months of his departure, Crosse was making special requests for data analysis of Fed staff that would inform his upcoming application for Franklin National's holding company status. After significant debate, the Board of Governors authorized the staff to develop and share the data, for a cost. Crosse had a habit of treating the line between the Fed and the private sector as very porous. Meeting Minutes, Board of Governors of the Federal Reserve System, December 23, 1965, Federal Reserve Bank of St. Louis, FRASER, https://fraser .stlouisfed.org/title/minutes-board-governors-federal-reserve-system-821/meeting-minutes -december-23-1965-516675.
53. Dee Wedemeyer, "Ex-Franklin Officer in Guilty Plea," *New York Times*, June 22, 1977, https:// www.nytimes.com/1977/06/22/archives/exfranklin-officer-in-guilty-plea.html.
54. Author's calculations. The rate between 1953 and 1971 was 7.3 percent, and between 1947 and 1953, the immediate postwar years, 7.6 percent. Fixed Private Investment data, Federal Reserve Bank of St. Louis, https://fred.stlouisfed.org/series/FPI.
55. William McChesney Martin, "Remarks before the Yale Club of Washington," March 21, 1968, Federal Reserve Bank of St. Louis, FRASER, https://fraser.stlouisfed.org/title/state ments-speeches-william-mcchesney-martin-jr-448/remarks-yale-club-washington-annual -dinner-honoring-charles-carroll-glover-jr-mayflower-hotel-washington-dc-7930.
56. Bremner, *Chairman of the Fed*, 275.

5: Crafting Health-Care Markets

1. Katherine H. Pollak, "Life-or-Death Struggle Looms in Coal Fields of W. Va.," *Labor Age*, July 1931, 5–7.
2. On Pollak's background, see Dorothy Sue Cobble, *The Other Women's Movement: Workplace Justice and Social Rights in Modern America* (Princeton, NJ: Princeton University Press, 2003), 35–37. On the CIO, see David Brody, *Workers in Industrial America: Essays on the 20th Century Struggle*, 2nd ed. (New York: Oxford University Press, 1993).
3. Katherine Ellickson, interview by Dennis East, January 10, 1976, transcript, 8, Archives of Labor History and Urban Affairs, Detroit, MI, copy in box 1, folder 5, Schlesinger Library, Harvard University: Labor oral history, January 10, 1976, Katherine Pollak Ellickson Papers, (hereafter KPEP).
4. Landon R. Y. Storrs, *The Second Red Scare and the Unmaking of the New Deal Left* (Princeton, NJ: Princeton University Press, 2013), 49.
5. Carl F. Ameringer, *The Health Care Revolution: From Medical Monopoly to Market Competition* (Berkeley: University of California Press, 2008), 23–24, 40–41.
6. Paul Starr, *The Social Transformation of American Medicine* (New York: Basic Books, 1982), 79–144.
7. Michael M. Davis, "The American Approach to Health Insurance," *Milbank Memorial Fund Quarterly* 12, no. 2 (1934): 203–17, reprinted in the *Milbank Quarterly* 83, no. 4 (2005): 537–47.
8. Paul Starr, *Remedy and Reaction: The Peculiar American Struggle over Health Care Reform* (New Haven, CT: Yale University Press, 2011), 36–37.
9. Katherine Ellickson, interview by Peter A. Corning, February 15, February 22, July 18, July 19, July 22, November 16, 1966, and June 15, 1967, transcript, 17–20, 42–43, Columbia Center for Oral History, Columbia University, New York, NY, https://dx.doi .org/10.7916/d8-zyhy-cn19; Nelson H. Cruikshank, interview with Lewis E. Weeks, 1983, transcript, 7–9, Hospital Administration Oral History Collection, American Hospital

Association, Chicago, IL, https://www.aha.org/system/files/media/file/2022/01/Cruikshank
.pdf, 7–9.

10. Elizabeth Wickenden, interview by Peter A. Corning, April 5, June 10, and October 24, 1966,
transcript, 25, Columbia Center for Oral History, https://dx.doi.org/10.7916/d8-7gsb-vf81.

11. Richard Harris, *A Sacred Trust* (New York: New American Library, 1966), 28; Ellickson, interview by Dennis East, 16.

12. Harry S. Truman, "Special Message to the Congress Recommending a Comprehensive
Health Program," November 19, 1945, Harry S. Truman Presidential Library, https://www
.trumanlibrary.gov/library/public-papers/192/special-message-congress-recommending
-comprehensive-health-program.

13. "For the People's Health," *Economic Outlook* [CIO] 7, no. 4 (April 1946). For Ellickson's authorship of the unsigned piece, see Jens Gorbahn, *Die amerikanischen Gewerkschaften zwischen
gesetzlicher und privater Krankenversicherung von der National Health Insurance zur betrieblichen
Absicherung im Krankheitsfall in den 40er und 50er Jahren* (Berlin: Lit Verlag, 2014), 133.

14. I. S. Falk, "Desk Diary Notes," November 10, 1948, box 64, folder 613: Redrafting S. 1320
and Development of S. 1679, I. S. Falk Papers (hereafter ISFP), Manuscripts and Archives
Repository, Sterling Memorial Library, Yale University; Ellickson to Stanley Ruttenberg, December 7, 1948, box 1, folder 22, KPEP.

15. Falk, "Desk Diary Notes," December 28, 1948. Leon's wife, Mary Dublin Keyserling, was an
economist in her own right as well as a member of the same New Deal women's networks as
Ellickson and Wickenden.

16. Falk, "Desk Diary Notes," December 28, 1948.

17. Ellickson, interview by Dennis East, 5–6.

18. Michael Davis quoted in Alan Derickson, *Health Security for All: Dreams of Universal Health
Care in America* (Baltimore, MD: Johns Hopkins University Press, 2005), 81.

19. Monte M. Poen, *Harry S. Truman versus the Medical Lobby: The Genesis of Medicare* (Columbia:
University of Missouri Press, 2014), 152.

20. Oscar Ewing, speech at the 1949 CIO convention, in *Proceedings of the Eleventh Constitutional
Convention of the Congress of Industrial Organizations*, 1949, 234–39.

21. Harris, *Sacred Trust*, 41.

22. Starr, *Social Transformation of American Medicine*, 285.

23. Harris, *Sacred Trust*, 43–44.

24. Alan B. Cohen, David C. Colby, Keith A. Wailoo, and Julian E. Zelizer, "Introduction: Medicare, Medicaid, and the Moral Test of Government," in *Medicare and Medicaid at 50: America's
Entitlement Programs in the Age of Affordable Care*, ed. Cohen, Colby, Wailoo, and Zelizer (Oxford, UK: Oxford University Press, 2015), 7.

25. Theodore Marmor, *The Politics of Medicare* (London: Routledge & Kagan Paul, 1970), 13–14.

26. Harry Truman, *Memoirs: Years of Trial and Hope*, vol. 2 (Garden City, NY: Doubleday, 1956), 23.

27. Marmor, *Politics of Medicare*, 12.

28. Jill Quadagno, *One Nation, Uninsured: Why the U.S. Has No National Health Insurance* (Oxford,
UK: Oxford University Press, 2006), 52.

29. Quadagno, *One Nation, Uninsured*, 50; Starr, *Remedy and Reaction*, 42.

30. Michael K. Brown, *Race, Money, and the American Welfare State* (Ithaca, NY: Cornell University Press, 1999), 162.

31. Brown, *Race, Money, and the American Welfare State*, 141.

32. Quadagno, *One Nation, Uninsured*, 69–71.

33. Katherine Ellickson, "The Social Security Approach to Health Services for the Aged,"
May 22, 1958, box 159, folder 2298: Correspondence, Katherine Ellickson, ISFP.

34. Marmor, *Politics of Medicare*, 17.

35. Quadagno, *One Nation, Uninsured*, 6.

36. Jonathan Oberlander and Theodor Marmor, "The Road Not Taken: What Happened to
Medicare for All?," in Cohen et al., *Medicare and Medicaid at 50*, 57; Jonathan Oberlander, *The
Political Life of Medicare* (Chicago: University of Chicago Press, 2003), 9.

37. Katherine Ellickson, "Outline Proposals and Questions Relating to Improvements in Health Benefits Legislation," January 13, 1959, reproduced in Ellickson, interview by Peter A. Corning, as Exhibit Z-1.
38. Oberlander and Marmor, "The Road Not Taken," 58.
39. Quadagno, *One Nation, Uninsured*, 54.
40. Edward D. Berkowitz and Wendy Wolff, "Disability Insurance and the Limits of American History," *Public Historian* 8, no. 2 (Spring 1986): 68–69.
41. Starr, *Social Transformation of American Medicine*, 368.
42. Nelson Cruikshank, interview by Peter A. Corning, November 18, 1965, February 15, February 22, August 16, and September 23, 1966, and August 29, 1967, transcript, 203, Columbia Center for Oral History, https://dx.doi.org/10.7916/d8-3a56-g414.
43. Rhode Island Representative Aime Forand first sponsored the bill. As momentum grew, Senator Clinton Anderson of New Mexico and Representative Cecil King of California played increasingly important roles.
44. "Social Security History—Chapter 4: The Fourth Round, 1957 to 1965," Social Security Administration, https://www.ssa.gov/history/corningchap4.html.
45. Cruikshank, interview by Peter A. Corning, 319.
46. Cohen et al., *Medicare and Medicaid at 50*, 7.
47. Quadagno, *One Nation Uninsured*, 59.
48. Cohen et al., *Medicare and Medicaid at 50*, 12; Ronald Reagan, "Ronald Reagan Speaks Out against Socialized Medicine," American Rhetoric, n.d., https://www.americanrhetoric.com/speeches/ronaldreagansocializedmedicine.htm.
49. On the Democratic convention march, see Natalie Shure, "How Medicare Was Won," *The Nation*, August 6, 2018, https://www.thenation.com/article/archive/how-medicare-was-won/.
50. Starr, *Social Transformation of American Medicine*, 46.
51. Ellickson, interview by Peter A. Corning, 24.
52. Cruikshank, interview by Peter A. Corning, 189.
53. Blue Carstenson, interview by Peter A. Corning, February 23, March 23, July 14, and September 19, 1966, transcript, 47, Columbia Center for Oral History, https://dx.doi.org/10.7916/d8-hg8q-7b84.
54. Oscar Ewing, interview by Peter A. Corning, August 26, 1966, transcript, 65, Columbia Center for Oral History, https://dx.doi.org/10.7916/d8-jztd-rs59.
55. Oscar R. Ewing, Oral History interview by J. R. Fuchs, May 2, 1969, transcript, 251, Harry S. Truman Presidential Library, https://www.trumanlibrary.gov/library/oral-histories/ewing4.
56. Derickson, *Health Security for All*, 89–102, 107.
57. Julian Zelizer, *Taxing America: Wilbur Mills, Congress, and the States, 1945–1975* (Cambridge, UK: Cambridge University Press, 2000), 134–36.
58. Wilbur Mills, Oral History Interview II by Michael L. Gillette, March 25, 1987, 2–3, Internet Copy, LBJ Library, https://www.discoverlbj.org/item/oh-millsw-19870325-2-94-18.
59. Oberlander and Marmor, "The Road Not Taken," 59.
60. Lyndon Johnson, "Remarks with President Truman at the Signing in Independence of the Medicare Bill," July 30, 1965, The American Presidency Project, https://www.presidency.ucsb.edu/documents/remarks-with-president-truman-the-signing-independence-the-medicare-bill.
61. Cobble, *The Other Women's Movement*.
62. Ellickson, interview by Dennis East, 10.
63. Cruikshank, interview by Peter A. Corning, 368–69.
64. Katherine Ellickson, interview by Philip Mason, December 15, 1974, transcript, 28, Archives of Labor History and Urban Affairs, Detroit, MI, copy in box 1, folder 4: Oral history, December 15, 1974, KPEP.
65. Marmor, *Politics of Medicare*, 25.
66. Ellickson, interview by Peter A. Corning, 53, 65–66.

67. Lisbeth Schorr and Leonard Lesser, interview by Peter A. Corning, June 15, 1967, transcript, 30, 74, Columbia Center for Oral History, https://dx.doi.org/10.7916/d8-57ge-f262.

68. Cruikshank, interview by Peter A. Corning, 371.

69. Quadagno, *One Nation, Uninsured*, 9.

70. Starr, *Social Transformation of American Medicine*, 52.

71. Quadagno, *One Nation, Uninsured*, 97.

72. David Barton Smith, "Stealth Capture: The Civil Rights Movement and the Implementation of Medicare," Poverty and Race Research Action Council, April–June 2016, https://www.prrac.org/stealth-capture-the-civil-rights-movement-and-the-implementation-of-medicare/.

73. David Barton Smith, *The Power to Heal: Civil Rights, Medicare, and the Struggle to Transform America's Health Care System* (Nashville: Vanderbilt University Press, 2016); Konczal, *Freedom from the Market*, 128–36.

74. Ellickson, interview by Peter A. Corning, 78.

75. Alice M. Rivlin, "Agreed: Here Comes National Health Insurance," *New York Times*, July 21, 1974, https://www.nytimes.com/1974/07/21/archives/agreed-here-comes-national-health-insurance-question-what-kind.html; Nancy Hicks, "National Health Insurance Now Considered Just Remote Possibility," *New York Times*, December 31, 1975, https://www.nytimes.com/1975/12/31/archives/national-health-insurance-now-considered-just-remote-possibility.html.

76. Starr, *Remedy and Reaction*, 74.

77. Cruikshank, interview by Peter A. Corning, 18–19.

78. Starr, *Social Transformation of American Medicine*, 63.

79. NHE by Age Group and Sex, Selected Years 2002, 2004, 2006, 2008, 2010, 2012, 2014, 2016, 2018, and 2020, National Health Expenditure Fact Sheet, Centers for Medicare and Medicaid Services, https://www.cms.gov/data-research/statistics-trends-and-reports/national-health-expenditure-data/nhe-fact-sheet#:~:text=Age%20and%20Sex,11%20percent%20of%20total%20NHE; Emma Wager, Matthew McGough, Shameek Rakshit, Krutika Amin, and Cynthia Cox, "How Does Health Spending in the U.S. Compare to Other Countries?," Petersen-KFF Health System Tracker, January 23, 2024, https://www.healthsystemtracker.org/chart-collection/health-spending-u-s-compare-countries/#GDP%20per%20capita%20and%20health%20consumption%20spending%20per%20capita,%202022%20(U.S.%20dollars,%20PPP%20adjusted).

RISE OF THE GLOBAL
6: In the Shadows of Bretton Woods

1. "Interview with Andrew F. Brimmer," Federal Reserve Board Oral History Project, 2007, 3–7, https://www.federalreserve.gov/aboutthefed/files/andrew-f-brimmer-interview-20070713.pdf.

2. "Interview with Andrew F. Brimmer," 5–6, 11–14.

3. "Interview with Andrew F. Brimmer," 25–28.

4. "Interview with Andrew F. Brimmer," 125–126.

5. Baker Library Special Collections and Archives, Harvard Business School, Box 425, folder 14, AFBP.

6. Nick Kotz, *Judgment Days: Lyndon Baines Johnson, Martin Luther King Jr., and the Laws That Changed America* (New York: Houghton Mifflin, 2006), 510.

7. "Interview with Andrew F. Brimmer," 127.

8. Joseph A. Califano, *The Triumph & Tragedy of Lyndon Johnson* (London: Atria Books, 2015), 190.

9. Richard F. Janssen, "Desire to Aid Negroes Could Make New 'Fed' Member More Liberal," *Wall Street Journal*, March 3, 1966.

10. Photo retrieved from Wikimedia, https://upload.wikimedia.org/wikipedia/commons/0/08/Andrew_Brimmer_Swearing_In.jpg.

11. Conversation with Sylvia Porter, February 2, 1966, Secret White House Tapes, Miller Center,

University of Virginia, https://millercenter.org/the-presidency/secret-white-house-tapes/con versation-sylvia-porter-february-2-1966.

12. "Interview with Andrew F. Brimmer," 147.

13. Barry Eichengreen, *Globalizing Capital: A History of the International Monetary System* (Princeton, NJ: Princeton University Press, 1996), 107, Kindle. Specifically, when countries other than the United States ran balance of payments deficits, they had to settle those balances in gold, thus draining their gold reserves. The United States could settle its deficits (at least in part) in its own currency by printing more money rather than drawing down its gold reserves.

14. Section 6 of the Gold Reserve Act of 1934 prohibited the conversion of dollars to gold for nonofficial purposes, so only officially held dollar reserves of IMF members could be presented to the Treasury for conversion to gold. The United States was never at risk of having the entire volume of outstanding dollars presented for conversion all at once. But the higher the proportion of offshore dollars that found their way into the accounts of foreign central banks, the greater would be the proportion of US gold reserves at risk.

15. Robert V. Roosa, *The Dollar and World Liquidity* (New York: Random House, 1967), 3.

16. The underlying tensions are often described as the "Triffin Dilemma." In 1959 testimony in the House, the economist Robert Triffin explained the tensions inherent in the dollar's dual role. As the international reserve currency, the dollar had to be strong and stable relative to gold, and its supply needed to increase elastically to meet the needs of global economic growth. Triffin pointed out that for the dollar to meet global liquidity needs, the United States had to run balance of payments deficits. However, if the US went too far—pursuing excessive deficit spending and low interest rates to stimulate the domestic economy—it could create a dollar overhang, putting pressure on the currency to devalue. Robert Triffin, "The Gold Shortage, the Dollar Glut, and the Future of Convertibility," *Hearings before the Joint Economic Committee Pursuant to S. Con. Res. 13*, 86th Cong., 1st Sess. (October 1959), part 9A, 2918–25, Federal Reserve Bank of St. Louis, FRASER, https://fraser.stlouisfed.org/title/employment-growth-price-levels-1242/part -9a--constructive-suggestions-reconciling-simultaneously-obtaining-three-objectives-maxi mum-employment-adequate-rate-growth-substantial-stability-price-level-3631?page=166.

17. Youn Ki and Yongwoo Jeung, "Ideas, Interests, and the Transition to a Floating Exchange System," *Journal of Policy History* 32, no. 2 (2020): 151.

18. Britain had been forced to devalue sterling twice by the end of the 1960s—first in 1949 and again in 1967—eliciting waves of popular resentment against sitting governments.

19. Theodore Sorensen quoted in John A. C. Conybeare, *United States Foreign Economic Policy and the International Capital Markets: The Case of Capital Export Countries, 1963–1974* (New York: Routledge, 1988), 79.

20. Roosa, *Dollar and World Liquidity*, 96–97.

21. "A Businessman's Letter to JFK and His Reply," *Life*, July 6, 1962, 30–31.

22. "Meeting with the President, April 18, 1963, 10:00 A.M. to 12 Noon—Balance of Payments," U.S. Department of State, Office of the Historian, https://history.state.gov/historicaldocu ments/frus1961-63v09/d24.

23. Ki and Jeung, "Ideas, Interests, and the Transition to a Floating Exchange System," 157.

24. James P. Hawley, *Dollars and Borders: U.S. Government Attempts to Restrict Capital Flows, 1960– 1980* (New York: Routledge, 2016), 48; see also Conybeare, *United States Foreign Economic Policy and the International Capital Markets*.

25. "Interview with Andrew F. Brimmer," 115.

26. Hawley, *Dollars and Borders*, 69.

27. Reported in "News Briefs," *Business Week*, January 1, 1966, 24.

28. On the effect of capital controls, see Hawley, *Dollars and Borders*, 109.

29. Offshore dollars existed well before the 1950s, and banks in multiple European financial centers held them in the 1920s. When sterling functioned as the global reserve currency in the nineteenth century, banks outside of the United Kingdom held offshore sterling deposits. For more on the emergence in London and its relationship with sterling, see Catherine R. Schenk, "The Origins of the Eurodollar Market in London: 1955–1963," *Explorations*

in Economic History 35, no. 2 (1998): 221–38, https://www.sfu.ca/~poitras/EEH_Eurodol lar_98.pdf.

30. The definition of "deposit" from the Federal Deposit Insurance Act of 1950 explicitly excludes offshore-dollar deposits: see section 3.l: "[A]ny obligation of a bank which is payable only at an office of the bank located outside the States of the United States, the District of Columbia, any Territory of the United States, Puerto Rico, and the Virgin Islands, shall not be a deposit for any of the purposes of this Act or be included as a part of total deposits or of an insured deposit."

31. Gary Burn, *The Re-emergence of Global Finance* (New York: Palgrave Macmillan, 2006), 6.

32. Ian M. Kerr, *A History of the Eurobond Market: The First 21 Years* (London: Euromoney, 1984).

33. Hawley, *Dollars and Borders*, 112.

34. Hawley, *Dollars and Borders*, 62, 90; Burn, *Re-emergence of Global Finance*, 147.

35. Robert N. McCauley and Catherine R. Schenk, "Central Bank Swaps Then and Now: Swaps and Dollar Liquidity in the 1960s," Bank for International Settlements Working Papers, no. 851, April 2020, https://www.bis.org/publ/work851.pdf.

36. Meeting Minutes, Board of Governors of the Federal Reserve System, May 4 and 25, 1960, Federal Reserve Bank of St. Louis, FRASER, https://fraser.stlouisfed.org/title/minutes -board-governors-federal-reserve-system-821/meeting-minutes-may-4-1960-515514 and https://fraser.stlouisfed.org/title/minutes-board-governors-federal-reserve-system-821/ meeting-minutes-may-25-1960-515525. See also Burn, *Re-emergence of Global Finance*, 141– 42. Treasury Secretary Douglas Dillon told the President in 1963: "[T]hese dollars have already left the US," so there would be "no immediate effect on our balance of payments nor will there necessarily be in the future," quoted in Burn, *The Re-emergence of Global Finance*, 150.

37. Andrew F. Brimmer, "Monetary Policy and the U.S. Balance of Payments," remarks at Wharton School of Finance and Commerce, University of Pennsylvania, October 5, 1966, 12, Federal Reserve Bank of St. Louis, FRASER, https://fraser.stlouisfed.org/title/statements-speeches -andrew-f-brimmer-463/monetary-policy-u-s-balance-payments-10321.

38. He also worried the offshore activity could interfere with domestic monetary policy, evidence of at least some ambiguity in posture. Meeting Minutes, Board of Governors of the Federal Reserve System, August 31, 1966, Federal Reserve Bank of St. Louis, FRASER, https://fraser .stlouisfed.org/title/minutes-board-governors-federal-reserve-system-821/meeting-minutes -august-31-1966-516815.

39. "Any comprehensive control program that prevents powerful industrial and financial interests from using available and sorely needed resources requires, for its own survival, a built-in escape valve," said one of Brimmer's colleagues at the Fed, Fred Klopstock, in a speech in 1968. "Otherwise, the pressures and strains that such a program tends to generate will eventually tear it apart, or at least cause compliance to fall to such a low level as to deprive it of much of its effectiveness. By leaving open the escape route to the [offshore-dollar market], the designers of our balance of payments program have stifled the inevitable opposition to its restraints, obtained a high degree of compliance, and made most businessmen and many bankers feel that they can somehow live with the program, even though not always comfortably." Fred H. Klopstock, "Impact of Euro-Markets on the United States Balance of Payments" [adapted from an address at Georgetown University, Washington, DC, September 26, 1968], in "Transatlantic Investment and the Balance of Payments," special issue, *Law and Contemporary Problems* 34, no. 1 (Winter 1969): 171.

40. Meeting Minutes, Board of Governors of the Federal Reserve System, October 3, 1966, Federal Reserve Bank of St. Louis, FRASER, https://fraser.stlouisfed.org/title/minutes-board-gov ernors-federal-reserve-system-821/meeting-minutes-october-3-1966-516837; and Brimmer, "Monetary Policy and the U.S. Balance of Payments."

41. Edward M. Bernstein, "The Eurodollar Market and National Credit Policy," *Quarterly Review and Investment Survey*, April 17, 1969.

42. Robert N. McCauley, "The Offshore Dollar and US Policy," *Policy Hub*, Federal Reserve Bank of Atlanta, May 2024, https://www.atlantafed.org/-/media/documents/research/pub lications/policy-hub/2024/05/15/02--offshore-dollar-and-us-policy.pdf; "Assets and Liabilities of Commercial Banks in the United States," Board of Governors of the Federal Reserve System, January 17, 2025, https://www.federalreserve.gov/releases/h8/current/.

43. "Interview with Andrew F. Brimmer," 37.

44. "Interview with Andrew F. Brimmer," 134.

45. For recent coverage of his efforts, see Brendan Greeley, "The Contentious Idea That Still Challenges the Fed," *Financial Times*, April 23, 2023, https://www.ft.com/content/9c2f28b6 -b31e-47ca-87a2-aa91340c083d.

46. Congress gives the Fed a broad statutory mandate, charging it with managing the growth of money and credit "to increase production, so as to promote effectively the goals of maximum employment, stable prices, and moderate long-term interest rates." Federal Reserve Act, section 2A, Board of Governors of the Federal Reserve System, "Section 2A. Monetary Policy Objectives," Federal Reserve Act, 12 U.S.C. § 225a, https://www.federalreserve.gov/about thefed/section2a.htm.

47. William McChesney Martin Jr., "Address before the New York Group of the Investment Bankers Association of America," October 19, 1955, Federal Reserve Bank of St. Louis, FRASER, https://fraser.stlouisfed.org/title/statements-speeches-william-mcchesney-martin -jr-448/address-new-york-group-investment-bankers-association-america-7800.

48. Brimmer said in a speech in 1972, "As monetary conditions swung from ease to restraint and back to ease in the last several years, commercial banks generally shifted the supply of credit away from households and governments and into the business sector. . . . Relying heavily on Euro-dollar inflows, they were able to maintain a high volume of lending to business in the face of severe attrition in time deposits." Andrew F. Brimmer, "Multi-national Banks and the Management of Monetary Policy in the United States," paper presented before a Joint Session of the Eighty-Fifth Annual Meeting of the American Finance Association, Toronto, Ontario, Canada, December 28, 1972, SSAFB, Federal Reserve Bank of St. Louis, https:// fraser.stlouisfed.org/title/statements-speeches-andrew-f-brimmer-463/multi-national-banks -management-monetary-policy-united-states-10415.

49. Andrew Brimmer, "Banking Structure and Monetary Management," remarks at the San Francisco Bond Club, Fairmont Hotel, April 1, 1970, SSAFB, Federal Reserve Bank of St. Louis, FRASER, https://fraser.stlouisfed.org/title/statements-speeches-andrew-f-brimmer-463/bank ing-structure-monetary-management-10376. Brimmer was not the only leader to explore a more nuanced credit allocation policy. Four years earlier, Johnson's Treasury Secretary Henry Fowler underlined the unfairness of a single policy rate. "[S]urely there is a better way to limit credit than by simply raising its price," he said in a public statement. "Raising the price of money should not be the sole means of determining who gets credit. When demands exceed a bank's resources, credit expansion can and should be restrained by bankers saying 'no' to borrowers on criteria other than that of who is willing to pay the highest rate." Press Release, U.S. Treasury Department, August 16, 1966, Federal Reserve Bank of St. Louis, FRASER, https://fraser.stlouisfed.org/title/press-releases-united-states-department-treasury-6111 /volume-155-586998.

50. *An Act to Lower Interest Rates and Allocate Credit: Hearings before the Subcommittee on Domestic Monetary Policy*, 94th Cong., 1st Sess. (February 4–6, 1975), 53.

51. Brimmer, "Multi-national Banks and the Management of Monetary Policy."

52. Statement of William Proxmire, *Hearings before the Subcommittee on Financial Institutions of the Committee on Banking, Housing, and Urban Affairs, United States Senate*, 92nd Cong., 1st Sess. (1971), 1, https://www.google.com/books/edition/Selective_Credit_Policies_and_Wage_prive /RiCjRDcOdS4C?hl=en&gbpv=1&dq=Proxmire+%22March+31,+1971%22+%22S+1201 %22&pg=PA1&printsec=frontcover.

53. Sherman J. Maisel, "Credit Allocation and the Federal Reserve," speech presented at the Banking Research Center at Northwestern University, Chicago, April 22, 1971.

54. Edwin L. Dale, "Reserve Opposes a Credit-Law Change," *New York Times*, April 1, 1971, https://www.nytimes.com/1971/04/01/archives/reserve-opposes-a-creditlaw-change -rejects-social-priority-as-a.html.

55. Greta Krippner, *Capitalizing on Crisis: The Political Origins of the Rise of Finance* (Cambridge, MA: Harvard University Press, 2011), 70.

56. *An Act to Lower Interest Rates and Allocate Credit, Hearings before the Subcommittee on Domestic Monetary Policy of the Committee on Banking, Currency, and Housing, U.S. House of Representatives*, 94th Cong., 1st Sess. (February 1975), 53.

57. James L. Rowe Jr., "Brimmer to Leave Fed," *Washington Post*, May 15, 1974, clipping in "Resignation from Board–1974," box 91, folder 7, AFBP.

58. "An Innovator Leaves the Fed," *Commercial and Financial Chronicle*, n.d., clipping in "Resignation from Board–1974."

59. Stan Strachan, "Brimmer Will Leave Economic Post in Aug.," *Journal of Commerce*, May 16, 1974, clipping in "Resignation from Board–1974."

60. *Act to Lower Interest Rates*, 53.

7: The Cost of Control

1. This chapter is based on an article previously published by the author, with revisions and expansions for this book. Chris Hughes, "Rethinking Arthur Burns, the 'Worst' Fed Chair in History," *Democracy Journal*, no. 67 (Winter 2023), https://democracyjournal.org/maga zine/67/rethinking-arthur-burns-the-worst-fed-chair-in-history/.

2. Wyatt Wells, *Economist in an Uncertain World: Arthur F. Burns and the Federal Reserve, 1970–1978* (New York: Columbia University Press, 1994), 61.

3. Erwin C. Hargrove and Samuel A. Morley, eds., *The President and the Council of Economic Advisers: Interviews with CEA Chairmen* (New York: Routledge, 1985), 100, 112, retrieved from Internet Archive, https://archive.org/details/presidentcouncilooocounse/page /112/mode/2up?q=%22+long-[…]ould+be+devoting+little+time+to+short-run+economic +problems.%22.

4. Wells, *Economist in an Uncertain World*, 29.

5. Richard M. Nixon, "U.S.A. Economy: Recession Ahead?," AP Archive, February 16, 1970, retrieved from YouTube, https://www.youtube.com/watch?v=UXn3eBGH3Xs.

6. Personal Consumption Expenditures data, Federal Reserve Bank of St. Louis, https://fred .stlouisfed.org/series/PCE; Unemployment Rate data, Federal Reserve Bank of St. Louis, https://fred.stlouisfed.org/series/UNRATE.

7. Robert H. Ferrell, *Inside the Nixon Administration: The Secret Diary of Arthur Burns, 1969–1974* (Lawrence: University of Kansas Press, 2010), 34.

8. For a brief study, see Malcolm Rutherford, "Institutional Economics, Then and Now," *Journal of Economic Perspectives* 15, no. 3 (Summer 2001): 173–94, https://pubs.aeaweb.org/doi/pdf plus/10.1257/jep.15.3.173. For a book-length treatment, see Geoffrey Hodgson, *The Evolution of Institutional Economics: Agency, Structure and Darwinism in American Institutionalism* (New York: Routledge, 2004); Malcolm Rutherford, *Institutional Economics: The Old and the New Institutionalism* (Cambridge, UK: Cambridge University Press, 1996).

9. Arthur F. Burns, "The Basis for Lasting Prosperity," address at Pepperdine College, December 7, 1970, Federal Reserve Bank of St. Louis, FRASER, https://fraser.stlouisfed.org/files /docs/historical/burns/Burns_19701207.pdf?utm_source=direct_download.

10. Richard M. Nixon, "Remarks at the Annual Meeting of the National Association of Manufacturers," December 4, 1970, The American Presidency Project, https://www.presidency.ucsb .edu/documents/remarks-the-annual-meeting-the-national-association-manufacturers.

11. Ferrell, *Inside the Nixon Administration*, 34.

12. Edwin L. Dale, "Burns Suggests Pay-Price Board to Cut Inflation," *New York Times*, December 8, 1970, https://timesmachine.nytimes.com/timesmachine/1970/12/08/78228395.html ?pageNumber=1.

13. Gallup Poll #1980-1159G: Presidential Election/Women's Rights [Roper #31088012]

July 11–14, 1980, and Gallup Poll #1200G [Roper #31088052], August 13–16, 1982, both in Longstanding Methods Collection, Roper Center for Public Opinion Research.

14. Robert L. Hetzel, *The Federal Reserve: A New History* (Chicago: University of Chicago Press, 2022), 363, 387.

15. Milton Friedman, "A New Chairman at the Fed," *Newsweek*, February 2, 1970, 68, https://miltonfriedman.hoover.org/internal/media/dispatcher/214051/full.

16. Arthur F. Burns, *The Business Cycle in a Changing World* (New York: National Bureau of Economic Research, 1969), 149, https://www.nber.org/books-and-chapters/business-cycle -changing-world. The essay in which this quote appears had appeared earlier in Arthur F. Burns, *Prosperity without Inflation* (New York: Fordham University Press, 1957).

17. Alan Blinder, *After the Music Stopped: The Financial Crisis, the Response, and the Work Ahead* (New York: Penguin, 2013).

18. James Tobin, "Stabilization Policy Ten Years After," Brookings Institution, 1980, 69–70, https://www.brookings.edu/wp-content/uploads/1980/01/1980a_bpea_tobin.pdf.

19. Employment data, Federal Reserve Bank of St. Louis, https://fred.stlouisfed.org/graph /?g=1aiJP.

20. Hugh Rockoff, *Drastic Measures: A History of Wage and Price Controls* (Cambridge, UK: Cambridge University Press, 2009), 201.

21. George S. Tavlas, *The Monetarists: The Making of the Chicago Monetary Tradition, 1927–1960* (Chicago: University of Chicago Press, 2023); Jennifer Burns, *Milton Friedman: The Last Conservative* (New York: Farrar, Straus and Giroux, 2023).

22. Just a few months into the job, Burns floated the idea of price and wage controls in a May 1970 speech. Arguing that America was relying "too heavily on monetary restriction as a device to curb inflation," he said for the first time that "there may be a useful—albeit a very modest—role for an incomes policy [i.e., wage and price controls] to play." Arthur F. Burns, "Inflation: The Fundamental Challenge to Stabilization Policies," remarks before the Seventeenth Annual Monetary Conference of the American Bankers Association, Hot Springs, Virginia, May 18, 1970, 6, 10, Federal Reserve Bank of St. Louis, FRASER, https://fraser .stlouisfed.org/title/statements-speeches-arthur-f-burns-449/inflation-fundamental-chal lenge-stabilization-policies-7953.

23. J. Bradford DeLong, "America's Peacetime Inflation: The 1970s," in *Reducing Inflation: Motivation and Strategy*, ed. Christina D. Romer and David H. Romer (Chicago: University of Chicago Press, 1997); Burton A. Abrams, "How Richard Nixon Pressured Arthur Burns: Evidence from the Nixon Tapes," *Journal of Economic Perspectives* 20, no. 4 (Fall 2006); Burns, *Milton Friedman*.

24. Ben S. Bernanke, *21st-Century Monetary Policy: The Federal Reserve from the Great Inflation to COVID-19* (New York: Norton, 2023).

25. In particular, some of Burns' critics have taken excerpts from his diary out of context, obscuring the bigger picture and suggesting a closer, more coordinated relationship than existed. Burns wrote privately in the diaries of his constant frustration with Nixon and the "sycophants" who surrounded him. He occasionally exhibited some interest in earning the President's affection, but he was just as often annoyed by the pressure campaigns from the White House. Ferrell, *Inside the Nixon Administration*.

26. Burns did share a commitment to general collaboration with the President, just as his predecessors Bill Martin and Marriner Eccles did. In March of 1971, inflation remained high, but the economy was struggling to move past the recession. The White House, anxious to build some economic momentum, had amped up its pressure campaign on Burns to lower interest rates from their historically high levels. Relating a private meeting with the President in the diary, Burns says that he told the President if a conflict arose between Nixon's priorities and the Fed's, he "would not lose a minute in informing RN and seeking a solution together." But even this seemingly clear statement of political fealty was actually a trade, as secretly recorded tapes of the conversation reveal. Burns buttered up the President at the start of the meeting. "I've done everything in my power, as I see it, to help keep pressing your reputation, your

standing in American life and in history," Burns said. "I've never seen a conflict between the two. But I want you to know this, if a conflict did arise, the moment a conflict arises, I'm going to be right here." After this preamble, the conversation dramatically turned, and Burns explained to the President why he refused to lower interest rates, which the President had been again requesting. He warned of an international monetary crisis, further inflation, a potential tailspin in housing policy, and dangerously higher rates in 1972. The message was clear: "I know what's best for you and the country, Mr. President, and it's to keep interest rates high."

From Burns' perspective, the tête-à-tête worked. The White House laid off its pressure campaign for a few weeks, and he kept rates where he wanted them. Burton A. Abrams and James L. Butkiewicz, "The Political Business Cycle: New Evidence from the Nixon Tapes," *Journal of Money, Credit and Banking* 44, no. 2/3 (March–April 2012): 385–99.

27. Transcript of Arthur F. Burns' Handwritten Journals, January 20, 1969–July 25, 1974, Journal I, 46–47, 103–6, Gerald R. Ford Presidential Library, https://www.fordlibrar ymuseum.gov/sites/default/files/pdf_documents/library/document/0428/burnstran script1.pdf.

28. Author interview with James Galbraith, October 4, 2023.

29. Burns' Handwritten Journals, Journal I, 107–9.

30. William Safire, *Before the Fall: An Inside View of the Pre-Watergate White House* (New York: Routledge, 2017 [1975]), 518.

31. Hawley, *Dollars and Borders*, 119.

32. C. A. Coombs, *The Arena of International Finance* (New York: Wiley, 1976), 212–14.

33. "Dollar Rate Sinks in Europe after Report on Devaluation," *Washington Post*, August 10, 1971, A1.

34. In reality, the British were asking for a guarantee to protect $745,000 of British reserves from a potentially devalued dollar. The message was garbled in transit. Jeffrey E. Garten, *Three Days at Camp David: How a Secret Meeting in 1971 Transformed the Global Economy* (New York: HarperCollins, 2022), 174–75.

35. Garten, *Three Days at Camp David*, 2, 169.

36. Safire, *Before the Fall*, 513–14.

37. Safire, *Before the Fall*, 513–14.

38. Ferrell, *Inside the Nixon Administration*, 116.

39. Garten, *Three Days at Camp David*, 211, quoting Haldeman diaries, 346.

40. Garten, *Three Days at Camp David*, 221.

41. Herbert Stein, *Presidential Economics: The Making of Economic Policy from Roosevelt to Reagan and Beyond American Enterprise Institute* (Washington, DC: American Enterprise Institute for Public Research Policy, 1988), Federal Reserve Bank of St. Louis, FRASER, https://fraser .stlouisfed.org/files/docs/meltzer/stepre88.pdf.

42. Rockoff, *Drastic Measures*, 205.

43. For an overview of the wage–price control dynamic since World War II, see Craufurd D. Goodwin, ed., *Exhortation and Controls: The Search for a Wage-Price Policy 1945–1971* (Washington, DC: Brookings Institution, 1975).

44. "Nixon's Convenient Vacuum," *Time*, February 21, 1972, 22.

45. Wells, *Economist in an Uncertain World*, 79.

46. From the start, Burns pushed back on any controls on interest, arguing that money markets were competitive and well functioning and not contributing to inflation. Congress balked at the perceived hypocrisy but did little. Burns did impose limits on dividends, capping them at 4 percent higher than previous years or a quarter of total earnings.

47. In 1971, the total expenses of the Federal Reserve Banks amounted to $405,700,561, including expenses of all of the regional reserve banks. *58th Annual Report, 1971*, Board of Governors of the Federal Reserve System, 252, table 7, Federal Reserve Bank of St. Louis, FRASER, https://fraser.stlouisfed.org/title/annual-report-board-governors-federal-reserve -system-117/1971-2426. For the cost of the price control program, see Rockoff, *Drastic Measures*, 221–22.

48. Personal Consumption Expenditures (PCE) Excluding Food and Energy (Chain-Type Price Index) data, Federal Reserve Bank of St. Louis, https://fred.stlouisfed.org/graph/?g=1aeeU.

49. Real Gross Domestic Product data, Federal Reserve Bank of St. Louis, https://fred.stlouisfed.org/graph/?g=1aeeR.

50. Arthur F. Burns, "Inflation: The Fundamental Challenge to Stabilization Policies," Seventeenth Annual Monetary Conference of the American Bankers Association, Federal Reserve Bank of St. Louis, FRASER, https://fraser.stlouisfed.org/title/statements-speeches-arthur-f-burns-449/inflation-fundamental-challenge-stabilization-policies-7953/fulltext.

51. Wells, *Economist in an Uncertain World*, 98.

52. Wells, *Economist in an Uncertain World*, 101.

53. Wells, *Economist in an Uncertain World*, 101.

54. "The 1972 Midyear Review of the Economy," *Hearings before the Joint Economic Committee, Congress of the United States*, 92nd Cong., 2nd Sess. (1972), https://www.jec.senate.gov/reports/92nd%20Congress/The%201972%20Midyear%20Review%20of%20the%20Economy%20(580).pdf.

55. "Interview with Andrew F. Brimmer," 176.

56. Rockoff, *Drastic Measures*, 214.

57. They ended 1973 by jumping 14.5 percent. Wells, *Economist in an Uncertain World*, 110.

58. Stein, *Presidential Economics*, 186.

59. Rockoff, *Drastic Measures*, 246.

8: Crisis Architect

1. Michael Lewis, *Liar's Poker: Rising through the Wreckage of Wall Street* (New York: Norton, 1989), 100.

2. Michael C. Jensen, *The Financiers: The World of the Great Wall Street Investment Banking Houses* (New York: Weybright and Talley, 1976), 8.

3. Lewis, *Liar's Poker*, 103.

4. William E. Simon, *A Time for Reflection: An Autobiography* (Washington, DC: Regnery, 2003), 67.

5. Simon, *Time for Reflection*, 66–72.

6. Simon, *Time for Reflection*, 4.

7. Simon did face meaningful personal adversity in this period, most prominently when his four-month-old baby, Timothy Charles, died from sudden infant death syndrome while in the care of Simon's mother-in-law. Simon, *Time for Reflection*, 26.

8. Simon, *Time for Reflection*, 21.

9. Simon, *Time for Reflection*, 2.

10. Simon, *Time for Reflection*, 53.

11. William E. Simon, *A Time for Truth* (New York: McGraw-Hill, 1978), 6.

12. On Simon's fundraising, see Ben A. Franklin, "Miss Woods's Gift List Links Donors to Corporations," *New York Times*, March 20, 1974, https://www.nytimes.com/1974/03/20/archives/miss-woodss-gift-list-links-donors-to-corporations-special-to-the.html. On vetting appointees, see Simon, *Time for Reflection*, 80–81.

13. In her history of the energy crisis, Meg Jacobs argues that Nixon's "market-oriented advisors" such as Simon consistently abhorred "New Deal–style controls" but were initially forced to act within the still-dominant New Deal consensus. Meg Jacobs, *Panic at the Pump: The Energy Crisis and the Transformation of American Politics in the 1970s* (New York: Hill and Wang, 2016), 31–32.

14. Simon, *Time for Reflection*, 5.

15. Simon, *Time for Reflection*, 51.

16. Simon, *Time for Reflection*, 61.

17. Simon, *Time for Reflection*, 72–74.

18. For example, Secretary of State William Rogers sent Nixon a memo in March 1972 on "the Impending Energy Crisis"; see "Memorandum from Secretary of State Rogers to President

Nixon," March 10, 1972, U.S. Department of State, Office of the Historian, https://history .state.gov/historicaldocuments/frus1969-76v36/d116. The Office of Emergency Preparedness issued a study titled "National Security Aspects of Alaskan Oil" in November 1971; see "Editorial Note," U.S. Department of State, Office of the Historian, https://history.state.gov /historicaldocuments/frus1969-76v36/d95.

19. Connally quoted in Jay Hakes, *Energy Crises: Nixon, Ford, Carter, and Hard Choices in the 1970s* (Norman: University of Oklahoma Press, 2021), 60.

20. Simon, *Time for Reflection*, 75.

21. Edwin L. Dale Jr., "Fight Is On over Oil Imports," *New York Times*, December 28, 1969, https://timesmachine.nytimes.com/timesmachine/1969/12/28/91296270.html?page Number=134.

22. John W. Frey and H. Chandler Ide, eds., *A History of the Petroleum Administration for War, 1941–1945* (Washington, DC: U.S. Government Printing Office, 1946), 1, https:// www.google.com/books/edition/A_History_of_the_Petroleum_Administration/KXc QqX6rLmAC?hl=en&gbpv=1.

23. David Painter, *Oil and the American Century: The Political Economy of U.S. Foreign Oil Policy, 1941–1954* (Baltimore, MD: Johns Hopkins University Press: 1986), 24–39, 97.

24. Richard H. K. Vietor, *Contrived Competition: Regulation and Deregulation in America* (Cambridge, MA: Belknap Press of Harvard University, 1994), 146–62.

25. Richard H. K. Vietor, *Energy Policy in America since 1945* (Cambridge, UK: Cambridge University Press, 2009), 115.

26. Hakes, *Energy Crises*, 36.

27. Hakes, *Energy Crises*, 18.

28. Vietor, *Energy Policy*, 194.

29. Hakes, *Energy Crises*, 78.

30. Hakes, *Energy Crises*, 64.

31. "Monthly Energy Review," U.S. Department of Energy, January 1977, 8–10, 2024, https:// www.eia.gov/totalenergy/data/monthly/archive/00357712.pdf.

32. Kissinger quoted in Hakes, *Energy Crises*, 54.

33. James Akins, "The Oil Crisis: This Time the Wolf Is Here," *Foreign Affairs*, April 1973, 469.

34. Akins quoted in Daniel Yergin, *The Prize: The Epic Quest for Oil, Money, and Power* (New York: Simon & Schuster, 1990), 572–73.

35. Jacobs, *Panic at the Pump*, 38.

36. Hakes, *Energy Crises*, 77.

37. Hakes, *Energy Crises*, 74.

38. Richard M. Nixon, Conversation with John A. Love, Alexander M. Haig, and others, Conversation 944-005, Taped Conversations, Richard Nixon Presidential Library, https://www .nixonlibrary.gov/white-house-tapes/944.

39. Hakes, *Energy Crises*, 81.

40. Yergin, *The Prize*, 585.

41. Stephen Wakefield, "The Fuel Crisis: An Energy Pearl Harbor," *Public Utilities Fortnightly*, December 6, 1973, 29–33.

42. Yergin, *The Prize*, 587.

43. Henry Kissinger, *Years of Upheaval* (New York: Simon & Schuster, 2011), 854.

44. Hakes, *Energy Crises*, 95.

45. Hakes, *Energy Crises*, 104.

46. Edward Cowan, "Love Quits Posts after A Shake-Up in Energy Agency," *New York Times*, December 4, 1973, https://www.nytimes.com/1973/12/04/archives/love-quits-posts-aftera shakeup-in-energy-agency-exczar-refuses-to.html.

47. Hakes, *Energy Crises*, 105.

48. Until May 1974, Simon held a dual appointment as head of the FEO and Deputy Treasury Secretary.

49. Statement of William E. Simon, *Federal Energy Administration, Hearings before a Subcommittee of the Committee on Government Operations, House of Representatives*, 93rd Cong., 1st Sess., on H.R. 11793 (December 10–11, 1973), 115–19.

50. Simon to Nixon, Subject: Energy Policy Framework (copy marked Bakke/draft, dated January 7, 1973), William Simon Papers 1, 1972–1977, Series IIIA, Special Collections and College Archives, Lafayette College: Drawer 13, Folder 22: FEO - Correspondence - White House: 1973–1974, https://archives.lafayette.edu/findingaids/simon-william-e-papers-1972-1977/.

51. Richard Nixon, "Address to the Nation about Policies to Deal with the Energy Shortages," November 7, 1973, The American Presidency Project, https://www.presidency.ucsb.edu/node/255503.

52. Jacobs, *Panic at the Pump*, 71.

53. Hakes, *Energy Crises*, 109.

54. Hakes, *Energy Crises*, 116–17.

55. Simon quoted in Edwin L. Dale Jr., "New Profit-Reducing Plan Would Keep Oil Incentive," *New York Times*, December 20, 1973, 30.

56. U.S. Energy Information Administration, Petroleum and Other Liquids, Landed Costs of Imported Crude by Area data, https://www.eia.gov/dnav/pet/pet_pri_land1_k_a.htm, and U.S. Energy Information Administration, Petroleum and Other Liquids, F.O.B. Costs of Imported Crude Oil by Area data, https://www.eia.gov/dnav/pet/pet_pri_imc1_k_m.htm.

57. Yergin, *The Prize*, 607.

58. Hakes, *Energy Crises*, 120.

59. Jacobs, *Panic at the Pump*, 91–93.

60. Simon, *Time for Truth*, 54.

61. Simon, *Time for Truth*, 53.

62. Hakes, *Energy Crises*, 123.

63. Hakes, *Energy Crises*, 124.

64. Hakes, *Energy Crises*, 130.

65. Some argued in the years following that prices should have been decontrolled in the midst of the global chaos, believing that higher prices of domestic producers would have incentivized additional American production. But energy producers in the United States and Canada were already pumping at capacity, and it would have taken years for new wells to come online, leaving Americans to pay record high prices. When decontrol did happen nearly seven years later, it triggered only modest exploration and drilling, and no significant sources of oil came online as a result. The opening of a pipeline to newly discovered oil fields in Alaska, already in development before the 1973 crisis began, was the only major event to bring online new reserves over the following decade.

66. U.S. Energy Information Administration, Petroleum and Other Liquids, Landed Costs of Imported Crude by Area data; and U.S. Energy Information Administration, Petroleum and Other Liquids, F.O.B. Costs of Imported Crude Oil by Area data.

67. Alan A. Tait and David Morgan, "Gasoline Taxation in Selected OECD Countries, 1970–79," *International Monetary Fund Staff Papers* 27, no. 2 (1980), https://www.elibrary.imf.org/view/journals/024/1980/002/article-A005-en.xml.

68. Hakes, *Energy Crises*, 129.

69. Simon quoted in Jacobs, *Panic at the Pump*, 113–14.

70. Simon, *Time for Truth*, 56.

71. In 1981, after leaving government service, Simon agreed to become the President of Nixon's foundation. In a speech celebrating the opening of the Richard Nixon Presidential Library, he spared no praise in commemorating the former President: "He left America leadership of character. Richard Nixon may have been the last casualty of Vietnam. Yet, he did not permit the tragedies that befell him to destroy his presidency or himself." Simon, forever loyal, was happy to collaborate in the attempted rewrite of Nixon's legacy. Simon, "Richard Nixon Presidential Library Dedication, Yorba Linda, California: 1990 (July 19)," box 7, folder 26, series VI, William Simon Papers 2, 1964–1971 and 1977–1992, Special

Collections and College Archives, Lafayette College, https://archives.lafayette.edu/findin gaids/simon-william-e-papers-1964-1971-1977-1992/.

72. Simon, *Time for Reflection*, 117.

73. Simon, *Time for Reflection*, 119.

74. By the summer, motorists were paying the peak price of fifty-six cents per gallon of gasoline, and global oil prices remained high, at thirteen dollars a barrel. Hakes, *Energy Crises*, 134–35.

75. Hakes, *Energy Crises*, 148.

76. Simon, *Time for Reflection*, 138.

77. Alan Greenspan, *The Age of Turbulence: Adventures in a New World* (New York: Penguin, 2008), 63.

78. William E. Simon, "Big Government and Our Economic Woes," *Reader's Digest*, April 1975, 18; Kim Phillips-Fein, *Fear City: New York's Fiscal Crisis and the Rise of Austerity Politics* (New York: Metropolitan Books, 2017); Simon, *A Time for Action* (New York: McGraw Hill, 1980), 95–96, 278–79.

79. Simon, *Time for Reflection*, 138–39.

80. Sebastian Mallaby, *The Man Who Knew: The Life and Times of Alan Greenspan* (New York: Penguin, 2017), 176.

81. "Strategic Petroleum Reserve Origins," U.S. Office of Cybersecurity, Energy, and Security, https://www.energy.gov/ceser/spr-origins.

82. *Project Independence Report*, Federal Energy Administration, November 1974, 58, https:// babel.hathitrust.org/cgi/pt?id=mdp.39015095120302&seq=86&q1=stockpile.

83. Prepared statement by William Simon, January 22, 1975, printed in *The Energy Crisis and Proposed Solutions: Panel Discussions before the House Committee on Ways and Means* (Washington, DC: U.S. Government Printing Office, 1975), 27.

84. *Government and the Nation's Resources: Report of the National Commission on Supplies and Shortages* (Washington, DC: U.S. Government Printing Office, December 1976), x, 51, 132. For Greenspan's approval of the document, see Greenspan to Dr. Donald B. Rice, December 13, 1976, U.S. Council of Economic Advisers during the Ford Administration, Part 1: Alan Greenspan Files, Correspondence, 1974–1977, Federal Agency Correspondence (Jul 1, 1975–Dec 31, 1976): Folder: Reports and Statistics on National Stockpiling Program, 5, https://pq-static-content.proquest.com/collateral/media2/documents/103345.pdf.

85. Hakes, *Energy Crises*, 162.

86. For more on the history of the SPR, see Bruce A. Beaubouef, *The Strategic Petroleum Reserve: U.S. Energy Security and Oil Politics, 1975–2005* (College Station: Texas A&M University Press, 2007); and Robert Bamberger, "The Strategic Petroleum Reserve: History, Perspectives, and Issues," *Congressional Research Service Report* (December 2009), RL33341, https:// apps.dtic.mil/sti/pdfs/ADA529737.pdf.

87. Hakes, *Energy Crises*, 308.

88. Simon, *Time for Action*, 109.

89. Alan Blinder estimates that the first oil shock increased retail energy prices by 26 percent and contributed 1.5 to 2 percentage points to inflation over a six-month period, while the second oil shock increased retail energy prices by 56 percent and contributed 5 to 6 percentage points to inflation over a fifteen-month period. Expressing the costs in terms of an "oil tax"— i.e., the amount of extra spending that would have occurred due to increased oil prices if consumption had remained constant—Blinder estimates that "the first OPEC shock amounted to a levy of about 2 1/2% of gross national product while the second shock amounted to about 6 1/2%." Alan S. Blinder, "The Anatomy of Double-Digit Inflation in the 1970s," in *Inflation: Causes and Effects*, ed. Robert E. Hall (Chicago: University of Chicago Press, 1983), 271.

90. The increase in crude oil imports was 101 percent (2.380 billion barrels in 1979 versus 1.184 billion barrels in 1973). It began dropping sharply in 1980, returning to 1.273 billion by 1982. "Petroleum and Other Liquids: U.S. Imports of Crude Oil" dataset, U.S. Energy Information Administration, https://www.eia.gov/dnav/pet/hist/LeafHandler.ashx ?n=PET&s=MCRIMUS1&f=M.

91. Beaubouef, *The Strategic Petroleum Reserve*, 97.

92. World Bank, "Energy Use (kg of oil equivalent per capita)—United States," https://data
.worldbank.org/indicator/EG.USE.PCAP.KG.OE?locations=US.

93. Jacobs, *Panic at the Pump*, 208.

94. Jimmy Carter, "Energy and National Goals: Address to the Nation," July 15, 1979, Jimmy
Carter Presidential Library (hereafter JCPL), https://www.jimmycarterlibrary.gov/the-cart
ers/selected-speeches/jimmy-carter-energy-and-national-goals-address-to-the-nation.

95. Philip K. Verleger Jr., "The U.S. Petroleum Crisis of 1979," Brookings Institution, 1979, 467,
https://www.brookings.edu/wp-content/uploads/1979/06/1979b_bpea_verleger_okun_law
rence_sims_hall_nordhaus.pdf.

96. Hakes, *Energy Crises*, 317.

97. Simon, *Time for Action*, 111.

98. World Bank, "Energy Use (kg of oil equivalent per capita)—United States."

99. Hakes, *Energy Crises*, 333–34.

THE LIBERTARIAN FANTASY
9: The Fight for Discretion

1. Transcript of swearing-in ceremony for Nancy H. Teeters, September 18, 1978, 2:30 p.m., Roo-
sevelt Room, the White House, Washington DC, 5, subgroup IV: Board of Governors - Federal
Reserve System, 1978–84, box 2, folder: Appointment Papers, 1978, Nancy H. Teeters Papers,
Oberlin College (hereafter NHTP).

2. "Combatting Role Prejudice and Sex Discrimination: Findings of the American Economic
Association Committee on the Status of Women in the Economics Profession," *American
Economic Review* 63, no. 5 (1973): 1049–61, http://www.jstor.org/stable/1813937.

3. Author interview with Ann Teeters Johnson, January 25, 2024.

4. Nancy H. Teeters to W. Dean Wolfe, February 20, 1979, subgroup IV, box 3, folder: FRB
Chron File, 1979, NHTP.

5. "Interview with Nancy H. Teeters," Federal Reserve Board Oral History Project, 2008,
19–20, https://www.federalreserve.gov/aboutthefed/files/nancy-h-teeters-interview-200810
25.pdf.

6. Office of Staff Secretary, "Memo to the President," series: Presidential Files, folder: 6/30/78
[2], container 83, JCPL, https://www.jimmycarterlibrary.gov/sites/default/files/pdf_documents
/digital_library/sso/148878/83/SSO_148878_083_09.pdf.

7. "Business People," *New York Times*, July 12, 1978, https://www.nytimes.com/1978/07/12/ar
chives/business-people-fed-chief-could-gain-an-ally-in-mrs-teeters.html.

8. Nancy Teeters, interview by Lynn S. Fox and Winthrop P. Hambley, October 25, 2008,
transcript, 15–17, https://www.federalreserve.gov/aboutthefed/files/nancy-h-teeters-inter
view-20081025.pdf.

9. Author interview with Ann Teeters Johnson, January 25, 2024.

10. Bill Neikirk, "Surging Prime Raises Fears of New Recession," *Chicago Tribune*, December 11,
1980, C9.

11. Spot Crude Oil Price: West Texas Intermediate data, Federal Reserve Bank of St. Louis,
https://fred.stlouisfed.org/series/WTISPLC.

12. For more, see *Economic Report of the President, 1979* (Washington, DC: U.S. Government Printing Office, 1979), Federal Reserve Bank of St. Louis, FRASER, https://fraser.stlouisfed.org/files
/docs/publications/ERP/1979/ERP_1979.pdf; and *Economic Report of the President, 1980* (Washington, DC: U.S. Government Printing Office, 1980), The American Presidency Project, https://
www.presidency.ucsb.edu/sites/default/files/books/presidential-documents-archive-guidebook
/the-economic-report-of-the-president-truman-1947-obama-2017/1980.pdf.

13. For an overview of this debate, see Blinder, "The Anatomy of Double-Digit Inflation"; Alan
S. Blinder and Jeremy B. Rudd, "The Supply-Shock Explanation of the Great Stagflation
Revisited," in *The Great Inflation: The Rebirth of Modern Central Banking*, ed. Michael D. Bordo
and Athanasios Orphanides (Chicago: University of Chicago Press, 2008); and DeLong,
"America's Peacetime Inflation."

14. In private correspondence with a Congressman, Teeters bemoaned the absence of institutions to help manage price instability, particularly when it came to labor relations. Contrasting America with West Germany and Japan, she wrote: "What the United States lacks is a mechanism for equitably distributing the loss in real income." Nancy H. Teeters to Rep. John LaFalce, March 11, 1980, subgroup IV, series 4, box 4, folder: FRB Chron File, 1980, NHTP.

15. Teeters to LaFalce, March 11, 1980.

16. See, for example, Nancy Teeters, "Statement before the House Budget Committee's Task Force on the Budget Process," November 13, 1979, Federal Reserve Bank of St. Louis, FRASER, https://fraser.stlouisfed.org/title/943/item/36631.

17. Peter T. Kilborn, "Consumer, Resigned to Inflation, Is Learning New Ways to Hedge," *New York Times*, April 22, 1979, https://www.nytimes.com/1979/04/22/archives/consumer -resigned-to-inflation-is-learning-new-ways-to-hedge.html.

18. Philip K. Verleger Jr., "The U.S. Petroleum Crisis of 1979," Brookings Institution, 1979, 467, https://www.brookings.edu/wp-content/uploads/1979/06/1979b_bpea_verleger_okun_law rence_sims_hall_nordhaus.pdf.

19. William Greider, *Secrets of the Temple: How the Federal Reserve Runs the Country* (New York: Simon & Schuster, 1989), 46.

20. The New York Fed President is unique among regional Reserve Bank Presidents in holding a permanent voting seat on the Federal Open Market Committee (hereafter FOMC).

21. Greg Conderacci and Richard F. Janssen, "Balm for Business: Volcker's Nomination as Chairman of the Fed Is Being Widely Hailed," *Wall Street Journal*, July 26, 1979. For details on the confirmation hearing, see Nomination of Paul A. Volcker, *Hearing before the Committee on Banking, Housing, and Urban Affairs*, United States Senate, 96th Cong., 1st Sess. (July 30, 1979), Federal Reserve Bank of St. Louis, FRASER, https://fraser.stlouisfed.org/title/ nomination-paul-a-volcker-272.

22. Steven Rattner, "Volcker's Rate Policy: 6 Weeks of Sharp Rises," *New York Times*, September 24, 1979.

23. Merrill Sheils and Rich Thomas, "Heading the Fed with Reserve," *Newsweek*, September 17, 1979, 78.

24. Steven Rattner, "A Look inside Paul Volcker's Fed," *New York Times*, May 3, 1981, F1.

25. Tim Barker and Chris Hughes, "Bigger than Penn Central: The Financial Crisis of 1970 and the Origins of the Federal Reserve's Systemic Guarantee," *Capitalism* 5, no. 1 (Winter 2024), https://muse.jhu.edu/pub/56/article/934538/pdf.

26. FOMC Minutes, August 14, 1979, 21.

27. "Fed, in a 4–3 Vote, Tightens Credit Reins by Lifting Discount Rate to Record 11%," *Wall Street Journal*, September 19, 1979; Robert A. Bennett, "Reserve Board, by 4–3, Raises Rate on Loans to Banks to Record 11%," *New York Times*, September 19, 1979.

28. Teeters, interview by Lynn S. Fox and Winthrop P. Hambley, 44.

29. Volcker to Ehrman V. Giustina, July 14, 1980, Chronological Correspondence: July 1980, box 2, item c22, Paul A. Volcker Papers, Federal Reserve Bank of St. Louis, https://fraser .stlouisfed.org/archival-collection/paul-a-volcker-papers-5297/chronological-correspon dence-588381?page=125.

30. In addition to the interest rate that banks lent to one another in the overnight federal funds market, the Fed also closely tracked the level of borrowed reserves and the rate on Treasuries.

31. For years, the Fed had been tracking the relationship between the monetary aggregates, the total reserve aggregates in the banking system, and short-term interest rates, including the federal funds rate. In 1976, when Volcker was President of the New York Fed and Burns had been chair, the board had debated whether to make moderate, steady growth in the money supply the primary goal of Fed monetary policy. The board understood that putting near exclusive emphasis on money growth would take a cue from monetarist policy frameworks, even if it didn't embrace the monetarist imperative to constrain the central bank to a consistent rate of growth.

The FOMC in 1976 rejected the idea, partially driven by Burns' skepticism. But it wasn't just Burns who didn't want to do it. In the discussions, Volcker had also been opposed. In

September of that year, he said the monetarist proposal for the Fed to exclusively target aggregate bank reserves as a way of controlling monetary growth was a step too far. Such a move
was based on inconclusive empirical evidence of the relationships and would introduce far
too much volatility into markets. "[T]he relationship between money and reserve aggregates,
particularly in the short run, appears no more reliable than the relationship between interest
rates and money," he said. It might be possible to improve the central bank's implementation
tactics, but Volcker did not "expect any startling breakthroughs."

See the FOMC Minutes, March 29, 1976; William L. Silber, *Volcker: The Triumph of Persistence* (London: Bloomsbury Press, 2012), 159; Paul Volcker, "The Contributions and Limitations of 'Monetary' Analysis," remarks before the American Economic Association and the
American Finance Association, Atlantic City, NJ, September 16, 1976; Paul Volcker, "The
Role of Monetary Targets in an Age of Inflation," *Journal of Monetary Economics* 4, no. 2 (April
1978): 330; and Paul Volcker, "A Broader Role for the Monetary Targets," remarks before the
Toronto Bond Traders Association, February 22, 1977, https://www.newyorkfed.org/mediali
brary/media/research/quarterly_review/1977v2/v2n1article6.pdf.

32. The next day, Volcker flew to Belgrade for an IMF conference on monetary policy. On the
plane ride over, Volcker told Treasury Secretary Bill Miller and CEA Chair Charles Schultze
that he was considering shifting the monetary-policy operational framework. The two were
resistant to the idea, fearing that interest rates could rise as high as 20 percent if the Fed were
not guiding them.

While in Belgrade, Volcker sat through a speech by Arthur Burns titled "The Agony of
Central Banking," in which Burns bemoaned the limited power of central banks to exercise
monetary control because of accelerating political pressure. Volcker, restless to chart a different path, returned to Washington early, landing on October 2 and igniting rumors in
financial markets that he might resign. Silber, *Volcker*, 164–69.

33. The primary monetary aggregate measures in use in 1979 were called M-1, M-2, and M-3.
M-1 measured the narrowest definition of money—currency in circulation, traveler's checks,
and checkable deposit accounts; M-2 included everything in M-1, plus savings deposits, small
time deposits, and other cash-like items such as overnight repurchase agreements; M-3 included everything in M-2 plus large time deposits, and other cash-like items such as term
repurchase agreements. The definitions of the various monetary aggregates have changed
over time, especially in response to the introduction of new cash-like financial products.

34. The initial Axilrod and Sternlight memo makes clear they understood that the new procedures would entail meaningful fluctuations in the Fed Funds rate. They noted, however, that
the FOMC might have placed some constraint on how widely it was allowed to fluctuate. The
FOMC chose such a broad band that it was effectively allowed to float.

35. "Interview with Stephen H. Axilrod," Federal Reserve Board Oral History Project, October 22,
2008, transcript, 34, https://www.federalreserve.gov/aboutthefed/files/stephen-h-axilrod-inter
view-20081022.pdf.

36. Greider, *Secrets of the Temple*, 106.

37. Stephen Axilrod and Peter Sternlight, "Proposal for Reserve Aggregates as Guide to Open
Market Operations," memorandum to the Federal Open Market Committee, October 4,
1979, https://www.federalreserve.gov/monetarypolicy/files/FOMC19791004Memo01.pdf.

38. Stephen Axilrod, *Inside the Fed: Monetary Policy and Its Management, Martin through Greenspan
to Bernanke* (Cambridge: MIT Press, 2009), 67 and 81.

39. "Interview with Stephen H. Axilrod," 32.

40. "Under the new system, we could say what we were doing was concentrating on the monetary aggregates," she later said of her vote. "It was perfectly obvious to me that if you set
the money growth too low, that would send interest rates up. That was never in doubt. The
problem with targeting the fed funds rate is that you had to set it. This did let us step back a
bit." Greider, *Secrets of the Temple*, 111.

41. Greider, *Secrets of the Temple*, 112.

42. Greider, *Secrets of the Temple*, 105–6.

43. FOMC Minutes, October 6, 1979, 43.

44. David E. Lindsey, Athanasios Orphanides, and Robert H. Rasche, "The Reform of October 1979: How It Happened and Why," Finance and Economics Discussion Series, Divisions of Research & Statistics and Monetary Affairs, Board of Governors of the Federal Reserve, February 2005, 20–21, https://www.federalreserve.gov/pubs/feds/2005/200502/200502pap.pdf.

45. Axilrod and Sternlight, "Proposal for Reserve Aggregates."

46. FOMC Minutes, October 6, 1979, 22.

47. FOMC Minutes, October 6, 1979, 14, 18.

48. FOMC Minutes, October 6, 1979, 17.

49. FOMC Minutes, October 6, 1979, 8.

50. FOMC Minutes, October 6, 1979, 50.

51. Author interview with Ann Teeters Johnson, January 25, 2024.

52. Greider, *Secrets of the Temple*, 125.

53. FOMC Conference Call, transcript, October 22, 1979, https://www.federalreserve.gov/monetarypolicy/files/FOMC19791022confcall.pdf.

54. FOMC Minutes, January 9, 1980, 35.

55. FOMC Minutes, November 18, 1980, 51–52. Also see Volcker private correspondence (from NHTP files), Volcker to Paul Armington, April 29, 1981.

56. FOMC Minutes, December 21, 1982, 40.

57. FOMC Minutes, November 18, 1980, 31.

58. Michael A. Urquhart and Marillyn A. Hewson, "Unemployment Continued to Rise in 1982 as Recession Deepened," *Monthly Labor Review* 106, no. 2 (February 1983): 3–12.

59. For a survey of various approaches to estimating output losses, see Robert J. Tetlow, "How Large Is the Output Cost of Disinflation?," Finance and Economics Discussion Series, Board of Governors of the Federal Reserve, 2022-079, November 2022, 5, table 1, https://www.federalreserve.gov/econres/feds/how-large-is-the-output-cost-of-disinflation.htm.

60. FOMC Minutes, July 7, 1981, 46–47.

61. The Reagan cuts brought the top rate to 50 percent in 1982, and it had been above this level since 1932. "Historical Highest Marginal Income Tax Rates," Tax Policy Center, May 11, 2023, https://www.taxpolicycenter.org/statistics/historical-highest-marginal-income-tax-rates.

62. William Greider, "The Education of David Stockman," *The Atlantic*, December 1981, https://www.theatlantic.com/magazine/archive/1981/12/the-education-of-david-stockman/305760/.

63. Greider, *Secrets of the Temple*, 355–56.

64. Teeters to Mrs. Ronald J. Koch, March 16, 1982, subgroup IV, series 4, box 4, folder: FRB Chron File, 1982, NHTP.

65. FOMC Minutes, November 17, 1981, 24.

66. Gallup Poll #1980-1159G, and Gallup Poll #1200G.

67. Daniel Yergin and Joseph Stanislaw, *The Commanding Heights: The Battle for the World Economy* (New York: Simon & Schuster, 2002), 347.

68. "Man Seized at Federal Reserve," *Washington Post*, December 8, 1981, B7.

69. FOMC Minutes, February 2, 1982, 92–93.

70. FOMC Minutes, February 1, 1982, 102. Teeters' sophisticated, empirically minded approach to economics informed her broad support for loosening policy in February 1982. The first econometric models were being developed while she was completing her graduate work in economics, and she brought them to bear in her many jobs in Washington before the Fed. She saw them as "valuable tools" in the pursuit of economic goals. "[T]hey are tools and not replacements for judgments," she wrote in private correspondence in early 1979. Teeters to W. Dean Wolfe, February 20, 1979, subgroup IV, series 4, box 3, folder: FRB Chron File, 1979, NHTP.

71. "Record of Policy Actions of the Federal Open Market Committee," FOMC, February 1, 1982, 11, https://www.federalreserve.gov/monetarypolicy/files/fomcropa19820202.pdf.

72. Greider, *Secrets of the Temple*, 446.
73. Teeters dissented on the monetary targets the committee was setting for the full year 1982. FOMC Minutes, February 1–2, 1982, 107.
74. Burns, *Milton Friedman*, 420–21.
75. Greider, *Secrets of the Temple*, 446. According to the historian Allan Meltzer, privately, Volcker was also growing doubtful about the effectiveness of the monetary aggregates. Because he did not wish for interest rates to decrease, he took no action. Allan Meltzer, *A History of the Federal Reserve*, vol. 2, book 2, *1970–1986* (Chicago: University of Chicago Press, 2010), 1091, 1123.
76. Bill Neikirk, "Fed Maverick Says Tight Money Ill-Advised," *Chicago Tribune*, February 22, 1982, D9.
77. FOMC Minutes, May 18, 1982, 27.
78. FOMC Minutes, May 18, 1982, 45.
79. Greider, *Secrets of the Temple*, 493.
80. Personal Consumption Expenditures: Chain-Type Price Index data, Federal Reserve Bank of St. Louis, https://fred.stlouisfed.org/series/PCEPI#.
81. Meltzer, *A History of the Federal Reserve*, vol. 2, book 2, *1970–1986*, 1109.
82. Meltzer, *A History of the Federal Reserve*, vol. 2, book 2, 1112.
83. Greider, *Secrets of the Temple*, 510.
84. FOMC Minutes, August 24, 1982, 26.
85. FOMC Minutes, August 24, 1982, 29
86. FOMC Minutes, October 5, 1982, 19
87. FOMC Minutes, October 5, 1982, 50.
88. Greider, *Secrets of the Temple*, 467.
89. Author interview with Ann Teeters Johnson, January 25, 2024.
90. Paul Vitello, "Nancy H. Teeters, First Woman on Federal Reserve Board, Dies at 84," *New York Times*, November 26, 2014, https://www.nytimes.com/2014/11/26/business/nancy-h-teeters-first-woman-on-federal-reserve-board-dies-at-84.html.
91. It is not clear whether Teeters herself saw this decision as a mistake in retrospect. The Fed could have raised rates aggressively using its existing tools. Volcker had the votes on the FOMC and Board of Governors for more rate rises, and some of Teeters' allies were already moving toward supporting Volcker's restrictive policy ahead of the adoption of the new operating procedures. At the same time, Teeters shared in the belief that a jolt to markets could help in the effort to fight inflation, ultimately causing her to cast her vote with her colleagues in support. Silber, *Volcker*, 172, 196–97.
92. "Moreover, even if the Federal Reserve were to adopt a looser monetary policy so as to prompt lenders to lend at lower interest rates, those lower rates would be a fleeting phenomenon. Private sector borrowers, attracted by the lower interest rates, would collide in the market with the federal government attempting to borrow huge amounts of money to finance the large federal deficit. As a result, interest rates would be bid up to record levels; savers and other lenders simply would not be willing to lend all the money that the federal government and private sector borrowers would want unless they were offered the inducement of very high rates of return." Teeters to Johnny C. Fang, May 13, 1982, subgroup IV, series 4, box 4, folder: FRB Chron File, 1982, NHTP.
93. FOMC Meeting Minutes, April 22, 1980.
94. Teeter to Dean Wolfe, February 20, 1979, subgroup IV, series 4, box 3, folder: FRB Chron File, 1979, NHTP. Emphasis in original.

10: Saving Silicon

1. Tom Wolfe, "The Tinkerings of Robert Noyce," *Esquire*, December 1983, 359–60.
2. Larry D. Browning and Judy D. Shelter, *Sematech: Saving the U.S. Semiconductor Industry* (College Station: Texas A&M University Press, 2000), 138.
3. Leslie Berlin, *The Man behind the Microchip* (New York: Oxford University Press, 2005), 21–22.

4. Berlin, *Man behind the Microchip*, 21–23; Wolfe, "Tinkerings of Robert Noyce," 353–54.

5. "Robert Noyce, Co-inventor of Microchip, Dies at 62," *Sacramento Bee*, June 4, 1990.

6. Berlin, *Man behind the Microchip*, 58–59.

7. Fairchild could make the purchase at any point before Fairchild Semiconductor had three successive years of net earnings greater than $300,000. If the parent company waited more than three years but bought within seven years, the company would have had to pay $5 million for Fairchild Semiconductor. Leslie Berlin, "Entrepreneurship and the Rise of Silicon Valley: The Career of Robert Noyce, 1956–1990" (PhD diss., Stanford University, 2001), 59.

8. In 1959, an engineer at Texas Instruments, Jack Kilby, simultaneously invented the integrated circuit. Kilby created the first working prototype using germanium, while Noyce developed a more practical version using silicon a few months later. That became the industry standard. Kilby eventually won the Nobel Prize for the invention, but it was awarded after Noyce's death. In 1964, the patent office split the claims for ownership between Texas Instruments and Fairchild, who eventually agreed to share the ownership. Berlin, *Man behind the Microchip*, 139–40.

9. The Army Ballistic Research Laboratory funded the University of Pennsylvania's 1946 development of the Electronic Numerical Integrator and Calculator (ENIAC) in 1946. As the first programmable computer, ENIAC was a breakthrough but operated without semiconductors. On this and other details, see Congressional Research Service, *Semiconductors: U.S. Industry, Global Competition, and Federal Policy*, 2020, 47, https://sgp.fas.org/crs/misc/R46581 .pdf.

10. The US government funded roughly half of all semiconductor research and development between 1958 and 1970, about $500 million or $5 billion today. Calculations from U.S. Department of Commerce, *Report on U.S. Semiconductor Industry, 1979* (Washington, DC: U.S. Government Printing Office, 1979), https://books.google.com/books?id=ykDvSrbZI-oC&p rintsec=frontcover&source=gbs_ge_summary_r&cad=0#v=onepage&q&f=false; *Semiconductors: U.S. Industry, Global Competition, and Federal Policy*, 47; and Berlin, "Entrepreneurship and the Rise of Silicon Valley," 82.

11. Berlin, *Man behind the Microchip*, 130.

12. Harry Sello quoted in Berlin, "Entrepreneurship and the Rise of Silicon Valley," 127.

13. Berlin, *Man behind the Microchip*, 130; Berlin, "Entrepreneurship and the Rise of Silicon Valley," 88.

14. *Semiconductors: U.S. Industry, Global Competition, and Federal Policy*, 47.

15. Berlin, "Entrepreneurship and the Rise of Silicon Valley," 88.

16. Berlin, "Entrepreneurship and the Rise of Silicon Valley," 161–62.

17. By 1963, fewer than 10 percent of sales were "directly contracted by the government." Berlin, "Entrepreneurship and the Rise of Silicon Valley," 125, quote at 126.

18. Chris Miller, *Chip War: The Fight for the World's Most Critical Technology* (New York: Simon & Schuster, 2022), 29.

19. Wolfe, "Tinkerings of Robert Noyce," 360.

20. Berlin, *Man behind the Microchip*, 190–91.

21. For an ethnographic analysis of the dynamics of consensus-oriented decision-making, see James R. Barker, "Tightening the Iron Cage: Concertive Control in Self-Managing Teams," *Administrative Science Quarterly* 38, no. 3 (1993): 408–37.

22. Berlin, *Man behind the Microchip*, 158.

23. Berlin, *Man behind the Microchip*, 158, 198.

24. By the time Noyce left in 1968, Fairchild had plants in Hong Kong, South Korea, Australia, Mexico, and the Navajo Nation. Because of its focus on cutting-edge chips, Intel had an above-average share of domestic employment. By 1974, however, the company employed 600 semiconductor production workers in California and 1,000 in Malaysia. "Intel Closes Two Plants in California for Week Due to Slowing Business," *Wall Street Journal*, September 4, 1974, 26; and Ramon C. Sevilla, "Employment Practices and Industrial Restructuring: A Case

Study of the Semiconductor Industry in Silicon Valley, 1955–1991" (PhD diss., University of California, Los Angeles, 1992).

25. Berlin, "Entrepreneurship and the Rise of Silicon Valley," 162.
26. World Bank national accounts data and OECD National Accounts data files, GDP Growth (annual %) - Japan, https://data.worldbank.org/indicator/NY.GDP.MKTP.KD.ZG?end=19 95&locations=JP&start=1961.
27. Andrew C. McKevitt, *Consuming Japan: Popular Culture and the Globalizing of 1980s America* (Chapel Hill: University of North Carolina Press, 2017), 23.
28. United States Department of Defense, *Report of the Defense Science Board Task Force on Semiconductor Dependency, February 1987*, 5, https://apps.dtic.mil/sti/pdfs/ADA178284.pdf; Larry D. Browning, Janice M. Beyer, and Judy C. Shetler, "Building Cooperation in a Competitive Industry: SEMATECH and the Semiconductor Industry," *Academy of Management Journal* 38, no. 1 (February 1995): 113.
29. Douglas Frantz, "U.S. Banks Pushed off List of Largest 25," *Los Angeles Times*, July 19, 1988, 3, https://www.latimes.com/archives/la-xpm-1988-07-19-fi-6035-story.html; Jonathan P. Hicks, "Inland, Nippon Sign Pact," *New York Times*, March 24, 1987, https://www.nytimes.com/1987/03/24/business/inland-nippon-sign-pact.html.
30. "1985: Trade in Goods with Japan," United States Census Bureau, 2024, https://www.census.gov/foreign-trade/balance/c5880.html#1985; Dominick Salvatore, "The Japanese Trade Challenge and the U.S. Response: Addressing the Structural Causes of the Bilateral Trade Imbalance," Economic Policy Institute, 1990, 10, https://files.epi.org/page/-/old/studies/japanese_trade-1990.pdf.
31. Gene Bylinsky, "The Japanese Spies in Silicon Valley," *Fortune*, February 27, 1978.
32. Berlin, *Man behind the Microchip*, 264.
33. Tom Nicholas, *VC: An American History* (Cambridge, MA: Harvard University Press, 2019), 173–75.
34. Nicholas, *VC*, 177–78.
35. Tom Redburn and Robert Magnuson, "Stung by Tax Bill, Electronics Firms Seek Broader Political Base," *Los Angeles Times*, November 15, 1981.
36. Redburn and Magnuson, "Stung by Tax Bill."
37. Robert S. Walters, ed., *Talking Trade: U.S. Policy in International Perspective* (New York: Routledge, 1993).
38. Browning and Shetler, *Sematech*, 12–13. Noyce is quoted in Berlin, "Entrepreneurship and the Rise of Silicon Valley," 286.
39. Gregory J. Benzmiller, "Assessing the Success of Dual Use Programs: The Case of DARPA's Relationship with SEMATECH—Quiet Contributions to Success, Silenced Partner, or Both" (PhD diss., University of Denver, 2011), 51.
40. Benzmiller, "Assessing the Success of Dual Use Programs," 51.
41. Jeff Bingaman, *Breakdown: Lessons for a Congress in Crisis* (Albuquerque: University of New Mexico Press, 2022), 65.
42. Berlin, *Man behind the Microchip*, 270.
43. Walters, *Talking Trade*.
44. Robert M. Uriu, *Clinton and Japan: The Impact of Revisionism on U.S. Trade Policy* (New York: Oxford University Press, 2009).
45. Those tariffs endured in some form for four years until George H. W. Bush's administration finally eliminated them. Douglas A. Irwin, "Trade Politics and the Semiconductor Industry," in *The Political Economy of American Trade Policy*, ed. Anne O. Krueger (Chicago: National Bureau of Economic Research/University of Chicago Press, 1996), 12–13, https://www.nber.org/system/files/chapters/c8703/c8703.pdf.
46. "Semiconductor Industry Association Proposal for Structuring a Healthy World Semiconductor Trading System," Semiconductor Industry Association memo, December 2, 1985, https://www.reaganlibrary.gov/public/2024-01/40-155-12007440-OA'12246-011-2023.pdf.

47. Douglas A. Irwin and Peter J. Klenow, "High Tech R&D Subsidies: Estimating the Effects of Sematech," *Journal of International Economics* 40 (1996): 326.

48. "Memorandum for Chairman, Defense Science Board," December 3, 1985, Office of the Under Secretary of Defense, printed in *Report of the Defense Science Board*, 96.

49. Louise Kehoe, "Technology: Natural Leader with a National Purpose—the Accomplishments of the Late Robert Noyce, Pioneer of the US Semiconductor Industry," *Financial Times*, June 12, 1990, 20.

50. Kyle Pope, "Sematech Opens with High Hopes," *Austin American Statesman*, November 16, 1988.

51. Berlin, *Man behind the Microchip*, 289.

52. Berlin, *Man behind the Microchip*, 289.

53. Janice M. Beyer and Larry D. Browning, "Transforming an Industry in Crisis: Charisma, Routinization, and Supportive Cultural Leadership," *Leadership Quarterly* 10, no. 3 (Autumn 1999): 492.

54. Beyer and Browning, "Transforming an Industry in Crisis," 498.

55. "Lessons Learned from SEMATECH," United States General Accounting Office, 1992, 5, https://www.gao.gov/assets/rced-92-283.pdf; Peter Grindley, David C. Mowery, and Brian Silverman, "SEMATECH and Collaborative Research: Lessons in the Design of High-Technology Consortia," *Journal of Policy Analysis and Management* 13, no. 4 (Autumn 1994): 730.

56. Browning and Shetler, *Sematech*, 100.

57. Berlin, "Entrepreneurship and the Rise of Silicon Valley," 352.

58. "SEMATECH's Technological Progress," United States General Accounting Office, 1992, 11, https://www.gao.gov/assets/rced-92-223br.pdf.

59. Valerie Rice, "Sematech's Activism Splits Industry," *San Jose Mercury News*, May 21, 1990, 1C.

60. Browning and Shetler, *Sematech*, 89.

61. Grindley, Mowery, and Silverman, "SEMATECH and Collaborative Research," 724.

62. "Lessons Learned from SEMATECH," 6.

63. Grindley, Mowery, and Silverman, "SEMATECH and Collaborative Research," 733–34; Charles W. Wessner, *Implementing the CHIPS Act: Sematech's Lessons for the National Semiconductor Technology Center* (Center for Strategic and International Studies, 2022), 2.

64. "Lessons Learned from SEMATECH," 6.

65. Grindley, Mowery, and Silverman, "SEMATECH and Collaborative Research," 734.

66. Grindley, Mowery, and Silverman, "SEMATECH and Collaborative Research," 732–33.

67. Grindley, Mowery, and Silverman, "SEMATECH and Collaborative Research," 730.

68. Of the nearly $1 billion of private and public money that Sematech spent between 1988 and 1992, a little over a third went to supporting collaborative research and development. Another third supported the construction and maintenance of Sematech's facilities for testing and refining manufacturing equipment and chip fabrication. The final third was for project equipment for its operations, employee salaries, and other operational expenses. "SEMATECH's Technological Progress," 3, 29.

69. Miller Bonner, W. Lane Boyd, and Janet A. Allan, *Robert N. Noyce, 1927–1990*, commemorative brochure (SEMATECH, 1990), 33, box 8, folder 2, Robert Noyce Papers, Stanford (hereafter Noyce Papers). Noyce had informed close colleagues a few months earlier that he intended to step down from an operational role at Sematech. No announcement had been made, but it is difficult not to speculate that individuals hoped to change his mind and organized the surprise celebration.

70. Berlin, *Man behind the Microchip*, 305. He had been a lifelong smoker, two packs a day. Berlin, *Man behind the Microchip*, 213.

71. Carla Lazzareschi, "Sematech Alliance Faces New Hurdle with Noyce's Death," *Los Angeles Times*, June 5, 1990, D1.

72. Valerie Rice, "Bush Gets Surprise from Noyce's Widow," *San Jose Mercury News*, June 5, 1990, 1A.

73. Valerie Rice, "Silicon Valley Says Goodbye to Noyce," *San Jose Mercury News*, June 19, 1990, 1A.

74. Browning and Shetler, *Sematech*, 142.

75. Browning and Shetler, *Sematech*, 150.

76. Browning and Shetler, *Sematech*, 186.

77. Douglas A. Irwin and Peter J. Klenow, "Sematech: Purpose and Performance," *Proceedings of the National Academy of Sciences of the United States of America* 93, no. 23 (November 12, 1996): 12741, https://www.jstor.org/stable/40689.

78. Francisco A. Moris, "Semiconductors: The Building Blocks of the Information Revolution," *Monthly Labor Review* 119, no. 8 (August 1996): 12, https://sci-hub.ru/https://www.jstor.org/stable/41844601, and "Annual Employment (Thousands of Jobs) for NAICS 334413, Semiconductor and Related Device Manufacturing, U.S. Total," U.S. Bureau of Labor Statistics, data extracted September 16, 2024, https://data.bls.gov/dataViewer/view/timeseries/IPUEN334413W200000000.

79. "Chipping Away at Japan," *Business Week*, December 7, 1992, 120.

80. "Lessons Learned from SEMATECH," 2.

81. Albert N. Link, David J. Teece, and William Finan, "Estimating the Benefits from Collaboration: The Case of SEMATECH," in *Market Failure in High-Technology Industries: Government and Industry Responses*, special issue, *Review of Industrial Organization* 11, no. 5 (October 1996): 748, https://www.jstor.org/stable/41798663?searchText=sematech&searchUri=%2Faction%2FdoBasicSearch%3FQuery%3Dsematech%26so%3Drel&ab_segments=0%2Fbasic_search_gsv2%2Fcontrol&refreqid=fastly-default%3Af1be279db29e0c36d00b201b93f6c907.

82. Irwin and Klenow, "Sematech: Purpose and Performance," 12741.

83. Wessner, *Implementing the CHIPS Act*, 3.

84. Miller, *Chip War*, 107–8.

85. Thomas McCarroll, "Chips Ahoy!," *Time*, November 23, 1992, https://time.com/archive/6721701/chips-ahoy/.

86. Steve Kaufman, "SEMATECH Is Breaking out of Doldrums," *Mercury News*, May 9, 1992, 10E.

87. Katie Hafner, "Does Industrial Policy Work? Lessons from Sematech," *New York Times*, https://www.nytimes.com/1993/11/07/business/does-industrial-policy-work-lessons-from-sematech.html.

88. *SEMATECH 1987–1997: A Final Report to the Department of Defense*, February 21, 1997, https://www.esd.whs.mil/Portals/54/Documents/FOID/Reading%20Room/Science_and_Technology/10-F-0709_A_Final_Report_to_the_Department_of_Defense_February_21_1987.pdf.

89. Browning and Shetler, *Sematech*, 182–83.

90. Evan Ramstad, "Five Foreign Firms to Increase Funding of Sematech Semiconductor Consortium," *Wall Street Journal*, February 4, 1998, https://carnegie-production-assets.s3.amazonaws.com/static/files/files__Schoff_US-Japan.pdf; https://www.wsj.com/articles/SB886549674320614500.

91. Alex Williams and Hassan Khan, "A Brief History of Semiconductors: How the US Cut Costs and Lost the Leading Edge," Employ America, March 20, 2021, https://www.employamerica.org/researchreports/a-brief-history-of-semiconductors-how-the-us-cut-costs-and-lost-the-leading-edge/.

92. Daniel Nenni, "How to Build a $20 Billion Semiconductor Fab," SemiWiki, May 6, 2024, https://semiwiki.com/forum/index.php?threads/how-to-build-a-20-billion-semiconductor-fab.20155/#:~:text=But%20at%20the%20same%20time,%2D%2420%20billion%20or%20more.

93. Raj Varadarajan, Iacob Koch-Weser, Christopher Richard, Joseph Fitzgerald, Jaskaran Singh, Mary Thornton, and Robert Casanova, "Emerging Resilience in the Semiconductor Supply Chain," Boston Consulting Group/Semiconductor Industry Association, May 2024, https://

web-assets.bcg.com/25/6e/7a123efd40199020ed1b4114be84/emerging-resilience-in-the
-semiconductor-supply-chain-r.pdf.

94. Richard D. Bingham, *Industrial Policy American Style: From Hamilton to HDTV* (New York: Routledge, 1998), 128–39.

95. Kehoe, "Technology: Natural Leader with a National Purpose," 20.

96. "Interview—Robert Noyce, regarding his work at SEMATECH," interview by Mary Burt Baldwin, transcript, 9, box 11, folder 13, Noyce Papers. This interview is dated March 5, 1996, which is after Noyce's death.

11: **The Maestro's Market**

1. Mallaby, *Man Who Knew*, xi, 58, 79.

2. Mallaby, *Man Who Knew*, 38.

3. Alan Greenspan, "Testimony of Alan Greenspan before the Committee on Banking, Housing & Urban Affairs," December 1, 1987, Federal Reserve Bank of St. Louis, FRASER, https://fraser.stlouisfed.org/files/docs/historical/greenspan/Greenspan_19871201.pdf.

4. Alan Greenspan, "Stock Prices and Capital Evaluation," *Proceedings of the Business and Economics Statistics Section, American Statistical Association* 6, no. 1 (1959): 2–26.

5. Mallaby, *Man Who Knew*, 699n20.

6. John Gurley and E. S. Shaw, "Financial Aspects of Economic Development," *American Economic Review* 45, no. 4 (September 1955): 515–38.

7. Greenspan, *Age of Turbulence*, 159.

8. Greenspan himself was careful to separate "black markets" that lacked the rule of law and property rights from "free markets" where they were present. Greenspan, *Age of Turbulence*, 138.

9. Gary Gerstle, *The Rise and Fall of the Neoliberal Order: America and the World in the Free Market Era* (New York: Oxford University Press, 2022).

10. Author interview with Oren Cass, May 20, 2024.

11. Nathaniel C. Nash, "Treasury Now Favors Creation of Huge Banks," *New York Times*, June 7, 1987, https://www.nytimes.com/1987/06/07/us/treasury-now-favors-creation-of-huge-banks.html.

12. See his testimony to the Senate Committee on Banking, Housing, and Urban Affairs, 100th Cong., 2nd Sess. (1988).

13. Bob Woodward, *Maestro: Greenspan's Fed and the American Boom* (New York: Touchstone/Simon & Schuster, 2000), 42.

14. William M. Isaac, *Senseless Panic: How Washington Failed America* (New York: Wiley, 2012) 64–85.

15. Mallaby, *Man Who Knew*, 301.

16. Mallaby, *Man Who Knew*, 303.

17. "The Federal Reserve's Role in the 1994 Mexican Peso Crisis," *Econ Focus*, First Quarter 2017, https://www.richmondfed.org/publications/research/econ_focus/2017/q1/federal_reserve.

18. Greenspan's biographer Sebastian Mallaby argues that by the time Greenspan had taken the Chair of the Fed, there was little evidence of an enduring libertarianism. He had become "a pragmatist capable of actively backing regulation." Mallaby, *Man Who Knew*, 678.

19. Alan Greenspan and Adrian Wooldridge, *Capitalism in America: An Economic History of the United States* (New York: Penguin, 2018), 405.

20. Michael Hirsh, *Capital Offense: How Washington's Wise Men Turned America's Future Over to Wall Street* (Hoboken, NJ: John Wiley & Sons, 2010), 1.

21. Financial Crisis Inquiry Commission, *The Financial Crisis Inquiry Report: Final Report of the National Commission on the Causes of the Financial and Economic Crisis in the United States*, authorized edition (New York: PublicAffairs, 2011), 132.

22. Hirsh, *Capital Offense*, 19.

23. As late as 2005, "complex orders were scribbled down in pen and faxed to unattended machines," according to former Treasury Secretary and New York Fed Chair Tim Geithner.

"Trades remained unconfirmed for months, and dealers often reassigned them without notifying counterparties." Timothy F. Geithner, *Stress Test: Reflections on Financial Crises* (New York: Crown, 2014), 102.

24. Brooksley E. Born, "Lessons Not Learned: The Derivatives Market and Continued Risk: A Conversation with Brooksley Born and Joseph Grundfest," *Legal Matters*, no. 88 (Spring 2013), https://law.stanford.edu/stanford-lawyer/articles/lessons-not-learned-the-derivatives-%E2%80%A8market-and-%E2%80%A9continued-risks/.

25. In 1994 and 1995, the General Accounting Office and the G30 issued two separate reports on the growth of and risks in the derivatives market and Congress debated a half-dozen bills to rein them in. "Prepared Statement of Alan Greenspan," *Hearings before the Committee on Banking, Housing, and Urban Affairs, United States Senate*, 104th Cong., 1st Sess. (January 5–6, 1995), 52.

26. As Greenspan saw it at the time, "today's markets and firms, especially those firms that deal in derivatives," were already "heavily regulated by private counterparties." They did not require public direction since they were already guided by their own instincts toward "self-protection." *Hearings before the Subcommittee on Telecommunications and Finance of the Committee on Energy and Commerce, House of Representatives*, 103rd Cong., 2nd Sess. (May 10, 19, and 25, 1994), 157.

27. Saul Hansell, "Market Place; Group Approves Use of Derivatives," *New York Times*, July 22, 1993, https://www.nytimes.com/1993/07/22/business/market-place-group-approves-use-of-derivatives.html; Lessons Learned Oral History Project interview with Brooksley Born, Yale School of Management, 2021, https://ypfsresourcelibrary.blob.core.windows.net/fcic/YPFS/Web_ready_YPFS_Transcript-final_7-14-22.pdf.

28. Nicholas Lemann, *Transaction Man: The Rise of the Deal and the Decline of the American Dream* (New York: Farrar, Straus and Giroux, 1999), 172.

29. Hans Trees, "The Political Economy of Financial Regulation of US Investment Banking" (PhD diss., Durham University, 2016), 161, http://etheses.dur.ac.uk/12265/1/PhD_Thesis_Hans_Trees.pdf?DDD35+. The SEC proposal, dubbed "Broker-Dealer Lite," would have allowed securities firms to engage in over-the-counter (OTC) derivatives trading without having to meet the capital and margin requirements that would typically apply to securities broker-dealers. Arthur Levitt, Testimony before the Senate Committee on Agriculture, Nutrition, and Forestry, July 30, 1998, https://www.sec.gov/news/testimony/testarchive/1998/tsty0998.htm.

30. Handwritten Notes from President's Working Group Meeting, April 21, 1998, FOIA 2010-0673-F - President's Working Group on Financial Markets, Clinton Library, https://clinton.presidentiallibraries.us/items/show/14635.

31. Peter Conti-Brown, *The Power and Independence of the Federal Reserve* (Princeton, NJ: Princeton University Press, 2017).

32. Greenspan, *Age of Turbulence*, 146.

33. Handwritten Notes from President's Working Group Meeting, April 21, 1998, 4.

34. Greenspan later denied saying this but continued to believe that rooting out fraud should be a concern for "law enforcement" rather than regulators. Excerpt from Hirsh, *Capital Offense*, *New York Times*, December 13, 2012, https://www.nytimes.com/2010/12/13/books/excerpt-capital-offense.html; Rick Schmitt, "Prophet and Loss," *Stanford Magazine*, March/April 2009, https://stanfordmag.org/contents/prophet-and-loss; Alan Greenspan, *The Map and the Territory: Risk, Human Nature, and the Future of Forecasting* (New York: Penguin Press, 2013).

35. Robert Rubin and Jacob Weisberg, *In an Uncertain World: Tough Choices from Wall Street to Washington* (New York: Random House, 2004), 251.

36. After a career at Goldman Sachs, Rubin joined the White House as the first Director of the National Economic Council. He moved to slash government deficits, which a Democratic Congress supported in 1993. When the government's cost of borrowing began to decline as deficits came down, Rubin saw this as a vindication of his policies. Subsequent evidence is more skeptical of the causality. See, for instance, Adam Tooze, "Chartbook Newsletter #14:

Are Bond Vigilantes Real? The Strange Case of the 1994 Bond Market Massacre," February 28, 2021, https://adamtooze.com/2021/02/28/chartbook-newsletter-14-are-bond-vigilantes-real-the-strange-case-of-the-1994-bond-market-massacre/.

37. Handwritten Notes from President's Working Group Meeting, April 21, 1998, 4.

38. Alan Greenspan, "Government Regulation and Derivative Contracts," remarks at the Financial Markets Conference of the Fed of Atlanta, February 21, 1997.

39. Geithner, *Stress Test*, 87.

40. "Joint Statement by Treasury Secretary Robert E. Rubin, Federal Reserve Board Chairman Alan Greenspan and Securities and Exchange Commission Chairman Arthur Levitt," Department of the Treasury, May 7, 1998, https://fcic-static.law.stanford.edu/cdn_media/fcic-docs/1998-05-07%20Joint%20Statement%20by%20Treasury%20Secretary%20Rubin,%20Federal%20Reserve%20Board%20Chairman%20Greenspan,%20and%20SEC%20Chairman%20Levitt%20(Treasury%20press%20release).pdf.

41. Roger Loewenstein, *When Genius Failed: The Rise and Fall of Long-Term Capital Management* (New York: Random House, 2001).

42. As a term, "financial innovation" is unwieldy and broad, encompassing the development of any new financial product or practice that affects the nature of credit and money. The creation of crop insurance for farmers in the nineteenth century, a pivotal financial innovation, changed farmers' ability to survive harvest-destroying seasons. The invention of the ATM in 1960, another meaningful financial innovation, scrambled the idea of branch banking. Both changed how individuals and institutions created and mediated money, credit, risk, and reward.

43. For an overview of the promise of financial innovation, see Peter Tufano, "Financial Innovation," in *Handbook of the Economics of Finance*, ed. G. M. Constantinides, M. Harris, and R. M. Stulz, vol. 1, part 1 (Amsterdam: North Holland, 2003); and Charles Calomiris, "Financial Innovation, Regulation, and Reform," *Cato Journal* 29, no. 1 (2009): 65–91.

44. For more on Greenspan's view of technology, see *Age of Turbulence*, 167–69.

45. "Remarks by Chairman Alan Greenspan," Financial Markets Conference, Federal Reserve Bank of Atlanta, February 21, 1997, https://www.federalreserve.gov/boarddocs/speeches/1997/19970221.htm.

46. Robert E. Litan with Jonathan Rauch, *American Finance for the 21st Century*, United States Department of the Treasury, November 17, 1997, https://www.google.com/books/edition/American_Finance_for_the_21st_Century/I4_9mvUzEowC?hl=en&gbpv=1&dq=american+finance+for+the+treasury&printsec=frontcover.

47. Peter Schwartz and Peter Leyden, "The Long Boom: A History of the Future, 1980–2020," *Wired*, July 1, 1997, https://www.wired.com/1997/07/longboom/.

48. Rudi Dornbusch, "Growth Forever," *Wall Street Journal*, July 30, 1998; James K. Glassman and Kevin A. Hassett, *Dow 36,000: The New Strategy for Profiting from the Coming Rise in the Stock Market* (New York: Crown, 1999).

49. Bill Winters interview, *Frontline*, February 27, 2012, https://www.pbs.org/wgbh/pages/frontline/oral-history/financial-crisis/bill-winters/.

50. Gillian Tett, *Fool's Gold: How the Bold Dream of a Small Tribe at J.P. Morgan Was Corrupted by Wall Street Greed and Unleashed a Catastrophe* (New York: Free Press, 2009), 53.

51. SPVs came in a variety of forms. Among the most prominent were Single-Seller Asset-Backed Commercial Paper (ABCP) Conduits, Securities Arbitrage Conduits, and Structured Investment Vehicles (SIVs). I use the term "SPVs" to encompass all of these forms. Zoltan Pozsar, Tobias Adrian, Adam Ashcraft, and Hayley Boesky, "Shadow Banking," *Federal Reserve Bank of New York Policy Review*, December 2003, https://www.newyorkfed.org/medialibrary/media/research/epr/2013/0713adri.pdf; and Matthias Thiemann, *The Growth of Shadow Banking* (Cambridge, UK: Cambridge University Press, 2018), chapter 2.

52. Frank Packer and Chamaree Suthiphongchai, "Sovereign Credit Default Swaps," *Bank for International Settlements Quarterly Review*, December 2003, 79; Tett, *Fool's Gold*, 58. See also Richard Spillenkothen, Director of FRB Division of Banking Supervision, to the Officer in

Charge of Supervision at Each Federal Reserve Bank, SR-96-17 (Gen): Supervisory Guidance for Credit Derivatives, August 12, 1996, Federal Reserve Bank of St. Louis, FRASER, https://fraser.stlouisfed.org/files/docs/historical/ny%20circulars/nycirc_1996_10868a .pdf?utm_source=direct_download.

53. Tett, *Fool's Gold*, 49. See also James R. Kraus, "Credit Derivatives Boom Seen Once Rules Are Clarified," *American Banker*, August 15, 1996.

54. "The J.P. Morgan Guide to Credit Derivatives," 1999, 59, http://www.defaultrisk.com/pp _crdrv121.htm.

55. "J.P. Morgan Guide," 3.

56. "[C]ooperative private-sector efforts to identify and implement sound risk-management practices have the potential to reinforce the efforts of individual firms and their prudential supervisors," Greenspan said. "Remarks by Chairman Alan Greenspan," Federal Reserve Bank of Chicago's Forty-First Annual Conference on Bank Structure, May 5, 2005, https://www.federalreserve.gov/boarddocs/speeches/2005/20050505/default.htm. See also Testimony of Michael Greenberger, Law School Professor, University of Maryland School of Law, *The Role of Derivatives in the Financial Crisis*, Financial Crisis Inquiry Commission Hearing, June 30, 2010, 13, https://digitalcommons.law.umaryland.edu/cgi/viewcontent .cgi?article=1036&context=cong_test.

57. When banks did explicitly take on some of the credit risk of their SPVs, they were required to hold capital reserves. But in 1996 and 2001, the Fed issued guidance allowing banks to decrease their capital reserves against credit guarantees on SPV assets if those assets received high ratings from the ratings agencies. One of the effects of these rulings was to incentivize banks to hold the highly rated tranches of an SPV's mortgage-related securitizations and sell off the higher-risk tranches to entities that did not have capital regulation obligations, like hedge funds and insurance funds. In this way, banks pushed risk out of the regulated banking industry into regulatory blind spots. Thiemann, *Growth of Shadow Banking*, 97–101.

58. Thiemann, *Growth of Shadow Banking*, 101.

59. Department of the Treasury (OCC & OTS), Federal Reserve, FDIC, "Risk-Based Capital Guidelines; Capital Adequacy Guidelines; Capital Maintenance: Capital Treatment of Recourse, Direct Credit Substitutes and Residual Interests in Asset Securitizations; Final Rules," part 2, November 29, 2001.

60. *Federal Register* 69, no. 144 (Wednesday, July 28, 2004), https://www.govinfo.gov/content/pkg /FR-2004-07-28/pdf/04-16818.pdf; "Agencies Issue Final Rule on Capital Requirements for Asset-Backed Commercial Paper Programs," Federal Reserve Board, July 20, 2004, https:// www.federalreserve.gov/boarddocs/press/bcreg/2004/20040720/default.htm.

61. Thiemann, *Growth of Shadow Banking*, 39–48. See also Marc Jarsulic, "Origins of the US Financial Crisis," in *The Handbook of The Political Economy of Financial Crisis*, ed. Gerald A. Epstein and Martin H. Wolfson (Oxford, UK: Oxford University Press, 2013), 32.

62. Barry Eichengreen, *Hall of Mirrors: The Great Depression, the Great Recession, and the Uses—and Misuses—of History* (Oxford, UK: Oxford University Press, 2016), 76.

63. "Risk-Based Capital Standards: Market Risk," published in the *Federal Register* on September 6, 1996 (see FIL-84-96, dated October 10, 1996), https://www.govinfo.gov/app/details/FR -1996-09-06/96-22546/context.

64. Thiemann, *Growth of Shadow Banking*, 100–102.

65. Mallaby, *Man Who Knew*, 9

66. "The Long Demise of Glass-Steagall," PBS, May 8, 2003, https://www.pbs.org/wgbh/pages /frontline/shows/wallstreet/weill/demise.html.

67. William J. Clinton, "Statement on Signing the Gramm-Leach-Bliley Act," November 12, 1999, The American Presidency Project, https://www.presidency.ucsb.edu/documents/state ment-signing-the-gramm-leach-bliley-act.

68. Susan Dudley and Melinda Warren, *Regulators' Budget Continues to Rise: An Analysis of the U.S. Budget for Fiscal Years 2004 and 2005*, Mercatus Center/Weidenbaum Center, Budget Report 26, 2004, https://www.mercatus.org/media/51236/download.

69. "Domestic Financial Sectors; Total Financial Assets; Level," Federal Reserve Bank of St. Louis, https://fred.stlouisfed.org/series/FBTFASQ027S.

70. "OTC Derivatives and Market Activity in the Second Half of 2007," Bank for International Settlements, May 2008, https://www.bis.org/publ/otc_hy0805.pdf.

71. Kelvin R. Utendorf, "The Upper Part of the Earnings Distribution in the United States: How Has It Changed?," *Social Security Bulletin* 64, no. 3 (2001/2002); Chye-Ching Huang and Chad Stone, "Average Income in 2006 Up $60,000 for Top 1 Percent of Households, Just $430 for Bottom 90 Percent," Center on Budget and Policy Priorities, October 2008.

72. Emmanuel Saez and Gabriel Zucman, "The Rise of Income and Wealth Inequality in America: Evidence from Distributional Macroeconomic Accounts," *Journal of Economic Perspectives* 34, no. 4 (Fall 2020), https://gabriel-zucman.eu/files/SaezZucman2020JEP.pdf.

73. Greenspan was sanguine about potential risks new technologies might introduce, particularly as global markets integrated, but he believed the benefits outweighed them. Government regulation would have only made things worse. Remarks by Alan Greenspan to the National Association for Business Economics Annual Meeting in Chicago, IL (via satellite), September 27, 2005; and "Remarks by Alan Greenspan," Financial Markets Conference of the Federal Reserve Bank of Atlanta, March 3, 1995, Federal Reserve Bank of St. Louis, FRASER, https://fraser.stlouisfed.org/title/statements-speeches-alan-greenspan-452/remarks-financial-markets-conference-federal-reserve-bank-atlanta-coral-gables-florida-8532.

74. "The Greenspan Era: Lessons for the Future," Federal Reserve Bank of Kansas City, 2005, https://www.kansascityfed.org/research/jackson-hole-economic-symposium/the-greenspan-era-lessons-for-the-future/.

75. Justin Lahart, "Mr. Rajan Was Unpopular (but Prescient) at Greenspan Party," *Wall Street Journal*, January 2, 2009, https://www.wsj.com/articles/SB123086154114948151.

76. Ben S. Bernanke, "Basel II: Its Promises and Its Challenges," Federal Reserve Bank of Chicago's 42nd Annual Conference on Bank Structure and Competition, Chicago, IL, May 18, 2006, https://www.federalreserve.gov/newsevents/speech/bernanke20060518a.htm.

77. "Remarks by Chairman Alan Greenspan," Financial Crisis Conference, Council on Foreign Relations, New York, New York, July 12, 2000, https://www.federalreserve.gov/boarddocs/speeches/2000/20000712.htm.

78. Christina D. Romer, "Macroeconomic Policy in the 1960s: The Causes and Consequences of a Mistaken Revolution," Economic History Association Annual Meeting, 2007, https://eml.berkeley.edu/~cromer/Lectures/MacroPolicy.pdf.

12: The Purist's Pitfall

1. Hank Paulson, *On the Brink: Inside the Race to Stop the Collapse of the Global Financial System* (New York: Hachette/Business Plus, 2010), 206.

2. William Cohan, *Money and Power: How Goldman Sachs Came to Rule the World* (New York: Knopf Doubleday, 2011), 409, Kindle.

3. For the first-person account of Paulson's sleeping pill drama, see Paulson, *On the Brink*, 205–6.

4. The Fed Chair often handled monetary policy and relations with Congress and the White House, leaving crisis management to the New York Fed President. This was no ordinary crisis, however, and by mid-September, Bernanke was aware of the extreme implications of a Lehman bankruptcy.

5. Laurence M. Ball, *The Fed and Lehman Brothers: Setting the Record Straight on a Financial Disaster* (Cambridge, UK: Cambridge University Press: 2018), 13.

6. Lehman CEO Dick Fuld and Paulson had a personal relationship but had never been friends even though they both ran major investment banks in the same city for years. Lehman's leadership was reckless, and Fuld and his people made up the "rear guard" of Wall Street, Paulson believed. Andrew Ross Sorkin, *Too Big to Fail: The Inside Story of How Wall Street and Washington Fought to Save the Financial System—and Themselves* (New York: Viking, 2009), 51.

7. Paulson did not have the power or authority to make the decision not to come to Lehman's aid. Without the support of the Treasury Secretary, however, Fed officials Geithner and Bernanke would have to be highly confident that they wanted to aid the struggling firm. The Fed had the power to provide Lehman liquidity, saving the bank in the short term, but its leaders chose not to use it.

8. Sorkin, *Too Big to Fail*, 345–50.

9. Ben S. Bernanke, "The Economic Outlook," Joint Economic Committee, United States Congress, March 28, 2007, https://www.federalreserve.gov/newsevents/testimony/bernanke20070328a.htm.

10. "Remarks by U.S. Treasury Secretary Henry M. Paulson, Jr., on the U.S., the World Economy and Markets before the Chatham House," U.S. Department of the Treasury, July 2, 2008, https://home.treasury.gov/news/press-releases/hp1064.

11. Paulson, *On the Brink*, 3.

12. FOMC Minutes, October 5, 1982, 4, Federal Reserve Bank of St. Louis, FRASER, https://fraser.stlouisfed.org/title/federal-open-market-committee-meeting-minutes-transcripts-documents-677/meeting-october-5-1982-23075.

13. Paulson, *On the Brink*, 411. See also "Greenspan: No Easy Answer for Fixing Lehman," NBC News, September 14, 2008, https://www.nbcnews.com/id/wbna26704633.

14. Paulson could have withstood the wave of political criticism. His team had demonstrated that they would pursue unpopular policies if they believed they were the right thing to do— particularly if they had the backing of the President. "Even though the predominant mood at the time, both generally and on the Hill, was against bailouts, President Bush didn't care," according to Paulson. "His goal was to leave the country in as strong a financial position as possible for his successor." The nationalization of Freddie and Fannie, like the package that helped ensure Bear Stearns' acquisition, was politically toxic, and yet the Treasury and Fed pursued them with the backing of the President because they believed the cost to the financial system would be much greater than the backlash. Paulson, *On the Brink*, 237.

15. Sorkin, *Too Big to Fail*, 359.

16. Sorkin, *Too Big to Fail*, 366.

17. Sorkin, *Too Big to Fail*, 367–70.

18. "Wall Street Casualties," *New York Times*, September 15, 2008, https://www.nytimes.com/2008/09/16/opinion/16tue1.html.

19. "Press Briefing by Dana Perino and Secretary of the Treasury Henry Paulson," The White House, September 15, 2008, https://georgewbush-whitehouse.archives.gov/news/releases/2008/09/20080915-8.html#:~:text=SECRETARY%20PAULSON%3A%20The%20situation%20in,line%20in%20resolving%20Lehman%20Brothers.

20. Mallaby, *Man Who Knew*, 667.

21. House Committee on Oversight and Government Reform, *The Financial Crisis and the Role of Federal Regulators: Hearing before the Committee on Oversight and Government Reform*, 2008, https://www.govinfo.gov/content/pkg/CHRG-110hhrg55764/html/CHRG-110hhrg55764.htm. For a video of their interaction, see https://www.youtube.com/watch?v=R5lZPWNFizQ.

22. "Looking Back in Disbelief," *New York Times*, October 24, 2008, A1.

23. Years later, in his final book, *The Map and the Territory*, Greenspan revised his Congressional testimony and relied on another explanatory framework for the crisis: tail risk. His fundamental ideology had not been flawed, he now said. Extreme events such as the ones that precipitated the 2008 crisis were in the "tails" of the distribution of probabilities, the 5 percent space that all the models had given for such an event.

24. Arthur E. Wilmarth Jr., "Citigroup: A Case Study in Managerial and Regulatory Failures," *Indiana Law Review* 47 (2013): 69–137.

25. "FDIC Temporary Liquidity Guarantee Program," Federal Deposit Insurance Corporation, https://www.fdic.gov/banker-resource-center/temporary-liquidity-guarantee-program#:~:text=The%20TLGP%20consisted%20of%20two,newly%20issued%20senior%20unsecured%20debt.

26. The Fed also lent Treasury securities to primary dealers in exchange for mortgage-backed securities through the Term Securities Lending Facility. "FOMC Statement: Federal Reserve and Other Central Banks Announce Specific Measures Designed to Address Liquidity Pressures in Funding Markets," Board of Governors of the Federal Reserve System, March 11, 2008, https://www.federalreserve.gov/newsevents/pressreleases/mon etary20080311a.htm.

27. McCauley and Schenk, "Central Bank Swaps Then and Now."

28. Adam Tooze, *Crashed: How a Decade of Financial Crises Changed the World* (New York: Viking, 2018), 9.

29. Jeanna Smialek, *Limitless: The Federal Reserve Takes on a New Age of Crisis* (New York: Penguin, 2023), 209.

30. The government's role gravitated back toward a long-term baseline. GM and Chrysler today are again private companies traded on stock exchanges. Many of the Fed's liquidity facilities were wound down, although some became a more permanent fixture of the implementation of monetary policy.

31. Joe Nocera and Edmund L. Andrews, "Struggling to Keep Up as the Crisis Raced On," *New York Times*, October 22, 2008, https://www.nytimes.com/2008/10/23/business/economy/23 paulson.html.

32. Bernanke did, however, sing a slightly different tune less than ten days after the bankruptcy. On September 23, he told Congress, "In the case of Lehman Brothers . . . the Federal Reserve and the Treasury declined to commit public funds to support the institution." Ben S. Bernanke, Testimony before the Committee on Financial Services, U.S. House of Representatives, on September 24, 2008, Board of Governors of the Federal Reserve System, https://www.federalreserve.gov/newsevents/testimony/bernanke20080923a1.htm. On having "essentially had no choice," see Ben S. Bernanke, Financial Crisis Inquiry Commission, Closed Session, November 17, 2009, 26, https://fcic-static.law.stanford.edu/cdn_media/fcic-docs/FCIC%20Interview%20with%20Ben%20Bernanke,%20Federal%20Reserve.pdf.

33. Meeting of the Federal Open Market Committee, September 16, 2008, 74, https://www.fed eralreserve.gov/monetarypolicy/files/FOMC20080916meeting.pdf.

34. Ball, *The Fed and Lehman Brothers*, 121.

35. Ball, *The Fed and Lehman Brothers*, 212.

36. Ball, *The Fed and Lehman Brothers*, 201.

37. Scott Alvarez, interview with FCIC staff, July 29, 2010, https://elischolar.library.yale.edu/ypfs-audio/278/.

38. Ball, *The Fed and Lehman Brothers*, 202.

39. Ball also reviewed the work that Bank of America, Barclays, and the consortium of other banks did over the fateful weekend, concluding that their calculations confirmed that "a resolution of Lehman was possible in which losses, if any, were absorbed by holders of subordinated debt, and all other creditors were repaid fully." Ball, *The Fed and Lehman Brothers*, 66.

40. See, for example, the discussion of the Franklin National bailout in 1974 in George C. Nurisso and Edward S. Prescott, "The 1970s Origins of Too Big to Fail," Federal Reserve Bank of Cleveland, October 18, 2017, https://www.clevelandfed.org/publications/economic -commentary/2017/ec-201717-origins-of-too-big-to-fail; "Continental Illinois: A Bank That Was Too Big to Fail," Federal Reserve History, May 15, 2023, https://www.federalreservehis tory.org/essays/continental-illinois; and Michael Fleming and Weiling Liu, "Near Failure of Long-Term Capital Management," Federal Reserve History, November 22, 2013, https://www.federalreservehistory.org/essays/ltcm-near-failure.

41. Lehman Brothers Chronology and Documents, Federal Reserve Bank of St. Louis, FRASER, https://fraser.stlouisfed.org/archival-collection/financial-crisis-inquiry-commission-4967 /lehman-brothers-chronology-documents-520702; and Brickler, Brodows, McCurdy, Schuermann to Tim Geithner, July 11, 2008, https://web.stanford.edu/~jbulow/Lehmandocs/docs /FRBNY/FRBNY%20to%20Exam.%20027043-027050.pdf.

42. Ball, *The Fed and Lehman Brothers*, 8. Fed staff in a summer memo before the crisis began had considered an option along these lines but noted that it exposed the Fed to the risk that Lehman may still find itself in bankruptcy. The Fed or the Treasury could be left with a permanent loss on its balance sheet if the collateral were to continue to fall in value.

   That kind of solution was not without precedent. In 1974, the New York Fed gave the bank Franklin National a lifeline to minimize the disruption its failure might cause in the markets. In 1984, a similar approach was taken with Continental Illinois. In those cases, the government had assessed the risk of a spectacular implosion and had chosen to pay for a softer landing.

43. There is little question that the expansion of the facility was critical in saving the two remaining independent investment banks, Goldman Sachs and Morgan Stanley. Both were at risk of failure without it. Two weeks after the announcement, usage of the facility peaked with borrowers pledging $164 billion of collateral, only about a quarter of which would have qualified before the program expansions to include riskier assets. Ball, *The Fed and Lehman Brothers*, 103.

44. Mark Van Der Weide, Federal Reserve Bank Email from Mark to Scott Alvarez Re Lehman Brothers, September 10, 2008, https://elischolar.library.yale.edu/cgi/viewcontent .cgi?article=6590&context=ypfs-documents; see also Michael Nelson to Christine Cumming and others, "Revised Liquidation Consortium Gameplan + Questions," in *Chronology of Selected Events Related to Lehman Brothers and the Possibility of Government Assistance*, Federal Reserve Bank of St. Louis, FRASER, https://fraser.stlouisfed.org/files/docs/historical/fct/ fcic/fcic_docs_lehman_20100901.pdf.

45. Geithner, *Stress Test*, 178.

46. "Greenspan: No Easy Answer for Fixing Lehman," NBC News, September 14, 2008, https:// www.nbcnews.com/id/wbna26704633.

47. Blinder, *After the Music Stopped*, 58.

A NEW MARKETCRAFT

13: The Realignment

1. Robin Bravender, "Obama's 4th-Quarter Climate Quarterback," *E&E News*, September 2, 2015, https://www.eenews.net/articles/obamas-4th-quarter-climate-quarterback/; Author interview with Brian Deese, April 10, 2024.

2. Author interview with Brian Deese, April 10, 2024.

3. Author interview with Jason Furman, May 9, 2024.

4. Author interview with Brian Deese, April 10, 2024.

5. Author interview with Jason Furman, May 9, 2024.

6. Coral Davenport and Julie Hirschfield Davis, "Obama Adviser during Recession Is Given New Challenge: Climate Change," *New York Times*, April 9, 2015, https://www.nytimes.com /2015/04/10/us/obama-adviser-during-recession-is-given-new-challenge-climate-change .html.

7. Barack Obama, *A Promised Land* (New York: Crown, 2020), 181.

8. John Carney, "America Lost $2.8 Trillion in 2008," *Business Insider*, February 3, 2009, https://www.businessinsider.com/2009/2/america-lost-102-trillion-of-wealth-in -2008#:~:text=Add%20together%20the%20loss%20of,GDP%20of%20the%20entire%20 world.

9. Ford burned through $6.3 billion in cash in the third quarter of 2008, which was $70 million per day. Because of liquidations and other financial restructuring, the quarterly loss amounted to $3 billion, or $33 million per day. GM's fourth-quarter 2008 loss was $9.6 billion, or more than $100 million per day. Chrysler's total 2008 losses were $1.75 billion, or roughly $5 million per day. Chris Isidore, "Ford: Massive Losses, Job Cuts," CNN Money, November 7, 2008, https://money.cnn.com/2008/11/07/news/companies/automakers_3q _results/index.htm; and "GM Lost Nearly $31 Billion in 2008," CBS News, February 26, 2009, https://www.cbsnews.com/news/gm-lost-nearly-31-billion-in-2008/.

10. Author interview with Larry Summers, May 13, 2024.

11. Austan D. Goolsbee and Alan B. Krueger, "A Retrospective Look at Rescuing and Restructuring General Motors and Chrysler," *Journal of Economic Perspectives* 29, no. 2 (Spring 2015): 3–24, https://pubs.aeaweb.org/doi/pdfplus/10.1257/jep.29.2.3.

12. Steve Rattner, *Overhaul: An Insider's Account of the Obama Administration's Emergency Rescue of the Auto Industry* (New York: Houghton Mifflin, 2010), 46.

13. George W. Bush, "President's Address to the Nation," The White House, September 24, 2008, https://georgewbush-whitehouse.archives.gov/news/releases/2008/09/20080924-10.html.

14. Jim Puzzanghera, "Auto Bailout Dies in Senate; Big 3 Could Opt for Bankruptcy after a Late Compromise Attempt Fails to Satisfy GOP Opponents," *Los Angeles Times*, December 12, 2008, A1.

15. Nicholas Kristof, "A Finger in the Dike," *New York Times*, December 14, 2008, WK11.

16. David E. Sanger, "The 31-Year-Old in Charge of Dismantling GM," *New York Times*, May 31, 2009, https://www.nytimes.com/2009/06/01/business/01deese.html.

17. Rattner, *Overhaul*, 65.

18. Noam Scheiber, *The Escape Artists: How Obama's Team Fumbled the Recovery* (New York: Simon & Schuster, 2012), 45.

19. Rattner, *Overhaul*, 55.

20. Author interview with Larry Summers, April 29, 2024.

21. David H. Gellis, "The First Word on Larry Summers," *Harvard Crimson*, May 4, 2001, https://www.thecrimson.com/article/2001/5/4/the-first-word-on-larry-summers/?page=single.

22. Brian Deese, Steven M. Shafran, and Dan Jester, "The Rescue and Restructuring of General Motors and Chrysler," in *First Responders: Inside the U.S. Strategy for the 2007–2009 Financial Crisis*, ed. Ben S. Bernanke, Nellie Liang, Henry M. Paulson Jr., and Timothy F. Geithner (New Haven, CT: Yale University Press, 2020), 375.

23. Jonathan Alter, *The Promise: President Obama, Year One* (New York: Simon & Schuster, 2010), 179.

24. Rattner, *Overhaul*, 68.

25. Obama, *Promised Land*, 301.

26. Deese et al., "The Rescue and Restructuring of General Motors and Chrysler," 379.

27. Rattner, *Overhaul*, 140; and Alter, *The Promise*, 181.

28. Rattner, *Overhaul*, 263.

29. Jody Freeman, "The Obama Administration's National Auto Policy: Lessons from the 'Car Deal,'" 35 *Harvard Environmental Law Review* 343 (2011).

30. "U.S. Exits GM Stake, Taxpayers Lose about $10 Billion," CBS News, December 9, 2013, https://www.cbsnews.com/news/us-exits-gm-stake-taxpayers-lose-about-10-billion/; Sean P. McAlinden and Debra Maranger Menk, "The Effect on the U.S. Economy of the Successful Restructuring of General Motors," Center for Automotive Research, December 5, 2013, https://www.cargroup.org/wp-content/uploads/2017/02/The-Effect-on-the-US-Economy-of-the-Succesful-Restructuring-of-General-Motors.pdf.

31. All Employees, Motor Vehicles and Parts data, Federal Reserve Bank of St. Louis, https://fred.stlouisfed.org/series/CES3133600101.

32. Author interview with Larry Summers, April 29, 2024.

33. Author interview with Brian Deese, April 10, 2024, and May 13, 2024.

34. Sanger, "The 31-Year-Old in Charge."

35. Author interview with Jen Harris, May 13, 2024.

36. Author interview with Brian Deese, April 10, 2024.

14: Revolution in the Ranks

1. Gilad Edelman, "The Democrats Confront Monopoly," *Washington Monthly*, October 29, 2017, https://washingtonmonthly.com/2017/10/29/the-democrats-confront-monopoly/.

2. Lina M. Khan, "Rethinking (In)action: World Alienation in the Thought of Hannah Arendt,"

(unpublished senior thesis, Williams College, 2010), https://librarysearch.williams.edu/dis covery/delivery/01WIL_INST:01WIL_SPECIAL/12288876020002786.

3. Sheelah Kolhatkar, "Lina Khan's Battle to Rein in Big Tech," *New Yorker*, November 29, 2021, https://www.newyorker.com/magazine/2021/12/06/lina-khans-battle-to-rein-in-big-tech.

4. Author interview with Barry Lynn, July 11, 2024.

5. David Halberstam, *The Best and the Brightest* (1972; repr., New York: Ballantine Books, 1993), 315–16.

6. Republican Senators Josh Hawley, elected at thirty-nine, and J. D. Vance, elected at thirty-eight, also went to Yale. Two of the most influential marketcrafting thinkers on the right, Julius Krein and Oren Cass, both went to Harvard, Krein as an undergrad and Cass as a law student. Rohit Chopra, the head of the Consumer Financial Protection Bureau (CFPB), led the student body at Harvard as an undergraduate.

7. Steven Brill, *America's Bitter Pill: Money, Politics, Backroom Deals, and the Fight to Fix Our Broken Healthcare System* (New York: Random House, 2015), 120.

8. Helene Cooper and Michael Barbaro, "Obama Says Election Offers a Clear Choice on the Economy's Long-Term Path," *New York Times*, June 14, 2012, https://www.nytimes.com/2012/06/15/us/politics/obama-speech-seeks-to-assert-stark-choice-for-voters.html.

9. Noam Scheiber, "The Biden Team Wants to Transform the Economy. Really," *New York Times*, February 11, 2021, https://www.nytimes.com/2021/02/11/magazine/biden-economy.html.

10. N. Gregory Mankiw, "A Carbon Tax That America Could Live With," *New York Times*, August 31, 2013, https://www.nytimes.com/2013/09/01/business/a-carbon-tax-that-america-could-live-with.html?_r=0.

11. Ryan Lizza, "As the World Burns," *New Yorker*, October 3, 2010, https://www.newyorker.com/magazine/2010/10/11/as-the-world-burns.

12. Brian Deese, "Crafting Presidential Climate Change Policy: The Paris Agreement and Beyond," lecture at Reed College, April 15, 2016, https://www.reed.edu/events/posts/2015-16/lecture-brian-deese.html; see video at https://www.youtube.com/watch?v=u5VfoMEoHLU.

13. Author interview with Ben Harris, May 3, 2024.

14. Author interview with Amy Kapczynski, April 29, 2024.

15. Kolhatkar, "Lina Khan's Battle."

16. Elizabeth Warren, "Reigniting Competition in the American Economy," keynote remarks at New America's Open Markets Program Event, June 29, 2016, https://www.warren.senate.gov/files/documents/2016-6-29_Warren_Antitrust_Speech.pdf.

17. Author interview with Lina Khan, May 22, 2024.

18. Lina Khan and Zephyr Teachout, "Market Structure and Political Law: A Taxonomy of Power," *Duke Journal of Constitutional Law and Public Policy* 9 (2014): 37.

19. Anne Alstott and Ganesh Sitaraman, *The Public Option: How to Expand Freedom, Increase Opportunity, and Promote Equality* (Cambridge, MA: Harvard University Press, 2019).

20. Lina Khan, "How to Reboot the FTC," *Politico*, April 13, 2016, https://www.politico.com/agenda/story/2016/04/ftc-antitrust-economy-monopolies-000090/.

15: The Odyssey

1. Gideon Lewis-Kraus, "Could Hillary Clinton Become the Champion of the 99 Percent?," *New York Times*, July 23, 2016, https://www.nytimes.com/2016/07/24/magazine/could-hillary-clinton-become-the-champion-of-the-99-percent.html.

2. Author interview with Felicia Wong, May 10, 2024.

3. Tom Perriello and Felicia Wong, "Bold vs. Old," *Democracy Journal*, May 18, 2018, https://democracyjournal.org/arguments/bold-versus-old/.

4. Author interview with Oren Cass, May 20, 2024.

5. Jennifer Schuessler, "Talking Trumpism: A New Political Journal Enters the Fray," *New York Times*, March 8, 2017, https://www.nytimes.com/2017/03/08/arts/american-affairs-journal-donald-trump.html.

6. Gideon Lewis-Kraus, "The Knight's Move," *The Nation*, April 19, 2017, https://www.thenation.com/article/archive/can-a-new-journal-make-sense-of-trumpism/.

7. Park MacDougald, "The New American Millennial Right," *Tablet*, February 5, 2020, https://www.tabletmag.com/sections/news/articles/the-new-millennial-american-right.

8. Author interview with Julius Krein, September 24, 2024.

9. Regina G. Lawrence and Amber E. Boydstun, "The Trump Conundrum," *Columbia Journalism Review*, October 11, 2017, https://www.cjr.org/special_report/trump-coverage-election-clinton.php.

10. Schuessler, "Talking Trumpism," https://www.nytimes.com/2017/03/08/arts/american-affairs-journal-donald-trump.html.

11. Eliana Johnson, "Meet the Harvard Whiz Kid Who Wants to Explain Trumpism," *Politico*, January 3, 2017, https://www.politico.com/story/2017/01/trump-intellectual-harvard-233150.

12. Author interview with Oren Cass, May 20, 2024.

13. Julius Krein, "James Burnham's Managerial Elite," *American Affairs* 1, no. 1 (Spring 2017), https://americanaffairsjournal.org/2017/02/james-burnhams-managerial-elite/.

14. Sridhar Kota and Tom Mahoney, "Reinventing Competitiveness: The Case for a National Manufacturing Foundation," *American Affairs* 3, no. 3 (Fall 2019), https://americanaffairsjournal.org/2019/08/reinventing-competitiveness/; Mehrsa Baradaran, "Postal Banking's Public Benefits," *American Affairs* 2, no. 3 (Fall 2018), https://americanaffairsjournal.org/2018/08/postal-bankings-public-benefits/; Timothy Meyer and Ganesh Sitaraman, "It's Economic Strategy, Stupid: The Case for a Department of Economic Growth and Security," *American Affairs* 3, no. 1 (Spring 2019), https://americanaffairsjournal.org/2019/02/its-economic-strategy-stupid/.

15. Julius Krein, "I Voted for Trump. And I Sorely Regret It," *New York Times*, August 17, 2017, https://www.nytimes.com/2017/08/17/opinion/sunday/i-voted-for-trump-and-i-sorely-regret-it.htm.

16. Philip Rucker and Robert Costa, "Bannon Vows a Daily Fight for 'Destruction of the Administrative State,'" *Washington Post*, February 23, 2017, https://www.washingtonpost.com/politics/top-wh-strategist-vows-a-daily-fight-for-deconstruction-of-the-administrative-state/2017/02/23/03f6b8da-f9ea-11e6-bf01-d47f8cf9b643_story.html.

17. Yale Bulletin and Calendar, "Yale Daily Editor Captures Academic 'Triple Crown,'" vol. 26, no. 18 (January 26–February 2, 1998), http://archives.news.yale.edu/ybc/v26.n18.news.03.html.

18. Elise Labott, "The Sullivan Model," *Foreign Policy*, April 19, 2021, https://foreignpolicy.com/2021/04/09/the-sullivan-model-jake-nsc-biden-adviser-middle-class/.

19. Julie Pace, "Vanishing Adviser Reappears as Iran Policy Player," Associated Press, December 23, 2013, https://apnews.com/united-states-government-07ab7ddd31c04d83be465dbf6bbfcbbc.

20. Pace, "Vanishing Adviser Reappears."

21. Alexander Ward, *The Internationalists: The Fight to Restore American Foreign Policy after Trump* (New York: Portfolio, 2024), 7.

22. Mark Leibovich, "Jake Sullivan, Biden's Adviser, a Figure of Fascination and Schadenfreude," *New York Times*, December 1, 2021, https://www.nytimes.com/2021/11/30/us/politics/jake-sullivan-biden.html.

23. Author interview with Jake Sullivan, April 23, 2024.

24. Salman Ahmed, ed., "U.S. Foreign Policy for the Middle Class: Perspectives from Ohio," Carnegie Endowment for International Peace, 2018, https://carnegie-production-assets.s3.amazonaws.com/static/files/files__USForeignPolicy_Ohio_final.pdf, 4.

25. Jake Sullivan, "The World after Trump: How the System Can Endure," *Foreign Affairs*, March 5, 2018, https://www.foreignaffairs.com/articles/2018-03-05/world-after-trump.

26. Jake Sullivan, "The New Old Democrats," *Democracy Journal*, June 20, 2018, https://democracyjournal.org/arguments/the-new-old-democrats/.

27. Steven Pearlstein, "Is Amazon Getting Too Big?," *Washington Post*, July 28, 2017, https://

www.washingtonpost.com/business/is-amazon-getting-too-big/2017/07/28/ff38b9ca-722e
-11e7-9eac-d56bd5568db8_story.html.

28. David Dayen, "This Budding Movement Wants to Smash Monopolies," *The Nation*, April 4,
2017, https://www.thenation.com/article/archive/this-budding-movement-wants-to-smash
-monopolies/.

29. Pearlstein, "Is Amazon Getting Too Big?"; Dana Mattioli, *The Everything War: Amazon's
Ruthless Quest to Own the World and Remake Corporate Power* (Boston: Little, Brown, 2024).

30. Author interview with Lina Khan, May 22, 2024.

31. Lina Khan, "Amazon Bites Off Even More Monopoly Power," *New York Times*, June 21, 2017,
https://www.nytimes.com/2017/06/21/opinion/amazon-whole-foods-jeff-bezos.html.

32. Dayen, "This Budding Movement Wants to Smash Monopolies."

33. "A Better Deal" proposal, 2017, https://appliedantitrust.com/00_basic_materials/hipster
_antitrust/A-Better-Deal-on-Competition-and-Costs.pdf.

34. Mattioli, *The Everything War*, 181.

35. Rana Foroohar, "Lina Khan: 'This Isn't Just about Antitrust. It's about Values,'" *Financial Times*,
March 29, 2019, https://www.ft.com/content/7945c568-4fe7-11e9-9c76-bf4a0ce37d49.

36. Cecilia Kang and David McCabe, "House Lawmakers Condemn Big Tech's 'Monopoly
Power' and Urge Their Breakups," *New York Times*, October 6, 2020, https://www.nytimes
.com/2020/10/06/technology/congress-big-tech-monopoly-power.html.

37. Chris Hughes, "It's Time to Break Up Facebook," *New York Times*, May 9, 2019, https://www
.nytimes.com/2019/05/09/opinion/sunday/chris-hughes-facebook-zuckerberg.html.

38. Author interview with Julius Krein, September 24, 2024.

39. John Harwood, "The Electoral Math of Romney's Stance on Trade with China," *New York
Times*, March 22, 2012, https://www.nytimes.com/2012/03/23/us/politics/mitt-romneys-sta
nce-on-china-trade.html.

40. "Romney Campaign Press Release—Barack in Time: When Obama Decried Borrowing
from 'the Bank Of China,'" September 16, 2012, The American Presidency Project, https://
www.presidency.ucsb.edu/node/302530.

41. Office of Marco Rubio, Press Release, March 2, 2023, https://www.rubio.senate.gov/rubio
-capitalism-didn-t-change-china-china-changed-capitalism/.

42. Office of Marco Rubio, Press Release.

43. Joanie Greve and Mariana Alfaro, "The Daily 202: Marco Rubio Slams CEOs for Bad
China Deals, Short-Term Thinking and Not Investing in U.S. Workers," *Washington Post*,
May 15, 2019, https://www.washingtonpost.com/news/powerpost/paloma/daily-202/2019
/05/15/daily-202-marco-rubio-slams-ceos-for-bad-china-deals-short-term-thinking-and
-not-investing-in-u-s-workers/5cdaf5841ad2e544f001dd1a/; "2025 and the Future of American Industry," United States Senate Committee on Small Business and Entrepreneurship
(2019), https://www.rubio.senate.gov/wp-content/uploads/_cache/files/d1c6db46-1a68-48
1a-b96e-356c8100f1b7/3EDECA923DB439A8E884C6229A4C6003.02.12.19-final-sbc
-project-mic2025-report.pdf; Marco Rubio, *American Investment in the 21st Century: Project for Strong Labor Markets and National Development*, https://www.rubio.senate.gov/wp-co
ntent/uploads/_cache/files/9f25139a-6039-465a-9cf1-feb5567aebb7/4526E9620A9A7DB
74267ABEA5881022F.5.15.2019.-final-project-report-american-investment.pdf.

44. "Josh Hawley Delivers Maiden Speech in the Senate," May 15, 2019, https://www.hawley
.senate.gov/senator-hawley-delivers-maiden-speech-senate/.

45. "Josh Hawley Delivers Maiden Speech."

46. Marco Rubio, "American Investment in the Twenty-First Century," United States Senate,
May 15, 2019, https://www.rubio.senate.gov/wp-content/uploads/_cache/files/9f25139a-60
39-465a-9cf1-feb5567aebb7/4526E9620A9A7DB74267ABEA5881022F.5.15.2019.-final
-project-report-american-investment.pdf. See also Lenore M. Palladino, "Ending Shareholder Primacy in Corporate Governance," Roosevelt Institute, February 8, 2019, https://
rooseveltinstitute.org/wp-content/uploads/2020/07/RI_EndingShareholderPrimacy_work
ingpaper_201902.pdf.

47. Eamon Javers, "Meet the Leaders of the Trump Era's New Conservative Economic Populism," CNBC, May 22, 2024, https://www.cnbc.com/2024/05/22/meet-the-leaders-of-the-trump-eras-new-conservative-economic-populism.html.

48. Roger Sollenberger, "Conservative Group Accidentally Reveals Its Secret Donors. Some of Them Are Liberal Orgs," *Daily Beast*, November 22, 2023, https://www.thedailybeast.com/conservative-group-accidentally-reveals-its-secret-donors-some-of-them-are-liberal-orgs.

49. "The Hewlett Foundation's Support of American Compass," Hewlett Foundation, December 2, 2023, https://hewlett.org/newsroom/hewletts-commitment-to-transparency-and-dialogue-across-difference/.

16: Bidenomics

1. Gabriel Debenedetti, "Biden Is Planning an FDR-Size Presidency," *New York Magazine*, May 11, 2020, https://nymag.com/intelligencer/2020/05/joe-biden-presidential-plans.html; and author interview with Ben Harris, May 3, 2024.

2. Steve Matthews, "U.S. Jobless Rate May Soar to 30%, Fed's Bullard Says," Bloomberg News, March 22, 2020, https://www.bloomberg.com/news/articles/2020-03-22/fed-s-bullard-says-u-s-jobless-rate-may-soar-to-30-in-2q?sref=hlHfgL28.

3. Brené Brown, "Brené with Joe Biden on Empathy, Unity, and Courage," *Unlocking Us with Brené Brown*, podcast, October 21, 2020, https://brenebrown.com/podcast/brene-with-joe-biden-on-empathy-unity-and-courage/.

4. Debenedetti, "Biden Is Planning an FDR-Size Presidency."

5. Author interview with Jake Sullivan, April 23, 2024.

6. Alexander Burns, "Seeking: Big Democratic Ideas That Make Everything Better," *New York Times*, May 17, 2020, https://www.nytimes.com/2020/05/17/us/politics/joe-biden-economy-democrats.html.

7. Farah Stockman, "The Queen Bee of Bidenomics," *New York Times*, June 17, 2024, https://www.nytimes.com/2024/06/17/opinion/jennifer-harris-bidenomics.html.

8. Author interview with Jen Harris, May 13, 2024.

9. Lawrence H. Summers, "The Age of Secular Stagnation: What It Is and What to Do about It," *Foreign Affairs*, March/April 2016, https://www.foreignaffairs.com/articles/united-states/2016-02-15/age-secular-stagnation.

10. Jennifer Epstein, "Larry Summers Plays Down Role as Adviser to His 'Friend' Biden," Bloomberg News, April 24, 2020, https://www.bloomberg.com/news/articles/2020-04-25/larry-summers-plays-down-role-as-adviser-to-his-friend-biden?sref=hlHfgL28.

11. Author interview with Brian Deese, April 10, 2024.

12. Kelsey Snell, "What's Inside the Senate's $2 Trillion Coronavirus Aid Package," NPR, March 26, 2020, https://www.npr.org/2020/03/26/821457551/whats-inside-the-senate-s-2-trillion-coronavirus-aid-package.

13. Amy Kapczynski, Reshma Ramachandran, and Christopher Morten, "How Not to Do Industrial Policy," *Boston Review*, October 2, 2023, https://www.bostonreview.net/articles/how-not-to-do-industrial-policy/.

14. "Fact Sheet: Two Years after the CHIPS and Science Act, Biden-Harris Administration Celebrates Historic Achievements in Bringing Semiconductor Supply Chains Home, Creating Jobs, Supporting Innovation, and Protecting National Security," The White House, August 9, 2024, https://www.whitehouse.gov/briefing-room/statements-releases/2024/08/09/fact-sheet-two-years-after-the-chips-and-science-act-biden-%E2%81%Aoharris-administration-celebrates-historic-achievements-in-bringing-semiconductor-supply-chains-home-creating-jobs-supporting-inn/#:~:text=America%20invented%20the%20semiconductor%2C%20and,of%20the%20most%20advanced%20chips. Employment in domestic production peaked in 2000 and then fell after the dot-com bubble burst in response to weak global demand. "All Employees, Durable Goods: Electrical Equipment, Appliance, and Component Manufacturing," Federal Reserve Bank of St. Louis, https://fred.stlouisfed.org/series/CES3133440001.

15. "Taiwan's Dominance of the Chip Industry Makes It More Important," *The Economist*, May 6, 2023, https://www.economist.com/special-report/2023/03/06/taiwans-dominance -of-the-chip-industry-makes-it-more-important.

16. As the Chinese economy took off, global demand rebounded, and by 2012, China was purchasing half of the world's chip production, making it very reliant on the United States and Taiwan. Chad P. Brown, "How the United States Marched the Semiconductor Industry into Its Trade War with China," *East Asian Economic Review* 24, no. 4 (December 2020).

17. David Sanger, *New Cold Wars: China's Rise, Russia's Invasion, and America's Struggle to Defend the West* (New York: Crown, 2024), 109.

18. Arthur Herman, "America Needs an Industrial Policy," *American Affairs* 3, no. 4 (Winter 2019), https://americanaffairsjournal.org/2019/11/america-needs-an-industrial-policy/.

19. "Young, Schumer Unveil Endless Frontier Act to Bolster U.S. Tech Leadership and Combat China," Office of Todd Young, May 27, 2020, https://www.young.senate.gov/newsroom /press-releases/young-schumer-unveil-endless-frontier-act-to-bolster-us-tech-leadership -and-combat-china/.

20. Jeanne Whalen, "To Counter China, Some Republicans Are Abandoning Free-Market Orthodoxy," *Washington Post*, August 26, 2020, https://www.washingtonpost.com/business/2020 /08/26/republicans-favor-industrial-policy/.

21. For a history of the beginning of the systemic guarantee, see Barker and Hughes, "Bigger than Penn Central."

22. Jared Bernstein, "The Time for America to Embrace Industrial Policy Has Arrived," *Foreign Policy*, July 22, 2020, https://foreignpolicy.com/2020/07/22/industrial-policy-jobs-climate-change/.

23. David Dayen, "BlackRock Executive Brian Deese Could Get Major White House Position," *American Prospect*, November 24, 2020, https://prospect.org/cabinet-watch/blackrock-execu tive-brian-deese-could-get-major-white-house-position.

24. Author interview with Felicia Wong, May 10, 2024.

25. Jake Sullivan, "Keynote Address," Washington Institute for Near East Policy, May 4, 2023, https://www.washingtoninstitute.org/policy-analysis/keynote-address-national-security-ad visor-jake-sullivan.

26. Author interview with Larry Summers, April 29, 2024.

27. Noam Scheiber, "The Memo That Larry Summers Didn't Want Obama to See," *New Republic*, February 22, 2012.

28. Elizabeth Warren, *A Fighting Chance* (New York: Henry Holt, 2014), 106.

29. Robert Kuttner, "Falling Upward: The Surprising Survival of Larry Summers," *American Prospect*, July 13, 2020, https://prospect.org/economy/falling-upward-larry-summers/.

30. Steve Matthews, "Larry Summers Rules Out Taking a Job in a Biden Administration," Bloomberg News, August 6, 2020, https://www.bloomberg.com/news/articles/2020-08-06 /summers-adviser-to-biden-says-his-time-in-government-is-over.

31. Larry Summers, "The Biden Stimulus Is Admirably Ambitious. But It Brings Some Big Risks, Too," *Washington Post*, February 4, 2021, https://www.washingtonpost.com/opinions/2021/02 /04/larry-summers-biden-covid-stimulus/.

32. Jordan Williams, "Larry Summers Blasts $1.9 T Stimulus as 'Least Responsible' Economic Policy in 40 Years," *The Hill*, March 20, 2021, https://thehill.com/policy/finance /544188-larry-summers-blasts-least-responsible-economic-policy-in-40-years/.

33. David J. Lynch, "How Larry Summers Went from Obama's Top Economic Adviser to One of Biden's Loudest Critics," *Washington Post*, March 29, 2021, https://www.washingtonpost.com /us-policy/2021/03/29/summers-biden-economy-inflation/.

34. Author interview with Ben Harris, May 3, 2024.

35. Franklin Foer, *The Last Politician: Inside Joe Biden's White House and the Struggle for America's Future* (New York: Penguin Press, 2023), 59.

36. J. W. Mason, "The American Rescue Plan as Economic Theory," March 15, 2021, https:// jwmason.org/slackwire/the-american-rescue-plan-as-economic-theory/.

37. Author interview with Brian Deese, April 10, 2024.

38. Author interview with Jen Harris, May 13, 2024.

39. "There's not a market-based solution to try to address some of the big weaknesses that we're seeing open up in our economy when we're dealing with competitors like China that are not operating on market-based terms," Deese said in April 2021, just as the United States was emerging from the most acute initial year of the pandemic. "That's, for me at least, a change in perspective from where I was a decade ago." "The Best Explanation of Biden's Thinking I've Heard," *The Ezra Klein Show*, April 9, 2021, https://www.nytimes.com/2021/04/09/opinion/ezra-klein-podcast-brian-deese.html.

40. Jen Harris, "Kamala Harris Begins to Sketch a New Economic Vision," *New York Times*, August 25, 2024, https://www.nytimes.com/2024/08/25/opinion/kamala-harris-economy-trade-antitrust.html.

41. Harris, "Kamala Harris Begins to Sketch a New Economic Vision."

42. Oren Cass, "Rebuilding U.S. Industry via Green Transition Makes No Sense," American Compass, October 18, 2023, https://americancompass.org/rebuilding-u-s-industry-via-green-transition-makes-no-sense/; Marco Rubio, "Why I Believe in Industrial Policy—Done Right," *Washington Post*, April 2, 2024, https://www.washingtonpost.com/opinions/2024/04/02/marco-rubio-industrial-policy-done-right/; Glenn Kessler, "JD Vance's False Claim That 'Green Energy Scam' Ships Jobs to China," *Washington Post*, August 12, 2024, https://www.washingtonpost.com/politics/2024/08/12/jd-vances-false-claim-that-green-energy-scam-ships-jobs-china/.

43. Scheiber, "The Biden Team Wants to Transform the Economy."

44. Atlantic Council, "Brian Deese on Biden's Vision for a 'Twenty-First-Century American Industrial Strategy,'" Atlantic Council, June 23, 2021, https://www.atlanticcouncil.org/commentary/transcript/brian-deese-on-bidens-vision-for-a-twenty-first-century-american-industrial-strategy/.

45. Lawrence H. Summers and Vinod Thomas, "Recent Lessons of Development," *World Bank Research Observer* 8, no. 2 (July 1993).

46. Author interview with Larry Summers, April 29, 2024.

47. "The Best Explanation of Biden's Thinking."

48. Eric Bradner, "Joe Biden: Breaking Up Facebook Deserves 'Really Hard Look,'" Associated Press, May 13, 2019, https://apnews.com/united-states-presidential-election-71c998ad3b39486ca1dcc220201b68b0.

49. Author interview with Tim Wu, April 25, 2024.

50. "The Grand Unified Theory of Antitrust Revival (and a Plan for Action)," 1, author's possession. On Wu's role in drafting the unsigned memo, see Michael Acton, "Biden Administration's Antitrust Overhaul Rested on Four-Point Internal Memo, Former Top Competition Advisor Says," MLex, October 5, 2023, .https://mlexmarketinsight.com/news/insight/biden-administration-s-antitrust-overhaul-rested-on-four-point-internal-memo-former-top-competition.

51. Author interview with Tim Wu, April 25, 2024.

52. Author interview with Tim Wu, April 25, 2024.

53. Josh Hawley, "A Trust-Busting Agenda for the 21st Century," https://www.hawley.senate.gov/senator-hawleys-trust-busting-agenda/.

54. Author interview with Lina Khan, May 22, 2024.

55. Mattioli, *The Everything War*, 315.

56. Leah Nylen, "Huge Win for Progressives As Lina Khan Takes Helm at FTC," *Politico*, June 15, 2021, https://www.politico.com/news/2021/06/15/khan-confirm-ftc-494609.

57. "Fact Sheet: Executive Order on Promoting Competition in the American Economy," The White House, July 9, 2021, https://www.whitehouse.gov/briefing-room/statements-releases/2021/07/09/fact-sheet-executive-order-on-promoting-competition-in-the-american-economy/#:~:text=The%20Order%20includes%2072%20initiatives,concrete%20improvements%20to%20people's%20lives.

58. "Remarks by President Biden at Signing of An Executive Order Promoting Competition

in the American Economy," The White House, July 9, 2021, https://www.whitehouse.gov
/briefing-room/speeches-remarks/2021/07/09/remarks-by-president-biden-at-signing-of
-an-executive-order-promoting-competition-in-the-american-economy/.

59. "Brian Deese Remarks on President Biden's Competition Agenda," The White House,
July 14, 2022, https://www.whitehouse.gov/briefing-room/statements-releases/2022/07/14
/brian-deese-remarks-on-president-bidens-competition-agenda/.

60. Lawrence H. Summers, post on X, May 22, 2022, https://x.com/LHSummers/status/1528
568277378662403.

61. "Summers: Antitrust Policy Needs to Avoid 1960's Horror Show," Bloomberg News,
June 25, 2021, https://www.bloomberg.com/news/videos/2021-06-25/summers-antitrust-policy
-needs-to-avoid-1960-s-horror-show-video.

62. "Press Briefing by Press Secretary Jen Psaki, Deputy Director of the National Economic
Council Sameera Fazili, and Senior Director for International Economics and Competitiveness Peter Harrell," The White House, June 8, 2021, https://bidenwhitehouse.archives
.gov/briefing-room/press-briefings/2021/06/08/press-briefing-by-press-secretary-jen
-psaki-deputy-director-of-the-national-economic-council-sameera-fazili-and-senior-direc
tor-for-international-economics-and-competitiveness-peter-harrell-june-8/.

63. "Consumer Price Index for All Urban Consumers: Used Cars and Trucks in U.S. City Average," Federal Reserve Bank of St. Louis, https://fred.stlouisfed.org/graph/?g=ISz2#o.

64. Jeanne Whalen, Reed Albergotti, and David J. Lynch, "Biden Can't Fix the Chip Shortage Anytime Soon. Here's Why," *Washington Post*, March 1, 2021, https://www.google.com
/url?q=https://www.washingtonpost.com/technology/2021/03/01/semiconductor-shortage
-halts-auto-factories/&sa=D&source=docs&ust=1719584708453046&usg=AOvVaw2P_pdE
sEETrvkuvynz-ACx.

65. Many corporations in concentrated markets exploited their pricing power to raise costs for
consumers, although there is little evidence this was a primary driver of the inflationary
surge. Mike Konczal and Niko Lusiani, "Prices, Profits, and Power: An Analysis of 2021
Firm-Level Markups," Roosevelt Institute, June 21, 2022, https://rooseveltinstitute.org/pub
lications/prices-profits-and-power/.

66. Jonathan Chait, "Maybe We Should Have Listened to Larry Summers's Warnings about Inflation," *New York Magazine*, November 10, 2021, https://nymag.com/intelligencer/2021/11
/inflation-larry-summers-biden-build-back-better-spending-manchin.html.

67. Lawrence H. Summers, "On Inflation, It's Past Time for Team 'Transitory' to Stand Down,"
Washington Post, November 15, 2021, https://www.washingtonpost.com/opinions/2021/11
/15/inflation-its-past-time-team-transitory-stand-down/.

68. Philip Aldrick, "Larry Summers Says US Needs 5% Jobless Rate for Five Years to Ease Inflation,"
Bloomberg News, June 20, 2022, https://www.bloomberg.com/news/articles/2022-06-20
/summers-says-us-needs-5-jobless-rate-for-five-years-to-ease-cpi?sref=hlHfgL28.

69. Foer, *The Last Politician*, 257.

70. Steven Pearlstein, "The Education of Lina Khan, Whose Superpower is Busting Monopolies," *Washington Post*, May 14, 2024, https://www.washingtonpost.com/opinions/2024/05/14
/lina-khan-antitrust-ftc/.

71. Author interview with Brian Deese, May 13, 2024.

72. Foer, *The Last Politician*, 323.

73. Foer, *The Last Politician*, 283.

74. Author interview with Brian Deese, May 13, 2024.

75. Ben White, "Larry Summers Emerges as the Unlikeliest Democratic Hero," *Politico*, August 15, 2022, https://www.politico.com/news/2022/08/15/larry-summers-emerges-as-the-un
likeliest-democratic-hero-00051433.

76. Foer, *The Last Politician*, 348.

77. Author interview with Brian Deese, April 10, 2024.

78. Sanger, *New Cold Wars*, 333.

79. Josh Boak, "Bumps, Bipartisanship in Long Fight for Semiconductor Bill," Associated Press,

August 1, 2022, https://apnews.com/article/abridged-content-5c8c698124da0188dee4f5d14c238432.

80. Oren Cass, "Pass the CHIPS, Please," American Compass, July 19, 2022, https://americancompass.org/pass-the-chips-please/.

81. Klon Kitchen, "The CHIPS Act: Far from Perfect, but Still Very Good," American Enterprise Institute, July 28, 2022, https://www.aei.org/articles/the-chips-act-far-from-perfect-but-still-very-good/.

82. "Total Construction Spending: Manufacturing in the United States," Federal Reserve Bank of St. Louis, https://fred.stlouisfed.org/series/TLMFGCONS.

83. "Global Landscape of Climate Finance, 2023," Climate Policy Initiative, https://www.climatepolicyinitiative.org/wp-content/uploads/2023/11/Global-Landscape-of-Climate-Finance-2023.pdf; Adam Tooze, "Chartbook Carbon Notes #3 Four Trillion Dollars per Annum—the Shock of Reality from Sustainable Development Thinking," April 9, 2023, https://adamtooze.substack.com/p/chartbook-carbon-notes-3-four-trillion.

84. For overviews, see Joseph E. Stiglitz and Ira Regmi, *The Causes of and Responses to Today's Inflation*, Roosevelt Institute (December 2022), https://rooseveltinstitute.org/wp-content/uploads/2022/12/RI_CausesofandResponsestoTodaysInflation_Report_202212.pdf; Ben Bernanke and Olivier Blanchard, "What Caused the U.S. Pandemic-Era Inflation?," Brookings Institution, May 2023, https://www.brookings.edu/wp-content/uploads/2023/04/bernanke-blanchard-conference-draft_5.23.23.pdf; and Thomas Ferguson and Servaas Storm, "Trump versus Biden: The Macroeconomics of the Second Coming," Institute for New Economic Thinking, Working Papers, no. 196 (2023), https://papers.ssrn.com/sol3/papers.cfm?abstract_id=4318174; Konczal and Lusiani, "Prices, Profits, and Power," https://rooseveltinstitute.org/publications/prices-profits-and-power/.

85. "Remarks on Executing a Modern American Industrial Strategy by NEC Director Brian Deese," City Club of Cleveland, October 13, 2022, .https://www.whitehouse.gov/briefing-room/speeches-remarks/2022/10/13/remarks-on-executing-a-modern-american-industrial-strategy-by-nec-director-brian-deese/.

86. Author interview with Larry Summers, April 29, 2024.

17: The New Marketcraft

1. Author interview with Mike Schmidt, April 22, 2024.

2. Author interview with Mike Schmidt, April 22, 2024.

3. Yuka Hayashi, "Why Washington Went to Wall Street to Revive the U.S. Chips Industry," *Wall Street Journal*, August 15, 2023, https://www.wsj.com/politics/policy/why-the-white-house-went-to-wall-street-to-revive-the-u-s-chips-industry-fe0a0aac.

4. Congressional Research Service, "Frequently Asked Questions: CHIPS Act of 2022 Provisions and Implementation," April 25, 2023, https://crsreports.congress.gov/product/pdf/R/R47523.

5. "Vision for Success: Commercial Fabrication Facilities," NIST, https://www.nist.gov/chips/vision-success-commercial-fabrication-facilities.

6. "CHIPS Act: Securing Semiconductor Supply," *Business Breakdowns* podcast, episode 167, May 31, 2024.

7. "Tracking the CHIPS Incentives Program Awards," Semiconductor Industry Association, October 10, 2024, https://www.semiconductors.org/chips-incentives-awards/; *State of the U.S. Semiconductor Industry*, 2024, Semiconductor Industry Association, 2024, https://www.semiconductors.org/wp-content/uploads/2024/09/SIA_State-of-Industry-Report_2024_final_091124.pdf.

8. Tim Culpan, "Apple Mobile Processors Are Now Made in America. By TSMC," Tim Culpan's Position, September 17, 2024, https://timculpan.substack.com/p/apple-mobile-processors-are-now-made.

9. Mackenzie Hawkins, "TSMC's Arizona Chip Production Yields Surpass Taiwan's in Win for US Push," Bloomberg News, October 24, 2024, https://www.bloomberg.com/news/articles/2024-10-24/tsmc-s-arizona-chip-production-yields-surpass-taiwan-s-a-win-for-us-push.

10. "Tracking the CHIPS Incentives Program Awards"; "State of the U.S. Semiconductor Industry."

11. Conversion to today's dollars is used by a percent of GDP. "Gross Domestic Product for United States," Federal Reserve Bank of St. Louis, https://fred.stlouisfed.org/series/NGDP SAXDCUSQ.

12. Mike Schmidt, "A Message from Mike Schmidt, Director of the CHIPS Program Office, on the Second Anniversary of the CHIPS and Science Act," August 7, 2024.

13. *Emerging Science in the Semiconductor Supply Chain*, Semiconductor Industry Association, May 2024, https://www.semiconductors.org/wp-content/uploads/2024/05/Report_Emerging -Resilience-in-the-Semiconductor-Supply-Chain.pdf, 11–13.

14. Schmidt, "Message from Mike Schmidt."

15. Bente Bouthier, "New Semiconductor Facility Opens in Odon, with Funding from CHIPS and Science Act," Indiana Public Media, January 19, 2024, https://indianapublicmedia.org /news/new-semiconductor-facility-opens-in-odon-with-funding-from-chips-and-science -act.php; Anne Lurea, "Senator Todd Young on Impact of Innovation Legislation and Research Funding," WSBT South Bend, April 25, 2024, https://www.wsbt.com/news/local /todd-young-sethuraman-panchanathan-chips-science-innovation-legislation-impact-nsf -grants-university-of-notre-dame-research-funding-technology-economy-south-bend -indiana.

16. "Schumer's CHIPS and Science Law Delivers Historic $6.1 Billion Federal Preliminary Chips Agreement for Micron," Office of Chuck Schumer, https://www.schumer.senate.gov /newsroom/press-releases/schumers-chips-and-science-law-delivers-historic-61-billion-fed eral-preliminary-chips-agreement-for-micron.

17. Stephen Groves, "House Speaker Johnson Says GOP May Try to Repeal CHIPS Act, Then Walks It Back," Associated Press, November 1, 2024, https://apnews.com/article/mike-john son-chips-act-d5504f76d3aa0d5b401216f3592c9a09.

18. For more, see Mariana Mazzucato, *Mission Economy: A Moonshot Guide to Changing Capitalism* (New York: Harper Business, 2001).

19. Author interview with Mike Schmidt, April 22, 2024.

20. "Warren, Jayapal Raise Concerns about Commerce Department Tasking Wall Street Financiers with Allocating $39 Billion in CHIPS Semiconductor Funding," January 10, 2024, https://www.warren.senate.gov/oversight/letters/warren-jayapal-raise-concerns-about-com merce-department-tasking-wall-street-financiers-with-allocating-39-billion-in-chips-semi conductor-funding.

21. Mackenzie Hawkins and Ian King, "US Needs More Chips Funding As AI Fuels Demand, Raimondo Says," Bloomberg News, February 21, 2024, https://www.bloomberg.com/news /articles/2024-02-21/raimondo-says-us-needs-more-chips-funding-as-ai-fuels-demand ?embedded-checkout=true.

22. David E. Sanger, "What $8.5 Billion Can Buy: Biden Aims to Bolster Chip Manufacturing," *New York Times*, March 20, 2024, https://www.nytimes.com/2024/03/20/us/politics/biden -chip-manufacturing.html.

23. Robert Langreth, "Sanofi Drops Rare Disease Drug Purchase After FTC Files Suit," Bloomberg News, December 11, 2023, https://www.bloomberg.com/news/articles/2023-12-11/ftc -sues-to-block-sanofi-purchase-of-maze-for-rare-disease-drug.

24. Gerry Smith, "Illumina Plans to Divest Grail after US Antitrust Ruling," Bloomberg News, December 18, 2023, https://www.bloomberg.com/news/articles/2023-12-17/illumina-plans -to-sell-grail-after-us-antitrust-appeal-ruling?sref=hlHfgL28.

25. Josh Eidelson and Max Chafkin, "Lina Khan Is Just Getting Started (She Hopes)," *Bloomberg Businessweek*, October 9, 2024, https://www.bloomberg.com/news/features/2024-10-09/lina -khan-on-a-second-ftc-term-ai-price-gouging-data-privacy?sref=hlHfgL28.

26. Danielle Kaye, "Federal Judge Blocks $25 Billion Kroger-Albertsons Grocery Merger," *New York Times*, December 10, 2024, https://www.nytimes.com/2024/12/10/business/kroger -albertsons-merger-ftc.html.

27. The FTC prevailed in three litigated victories, secured seventeen consent agreements where deals were restructured or meaningful limitations applied, and in eight instances the acquiring company abandoned the effort. K. J. Boyle, "Matt Yglesias Is Wrong About Lina Khan's Record," Revolving Door Project, August 13, 2024, https://therevolvingdoorproject.org/matt-yglesias-is-wrong-about-lina-khans-record/; Anna Langlois, "Merger Abandonments Soar in 2024," *Global Competition Review*, August 9, 2024, https://globalcompetitionreview.com/gcr-usa/article/dechert-merger-abandonments-soar-in-2024; Douglas Farrar, post on X, August 15, 2024, https://x.com/DouglasLFarrar/status/1824125874918265093.

28. Evan Starr, J. J. Prescott, and Norman D. Bishara, "Noncompete Agreements in the U.S. Labor Force," *Journal of Law and Economics* 64, no. 1 (2021): https://ssrn.com/abstract=2625714.

29. "United States—M&A Statistics," Institute for Mergers, Acquisitions, and Alliances, https://imaa-institute.org/mergers-and-acquisitions-statistics/united-states-ma-statistics/.

30. Justin Wise and Mahira Dayl, "Failed Deals Climb As Antitrust Enforcers Push Aggressive Agenda," Bloomberg Law, September 23, 2024, https://news.bloomberglaw.com/antitrust/failed-deals-climb-as-antitrust-enforcers-push-aggressive-agenda.

31. Author interview with Brian Deese, April 10, 2024, and May 13, 2024.

32. Molly Ball and Brody Mullins, "Biden's Trustbuster Draws Unlikely Fans: 'Khanservative' Republicans," *Wall Street Journal*, March 25, 2024, https://www.wsj.com/politics/policy/lina-khan-ftc-antitrust-khanservatives-a6852a8f.

33. Ball and Mullins, "Biden's Trustbuster Draws Unlikely Fans."

34. Adam Candeub, "Federal Trade Commission," *Mandate for Leadership: The Conservative Promise* (Project 2025), ed. Paul Dans and Steven Groves (Washington, DC: Heritage Foundation, 2022, https://static.project2025.org/2025_MandateForLeadership_CHAPTER-30.pdf.

35. Dans and Groves, *Mandate for Leadership.*

36. "The Wall Street Grumble," American Economic Liberties Project, https://www.economicliberties.us/the-wall-street-grumble/.

37. Christine Wilson, "Why I'm Resigning as an FTC Commissioner," *Wall Street Journal*, February 14, 2023, https://www.wsj.com/articles/why-im-resigning-from-the-ftc-commissioner-ftc-lina-khan-regulation-rule-violation-antitrust-339f115d.

38. In a survey of the best places to work in the federal government, the FTC had historically come in close to the top in its category. In Khan's first year, the FTC fell from the second-best government agency for employee satisfaction to the twenty-second. It crept up a bit in 2022, and by 2023 it had meaningfully rebounded to the ninth spot. That was still not where it had been in the years before Khan's arrival, but a marked improvement from its low. "2023 Best Places to Work in the Federal Government Rankings," Partnership for Public Service, https://bestplacestowork.org/rankings/?view=overall&size=mid&category=overall&; and Cat Zakrzewski, "Sinking FTC Workplace Rankings Threaten Chair Lina Khan's Agenda," *Washington Post*, July 13, 2022, https://www.washingtonpost.com/technology/2022/07/13/ftc-lina-khan-rankings/.

39. Pearlstein, "The Education of Lina Khan."

40. "Biden-Harris Administration Announces $20 Billion in Grants to Mobilize Private Capital and Deliver Clean Energy and Climate Solutions to Communities across America," Environmental Protection Agency, April 4, 2024, https://www.epa.gov/newsreleases/biden-harris-administration-announces-20-billion-grants-mobilize-private-capital-and-o.

41. John Bistline, Neil R. Mehrotra, and Catherine Wolfram, "Economic Implications of the Climate Provisions of the Inflation Reduction Act," Brookings Institution, March 29, 2023, https://www.brookings.edu/articles/economic-implications-of-the-climate-provisions-of-the-inflation-reduction-act/; "The U.S. Is Poised for an Energy Revolution," Goldman Sachs, April 17, 2023, https://www.goldmansachs.com/intelligence/pages/the-us-is-poised-for-an-energy-revolution.html.

42. Brian Deese, post on X, February 29, 2024, https://x.com/BrianCDeese/status/1763247502780698853.

43. "Q3 2024 Update," Clean Investment Monitor, https://www.cleaninvestmentmonitor.org/reports/clean-investment-monitor-q3-2024-update.

44. John Bistline, Geoffrey Blanford, Maxwell Brown et al., "Emissions and Energy Impacts of the Inflation Reduction Act," *Science* 380, no. 6652 (June 29, 2023), https://www.science.org/doi/full/10.1126/science.adg3781.

45. Lael Brainard, "Consumer Interests in the Global Trading System," remarks to Consumer Federation of America, March 16, 2000, https://clintonwhitehouse4.archives.gov/textonly/WH/EOP/nec/html/BrainardCfaSpeech.html.

46. Lael Brainard, "Trade Policy in the 1990s," Brookings Institution, June 29, 2001, https://www.brookings.edu/wp-content/uploads/2016/06/20010629.pdf.

47. "Remarks by National Economic Advisor Lael Brainard on Responding to the Challenges of China's Industrial Overcapacity," The White House, May 16, 2024, https://www.whitehouse.gov/briefing-room/speeches-remarks/2024/05/16/remarks-by-national-economic-advisor-lael-brainard-on-responding-to-the-challenges-of-chinas-industrial-overcapacity/.

48. "Remarks by National Economic Advisor Lael Brainard."

49. "Remarks by National Security Advisor Jake Sullivan on Renewing American Economic Leadership at the Brookings Institution," The White House, April 27, 2023, https://www.whitehouse.gov/briefing-room/speeches-remarks/2023/04/27/remarks-by-national-security-advisor-jake-sullivan-on-renewing-american-economic-leadership-at-the-brookings-institution/.

50. J. D. Vance, "Rebuilding American Capitalism: An American Compass Forum," YouTube video, 5:01, posted by American Compass, June 13, 2023, https://www.youtube.com/watch?v=J8I2YcSgo8c.

51. Marco Rubio, "Decades of Decadence: An American Compass Forum," YouTube video, 6:45, posted by American Compass, August 16, 2023, https://www.youtube.com/watch?v=yoXhRaT3VN8.

52. Marco Rubio, "Industrial Policy, Right and Wrong," *National Affairs*, no. 60 (Spring 2024): https://www.nationalaffairs.com/publications/detail/industrial-policy-right-and-wrong.

53. Rubio, "Industrial Policy."

54. Federal Trade Commission, "FTC and State Partners Sue Pesticide Giants Syngenta and Corteva for Using Illegal 'Pay to Block' Scheme to Inflate Prices," Federal Trade Commission, September 29, 2022, https://www.ftc.gov/news-events/news/press-releases/2022/09/ftc-state-partners-sue-pesticide-giants-syngenta-corteva-using-illegal-pay-block-scheme-inflate.

55. Federal Trade Commission, *Nixing the Fix: An FTC Report to Congress on Repair Restrictions*, May 2021, https://www.ftc.gov/system/files/documents/reports/nixing-fix-ftc-report-congress-repair-restrictions/nixing_the_fix_report_final_5521_630pm-508_002.pdf; and Federal Trade Commission, "FTC Approves Final Orders in Right to Repair Cases against Harley-Davidson, MWE Investments, and Weber," Federal Trade Commission, October 27, 2022, https://www.ftc.gov/news-events/news/press-releases/2022/10/ftc-approves-final-orders-right-repair-cases-against-harley-davidson-mwe-investments-weber.

Conclusion

1. The work of Marianna Mazzucato and Stephen Vogel was particularly helpful in my early conceptual journey. Marianna Mazzucato, *The Entrepreneurial State: Debunking Public vs. Private Sector Myths* (London: Anthem Press, 2013); Mazzucato, *Mission Economy*; and Vogel, *Marketcraft*.

2. There is an ideologically diverse effort to rethink state capacity and how to make government more effective, led by people like Jen Pahlka, Ezra Klein, Derek Thompson, and Sabeel Rahman. Much of this literature focuses on creating clear structures for streamlining decision-making and accountability. See, for instance, Jen Pahlka, *Recoding America: Why Government Is Failing in the Digital Age and How We Can Do Better* (New York: Metropolitan Books, 2023);

and K. Sabeel Rahman, "Building the Government We Need: A Framework for Democratic State Capacity," Roosevelt Institute, June 6, 2024.

3. Michael Strain, "Trump Victory Kicks off the Battle for the Right's Future," *Financial Times*, November 8, 2024, https://www.ft.com/content/42c723a0-9ff3-437c-83ee-cae17c5cdb68.

4. "Fiscal, Macroeconomic, and Price Estimates of Tariffs Under Both Non-Retaliation and Retaliation," The Budget Lab, Yale University, October 16, 2024, https://budgetlab.yale .edu/research/fiscal-macroeconomic-and-price-estimates-tariffs-under-both-non-retaliation -and-retaliation.

5. For a thorough accounting of Trump's trade policies, see Robert Lighthizer, *No Trade is Free* (New York: Broadside Books, 2023); Geoffrey Gertz, "Did Trump's Tariffs Benefit American Workers and National Security?," Brookings Institution, September 10, 2020; and Erica York, "Tracking the Economic Impact of the Trump Tariffs," Tax Foundation, June 26, 2024.

6. "Fact Sheet: President Biden Takes Action to Protect American Workers and Businesses from China's Unfair Trade Practices," The White House, May 14, 2024, https://www.whitehouse .gov/briefing-room/statements-releases/2024/05/14/fact-sheet-president-biden-takes-ac tion-to-protect-american-workers-and-businesses-from-chinas-unfair-trade-practices/.

7. There are many provisions of the tax code—including important and popular ones—that are not designed to guide a market in a certain direction. In 1997, a Republican Congress and President Bill Clinton created the child tax credit to lower the tax burden on working families. Some legislators hoped that it might encourage families to have more children by making it more affordable. In the nearly thirty years since, the tax credit has been expanded multiple times, including most recently in Biden's American Rescue Package. Both Trump and Kamala Harris, the Democratic nominee in 2024, advocated for its expansion, although in different ways. But the push for an expanded child tax credit doesn't shape a particular market for political reasons. Its goal is broad: to lower the cost of living for American families. Indirectly, it might subsidize childcare providers or boost sales of car seats and cribs, but that's not what policymakers set out to do when they created it. For an overview of the child tax credit, see Congressional Research Service, "The Child Tax Credit: Legislative History," December 23, 2021, https://sgp.fas.org/crs/misc/R45124.pdf.

8. Marie Boran, "What Donald Trump's Strategic Bitcoin Reserve Could Look Like," *Newsweek*, November 18, 2024, https://www.newsweek.com/what-donald-trumps-strategic-bit coin-reserve-could-look-like-1986360; David Yaffe-Bellany, "A First-Day Trump Order: A Federal Stockpile of Bitcoin?," *New York Times*, January 16, 2025, https://www.nytimes .com/2025/01/16/technology/trump-bitcoin-stockpile.html.

9. Jigar Shah, interviewed by Robinson Meyer, "Yes, Biden's Green Future Can Still Happen Under Trump," *Ezra Klein Show*, December 20, 2024, https://www.nytimes.com/2024/12/20 /opinion/ezra-klein-podcast-jigar-shah-robinson-meyer.html; and U.S. Department of Energy, "Monthly Application Activity Report," Energy Loan Programs Office, accessed January 6, 2025, https://www.energy.gov/lpo/monthly-application-activity-report.

10. Robinson Meyer, "The Bill That Could Truly, Actually Bring Back U.S. Manufacturing," *The Atlantic*, August 18, 2021, https://www.theatlantic.com/science/archive/2021/08/america -into-the-worlds-factory-again-industrial-finance-corporation/619793/.

11. Jeff Stein, "J. D. Vance Broke Off Talks on Bipartisan Childbirth Plan Amid VP Search," *Washington Post*, July 24, 2024, https://www.washingtonpost.com/business/2024/07/24/jd -vance-bipartisan-child-plan-trump/.

12. Governments usually create sovereign wealth funds to grow a country's wealth or tie off profits from natural resources to fund government services in the future once the resource is depleted or no longer valuable. The portfolio of the fund is optimized for financial performance, not political goals. A national investment bank, by contrast, uses the power of credit provision and equity investment to support particular industries and initiatives important to economic and geopolitical goals. For Trump's comments, see remarks by Donald J. Trump at the Economic Club of New York, September 5, 2024, https://www.econclubny.org/docu ments/10184/109144/20240905_Trump_Transcript.pdf.

13. Alan Rappeport, "Trump and Democrats Agree: U.S. Needs a National Wealth Fund for Investments," *New York Times*, September 10, 2024, https://www.nytimes.com/2024/09/10/us /politics/us-sovereign-wealth-fund.html.

14. Donald Trump, "A Plan for Establishing a United States Sovereign Wealth Fund," Executive Order, issued February 3, 2025, The White House, https://www.whitehouse.gov/preside ntial-actions/2025/02/a-plan-for-establishing-a-united-states-sovereign-wealth-fund/.

15. "A Bill to Establish the Industrial Finance Corporation of the United States, and for Other Purposes," 117th Cong., 1st Sess. (2021), https://www.coons.senate.gov/imo/media/doc /text_ifcus_117.pdf.

16. If Democrats ended up passing the legislation in future Congressional sessions, they might assign it the mission of mitigating climate change by investing in cutting edge technologies and research to prevent further climate harm.

17. Setting these expectations is critical, as we saw with the disasters of Lustron for the RFC (see Chapter 3) or the Solyndra scandal for the Loan Program Office. On Solyndra, see Matthew L. Wald, "Solar Firm Aided by Federal Loans Shuts Doors," *New York Times*, August 31, 2011, https://www.nytimes.com/2011/09/01/business/energy-environment/solyndra-solar -firm-aided-by-federal-loans-shuts-doors.html; and Congressional Research Service, "Market Dynamics That May Have Contributed to Solyndra's Bankruptcy," October 25, 2011, https://crsreports.congress.gov/product/pdf/R/R42058/3.

18. For a broader institutional blueprint of how the national investment bank might work, see Saule Omarova, "The National Investment Authority: An Institutional Blueprint," March 22, 2022, https://papers.ssrn.com/sol3/papers.cfm?abstract_id=4685133.

Image Credits

1. Courtesy of the Woodson Research Center Special Collections and Archives, Rice University
2. Myron Davis / The LIFE Picture Collection/Shutterstock
3. Bettman via Getty Images
4. Bettman via Getty Images
5. Federal Reserve Bank of New York
6. Courtesy of the Walter P. Reuther Library, Archives of Labor and Urban Affairs, Wayne State University
7. Courtesy of the Lyndon Johnson Presidential Library and Museum, National Archives and Records Administration
8. United Press International
9. Byron Schumaker / Courtesy of the Richard Nixon Presidential Library and Museum, National Archives and Records Administration
10. Bettmann via Getty Images
11. James K. W. Atherton / Washington Post via Getty Images
12. Wayne Miller / Grinnell Office of College Relations. Courtesy of Grinnell College Special Collections and Archives.
13. Sematech
14. Pete Souza via Flickr Commons
15. Courtesy of Lindsey Toomer / Colorado Newsline
16. Cameron Smith via Flickr Commons

Index

440   INDEX

Federal Trade Commission (FTC), 285, 300, 360
  conditions for marketcraft and, 351
  creation of, xix
  increase in funding, 350
  Larry Summers on, 329
  Lina Khan as a fellow at, 300
  Lina Khan as Chair of, 327, 328, 332–33
  Lina Khan as commissioner of, 326
  on mergers and acquisitions, 347–50
  "noncompete" agreements, 348
  Rohit Chopra and, 283, 300
  working for farmers, 356–57
Fed Funds rate, 179–80
Feldstein, Martin, 268
Fiat, 269, 271
Financial Accounting Standards Board, 233
Financial Crisis Inquiry Commission (FCIC),
  221, 253, 256
financial innovation
  Alan Greenspan and, 215, 216, 220
  Ben Bernanke and, 237
  Congressional legislation for, 234–35
  credit default swaps, 229–32
  derivatives and, 223
  Gramm-Leach-Bliley Act (1999) and, 234–35
  Great Financial Crisis and, 244, 256–57
  Greenspan on, 221–22
  Greenspan's theory on, 227–28
  Hank Paulson on, 256
  impact of, 235–36
  inequality resulting from, 236
  special purpose vehicles (SPVs), 229, 231, 232–33
  "value at risk" models for banks, 233–34
Financial Services Authority, 243
Financial Times, 301
First National City Bank, 62–63, 65–66
First World War, 98
Fisher, Carl, 24
Fisher, Todd, 343–46
Florida, 24, 25, 148, 286
FOMC. See Federal Open Market Committee
  (FOMC)
Food and Drug Administration (FDA), xxv, 313
food prices, 128, 168, 169, 192, 339
Ford, Gerald (administration of), 130, 150, 152,
  154, 155, 156, 158, 216
Ford Motor Company, 35
Foreign Affairs, 139, 297
foreign investment, 100–102, 103, 108
foreign policy
  foreign oil production and, 139
  Jake Sullivan on domestic policy and, 296, 311,
    317
  oil production/supplies and, 139
Foreign Policy, 311
"The Forgotten Man Speech" (Roosevelt), 7
Fortnite, 348
Fortune, 30, 39, 128, 202
fossil-fuels, 137–38, 282

Fox News, 332
France, xxiii, 34, 42, 121
Franklin National Bank, 67, 172
Freddie Mac, 239, 241, 245–46
free-market ideology/policies
  in the 1980s, 217
  Alan Greenspan and, 216–17, 220
  Allan Sproul on, 60
  Bill Martin Jr. on, 56–57, 60
  debate over government regulation and, ix–x
  Federal Reserve's role and, 56
  Great Financial Crisis and, 257
  Hank Paulson and, 244–45
  Julius Krein on, 293–94
  Lehman Brothers collapse and, 244–45
  marketcraft and, xii
  pegged interest rates and, 56
  skepticism of, by new generation of policy
    leaders, 277
Friedman, Milton, 61, 115–16, 117–18, 153, 157,
  186
FTC. See Federal Trade Commission (FTC)
Fulbright, J. William, 45
Fuld, Dick, 247
Furman, Jason, 261, 263, 264, 265, 266, 279, 285,
  319, 329

Gaetz, Matt, 350
Galbraith, James, 120
Galbraith, John Kenneth, 116–17
Gamble, Joelle, 316
garden, comparison of markets to a, xv–xvii
Garner, John Nance, 6, 13, 19–20
gasoline, rationing of, 140, 146–47
gasoline prices, 138, 140, 147, 148, 149, 150, 159,
  169–70
gasoline production, 138, 139
gasoline supplies/shortages, 138, 148–49, 159
GCA (company), 211
Geithner, Tim, 226, 241, 242–43, 246–47, 252–55,
  257, 266, 269, 280
Gelsinger, Patrick, 346
General Electric, 62
genocide, xi
geothermal wells, 351
germanium, 197
Germany, 32, 34, 36, 37, 121, 122, 144–45, 291
Gingrich, Newt, 212
Glass, Carter, 49, 50
Glass-Steagall law, 234
global currency. See Bretton Woods
globalization, 211, 292, 297, 304
global minimum tax, 331
global reserve currency, 97
GM, 70, 265, 269–70, 271
Goldman Sachs, 239, 240, 241, 255, 344, 352
gold reserves, American, 98–99
gold standard, 97, 98, 123, 124
Goldwater, Barry, 79

About the Author

CHRIS HUGHES is the co-founder and Chair of the Economic Security Project. He holds degrees in history and economics from Harvard University and the New School of Social Research and is completing his PhD at the Wharton School at the University of Pennsylvania. His research focuses on the history of central banking, antimonopoly policy, guaranteed income studies, and tax policy.

Hughes' essays and articles have appeared in *The New York Times*, *Financial Times*, *Washington Post*, *The Wall Street Journal*, and *Time*. His first book, *Fair Shot: Rethinking Inequality and How We Earn*, was published by St. Martin's Press in 2018.

In 2004, Hughes co-founded Facebook and later went on to direct Barack Obama's digital organizing efforts in 2008. Hughes chairs the board of the Brooklyn-based Foundation for Community Psychoanalysis and serves on the boards of the New York Public Library and the Chamber Music Society of Lincoln Center. He lives in New York's Greenwich Village with his husband and their two children.